IF FOUND, please notify and arrange return to owner. This text is an important study guide for the owner's career and/or exam preparation.

Name: _____

Address: _____

City, State, ZIP: _____

Telephone: (____) _____ Email: _____

Gleim Publications, Inc., offers five university-level study systems:

Auditing & Systems Exam Questions and Explanations with Test Prep CD-Rom
Business Law/Legal Studies Exam Questions and Explanations with Test Prep CD-Rom
Federal Tax Exam Questions and Explanations with Test Prep CD-Rom
Financial Accounting Exam Questions and Explanations with Test Prep CD-Rom
Cost/Managerial Accounting Exam Questions and Explanations with Test Prep CD-Rom

The following is a list of Gleim examination review systems:

CIA Review: Part I, Internal Audit Role in Governance, Risk, and Control
CIA Review: Part II, Conducting the Internal Audit Engagement
CIA Review: Part III, Business Analysis and Information Technology
CIA Review: Part IV, Business Management Skills

CMA Review: Part 1, Business Analysis
CMA Review: Part 2, Management Accounting and Reporting
CMA Review: Part 3, Strategic Management
CMA Review: Part 4, Business Applications

CPA Review: Financial
CPA Review: Auditing
CPA Review: Business
CPA Review: Regulation

EA Review: Part 1, Individuals
EA Review: Part 2, Businesses
EA Review: Part 3, Representation, Practice, and Procedures

D1484657

An order form is provided at the back of this book or contact us at www.gleim.com or (800) 87-GLEIM.

Groundwood Paper and Highlighters — All Gleim books are printed on high quality groundwood paper. We recommend you use a non-bleed-through (dry) highlighter (e.g., the Avery *Glidestick*™ -- ask for it at your local office supply store) when highlighting page items within these books.

REVIEWERS AND CONTRIBUTORS

Garrett Gleim, B.S., CPA (not in public practice), University of Pennsylvania, is one of our vice presidents. Mr. Gleim coordinated the production staff, reviewed the manuscript, and provided production assistance throughout the project.

Grady M. Irwin, J.D., is a graduate of the University of Florida College of Law, and he has taught in the University of Florida College of Business. Mr. Irwin provided substantial editorial assistance throughout the project.

John F. Rebstock, B.S.A., is a graduate of the Fisher School of Accounting at the University of Florida. He has passed the CIA and CPA exams. Mr. Rebstock reviewed portions of the manuscript.

Stewart B. White, B.M., *Cum Laude*, University of Richmond, B.S., Virginia Commonwealth University, has passed the CPA and CISA exams and has worked in the fields of retail management, financial audit, IT audit, COBOL programming, and data warehouse management. He extensively revised portions of this manuscript.

A PERSONAL THANKS

This manual would not have been possible without the extraordinary effort and dedication of Jacob Brunny, Kyle Cadwallader, Julie Cutlip, Mumbi Ngugi, Eileen Nickl, Teresa Soard, and Joanne Strong, who typed the entire manuscript and all revisions and drafted and laid out the diagrams and illustrations in this book.

The authors appreciate the proofreading and production assistance of Christine Bertrand, Ellen Buhl, Kimberly Ferrero, Katherine Goodrich, James Harvin, Jean Marzullo, Shane Rapp, Victoria Rodriguez, and Martha Willis.

The authors also appreciate the critical reading assistance of Christy Carlson, Will Clamons, Margaret Curtis, Ellie Gonzalez, and Holly Johnson.

Finally, we appreciate the encouragement, support, and tolerance of our families throughout this project.

NONDISCLOSED EXAM

The CMA is a nondisclosed exam, and you will encounter questions that may be totally unfamiliar to you. That is the nature of nondisclosed exams. Please follow the study suggestions on pages 11 through 14. We have the best and most efficient CMA exam prep system for success.

FOURTEENTH EDITION

GLEIM's

CMA Review

Part 4
Business Applications

by

Irvin N. Gleim, Ph.D., CPA, CIA, CMA, CFM

and

Dale L. Flesher, Ph.D., CPA, CIA, CMA, CFM

ABOUT THE AUTHORS

Irvin N. Gleim is Professor Emeritus in the Fisher School of Accounting at the University of Florida and is a member of the American Accounting Association, Academy of Legal Studies in Business, American Institute of Certified Public Accountants, Association of Government Accountants, Florida Institute of Certified Public Accountants, The Institute of Internal Auditors, and the Institute of Management Accountants. He has had articles published in the *Journal of Accountancy, The Accounting Review,* and *The American Business Law Journal* and is author/coauthor of numerous accounting and aviation books and CPE courses.

Dale L. Flesher is the Arthur Andersen Alumni Professor in the School of Accountancy at the University of Mississippi and has written over 300 articles for business and professional journals, including *Management Accounting, Journal of Accountancy*, and *The Accounting Review*, as well as numerous books. He is a member of the Institute of Management Accountants, American Institute of Certified Public Accountants, The Institute of Internal Auditors, American Accounting Association, and American Taxation Association. He is a past editor of *The Accounting Historians' Journal* and is a trustee and past president of the Academy of Accounting Historians.

Gleim Publications, Inc.
P.O. Box 12848
University Station
Gainesville, Florida 32604
(800) 87-GLEIM or (800) 874-5346
(352) 375-0772
FAX: (352) 375-6940
Internet: www.gleim.com
Email: admin@gleim.com

This is the first printing of the fourteenth edition of **CMA Review: Part 4**. Please email update@gleim.com with **CMA 4 14-1** included in the subject or text. You will receive our current update as a reply. Updates are available until the next edition is published.

EXAMPLE:

To: update@gleim.com
From: *your email address*
Subject: **CMA 4 14-1**

ISSN: 1093-2577

ISBN: 978-1-58194-664-2

ACKNOWLEDGMENTS

The authors are indebted to the Institute of Certified Management Accountants for permission to use problem materials from past CMA examinations. Questions and unofficial answers from the Certified Management Accountant Examinations, copyright © 1982 through 1997 by the Institute of Management Accountants, are reprinted and/or adapted with permission.

The authors are also indebted to The Institute of Internal Auditors, Inc. for permission to use Certified Internal Auditor Examination Questions and Suggested Solutions, copyright © 1985 through 1996 by The Institute of Internal Auditors, Inc.

The authors also appreciate and thank the American Institute of Certified Public Accountants, Inc. Material from Uniform Certified Public Accountant Examination questions and unofficial answers, Copyright © 1981-2006 by the American Institute of Certified Public Accountants, Inc., is reprinted and/or adapted with permission.

This publication was printed and bound by Corley Printing Company, St. Louis, MO, a registered ISO-9002 company. More information about Corley Printing Company is available at www.corleyprinting.com or by calling (314) 739-3777.

Visit our website (www.gleim.com) for the latest updates and information on all of our products.

This publication is designed to provide accurate and authoritative information with regard to the subject matter covered. It is sold with the understanding that the publisher is not engaged in rendering legal, accounting, or other professional service.

If legal advice or other expert assistance is required, the services of a competent professional person should be sought.

(From a declaration of principles jointly adopted by a Committee of the American Bar Association and a Committee of Publishers.)

TABLE OF CONTENTS

PREFACE FOR CMA PART 4 CANDIDATES

CONGRATULATIONS on passing Parts 1, 2, and 3. You only have Part 4 to go. We will make it easy with this book, our Test Prep CD-Rom, Gleim Online, and our audios.

The purpose of this book is to help **you** prepare **yourself** to pass Part 4 of the CMA examination. The overriding consideration is to provide an inexpensive, effective, and easy-to-use study program. This manual

1. Defines topics tested on Part 4 of the CMA exam.

2. Explains how to optimize your exam score by analyzing how Part 4 of the CMA exam is constructed, administered, and graded.

3. Lists the IMA Learning Outcome Statements of the Parts 1, 2, and 3 subject matter, which is the material tested on Part 4 of the CMA exam, and outlines them into 20 easy-to-use study units.

4. Presents scenarios with 292 essay questions to prepare you to answer questions on Part 4 of the CMA exam. The answer explanations are presented on the page following the question for your convenience.

5. Illustrates individual question-answering techniques to minimize selecting incorrect answers and to maximize your exam score.

6. Suggests exam-taking techniques to help you maintain control and achieve success.

This is the Fourteenth Edition of *CMA Review* for Part 4, which covers only Part 4 of the CMA exam. This new edition includes the following features and benefits:

1. Gleim's content and structure are organized to closely follow the IMA's Learning Outcome Statements (LOSs), thus ensuring your study time is spent preparing to Pass the Exam!

2. Core Concepts at the end of each Knowledge Transfer Outline (or, for the review study units, after the LOSs) allow CMA candidates to obtain an overview of each study unit, as well as ensure that they understand the basic concepts.

3. Many examples throughout the Knowledge Transfer Outlines in Study Units 1-9 clarify harder-to-understand concepts.

4. Comprehensive coverage of all topics, including Statement of Financial Accounting Standards 154, the IMA's *Statement of Ethical Professional Practice*, and information technology.

To maximize the efficiency of your review program, begin by **studying** (not reading) the introduction in this book. "Preparing for and Taking the CMA Exam" is very short but very important. It has been carefully organized and written to provide you with important information to assist you in successfully completing Part 4 of the CMA examination.

Thank you for your interest in our review materials. We very much appreciate the thousands of letters and suggestions we have received from CIA, CMA, and CPA candidates since 1974. Please give us feedback concerning this book. Do NOT disclose information about individual questions beyond subject matter not covered in our books. Tell us which part and which topics were NOT covered or were inadequately covered. The last page has been designed to help you note corrections and suggestions throughout your study process. Please tear it out and mail or fax it to us with your comments.

Finally, THANK YOU for recommending our products to others.

Good Luck on the Exam,

Irvin N. Gleim
Dale L. Flesher
June 2008

PREPARING FOR AND TAKING THE CMA EXAM

ABOUT THE CMA EXAM

Introduction

CMA is the acronym for Certified Management Accountant.

The CMA examination has been and will continue to be developed and offered by the Institute of Certified Management Accountants (ICMA) in approximately 200 locations in the U.S. and an additional 200 international locations.

The CMA exam consists of four parts: Business Analysis, Management Accounting and Reporting, Strategic Management, and Business Applications. Parts 1, 2, and 3 must be successfully completed before the candidate can register for Part 4. Holders of certain professional certifications may be granted a waiver for Part 1 (Business Analysis).

CMA Review: Part 4 contains this 20-page Introduction and 20 study units of outlines, multiple-choice questions, and essay questions that cover all of the material tested on Part 4 of the CMA exam. This Introduction discusses exam content, pass rates, administration, organization, background information, preparing for the CMA exam, and taking the CMA exam. We urge you to read the next 19 pages carefully because they will help you dramatically improve your study and test-taking procedures.

Objectives of the CMA Examination

The CMA certification program has four objectives:

- *To establish management accounting as a recognized profession by identifying the role of the management accountant and financial manager, the underlying body of knowledge, and a course of study by which such knowledge is acquired;*
- *To encourage higher educational standards in the management accounting field;*
- *To establish an objective measure of an individual's knowledge and competence in the field of management accounting; and*
- *To encourage continued professional development by management accountants.*

The exam tests the candidates' knowledge and ability with respect to the current state of the fields of management accounting and financial management.

We have arranged the subject matter tested on the CMA examination into 20 study units for each part. Each part is presented in a separate book. All of these books contain review outlines and prior CMA exam questions and answers.

Requirements to Attain the CMA Designation

The CMA designation is granted only by the ICMA. Candidates must complete the following steps to become a CMA:

1. Become a member of the Institute of Management Accountants. You can submit an application for IMA membership with your application for certification.

2. Complete the certification information section on the IMA application and register for the CMA examination.

3. Pass all four parts of the CMA examination. "Continuous candidacy" is required to retain credit after successful completion of one or more parts. "Continuous candidacy" includes IMA membership, and candidates must pass all four parts of the exam within 4 years. The 4-year period begins with the first part passed.

4. Fulfill or expect to fulfill the education requirements (see next page).

5. Be employed or expect to be employed in a position that meets the experience requirement (see below).

6. Provide two character references proving you are of good moral character.

7. Comply with the IMA's Statement of Ethical Professional Practice.

Credit can be retained indefinitely as long as these requirements are fulfilled. Once a designation is earned, the CMA is a member of the Institute of Certified Management Accountants and must comply with the program's CPE requirement and maintain IMA membership in good standing.

Education and Experience Requirements

Candidates seeking admission to the CMA program must meet one of the following educational credentials:

1. Hold a bachelor's degree, in any area, from an accredited college or university. Degrees from foreign institutions must be evaluated by an independent agency approved by the ICMA (visit www.imanet.org/certification_started_education_partial_Int.asp for a list of foreign universities that are acceptable without an evaluation); or

2. Pass the U.S. CPA examination or hold another professional qualification issued in a foreign country that is comparable to the CPA, CMA, etc.; or

3. Achieve a score in the 50th percentile or higher on either the Graduate Management Admission Test (GMAT) or the Graduate Record Examination (GRE).

NOTE: Educational credentials may be submitted when applying or within 7 years of passing the examination. The educational credentials must qualify in order to be certified.

Two continuous years of **professional experience** in financial management and/or management accounting are required any time prior to or within 7 years of passing the examination.

1. Professional experience shall be defined as full-time continuous experience at a level where judgments are regularly made that employ the principles of financial management and/or management accounting, e.g.,

    a. Financial analysis
    b. Budget preparation
    c. Management information systems analysis
    d. Financial management
    e. Management accounting
    f. Auditing in government, finance, or industry
    g. Management consulting
    h. Auditing in public accounting
    i. Research, teaching, or consulting related to management accounting (for teaching, a significant portion required to be above the principles level)

2. Employment in functions that require the occasional application of financial management or management accounting principles, but are not essentially management accounting oriented, will not satisfy the requirement, e.g.,

    a. Computer operations
    b. Sales and marketing
    c. Manufacturing
    d. Engineering
    e. Personnel
    f. Employment in internships, trainee, clerical, or nontechnical positions

3. Continuous part-time positions of 20 hours per week meeting the definition of qualified experience will count toward the experience requirement at a rate of one year of experience for every two years of part-time employment.

If you have any questions about the acceptability of your work experience or bachelor's degree, please write or call the ICMA. Include a complete description of your situation. You will receive a response from the ICMA as soon as your request is evaluated.

Institute of Certified Management Accountants
10 Paragon Drive
Montvale, NJ 07645-1759
(201) 573-9000
(800) 638-4427

NOTE: The ICMA Board of Regents has compiled a list of U.S. and international certifications for which they will grant a waiver of Part 1. To be granted the waiver, acceptable proof must be supplied to the ICMA along with the appropriate waiver fee of $190. For example, you can waive Part 1 of the CMA exam if you have passed the U.S. CPA exam. To receive the waiver, you must request that a letter from your state board be sent directly to the ICMA confirming your licensure or passing of the U.S. CPA exam; copies are not acceptable. Visit www.imanet.org/certification_started_waivers.asp for the complete listing of accepted certifications.

Content Specification Outlines

The ICMA has developed content specification outlines and has committed to follow them on each examination. Thus, each examination will cover the major topics specified below; e.g., Business Applications will test all of the material on Parts 1, 2, and 3, plus Organization Management, Organization Communication, Behavioral Issues, and Ethics. We predict 6 scenarios with at least one scenario on ethics. Note that each scenario will have about 3 questions.

Candidates for the CMA designation are expected to have a minimum level of business knowledge that transcends all examination parts. This minimum level includes knowledge of basic financial statements, time value of money concepts, and elementary statistics. Specific discussion of the ICMA's Levels of Performance (A, B, and C) is provided below.

ICMA'S CMA CONTENT SPECIFICATION OVERVIEW						
Part 1: Business Analysis			**Part 3: Strategic Management**		
(3 hours – 110 questions)			**(3 hours – 110 questions)**		
Business Economics	25%	Level B	Strategic Planning	15%	Level B
Global Business	20%	Level B	Strategic Marketing	15%	Level A
Internal Controls	15%	Level A	Corporate Finance	25%	Level B
Quantitative Methods	15%	Level B	Decision Analysis	25%	Level C
Financial Statement Analysis	25%	Level B	Investment Decisions	20%	Level C
Part 2: Management Accounting and Reporting			**Part 4: Business Applications (Level C)**		
(4 hours – 140 questions)			**(3 hours – 3-7 scenarios)**		
Budget Preparation	15%	Level C	All topics from Parts 1, 2, and 3 plus:		
Cost Management	25%	Level C	Organization Management		
Information Management	15%	Level A	Organization Communication		
Performance Measurement	20%	Level C	Behavioral Issues		
External Financial Reporting	25%	Level B	Ethical Considerations		

Level of Performance Required

All parts of the exam appear to be tested at the skill level of a final examination for the appropriate course at a good school of business. The ICMA has specified three levels of coverage as reproduced on the next page and indicated in its content specification outlines. You will evaluate and compare the difficulty of each part of the CMA exam as you work the questions in this book.

Authors' Note: Rely on the questions at the end of each study unit in each *CMA Review* book and in *CMA Test Prep* CD-Rom and *CMA Gleim Online*.

Level A: Requiring the skill levels of knowledge and comprehension.

Level B: Requiring the skill levels of knowledge, comprehension, application, and analysis.

Level C: Requiring all six skill levels: knowledge, comprehension, application, analysis, synthesis, and evaluation.

Gleim Study Unit Listing

LISTING OF GLEIM STUDY UNITS*

Part 1: Business Analysis

1. Factors Affecting the Firm
2. Consumption and Production
3. Market Structures and the Market for Inputs
4. Macroeconomic Issues, Measures, and Cycles
5. Government Participation in the Economy
6. Comparative Advantage and Free Trade
7. Trade Barriers and Agreements
8. Foreign Exchange
9. Other Global Business Topics
10. Risk Assessment and Controls
11. Internal Auditing
12. Systems Controls and Security Measures
13. Forecasting Analysis
14. Linear Programming and Network Analysis
15. Probability, Decision Trees, and Other Techniques
16. The Development of Accounting Standards
17. Financial Statement Assurance
18. Liquidity, Capital Structure, and Solvency
19. Return on Investment, Profitability, and Earnings
20. Other Analytical Issues

Part 2: Management Accounting and Reporting

1. Budgeting Concepts and Budget Systems
2. Annual Profit Plan and Supporting Schedules
3. Cost Management Terminology and Concepts
4. Cost Accumulation Systems
5. Cost Allocation Techniques
6. Overview of Information Systems and Systems Development and Design
7. Technology of Information Systems
8. Electronic Commerce and Other Topics
9. Cost and Variance Measures
10. Responsibility Accounting and Financial Measures
11. The Balanced Scorecard and Quality Considerations
12. Overview of External Financial Reporting
13. Cash and Receivables
14. Inventories and Investments
15. Long-Lived Assets
16. Liabilities
17. Equity and Revenue Recognition
18. Other Income Statement Items
19. Business Combinations and Derivatives
20. SEC Requirements and the Annual Report

*WARNING!!!
About 30% of CMA test questions will require mathematical calculations.
Practice computational questions to prepare for exam success!

Part 3: Strategic Management

1. Strategic and Tactical Planning
2. Manufacturing Paradigms
3. Business Process Performance
4. Marketing's Strategic Role within the Firm
5. Marketing Information and Market Segmentation
6. Other Marketing Topics
7. Risk and Return
8. Financial Instruments
9. Cost of Capital
10. Managing Current Assets
11. Financing Current Assets
12. The Decision Process
13. Data Concepts Relevant to Decision Making
14. Cost-Volume-Profit Analysis
15. Marginal Analysis
16. Cost-Based Pricing
17. The Capital Budgeting Process
18. Discounted Cash Flow and Payback
19. Ranking Investment Projects
20. Risk Analysis and Real Options

Part 4: Business Applications

1. Organization Structures
2. Jobs and Teams
3. Leadership Styles and Sources of Power
4. Motivational Theories and Diversity Issues
5. Organization Communication
6. Behavior – Alignment of Organizational Goals
7. Behavior – Budgeting and Standard Setting
8. Behavior – Reporting and Performance Evaluation
9. Ethics as Tested on the CMA Exam
10. Part 1 Review – Business Economics and Global Business
11. Part 1 Review – Internal Controls and Quantitative Methods
12. Part 1 Review – Financial Statement Analysis
13. Part 2 Review – Budget Preparation and Cost Management
14. Part 2 Review – Information Management and Performance Measurement
15. Part 2 Review – External Financial Reporting I
16. Part 2 Review – External Financial Reporting II
17. Part 3 Review – Strategic Planning and Strategic Marketing
18. Part 3 Review – Corporate Finance
19. Part 3 Review – Decision Analysis
20. Part 3 Review – Investment Decisions

Each study unit begins with the Learning Outcome Statements from the Institute of Management Accountants, followed by our Knowledge Transfer Outline, then our Core Concepts, and finally essay questions.

The *CMA Review* study unit titles and organization differ somewhat from the subtopic titles used by the ICMA in its content specification outlines (see the next page) for the CMA exam. The selection of study units for *CMA Review: Part 4* is based on the types and number of questions that have appeared on past CMA exams, as well as the extensiveness of past and expected future exam coverage as defined in both the ICMA Content Specification Outlines and Learning Outcome Statements.

Learning Outcome Statements

In addition to the Content Specification Outlines, the ICMA has published Learning Outcome Statements (LOSs) that specify what you should be able to do. Before you study our knowledge transfer outline, read the LOS at the beginning of each study unit. This will alert you to what is expected and required of you.

Conceptual vs. Calculation Questions

About 30% of CMA test questions will be calculations in contrast to conceptual questions. When you take the test, it may appear that more than 40% of the questions are calculation-type because they take longer and are "more difficult." The ICMA has approved the use of two new calculators (see page 18) to assist in this area. As an additional benefit, beginning in Spring of 2009, the exam will include a new spreadsheet function to assist with calculations, including net present value.

How Ethics Are Tested

Ethical issues and considerations will be tested on Part 4, Business Applications. At least one (essay) question in this part will be devoted to an ethical situation presented in a business-oriented context. Candidates will be expected to evaluate the issues involved and make recommendations for the resolution of the situation.

The Institute of Management Accountants (IMA)

Conceived as an educational organization to develop the individual management accountant professionally and to provide business management with the most advanced techniques and procedures, the IMA was founded as the National Association of Cost Accountants in 1919 with 37 charter members. It grew rapidly, with 2,000 applications for membership in the first year, and today it is the largest management accounting association in the world, with approximately 67,000 members and more than 230 chapters in the U.S. and 10 abroad.

The IMA has made major contributions to business management through its continuing education program, with courses and seminars conducted in numerous locations across the country; its two magazines, *Strategic Finance*, which is a monthly publication, and *Management Accounting Quarterly*, which is a new online journal; other literature, including research reports, monographs, and books; a technical inquiry service; a library; the annual international conference; and frequent meetings at chapter levels.

Membership in the IMA is open to all persons interested in advancing their knowledge of accounting or financial management. It is required for CMA candidates and CMAs.

IMA Dues in the USA, Canada, and Mexico* (as of January 1, 2008)

1. **Regular:** 1 year, $195
2. **Associate:** 1st year, $65
3. **Associate:** 2nd year, $130
4. **Educator:** $98; must be a full-time faculty member and reside in the U.S., Canada, or Mexico
5. **Student:** $39; must have 6 or more equivalent hours per semester and reside in the U.S., Canada, or Mexico

* All new members (except Students and Associates) also pay a one-time registration fee of $15.

Membership application forms may be obtained by writing the Institute of Management Accountants, 10 Paragon Drive, Montvale, NJ 07645-1718, or calling (201) 573-9000 or (800) 638-4427. A sample of the two-page form appears in Appendix A on pages 480 and 481. Or, visit the IMA's website and complete the form online.

The Institute of Certified Management Accountants (ICMA)

The ICMA is located at the IMA headquarters in Montvale, New Jersey. The only function of the ICMA is to offer and administer the CMA designations. The staff consists of the managing director, the director of examinations, and support staff. The ICMA occupies about 2,000 square feet of office space in the IMA headquarters. This office is where new examination questions are prepared and where all records are kept.

ICMA Board of Regents Staff

The ICMA Board of Regents is a special committee of the IMA established to direct the CMA programs for management accountants through the ICMA.

The Board of Regents consists of 16 regents, one of whom is designated as chair by the president of the IMA. The regents are appointed by the president of the IMA to serve 3-year terms. Membership on the Board of Regents rotates, with one-third of the regents being appointed each year. The regents usually meet twice a year for 1 or 2 days.

The managing director of the ICMA, the director of examinations, and the ICMA staff are located at the ICMA office in Montvale, NJ. They undertake all of the day-to-day work with respect to the CMA programs.

How to (1) Apply and (2) Register for the CMA Exam

First, you are required to **apply both for membership** in the IMA **and for admission** into the Certification Program (see sample application form in Appendix A on pages 482 and 483).

Apply to join the IMA and the Certification Program **today** -- it takes only a few minutes. Application to the certification program requires education, employment, and reference data. The educational and experience requirements are discussed on pages 3 and 4. You must provide two references if requested: one from your employer and the second from someone other than a family member or fellow employee. An official transcript providing proof of graduation also is required after you have completed the exams. There is a $200 Certification Entrance Fee ($75 for students), and everyone who enters the certification program by paying the fee receives four electronic books in .pdf format that contain sample questions and exam content information and a knowledge assessment exam. Once a person has become a candidate, there is no participant's fee other than IMA membership dues, unless a candidate does not complete the exam within 4 years, in which case the entrance fee must be paid again to take the exam.

Second, it is necessary to **register** each time you wish to sit for the exams. The exam registration form (see pages 480 and 481) is very simple (it takes about 2 minutes to complete). The registration fee for each part of the exam is $190. Graduating seniors, full-time graduate students, and full-time faculty are charged special rates as discussed below.

Order a registration booklet and IMA membership application form from the ICMA at (800) 638-4427, extension 510. The IMA encourages candidates to view information and complete an IMA application and exam registration forms online. Visit the IMA's website at www.imanet.org for more information.

Special Student Examination Fee

U.S., Canadian, and Mexican college students may take up to four examinations at $95 per part (versus the normal $190). These discounts must be used within the year following application or they will be forfeited. To be eligible for this discount, students must

1.   Provide the name of someone who can verify student status.
2.   Apply to the ICMA while enrolled in school.
3.   Upon graduation, arrange for an official copy of your transcript to be sent to the ICMA.

Fees for Full-Time Professors

Full-time faculty members are permitted to take up to four examination parts once at no charge. The fee for any parts that must be retaken is 50% of the normal fee. To qualify, a faculty member must submit a letter on school stationery affirming his/her full-time status. Faculty should sit for the CMA examinations because a professor's status as a CMA encourages students to enter the program. Full-time doctoral students who plan to pursue a teaching career are treated as faculty members for purposes of qualifying for the free examination.

CMA Test Administration

After registering for an exam part, the ICMA will send you authorization to take the exam. Until December 31, 2008, candidates have 120 days from receipt of authorization to sit for the exam, and the exam is offered year-round (except for Part 4, which is only offered in the second month of every calendar quarter). Beginning January 1, 2009, however, the authorization period will shorten so that candidates will have a 60-day window for Parts 1, 2, and 3 and a 30-day window for Part 4. The periods during which the exam parts are available will also change (see table below for testing windows as of January 1, 2009). The authorization will instruct you to call the Prometric registration office at (800) 479-6370 and register for your test at a local Prometric testing center. You may also register online at www.prometric.com. Call your testing center a day or two before your test to confirm your time and obtain directions to the testing center or visit www.prometric.com.

January and February:	Parts 1, 2, and 3
March:	No exam parts
April:	Part 4 only
May and June:	Parts 1, 2, and 3
July:	No exam parts
August:	Part 4 only
September and October:	Parts 1, 2, and 3
November:	No exam parts
December:	Part 4 only

DOMESTIC INSTRUCTIONS TO CANDIDATES

The letter accompanying these instructions is your authorization to schedule the taking of your examination part(s) with Prometric. Please note that you have a separate authorization number for each part that you registered to take. Questions regarding your registration with ICMA should be directed to 800-638-4427, ext. 1521.

You should contact Prometric for your appointment(s) **at your earliest convenience**, as ICMA is not responsible if you delay scheduling and there are no longer appointments available within your authorization period.

Scheduling with Prometric

The interval dates shown on your authorization letter represent the time/authorization period during which you are authorized to take CMA examination part(s).

- Before contacting Prometric, select two or three dates during your authorization period that are convenient for you to take the examination in case your first choice is not available. Please be aware that Saturdays fill quickly and you may not be able to get a Saturday appointment.
- Choose a Prometric Center by checking the list of sites at www.prometric.com or ask the Prometric Call Center representative to suggest a center close to your home or office.
- Be sure you have your authorization number(s) from the accompanying letter handy, as you will be required to provide this information.
- To schedule your examination, you can log onto the Internet 24 hours, 7 days a week by visiting www.prometric.com. You can also call Prometric's Candidate Service Call Center at 800-479-6370 or the local Prometric Testing Center of your choice. Online is the recommended choice to schedule your test.
- Once you have scheduled your appointment, it is strongly suggested that you confirm the date and time of your appointment by visiting www.prometric.com and selecting the View/Print Appointment option.

Reschedule or Cancellation of a Scheduled Appointment

If you find that you are unable to keep a scheduled appointment at Prometric or wish to move your appointment to another date, **you must do so three business days** before the appointment. To cancel or reschedule your appointment, please have your confirmation number ready and visit www.prometric.com or call 800-479-6370 and select option 1 to be directed to the automated system. Both options are available 24 hours, 7 days a week. If you cancel an appointment, you must wait 72 hours before calling to make a new appointment. If you do not comply with this **reschedule/cancellation policy**, you will be considered a "no-show" and you will need to reregister with ICMA and REPAY the examination fee.

Cancellation Examples

- If your exam date is on Friday at 3 pm, you must cancel by noon on the Tuesday before your scheduled appointment date.
- If your exam date is on Thursday at 8 am, you must cancel by 8 am on the Monday before your scheduled appointment date.
- If your exam date is on Saturday at 10 am, you must cancel by 10 am on the Wednesday before your scheduled appointment date.
- Upon written request, ICMA will consider limited time period extensions of the authorization period. For a processing fee of $60, ICMA can grant a one-time 60-day extension for parts 1, 2, and 3. For a processing fee of $50, ICMA can grant a one-time extension to the following monthly testing window for part 4.

ICMA Credit Policy

If you do not take an examination within the authorized time period, you will not receive any credit for your exam fees. However, students and faculty who registered at a discounted fee will have their discounts restored for future use.

General Instructions

- You should arrive at the Prometric Testing Center **30 minutes** before the time of your appointment. If you are more than 15 minutes late for your scheduled appointment, you may lose your scheduled sitting and be required to reschedule at a later date at an additional cost.
- You will be required to sign the Prometric Log Book when you enter the center.
- For admission to the examination, you will be required to present **two** forms of identification, one with a photograph, both with your signature. Approved IDs are a passport, driver's license, military ID, credit card with photo, or company ID. Student IDs are **not** acceptable. You **will not be** permitted into the examination without proper identification.
- Small lockers are available at the test centers for personal belongings. Items such as purses, briefcases, and jackets will not be allowed in the testing room.
- Small battery or solar powered electronic calculators restricted to a maximum of six functions - addition, subtraction, multiplication, division, square root, and percent - are allowed. The calculator must be non-programmable and must not use any type of tape. Candidates may alternatively choose to bring either a Texas Instruments BAII Plus or a Hewlett Packard 10bII calculator. Candidates **will not** be allowed to use calculators that do not comply with these restrictions.
- Candidates will receive ONE scratch paper booklet initially during their examination. However, if you require more sheets during the exam in order to complete calculations, you should raise your hand and ask the test center personnel for ONE additional booklet. Candidates are able to keep one used booklet in case they need to refer back to previous calculations. Candidates will be permitted to trade in ONE or TWO used booklets for ONE or TWO new booklets. Candidates are only permitted to have TWO booklets at any given time. The test center personnel will then collect and destroy ALL booklets from each candidate at the end of their testing session.
- The test center will provide pencils for use in making calculations, etc., on the provided scratch paper booklet(s).
- The staff at the Prometric Testing Center is not involved in the development of the examination or the procedures governing the evaluation of your performance. Questions or comments on the examination content or performance evaluation should be directed only to the ICMA, as this is a nondisclosed examination.
- At the beginning of your test administration, you will be given the opportunity to take a tutorial that introduces the testing screens; the tutorial is not part of your testing time and may be repeated if the candidate wishes; however, total tutorial time is limited.
- Upon completion of each examination part, your performance results will be displayed on the screen, and you will also receive a printed and embossed copy of your results before leaving the testing center. (Part 4 "Revised" - Business Applications is graded offline and there is no immediate performance feedback. Grades are mailed to candidates approximately 30 days after each testing period.)

Computer Testing Procedures

When you arrive at the computer testing center, you will be required to check in. Be sure to bring your authorization letter and two forms of identification, one with a photograph, both with your signature. If you have any questions, please call the IMA at (800) 638-4427.

Next, you will be taken into the testing room and seated at a computer terminal. You will be provided with pencils and scrap paper. You are permitted to use a 6-function, non-programmable calculator; a Texas Instruments BAII Plus calculator; or a Hewlett Packard 10bII calculator. A person from the testing center will assist you in logging on the system, and you will be asked to confirm your personal data. Then you will be prompted and given an online introduction to the computer testing system and you will view a tutorial.

If you have used our *CMA Test Prep* CD-Rom, you will be conversant with the computer testing methodology and environment, and you will probably want to skip the tutorial and begin the actual test immediately. Once you begin your test, you will be allowed 3 hours to complete the actual test. You may take a break during the exam, BUT the clock continues to run during your break. Before you leave the testing center, you will be required to check out of the testing center.

ICMA Refund Policy

If you do not take an examination within the authorized time period, you will not receive any credit for your exam fees. However, students and faculty who registered at a discounted fee will have their discounts restored for future use.

Pass/Fail and Grade Reports

"Candidates are given different 'forms' of the exam and it is therefore necessary to establish a passing score for each form, taking into consideration the relative difficulty of the items contained in each form. In order to equate all scores for all forms of the exam, the scores for each part are placed along a scale from 200 to 700. On this scale, a score of 500 represents the minimum passing scaled score. One form of the exam might require a passing percentage of 70% and another a passing percentage of 65%; both of these passing percentages would represent a scaled score of 500. The scaled score allows candidates to know how they performed in relation to the passing standard of 500." If you fail the exam, you may register to take it again as soon as you like. However, you may not sit for any part more than three times in a one-year period.

Maintaining Your CMA Designation

Membership in the IMA is required to maintain your CMA certificates. The general membership fee is $195. There is no additional participant fee.

Continuing professional education is required of CMAs to maintain their proficiency in the field of managerial accounting. Beginning the calendar year after successful completion of the CMA exams, 30 hours of CPE must be completed, which is about 4 days per year. Qualifying topics include management accounting, corporate taxation, statistics, computer science, systems analysis, management skills, marketing, business law, and insurance.

Credit for hours of study will be given for participation in programs sponsored by businesses, educational institutions, or professional and trade associations at either the national or local level.

Programs conducted by an individual's employer must provide for an instructor or course leader. There must be formal instructional training material. On-the-job training does not qualify. An affidavit from the employer is required to attest to the hours of instruction. The programs may be seminars, workshops, technical meetings, or college courses under the direction of an instructor. The method of instruction may include lecture, discussion, case studies, and teaching aids such as training films and cassettes.

Credit for hours of study may be given for technical articles published in business, professional, or trade journals, and for major technical talks given for the first time before business, professional, or trade organizations. The specific hours of credit in each case will be determined by the Institute.

PREPARING FOR THE CMA EXAM

How Many Parts to Take

We suggest that you take one part at a time. For a list of the Gleim/Flesher study units in each part, see page 5. See page 4 for the ICMA Content Specification Overview for all parts.

CMA Part 1:   Business Analysis
CMA Part 2:   Management Accounting and Reporting
CMA Part 3:   Strategic Management
CMA Part 4:   Business Applications

Candidates can maintain credit for passed parts as long as they maintain continuous candidacy. "Continuous candidacy" includes IMA membership, and candidates must pass all four parts of the exam within 4 years. Note that a candidate receives 12 hours of continuing professional education for each exam part passed.

How to Study a Study Unit Using Gleim's Complete System

To ensure that you are using your time effectively, we recommend that you follow the steps listed below when using all of the materials together (books, CD-Rom, audios, and Gleim Online):

1. (25-30 minutes) In Gleim Online, complete Multiple-Choice Quiz #1 in 20-25 minutes (excluding the review session). It is expected that your scores will be low on the first quiz.

   a. Immediately following the quiz, you will be prompted to review the questions you marked and/or answered incorrectly. For each question, analyze and understand why you answered it incorrectly. This step is an essential learning activity.

2. (15-30 minutes) Use the audiovisual presentation for an overview of the study unit. The Gleim *CMA Review Audios* can be substituted for audiovisual presentations and can be used while driving to work, exercising, etc.

3. (30-45 minutes) Complete the 30-question True/False quiz. It is interactive and most effective if used prior to studying the Knowledge Transfer Outline.

4. (60 minutes) Study the Knowledge Transfer Outline, specifically the troublesome areas identified from the multiple-choice questions in Gleim Online. The Knowledge Transfer Outlines can be studied either online or from the books.

5. (25-30 minutes) Complete Multiple-Choice Quiz #2 in Gleim Online.

   a. Immediately following the quiz, you will be prompted to review the questions you marked and/or answered incorrectly. For each question, analyze and understand why you answered it incorrectly. This step is an essential learning activity.

6. (40-50 minutes) Complete two 20-question quizzes while in Test Mode from the *CMA Test Prep* CD-Rom.

7. (30-90 minutes) Complete all of the essay questions in at least two scenarios in Gleim Online. (This only applies to Part 4 since there are no essays in Parts 1, 2, and 3.)

When following these steps, you will complete all 20 units in about 80-90 hours. Then spend about 10-20 hours using the *CMA Test Prep* CD-Rom to create customized tests for the problem areas that you identified. To review the entire part before the exam, use the *CMA Test Prep* CD-Rom to create 20-question quizzes that draw questions from all 20 study units. Continue taking 20-question quizzes until you approach a 75%+ proficiency level.

Avoid studying Gleim questions to learn the correct answers. Use questions to help you <u>learn</u> how to answer CMA questions <u>under exam conditions</u>. Expect the unexpected and be prepared to deal with the unexpected. Always take one 20-question test in test mode *before* studying the material in each study unit. These test sessions will allow you to practice answering questions you have not seen before. Become an educated guesser when you encounter questions in doubt; you will outperform the inexperienced exam taker.

After you complete each 20-question test, ALWAYS do a study session of questions you missed. FOCUS on why you selected the incorrect answer, NOT the correct answer. You want to learn from your mistakes during study so you avoid mistakes on the exam.

CMA Gleim Online

CMA Gleim Online is a versatile, interactive, self-study review program delivered via the Internet. With *CMA Gleim Online*, Gleim guarantees that you will pass the CMA exam on your first sitting. It is divided into four courses (one for each part of the CMA exam).

Each course is broken down into 20 individual, manageable study units. Completion time per study unit will vary from 1-5 hours. Each study unit in the course contains an audiovisual presentation, 30 true/false study questions, 10-20 pages of Knowledge Transfer Outlines, and two 20-question multiple-choice quizzes. Essay questions also are included with each study unit in Part 4.

CMA Gleim Online provides you with a Personal Counselor, who will provide support to ensure your competitive edge. *CMA Gleim Online* is a great way to get confidence as you prepare with Gleim. This confidence will continue during and after the exam.

Gleim/Flesher Audio Reviews

Gleim/Flesher *CMA Review* Audios provide a 15- to 40-minute introductory review for each study unit. Each review provides a comprehensive overview of the outline or (for the review study units in Part 4) the LOSs and Core Concepts in the *CMA Review* book. The purpose is to get candidates "started" so they can relate to the questions they will answer before reading the study outlines and/or Core Concepts in each study unit.

The audios are short and to the point, as is the entire Gleim System for Success. We are working to get you through the CMA exam with the minimum time, cost, and frustration. You can listen to an informative discussion about the CMA exam and hear a sample of two audio reviews (Cost-Volume-Profit Analysis and CVP Applications) on our website at www.gleim.com/accounting/demos/.

How to Study a Study Unit (Books and CD-Rom)

1. Gain an overview of the study unit in the book.

   a. Think about the subunit titles on the first page. Study Units 1-9 cover new material and therefore have unique subunits with outlines. Study Units 10-20 are reviews of study units from other parts of the exam. We have reproduced only the IMA's Learning Outcome Statements and Gleim's Core Concepts from our *CMA Review* books for these review study units.

   b. Note the number of pages of outline or the number of LOSs and Core Concepts.

   c. Flip through the outlines or Core Concepts and the essay questions.

   d. Visualize a plan based on 2. and 3. below.

2. Work through the outline or review the Core Concepts. Learn and understand the concepts. Remember, you are aiming toward the analysis, synthesis, and evaluation levels of knowledge, not rote memorization. Study the outlines or Core Concepts with the objective of being able to explain the subject matter to third parties. The actual exam questions will be presented and written differently than the material in this book.

3. After you are comfortable with the outlines or Core Concepts, apply your essay question-answering technique to answer each of the essay questions under simulated exam conditions.

   a. We present the questions on odd-numbered pages and the answers on even-numbered pages.

      1) There will be 2–6 questions about what the ICMA refers to as a "scenario." Expect the same on the exam. Unlike the exam, though, Gleim also provides clarification on the subtopic that each scenario is testing. This addition is to allow you to better pinpoint the concepts you are having difficulty understanding.

   b. Note that the requirements of all questions in each study unit are numbered sequentially (just as you will experience on your exam).

   c. For each scenario, begin by reading each of the requirements carefully.

   d. Visualize how each response will appear, e.g., a list of numbered sentences; one or more short paragraphs; a memo; etc.

   e. Read and study the scenario. You have already read and studied the requirements so you can analyze the scenario with your understanding of the requirements.

   f. At the bottom of the page (following the questions), make an outline of your answer: one or several words to reflect each "grading concept."

   g. Type your answer on your computer (optional).

   h. Proofread and edit your answer just as you will on the exam.

   i. Turn the page and view the "Unofficial Answers."

   j. Underline all of the grading concepts in the Unofficial Answers.

   k. Compare the grading concepts in your answer outline to the grading concepts in the Unofficial Answers.

   l. Compute your grade as the ratio of the number of your appropriate grading concepts over the number of Unofficial Answers grading concepts.

   m. Analyze your performance and how you could have developed a better answer. Does your answer look like the Unofficial Answer?

4. Learning from questions you answer less than 100% is very important. Analysis of each question you answer is an <u>opportunity</u> to improve your results on the CMA exam. Thus, you should carefully analyze the differences between your answer and the Unofficial Answer provided so you can recognize any weaknesses and take the appropriate corrective action. This study technique may prove to be the difference between passing and failing.

You **must** work on how to improve your essay question-answering technique. Reasons for poor performance include

   a.   Misreading the requirement
   b.   Failing to understand what is required
   c.   Making a math error
   d.   Applying the wrong rule or concept
   e.   Being distracted by other essay questions or scenarios
   f.   Not knowing the subject matter or topic tested
   g.   Inadequate essay question-answering technique

5.   Twenty-question tests in *CMA Test Prep* CD-Rom will help you to focus on your weaker areas. Make it a game: How much can you improve?

Our *CMA Test Prep* forces you to commit to your answer choice before looking at answer explanations; thus, you are preparing under true exam conditions. It also keeps track of your time and performance history for each study unit, which is available in either a table or graphical format.

Simplify the exam preparation process by following our suggested steps below and on the next page. DO NOT omit the step in which you diagnose the reasons for answering questions incorrectly; i.e., learn from your mistakes while studying so you avoid making similar mistakes on the CMA exam.

   a.   In test mode, answer a 20-question diagnostic test from each study unit before studying any other information.

   b.   Study the Knowledge Transfer Outline for the corresponding study unit in your Gleim/Flesher book. Place special emphasis on the weaker areas that you identified with the initial diagnostic quiz in Step 1.

   c.   Take two or three 20-question tests in test mode after you have studied the Knowledge Transfer Outline.

   d.   Immediately following the quiz, you will be prompted to review the questions you marked and/or answered incorrectly. For each question, analyze and understand why you answered it incorrectly. This step is an essential learning activity.

   e.   Continue this process until you approach a predetermined proficiency level, e.g., 75%+.

   f.   Modify this process to suit your individual learning process.

Study Plan and Time Budget

Complete one study unit at a time. For Study Units 1-8, initially budget 2 hours per study unit (90 minutes on the learning outcome statements and studying the outline, plus 30 minutes on one scenario from each study unit). Allocate 3 hours for Study Unit 9 on ethics (90 minutes on the outline, plus 30 minutes each on 3 scenarios). For Study Units 10-20, select 11 scenarios in total, and budget 30 minutes for each of the 11 selected scenarios. Depending on your background, you may need more or less time to prepare.

This Introduction	2
Study Units 1-8 at an average of 2 hours each	16
Study Unit 9 at 3 hours	3
Study Units 10-20 at 2 hours each	22
General review	10
Total Hours	53

Each week, you should evaluate your progress and review your preparation plans for the time remaining prior to the exam. Use a calendar to note the exam dates and the weeks to go before the exam. Marking a calendar will facilitate your planning. Review your commitments, e.g., out-of-town assignments, personal responsibilities, etc., and note them on your calendar to assist you in keeping to your schedule.

Control: How To Be in

You have to be in control to be successful during exam preparation and execution. Control can also contribute greatly to your personal and other professional goals. The objective is to improve performance as well as be confident that the best possible performance is being generated. Control is a process whereby you improve performance as well as

1. Develop expectations, standards, budgets, and plans.
2. Undertake activity, production, study, and learning.
3. Measure the activity, production, output, and knowledge.
4. Compare actual activity with expected and budgeted activity.
5. Modify the activity, behavior, or study to better achieve the desired outcome.
6. Revise expectations and standards in light of actual experience.
7. Continue the process or restart the process in the future.

Most accountants study this process in relation to standard costs, i.e., establish cost standards and compute cost variances. Just as it helps them in their jobs, the control process will help you pass the CMA exam.

Every day you rely on control systems implicitly. For example, when you groom your hair, you use a control system. You have expectations about the desired appearance of your hair and the time required to style it. You monitor your progress and make adjustments as appropriate. The control process, however, is applicable to all of your endeavors, both professional and personal. You should refine your personal control processes specifically toward passing the CMA exam.

Unless you are a natural at something, most endeavors will improve with explicit control. This is particularly true with the CMA exam.

1. Develop an explicit control system over your study process.

2. Practice your question-answering techniques (and develop control) as you prepare solutions to practice questions/problems during your study program.

3. Plan to use the Gleim Time Management System at the exam.

Essay Question-Answering Technique

The following tactical suggestions are to assist you in maximizing your score on Part 4 of the CMA exam. Remember, knowing how to take the exam and how to answer individual questions is as important as studying/reviewing the subject matter tested on the exam.

1. **Budget your time.**

    a. We make this point with emphasis. Just as you would fill up your gas tank prior to reaching empty, so too should you finish your exam before time expires.

    b. You have 180 minutes to answer about 18 questions on six scenarios. Time will be allocated to scenarios, not questions. For example:

        1 scenario @ 30 min. =   30 min.
        2 scenarios @ 45 min. =   90 min.
        3 scenarios @ 20 min. =   60 min.
        6 scenarios @ 30 min. = 180 min.

    NOTE: It is probable that some scenarios will have one, two, or four questions rather than three questions.

c.   Use your first sheet of scratch paper to prepare a Gleim Time Control Sheet (see below). Along the top of the sheet, write:

<u>Scenario</u>   <u>Questions</u>   <u>Time</u>   <u>Start</u>   <u>Finish</u>   <u>Comments</u>

Number the scenarios one inch apart to leave you plenty of space for your notes. One of Prometric's introductory screens will provide a list of scenarios (with the number of questions) and suggested time for each.

Fill out the first three columns in the Gleim Time Control Sheet (GTCS).

d.   On your Prometric computer screen, the time remaining (starting with 3:00:00, or 180 minutes) appears at the upper right corner of your screen. Enter 180 on your GTCS.

Gleim Time Control Sheet

Fill in these three columns when you begin the exam (from the Prometric Intro Screen)   *Fill in these columns as you start and complete each scenario.*

Scenario	Questions	Time	Start	Finish	Comments
1	1 2	20	180		
2	3 4	20			
3	5 6 7	20			

Note that the image above is an example only. The number of scenarios, number of questions per scenario, and suggested times will vary. It is important to use a sheet of scratch paper as your GTCS to help you manage your time at the exam.

2.   **For each scenario, note the suggested time allocation and number of questions** on your GTCS.

a.   **Read requirements for each question** carefully.

1)   Focusing on what is required enables you to ignore extraneous information.

b.   Allocate 20, 30, or 45 minutes as specified to the scenario amongst the questions associated with the scenario.

c.   On a separate sheet of scratch paper, outline the grading concepts for each of the requirements. Plan on using one sheet for each scenario. Thus, you will need six additional sheets of scratch paper.

d.   Type your answer one question at a time.

e.   Proofread and edit.

3. **Answer questions in sequential order.**

    a. Do **not** agonize over any one question or scenario. Stay within your time budget.

    b. As time permits, you can return to questions previously completed.

4. **Time is precious.** You will likely need all 180 minutes to answer all of the questions. Be prepared to stay at your Prometric computer for the entire 3 hours (i.e., no breaks).

5. **Prometric Computer Screen Layout**

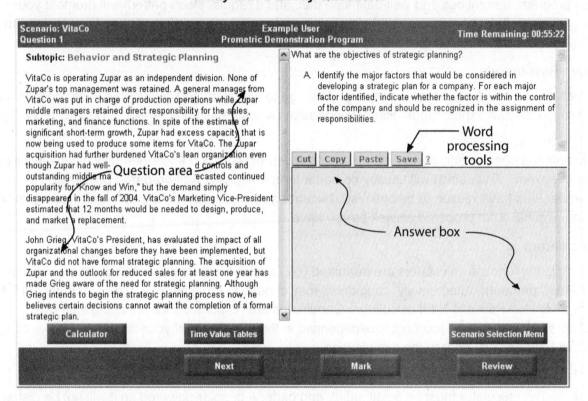

TAKING THE CMA EXAM

CMA Examination Checklist

1. Acquire your study materials. Rely on this book, *CMA Test Prep* CD-Rom, and *CMA Gleim Online*. Consider our audios as a supplement, which can be used while you commute, exercise, etc.

2. **Apply** for membership in the IMA (see pages 480 and 481). **Register** to take the desired part of the exam using the examination registration form (pages 482 and 483) and send it with your applications to the ICMA. Take one part at a time. When you register and pay $190 for a part, you have 60 days to take Parts 1, 2, and 3 and 30 days to take Part 4.* Upon receipt of authorization to take the exam, call Prometric to schedule your test.

3. Plan your preparation process. It's easy. You have 20 study units to complete.

4. Orderly, controlled preparation builds confidence, reduces anxiety, and produces success!

5. PASS THE EXAMINATION (study this Introduction)!

* Authorization periods effective January 1, 2009. Through December 31, 2008, the authorization period is 120 days for all 4 parts.

Logistical and Health Concerns

As soon as the ICMA sends you a computer-based test authorization, call and schedule your test at a convenient time and convenient Prometric testing center. In almost all cases, you should be able to drive to your testing site, take the test, and return home in one day. If the exam is not being given within driving distance of your home, call Prometric Technology Centers to inquire about accommodations. Stay by yourself at a hotel to be assured of avoiding distractions. The hotel room should be soundproof and have a comfortable bed and desk suitable for study. If possible, stay at a hotel with the recreational facilities you normally use, e.g., a swimming pool.

Proper exercise, diet, and rest in the weeks before you take your exam are very important. High energy levels, reduced tension, and an improved attitude are among the benefits. A good aerobic fitness program, a nutritious and well-balanced diet, and a regular sleep pattern will promote your long-term emotional and physical well-being, as well as contribute significantly to a favorable exam result. Of course, the use of health-undermining substances should be avoided.

Exam Psychology

Plan ahead and systematically prepare. Then go to the exam and give it your best: neither you nor anyone else can expect more. Having undertaken a systematic preparation program, you will do fine.

Maintain a positive attitude and do not become depressed if you encounter difficulties before or during the exam. An optimist will usually do better than an equally well-prepared pessimist. Remember, you have reason to be optimistic because you will be competing with many less-qualified persons who have not prepared as well as you have.

Calculators

Simple six-function calculators are permitted (i.e., addition, subtraction, multiplication, division, square root, percent). Alternatively, candidates may choose to bring either a Texas Instruments BAII Plus or a Hewlett Packard 10bII calculator. Candidates are responsible for providing their own calculators. You should be thoroughly experienced in the operations of your calculator. Make sure it has fresh batteries just prior to the examination.

1. Consider bringing a backup calculator with you.
2. The calculator must be small, quiet, and battery- or solar-powered so it will not be distracting to other candidates.
3. The calculator may have a memory. However, the memory must be temporary and erase when the memory is cleared or the calculator is turned off.
4. The calculator must not use any type of tape.
5. The calculator must be nonprogrammable.
6. Nonconforming calculators and calculator instruction books are not permitted.
7. We suggest that you study using the calculator that you will be bringing to the exam so that you are completely comfortable using it.

Examination Tactics

1. Remember to bring your authorization and appropriate identification to the exam site. The photo ID requirement is strictly enforced.

2. Arrive at the test center at least 30 minutes prior to the scheduled exam time to allow for orientation and check-in procedures. Your appointment may be canceled if you are more than 15 minutes late.

3. Dressing for exam success means emphasizing comfort, not appearance. Be prepared to adjust for changes in temperature, e.g., to remove or put on a sweater.

4. Do not bring notes, this text, other books, etc., into the Prometric testing center. You will only make yourself nervous and confused by trying to cram the last 5 minutes before the exam. Books are not allowed in the testing room, anyway. You should, however, bring an appropriate calculator.

5. Adequate scratch paper and pencils are provided. You must turn in your scratch paper as you leave the exam site. Any breath mints, gum, etc., should be in your pocket as they may distract other persons taking the test.

6. As soon as you complete the exam, we would like you to email, fax, or write to us with your comments on our books, CD-Rom, audios, and Gleim Online. We are particularly interested in which topics need to be added or expanded in our materials. We are NOT asking about specific CMA questions; rather, we are asking for feedback on our materials.

Recap of CMA Part 4 Exam Coverage

ICMA Major Topics

A. Organization Management

B. Organization Communication

C. Behavioral Issues

D. Ethical Considerations

E. All Topics from Part 1

F. All Topics from Part 2

G. All Topics from Part 3

Gleim/Flesher Study Units

1. Organization Structures
2. Jobs and Teams
3. Leadership Styles and Sources of Power
4. Motivational Theories and Diversity Issues

5. Organization Communication

6. Behavior – Alignment of Organizational Goals
7. Behavior – Budgeting and Standard Setting
8. Behavior – Reporting and Performance Evaluation

9. Ethics as Tested on the CMA Exam

10. Business Economics and Global Business
11. Internal Controls and Quantitative Methods
12. Financial Statement Analysis

13. Budget Preparation and Cost Management
14. Information Management and Performance Measurement
15. External Financial Reporting I
16. External Financial Reporting II

17. Strategic Planning and Strategic Marketing
18. Corporate Finance
19. Decision Analysis
20. Investment Decisions

WARNING!!!

About 30% of CMA test questions will require mathematical calculations. Practice computational questions to prepare for exam success!

GO FOR IT!
IT'S YOURS TO PASS!

STUDY UNIT ONE
ORGANIZATION STRUCTURES

(23 pages of outline)

The relative weight range assigned to any particular topic is not given for Part 4 of the CMA examination. Thus, you will want to prepare well for all subjects. Also, the material in Study Units 1 through 9 are to be incorporated along with the material tested in the first three parts of the examination. Therefore, memorization is less important than integration of subject matter.

This study unit is the **first of four** on **organization management**. The four study units are

Study Unit 1: Organization Structures
Study Unit 2: Jobs and Teams
Study Unit 3: Leadership Styles and Sources of Power
Study Unit 4: Motivational Theories and Diversity Issues

After studying the outline and answering the essay questions, you will have the skills necessary to address the following topics listed in the IMA's Learning Outcome Statements:

Part 4 - Section A. Organization Management, 1. Organization structures

The candidate should be able to:

a. define departmentalization, division of labor, and task specialization
b. identify the various ways to departmentalize tasks, including by process, by product or service, by customer, and by geography
c. define span of control
d. distinguish between line and staff authority
e. distinguish between centralization and decentralization
f. define matrix organization and determine when it might be appropriate to use this organizational structure
g. define bureaucracy
h. identify and define the four management functions of planning, organizing, directing, and controlling
i. define reengineering and determine the best way to reengineer a process
j. demonstrate an understanding of how strategic partnering and outsourcing can benefit a business firm
k. define lean thinking and demonstrate an understanding of its implications for organizational structure
l. apply the principles of organizational design to a managerial scenario
m. analyze a management structure and recommend improvements

1.1 DEPARTMENTALIZATION AND SPAN OF CONTROL

1. **Division of labor** breaks complex processes into their simpler components. This makes **task specialization** by employees possible. However, dividing labor creates a need for efficient coordination of those performing the separate tasks. One response to the problem is departmentalization, which is a form of organizational integration intended to promote coordination. It is the grouping of related activities into significant organizational subsystems.

    a. **Departmentalization by function** is the most widely used. It is found in almost every organization at some level, whether profit-making or nonprofit. The most common departments in profit-making organizations are marketing, production, and finance (though other terms may be used). These often extend upward in the organizational chart to the level below the chief executive.

        1) Advantages include occupational specialization, simplified training, and representation of primary functions at the top level of the organization.

        2) Disadvantages include lack of coordination between primary functions and absence of profit centers within the organization.

    b. **Departmentalization by product** is growing in importance for multiline, large-scale enterprises. It is often an outgrowth of functional departmentalization and permits extensive authority for a division executive over a given product or product line.

        1) Advantages include better use of specialized capital and skills, ease of coordination, simpler assignment of profit responsibility, compatibility with a decentralization strategy, and a basis for allocating capital efficiently to products likely to achieve the best returns.

        2) Disadvantages include the requirement for a greater number of persons with managerial ability, duplication of staff functions, and difficulty in maintaining top management control over operations.

    c. **Departmentalization by customer** allows for service to a particular customer to be provided under the management of a department head. This form of departmentalization seldom appears at the top level of an organizational structure, but it·is often found at middle levels (e.g., the loan officer of a large bank who handles one account exclusively). Customer departmentalization is often found within the sales department of a firm organized by function.

        1) Advantages include increased customer service as a result of the expertise gained in that customer's business and ease in identifying contributions to profit made by different types and locations of customers.

        2) Disadvantages include difficulties in coordination with other units in the organization and pressure to give preferential treatment to any given manager's customers.

    d. **Departmentalization by territory** is favored by national or multinational firms and government agencies with scattered offices or plants.

        1) Advantages include quicker reaction to local market changes, greater familiarity with local problems or unique geographic concerns, and logistical savings in freight costs and travel time.

        2) Disadvantages include more delegation of authority to regional managers, problems of control for headquarters, and duplication of service functions (personnel, purchases, etc.).

    e. **Departmentalization by project** is appropriate for experimental or one-time activities, e.g., the construction of a ship, a large building, or a major design project (such as a military weapons system).

1) Advantages include specialization and ease of communication and coordination of efforts required within a particular project.

2) Disadvantages include need for reorganization at the end of the project, problems of recruitment at the start of the project, and difficulty of maintaining control at the central office.

2. **Span of Control**

a. **Span of control** (span of management or span of authority) is an upper limit to the number of subordinates who can be effectively supervised by one person. Beyond a certain number of subordinates, the effectiveness and efficiency of supervision decreases.

b. The **classical view** holds that the universal span of control is five or six subordinates.

c. The **behavioral school** advocates expanding the span of control if possible. The advantages are

1) Increasing the autonomy and morale of individual workers by reducing the time available to a manager to direct them (the more subordinates per manager, the less time available per subordinate)

2) Decreasing communication problems by reducing organizational levels (given a fixed number of employees, the narrower the span of control, the taller the organization, and the greater the number of levels)

d. The **modern or contingency approach** to span of control identifies the situational variables that determine the span of control, including the

1) Supervisor's training, interests, abilities, personality, time available to supervise, etc.

2) Subordinates' interests, drives, commitment to the job, training, attitudes, aptitudes, etc.

3) Work situation, including the technological process used (job shop, mass production, continuous process), frequency of change in job method, complexity of the task, dependence on the work of others, and supervision required.

4) Organization's environment, including how rapidly it is compelled to change by technological innovation or market pressure and the amount of uncertainty in the environment.

NOTE: Current research indicates that the appropriate span of control varies widely depending on the situation as defined by the factors previously listed.

e. The number of levels in an organization will be greatly influenced by the span of control.

1) **Flat** organizational structures have relatively few levels from top to bottom. Thus, they have wide spans of control.

a) Flat structures provide fast information flow from top to bottom of the organization and increased employee satisfaction.

2) **Tall** organizational structures have many levels between top and bottom. Hence, they have relatively narrow spans of control.

a) Tall structures are faster and more effective at problem resolution than flat structures because of increased frequency of interaction between superior and subordinate and the greater order imposed by the hierarchical structure.

3) Studies do not indicate great advantages for either flat or tall structures.

1.2 LINE AND STAFF RELATIONSHIPS

1.   **Major Approaches to Line and Staff Distinctions**

    a.   The **classical approach** views **line** activities as those directly responsible for the primary function, product, or service of the organization, whereas **staff** members provide support services.

        1)   Production is ordinarily classified as a line activity, although more current writers include sales (marketing) and sometimes finance, depending on the goals of the organization.

        2)   Staff activities are those necessary to the organization but secondary or peripheral to the line functions. These functions assist or advise the line function.

        3)   Confusion arises from this concept because most staff activities are, in fact, essential to the accomplishment of the organization's purpose as recognized in modern (systems) theory.

        4)   Because early classical writers were describing production organizations, the holders of formal line authority were those producing the product.

        5)   Staff were merely hired hands to take the burden of secondary tasks off the shoulders of the production people.

    b.   Behavioral theorists' concerns with authority and its acceptance distinguish their approach to line and staff relationships.

        1)   The **behavioral school** sees exercise of **informal authority** as a very important constraint on formal chains of command.

            a)   Advice offered by senior staff members is akin to a command because they have access to top management and can exercise more informal authority than a junior-level line manager.

            b)   Staff assistants may be perceived as spies rather than assistants.

        2)   Even the classical school acknowledged the dilemma of how to ensure adoption of specialized staff advice without subverting line authority.

            a)   If line management refuses to accept staff's advice, what can top management do?

        3)   A staff group with **advisory** authority can only offer suggestions, prepare plans for consideration by line managers, and study and evaluate organizational performance.

            a)   A staff member often has an area of technical expertise, such as law, industrial labor relations, operations research, or personnel.

            b)   Line managers are not obligated to follow staff advice.

            c)   The staff member's goal is the approval (or rejection) of a complete recommended solution, but a line manager may want a quick fix to a problem rather than a complete solution.

            d)   Consultation by staff members with line personnel while preparing a solution is essential.

            e)   The concept of completed staff work requires that all loose ends be tied up by the staff member.

        4)   A staff group may be given **concurrent** authority, meaning that line management is required to induce the staff experts in specified areas to agree to an action or decision.

            a)   EXAMPLE: A line production manager may be required to obtain a second signature on a lease agreement from the law department, which must concur with terms in the lease.

5) A staff group may be given complete authority in a specialized area, and its specialized activities are separated from line.

    a) Unlike advisory activities, the line manager must use the services of the staff organization.

    b) Examples include information systems, purchasing, and personnel.

6) A staff group may occasionally be given **control** authority. Thus, line authority may be superseded by that of the specialist staff designated by higher levels of management to make certain decisions in the area of staff expertise.

    a) Control staff authority appears to violate classical principles of unity of command.

    b) Ideally, however, there is no violation because the control staff act as agents for the higher-level line manager who has delegated authority to the staff.

        i) EXAMPLE: Quality-control inspectors have the authority to reject marginal products, but because this authority is exercised on behalf of the manufacturing manager, the chain of command actually remains intact.

7) If the organization adopts TQM concepts (see item 12. in Subunit 1.5) with an emphasis on internal as well as external service, line managers and staff personnel may be viewed as having a customer-service provider relationship.

2. A hybrid of the control authority relationship of staff and line is called a **functional** relationship.

    a. Functional authority exists when an individual is given authority outside the normal chain of command for certain specified activities. The individual may be either a line or a staff manager who is a specialist in a particular field.

        1) EXAMPLE: The vice president in charge of sales may be given functional authority over manufacturing executives in scheduling customer orders, packaging, or making service parts available.

    b. Functional authority may be created for numerous reasons when a line manager is not the person best suited to oversee a given activity. Examples are a lack of special knowledge, a lack of ability to supervise processes, a danger of diverse interpretations of policies, etc.

        1) EXAMPLE: The vice president for industrial labor relations may have functional authority over the production manager for the purpose of negotiating a new labor contract, though no line relationship exists at other times.

    c. Functional specialists have the authority to determine the appropriate standards in their own field of specialization and to enforce those standards.

        1) EXAMPLE: The chief engineer of an airline may have the authority to remove airplanes from service, overriding the wishes of the vice president for operations.

3. **Line and Staff Conflicts**

    a. Conflict between line and staff personnel is almost inevitable given the considerable difference in their backgrounds and activities.

        1) These individuals tend to have different training and education, perspectives on the organization, and career and other objectives.

       2)   Line and staff personnel also tend to have different temperaments.

           a)   Line managers are immediately responsible for operating activities. Thus, they place an emphasis on decisive action.

           b)   Staff members have a preference for thorough research and analysis of problems.

   b.   Operating executives with line authority often see a high potential for harm in staff activity. A staff member with vaguely defined authority from a chief executive effectively usurps the authority of departmental managers.

   c.   Staff is not responsible for the success of a line department but only for generating suggestions. If an implemented suggestion fails,

       1)   Line managers will blame the suggestion.
       2)   Staff will blame the poor implementation of the suggestion.

   d.   Setting staff apart from line responsibilities gives them the time and environment in which to think.

       1)   Unfortunately, this separation can also lead to thinking in a vacuum and resultant impracticable or inappropriate suggestions by staff.

   e.   Excessive staff activity may violate the principle of unity of command.

       1)   Subordinates may become confused and wonder whether they are primarily responsible to the staff member or to their line manager.

4.   Line-staff conflicts may be minimized by

   a.   Clearly defining areas of activity and authority.

   b.   Sharply defining the nature and place of line and staff. For example,

       1)   Line may have authority and responsibility.
       2)   Staff may be required to sell their ideas to line.

   c.   Stressing the systems approach to all employees, whether line or staff, to encourage them to work together towards organizational goals.

   d.   Minimizing areas of possible conflict, e.g.,

       1)   Keeping functional authority to a minimum and
       2)   Providing feedback to staff of line's reaction to proposals.

   e.   Using the concept of completed staff work if possible.

       1)   Recommendations should be complete enough to make possible a simple yes-or-no response from line managers.

       2)   Staff members should be problem solvers, not problem creators.

           a)   Incomplete or vague advice creates problems for line managers.

       3)   The essential task of staff is to make the line manager involved look good. This result cannot be accomplished by staff members who insist on taking credit for the success of their ideas.

5.   The **modern approach** to line and staff is based on systems thinking.

   a.   Every position and every task must contribute to the organizational purpose or it should not exist.

   b.   Distinctions between producers and helpers are therefore irrelevant.

   c.   The changing nature of work environments from predominantly production firms to predominantly service providers makes it harder to pinpoint who exactly is responsible for producing.

       1)   EXAMPLE: At a motor inn with the purpose of people-pleasing, who is line and who is staff?

1.3 CENTRALIZATION AND DECENTRALIZATION

1. Centralization concerns the concentration of authority in an organization and the degree and levels at which it occurs.

   a. Centralization and decentralization are relative terms. Absolute centralization or decentralization is impossible.

2. **Classicists** view decentralization with some distrust because they seek to avoid any dilution of control by top managers.

3. **Behaviorists** view decentralization in the same way as delegation, that is, as a good way to improve motivation and morale of lower-level employees.

4. The **modern or contingency view** is that neither centralization nor decentralization is good or bad in itself. The degree to which either is stressed depends upon the requirements of a given situation.

   a. Information. Decisions cannot be decentralized to those who do not have necessary information, e.g., knowledge of job objectives or measures for evaluation of job performance.

   b. Ability. Decisions cannot be decentralized to people who do not have the training, experience, knowledge, or ability to make them.

   c. Timeliness. Decisions requiring a quick response should be decentralized to those near the action.

   d. Degree of coordination. Decentralization should not occur below the organizational level at which coordination must be maintained (e.g., each supervisor on an assembly line cannot be allowed to decide the reporting time for employees).

   e. Significance of decision. Decisions that are of critical importance to the survival of the organization should not be decentralized.

   f. Morale. Decentralization has a positive influence on morale.

5. Decentralization is a philosophy of organizing and managing. Careful selection of which decisions to push down the hierarchy and which to hold at the top is required. There will be a greater degree of decentralization if

   a. The greater number of decisions are made lower down the management hierarchy.
   b. The more important decisions are made lower down the management hierarchy.
   c. Most functions are affected by decisions made at lower levels.
   d. Review or prior approval is required before implementation of a decision.

6. **Implementing Decentralization**

   a. Decentralized structures typically use **return on investment** (ROI) or **profit center** accounting methods. ROI accounting has the following advantages:

      1) It gives an objective measure of the performance of individual managers of decentralized units.
      2) It allows monitoring of performance through **management by exception**.
      3) It permits comparison of performance of decentralized divisions.
      4) It facilitates allocation of resources and rewards to the decentralized divisions.

    b.   ROI measures for decentralized divisions have some limitations, as do other profit-center approaches.

        1)   ROI measures encourage short-run performance to the detriment of long-run survival.

        2)   They encourage division managers to maximize subunit goals to the possible detriment of the total organization.

        3)   Transfer prices between units may be unjust.

        4)   Top management may adversely influence divisional performance by indirect cost allocation decisions.

        5)   Some parts of an organization do not lend themselves to 1-year evaluations (e.g., new product divisions).

        6)   Annual profit objectives in a cyclical industry or economy may be difficult to determine.

        7)   It is frequently impossible to assign responsibilities for deviations from profit objectives beyond the manager's control.

    c.   Decentralization is most easily implemented in organizations with product departmentation based on clearly divisible units. It eliminates extensive transfer-price problems and allows for easier allocation and isolation of overhead.

7. **Advantages of Decentralization**

    a.   Allows greater speed in making operational decisions

    b.   Encourages better communication

    c.   Necessitates understanding of goals throughout the organization (goal congruence)

    d.   Enables identification and training of good decision makers at lower levels

    e.   Builds a large pool of experienced management talent

    f.   Provides many behavioral advantages

        1)   Gains advantages of participation in management

        2)   Gives responsibility and authority to lower-level managers

            a)   Job autonomy is desired by many employees.

            b)   Specific feedback is important for goal-directed people.

        3)   Provides objective feedback

    g.   Frees top management from operating problems, thus allowing them to concentrate on long-term strategy

    h.   Provides a mechanism for allocating resources to profit centers based on ROI applications

    i.   Permits determination of a single comprehensive figure, e.g., ROI or net income, that measures the financial status of the decentralized unit

8. **Disadvantages of Decentralization**

    a.   Strong tendency to focus on short-run results to the detriment of long-run health

    b.   Increased risk of loss of control by top management

    c.   More difficulty in coordinating highly interdependent units

        1)   EXAMPLE: A conglomerate that is highly decentralized, i.e., operates its divisions as totally separate companies, will find it difficult to establish a transfer price for goods manufactured in one division and consumed in another. The consuming division will not believe market prices are equitable, and the producing division will not want to sell for less.

d.   Greater danger of **satisficing** decisions (those that satisfy or suffice but are not optimal) made by a manager who is unable or unwilling to see overall organizational goals and is rewarded for maximizing the performance of the decentralized unit

e.   Less cooperation and communication between competing unit managers

1.4 THE ORGANIZING PROCESS

1.   In *Management*, 9th ed. (Boston: Houghton Mifflin, 2004, pp. 264-265), Robert Kreitner classifies organizations as follows:

   a.   Businesses are engaged in economic activities with the intent to make a profit.

   b.   Nonprofit service organizations, such as charities and universities, serve particular groups of clients. Money may come from donations, appropriations, or grants.

   c.   Mutual benefit organizations are groups that exist to serve their members, e.g., labor unions or political parties.

   d.   Commonweal entities provide a standard service to all members of a population. A public school system is an example.

2.   Organizing is the **design and structuring of tasks and roles** to accomplish organizational goals.

   a.   The roles define the relationships among individuals and groups of individuals within an organization.

   b.   The structuring reflects the division of activities into subactivities. Structuring also integrates these divided activities into a cohesive whole.

3.   The **traditional approach** (also known as classical, structural, or formal) emphasizes authority, responsibility, tasks, hierarchy, span of control, etc.

   a.   The traditional approach to organizing sets up prescribed (or dictated) relationships and then places people in them. "The person is selected to fill the job."

   b.   Management's primary goal is to create profit for the firm.

   c.   Under classical theory, workers are motivated by economic forces, but under modern theory, there are a variety of things that motivate workers.

   d.   Under classical management, workers are viewed more from the viewpoint of McGregor's Theory X (see item 9.a. in Subunit 4.3), while modern theory views workers as being akin to those described under Theory Y (see item 9.b. in Subunit 4.3).

4.   The **behavioral approach** emphasizes the limits, strengths, availability, and interests of the people available.

   a.   The participants provide feedback in the role-definition process.

   b.   This approach is less deterministic than the traditional approach because group dynamics and the feelings of subordinates are included in the process.

   c.   "The job is designed to fit the person."

5.   The **modern (contingency) approach** emphasizes the tailoring of the organization to its unique situation.

   a.   It combines classical and behavioral principles of organization.

   b.   "The job and the person must fit each other."

6. **Unity of objective.** An organizational structure is effective if it facilitates the contribution of individuals toward the attainment of enterprise objectives. Hence, organizational objectives must have been clearly formulated in the planning process.

   a. In other words, the purpose of organizing is goal congruence, ensuring that all individuals in the organization are working toward the same organizational goals.

   b. Organizing also allows management to perform a monitoring function by determining when goals are not achieved and where the problems exist within the organization.

      1) Organizing is the beginning of control.

7. **Efficiency.** An organizational structure is efficient if it facilitates the accomplishment of organizational objectives with minimum resources and fewest unsought consequences. An efficient organizational structure

   a. Maximizes output for a given amount of input
   b. Provides all resources required, whether physical, financial, or human

8. **Effectiveness.** An organization that reaches its goals is effective. However, effectiveness does not consider the cost-benefit criterion. Thus, a process may be both very effective and very inefficient.

   a. Goals usually include being efficient and may include social responsibility.

   b. Effectiveness in meeting organizational objectives and social expectations should occur in the near future, the intermediate future, and the distant future.

9. **Decision making.** The formal decision-making process in organizations is essential to organizing. For coverage of this process, see Gleim's *CMA Review*, Part 3, Study Unit 12.

10. **Elements of organizational structure.** Structure can be defined in terms of complexity, formalization, and centralization.

    a. The following are three kinds of differentiation that contribute to complexity:

       1) **Vertical differentiation** concerns the depth of the organizational hierarchy. The greater the number of levels, the more complex the organization, the greater the potential for information distortion, the more difficult the coordination of management activities, and the slower and less effective the response to changing conditions.

       2) **Horizontal differentiation** concerns the extent to which tasks require special skills and knowledge. The greater the diversity of skills and knowledge, the greater the organizational complexity, and the more difficult communication and coordination become.

       3) **Spatial differentiation** concerns the extent of the geographical separation of the organization's operations.

    b. **Formalization** concerns the extent to which job performance is standardized by job descriptions and clear procedures that define how tasks are to be accomplished. Low formalization enhances worker discretion.

    c. **Centralization** (See Subunit 1.3.)

11. **Mechanistic versus organic structures.** The extremes of the structural continuum are mechanistic and organic organizations.

    a. A **mechanistic structure** is appropriate for organizations focusing on a cost-minimization strategy through tight controls, extensive division of labor, high formalization, and centralization. The information network is limited, and employees rarely participate in decision making.

    b. An **organic structure** is characterized by low complexity, low formalization, and decentralization. It has an extensive information system, and employees participate in decision making. Organic organizations tend to be flexible and adaptive to change.

12. Structure is a function of the organization's fundamental strategy.

   a. An **innovation strategy** concentrates on developing important new products or services. An organic structure provides the flexibility for this strategy.

   b. A **cost-minimization strategy** imposes tight controls over expenditures and attempts to reduce prices of products. The mechanistic structure is appropriate.

   c. An **imitation strategy** is not adopted by true innovators but rather by companies that move into new markets only after smaller competitors have demonstrated the potential for success. Imitation strategies are best suited to a structure that combines mechanistic and organic components.

13. Structure is also a function of

   a. **Organizational size.** Larger organizations tend to be mechanistic because greater formalization is needed. Strategies also change as organizations change size. Growing organizations often expand their activities within their industry.

   b. **Technology.** An organic structure may be best for coping with nonroutine technology because formalization is low.

   1) British professor of industrial sociology Joan Woodward (1916-1971) classified technology as follows:

      a) Job shop
      b) Mass production
      c) Continuous process

   2) Woodward concluded that organizations with more complex technology have more management levels, more administrative and clerical personnel, more coordination by committees, and a larger span of control at the chief-executive level.

   c. **Environment.** In general, the more stable the environment, the more mechanistic the organization. A mechanistic structure is also appropriate when the environment has little capacity for growth. Dynamic environments require an organic structure because of their unpredictability. Moreover, a complex environment (e.g., one with numerous and constantly changing competitors) also requires the flexibility and adaptability of an organic structure.

   1) Every organization's environment has three key dimensions: capacity, volatility, and complexity. Capacity is the degree of growth an environment can support. Volatility concerns the relative instability in the environment. Complexity refers to the amount of heterogeneity and concentration in the environment; e.g., an industry with a few very large firms is homogeneous and concentrated.

      NOTE: Uncertainty is not a specific environmental factor. Rather, the foregoing factors determine the level of uncertainty present in the environment. However, entities that cope with high uncertainty or rates of change have design strategies different from those of stable organizations.

   d. **Stage in life cycle.** Older organizations have structures different from those of newer ones.

14. According to Henry Mintzberg, an organization has five components. Depending on which is in control, one of five different structures will evolve. The five organizational components include the

   a. **Operating core** – workers who perform the basic tasks related to production
   b. **Strategic apex** – top managers
   c. **Middle line** – managers who connect the core to the apex
   d. **Technostructure** – analysts who achieve a certain standardization in the organization
   e. **Support staff** – indirect support services

15. Mintzberg's five organizational structures include the following:

   a. A **simple structure**, such as that of a small retailer, has low complexity and formality, and authority is centralized. Its small size and simplicity usually preclude significant inefficiency in the use of resources. The strategic apex is the dominant component.

   b. A **machine bureaucracy** is a complex, formal, and centralized organization that performs highly routine tasks, groups activities into functional departments, has a strict chain of command, and distinguishes between line and staff relationships. The technostructure dominates.

   c. A **professional bureaucracy** (e.g., a university or library) is a complex and formal but decentralized organization in which highly trained specialists have great autonomy. Duplication of functions is minimized. For example, a university would have only one history department. Thus, the operating core is in control.

   d. A **divisional structure** is essentially a self-contained organization. Hence, it must perform all or most of the functions of the overall organization of which it is a part. It is characterized by substantial duplication of functions compared with more centralized structures. The middle line dominates.

   e. An **adhocracy** (an organic structure) has low complexity, formality, and centralization. Vertical differentiation is low and horizontal differentiation is high. The emphasis is on flexibility and response. Thus, the support staff dominates.

16. **Matrix organization** is a combination of any of the previously mentioned approaches to departmentalization. For example, a manager for each product may be appointed to supervise personnel who simultaneously report to a manager for each function. This form is used in R&D and in project management.

   a. The emphasis of the arrangement is on the result or the product. The functional organization remains, while parts of it are temporarily lent or assigned to a given project.

      1) The project may be to make a product indefinitely or to accomplish a limited but lengthy task, such as construction of a submarine.

   b. Matrix organization provides the security and accountability of the functional form while providing expert personnel to the project only when needed and only to the extent required. It allows personnel as well as functions to be most effectively and efficiently used.

   c. Technical ability of employees is better appraised by the functional managers than by the project manager.

   d. Practical applications skills can be appraised by the project manager on-site.

   e. Unnecessarily large swings in levels of personnel and equipment are minimized.

   f. The major disadvantage is that the principle of unity of command is violated. Hence, the authority, responsibility, and accountability of the parties involved must be clearly defined to avoid confusion and employee dissatisfaction.

   g. A second disadvantage is the possible inefficient use of employees. Individuals may be idle while waiting for project assignments that require their specific talents.

      1) It is difficult for large organizations to use matrix organization because they typically have many levels (both vertical and horizontal), thus slowing communications.

17. **Bureaucracy** is a term applied by German sociologist Max Weber (writing in the 1900s) to a type of organizational hierarchy characterized by clear rules, sharply defined lines of authority, and a high degree of specialization. He insisted that bureaucracy was the most rational and efficient form of organization.

    a. The basic **characteristics** of a bureaucratic organization are as follows:

       1) The organization is efficient, logical, mature, and formal with distinct divisions of labor ensuring task performance, uniformity, and definition. It operates mechanically according to established laws, rules, or procedures which are consistent.

       2) The organization is typically large and complex where members are easily replaceable and treated impersonally as positions rather than unique individuals. Employees have no sense of "ownership" in the organization, having little impact on organizational goals.

       3) Highly specialized and repetitive functions are performed by experts who have a limited sphere of competence and whose obligations, authority, and obedience are strictly defined.

       4) The organization offers career growth and promotions based on seniority or on achievement determined by the judgment of immediate superiors.

       5) The flow of communication is strictly related to the organizational chart, moving top-down, allowing communication to become distorted or misinterpreted.

    b. **Advantages** that an organization might realize from the bureaucratic design are as follows:

       1) The routines and procedures of a job function are established and consistent, with certainty in the job's description and definition.

       2) The division of labor promotes high efficiency and provides consistency in organizational performance, unifying the focus on organizational objectives while enabling greater attention and quick response time to local issues.

       3) Due to the clear lines of reporting relationships, centralization, and responsibility, there is a strong code of discipline.

    c. **Disadvantages** that an organization might realize from the bureaucratic design are as follows:

       1) Action in the organization is slow and generates problems of control due to the elaborate level of paperwork required to ensure adequate checks and balances.

       2) The organization is typically inflexible with a rigid design, limiting the performance of individuals within the organization.

       3) Communication is limited due to the top-down nature of the hierarchical structure and may lead to duplication of efforts by different departments.

    d. The effect of the bureaucratic design on the motivation of an employee within the organization is as follows:

       1) Due to the impersonal environment, the employee is poorly motivated because (s)he feels unimportant, having no incentive for extraordinary performance.

       2) There is little participation in the decision-making process and therefore a lack of commitment to organizational goals.

       3) Having no sense of ownership or belonging to the organization, the employee will tend to be dissatisfied and more alienated, causing an unfavorable attitude that could be disruptive to others.

18. The method of departmentalization chosen is contingent upon

    a. Organizational plans, programs, policies, and purposes
    b. Environmental constraints
    c. Training and preferences of available personnel

1.5 OVERVIEW OF MANAGEMENT

1. Management can be characterized in many ways, each view reflecting one or more aspects of the development of management theory:

    a. Management is accomplishing work through people.

    b. Management is the process of planning, organizing (staffing), directing, and controlling resources to reach organizational goals.

    c. Management is a set of scientific tools used to produce rational solutions to organizational problems in a changing environment.

    d. Management is making and implementing decisions in an organizational setting.

    e. Kreitner (op. cit., p. 5) defines management as "the process of working with and through others to achieve organizational objectives in a changing environment. Central to this process is the effective and efficient use of limited resources."

        1) Thus, management is a social process that attempts to use scarce resources to achieve organizational objectives while anticipating environmental changes and balancing effectiveness against efficiency.

            a) The physical, social, political, moral, and informational environments external to the organization are the sources of change that managers must anticipate.

        2) Kreitner (pp. 20-22) also states that the variables in the basic formula for effective management are ability, motivation, and opportunity. Ability is the "capacity to achieve organizational objectives both effectively and efficiently." Motivation is "a persistent desire to move ahead." Opportunity has two components according to Kreitner: a suitable job in management and a supportive climate.

2. The management function is universal. Managers at every level of every organization perform four functions:

    a. **Planning**
    b. **Organizing**
    c. **Directing**
    d. **Controlling**

3. The amount of time spent on each function varies by level of manager.

    a. The higher the level, the more planning and organizing.
    b. The lower the level, the more directing.
    c. All levels of management must spend time controlling.

4. The proportionate time also varies with the size of the organization. Larger entities must make long-range plans, whereas smaller ones can be more flexible. Large amounts of invested assets often cannot respond to change as quickly.

5. Managers can be classified variously.

    a. An **executive or general manager**, such as a chair of the board, has policy-making as well as operational authority. A general manager has responsibility for multiple operational functions in a specific organizational unit.

    b. A **functional manager** has authority over a specific operational area (e.g., accounting) and is responsible for intermediate planning with a time line of approximately 6 months to 1 year.

    c. A **first-line or middle manager** directly supervises employees who are not managers. These managers deal with day-to-day operations.

6. Canadian professor of management studies Henry Mintzberg (writing in 1973) disagreed with the functional method of describing management's roles. He observed that the actual activities of managers could be classified as follows:

    a. **Interpersonal Roles**

        1) Figurehead or ceremonial symbol of legal authority
        2) Leader who motivates subordinates
        3) Liaison in both horizontal and vertical chains of communication

    b. **Informational Roles**

        1) Nerve center of nonroutine information and a recipient of all kinds of information
        2) Disseminator of information to subordinates
        3) Spokesperson who transmits information to outsiders

    c. **Decisional Roles**

        1) Entrepreneur who devises and brings about organizational change
        2) Disturbance handler who takes nonroutine corrective action
        3) Resource allocator who determines who receives what
        4) Negotiator with outside parties who protects the organization's interests

7. The **scientific school of management** was the first major school to develop.

    a. Scientific management focuses on the production process and ways to make it more efficient. The field was founded by American engineer Frederick W. Taylor. In *The Principles of Scientific Management* (1911), he advocated a systematic, quantitative approach oriented towards individual job design.

        1) Taylor's four principles of scientific management are

            a) Scientific analysis of work
            b) Scientific selection, training, and development of workers
            c) Cooperation between work planners and operators
            d) Equal sharing of responsibility by labor and management who perform the tasks for which they are best suited

        2) Taylor also pioneered the use of time and motion analysis, stopwatch measurement, and systematic shop management.

        3) Scientific management holds that there is "one best way" to do each job. Management should discover the best way and teach it to workers.

            a) Each job/task should be designed for maximum efficiency.
            b) Management should teach workers new habits. Old habits are often inefficient.

        4) Taylor designed incentive programs based on the prevailing management philosophy that the best way to get worker cooperation in performing a job in the prescribed efficient manner was to offer monetary rewards.

            a) If workers produce more, they should share in benefits.
            b) Productivity increased because the workers' incremental bonus usually was less than their productivity increase.

        5) Separation of tasks into simple subtasks, close supervision, and reliance on economic motivation are all characteristics of the scientific school later attacked by human relations researchers.

        6) Taylor coined the phrase "the one best way" to describe his conclusion that all processes have a single optimal solution.

8.   The **administrative school of management** emphasized principles, concepts, and ideas from past organizational experience. It paralleled the scientific school of management in seeking one best way to organize, but its focus was on the overall organization. The scientific school had focused on shop management and individual workers.

    a.   The administrative school attempted to distill universal principles from practical experience. A principle is a statement of valid causal relationships that is useful in predicting the outcome of a pending relationship. The administrative school believed in the existence of certain valid principles of organization, such as the following:

       1)   **Principle of span of control.** The number of subordinates a superior can effectively supervise is limited.

       2)   **Principle of unity of command.** Each subordinate should have only one superior (though a superior may have as many subordinates as allowed by the superior's span of control). Violation of this principle (unity of command) leads to confusion and frustration for the subordinate.

    b.   The value of a management principle is to give the manager guidelines for improving decisions, minimizing inefficiency, and reducing unnecessary conflict.

       1)   Principles based on successful practices or careful observation did help managers learn to apply useful knowledge about organizational design.

    c.   The administrative school of management is considered mechanistic in that it seeks to build static models of organizations and the people in them (as opposed to organic or dynamic models).

       1)   It reflects the same lack of concern with human relations as the scientific school.

       2)   It assumes away the need of the organization to adapt to human, social, and technological changes.

    d.   The difficulty with administrative school of management principles is that they do not always hold true in actual organizations. For example, different organizations use different spans of control and are still successful.

9.   French management theorist Henri Fayol (publishing in 1916), sometimes called the Father of Administration, advocated the separation of administration from technical, commercial, financial, and accounting operations.

    a.   Fayol's **functions of management** listed below form the foundation for the modern functional or process approach to classifying a manager's activities.

       1)   Planning
       2)   Organizing
       3)   Commanding
       4)   Coordinating
       5)   Controlling

10.   **Behaviorism** views management as accomplishing results through people, both as individuals and in groups. Thus, the stress is on applying findings from psychology, anthropology, and sociology.

    a.   Australian management theorist Elton Mayo (working in the 1920s and 1930s) is referred to as the Father of Human Relations. His initial experiments studied the relationship of workshop lighting levels to levels of productivity.

1) These experiments, conducted at the Western Electric Company's Hawthorne plant near Chicago from 1927 to 1932, are known as the Hawthorne experiments. The results astounded researchers by revealing that increased worker productivity resulted from the workers' willingness to cooperate, not from the level of lighting. The researchers concluded that

    a) The workers' individual needs and their social relationships with peers on the job were more important to productivity than the physical working conditions.

    b) Work is a group activity.

    c) Informal relationships are important parts of organizational systems.

b. Key elements recognized by the behavioral school include

  1) Participation

    a) Permits more involvement of subordinates in the organization

    b) Encourages communication up as well as down the organizational hierarchy

    c) Leads to better decisions

  2) Group influences

    a) Informal communication processes are important.

    b) Group pressure shapes individual behavior, beliefs, values, and job attitudes.

  3) Individual needs

    a) Individuals are not solely motivated by financial incentives.
    b) People get bored doing routine, simple, and repetitive jobs.
    c) People have a variety of needs that the job setting should satisfy.

11. The **systems school** stresses interrelationships and interdependence of managerial problems. It emphasizes chains of events and how components relate to one another. The systems school is considered the modern approach to management.

a. An organizational system is a group or set of things that are interrelated or interdependent so as to form a part of a larger whole. The systems school recognizes that understanding an organization is impossible without considering the larger context or system of which it is a part.

  1) It also considers both human relations and structural issues.

  2) Systems may be closed or open. **Closed systems** are closed to the external environment. Few systems are truly closed, but boundaries may be artificially drawn to facilitate analysis by treating a system as if it were closed.

    a) Classical viewpoints treated management as a closed system and ignored most things external to the organization. Such policy is limited and dangerous in that effective management of a social system is not deterministic or mechanistic.

  3) **Open systems** are open to and have interaction with an external environment. The system boundaries are drawn to reflect external inputs and system outputs.

    a) A closed system suffers entropy, but an open system seeks replenishment through its boundaries with the larger system (environment).

    b) Closed-systems management writers viewed the environment as beyond their concern; open-systems writers see the environment as vital.

    b.   The **contingency approach** derived from systems thinking stresses that the search for answers to organizational problems depends on contingencies that can be discovered and studied.

        1)   Because this approach argues for situationally determined answers to management concerns, the key is finding the relevant factors in the organization's environment.

        2)   The same argument applies to individuals' motivations, needs, and wants because people are subsystems within the larger organizational system.

    c.   Management should be studied as an open social system because of its continual interaction with its external environment. Factors include:

        1)   Technological change
        2)   Social responsibilities to other institutions
        3)   Relationships of employee needs and organizational requirements
        4)   Organizational growth and development
        5)   Individual and organizational reasons for resisting change

    d.   The recognition of social responsibilities is a logical outgrowth of systems thinking. If the organization is part of a larger social system, it must recognize its subordination to and interdependence with this larger system. This recognition requires accepting the responsibility to make decisions with thoughtful consideration of their impact on society, the larger system.

    e.   Managers who recognize the interrelatedness of the business environment also recognize and take advantage of the principle of **synergy** -- the joint action of two or more parties that, taken together, enhances each other's effectiveness.

12.   The emergence of the **total quality management (TQM)** concept is one of the most significant developments in recent years. TQM recognizes that quality improvement can increase revenues and decrease costs significantly.

    a.   TQM is a comprehensive approach to quality. It treats the pursuit of quality as a basic organizational function that is as important as production or marketing.

    b.   TQM is the continuous pursuit of quality in every aspect of organizational activities through a philosophy of doing it right the first time, employee training and empowerment, promotion of teamwork, improvement of processes, and attention to satisfaction of customers, both internal and external.

    c.   TQM emphasizes the supplier's relationship with the customer, identifies customer needs, and recognizes that everyone in a process is at some time a customer or supplier of someone else, either within or without the organization.

    d.   American statistician W. Edwards Deming pioneered the concept of TQM in the 1940s. Deming listed 14 quality points in his 1986 book *Out of the Crisis*:

        1)   Create constancy of purpose for improvement of products and services. Companies must downplay the emphasis on profits, especially short-term profits, and emphasize innovation, research, and constant quality improvement.

        2)   Adopt the new philosophy. This means the organization and its workers cannot be tolerant of poor workmanship and sullen service. TQM is a religion in which mistakes and negativism are unacceptable.

        3)   Cease dependence on mass inspection. Inspection leads to defective products being thrown out or reworked, both of which are expensive. When products are rejected, it means that the company has paid workers to make defects, and then pays them again to correct their own mistakes. Quality comes from process improvement, not from inspection.

4) End the practice of awarding business on price tag alone. A purchasing department which bases decisions solely on price will end up with some low quality components. The objective should be to purchase the best quality and then negotiate for the best price on the best quality.

5) Improve constantly and forever the system of production and service. Quality improvement is not a one-time effort.

6) Institute training and retraining. Workers must be trained to do their jobs properly.

7) Institute leadership. The job of a supervisor is to lead. Leading consists of helping people do a better job and of recognizing those workers who need special help.

8) Drive out fear. Workers should not be afraid to ask questions or point out problem areas. Every worker should have the responsibility to shut down the entire production line when quality problems arise. This is typical in just-in-time (JIT) systems, which leads many people to conclude that JIT is a quality control system as well as an inventory control system.

9) Break down barriers between staff areas. All workers must function as a team, even though they may be separated by divisional lines.

10) Eliminate slogans, exhortations, and targets for the workforce. Let individual workers put up their own slogans. The overall concept of quality is the only overriding exhortation.

11) Eliminate numerical quotas. Quotas take into account only numbers, not quality. Numerical quotas are normally a cause of poor quality. If a worker is required to maintain a numerical quota, quality takes a back seat.

12) Remove barriers to pride of workmanship. People want to do good work, and management should do everything possible to give employees the tools they need to produce outstanding products.

13) Institute a vigorous program of education and retraining. When a new quality program is implemented, workers will have to be given training in teamwork and statistical methods because they have not been asked to use such skills in the past.

14) Take action to accomplish the transformation. Top management must have a plan of action to carry out the TQM mission. A critical mass of people must be involved.

1.6 OTHER ORGANIZATIONAL ISSUES

1. **Reengineering** involves **starting from scratch** to **redesign** a company's core processes rather than attempting to improve the current system.

    a. Kreitner (p. 239) says of reengineering that "Its chief tool is a clean sheet of paper." Reengineering is not incremental improvement of current processes, nor is it simple downsizing. As Kreitner goes on to say, "reengineers start from the future and work backward..."

    b. The scientific school of management focused on breaking tasks down into ever smaller subtasks, resulting in greater specialization by each worker. One of the drawbacks of this technique was the inevitable tunnel vision as each employee dwelled only on the inputs and outputs of his/her particular task.

    c. Reengineering, by contrast, focuses on entire processes, not the individuals performing them. For instance, attempting to improve the timeliness of paying vendor invoices by looking only at the accounts payable department is useless. The entire purchases-payables-disbursements cycle should be examined and rethought from the ground up.

d.   In the modern, highly competitive business environment, a company may need to adapt quickly and radically to change. Thus, reengineering is usually a cross-departmental process of innovation requiring substantial investment in information technology and retraining. Successful reengineering may bring dramatic improvements in customer service and in the speed with which new products are introduced.

2.   **Strategic partnerships** (also called strategic alliances or joint ventures) are associations between **competitors** to accomplish a specific business purpose or objective. Competitors may form an alliance to design a new automobile or set a new standard for video reproduction.

    a.   Such arrangements can be **contrasted** with ordinary loyalty between a customer and supplier, which has long been standard practice in business settings.

    b.   Strategic partnerships are very often created between **firms in different countries**.

    c.   **Advantages** of strategic partnerships are:

        1)   A strategic partnership may be the only way to enter a difficult foreign market.

        2)   The fixed costs and risks of the venture are shared.

        3)   The partners can share skills and technology.

        4)   The partners together have a greater chance of setting a technological standard.

    d.   The **disadvantage** of a strategic partnership is that the arrangement must be closely monitored. One of the partners might be in a weaker position and could "give away" its competencies without gaining anything in return.

3.   **Outsourcing** is a way for a company to gain cost savings by "farming out" business functions that it doesn't consider core competencies.

    a.   For instance, a manufacturer may determine that payroll activities are not ones it performs with much efficiency. The company may then contract out those activities to a company that specializes in payroll processing.

    b.   The most renowned **example** of outsourcing is Cisco Systems, a California-based company known for being "a hardware vendor that doesn't make hardware."

        1)   Cisco designs and markets routers and switches for Internet communications and manages its supply chain, but it has delegated all manufacturing of products to several other companies.

        2)   This relieves the company of both the need to tie up working capital in inventory and the need for a huge capital investment in manufacturing equipment.

        3)   Cisco can be thought of as a **networked corporation**, designing and marketing the product at the center, while others in the network supply the parts, assemble them into the finished product, store the product as inventory, and ship it to the final customer.

4.   **Lean production** is a management concept that encourages minimizing everything, from inventories to labor hours. Invented by Toyota, lean production was considered the crucial factor in making that company the world's most efficient automaker. It has been driving many of the performance improvements now taking place in industry.

    a.   The object is to **identify and eliminate waste**. These improvements benefit all of the organization's stakeholders, including customers and shareholders. Society as a whole also benefits, as the waste traditionally embedded in the manufacturing process is removed, which frees up resources for other uses.

    b.   Lean production includes a basic premise that doing a better job in designing products, avoiding defects, increasing speed and flexibility, and reducing inventory buffers translates to decreased costs of doing business. Many companies use bench-marking as a tool to determine how low inventories and costs can be.

    c.   A company cannot become a lean producer overnight. Management must build and nurture the logic and machinery that drive lean production. Implementing lean production usually means breaking old patterns and installing new ones. Strategic planning is an important cornerstone of lean production.

    d.   Effective lean production requires partnering with suppliers.

5. **Organizational Charts**

    a.   Organizational charts used to represent the organizational structure often resemble a pyramid, with the chief executive on top and the operating workforce on bottom. Recent trends in management, including increased span of control and decreased hierarchy, have resulted in flatter organizational charts. The typical organizational chart can be designed to

        1)   Reflect classical, formal authority channels (chain of command)
        2)   Show reporting relationships and task groupings (departmentation)
        3)   Describe communication channels
        4)   Identify location of sources of organizational expertise
        5)   Show promotional or career tracks
        6)   Depict span of control and number of organizational levels
        7)   Show major functions and their respective relationships

    b.   Shortcomings of Organizational Charts

        1)   Limited presentation of information, a shortcoming that can be overcome by supplementing the chart with a detailed manual
        2)   Tendency to become quickly obsolete because of rapid change
        3)   Failure to show informal communication, influence, power, or friendships
        4)   Tendency to ignore informal job trade-offs between titles on the chart
        5)   Possibility of misleading management by giving an appearance of structure and order that might not exist
        6)   Possibility that position titles do not reflect actual functions

1.7 CORE CONCEPTS

Departmentalization and Span of Control

- **Division of labor** breaks complex processes into their simpler components. This makes task specialization by employees possible. One response to the resulting need for efficient coordination is **departmentalization**.

- Departmentalization can be by **function**, by **product**, by **customer**, by **territory**, or by **project**.

- **Span of control** is an upper limit to the number of subordinates who can be effectively supervised by one person. Beyond a certain number of subordinates, the effectiveness and efficiency of supervision decreases.

- **Flat** organizational structures have relatively few levels from top to bottom and thus have wide spans of control. **Tall** organizational structures have many levels between top and bottom and thus have relatively narrow spans of control.

Line and Staff Relationships

- The **classical approach** views **line** activities as those directly responsible for the primary function, product, or service of the organization, whereas **staff** members provide support services.
- The **behavioral school** sees exercise of informal authority as a very important constraint on formal chains of command.
- **Conflict** between line and staff personnel is almost inevitable given the considerable difference in their backgrounds and activities. These individuals tend to have different training and education, perspectives on the organization, and career and other objectives.
- Line-staff conflicts may be **minimized** by clearly defining areas of activity and authority and by sharply defining the nature and place of line and staff.
- The **modern approach** to line and staff is based on systems thinking. Every position and every task must contribute to the organizational purpose or it should not exist. Distinctions between producers and helpers are therefore irrelevant.

Centralization and Decentralization

- **Centralization** concerns the concentration of authority in an organization and the degree and levels at which it occurs.
- **Classicists** view decentralization with some distrust because they seek to avoid any dilution of control by top managers.
- **Behaviorists** view decentralization in the same way as delegation, that is, as a good way to improve motivation and morale of lower-level employees.
- The **modern or contingency view** is that neither centralization nor decentralization is good or bad in itself. The degree to which either is stressed depends upon the requirements of a given situation.
- **Decentralization** is a philosophy of organizing and managing. Careful selection of which decisions to push down the hierarchy and which to hold at the top is required.
- Among the **advantages** of decentralization are greater speed in making operational decisions and encouraging better communications.
- Among the **disadvantages** of decentralization are a strong tendency to focus on short-run results to the detriment of long-run health, and increased risk of loss of control by top management.

The Organizing Process

- Organizing is the **design and structuring of tasks and roles** to accomplish organizational goals.
- The **traditional approach** (also known as classical, structural, or formal) emphasizes authority, responsibility, tasks, hierarchy, span of control, etc. The traditional approach to organizing sets up prescribed (or dictated) relationships and then places people in them. "The person is selected to fill the job."
- The **behavioral approach** emphasizes the limits, strengths, availability, and interests of the people available. The participants provide feedback in the role-definition process. This approach is less deterministic than the traditional approach because group dynamics and the feelings of subordinates are included in the process. "The job is designed to fit the person."
- The **modern (contingency) approach** emphasizes the tailoring of the organization to its unique situation. It combines classical and behavioral principles of organization. "The job and the person must fit each other."
- A **mechanistic structure** is appropriate for organizations focusing on a cost-minimization strategy through tight controls, extensive division of labor, high formalization, and centralization. The information network is limited, and employees rarely participate in decision making.

- An **organic structure** is characterized by low complexity, low formalization, and decentralization. It has an extensive information system, and employees participate in decision making. Organic organizations tend to be flexible and adaptive to change.
- Structure is also a function of **organizational size, technology, and environment**.
- Mintzberg's **five organizational structures** are: simple structure, machine bureaucracy, professional bureaucracy, divisional structure, and adhocracy.
- A **matrix organization** is a combination of any of the previously mentioned approaches to departmentalization. The emphasis of the arrangement is on the result or the product.
- **Bureaucracy** is a type of organizational hierarchy characterized by clear rules, sharply defined lines of authority, and a high degree of specialization.

Overview of Management

- **Management** can be characterized in several ways. In the most basic sense, management is accomplishing work through people.
- Managers at every level of every organization perform **four functions**: planning, organizing, directing, and controlling.
- Henry Mintzberg disagreed with the functional model and defined **three roles** of managers: interpersonal, informational, and decisional.
- Frederick W. Taylor founded the **scientific school of management**, which urged breaking down every task into its smallest components and having workers specialize in the performance of each subtask. He also insisted that there was "one best way" to perform every job.
- The **administrative school of management** paralleled the scientific school of management in seeking one best way to organize, but its focus was on the overall organization rather than on shop management and individual workers.
- Henri Fayol advocated the **separation of administration** from technical, commercial, financial, and accounting operations.
- **Behaviorism** views management as accomplishing results through people, both as individuals and in groups. Thus, the stress is on applying findings from psychology, anthropology, and sociology.
- The **systems school** stresses interrelationships and interdependence of managerial problems. It emphasizes chains of events and how components relate to one another. The systems school is considered the modern approach to management.
- The **contingency approach**, derived from systems thinking, stresses that the search for answers to organizational problems depends on contingencies that can be discovered and studied.
- The emergence of the **total quality management** (TQM) concept is one of the most significant developments in recent years. TQM is a comprehensive approach to quality. It treats the pursuit of quality as a basic organizational function that is as important as production or marketing.

Other Organizational Issues

- **Reengineering** involves **starting from scratch** to **redesign** a company's core processes rather than attempting to improve the current system. Reengineering is not incremental improvement of current processes, nor is it simple downsizing.
- **Strategic partnerships** (also called strategic alliances or joint ventures) are associations between **competitors** to accomplish a specific business purpose or objective. Competitors may form an alliance to design a new automobile or set a new standard for video reproduction.
- **Outsourcing** is a way for a company to gain cost savings by "farming out" business functions that it doesn't consider core competencies.
- **Lean production** is a management concept that says to minimize everything, from inventories to labor hours. The object is to **identify and eliminate waste**.

This page intentionally left blank.

1.8 ESSAY QUESTIONS

Recall that your CMA Part 4 exam will probably contain six scenarios, with about three questions per scenario. There will be a recommended time allocation of 20 minutes, 30 minutes, or 45 minutes for each scenario and related questions.

One scenario will involve ethics, and probably one or two scenarios will include calculations and responses on a worksheet. Also, expect at least one scenario on organizational/behavioral topics. The remaining scenarios cover Parts 1, 2, and 3.

Scenario Title	Subtopic	Questions	Suggested Time
Delaware City	Bureaucratic Organizational Design	1, 2, 3	30 minutes
Management Accountants	Mintzberg's Roles for Managers	4, 5	30 minutes
Comparison of Theories	Classical vs. Modern Theories	6, 7, 8, 9	30 minutes
Parker Machine Company	Flat Organizational Structure and Span of Control	10, 11, 12	30 minutes

Scenario for Essay Questions 1, 2, 3

The government of Delaware City is organized in a similar manner to most other United States city governments and employs several thousand people in various functions. As prescribed by law, the city follows a formal organizational structure with very specific position descriptions outlining decision-making authority and expenditure limitations. In reality, only elected officials can authorize expenditures and make decisions; however, in some cases, elected officials delegate minimal decision-making authority to positions within the organization. This type of organizational structure is often called "bureaucratic."

Questions

1. Describe the basic characteristics of the bureaucratic organizational design. Be sure to include in your discussion comments on organizational structure, communication, and employment environment.

2. a. Identify four advantages that Delaware City might realize from the bureaucratic organizational design.

   b. Identify four disadvantages that Delaware City might realize from the bureaucratic organizational design.

3. Describe the effect of the bureaucratic organizational design on the motivation of an employee within the organization.

Essay Questions 1, 2, 3 — Unofficial Answers

1.   The basic characteristics of a bureaucratic organization are as follows:

    a.   The organization is efficient, logical, mature, and formal with distinct divisions of labor ensuring task performance, uniformity, and definition. It operates mechanically according to established laws, rules, or procedures which are consistent.

    b.   The organization is typically large and complex where members are easily replaceable and treated impersonally as positions rather than unique individuals. Employees have no sense of "ownership" in the organization, having little impact on organizational goals.

    c.   Highly specialized and repetitive functions are performed by experts who have a limited sphere of competence and whose obligations, authority, and obedience are strictly defined.

    d.   The organization offers career growth and promotions based on seniority or achievement determined by the judgment of the immediate superiors.

    e.   The flow of communication is strictly related to the organizational chart, moving top-down, allowing communication to become distorted or misinterpreted.

2.   a.   Advantages that Delaware City might realize from the bureaucratic organizational design are listed below.

       1)   The routines and procedures of a job function are established and consistent, with certainty in the job's description and definition.

       2)   The division of labor promotes high efficiency and provides consistency in organizational performance, unifying the focus on organizational objectives while enabling greater attention and quick response time to local issues.

       3)   Due to the clear lines of reporting relationships, centralization, and responsibility, there is a strong code of discipline.

    b.   Disadvantages that Delaware City might realize from the bureaucratic organizational design are listed below.

       1)   Action in the organization is slow and generates problems of control due to the elaborate level of paperwork required to ensure adequate checks and balances.

       2)   The organization is typically inflexible with a rigid design, limiting the performance of individuals within the organization.

       3)   Communication is limited due to the top-down nature of the hierarchical structure and may lead to duplication of efforts by different departments.

3.   The effect of the bureaucratic organizational design on the motivation of an employee within the organization is described below.

    a.   Due to the impersonal environment, the employee is poorly motivated because (s)he feels unimportant, having no incentive for extraordinary performance.

    b.   There is little participation in the decision-making process and, therefore, a lack of commitment to organizational goals.

    c.   Having no sense of ownership or belonging to the organization, the employee will tend to be dissatisfied and more alienated, causing an unfavorable attitude that could be disruptive to others.

Scenario for Essay Questions 4, 5

Managers are a separate and distinct category of employees whose primary activities are a part of the management process. Certain roles and skills are usually required of all managers, no matter what their specialty. During the 1970s, Henry Mintzberg closely observed the day-to-day activities of a group of managers and concluded that general managerial roles fall into three basic categories:

- Interpersonal roles that are directly related to the status of the manager
- Informational roles involving the flow of information and stemming from the interpersonal roles
- Decisional roles involving strategy formulation and stemming from the informational roles

Management accountants are actively involved in the process of managing the entity. The process includes making strategic, tactical, and operating decisions while helping to coordinate the efforts of the entire organization. In order to fulfill these objectives, the management accountant accepts certain responsibilities which can be identified as:

- Planning
- Evaluating
- Controlling
- Assuring accountability of resources
- External reporting

Questions

4. Referring to the general roles of all managers,

   a. Describe two interpersonal roles.
   b. Describe two informational roles.
   c. Describe three decisional roles.

5. Describe each of the five responsibilities of the management accountant, identifying examples of practices and techniques.

Essay Questions 4, 5 — Unofficial Answers

4.   In referring to the general roles of managers,

    a.   Two interpersonal roles include acting as a

        1)   Leader who hires, trains, motivates employees by integrating individual and organization goals by using effective communication

        2)   Liaison who deals with people outside the organization

    b.   Two informational roles include acting as a

        1)   Monitor who seeks information about other internal departments, the external environment, and other organizations

        2)   Disseminator who communicates outside information internally, and internal information to the subordinates, while exercising judgment so there is minimal information overload

    c.   Three decisional roles include acting as a

        1)   Negotiator between subordinates, suppliers, contracts, and union

        2)   Resource allocator who distributes funds, equipment, time, etc., in accordance with organizational objectives

        3)   Disturbance handler who solves issues of conflict within and without the organization

5.   Descriptions of the five responsibilities of the management accountant, as well as examples of practices and techniques of each, include the following:

    a.   **Planning.** The manager gains an understanding of the impact on the organization of planned transactions (i.e., analyzing strengths and weaknesses) and economic events, both strategic and tactical, and sets obtainable goals for the organization. The development of budgets in a bottom-up or top-down approach for both the short and long term is an example of planning.

    b.   **Evaluating.** The manager judges and analyzes the implication of various past and expected events, and then chooses the optimum course of action. The manager also translates data and communicates the conclusions. Graphical analysis (such as trend, bar charts, or regression) and net present value analysis are examples of evaluating.

    c.   **Controlling.** The manager ensures the integrity of financial information, monitors performance against budgets and goals, and provides information internally for decision making. The successful implementation of internal control procedures is an example of controlling.

    d.   **Accountability.** The manager implements a reporting system closely aligned to organizational goals that contributes to the measurement of the effective use of resources and safeguarding of assets. Internal reporting, such as comparisons of actuals to budget, is an example of accountability.

    e.   **External reporting.** The manager prepares reports in accordance with generally accepted accounting principles and then disseminates this information to shareholders (both current and potential), creditors, and regulatory and tax agencies. An annual report or a credit application are examples of external reporting.

Scenario for Essay Questions 6, 7, 8, 9

Classical management theory was developed from the input of many theoreticians and gained widespread acceptance in the early 1900s. Classical management theory emphasizes that economic factors are the primary means of motivation. The development of the classical management theory was strongly influenced by classical economists. While times and circumstances have changed dramatically since the early 1900s, many features of this approach, such as the primary functions of management, have withstood the test of time and are accepted today.

Modern organization theory has evolved from the contributions of the earlier theoreticians as well as more contemporary theoreticians. The modern organization theory is generally considered to have come into prominence by the 1930s. A basic component of modern organization theory is that an individual's behavior is adaptive and that a variety of needs and drives are the means of motivation.

While both the classical management theory and modern organization theory are accepted and followed, there are specific basic conflicts between the two schools of thought. These conflicts can be elaborated upon in the areas of organization goals, behavior of employees, behavior of management, and the role of accounting. Your supervisor, who is considering implementing a new managerial philosophy, has asked for your advice on the difference between classical management and modern organization theory.

Questions

Contrast the classical management theory and the modern organization theory in each of the following four areas:

6. Organization goals
7. Employee behavior
8. Management behavior
9. Role of accounting

Essay Questions 6, 7, 8, 9 — Unofficial Answers

6.   Classical management theory can be contrasted with modern organizational theory in the area of organizational goals as follows:

Issue	Classical	Modern
Principal objective	The principal objective of business activity is profit maximization.	In the modern complex business enterprise, there are many diverse goals.
Goal structure and development	Goals are set by a few people because they are the only ones knowledgeable to do so.	Organizations are coalitions of individual participants. The organization itself cannot have goals, only individuals can have goals. Those goals are, in fact, the objectives of the dominant members of the coalition.
	Goals are additive – what is good for the parts of the business is also good for the whole.	There appears to be no valid basis for the assumption that goals are homogeneous and thus additive – what is good for the parts of the organization is not necessarily good for the whole.

7.   Classical management theory can be contrasted with modern organizational theory in the area of employee behavior as follows:

Issue	Classical	Modern
Motivation	Organization participants are motivated primarily by economic forces.	Organization participants are motivated by a wide variety of psychological, social, and economic needs and drives.
Behavior	Employees have the capacity to behave in only a few ways and are not adaptive to specific situations or self-initiative.	Human behavior within an organization is essentially an adaptive, problem-solving, decision-making process.
	Employees behave in ways which only satisfy individual primary needs.	The efficiency and effectiveness of human behavior is usually directed toward attempts to find satisfactory need gratification.
Productivity	Work is essentially an unpleasant task which people will avoid whenever possible. Therefore, productivity improvements must be realized through control of the technical elements of the job, such as rate and quality of work and incentive pay.	Productivity improvements are realized by managing antecedents and consequences of effort, such as total work setting, climate, socialization, and non-monetary rewards.

8. Classical management theory can be contrasted with modern organizational theory in the area of management behavior as follows:

Issue	Classical	Modern
Role of business manager	The role of the business manager is to maximize the profits of the firm.	The management role is essentially a decision-making process subject to the limitations on human rationality and cognitive ability, and favorable for the organization.
	The manager uses employees as necessary components of the technical system.	The primary role of the business manager is to maintain a favorable balance between: (1) the contributions required from the participants and (2) the inducements (i.e., perceived need satisfactions) which must be offered to secure those contributions.
Management control	The essence of management control is authority. The ultimate authority of management stems from its ability to affect the economic reward structure.	The essence of management control is the willingness of other participants to accept their authority of management. This willingness appears to be a nonstable function of the inducement-contribution balance.
Authority versus responsibility	Responsibility is assigned from above and authority is accepted from below.	There must be a balance between the authority a person has and the responsibility for performance.

9. Classical management theory can be contrasted with modern organizational theory in the area of accounting as follows:

Issue	Classical	Modern
Primary function of accounting	The primary function of management accounting is to aid management in the process of profit maximization.	The management accounting process is an information system whose major purposes are (1) to provide the various levels of management with data which will facilitate the decision-making functions of planning and control and (2) to serve as a communications medium within the organization.
Accounting system	The accounting system is a goal-allocation (planning) device which permits management to select its operating objectives and to divide and distribute them throughout the firm. The accounting system is also a control device which permits management to identify and correct undesirable performance.	The effective use of budgets and other accounting planning and control techniques requires an understanding of the interaction between these techniques and the motivations and aspiration levels of the individuals to be controlled.
	There is sufficient certainty, rationality, and knowledge within the system to permit an accurate comparison of responsibility for performance and the ultimate benefits and costs of that performance.	The objectivity of the management accounting process is largely a myth. Accountants have wide areas of discretion of the selection, processing, and reporting of data.
	The accounting system is neutral in its evaluations – personal bias is eliminated by the objectivity of the system.	In performing their function within an organization, accountants can be expected to be influenced by their own personal and departmental goals in the same way that other participants are influenced.

Scenario for Essay Questions 10, 11, 12

Barnes Corporation recently purchased Parker Machine Company, a manufacturer of sophisticated parts for the aircraft industry. Donald Jenkins has been appointed vice president of production of Parker and has been asked by Beverly Kiner, president of Barnes, to prepare an organizational chart for his department at Parker. The chart that Jenkins prepared is presented in Chart A below.

When Jenkins presented his chart to Kiner, she told him that she preferred a flat organizational structure and showed him how she envisioned his department at Parker by drawing the chart presented in Chart B below. Kiner's chart reduced a layer of management personnel and increased the number of people reporting directly to the manager of planning and control and the manager of manufacturing.

Jenkins expressed concern about the broad span of control depicted in Kiner's chart, as he believed this might cause problems for the two managers. Kiner said that she believed the benefits of a flat organization outweighed the problems that could arise from too great a span of control.

Chart A

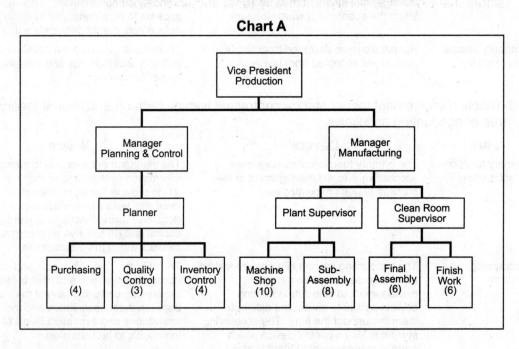

Chart B

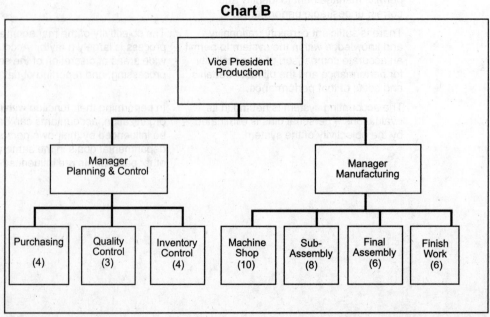

Questions

10. For the original organizational structure proposed by Donald Jenkins, vice president of production, describe

    a. The advantages and disadvantages of the organizational structure
    b. The impact of the resulting span of control
    c. The effect of the organizational structure on employee behavior

11. For the flat organizational structure proposed by Beverly Kiner, president, describe

    a. The advantages and disadvantages of the organizational structure
    b. The impact of the resulting span of control
    c. The effect of the organizational structure on employee behavior

12. When determining the appropriate span of control for Parker Machine Company, discuss the factors that Donald Jenkins and Beverly Kiner should consider.

Essay Questions 10, 11, 12 — Unofficial Answers

10. For the original organizational structure proposed by Donald Jenkins,

   a. Advantages include
   - Centralized decision making
   - Close supervision of subordinates
   - Increased opportunities for promotion

   Disadvantages include
   - Lack of flexibility/creativity
   - More difficult vertical communication
   - Increased costs for additional management personnel

   b. The span of control will
   - Allow for tighter control over employees
   - Afford timelier task completion and problem resolution, as the supervisors are closer to everyday operations

   c. As a result of the organizational structure proposed by Donald Jenkins, the employees are likely to have a clear understanding of what is expected of them. However, because of the tighter span of control, the employees may avoid making decisions and taking risks.

11. For the flat organizational structure proposed by Beverly Kiner,

   a. Advantages include
   - Quicker decision making
   - Lower costs resulting from fewer management personnel

   Disadvantages include
   - Increased risk of inaccuracy in performing tasks due to reduced supervision
   - Fewer available promotional opportunities, which may lead to increased employee turnover

   b. The span of control will
   - Afford employees greater autonomy
   - Result in increased creativity

   c. As a result of the organizational structure proposed by Beverly Kiner, employees are likely to be motivated by greater participation, as their input has greater value. However, employees may not be adequately trained for additional responsibilities.

12. The factors that Donald Jenkins and Beverly Kiner should consider when determining the appropriate span of control include the
   - Competence and qualifications of the employees
   - Corporate culture and preferred style of management of the organization

---

Consider using Gleim's **CMA Test Prep** for interactive testing with **hundreds of multiple-choice questions** as an additional method of knowledge transfer in your quest to pass Part 4.

STUDY UNIT TWO
JOBS AND TEAMS

(9 pages of outline)

This study unit is the **second of four** on **organization management**. The four study units are

Study Unit 1: Organization Structures
Study Unit 2: Jobs and Teams
Study Unit 3: Leadership Styles and Sources of Power
Study Unit 4: Motivational Theories and Diversity Issues

After studying the outline and answering the essay questions, you will have the skills necessary to address the following topics listed in the IMA's Learning Outcome Statements:

Part 4 - Section A. Organization Management. 2. Jobs and teams

The candidate should be able to:

NOTE: Statements a. and b. are covered in Study Unit 4.

    c.   differentiate teams from groups
    d.   contrast formal and informal teams
    e.   summarize the benefits and costs of teams in organizations
    f.   identify different types of teams
    g.   explain issues inherent in the team model, including empowerment, leadership issues, consensus building, and decision making
    h.   identify top management support as one of the critical factors in the success of a team
    i.   analyze the effectiveness of a team and recommend changes to improve performance

2.1 GROUPS

1.   A **group** is a set of two or more people who interact. Note that mere proximity does not make for a group; people can work next to each other but if they do not interact, they do not form a group. Also, people form a group whenever they interact, even if they are working at cross purposes.

    a.   A **team** is a type of group in which the members (1) are committed to a common goal and (2) have expectations of each other's performance in pursuit of that goal.

2.   **Informal groups**, ignored by classical school writers, were the major focus of the behavioral school.

    a.   People naturally seek association and group acceptance and tend to form both formal and informal groups as a result. Thus, effective managers recognize, accept, and take advantage of informal organization. Informal groups are created within organizations because of

        1)   Authority interrelationships that cannot be charted
        2)   Unwritten rules of conduct
        3)   Group preferences

b. **Characteristics of informal groups** (informal organization)

1) Almost all employees, including managers, are members of some informal group(s).

2) Members of informal groups react to the pressures of these groups.

   a) These pressures are difficult to resist, and most members do tend to conform.

3) These groups tend to be small and are often very complex. They tend to develop their own leaders, exist to fill the needs of the members, and usually result from the frequent interaction among individuals in the course of their work.

c. **Favorable effects of informal groups**

1) Reduce tension and encourage production
2) Improve coordination and reduce supervision required
3) Aid in problem-solving situations
4) Provide another (often faster) channel of communication

   a) The grapevine is the informal, unofficial communication system found in every kind of organization. The emergence of computer networks in the workplace has only served to strengthen the grapevine.

5) Provide social satisfactions that supplement job satisfactions

d. **Some potentially unfavorable effects of informal groups**. They can

1) Work to circumvent managerial actions
2) Serve to reduce production levels (slowdowns caused by counterproductive social interactions)
3) Generate dissension in the formal organization
4) Spread rumors and distort information
5) Add to the cost of doing business
6) Form subgroups that hinder group cohesiveness
7) Pressure members to adopt group norms that may be contrary to the main goals of the organization
8) Develop dominant members

3. A **team** is a group whose members work intensively with each other to achieve a specific common goal, whereas a group is two or more people who merely interact. Thus, all teams are groups, but not all groups are teams. Teams can improve organizational performance, but are often difficult to form because it takes time for members to work together. Normally, the smaller the team, the better; from two to nine members is recommended. A team differs from a group in that team leadership often rotates and team members are accountable to each other.

a. A team may be

1) **Functional**, which includes a manager and some of his or her subordinates in the same department.

2) **Cross-functional (or horizontal)**, meaning that the team includes members of different departments who have different areas of expertise. A **research-and-development team** is an example of a team that is typically cross-functional in that many skills are needed to identify and create a new product.

3) **Cross-cultural**, which includes members of different cultures. Diversity is believed to enhance group work because there are more viewpoints that can be brought forth.

4) A **command group**, which is a team composed of members who report to the same manager.

5) **Top-Management**, which helps develop the organization's direction.

6) **Problem-solving**, which is formed to solve a specific problem. An example is a quality circle. Such teams are usually disbanded after the problem has been solved.

7) **Virtual**, which is a team that uses computer technology so that geographically distant members can work together on projects and reach common goals.

b. Teams may also be classified by purpose (goal or objective), duration (permanent or temporary), membership (functional versus cross-functional), and structure (supervised versus self-managed).

c. The benefits of teams include the synergy (i.e., the total is more than the sum of the parts) that is created by talented people working together. Workers on a team have the opportunity to produce more or better output than separate workers because members correct each other's mistakes and bring new ideas to the forefront. Innovation is another benefit since individuals rarely possess the wide variety of skills needed to develop flawless new ideas. Motivation is also a benefit because team members are often better motivated and satisfied than individuals. The benefits are dependent upon the existence of able team **leadership**, full **empowerment** from management, and a group that is able to **build consensus** and **come to a decision**. Teams also provide social interaction to members.

d. Empowerment is an important aspect of team success. First, management must recognize the need to support teams, and secondly must give the teams full empowerment to achieve the established goals.

e. Management must periodically evaluate teams and provide recommendations for improvement when needed.

f. A problem with teams is the situation known as **social loafing**, which is the human tendency to put forth less effort in a group than individually. To avoid social loafing, individual efforts should be identifiable and subject to evaluation. Social loafing is less of a problem in small groups where every member knows what the others are supposed to be doing.

g. **Brainstorming** is sometimes an important team activity. Brainstorming involves a group getting together and developing ideas. Ideally, ideas will not be judged initially, but all ideas are written down and are later either discarded or are more fully developed. Thus, a nonjudgmental environment is essential for effective brainstorming.

1) To create a nonjudgmental environment or to avoid letting personalities affect the evaluation of ideas, some means of conferring anonymity is sometimes used, such as the Delphi Method, which allows for the anonymous evaluation of ideas.

4. A **committee** is a group that considers a particular problem or class of problems. The committee's objective is to educate, to inform, or to make a decision. The committee is one of the most universal, and most controversial, devices of the organization. Other names include task force, team, commission, and board.

a. The classical position is to avoid the committee. The behavioral position is to encourage its use because of positive morale benefits. The modern position is to determine both the type and the nature of committees by situational factors.

b.   Committees may

1)   Undertake managerial functions

2)   Make decisions or participate in one or more parts of the decision process (e.g., identifying problems, searching for alternatives, evaluating alternatives, making recommendations, helping to implement choices)

3)   Be formed merely to receive information, without making decisions or recommendations

4)   Be either line or staff, depending upon authority

5)   Be formal, if designated as part of the organizational structure

    a)   Formal committees can be standing (permanent) or ad hoc (temporary), i.e., formed to consider a one-time situation.

6)   Be informal, if organized without specific delegation of authority

    a)   Informal committees are often formed by individuals desiring input for decision making in the form of advice from other managers or specialists.

c.   **Principles for the use of committees**

1)   **Balance.** Members should be selected to obtain optimum input bearing on the problem; the selection entails consideration of members' knowledge, time, and communication skills.

2)   **Efficiency.** The benefits should exceed the cost.

3)   **Time.** Scheduling and time away from regular work should be considered.

4)   **Objective.** The objective should guide the committee and limit its actions in solving a problem, coordinating activities, selling an idea, educating, etc.

5)   **Leadership.** The chair should act as a moderator and not be considered threatening or overbearing by the members.

6)   **Groupism.** A tendency toward mediocrity and compromise should be avoided. **Groupthink**, i.e., the tendency to conform and ignore relevant individual input that is at variance with the perceived group opinion, is to be avoided. At the same time, consensus is desirable.

7)   **Size.** The size of a committee is determined by its needed input, but in any event it should be kept small. Five members are often considered maximum for effective work.

8)   **Individualism.** An overriding question is whether an individual should make the decision rather than the committee.

d.   Misuse of committees has caused some organizations to neglect this form of management. The following abuses of committees should be avoided:

1)   The committee should not be used as a managing device. Leadership is essentially a quality of individuals rather than groups. Clear, prompt decisions subject to unquestioned responsibility are better made by individuals.

2)   Use of the committee for research or study is ineffective. The primary purpose of a committee is to discuss or exchange views on information already known to the members. A committee may use a research staff if research and study are needed.

3)   Unimportant decisions are not appropriate for the committee forum. The feeling that time is being wasted on insignificant matters frustrates and alienates intelligent managers and specialists.

        4)   One of the most common abuses of committees is to make decisions that are beyond the authority of the participants. Delays occur while matters are referred to the appropriate superior authority, and much of the advantage of group decision making is lost.

        5)   The consolidation of divided authority is better accomplished through changes in the organizational structure than through committees.

5.   **Quality circles** are groups, usually of five to ten employees (management or subordinates), doing similar work who volunteer to meet at a specified time (e.g., once a week) to discuss and solve problems associated with their work areas.

    a.   The objectives of quality circles are to use employee capabilities more fully, build a more congenial workplace, and contribute to the improvement and development of both the company and individual employees.

    b.   The mechanics of a quality circle include the following problem-solving steps:

        1)   Circle members bring problems before the group.

        2)   The problems or projects are analyzed.

        3)   Solutions are developed and presented to management.

        4)   Management follows up on the suggestions by either approving or disapproving the ideas, with feedback to circle members.

    c.   **Advantages of quality circles**

        1)   Easy implementation without major organizational change

        2)   More efficient and effective operation of the company

        3)   Better-quality products

        4)   Improved employee morale and better cohesion among coworkers

    d.   **Disadvantages of quality circles**

        1)   Objections from unions

        2)   Reduced morale if suggestions are not accepted by management and management fails to adequately explain nonacceptance

        3)   Potential loss of management control

6.   **Self-managed teams** are a facet of TQM. They are autonomous groups that go beyond quality circles because they represent a major organizational change.

    a.   Team members are not volunteers but have been assigned to the teams.

    b.   Teams are assembled to produce a complete product or service. Accordingly, they are empowered to perform traditional management tasks, such as scheduling, ordering materials, and even hiring.

    c.   A **self-managed team** is one with autonomy and control over its work. The team decides how to perform the assigned task. Keys to the effectiveness of self-managed teams include:

        1)   The team should have enough **responsibility and autonomy** to be self managing.

        2)   Members should have **diversity, skills, and enthusiasm** for the project. Diversity is important to avoid group-think. Workforce diversity is not limited to gender, sex, or national origin; it also includes differences in style, cultures, age, education, kinds of work performed, length of time in the organization, religious affiliation, sexual orientation, geographic origin, and more.

        3)   The task should be complex enough to include several different steps.

        4)   Managers should only guide and coach, not supervise.

        5)   Top management should support the team.

7. The **benefits of teams** flow from the principle that employee self-management is the best management.

    a. Motivation is improved because decision making is decentralized. The increased authority of autonomous work groups is intended to create a sense of ownership in the work product. Better decision making, productivity, quality, and goal congruence should be the results.

    b. An advantage of cross-functional teams is improved communication because all members have a better understanding of all facets of team activities.

    c. If teams are staffed appropriately and have the necessary resources and support from management, they should be able to improve the processes of production. The individuals who perform the work have the power to make decisions about the way it is done.

2.2 GROUP DYNAMICS

1. Many problems in management stem from group behavior patterns, attitudes, and desires.

    a. Any organized enterprise is also a social structure that includes a number of subunits.

        1) Each social structure is a complex of interacting attitudes, pressures, and conflicts arising from the cultural background of the individuals making up the subunit.

    b. Some problems arise from the work group (inside the enterprise).

    c. Other problems result from the differing backgrounds of people (outside of the enterprise), i.e., attitudes they bring with them to work. Examples are individual prejudices about race or religion.

2. German-American psychologist Kurt Lewin (late 1930s) identified **group dynamics** as a working model for describing human behavior. He stressed studying people where they were, not where someone believed they ideally should have been.

    a. Lewin's work provided the theoretical framework for modern **sensitivity training** and training laboratories.

3. Several common **characteristics of groups** influence behavior.

    a. Leadership. All groups have leaders, formal and/or informal, who initiate interrelationships and act as communication centers.

    b. Norms. From earliest observations, groups have been found to be guided by self-set standards of performance and behavior, usually based on a composite of the personal and social backgrounds of the individuals on the job as well as those of people outside the group and outside the job.

    c. Status systems. There is a ranking within the group; it may be based on skill, age, ethnic background, seniority, and/or personality.

    d. Roles. Certain behavior patterns are expected of the individual by the group.

    e. Goals. The group becomes an entity and develops its own goals, its own survival and recognition needs, etc.

    f. Activity. Action by the members of the group identify them as a group.

    g. Bias. The group shares common beliefs and values about the world in which the group operates.

4. **Group behavior** is a distinct phenomenon. It is not merely the sum of the behaviors of the individuals making up the group. However, groups conceal the relationship between individual effort and outcome.

   a. A group as a whole tends to be riskier and more emotional than most of its individuals.

   b. A group has values of its own, as expressed by group behavior.

   c. Groups tend to normalize behavior, bringing deviant individuals into line through pressure to conform to group norms.

      1) The strength of this normalizing pressure is correlated to group cohesiveness. Increased cohesiveness may either increase or decrease productivity.

      2) Workers who exceed the group norm will also be pressured to conform so as not to embarrass the other group members.

      3) Workers who produce below the norm will be pressured to improve so as not to overburden the others.

      4) Cohesiveness in the organization of a labor union may allow the group to halt production completely until their demands are met.

   d. Work groups have a positive effect on the organization if management arranges for congruence between group goals and organizational goals. Management may encourage the development of a **corporate or organizational culture**, that is, a sense of shared customs, values, rituals, history, and style. It may operate through both formal procedures and implicit means of social control.

      1) An organizational culture should enhance stability, goal congruence, morale, and performance.

      2) Organizational socialization is the formal or informal process of training new employees to conform to the organizational culture.

      3) The increasing rate of globalization has complicated the development of unique organizational cultures. The problems of dealing with foreign customers, branches, and subsidiaries means socialization must consider country-specific cultural differences.

5. **Commitment** to a group depends on its **attractiveness and cohesiveness**.

   a. Attractiveness is a favorable view from the outside.

   b. Cohesiveness is the tendency of members to adhere to the group and resist outside influences.

   c. Factors that enhance group attractiveness and cohesiveness are prestige, status, a cooperative relationship, a high degree of interaction, small size, the similarity of members, a superior public image, and a common threat in the environment.

   d. The process of group development proceeds through a succession of stages in which conflicts over power, authority, and interpersonal relationships must be overcome.

      1) Groups that evolve into the acceptance stage of group development tend to be both effective and efficient. This stage is characterized by personal and mutual understanding, tolerance of individual differences, constructive conflict about substantive matters, realistic expectations about group performance, and acceptance of the authority structure. The resulting trust engenders cohesiveness and a free exchange of information between group members.

6. **Role playing** is an important concept that emerged from the group dynamics theory. A role is the behavior expected of a person who occupies a particular position. Everyone is expected to play or assume different roles in different situations.

7. **Role conflict** emerges when two or more roles, making conflicting demands, are simultaneously expected of, or imposed on, a person.

    a. For example, a manager may expect an employee to work late (employee role) on the night of his/her child's birthday party (parent role). An example of conflict between an employer role and a coworker role occurs when a person is promoted to supervisor (employer role) of a department in which (s)he was previously on the same level with other employees (peer or coworker role).

    b. Types of role conflict

        1) Conflict between role and self occurs when personal characteristics are incompatible with the expected role.

        2) Interrole conflict involves having different roles, each with different behavioral expectations.

        3) Intersender conflict results from being expected to behave differently by different people, although having the same role, e.g., a manager who has to be a leader (of subordinates) and a follower (of top management).

        4) Intrasender conflict arises from being sent different **messages** (roles) by the same person (e.g., a manager who expects an employee to behave one way one day and another the next).

8. Ambiguous or contradictory role demands cause stress to the individual. Recognition of the causes of role conflict helps to minimize its effect.

2.3 CORE CONCEPTS

Groups

- A **group** is a set of two or more people who interact. Note that mere proximity does not make for a group; people can work next to each other but if they do not interact, they do not form a group. Also, people form a group whenever they interact, even if they are working at cross purposes.

- **Informal groups**, ignored by classical school writers, were the major focus of the behavioral school. People naturally seek association and group acceptance and tend to form both formal and informal groups as a result. Thus, effective managers **recognize, accept, and take advantage** of informal organization.

- **Almost all employees**, including managers, are members of some informal group(s). Members of informal groups **react to the pressures** of these groups.

- Informal groups have **both beneficial and negative aspects** for the organization.

- A **team** is a group whose members work intensively with each other to achieve a specific common goal, whereas a group is two or more people who merely interact. Thus, all teams are groups, but not all groups are teams.

- A **committee** is a group that considers a particular problem or class of problems. The committee's objective is to educate, to inform, or to make a decision. The committee is one of the **most universal, and most controversial**, devices of the organization.

- The **classical** position is to avoid the committee. The **behavioral** position is to encourage its use because of positive morale benefits. The **modern** position is to determine both the type and the nature of committees by situational fact.

- The committee should **not be used as a managing device**. Leadership is essentially a quality of individuals rather than groups. Clear, prompt decisions subject to unquestioned responsibility are better made by individuals.

- Use of the committee **for research or study is ineffective**. The primary purpose of a committee is to discuss or exchange views on information already known to the members. A committee may use a research staff if research and study are needed.

- **Quality circles** are groups, usually of five to ten employees (management or subordinates), doing similar work who volunteer to meet at a specified time (e.g., once a week) to discuss and solve problems associated with their work areas.

- **Self-managed** teams are autonomous groups that go beyond quality circles because they represent a major organizational change. Team members are not volunteers but have been assigned to the teams. A self-managed team is one with autonomy and control over its work.

- The **benefits** of teams flow from the principles that employee self-management is the best management. Motivation is improved because decision making is decentralized. The increased authority of autonomous work groups is intended to create a sense of ownership in the work product. Better decision making, productivity, quality, and goal congruence should be the results.

Group Dynamics

- **Group dynamics** is a working model for describing human behavior. It stresses studying people where they were, not where someone believed they ideally should have been. Group dynamics has provided the theoretical framework for modern **sensitivity training** and training laboratories.

- **Group behavior** is a distinct phenomenon. It is not merely the sum of the behaviors of the individuals making up the group. However, groups conceal the relationship between individual effort and outcome.

- A group as a whole tends to be **riskier and more emotional** than most of its individuals. A group has values of its own, as expressed by group behavior. Groups tend to **normalize behavior**, bringing deviant individuals into line through pressure to conform to group norms.

- **Attractiveness** is a favorable view of a group from the outside. **Cohesiveness** is the tendency of members to adhere to the group and resist outside influences.

- **Role playing** is an important concept that emerged from the group dynamics theory. A role is the behavior expected of a person who occupies a particular position. Everyone is expected to play or assume different roles in different situations. **Role conflict** emerges when two or more roles, making conflicting demands, are simultaneously expected of, or imposed on, a person.

2.4 ESSAY QUESTIONS

Recall that your CMA Part 4 exam will probably contain six scenarios, with about three questions per scenario. There will be a recommended time allocation of 20 minutes, 30 minutes, or 45 minutes for each scenario and related questions.

One scenario will involve ethics issues, and probably one or two scenarios will include calculations and responses on a worksheet. Also, expect at least one scenario on organizational/behavioral topics. The remaining scenarios cover Parts 1, 2, and 3.

Scenario Title	Subtopic	Questions	Suggested Time
Askew, Inc.	Behavior and Organizational Structure	1, 2, 3	30 minutes
Goliath Systems Corporation	Groups and Motivation	4, 5, 6	30 minutes

Scenario for Essay Questions 1, 2, 3

Askew, Inc. manufactures machines that produce precision tools. Askew has been in business for over 70 years and has been unionized. Askew has been hurt by foreign competitors who have captured large shares of the United States domestic market. To survive, Askew invested considerable effort in developing an advanced hi-tech machine. As a result of this revolutionary design, Askew is planning to build a new, modernized manufacturing plant to meet the predicted demand.

Askew is conscious of costs and has requested the union to participate in the planning process for the new facility. After discussing the matter with the union leadership, an innovative agreement was reached to help contain costs. Highlights of the agreement are presented below.

- The union has made wage concessions and agreed to eliminate restrictive work rules, including seniority rights, in return for greater participation in management decisions and job security for the majority of the workers.
- The union has agreed to a specified level of robotics and subcontracting to meet the foreign competition's lower labor costs.
- All workers will participate in a profit-sharing plan.

Both management and union leaders recognized that it was in the best interests of both to have a profitable company. The result was an organizational structure different from Askew's hierarchical one. The new structure provides for union representation on all committees and with consensus decision making at all levels. The following represents the basic elements of the structure:

- Team-directed Work Force. Groups or cells of workers who discuss and plan the day's activities including workloads, job assignments, ordering, production, etc. The team is responsible for quality control, controlling costs, and budgeted expenditures. New ideas developed by the team must be considered by management. The teams have coaches-facilitators who help to direct and support the team, but they do not control it.
- Business Unit. A committee that coordinates plant level operations, with company and union advisors participating at this level.
- Manufacturing Advisory Committee. Top company and union officials who oversee the entire business and are charged with reaching consensus decisions on salary and benefit changes, as well as promotions, without formal collective bargaining.
- Strategic Advisory Committee. A committee that performs long-range planning, comprised of Askew's president, a top union official, and appropriate staff members.

Both labor and management have critics of the plan. Union factions believe that turning workers into managers and de-emphasizing collective bargaining will undermine the union, while management has reservations as to whether the advantages are worth the loss of many management prerogatives.

Questions

1. With respect to the organizational structure introduced at Askew, Inc.'s new facility, discuss at least two advantages and at least two disadvantages to

   a. The employees.
   b. Askew, Inc.

2. Discuss the likely behavior of all affected personnel under the following two situations:

   a. Several management level employees will be transferred from other Askew plants to the new facility.

   b. To provide a technical base for a start-up operation, management and union officials have agreed to employ several workers who recently retired at other locations. These workers are not expected to remain employed for more than 2 years.

3. a. Describe actions that must be taken to ensure that a team-directed, workforce approach can be successful.

   b. Describe the negative behavioral issues that can be expected to surface in the initial stages of a team-directed, workforce approach.

Essay Questions 1, 2, 3 — Unofficial Answers

1. a. Advantages to employees include

    1) Profit-sharing and incentive bonuses
    2) Increased job satisfaction from increased responsibilities and greater challenges

    Disadvantages to employees include

    1) Loss of seniority rights
    2) Loss of collective bargaining and grievance procedures

    b. Advantages to Askew, Inc. include

    1) Lower costs and higher profit potential through wage concessions, elimination of restrictive work rules and seniority rights, and ability to use robotics and subcontract work
    2) Greater employee loyalty and higher quality work through team responsibility

    Disadvantages to Askew, Inc. include

    1) Loss of management prerogatives through power sharing with union members
    2) Loss of flexibility and adaptability because of the time involved in consensus decision making

2. a. The management level employees transferred to the new Askew Plant, having come from the more traditional management-employee environment, are likely to resent the loss of management authority and the requirements of consensus decision making. The union employees at the new plant may not trust the transferred-in managers until they have been time-tested.

    b. Because of their long association with the union, the skilled workers hired to assist with the start-up may find the structure difficult to work in and may try to undermine the new organizational structure.

3. a. The actions that must be taken to assure that a team-directed work-force approach can be successful include

    1) Training all employees on at least two levels: skill-based training to make all employees cross-functional and communication training. Also there should be training for all employees on all functions of business, focused primarily on the non-physical skills of business, problem-solving, and team dynamics.
    2) Ensuring that changes do not negatively affect customer service or productivity.
    3) Defining goals and operating parameters for the business unit, as well as determining exactly what constitutes "acceptable performance."

    b. The negative behavioral issues that can be expected to surface in the initial stages of a team-directed, workforce approach include

    1) Fear. At the outset, managers will fear the loss of control because, under the old system, control equaled power. First-line managers may fear losing their jobs as teams take on the traditional managerial responsibilities.
    2) Stress, as emotions run high in the beginning. Issues that were buried for many years come out into the open.
    3) Potentially high losses of first-line supervisors should efforts to retrain and transform them fail.

Scenario for Essay Questions 4, 5, 6

Roy Nelson has been hired as the new controller of Goliath Systems Corporation. His previous job and all of his experience was in another region of the country more than a thousand miles away. He has noticed that the employees at Goliath seem to operate somewhat differently than at the smaller companies where he had previously worked.

One characteristic common to many organizations is the existence of informal groups within the organization. These groups often fill an important role in the operation of an organization.

Questions

4. Define an "informal group."

5. Enumerate and briefly describe the hierarchy of needs which are said to motivate workers.

6. Identify the need(s) that an informal group helps to satisfy and explain how informal groups meet the need(s).

Essay Questions 4, 5, 6 — Unofficial Answers

4. An informal group is a number of individuals attracted to one another by common geography, identity, values, and/or goals. The group identifies, then enforces, a set of behavior standards via sanctions and rewards. The informal group exists supplementary to the formal management system within which it is normally found.

5. Maslow, among others, has identified a framework or hierarchy of human needs to help explain human motivation in the work situation. His hierarchy has five levels as follows:

   a. Physiological needs -- food, clothing, shelter; the most basic survival requirements
   b. Safety needs -- freedom from fear of physical threats or loss of means to satisfy the physiological needs
   c. Social needs -- the desire to give and receive acceptance, friendship, and affection; the desire to feel needed
   d. Esteem needs -- to have recognition and respect shown by others; the desire to feel important or have power
   e. Self-actualization needs -- the desire to achieve one's potential

6. Needs satisfied through the informal group include

   a. Social needs -- The formal work environment does not necessarily provide social needs, but the primary reason for the formation and existence of informal groups is the desire for social relationships and acceptance
   b. Safety needs -- Safety needs help protect the worker against real or imagined threats from the formal organization
   c. Esteem needs -- Persons receive respect or recognition of importance within the informal group whether it be by leadership or some other mechanism
   d. Self-actualization needs -- Persons achieve self-actualization through leadership, influence, and goal accomplishment within the informal group

---

Consider using Gleim's *CMA Test Prep* for interactive testing with **hundreds of multiple-choice questions** as an additional method of knowledge transfer in your quest to pass Part 4.

STUDY UNIT THREE
LEADERSHIP STYLES AND SOURCES OF POWER

(10 pages of outline)

This study unit is the **third of four** on **organization management**. The four study units are

Study Unit 1: Organization Structures
Study Unit 2: Jobs and Teams
Study Unit 3: Leadership Styles and Sources of Power
Study Unit 4: Motivational Theories and Diversity Issues

After studying the outline and answering the essay questions, you will have the skills necessary to address the following topics listed in the IMA's Learning Outcome Statements:

Part 4 - Section A. Organization Management. 3. Leadership styles and sources of power

The candidate should be able to:

a. distinguish between management and leadership

b. identify and explain the various types of leadership styles, including autocratic and democratic leadership

c. contrast task or job-centered leader behavior with employee-centered leader behavior

d. infer the leadership style and/or behavior given an organizational situation

e. explain the major features of Fiedler's contingency (or LPC) theory of leadership, the path-goal theory of leadership, and the Vroom-Yetton-Jago model of leadership

f. define transformational leadership

g. apply theories of leadership to organizational scenarios

h. identify the types and sources of power, including legitimate power, reward power, coercive power, expert power, and referent or charismatic power

i. discuss the importance of informal power and influence

j. define and explain delegation of authority

k. identify sources of resistance to change at an individual level, as well as at the group level and the organizational level

l. recommend methods to accept, encourage, and bring about change from a leadership perspective

3.1 LEADERSHIP

1. **Management** is arranging the work of others toward organizational objectives. **Leadership** is the act or process of influencing people so they will strive willingly toward the objectives. Leadership, then, is a special type of management, one that inspires enthusiastic cooperation in pursuit of the objectives, not mere assent.

    a. The classical position focused on the idea that authority, decision making, and responsibility may all be decentralized in the organization to some extent, but leadership is a characteristic of the individual's personality and cannot be subdivided.

    b. The **traitist approach** was characteristic of studies before 1949, in which attempts were made to identify traits possessed by leaders. Starting with the theory that leaders are born, not made, attempts were made to identify the physical, mental, and psychological traits of various leaders. The traitist approach has produced such a long list of leadership traits that, in effect, it identifies nothing. A few traits do seem to have significant correlation with a leader's effectiveness, however.

        1) Intelligence
        2) Maturity
        3) Social participation and interest
        4) Socioeconomic status (in comparison to nonleaders)

2. With so little useful guidance from the leader characteristics approach, behavior-oriented researchers examined **leader behavior** to see if leaders conducted themselves in certain ways.

    a. **Styles of leadership** are emphasized in behavioral approaches. The proper leadership style depends on the situation. The personal background of the manager is also a determining factor, as are the personalities and backgrounds of the employees being supervised.

        1) These styles have been characterized as

            a) **Autocratic.** The manager dictates all decisions to the employees. This is considered the classical approach to leadership. Employees are not allowed to give input. Autocratic leaders rely on threats and punishment and do not trust workers. However, autocratic leadership can sometimes be the most effective, such as when there is limited time to make a decision or when workers do not respond to any other leadership style.

            b) **Consultative.** The manager takes the employee's view into account but still makes the decisions.

            c) **Participative** (also known as **democratic**). The employee has a definite input into decision making and the manager must include subordinates' views in the decision. The employee is encouraged to grow on the job and be promoted.

                i)   But not all employees are willing to participate.
                ii) Many employees like the trust they receive.

            d) **Free-rein** (also known as **laissez-faire**). The employees make their own decisions.

            e) **Bureaucratic.** A manager manages "by the book." Everything must be done according to procedure or policy. If there is no policy to cover a situation, the manager refers to the next level above himself.

                i)   Bureaucratic leaders are essentially policemen rather than leaders. Bureaucratic leaders are sometimes necessary when employees are working with dangerous or highly delicate equipment or chemicals. Cash handling functions are sometimes policed by a bureaucratic leader.

ii) German sociologist Max Weber argued that bureaucracy is essential in structuring governments and administrations. He viewed it as functional, efficient, and necessary for capitalism to be successful. Within the bureaucratic type there are specific rules and regulations for every goal. These rules must be followed by employees. Officials are subject to a hierarchy, and fulfill their duties impersonally.

iii) Weber began by discussing how work is carried out within the bureaucratic organization. Activities for governing are official duties and are assigned by a set of rules that determine who will perform what specialized task. These are completed only by employees who have received the adequate education. In this manner, the functions become bureaucratic authority.

iv) Within the bureaucracy there exists a labor hierarchy directed by more regulations. That is, there are levels of authority. Supervision by a higher official ensures that management remains orderly. Also, subordinate officials have the opportunity to appeal a decision to a higher authority.

2) The behaviorists feel that leadership traits are not hereditary, except for physical characteristics like stature or health.

b. **Employee vs. task orientation.** A greater concern for people than for task accomplishment (although a certain degree of task orientation is vital) is believed to be more productive than the opposite. The leader must balance the personal needs of subordinates with task accomplishment.

c. **Initiating-structure behavior vs. consideration behavior.** Two behavior patterns that are consistently found in the study of leadership are the initiation of structure and consideration by the leader (production-centered versus employee-centered behavior).

1) Initiating-structure behavior is directed towards accomplishing tasks. Structure includes

   a) Defining duties
   b) Establishing procedures
   c) Planning and organizing the work

2) Consideration behavior is the establishment of a personal relationship between the leader and the subordinate. High consideration by the leader includes

   a) Warmth toward the employee as a person
   b) Psychological support for the employee
   c) Helpfulness with problems in the work

3) Both structure initiation and consideration behavior are present in all job situations, and the relative amounts of each must be appropriate to the situation.

   a) EXAMPLES:

      i) A highly structured situation (like assembly-line work) may respond negatively to further structure initiated by the manager but positively to increased consideration.

      ii) A manager of research and development may find the initiation of structure much more productive than increased consideration. Creative personnel working on a disorganized project may find a better-defined project plan much more satisfying than a demonstration of concern by the manager.

3.   The modern view follows a **contingency approach** in looking for even better answers to the questions, "What is an effective leader?" and "How do we train and identify leaders?".

   a.   According to Austrian-American organizational psychologist Fred E. Fiedler's contingency theory, people become leaders not only because of personality attributes but also because of various situational factors and the interaction between the leaders and the situation.

      1)   Thus, the right person at the right time may rise to a position of leadership if his/her personality and the needs of the situation complement each other. The same person might not become a leader in different circumstances because of failure to interact successfully with that situation.

      2)   There are three dimensions to the contingency theory model:

         a)   **Position power** is a function of the formal authority structure and is the degree to which the position held enables a leader to evaluate, reward, sanction, or promote the group members independent of other sources of power, such as personality or expertise.

         b)   **Task structure** is how clearly and carefully the worker's responsibilities for various tasks are defined. Quality of performance is more easily controlled when tasks are clearly defined.

         c)   **Leader-member relations** reflect the extent to which group members like and trust and are willing to follow a leader.

            i)   Relationship to group members is the most important dimension from the leader's point of view, since position power and task structure may be largely under the control of the enterprise.

            ii)   The "least preferred coworker" test is one way to assess the optimal arrangement of group members by asking the leader to rank possible subordinates from least to most preferred. Previously unrecognized biases may surface that the leader can evaluate and learn to deal with.

      3)   **Fiedler's research** showed two types of leaders:

         a)   **Task-oriented** style is most effective when the situation is very favorable or very unfavorable.

         b)   **Relationship-oriented** style is most effective in the middle, less extreme situations.

      4)   The most effective leadership style is contingent upon the definition of the three dimensions.

      5)   Leadership is therefore as much a responsibility of the organization's placement of leaders as it is of the leaders themselves. An organization should identify leadership situations and its managers' leadership styles and engineer the job to suit the manager if necessary.

   b.   According to Hersey and Blanchard's **situational leadership theory**, the appropriate leadership style depends on followers' maturity, which is their degree of willingness to be responsible for directing their behavior.

      1)   Maturity includes both job and psychological maturity. For example, experienced and knowledgeable workers who are highly motivated need little external direction.

2) The dimensions of leadership involve task and relationship behaviors.

    a) One leadership style is participative. Task emphasis should be low, but relationship emphasis should be high. The leader's primary activities are facilitating and communicating, and decisions should be shared.

    b) The delegating style does not emphasize tasks or relationships.

    c) The selling style emphasizes both tasks and relationships.

    d) A directive (telling) leadership style is characterized by a high task, low relationship emphasis.

c. **Path-goal theory** combines the research on initiating structure and consideration with expectancy theory. According to path-goal theory, **situational factors** and **leader behaviors** interact to influence worker motivation.

1) Situational factors fall into two categories, **personal characteristics of subordinates** and **environmental characteristics**.

    a) Subordinates' personal characteristics include locus of control, level of experience, and perceived ability.

    b) Environmental factors are those beyond subordinates' control, such as task structure, the formal authority system, and the work group.

2) A **leadership style should be chosen** that complements but does not duplicate the factors in the environment and is consistent with subordinates' characteristics.

    a) The **directive** leader lets subordinates know what is expected of them, schedules work to be done, and gives specific guidance on how to accomplish tasks.

        i) A directive style is most effective when the subordinate's locus of control is external, tasks are ambiguous or stressful, and substantial conflict exists in the work group. Thus, a directive style is appropriate when subordinates do not have high perceived ability or experience.

    b) The **supportive** leader is friendly and shows concern for the needs of the subordinates.

        i) Supportive style is best when tasks are highly structured and the authority relationships are clear and bureaucratic.

        ii) This approach depends on people who want to work, grow, and achieve.

    c) The **participative** leader consults with subordinates and uses their suggestions before making a decision.

        i) Participative style is most useful when subordinates believe they control their own destinies, that is, when they have an internal locus of control. Such individuals may be resentful if they are not consulted.

    d) The **achievement-oriented** leader sets challenging goals and expects subordinates to perform at their highest level.

        i) Achievement-oriented leadership is appropriate when tasks are nonrepetitive and ambiguous and employee competence is high.

4. The **Vroom-Yetton-Jago** model describes leadership as a decision making process. The model helps leaders to determine how to arrive at, communicate, and implement decisions for various situations in an organization.

    a. The model identifies five decision-making styles and provides tools for reaching decisions under each style. Two of the decision-making styles are autocratic, two are consultative, and the fifth is group-directed. The degree of subordinate participation ranges from none or low (the autocratic styles), to moderate (the consultative styles), to high (the group-directed style).

    b. Computer software programs or decision-trees are used to guide leaders in the decision making process, including the choice of the decision-making style that is appropriate to a given situation.

        1) The guidance consists of diagnostic questions concerning such issues as the significance of the technical quality of the decision, the need for subordinates' commitment to the decision, the sufficiency of information available to the leader and to subordinates, the degree to which the problem is structured, potential conflict among subordinates regarding solutions, the probability that subordinates will be committed to a decision made by the leader, and the degree to which subordinates' goals and those of the organization are congruent.

5. A **transformational leader** is an agent of change. The transformational leader is able to inspire the members of the organization to aspire to and achieve more than they thought was possible.

    a. Transformational leadership emphasizes vision, development of the individual, empowerment of the worker, and the challenging of traditional assumptions.

    b. Transformational leaders articulate a vision, use nontraditional thinking, encourage individual development, provide workers with regular feedback, use participative decision-making, and promote a cooperative and trusting work environment.

    c. The transformational leader normally has charisma, is inspirational, motivational, provides intellectual stimulation to workers, and gives individualized consideration.

6. **Power** is the ability to influence employees to do what they would not ordinarily do. Power and influence may be wielded informally. Thus, power sources include

    a. **Legitimate or position power** (of the person with formal status). For example, a policeman or an elected official would have legitimate power because of their position.

    b. Control of rewards (**reward power**). A person may have power because they have the ability to give rewards.

    c. Ability to punish (**coercive power**). A manager who can fire employees has coercive power over those employees.

    d. **Expert power**, or expertise, is the power derived through advanced knowledge or experience in a particular subject. People look to such individuals to be the leader when a knowledge of the subject matter is lacking among the other participants.

    e. **Referent or charismatic power** (derived from the leader's charisma or employees' identification with the leader). For example, pop stars or actors might have referent power because others want to be like them.

7. **Influence** is an attempt to change the behavior of others in the workplace, whether they are superiors, subordinates, or coworkers. The following categories of influence tactics have been identified:

    a. **Consultation** permits the other person(s) to participate in the decision or change.

    b. **Rational persuasion** tries to convince others by reliance on a detailed plan, supporting evidence, and reason.

    c. **Inspirational appeals** are calls to superordinate goals. They are appeals to emotions, values, or ideals.

    d. **Ingratiating tactics** attempt to raise the other person's self-esteem prior to a request.

    e. **Coalition tactics** seek the aid of others to persuade someone to agree.

    f. **Pressure tactics** involve intimidation, threats, and demands.

    g. **Upward appeals** are based on the formal or informal support of higher management.

    h. **Exchange tactics** entail an exchange of favors, a reminder of a past favor, or an offer of a personal sacrifice.

8. **Delegation of authority** is the formal process of passing power downward from one individual to a subordinate. Delegation is similar to decentralization in philosophy, process, and requirements.

    a. The classical approach is to avoid delegation because the superior is deemed to be both responsible and knowledgeable. Under that view, delegation avoids responsibility.

    b. The behavioral view sees delegation as useful in every organization because no one has time to make every decision, and subordinates like to make decisions affecting their work.

    c. The modern approach is to view delegation as dependent on the situation and the people involved. Delegation requires

        1) Skill, self-confidence, and knowledge of organizational goals
        2) A feedback system to allow objective assessment of performance
        3) Faith in subordinates' abilities
        4) Clear recognition of the basic need to delegate
        5) Willingness to accept risk
        6) Desire to develop and train subordinates

    d. The delegation process involves

        1) Determination of results expected
        2) Assignment of tasks and responsibilities
        3) Delegation of authority for accomplishing these tasks
        4) Recruitment of responsible subordinates for the accomplishment of tasks
        5) Clear communication of what is expected in objective terms to subordinates
        6) Follow-up because ultimate responsibility still resides with the delegator

    e. Under the **Scalar Principle**, employees should respect the chain of direct authority relationships from superior to subordinate throughout the organization (the chain of command). The clearer the line of authority from top management to every subordinate position, the more effective the responsible decision making and organizational communication will be. Failure to define the chain of command with care leads to inefficiency.

3.2 ORGANIZATIONAL CHANGE

1. **Organizational change** anticipates expected changes in circumstances or may be a reaction to the unexpected. The nature of the change may be incremental, or it may entail a strategic alteration of the structure or purpose of the organization.

    a. Organizational and procedural changes often are resisted by the individuals and groups affected. **Resistance** may be caused by simple surprise or by inertia, but it also may arise from fear of

    1) Personal adjustments that may be required

        a) Concern about usefulness
        b) Apparent disregard for workers' feelings
        c) Deviations from past procedures for implementing change (especially if procedures used are less participative than before)
        d) Downgrading of job status

    2) Social adjustments that may be required

        a) Potential violation of the behavior norms of informal groups
        b) Disruption of the social situation within groups

    3) Economic adjustments, e.g., potential economic loss and insecurity based on perceived threats to jobs

    4) In general, any perceived deterioration in the work situation that is seen as a threat to needs -- economic, social, or psychological

    b. **Resistance may be overcome** by a participative management approach that

    1) Communicates fully to reduce fear of adjustments
    2) Avoids arbitrary, capricious, or prejudicial actions
    3) Times the change so ample notice is given, including the reasons for the change, the precise nature of the change, and expected outcomes or results of the change
    4) Allows participation in the implementation of changes by those affected
    5) Includes informal and formal conferences and problem-solving groups
    6) Provides express guarantees against economic loss
    7) Anticipates and accommodates the perceived impact of a change on the needs -- economic, social, or psychological -- of those involved

    c. Nadler and Tushman developed a model for **categorizing organizational changes**.

    1) Change is either anticipatory or reactive.

        a) Anticipatory changes are systematically planned changes intended to take advantage of expected situations.
        b) Reactive changes are necessitated by unexpected environmental events or pressures.

    2) The scope of change is either incremental or strategic.

        a) Incremental changes involve subsystem adjustments needed to keep the organization on its chosen path.
        b) Strategic changes alter the overall shape or direction of the organization.

    3) Tuning is an incremental anticipatory change. Preventive maintenance and continuous improvement (kaizen) are examples.

    4) Adaptation is an incremental reactive change. An example is a change in the styling of an automobile to meet competition.

5) Reorientation is a strategic anticipatory change. It is "frame bending" because it is a redirection. For example, some fast food companies are offering their products in dramatically different locations, such as department stores.

6) Re-creation is a strategic reactive change. It is risky because it is "frame breaking." Moving into an entirely new business is an example.

3.3 CORE CONCEPTS

Leadership

- **Management** is arranging the work of others toward organizational objectives. **Leadership** is the act or process of influencing people so they will strive willingly toward the objectives. Leadership, then, is a special type of management, one that inspires enthusiastic cooperation in pursuit of the objectives, not mere assent.

- **Styles of leadership** are emphasized in behavioral approaches. The proper leadership style depends on the situation. These styles have been characterized as autocratic, consultative, participative (also known as democratic), free-rein (also known as laissez-faire), and bureaucratic.

- A greater concern for people than for task accomplishment (although a certain degree of task orientation is vital) is felt to be more productive. The **leader must balance** the personal needs of subordinates with task accomplishment.

- Two behavior patterns that are consistently found in the study of leadership are the **initiation of structure** and the **initiation of consideration** by the leader (production-centered versus employee-centered behavior).

- The modern view follows a **contingency approach** in looking for even better answers to the questions, "What is an effective leader?" and "How do we train and identify leaders?". The **right person at the right time** may rise to a position of leadership if his/her personality and the needs of the situation complement each other.

- There are **three dimensions** to the contingency theory model (position power, task structure, and leader-member relations), and **two types** of leaders (task-oriented style and relationship-oriented style).

- According to **situational leadership theory**, the appropriate leadership style depends on followers' maturity, which is their degree of willingness to be responsible for directing their behavior.

- According to **path-goal theory**, two groups of contingency factors affect the relationship between leadership behavior and outcomes (performance and satisfaction). Environmental factors are those beyond subordinates' control (task structure, the formal authority system, and the work group). Subordinate factors include the subordinate's locus of control, experience, and perceived ability.

- **Path-goal theory** combines the research on initiating structure and consideration with expectancy theory. According to path-goal theory, **situational factors** and **leader behaviors** interact to influence worker motivation. The four leadership styles identified in path-goal theory are directive, supportive, participative, and achievement-oriented.

- The **Vroom-Yetton-Jago** model describes leadership as a decision-making process. The model identifies **five decision-making styles** and provides tools for reaching decisions under each style. Two of the decision-making styles are autocratic, two are consultative, and the fifth is group-directed.

- A **transformational leader** is an agent of change. The transformational leader is able to inspire the members of the organization to aspire to and achieve more than they thought was possible.

- **Power** is the ability to influence employees to do what they would not ordinarily do. Power and influence may be wielded informally. **Power sources** include legitimate power, reward power, coercive power, expert power, and referent or charismatic power.

- **Delegation of authority** is the formal process of passing power downward from one individual to a subordinate. Delegation is similar to decentralization in philosophy, process, and requirements.

- The **classical approach** is to avoid delegation because the superior is deemed to be both responsible and knowledgeable. Under that view, delegation avoids responsibility. The **behavioral view** sees delegation as useful in every organization because no one has time to make every decision, and subordinates like to make decisions affecting their work. The **modern approach** is to view delegation as dependent on the situation and the people involved.

Organizational Change

- **Organizational change** anticipates expected changes in circumstances or may be a reaction to the unexpected. The nature of the change may be incremental, or it may entail a strategic alteration of the structure or purpose of the organization.

- Organizational and procedural changes often are **resisted by the individuals and groups** affected. Resistance may be caused by simple surprise or by inertia, but it also may arise from fear of personal adjustments, social adjustments, and economic adjustments.

- Resistance may be **overcome** by a participative management approach.

- Organizational changes can be **categorized**: Change is either anticipatory or reactive. The scope of change is either incremental or strategic. Tuning is an incremental anticipatory change. Adaptation is an incremental reactive change. Reorientation is a strategic anticipatory change. Re-creation is a strategic reactive change.

3.4 ESSAY QUESTIONS

Recall that your CMA Part 4 exam will probably contain six scenarios, with about three questions per scenario. There will be a recommended time allocation of 20 minutes, 30 minutes, or 45 minutes for each scenario and related questions.

One scenario will involve ethics, and probably one or two scenarios will include calculations and responses on a worksheet. Also, expect at least one scenario on organizational/behavioral topics. The remaining scenarios cover Parts 1, 2, and 3.

Scenario Title	Subtopic	Questions	Suggested Time
Cromwell University	Leadership Styles	1, 2, 3	30 minutes

Scenario for Essay Questions 1, 2, 3

Until recently, Cromwell University maintained a low turnover rate in the nonprofessional work force. However, in each of the last 3 years, the turnover rate has increased to where it is now, well above the industry average.

Brian Smythe, personnel manager, has been asked by the university president to analyze the situation. Smythe reviewed turnover rates on a departmental basis and discovered that the Accounts Payable Department had the highest turnover rate, while the Admissions Department had the lowest turnover rate. Although employees of both departments are compensated equally, productivity and work efficiency are at the expected level for the Accounts Payable Department and above the expected level for the Admissions Department. Upon further investigation, Smythe determined that there was a significant difference in the leadership styles of the accounts payable manager, Wendy Drumman, and the admissions director, Paul Browne. Both Drumman and Browne had joined the university 3 years ago.

Drumman is task-oriented in her management approach, constantly checking on her employees and monitoring their progress. She allows no feedback, comments, or objections by her employees. These employees mistrust Drumman.

Browne's method is to use the relationship-oriented management style and have his employees involved in day-to-day decisions. Consequently, not only does Browne's department have a lower turnover rate, but his employees are willing to put forth extra effort to get the job done.

Questions

1. Compare the leadership styles of Wendy Drumman and Paul Browne,

    a. Explaining why one style appears more successful than the other and
    b. Discussing the behavioral effects on the employees of the leadership styles employed.

2. Of the five sources of power (reward, coercive, expert, charismatic, and legitimate), describe the main source(s) of power for

    a. Wendy Drumman
    b. Paul Browne

3. Describe the working environment where it would be most appropriate to use the

    a. Task-oriented leadership style
    b. Relationship-oriented leadership style

Essay Questions 1, 2, 3 — Unofficial Answers

1.   a.   Paul Browne's democratic (Theory Y) style of management appears to be more successful than Wendy Drumman's autocratic, task-oriented style. Browne is a participative, relationship-oriented manager who involves employees in the entire process, allowing them to have some influence in the decision process.

Comparatively, Drumman is an autocratic (Theory X) type of manager who makes all the decisions and does not permit her subordinates to have any influence in decision making. Although this style is concerned with reaching high levels of production in the short run, it usually uses high pressure on the employees to accomplish the desired performance.

   b.   Browne's employees are content in their work. Employees react more favorably to treatment that views them as humans; they identify with the organization and with each other. They are more highly motivated to perform cheerfully and are more likely to be a productive group, as there is greater opportunity for personal growth and satisfaction.

The employees working under Wendy Drumman are likely to regard work as unpleasant. They will have little trust in Drumman's leadership and will not be motivated to offer suggestions or improved productivity. In general, morale will be low, and employees will do only what is needed to get by.

2.   Of the five sources of power (reward, coercive, expert, charismatic, and legitimate) the main sources for

   a.   Wendy Drumman are

   1)   Legitimate power, which results from her position as manager of the Accounts Payable Department

   2)   Coercive power, which comes from being able to exert high pressure, if needed, to achieve desired performance

   3)   Reward power, which depends on her ability to provide rewards, usually monetary

   4)   Expert power, which may result from assumed or actual overall departmental knowledge

   b.   Paul Browne are

   1)   Legitimate power, which results from his position as manager of the Admissions Department.

   2)   Charismatic power. By treating employees with consideration and respect, Browne has earned the respect, trust, and admiration of his employees.

   3)   Reward power, which depends on his ability to provide rewards. Browne's reward power is greater because, in addition to monetary rewards, he can provide social rewards of recognition.

   4)   Expert power, which may result from assumed or actual overall departmental knowledge.

3.   The working environment where it would be most appropriate to use the task-oriented and relationship-oriented leadership styles, respectively, are as follows:

   a.   The task-oriented leadership style, to some extent, is necessary to make all work groups function effectively. It is usually used where the job is repetitive, under time pressure, and requires accuracy.

   b.   The relationship-oriented leadership style is used when the work environment is open or unstructured, or the methodology for accomplishing a task is loosely defined and the exercise of judgment is important.

STUDY UNIT FOUR
MOTIVATIONAL THEORIES AND DIVERSITY ISSUES

(12 pages of outline)

This study unit is the **last of four** on **organization management**. The four study units are

Study Unit 1: Organization Structures
Study Unit 2: Jobs and Teams
Study Unit 3: Leadership Styles and Sources of Power
Study Unit 4: Motivational Theories and Diversity Issues

After studying the outline and answering the essay questions, you will have the skills necessary to address the following topics listed in IMA's Learning Outcome Statements:

Part 4 – Section A. Organization Management, 2. Jobs and teams

The candidate should be able to:

NOTE: Statements c. through i. are covered in Study Unit 2.

    a.   define job design, job specialization, and job rotation
    b.   compare and contrast job enlargement and job enrichment

Part 4 – Section A. Organization Management, 4. Motivational theories

The candidate should be able to:

    a.   explain Frederick Taylor's scientific approach to motivation in the business organization
    b.   demonstrate an understanding of the need-based theories of motivation, including Maslow's hierarchy, Existence-Relatedness-Growth theory, Herzberg's two-factor (or dual-structure) theory, and McClelland's achievement/power theory
    c.   apply the above need-based theories to organizational situations and recommend a course of action based on a particular theory
    d.   demonstrate an understanding of the process-based theories of motivation, including equity theory, expectancy theory, reinforcement theory, intrinsic motivation, and goal-setting theory
    e.   apply process-based theories to organizational situations and recommend a course of action based on a particular theory
    f.   explain and interpret McGregor's Theory X and Theory Y and Ouchi's Theory Z

Part 4 – Section A. Organization Management, 5. Diversity issues

The candidate should be able to:

    a.   discuss the importance of organizational culture
    b.   define workforce diversity and infer some of the possible organizational advantages and disadvantages of cultural diversity
    c.   identify management issues resulting from the increasing rate of globalization

4.1 THEORIES OF MOTIVATION – SCIENTIFIC

1.   Frederick Taylor's scientific approach to motivation in the business organization centered around incentive programs based on the prevailing management philosophy that the best way to get worker cooperation was to offer monetary rewards. If workers produced more, they would share in the benefits.

    a.   Productivity increased because the workers' incremental bonus was usually less than their productivity increase. In addition to the economic motivation, the scientific approach used separation of duties to divide tasks into simple subtasks to make jobs easier (but more boring). Close supervision was also required.

    b.   For a fuller discussion of Taylor's scientific approach, see item 7. in Subunit 1.5.

4.2 THEORIES OF MOTIVATION – NEED-BASED

1.   American psychologist Abraham Maslow (1940s and 1950s) presented one of the most widely cited theories of motivation. He saw human needs as a hierarchy, from lowest to highest. Lower-level needs must be satisfied before higher-level needs can influence the individual. He concluded that, as the set of needs on each level was satisfied, those needs ceased to be a motivator.

    a.   **Maslow's hierarchy of needs** is listed below, from lowest to highest:

        1)   **Physiological needs** are the basic requirements for sustaining human life, such as water, food, shelter, sleep, and sexual satisfaction. Maslow took the position that, until these needs are satisfied to the degree needed to maintain life, higher-level needs will not serve as motivators.

        2)   **Security or safety needs** are freedom from physical danger, or from loss of job, property, food, or shelter.

        3)   **Affiliation or acceptance needs** are the needs of people as social beings to belong to groups and be accepted by others.

        4)   **Esteem** is the need to be valued, including the need to be esteemed by both one's self and others. These needs are satisfied by power, prestige, status, and self-confidence.

        5)   **Self-actualization** is the highest need in the hierarchy. It is the desire to become what one is capable of becoming, to realize one's potential, then to accomplish to the limit of one's ability. In other words, the job itself is an **intrinsic** motivation; no **extrinsic** motivation (such as rewards or reinforcements) is needed. Intrinsic motivation provides the worker with a psychic income.

    b.   Research does not support the concept of a strict hierarchy in all situations (beyond the requirement that biological needs must be satisfied before other needs begin to serve as motivators).

        1)   Physiological and safety needs tend to decrease in importance as managers advance in organizations, whereas needs for acceptance, esteem, and self-actualization tend to increase.

        2)   Higher-level needs, esteem and self-actualization, are variable in their identity, depending upon the individual.

    c.   Maslow's hierarchy does not apply equally to all situations. It is dependent on the social, cultural, and psychological backgrounds of the people involved.

        1)   People of different cultures respond differently.

        2)   Professional workers, skilled workers, and unskilled workers react differently.

        3)   Other social, ethnic, and cultural factors make people react differently.

        4)   The hierarchy is not a smooth, step-by-step path; it is a complicated, intermingled, and interdependent set of relationships.

            a)   The tendency to move upward as lower needs are satisfied does exist.

2.   The **Existence-Relatedness-Growth (ERG) theory** developed by American psychologist Clayton Alderfer in 1969 states that the core needs are existence (physiological and security needs), relatedness (affiliation and external esteem needs), and growth (self-actualization and internal esteem needs).

    a.   ERG theory argues that multiple needs may serve as motivators at the same time.

    b.   Frustration of a higher need may lead to regression to a lower need. For example, frustration of growth needs through inability to find more fulfilling work may result in a heightened need to make money.

3.   American management professor Frederick Herzberg's **two-factor theory of human behavior** (late 1950s) postulated that there are two classes of factors in the job situation.

    a.   **Dissatisfiers (maintenance or hygiene factors)** are found in the job context. Their presence will not especially motivate people, but their absence will diminish performance. They include company policy, supervision, working conditions, interpersonal relations, salary, status, and job security.

    b.   **Satisfiers (motivational factors)** relate to job content. Their absence will not diminish performance, but their addition will motivate employees. These include achievement, recognition, challenging work, advancement, and responsibility.

    c.   If Herzberg is correct, considerable attention should be given to upgrading job content through the use of job enrichment strategies.

    d.   Herzberg's work has not gone unchallenged. Other researchers have found hygiene factors to be potent in yielding both satisfaction and dissatisfaction and therefore motivation. Nevertheless, Herzberg's ideas have been well received by practicing managers because many of them hold similar beliefs about motivation.

        1)   Based on Herzberg's analysis, some jobs obviously do not contain many motivators, whereas others have more than are being fully used by management. For example,

            a)   Routine, low-status work such as mail sorting has few motivators.

            b)   A company that may be paying above the industry average (maintenance factor) could also increase satisfaction by openly acknowledging sales or other efforts by initiating a salesperson of the week recognition program.

4.   According to American psychologist **David McClelland** (writing in the 1960s and 1970s), motivation is based on the needs for achievement, power, and affiliation.

    a.   The **need for achievement** is the drive to succeed in relation to a set of standards. Thus, high achievers wish to do something better than it has been done before. They thrive when the job provides personal responsibility, feedback, and moderate risks. They avoid very easy or very difficult tasks, and they do not like to succeed by chance.

    b.   The **need for power** is a desire to compel others to behave in certain ways, to influence or control others. Individuals with a high need for power are concerned with prestige and status and prefer to be in charge.

    c.   The **need for affiliation** is the need for close, amicable interpersonal relationships. Individuals with a high need for affiliation seek friendship, cooperative rather than competitive situations, and mutual understanding.

5.   American psychologist Rensis Likert (1967) stressed participation as the key to motivation. The manager is the **supportive mechanism** or device used in building toward the environment most conducive to participation and a resulting increase in productivity.

    a.   He outlined four systems of management, the effects of which range from low productivity to high productivity.

        1)   System 1 -- Exploitive-authoritative
        2)   System 2 -- Benevolent-authoritative
        3)   System 3 -- Consultative
        4)   System 4 -- Participative

    b.   As the management style moves from System 1 to System 4 (from autocratic to participative), some of the following shifts in variables are observed:

        1)   Motivational forces move from security, fear, threats, conflict of goals, responsibility felt only at the top, and subservience to group processes in goal setting, a high level of satisfaction, feelings of responsibility, and high satisfaction with achievement.

        2)   Communications move from little, all downward, inaccuracy, and no questioning to up-and-down freely, initiated by all levels as needed, accuracy, and no need for supplementary means.

        3)   Personal interaction (influence) moves from little interaction, fear, distrust, and no teamwork to friendliness, trust and confidence, and much teamwork. Effective participation is impossible if either party feels threatened.

        4)   Decision making moves from decisions made at the top without lower-level input, decisions made by individuals only, or decisions made at too-high levels, to decision making spread throughout the organization, full information input, and group decisions.

        5)   Goal setting moves from goals by edict and orders from the top and rejection by many to group participation, input from all levels, and full acceptance.

        6)   Control processes move from a top-heavy concentration and inaccurate measurements to concern felt throughout the organization and widespread responsibility.

6.   **Individual values**

    a.   Values are specific to each individual person and involve moral and personal issues.
    b.   Values are learned from family, friends, school, and life experience in general.
    c.   Values can be modified throughout life but ordinarily tend to stay the same.
    d.   It is important to reward good values in a corporation to prevent fraud, theft, and deception and improve worker morale.

        1)   The value structure is an important part of the corporate culture.

    e.   Personal beliefs, such as those on religious and political matters, cannot be the basis of personnel actions. Discrimination on the basis of personal beliefs could expose the organization to legal action.

7.   **Human defense mechanisms**

    a.   Defense mechanisms come into play when an employee feels jeopardized or threatened. Some of the most common methods of defense are listed below.

        1)   Rationalization entails giving more acceptable reasons for behavior than the actual ones.
        2)   Regression involves reversion to child-like behavior.
        3)   Repression eliminates stressful items from working memory.

4) Projection is the attribution of one's own ideas, feelings, or attitudes to others, especially the externalization of blame, guilt, or responsibility as a defense against anxiety.

5) Compensation attempts to offset bad qualities with good qualities.

6) Withdrawal is simply avoidance.

7) Aggression involves a direct attack on the perceived causes of the problem.

4.3 THEORIES OF MOTIVATION – PROCESS-BASED

1. Motivation is a general term used to describe an entire class of drives, desires, needs, fears, and similar forces that cause behavior.

   a. The ideal management action motivates subordinates by structuring situations and requiring behaviors of subordinates that will simultaneously satisfy both the subordinates' needs and the organization's requirements.

   b. There is no reason that the organization's needs and those of the individual **must** conflict.

   c. Level of motivation is determined by individuals' opportunity to satisfy their needs and wants within the organizational setting (i.e., the greater the ability to satisfy these needs, the greater the motivational level).

      1) The inducements that an organization offers an individual member should be matched with the contributions expected from that individual (i.e., each is willing to give up something to get something it wants).

      2) The task of a leader is to make available the kinds and amounts of inducements an individual requires as a trade for the kinds and amounts of contributions the organization requires.

2. **Classical views** stress fear and economics as motivators, i.e., the carrot-and-stick approach. For example, economic incentive programs or bonuses (carrots), and losing one's job or being demoted (sticks).

   a. Frederick Taylor's scientific approach to motivation in the business organization was rather crude when compared to later ideas. His concept of motivation began and ended with monetary incentives. He felt that money was the common ground between workers and management. Prosperity for the company must be accompanied by prosperity for the worker and vice versa.

3. **Behaviorists** believe that these motivational strategies are effective only for the short run or for people who don't have job alternatives. The behaviorist approach focuses on participation and personal involvement in the work situation as motivational factors.

4. **Equity theory** states that employee motivation is affected significantly by relative as well as absolute rewards. An employee compares the ratio of what (s)he receives from a job (outcomes, such as pay or recognition) to what (s)he gives to the job (inputs, such as effort, experience, ability, or education) with the ratios of relevant others.

   a. If the ratios are equal, equity exists, but if they are unequal, equity tension exists, and the employee will be motivated to eliminate the tension.

   b. The referent chosen (the employee's experience inside or outside the organization or the experiences of others inside or outside the organization) tends to be affected by the employee's job tenure, education, and salary level. For example, better-educated employees are more likely to make comparisons with outsiders, and longer-tenured employees may rely on coworkers.

   c. Equity tension leads to changes in inputs or outcomes, distorted perceptions of one's effort or of the referent, choice of a different referent, or abandonment of the job.

5.   **Expectancy theory** (Victor Vroom, 1960s) is a commonsense notion that people have expectations of rewards derived from their unique personal motive structure (achievement, affiliation, power, etc.), from their beliefs as to what is important (a trip to Acapulco, a gold watch, a pat on the back), and from their expectations of getting these incentives if they exert effort (probability assessments, such as, "If I do this, will I get that reward?").

    a.   High effort expended, ability, and accurate role assessment will lead to a high performance level (i.e., putting the effort into the task and having the right amount of ability to do it will lead to high performance).

        1)   Insufficient ability will impede performance despite effort.

        2)   Executing a task that is not desired or is improperly performed according to role definition will impede performance despite effort or ability.

    b.   Motivation is a product of the values an individual seeks and his/her estimation of the probability that a certain action will lead to those values. This relationship can be expressed as the following equation:

$$Motivation = Valence \times Expectancy$$

    c.   **Valence** is the strength of an individual's preference for one outcome in relation to others. Valence is a personal value unique to each employee that cannot be controlled by management.

    d.   **Expectancy** results from past experiences and measures the strength of belief that a particular act will be followed by a specific outcome.

    e.   Management is more able to control the expectancy factor than the valence factor because expectations are based on past experiences. A consistent management policy will reinforce employee expectations.

    f.   Performance leads to rewards.

        1)   Individuals evaluate rewards on the basis of equity ("Did I get what I deserved for what I did?") compared with others in similar jobs.

        2)   If inequity exists, individuals react, usually negatively.

        3)   Perception of the equity of rewards leads to satisfaction ("I got what I earned.")

    g.   Level of satisfaction or dissatisfaction feeds back into the next cycle's estimates of reward values, individual abilities, and role perceptions.

6.   **Behavior modification** is the management of environmental factors to encourage desirable behavior and to discourage undesirable behavior.

    a.   Environmental factors include antecedents and consequences of behavior. Antecedents are cues that encourage but do not cause a given behavior. Barriers to good performance should be eliminated and replaced with helpful aids.

    b.   Consequences include the following:

        1)   **Positive reinforcement** provides rewards for certain responses. It focuses on desirable rather than undesirable behavior. Theorists regard positive reinforcement as the most effective approach.

            a)   Examples are the awarding of merit-based salary bonuses or paying on a sliding scale relative to production.

            b)   Continuous reinforcement rewards every occurrence of a desirable new behavior, and intermittent reinforcement provides occasional rewards for an established behavior.

            c)   Variable-interval schedules of intermittent reinforcement lead to better performance. Employees are more alert because of the uncertainty involved, and performance and reward are connected. Fixed-interval schedules of reinforcement do not clearly link performance and reward.

      2)   **Negative reinforcement** is the withdrawal of an existing unpleasant condition when the desired behavior occurs.

      3)   **Extinction** discourages a behavior by ignoring it (not reinforcing it).

      4)   **Punishment** discourages a behavior by immediately following it with a negative consequence.

7.   **Cognitive evaluation theory** holds that **intrinsic rewards** (such as competence, responsibility, and achievement) tend to be reduced when extrinsic rewards (such as higher pay, promotion, and better working conditions) are provided for superior performance.

   a.   The reason may be that the individual perceives a loss of control over his/her behavior. However, research suggests that the negative effects of extrinsic rewards on motivation do not apply when a job provides either a very high or a very low level of intrinsic rewards. In the latter case, extrinsic rewards may actually increase intrinsic motivation.

8.   American management professor Chris Argyris (1964) proposed a **theory of action** that involves integrating the needs of the individual with those of the organization.

   a.   Conflict arises when a mature, independent adult who seeks self-actualization joins a highly structured, demanding, and limiting organization.

      1)   EXAMPLE: A highly competent aeronautical engineer who takes a job with the federal government may find his/her attempts to pursue technical excellence through intellectual effort stifled by the rules and procedures that are characteristic of a bureaucracy.

      2)   Self-actualization is the process of accomplishing goals to the limit of one's ability because of the personal need to excel.

9.   American management professor Douglas McGregor's **Theory X and Theory Y**, set forth in *The Human Side of Enterprise* (1960), are simplified models that define the extremes of managers' views on employee conduct. They permit a manager to evaluate his/her own tendencies.

   a.   **Theory X** is the viewpoint of the autocratic manager. It is thought to be very common.

      1)   "Average human beings have an inherent dislike of work and will avoid it if possible."

      2)   "Because of this dislike for work, most people must be coerced, controlled, directed, and threatened with punishment to get them to put forth adequate effort toward the achievement of organizational objectives."

      3)   "Average human beings prefer to be directed, have relatively little ambition, and want security above all."

   b.   **Theory Y** is the extreme opposite of Theory X. The permissive manager assumes that

      1)   "The expenditure of physical and mental effort in work is as natural as play or rest -- to average human beings."

      2)   "External control and the threat of punishment are not the only means for bringing about individual effort toward organizational objectives. Employees will exercise self-direction and self-control in their efforts to accomplish goals thought to be worthwhile."

      3)   "Commitment to objectives is proportional to the rewards associated with their achievement."

      4)   "Average human beings learn, under proper conditions, not only to accept responsibility, but to seek it."

     5)   "The capacity to exercise a relatively high degree of imagination, ingenuity, and creativity in the solution of organizational problems is widely, not narrowly, distributed in the population."

     6)   "Under the conditions of modern industrial life, the intellectual potentialities of the average human being are only partially realized."

  c.   McGregor did not suggest that Theory Y was the only correct managerial behavior. He suggested these theories as starting points from which a manager can examine his/her own views about human nature.

10.   In his book ***Theory Z: How American Management Can Meet the Japanese Challenge*** (Addison-Wesley, 1981), William Ouchi described the characteristics at Japanese companies that produce high employee commitment, motivation, and productivity. At many Japanese companies, employees are guaranteed a position for life, increasing their loyalty to the organization. Careful evaluation occurs over a period of time, and the responsibility for success or failure is shared among employees and management. Most employees do not specialize in one skill area, but work at several different tasks, learning more about the company as they develop. The Japanese companies are often concerned about all aspects of their employees' lives, on and off the job. According to Ouchi, Theory Z organizations tend to have stable employment, high productivity, and high employee morale and satisfaction. These outcomes are similar to Theory Y.

  a.   The goal of Theory Z is to achieve a long-range orientation among workers.

  b.   The promise of long-term employment creates intense job loyalty. This opportunity for life-time employment is the foundation of Theory Z.

  c.   Teamwork is a key requirement of a Theory Z organization. There is collective decision making in all activities.

     1)   This results in a "bottom-up" process, which is slower than a "top-down" approach.

  d.   Promotion and performance evaluation occurs more slowly than is typically the case in American companies.

     1)   The result is that a long-range orientation is rewarded and there is less emphasis on short-term successes.

     2)   However, since most workers in Western companies are accustomed to more frequent promotions, there must be some other recognition of performance.

  e.   Despite the emphasis on group decision making, Theory Z still places an emphasis on individual responsibility. Because sole reliance on a group decision is hard for Western businesses to accept, Theory Z recommends that an individual be assigned responsibility for carrying out the group's decision.

  f.   Theory Z requires trust among employees and between employees and management.

     1)   The concept of egalitarianism says each person can work autonomously, without supervision, because they are to be trusted.

  g.   The holistic orientation of Theory Z organizations includes employees and their families in all decisions. Work and social life are integrated.

  h.   Criticisms of Theory Z include:

     1)   Japanese success is due to their work ethic, not their management style. Adopting this style will not alter the basic values of the American worker.

     2)   Theory Z creates a work atmosphere that is resistant to change, crushes individual expression through conformity, and lacks the ability to make quick decisions.

     3)   Theory Z is just a new name for practices that have existed for many years.

11. **Job Enrichment vs. Job Enlargement**

    a. **Job enrichment** attempts to apply the findings of Maslow, Likert, and McGregor by structuring the job so that each worker participates in planning and controlling. The purpose is to maximize the satisfaction of both social and ego needs and avoid the disadvantages of routine, highly specialized work. Job enrichment includes

        1) Allowing and encouraging more worker discretion over work methods, sequence, and pace
        2) Encouraging interactions between workers
        3) Giving workers a feeling of personal responsibility for their tasks
        4) Making sure workers understand how their tasks contribute to the finished product
        5) Giving people feedback on their job performance
        6) Involving workers in changes in physical aspects of the work environment

    b. **Job enlargement** is primarily a technique for combating boredom at repetitive or highly paced jobs through the assignment of a wide variety of tasks. Job enrichment may result from job enlargement. **Job specialization** is the opposite of job enlargement in that an employee works in only a specialized area. Under job specialization, each worker performs only small, simple tasks.

    c. **Job design** is the process of linking specific tasks to specific jobs and deciding which techniques, equipment, and procedures should be used to perform those tasks.

    d. **Job rotation** is where workers perform a variety of different jobs that are not necessarily related. They may rotate weekly, monthly, or during their work day/shift. A good job rotation scheme will be designed to allow each worker to be exposed to a variety of physical and mental demands during the shift. The advantage of job rotation is that all employees learn all of the jobs, which makes it easier to find a replacement when a worker is ill or quits unexpectedly.

12. **Quality of Work Life (QWL).** According to Robert Guest (*Harvard Business Review*, Vol. 57, July-August 1979, pp. 76-77), quality of work life (QWL) is "a process by which an organization attempts to unlock the creative potential of its people by involving them in decisions affecting their lives."

    a. The domain of QWL includes pay, employee benefits, job security, alternative work schedules, occupational stress, participation, and workplace democracy.

    b. The major categories of QWL programs are flexible work schedules, participative management, and workplace democracy.

13. **Satisfaction and Productivity**

    a. The proposition that "a happy worker is a good worker" has **not** been supported by research. Evidence tends to indicate that increased rewards bring increased satisfaction, but not necessarily increased productivity.

    b. Increased productivity, when followed by increased rewards, has been shown to produce increased satisfaction. Productivity is affected by many factors other than satisfaction; that is, there is no direct relationship between satisfaction and productivity.

    c. Job satisfaction has an economic importance only indirectly related to productivity. Satisfied workers exhibit lower rates of absenteeism and turnover, and reduced tardiness, apathy, and sabotage.

    d. Nevertheless, it remains a basic belief of the human relations position that satisfaction and productivity must bear some relationship despite the lack of empirical evidence.

14. **Job Characteristics Model.** The JCM (developed by J.R. Hackman and G.R. Oldham) defines five core job characteristics and their relationship to behavioral outcomes.

    a.   The first three of the following five job dimensions determine the meaningfulness of work.

        1) Skill variety
        2) Task identity (requires completion of a whole, identifiable unit of work)
        3) Task significance
        4) Autonomy (worker discretion in carrying out the work)
        5) Feedback

    b.   High motivation, performance, and satisfaction and low turnover and absenteeism result when a worker views the job as important, feels responsible for outcomes as a result of autonomy, and knows how effectively (s)he performed because of feedback.

    c.   The model computes a **motivating potential score** (MPS) as follows:

$$\left[\frac{Skill\ Variety \times Task\ Identity \times Task\ Significance}{3}\right] \times Autonomy \times Feedback$$

4.4 DIVERSITY ISSUES

1.   **Diversity issues** have become important in recent years as organizations have implemented policies that require respect for individuals, regardless of their race, religion, or sexual orientation. The objective is to create a positive environment of diversity that will allow people of all backgrounds to feel welcome, to excel, and to make a positive contribution to society.

    a.   This objective has led to **sensitivity** sessions, or sensitivity awareness education.

    b.   One advantage of diversity is that a broader range of ideas is available to develop new products and solve workplace problems.

4.5 CORE CONCEPTS

Theories of Motivation – Scientific

- **Frederick Taylor's scientific approach** to motivation in the business organization centered around incentive programs based on the prevailing management philosophy that the best way to get worker cooperation was to offer monetary rewards.

- If workers produced more, they would share in the benefits. Productivity increased because the workers' incremental bonus was usually less than their productivity increase.

- In addition to the economic motivation, the scientific approach used separation of duties to divide tasks into simple subtasks to make jobs easier (but more boring). Close supervision was also required.

Theories of Motivation – Need-Based

- **Abraham Maslow** presented one of the most widely cited theories of motivation. He saw **human needs as a hierarchy**, from lowest to highest. Lower-level needs must be satisfied before higher-level needs can influence the individual. He concluded that as the set of needs on each level was satisfied, those needs ceased to be a motivator. **Maslow's hierarchy of needs**, from lowest to highest, consists of physiological needs, security or safety needs, affiliation or acceptance needs, esteem, and self-actualization. Maslow's hierarchy does not apply equally to all situations. It is dependent on the social, cultural, and psychological backgrounds of the people involved.

- The **Existence-Relatedness-Growth (ERG) theory** developed by American psychologist Clayton Alderfer in 1969 states that the core needs are existence (physiological and security needs), relatedness (affiliation and external esteem needs), and growth (self-actualization and internal esteem needs). ERG theory argues that **multiple needs** may serve as motivators **at the same time**. Frustration of a higher need may lead to regression to a lower need.

- American management professor Frederick Herzberg's **two-factor theory** of human behavior postulated that there are two classes of factors in the job situation. **Dissatisfiers** (maintenance or hygiene factors) are found in the **job context**. Their presence will not especially motivate people, but their absence will diminish performance. They include company policy, supervision, working conditions, interpersonal relations, salary, status, and job security. **Satisfiers** (motivational factors) relate to **job content**. Their absence will not diminish performance, but their addition will motivate employees. These include achievement, recognition, challenging work, advancement, and responsibility.

- According to American psychologist **David McClelland**, motivation is based on the need for achievement, the need for power, and the need for affiliation.

- American psychologist Rensis Likert stressed participation as the key to motivation. The manager is the **supportive mechanism** or device used in building toward the environment most conducive to participation and a resulting increase in productivity. He outlined **four systems of management**, the effects of which range from low productivity to high productivity: exploitive-authoritative, benevolent-authoritative, consultative, and participative.

- **Values are specific to each individual person** and involve moral and personal issues. Values are learned from family, friends, school, and life experience in general. Values can be modified throughout life but ordinarily tend to stay the same.

- **Human defense mechanisms** come into play when an employee feels jeopardized or threatened. Some of the most common methods of defense are rationalization, regression, repression, projection, compensation, withdrawal, and aggression.

Theories of Motivation – Process-Based

- **Motivation** is a general term used to describe an entire class of drives, desires, needs, fears, and similar forces that cause behavior. The ideal management action motivates subordinates by structuring situations and requiring behaviors of subordinates that will **simultaneously satisfy** both the subordinates' needs and the organization's requirements. There is no reason that the organization's needs and those of the individual **must** conflict.

- **Classical views** stress fear and economics as motivators, i.e., the carrot-and-stick approach. **Behaviorists** believe that these motivational strategies are effective only for the short run or for people who don't have job alternatives. The behaviorist approach focuses on participation and personal involvement in the work situation as motivational factors.

- **Equity theory** states that employee motivation is affected significantly by relative as well as absolute rewards. An employee compares the ratio of what (s)he receives from a job (outcomes such as pay or recognition) to what (s)he gives to the job (inputs such as effort, experience, ability, or education) with the ratios of relevant others.

- **Expectancy theory**, developed by Victor Vroom, is a commonsense notion that people have expectations of rewards derived from their unique personal motive structure (achievement, affiliation, power, etc.), from their beliefs as to what is important (a trip to Acapulco, a gold watch, a pat on the back), and from their expectations of getting these incentives if they exert effort (probability assessments, such as, "If I do this, will I get that reward?").

- **Behavior modification** is the management of environmental factors to encourage desirable behavior and to discourage undesirable behavior. Environmental factors include **antecedents and consequences** of behavior. Antecedents are cues that encourage but do not cause a given behavior. Barriers to good performance should be eliminated and replaced with helpful aids. Consequences include positive reinforcement, negative reinforcement, extinction, and punishment.
- **Cognitive evaluation theory** holds that intrinsic rewards (such as competence, responsibility, and achievement) tend to be reduced when extrinsic rewards (such as higher pay, promotion, and better working conditions) are provided for superior performance.
- American management professor Chris Argyris (1964) proposed a **theory of action** that involves integrating the needs of the individual with those of the organization.
- American management professor Douglas McGregor's **Theory X and Theory Y** are simplified models that define the extremes of managers' views on employee conduct. They permit a manager to evaluate his/her own tendencies. **Theory X** is the viewpoint of the autocratic manager. It is thought to be very common. **Theory Y** is the extreme opposite of Theory X, i.e., the permissive manager.
- In his book *Theory Z*, William Ouchi described the characteristics at Japanese companies that produce high employee commitment, motivation, and productivity. The goal of Theory Z is to achieve a long-range orientation among workers.
- **Job enrichment** attempts to apply the findings of Maslow, Likert, and McGregor by structuring the job so that each worker participates in planning and controlling. The purpose is to maximize the satisfaction of both social and ego needs and avoid the disadvantages of routine, highly specialized work. **Job enlargement** is primarily a technique for combating boredom at repetitive or highly paced jobs through the assignment of a wide variety of tasks. Job enrichment may result from job enlargement. **Job specialization** is the opposite of job enlargement in that an employee works in only a specialized area. Under job specialization, each worker performs only small, simple tasks. **Job rotation** is where workers perform a variety of different jobs that are not necessarily related. They may rotate weekly, monthly, or during their work day/shift.
- The proposition that **"a happy worker is a good worker"** has **not been supported** by research. Evidence tends to indicate that increased rewards bring increased satisfaction, but not necessarily increased productivity. Increased productivity, when followed by increased rewards, has been shown to produce increased satisfaction.
- The **job characteristics model** defines five core job characteristics and their relationship to behavioral outcomes. The first three of the following **five job dimensions** determine the meaningfulness of work: skill variety, task identity (requires completion of a whole, identifiable unit of work), task significance, autonomy (worker discretion in carrying out the work), and feedback.

Diversity Issues

- **Diversity issues** have become important in recent years as organizations have implemented policies that require respect for individuals, regardless of their race, religion, or sexual orientation. The objective is to create a positive environment of diversity that will allow people of all backgrounds to feel welcome, to excel, and to make a positive contribution to society.
- This objective has led to **sensitivity** sessions, or sensitivity awareness education.

4.6 ESSAY QUESTIONS

Recall that your CMA Part 4 exam will probably contain six scenarios, with about three questions per scenario. There will be a recommended time allocation of 20 minutes, 30 minutes, or 45 minutes for each scenario and related questions.

One scenario will involve ethics, and probably one or two scenarios will include calculations and responses on a worksheet. Also, expect at least one scenario on organizational/behavioral topics. The remaining scenarios cover Parts 1, 2, and 3.

Scenario Title	Subtopic	Questions	Suggested Time
Myland Corporation	Job Design	1, 2, 3	30 minutes
Midwest Electronics	Theories of Motivation	4, 5, 6	30 minutes
Welsteel Corporation	Maslow's Hierarchy of Needs	7, 8, 9, 10	30 minutes
Global Telecommunications	Organizational Change	11, 12, 13	30 minutes

Scenario for Essay Questions 1, 2, 3

Myland Corporation manufactures desktop computers for both business and home use and employs more than 1,000 employees. The manufacturing facility is 50 years old and is located in an industrial city. The manufacturing process uses multiple assembly lines, and each line produces 120 computers per day, allowing 4 minutes for each specialized process on the line. There are 30 employees, each of whom performs a specific task on the assembly line. In addition, there are six inspectors placed appropriately along the assembly line. There is a production supervisor in each manufacturing room, which houses four assembly lines. The specialized process performed at each station was designed by an engineering consultant trained in assembly-line production.

A new employee needs 2 weeks to learn the specialized process and reach an effective level of production. Each inspector checks the computer to ensure that the five prior processes have been performed correctly; poor workmanship is noted on a production sheet for each individual production worker. At the end of the day, the supervisor reviews these sheets. If the incidence of poor workmanship reaches prescribed levels repeatedly, the supervisor will place the employee on probation; if there is no improvement, the employee will be dismissed.

A "floater," an experienced line worker, moves up and down the line to fill in when a production worker needs a break and to help out when a production worker falls behind schedule. Employees must enter all time away from the assembly line on their timecards; if this time is excessive, their pay is reduced.

Although union activity has been minimal, the management at Myland is concerned about a recent upsurge in poor employee attitude, poor performance, and high employee turnover. Myland wants to remain competitive and therefore needs to minimize scrap costs and training costs for new employees. The company would like to explore the use of job design, which has been instituted successfully at other manufacturing companies.

Questions

1. Discuss the principal reasons why the interest in job design techniques continues to grow.

2. Define each of the four components of job design:
    a. Job rotation
    b. Job enlargement
    c. Job enrichment
    d. Work redesign

3. Describe how Myland Corporation could use job design techniques to improve employee performance.

Essay Questions 1, 2, 3 — Unofficial Answers

1. The principal reasons why the interest in job design techniques continues to grow is because a company can increase overall organizational performance by increasing individual motivation and productivity. Specifically, a company can

    a. Resolve the problems of monotony and boredom associated with repetitive work
    b. Decrease excessive employee turnover
    c. Reduce the costs of poor workmanship
    d. Improve employee training

2. Definitions of the four components of job design are as follows:

    a. **Job rotation** is an attempt to reduce monotony and boredom by systematically moving employees from one job to another. Employees perform similar but different job functions on a regular basis. The employees are given a greater variety of tasks to perform.

    b. **Job enlargement** is the horizontal expansion of an employee's job by increasing the variety and number of similar tasks performed.

    c. **Job enrichment** is a vertical expansion of the employee's job by increasing the number of different tasks and the control over his/her job. The worker assumes more responsibility for planning and controlling the job function.

    d. **Work redesign** is the reorganization of job content. Jobs are redesigned to incorporate an individual's differences and motivational factors. The emphasis is to achieve a proper fit between job requirements and individual talent and meet individual needs for growth and development.

3. Myland Corporation could use job design techniques to improve performance and reduce the turnover of the assembly-line workers in the following ways:

    a. The production workers' responsibilities could be increased to include the quality-control checking of their own work and the correction of errors. An incentive system that rewards reduced or no errors could be established.

    b. Assembly-line jobs could be expanded to encompass two or more operations on the line, providing greater work diversity for the employees.

    c. The production worker's job could be redesigned to include the review or handling of customer complaints.

Scenario for Essay Questions 4, 5, 6

Midwest Electronics Corp. manufactures computers. Recently, its products have met competition from lower-priced imports, and the firm is seeking ways to improve its workers' productivity in order to maintain its market share. Alice Kumar, manager of the Accounting Department, and Greg Mossman, manager of the Sales Department, recently discussed a presentation made to management of Midwest by a consultant on employee motivation. This consultant had talked about content and process theories of motivation. The content theories seek to answer what motivates people, while process theories focus on why people choose certain behavioral options and how they judge their success.

In the course of the conversation, Kumar recalled what happened at Spokane Computer associates, her former employer. A national labor union had sought repeatedly to unionize the workers at the plant but had never succeeded. There was little turnover among the workers, and the plant was considered a safe and pleasant place to work. Salaries were relatively high, and workers earned not only a base salary but also incentive bonuses based on their individual output and company profits.

Mossman recalled his experience at Pullman Lighting Inc. during the late 1970s and 1980s. The firm developed a light fixture that conserved energy and was a tremendous success. Mossman recalled that most of his salespeople did well without undue exertion; the product sold itself. Initially, the company had trouble obtaining market share outside the Northeast; it appeared that the salespeople were reluctant to make contacts outside their immediate region. Mossman commented, "We started by promising them higher commissions, and that didn't work. But when we started giving the top performers special recognition awards at sales meetings and sending them on cruises, sales spread beyond the Northeast all the way to the Pacific Northwest."

Alice and Greg were joined by Zach Chaudry, Research Department supervisor. He informed them that he was leaving the company to take a research and teaching position with a university. He would be taking a pay cut but would be in control of selecting the type of research he would undertake.

After the meeting, they greeted Lon Noll. Noll, who is an immigrant, had started working at Midwest as a lab assistant and had recently been promoted to a supervisory position. He also attends a graduate program at a nearby university and is seeking a doctoral degree in computer science. Chaudry commented, "There's a guy who knows what he wants and then goes after it. And he will get what he wants!"

Questions

4. Using Maslow's theory of motivation, explain

   a. Why the efforts to unionize Spokane Computer Associates failed
   b. What allowed the sales of Pullman Lighting Inc. to spread beyond the Northeast region
   c. Why Zach Chaudry is moving to the university and taking a pay cut

5. Using Herzberg's two-factor theory of motivation, explain

   a. Why the efforts to unionize Spokane Computer Associates failed
   b. What allowed the sales of Pullman Lighting Inc. to spread beyond the Northeast region
   c. Why Zach Chaudry is moving to the university and taking a pay cut

6. a. Explain the expectancy theory of motivation.

   b. Use the expectancy theory of motivation to explain the comments concerning Lon Noll.

   c. Describe the implications of the expectancy theory of motivation on Midwest Electronics Corp.'s effort to increase worker productivity.

Essay Questions 4, 5, 6 — Unofficial Answers

4. According to Maslow's theory of motivation, human needs exist in a hierarchy of importance, namely, physiological, security, social, esteem, and self-actualization. Once the first level of physiological needs is satisfied, the individual is no longer motivated by them and moves to the next level. The process continues until the individual reaches self-actualization.

    a. Unions are often associated with the ability to satisfy the lower level needs by providing competitive salaries, safe working conditions, job security, and social belonging. It appears that these needs were already being satisfied at Spokane Computer Associates, as salaries were relatively high, there was little turnover, and the plant was considered a safe and pleasant place to work.

    b. The products at Pullman were successful and sold without much effort on the part of the salespeople. As a result, the salespeople were doing well financially, and their lower needs were satisfied. By offering the top performers recognition, the firm was appealing to them through a higher level motivator, esteem. The salespeople were motivated to increase sales by the need for recognition and respect from their peers and others.

    c. Zach Chaudry is leaving Midwest Electronics to accept a teaching and research position at the university to satisfy the highest level need, self-actualization. In this new position, Chaudry will have the opportunity to control his own research.

5. Herzberg's two-factor theory of motivation identifies two sets of factors, hygiene factors and motivation factors. Hygiene factors, such as salary, job security, and working conditions, do not motivate employees but can cause dissatisfaction if they are deficient. Employees must be given the opportunity to experience the motivation factors, such as achievement, recognition, advancement, and growth.

    a. The efforts to unionize Spokane Computer Associates failed because the union did not offer anything new to the workers. The management of Spokane had seen to it that the dissatisfiers were absent by providing good wages, a pleasant environment, and reasonable job security. Since the union could not capitalize on the workers' dissatisfaction, it failed in its effort.

    b. Recognition and awards are motivators, while increased commissions are a hygiene factor. The salespeople at Pullman were not dissatisfied with their income level and working environment, and increased commissions only meant more of the same. However, the offer of recognition and awards motivated the salespeople.

    c. Zach Chaudry's move to the university may offer as many as four motivational factors, namely, the job itself, personal growth, responsibility, and personal achievement. As long as Chaudry is not dissatisfied with his income, he will be motivated to perform.

6. a. Expectancy theory suggests that motivation depends on two things: how much we want something and how likely we think we are to get it. The model suggests that motivation leads to effort, which results in performance. Performance, in turn, leads to various outcomes, each of which has an associated value called its valence. The individual must have the expectation that performance will lead to outcomes.

    b. Lon Noll expects that certain performance activities, such as advanced education and a doctoral degree, will result in a particular outcome or goal which has value to him.

    c. In accordance with expectancy theory, Midwest Electronics should take the following steps to increase worker productivity;

        1) Since employees have different levels of expectation and exert different levels of effort, management must determine the rewards valued by the employees.

        2) The rewards must be clearly connected to the goal of increased productivity.

        3) The goal of increased productivity must be perceived as attainable by the employees.

Scenario for Essay Questions 7, 8, 9, 10

Welsteel Corporation is a steel foundry that produces hardware for electrical and telephone pole needs. The company has 550 employees, 75 of whom are professional or management employees, 375 assembly-line employees, and 100 clerical employees. In the past, Welsteel has responded positively to employees' compensation needs and has avoided any union activity by the assembly-line employees.

Welsteel has an established annual review process for all of its employees. The performance evaluation is initiated by all departments in November and completed in December so that any associated raises or promotions can be reflected in January, the beginning of the company's fiscal year.

The evaluation process begins with the manager (or supervisor) preparing a checklist document that evaluates all employees on a one-to-five rating scale (one being excellent and five being poor). Characteristics evaluated include attitude, loyalty, accuracy, attendance, dependability, maturity, confidence, time management, and communication skills. There is also a blank section on the form where the manager can report any improvements since the employee's last performance review.

The manager then has his/her superior approve the review, and together they recommend the employee's raise. This form is passed on to the personnel director for approval who then returns the evaluation form to the manager.

The manager arranges a meeting with the employee to privately discuss the evaluation form. This meeting, on average, is fifteen minutes in length, allowing five minutes for the employee to read the form. The manager and employee discuss the written form and may have an informal discussion about problem areas that need improvement. The manager will then inform the employee of the raise that is associated with the performance review, being sure to let the employee know in which pay period to expect the raise. The meeting finishes with the employee signing the form and the manager stating that a copy of the signed form will be given to the employee.

Questions

7. According to Maslow's Hierarchy of Needs, humans share a concern for five levels of need satisfaction: physiological, safety, social, esteem, and self-actualization. Describe the five basic need categories associated with Maslow's theory of motivation.

8. By referring to the need categories in Question 8, identify the need category or categories most closely associated with the following groups of employees, and explain why each category identified applies to each group of employees.

   a. Professional employees
   b. Assembly-line employees

9. Discuss whether or not Welsteel Corporation's evaluation system fulfills the needs of the

   a. Professional employees
   b. Assembly-line employees

10. Recommend at least three actions Welsteel Corporation can take to improve its employee evaluation system.

Essay Questions 7, 8, 9, 10 — Unofficial Answers

7. The five basic need categories associated with Maslow's Hierarchy of Needs theory of motivation can be described as follows:

   a. **Physiological.** These needs represent the basic issues of survival and include the need for food, water, and shelter.

   b. **Safety.** These needs are concerned with a safe and secure physical and emotional environment and include protection against danger and freedom from threat.

   c. **Social.** The needs are for love, affection, and acceptance and can be fulfilled by social belonging, membership, and affiliation.

   d. **Esteem.** This level includes the need for a positive self-image and the need to receive recognition, respect, and appreciation from others for one's contributions.

   e. **Self-actualization.** In fulfilling these needs, an individual seeks to maximize the use of abilities, skills, and potential and focuses on continued growth and individual development.

8. a. The need categories most often associated with professional employees are esteem and self-actualization, since the lower level needs are usually satisfied by professional employment and are no longer motivators (satisficers).

   b. The need categories most often associated with assembly-line workers (skilled labor) are the physiological, safety, and social needs. The physiological and safety needs are usually satisfied by employment and are no longer motivators (satisficers). The social needs such as acceptance and affiliation must continue to be fulfilled.

9. a. Welsteel Corporation's evaluation system does not fulfill the needs of the professional employees, as it does not provide for the evaluation of such characteristics as initiative, creativity, etc., that are important to professional employees. The characteristics evaluated are those associated with lower level needs, and there is no recognition of accomplishments or the achievement of goals previously established. There is no consideration of personal objectives or plans for future growth in the performance evaluation.

   b. Although Welsteel's performance will fulfill the psychological and safety needs of the assembly-line workers, it will stop there. The evaluation process does not address social or esteem needs. Associating the raise with the performance evaluation will lead to the employee being concerned only with the lower level needs.

10. At least three actions that Welsteel Corporation can take to improve its evaluation process include the following:

   a. Provide different evaluation forms for the different groups of employees so that the employees' individual needs are fulfilled.

   b. Motivate employees by identifying strengths and weaknesses in performance and provide employees with a sense of satisfaction for a job well done.

   c. Encourage employees to participate in establishing personal objectives as well as departmental and organizational objectives.

Scenario for Essay Questions 11, 12, 13

During the 1990s, Global Telecommunications, whose main business is telephone services, set up a division devoted to the production and marketing of personal computers. Even though its computer products received high marks from experts, Global failed to capture a major share of the growing market. In 2004, George Hanover became Global's president and chief executive officer. His perception was that computer technology would have an ever-increasing impact on telecommunications. Given that perception, he believed the firm ought to be doing more in the field of computer development. Accordingly, Hanover decided that Global should acquire Palouse Electronics, a firm engaged in computer development whose products competed with Global's own line of personal computers. The Board of Directors agreed and made a tender offer to purchase Palouse.

The tender offer resulted in considerable unrest in the Computer Division of Global. Rumors flourished, alleging that the current staff was to be replaced by those working for Palouse. The Global employees joined together and voiced their concerns to Hanover. Hanover issued a memorandum to the effect that, while organizational discussions are occurring, nothing has been determined, and he will inform the employees when the decision had been made.

Questions

11. Describe the general steps an organization should follow before undertaking a major organizational change.

12. Describe at least three reasons employees generally resist organizational change.

13. Discuss how an organization can best manage changes like the one contemplated by Global Telecommunications in order to encourage employee acceptance.

Essay Questions 11, 12, 13 — Unofficial Answers

11. When a firm is contemplating an organizational change, management should ensure that the change is properly planned and communicated to those affected in order to assure success. The general steps that an organization should follow before undertaking a major organizational change include the following:

   a. Recognize the need for change and understand the factors that caused the need for change.

   b. Evaluate the relevant variables and alternative courses of action available.

   c. Evaluate the results of the implementation and make adjustments as necessary.

12. At least three reasons why employees generally resist organizational change include

   a. Feelings of uncertainty or insecurity. Employees are likely to become anxious about impending changes. They may believe that their jobs are threatened by the change or be concerned about their ability to meet any new demands made on them.

   b. Threatened self-interests. Employees may fear losing their power or influence within the organization.

   c. Feelings of personal loss stemming from the disruption of existing social relationships.

13. Ways to manage changes like the one contemplated by Global Telecommunications in order to encourage employee acceptance include the following:

   a. **Participation.** Employees should be encouraged to participate in the planning and implementation of changes as they are more likely to accept change when they have had the opportunity to express their own ideas and hear the position of others.

   b. **Education.** Management should educate employees concerning the need for and the expected results of future changes.

   c. **Communication.** Initially, in changes such as Global Telecommunications is undertaking, face-to-face meetings with the affected divisional personnel should be held, as opposed to a memorandum, to address the employees' questions and concerns as soon as possible. Open lines of communication must be established and maintained to address ongoing concerns.

   d. **Facilitation.** Support should be given to those employees directly impacted by the change, i.e., retraining, placement in other positions within the firm, outplacement services, retention of key employees, etc.

STUDY UNIT FIVE
ORGANIZATION COMMUNICATION

(14 pages of outline)

Being a good communicator does not ensure that a person will be a good manager, but virtually every good manager is a good communicator. Communication should not be viewed as a separate managerial activity. Every aspect of management requires effective communication.

After studying the outline and answering the essay questions, you will have the skills necessary to address the following topics listed in the IMA's Learning Outcome Statements:

Part 4 - Section B. Organization Communication, 1. Communication models, 2. Deterrents to effective communication

The candidate should be able to:

a. describe the basic communication model of sender – communication method – receiver

b. define encoding, transmission, decoding, noise, and feedback

c. classify the different types of communication networks, including the wheel, chain, circle, Y, and all-channel networks and identify which network is present within an organizational context

d. identify different roles within communication networks, including the gatekeeper, the opinion leader, and the liaison

e. distinguish between formal and informal channels of communication

f. identify deterrents to effective communication, including semantics, noise, the grapevine, inadequate listening skills, screening, bias, stereotyping, organizational structure, cultural context, perception, skill level, overload, and lack of feedback

g. explain how a particular communication process could be improved by eliminating deterrents to communication, understanding the other's viewpoint, and using other communication skills

5.1 NATURE OF COMMUNICATION

1. **Communication** is the process of conveying meaning or understanding from one person to another by any of a variety of methods. It permeates all segments of an organization and moves in many directions.

   a. Because all managerial functions require communication, it is the secret to the success of any manager. A manager's ability to understand other people and their ability to understand the manager are crucial to accomplishing organizational objectives. Communication is the link that ties an organization together and transforms a diverse group of people into a cohesive whole.

   b. An organization's internal communications network is designed to facilitate decision making among managers, promote goal congruence among employees, integrate the efforts of all employees, and build high morale and mutual trust.

    c.   **Formal communication** is conducted through the formal structure of the organization, e.g., budgets, bonus programs, memoranda, internal variance reports, or technical manuals.

    d.   **Informal communication** (the **grapevine**) operates outside of formal structural channels.

        1)   The grapevine exists wherever there are people.

        2)   Grapevines can exist in several patterns. For example, one person may tell one other person who tells one other person, etc.; one person may tell all people in a group; individuals may tell selected others; or individuals may tell others at random.

        3)   Although the grapevine is usually accurate, it can carry gossip and rumor. Managers can minimize the damage that a grapevine can cause by transmitting accurate and timely information and maintaining open channels of communication.

        4)   The effective manager stays tuned in to the grapevine and uses it constructively.

    e.   **Written communication** provides a permanent record of the message and tends to be accurate but can be time-consuming to prepare. An inherent weakness of written communication is that it inhibits feedback because the sender and the receiver are not in simultaneous communication.

    f.   **Oral communication** is less formal and less accurate than written communication but permits immediate feedback. It also permits messages to be transmitted rapidly. Most managers spend more of their time in oral than in written communication.

    g.   **Electronic communication.** Modern technology (e.g., voice mail, fax, and email) blurs the distinction between written and oral communications. The benefits of electronic communication include better control of information, more timely information, elimination of tedious tasks, improvement of competitiveness due to improved technology, standardization of procedures by computer programs, assistance for strategic planning, and optimization of organizational resources to improve productivity.

    h.   Although communication was defined on the previous page as a process, it is also sometimes defined as the message. However, when so defined, communication is the message that is received, which is not necessarily the same as the message that was sent.

2.   **Directions of Communication**

    a.   **Downward communication** (from superior to subordinate) is vertical communication consisting of orders, instructions, notices, memos, bulletins, newsletters, handbooks, loudspeakers, and the chain of command.

    b.   **Upward communication** is vertical communication consisting of morale surveys, grievance procedures, interviews, and conferences. Upward communication must overcome more barriers and is slower than downward communication.

    c.   **Horizontal (lateral) communication** is from one peer to another.

3.   The communication process has five elements (the mnemonic is SSMRF):

    a.   **Sender**, who originates the message

    b.   **Symbols**, in which the message is encoded

    c.   **Medium**, the channel through which the message flows

    d.   **Receiver**, the person who decodes the message and interprets the sender's meaning

    e.   **Feedback**, acknowledging to the sender that the message was correctly understood

f. EXAMPLE:

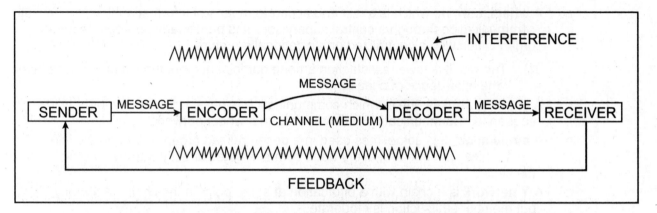

4. The effectiveness of communication can be determined only when the sender observes the impact of the communication on the receiver and seeks feedback.

   a. The sender is obligated to solicit feedback to ensure the communication process is complete.

   b. The receiver is obligated to give feedback to the sender.

   c. The importance of feedback to check on the effectiveness of the communication process indicates the limitations of one-way communications (e.g., memos).

5. Managers must consider the nature of the message receiver. Receivers vary in their perception of messages because of language, education, culture, attitudes toward the sender and job, etc. This variance may result in communication distortion.

   a. EXAMPLES:

      1) In some cultures, to move toward a person while speaking is expected; in others, it is considered an act of aggression.

      2) In some cultures, consistently being late to appointments means laxness, lack of concern, discourtesy, and disinterest; in others, it is normal and expected and carries no particular meaning.

6. Organizational structure is a determinant of how communication is transmitted.

   a. **Traditional or classical management** stresses the sending of one-way communications from top management down to the subordinates. This military model of organization is autocratic or mechanistic and ignores the need for feedback.

   b. **Participative management** stresses multidirectional communication. All parts of the organization are allowed and expected to communicate with each other and not merely along lines of authority.

   c. **Systems theory** stresses the importance of feedback in determining the effectiveness of communications. Without a channel from the receiver back to the sender, the sender has no idea how the information has affected the performance or actions of the receiver, if at all.

7.   Research shows that communications networks have various characteristics.

   a.   A **wheel** network, which is a fast and accurate means of information flow, funnels all communication through a central supervisor. It is particularly appropriate for an organization with a centralized organizational structure.

      1)   The result is lower satisfaction among participants, but the circumstances favor the emergence of a leader.

   b.   A **chain** network is one in which communication is passed from party to party in sequence. Communication is slower than in a wheel network.

   c.   A **circle** network is sometimes used in a decentralized organization. In a circle communication structure, every node communicates directly with every other node on the circle.

   d.   A **Y network** is a chain with a bifurcation at some point in the chain. Accuracy is high, but member satisfaction is moderate.

   e.   Extensive cross-communication in an **all-channel network** results in moderate accuracy but with free-flow, more innovation, and member satisfaction.

8.   **Nonverbal Communication**

   a.   **Nonverbal signals** occur in clusters, whether or not accompanied by verbal communication. They include such nonverbal nuances as

      1)   Vocal characteristics, such as tone of voice
      2)   Facial expressions and eye contact
      3)   Hand and body gestures and other movements
      4)   Breathing, sighs, and other noises that are not words
      5)   Physical distance between the sender and the receiver
      6)   Posture and other aspects of physical appearance
      7)   Touch
      8)   Mode of attire
      9)   Decoration and layout of rooms

   b.   Nonverbal communication is easily misunderstood because

      1)   Different cultures and languages employ different nonverbal signals.
      2)   Clarifying the ambiguities inherent in nonverbal communication is difficult.

   c.   Interpreting nonverbal communication requires the establishment of the norms in a particular person's nonverbal repertoire.

      1)   For example, folded arms may signify resistance or inflexibility or may simply be a habit.
      2)   People should not be judged solely on established or learned norms of nonverbal communication but instead on an individual basis.

   d.   For any communication to be effective, verbal and nonverbal messages should complement each other.

5.2 PROBLEMS IN COMMUNICATION

1. **Poorly encoded messages.** Encoding refers to the way that meaning is transmitted in communication.

   a. Inappropriate choice of words or phrases for the receiver

      1) An example is using technical language (jargon) in speaking with a lay person. The skill levels of both the sender and the recipient are keys to the manner in which a message should be encoded.

   b. Careless omissions of key ideas

   c. Lack of coherence in forming the message

   d. Inconsistency between verbal and nonverbal messages

   e. Incomplete ideas or ideas out of the receiver's context

   f. **Projection**, which is the tendency of the sender to attribute his/her traits, values, and emotions to the receiver, and vice versa

   g. **Filtering** the message so that it reflects more favorably on the sender, a typical problem in upward communication

2. **Faulty Channel Selection**

   a. Trying to speak while a loud airplane flies overhead

   b. Gesturing to someone who cannot see the gesture

3. **Noise in the communications channel** is an outside disruption that impedes the flow of a message. It can be literally "noise"; in other words, the listener cannot hear the sender of the message. Noise can also be psychological or in other forms, for example,

   a. Asking for a raise during discussion of an operational problem.

   b. Random events that cause a breakdown in communication (lost mail, phone service disruption, etc.).

   c. Receipt of phone calls during a meeting. Although the ringing of the phone is literally noise, the disruption in the thinking process is equally a noise.

4. **Perceptual Problems**

   a. Sender's dislike of receiver or vice versa.

   b. Distortion created by personal enthusiasm for embellishing good news and downplaying the bad or vice versa. Bias can lead to people overemphasizing in one direction or the other.

   c. Status differences between people that impede free and open communication.

      1) Few people are secure enough to tell a superior that what was just said was not understood.

   d. **Selective perception** arising from the receiver's needs, motives, projections, experiences, and expectations.

      1) People tend to interpret what they see and hear in the light of their own needs, etc., and to regard that interpretation as reality.

      2) Moreover, people necessarily must narrow their perception to avoid sensory overload. Such screening is required to organize and interpret experience.

   e. **Stereotyping** or attributing to another person traits that are commonly associated with a category or group to which that person belongs.

   f. Semantics can be a problem when a highly educated person is talking to a less educated individual. One or both may not understand the words used by the other.

   NOTE: Perceptual errors can be minimized with feedback from the receiver concerning his/her perceptions and interpretations of the message, understanding of the sender's perspective by the receiver, the sender's sensitivity to the receiver's problems, and implementation of a company-wide training program to improve communication skills.

5.   **Use of communication channels for enhancement of personal status.** Some lower-level employees who have the ear of management become influential among their peers. These individuals are, in effect, **gatekeepers** in that they can determine which messages will be communicated.

    a.   An organization can use the opposite of this phenomenon to good effect, that is, use personal status to enhance a communication. For example, a firm can use a respected celebrity in an ad campaign. Such **opinion leaders** can be used to enhance the reception that a message obtains.

6.   **Loss in Transmission and Poor Retention**

    a.   As much as 30% of the information in oral communication is lost in each transmission. Even written communications are subject to some loss. After passing through a chain of command, little of the message may have been retained.

    b.   Poor retention. One study found that as little as 50% of communicated information was retained by employees.

7.   **Nonreception.** The receiver commonly fails to receive any communication.

    a.   Inattention or disinterest in the message -- Messages are sometimes screened, and those in which the recipient has no interest are ignored.

    b.   Information overload -- The receiver is already receiving so many messages that (s)he cannot process what (s)he is hearing.

    c.   Confusing messages -- The sender is not sending enough information to fully communicate thoughts, and the receiver must allocate too much time to interpreting what the sender is saying.

8.   **Formal Organization Channel Breakdowns**

    a.   EXAMPLE: Omissions from mailing lists

9.   **Solutions to Communications Problems**

    a.   The message should be in the context of the receiver's perceptions.

        1)   Explaining an accounting concept to a nonaccountant will require terms different from those used with someone who has an accounting background.

    b.   The sender must monitor channels to ensure they are free from distortion or breakdown.

    c.   The sender must actively solicit feedback to ensure reception and understanding.

    d.   The organizational climate should encourage the elimination of interpersonal barriers to communication.

    e.   The sender should look for nonverbal cues or feedback (such as body language).

    f.   The sender must remember that it is his/her responsibility to deliver the communication with appropriate symbols over appropriate channels and never to make assumptions about the receiver's reaction.

    g.   Two-way communication should be used whenever possible to permit ease of feedback.

    h.   Communication can be improved through redundancy, that is, by repeating the message in several different formats and in several media.

5.3 LISTENING AND OTHER FORMS OF COMMUNICATION

1. **Listening** is the responsibility of both the speaker (sender) and the listener (receiver). Listening is one of the problems in communication that can be improved by the manager. The art of listening must be exercised effectively to

    a. Gain more information about the work situation
    b. Have a positive effect on both superiors and subordinates through showing concern for their views

2. **Problems in Listening**

    a. People can listen several times faster than words can be spoken, which may result in inattention and mind-wandering.
    b. Prejudgment of the message before or during the communication process may reduce the ability to listen objectively. In other words, the recipient could be biased and fail to give the message adequate consideration. Essentially, a listener screens out what he or she does not want to hear.
    c. Concentration may be focused on the words used to the exclusion of the ideas. In other words, there is a decoding problem.

3. **Guides to More Effective Listening**

    a. **Empathy** is the process of mentally putting oneself in another person's position to better understand his/her feelings, attitudes, and thoughts. Empathy

        1) Enables the sender and the receiver to take into account each other's backgrounds, biases, beliefs, and values
        2) Aids in anticipating others' reactions to messages
        3) Aids in effective communication by guiding the choice of

            a) Words used and their meanings
            b) Word inflection and emphasis
            c) Tone of voice and gestures

    b. **Sensitivity training** gives managers a greater awareness of, or sensitivity to, their own attitudes, feelings, and beliefs. This understanding helps them perceive how their behavior affects the people with whom they communicate.

        1) Such training is designed to result in better listening skills, tolerance for individual differences, and an awareness of the impact of one's personality on other people.
        2) The disadvantage is that some managers may spend a disproportionate amount of time focusing on relationships rather than on the day-to-day problems of the job.

    c. **Interpersonal communications training.** Supervisors and their subordinates receive formal training in how to give and receive both written and oral communication. The advantage is that everyone has the same training and can practice working together using specific problems.

    d. To enhance listening abilities, a listener should stop working on other activities and concentrate on what is being said. Listening entails decoding and understanding the first message sent. The sender then becomes a listener with respect to the feedback. Hence, listening is necessary at both ends of the communication channel.

    e. Other aids to effective listening are using body language to encourage the speaker, showing appropriate emotion to signify sympathy, understanding and correcting for one's biases, avoiding making premature judgments, and briefly summarizing what has been said.

4. **Other Forms of Communication**

    a. **Audit reports** and other documents are forms of communication.

        1) Internal audit reports are expected to communicate audit results to management and create desired actions.
        2) Audit reports should be timely, clear, concise, objective, and constructive.
        3) A corporate annual report is a one-way communication device.

            a) Clarity and conciseness must be emphasized because no immediate feedback from readers is possible.
            b) A logical organization of the report's contents facilitates transmission of the message.

    b. **Employee handbooks and accounting manuals** are also forms of communication.

        1) The employee handbook communicates company policies and provides employees and management with quick and consistent answers to employment-related questions.

            a) It provides a store of knowledge and outlines the responsibilities and levels of authority within an organization.
            b) It can be the basis of a contract between the company and its employees.
            c) It should include information about

                i)   Benefit packages
                ii)   Holiday and vacation policies
                iii) Sick pay provisions
                iv)   Severance policy
                v)   Retirement benefits
                vi)   Grievance procedures
                vii) Promotion and transfer policies

        2) An accounting manual promotes equitable and consistent treatment of similar transactions.

            a) It should define accounting and technical terms in language that all employees can understand.

        3) Both employee handbooks and accounting manuals should be prepared so that revisions and updates are facilitated (e.g., kept in a ring binder).

            a) Specific individuals should be responsible for periodic updating of handbooks and manuals.

    c. **Business memos**

        1) Memos vary in form and content but often begin in the following way:

            TO: All employees
            FROM: Irv Gleim
            SUBJECT: Format and content of memos
            DATE: July 30, 2008

            a) Most companies have prepared stationery with a logo and their desired format.
            b) Memos may be signed or unsigned, convey good or bad news, or give information necessary to facilitate smooth daily business.

2) Memos should have the characteristics of good writing. They should avoid unnecessary verbiage, and readers should grasp the meaning quickly and easily. Good business writing style is concise, clear, coherent, correct, credible, natural, positive, interesting, and readable.

    a) It treats receivers with respect by sending a courteous message.

    b) It is also suitable to the medium of presentation and delivery.

    c) Good business writing style provides clear, developed ideas but avoids overstatement.

        i) It also conveys the message unobtrusively. The writing should not call attention to itself.

3) The details for a memorandum announcing a mandatory meeting include the purpose and goals of the meeting, a list of who must attend, the information or reports required for the meeting, the expected length of the meeting, and the person to contact regarding any questions or problems.

    a) The writer-chairperson should take preliminary actions after announcing the meeting, including distributing the planned agenda, providing copies of information to prepare the participants, and calling the participants to remind them of their required attendance.

    b) During the meeting, the writer-chairperson should state the purpose and objectives of the meeting, maintain a list of assignments decided on during the meeting, focus the discussion by giving direction, curtail repetition and triviality, encourage individual responses, and summarize and review the discussion at the meeting's conclusion.

    c) After the meeting, the writer-chairperson should follow up the special assignments made to individuals at the meeting. A request for periodic reports on the status of these assignments may be made, or the individuals can be contacted directly.

d. **Persuasive communications**

1) Persuasive communication, whether for internal or external purposes, requires clarity of presentation. Arguments should be focused on the ultimate objective, organized in a logical manner that leads inevitably to the desired conclusion, and shaped with regard to the attitudes, opinions, and information needs of the specific recipient. Unrelated and unnecessary subjects should be avoided.

    a) The credibility of the message is also important in changing attitudes. Trust, competence, objectivity, and high ethical standards are persuasive.

    b) Although objective evidence is important, emotional appeals may also be effective. However, they must be carefully designed to appeal to the recipient's emotional structure. Otherwise, they may backfire.

        i) High connotation words should be used with care in persuasive communication because such language has strong but unpredictable effects. Emotion-laden words should be chosen to appeal to the particular recipient.

2)   A typical sequence of arguments in a persuasive message places strong arguments first and last, with weaker arguments and refutations of opposing arguments in the middle. The reasons for this ordering are the primacy and recency principles. People tend to remember best what they read or hear first and last.

    a)   The middle section includes weaker arguments. It also is the appropriate location of counterarguments.

        i)   Selective choice of the opponent's arguments that can be successfully rebutted can be very effective. However, mention of the opponent's arguments that cannot be refuted will weaken the persuader's case.

e.   **Telecommuting.** People who are computer literate have in recent years begun working from their homes. They correspond with their offices by means of telecommunication.

    1)   Problems associated with these employees include a tendency to fall behind in their fields of specialization, a lack of strong working relationships with other employees, a loss of career opportunities, and inadequate organizational socialization.

    2)   The primary strength of these individuals, however, has been their communication skills.

    3)   Many corporations have taken advantage of email, file transfer protocol (FTP), the Internet, and various network configurations to make telecommuting more practical and useful.

5.4 NEGOTIATION AND CONFLICT MANAGEMENT

1.   **Negotiation**, or bargaining, strives for an exchange of goods or services and an agreement as to the rate of exchange.

    a.   According to Walton and McKensie, *A Behavioral Theory of Labor Negotiations: An Analysis of a Social Interaction System*, the general approaches to negotiation are distributive bargaining and integrative bargaining.

        1)   **Distributive bargaining** is typical of negotiators who are in a zero-sum situation, such as labor-management negotiations about wages. What one side gains, the other loses. Thus, the interests of the parties diverge because they are competing for shares of a fixed amount of resources.

            a)   The negotiators in distributive bargaining operate with a maximum desired result and a minimum acceptable result in mind. If the ranges of feasible outcomes of the parties overlap, an agreement is possible.

        2)   **Integrative bargaining** occurs in a positive sum situation; that is, the parties believe that a solution exists that permits both sides to win. The parties have shared interests, the amount of resources to be allocated is not fixed, and the relationship tends to be long-term.

            a)   Integrative bargaining is the preferable mode within an organization because it fosters cooperation, minimizes conflict, and develops constructive long-term relationships. However, it works only when the negotiators are open, flexible, able to trust the other side, sympathetic to each other's concerns, and committed to finding creative solutions.

        b) Effective negotiators are good listeners, ask frequent questions, avoid defensiveness and attacks on the opponents, do not use language calculated to be irritating, and phrase their arguments clearly and directly.

           i) They also understand that reciprocity is often a characteristic of negotiation. A tough stance encourages a similar response, and concessions usually result in reciprocal concessions. In the latter case, however, the amount of concessions received will usually be less than those offered.

        c) Third parties as negotiators

           i) **Mediation** is an intervention between conflicting parties by a neutral and noncoercive agency to facilitate an agreement. A mediator offers solutions, facilitates communications, and presents arguments.

           ii) **Arbitration** is the hearing and determination of a case in controversy by a person chosen by the parties or appointed under statutory authority. The results of arbitration are binding, although the process may be entered voluntarily or compulsorily (under law or contract).

           iii) **Conciliation** overlaps with mediation. A conciliator is a trusted individual who provides an informal communication link, interprets messages, etc.

           iv) **Consultation** is performed by a neutral individual whose expertise is in conflict management. The consultant's function is less to arrive at a settlement than to improve interactions between the parties.

    b. The benefits of negotiating include resolving an issue without litigation, recognizing that each party values the other party's needs and rights, and impartially treating tension while finding compromise solutions.

2. **Conflict management.** Conflict may be constructive or destructive.

    a. Communication, structure, and personal variables are the broad categories of conditions that may result in conflict.

      1) Communication variables pertain to semantical issues, noise in communication channels, and other problems in communication that impair cooperation and cause misunderstanding.

      2) Structural conditions include the size of the work group, specialization of tasks, the clarity of lines of authority, leadership practices, compensation schemes, and the interdependence of groups.

      3) Personal variables include individual personality characteristics and value systems.

    b. Conflict triggers include ambiguous jurisdictions (unclear job boundaries); competition for scarce resources; status differentials; time pressures; personality clashes; unreasonable standards, rules, etc.; communication breakdowns; and unrealized expectations.

    c. **Interactionist theory** regards conflict as potentially beneficial. Functional conflict improves performance and helps the organization to achieve its objectives.

d.   Whether conflict is functional depends on the intentions of the parties.

    1)   In **competition**, individuals display the maximum of assertiveness (behavior intended to achieve one's own objectives) and the minimum of cooperativeness (behavior intended to meet the concerns of others). Generally, this technique does not effectively resolve conflict.

    2)   **Collaboration** is an attempt by all parties to the conflict to attain everyone's objectives.

    3)   **Avoidance** is withdrawal from the conflict (the minimum of both cooperation and assertiveness).

    4)   **Compromise** is a position in which each party to the conflict both gains and loses. It is characterized by moderate cooperation and moderate assertiveness.

    5)   **Accommodation** is an intention that reflects a high degree of cooperation and a low degree of assertiveness.

e.   Conflict may result in better decision making, a reduction in complacency, more self-criticism, greater creativity, and solutions to problems. Functional conflict drives the change processes that all organizations need to survive and prosper.

    1)   Thus, intentional stimulation of conflict may be desirable. For example, management may intentionally trigger conflict by issuing threatening communications; by making changes in the organizational structure; by hiring new employees with different values, managerial styles, attitudes, and backgrounds; or by designating individuals to oppose the majority views of the group.

f.   Conflicts may be resolved in a variety of ways.

    1)   **Problem solving** is a means of confronting the conflict and removing its causes. The emphasis is on facts and solutions, not personalities and assignment of blame. The disadvantage is that problem solving takes time.

    2)   **Smoothing** is a short-term avoidance approach. The parties in conflict are asked by management to submerge their differences temporarily.

    3)   **Forcing** occurs when a superior uses his/her formal authority to order a particular resolution of the conflict.

    4)   **Superordinate goals** are the overriding goals of the entity to which subunit and personal goals are subordinate. An appeal to these goals is another short-term solution.

    5)   **Compromise** entails negotiation by the parties in conflict. The conflict is avoided rather than solved through a process by which each side makes concessions. Thus, the parties both gain and lose.

    6)   **Expanding resources** resolves conflicts that result from scarcity.

    7)   **Avoidance** withdraws from and suppresses the conflict but does not solve the underlying problem.

    8)   **Changing the human element** involves use of behavioral techniques to change attitudes and behavior.

    9)   **Changing structure** alters formal organizational arrangements.

    10) **Diffusion** is an approach to resolving conflict whereby critical issues are temporarily set aside while an attempt is made to reach an agreement on less controversial issues first.

    11) The **public media** hinders communication because issues are addressed to the public, not the other party. However, the media may help resolve the problem through public pressure.

5.5 CORE CONCEPTS

Nature of Communication

- **Communication** is the process of conveying meaning or understanding from one person to another by any of a variety of methods. It permeates all segments of an organization and moves in many directions. Because all managerial functions require communication, it is the secret to the success of any manager.

- Communication can take multiple **forms**: formal vs. informal, written vs. oral, electronic.

- Communication has a **direction**: downward (from superior to subordinate), upward (from subordinate to superior), or horizontal (from one peer to another).

- The communication process has **five elements** (the mnemonic is SSMRF): sender, symbols, medium, receiver, feedback. The **effectiveness** of communication can be determined only when the sender observes the impact of the communication on the receiver and seeks **feedback**.

- Organizational structure is a determinant of how communication is transmitted. **Traditional or classical management** stresses the sending of one-way communications from top management down to the subordinates. **Participative management** stresses multidirectional communication. **Systems theory** stresses the importance of feedback in determining the effectiveness of communications.

- Research shows that communications networks have various characteristics. **Models** include the wheel, the chain, the circle, the Y network, and the all-channel network.

- **Nonverbal signals** occur in clusters, whether or not accompanied by verbal communication. They include such nonverbal nuances as (1) vocal characteristics, such as tone of voice, (2) facial expressions and eye contact, and (3) hand and body gestures and other movements.

- Nonverbal communication is **easily misunderstood** because different cultures and languages employ different nonverbal signals, and clarifying the ambiguities inherent in nonverbal communication is difficult. For any communication to be effective, verbal and nonverbal messages should complement each other.

Problems in Communication

- Messages can be **poorly encoded** by, among other things, inappropriate choice of words or phrases for the receiver, careless omissions of key ideas, projection, and filtering.

- **Noise in the communications channel** is an outside disruption that impedes the flow of a message. It can be literally "noise"; in other words, the listener cannot hear the sender of the message. Noise can also be psychological or in other forms.

- **Perceptual problems** sometimes arise, such as selective perception (arising from the receiver's needs, motives, projections, experiences, and expectations), and stereotyping (attributing to another person traits that are commonly associated with a category or group to which that person belongs).

- Communication channels are sometimes used for the **enhancement of personal status**. Some lower-level employees who have the ear of management become influential among their peers. These individuals are, in effect, **gatekeepers** in that they can determine which messages will be communicated. **Opinion leaders** can be used to enhance the reception that a message obtains.

- As much as **30%** of the information in oral communication is **lost** in each transmission. Even written communications are subject to some loss. After passing through a chain of command, little of the message may have been retained. One study found that as little as 50% of communicated information was retained by employees.

- The receiver sometimes **fails to receive** a communication. Inattention or disinterest in the message, information overload, and confusing messages are causes.

- **Solutions to communications problems include** the sender monitoring channels to ensure they are free from distortion or breakdown, and the sender actively soliciting feedback to ensure reception and understanding.

Listening and Other Forms of Communications

- **Listening** is the responsibility of both the speaker (sender) and the listener (receiver). Listening is one of the problems in communication that can be improved by the manager.
- People can listen several times faster than words can be spoken, which may result in **inattention** and **mind-wandering**. **Prejudgment** of the message before or during the communication process may reduce the ability to listen objectively. Concentration may be **focused on the words** used to the exclusion of the ideas.
- **Empathy** is the process of mentally putting oneself in another person's position to better understand his/her feelings, attitudes, and thoughts. **Sensitivity training** gives managers a greater awareness of, or sensitivity to, their own attitudes, feelings, and beliefs. This understanding helps them perceive how their behavior affects the people with whom they communicate. Supervisors and their subordinates can receive formal **interpersonal communications training** in how to give and receive both written and oral communication.
- **Persuasive communication**, whether for internal or external purposes, requires clarity of presentation. Arguments should be focused on the ultimate objective, organized in a logical manner that leads inevitably to the desired conclusion, and shaped with regard to the attitudes, opinions, and information needs of the specific recipient.

Negotiation and Conflict Management

- **Negotiation** or bargaining strives for an exchange of goods or services and an agreement as to the rate of exchange.
- **Distributive bargaining** is typical of negotiators who are in a zero-sum situation, such as labor-management negotiations about wages. What one side gains, the other loses. Thus, the interests of the parties diverge because they are competing for shares of a fixed amount of resources.
- **Integrative bargaining** occurs in a positive sum situation; that is, the parties believe that a solution exists that permits both sides to win. The parties have shared interests, the amount of resources to be allocated is not fixed, and the relationship tends to be long-term.
- **Effective negotiators** are good listeners, ask frequent questions, avoid defensiveness and attacks on the opponents, do not use language calculated to be irritating, and phrase their arguments clearly and directly.
- **Third parties negotiations** can take the form of mediation, arbitration, conciliation, and consultation.
- **Conflict** may be constructive or destructive. **Interactionist theory** regards conflict as potentially beneficial. Functional conflict improves performance and helps the organization to achieve its objectives. Whether conflict is functional depends on the **intentions** of the parties. Competition, collaboration, avoidance, compromise, and accommodation are the modes of intent.
- **Conflict-resolution methods** include problem solving, smoothing, forcing, superordinate goals, compromise, expanding resources, avoidance, changing the human element, changing structure, and diffusion.

5.6 ESSAY QUESTIONS

Recall that your CMA Part 4 exam will probably contain six scenarios, with about three questions per scenario. There will be a recommended time allocation of 20 minutes, 30 minutes, or 45 minutes for each scenario and related questions.

One scenario will involve ethics, and probably one or two scenarios will include calculations and responses on a worksheet. Also, expect at least one scenario on organizational/behavioral topics. The remaining scenarios cover Parts 1, 2, and 3.

Scenario Title	Subtopic	Questions	Suggested Time
Tabor Industries	Problems in Communication	1, 2, 3	30 minutes
Seth Varner	The Annual Report as a Communication Device	4, 5, 6	30 minutes
Northside Health Club	Medium and Message	7, 8, 9	30 minutes

Scenario for Essay Questions 1, 2, 3

Tabor Industries is an established manufacturer of refrigeration equipment for supermarkets. While gross sales have been steadily increasing, net profits have not kept pace. It is generally believed that production is not as efficient as possible and that better cost controls need to be instituted.

To help address these problems, Warren Renson, vice president and production manager, decided to involve the workforce in making suggestions. He sent the following memo to all production line and staff employees.

Date: December 1, 2008

To: Production Line and Staff Employees

From: Warren Renson

Let's improve production together. We need your input. I know we can make production more efficient. A suggestion box system is hereby implemented. We will pay an appropriate percentage of the savings to the employee who makes any suggestion that is implemented. Send your suggestions to my office. I look forward to hearing from you.

The suggestion box system has been in operation for a full year now, and Renson is annoyed and disappointed with the results. Only three worthwhile suggestions have been received, and only one of them had any measurable impact on production efficiency. Many other suggestions were submitted, but they were all for the benefit of the employees.

Questions

1. Communications can be misunderstood at various levels.

   a. Describe at least four personal characteristics, attributable to both senders and receivers, that can cause communication problems.

   b. Describe at least three organizational characteristics that may be barriers to effective communication.

2. Explain why the suggestion box system failed at Tabor Industries.

3. Recommend at least four ways in which Tabor Industries might improve its communication with employees in order to increase production efficiency.

Essay Questions 1, 2, 3 — Unofficial Answers

1. a. Four personal characteristics, attributable to both senders and receivers, that can cause communications problems include

   1) Listening problems resulting from the receiver misunderstanding the intended message
   2) Poor channel or media selection, e.g., sender has chosen a communication carrier that does not get to the receivers, or faulty encoding, e.g., the use of jargon
   3) The influence that knowledge level, attitude (lack of interest), and background (demographics) will play in sending and receiving an effective message
   4) Interpersonal dynamics and emotions, including trust in the sender

   b. Three organizational characteristics that may be barriers to effective communications include

   1) Organizational status and power differences, e.g., lower levels reluctant to communicate with upper levels or upper level perception that lower levels have little to contribute
   2) Lack of formal channels, i.e., organization must provide adequate upward, downward, and horizontal communications in the form of surveys, open-door policies, newsletters, memos, task force, and liaison personnel
   3) Departmental needs and goals; each one views problems and needs in its own terms

2. The reasons why the suggestion box failed at Tabor Industries include

   a. Use of the wrong communication channel; more personal communication, such as meeting(s), should have been held to obtain more impact
   b. Brevity of the memo did not allow for an understandable explanation of the company's expectations
   c. The lack of an explanation of the problems the company is facing so the employees would be able to direct their efforts more effectively
   d. The rewards or incentives were not clearly stated in order to capture employee attention as to the benefits to them rather than to management

3. Four ways in which Tabor Industries might improve its communication with employees in order to increase efficiency include

   a. Use of a company newsletter for employee updates to publicize employees receiving awards for appropriate suggestions
   b. Group meetings to discuss expectations for suggestions and request feedback
   c. Management communicating directly by visiting the production area to meet the employees at the day-to-day operations to find out what is wrong and exchange ideas
   d. Creating a climate of trust and openness that will encourage employees to communicate freely

Scenario for Essay Questions 4, 5, 6

Seth Varner has recently been assigned the responsibility of preparing his company's corporate annual report. The CEO has made a big deal out of this assignment and has told Seth that this may be the most important job he ever undertakes.

The annual report is considered by some to be the single most important printed document that companies produce. It provides information used in making both economic investments and business decisions. The content of the annual report has expanded considerably in recent years in an effort to satisfy a growing audience that includes not only shareholders but also financial analysts, investors, and customers. The future of most companies depends on acceptance by the investing public and by its customers; therefore, companies should take this opportunity to communicate well-defined corporate strategies.

Questions

4. In viewing the annual report as a communication device, analyze the six basic parts of the communication model (sender, encoded message, channel, receiver, feedback, and noise) as they relate to the preparation of an annual report.

5. a. Describe four types of information found in an annual report, other than the financial statements and accompanying footnotes, that are useful to the users of annual reports.

    b. Discuss at least two advantages and two disadvantages of stating well-defined corporate strategies in the annual report.

6. Evaluate the effectiveness of annual reports in fulfilling the information needs of current and potential

    a. Shareholders
    b. Creditors
    c. Employees
    d. Customers

Essay Questions 4, 5, 6 — Unofficial Answers

4.   **Sender.** The sender of the information (the management of the company who is responsible for the annual report) wishes to inform the external readers, viz., the shareholders, creditors, investors, and other interested parties, about the company's financial performance, organizational objectives, and product information.

Encoded Message. The message sent from the company is encoded via a form of communication, in this case, a written format.

Channel. The channel or avenue of communication for a company's annual report is the printed, formal, written report including graphic presentations.

Receiver. Each individual listener or receiver has his/her own perceptions and expectations in reading the annual report, as well as variant skill levels in interpreting the detailed information (e.g., knowledge of finance, comparative industry information, SEC law, etc.).

Feedback. An essential element of communication is feedback. The company issuing an annual report does not usually receive feedback or a response to the information communicated in the annual report, thereby forcing the preparers to be clear, concise, and complete.

Noise. The company's annual report could suffer noise from the impact of uncontrollable, external environmental factors.

5.   a.   Other than the financial statements and accompanying footnotes, an annual report provides information concerning

1)   Management's discussion and analysis of results
2)   Organizational objectives, strategies, and management's outlook for the future
3)   The members of the board of directors and the officers of the organization
4)   Segment data and performance information
5)   New initiatives and research information
6)   Recent stock price history and stock information

b.   In stating well-defined corporate strategies in the annual report, the company will experience the following advantages:

1)   Communicates the company's plan for the future and resolves any disparate issues
2)   Provides a vehicle for communicating the company's strengths
3)   Builds investor confidence and portrays a positive image

Disadvantages include the following:

1)   Locks management into fulfilling the stated objectives, causing inflexibility
2)   Communicates to unintended users who could put the company at risk (e.g., competitors)

6.   Annual reports fulfill information needs as discussed below.

a.   Shareholders. The annual report gives current and potential shareholders financial information, such as income from operations, earnings per share, the balance sheet, cash flows, and related footnote disclosure, to make investment decisions.

b.   Creditors. The annual report of public companies provides financial information that allows creditors to project financial solvency to evaluate the ability to repay.

c.   Employees. The annual report gives the employees information, specifically the description of the company's pension plan and employees' stock incentive plans.

d.   Customers. The annual report provides trend information and management performance for the customer to assess the company's and product's past performance and to evaluate the company's longevity.

Scenario for Essay Questions 7, 8, 9

Rashid Ahmed is the director of the Northside Health Club. Ahmed has monthly meetings with the administrative staff of the club to coordinate activities, discuss problems that have arisen in the past month, and outline plans for the coming months. The following items were discussed during the most recent meeting:

- Jeffrey Stram, membership supervisor of the club, reported that a clerical position is vacant in his department, as Peter Price resigned because of a family emergency. Stram asked to have the job opening announced at the next meeting of the full staff.

- Ahmed reported that stricter staff licensing requirements were going into effect that might require additional staff training and suggested that this information be included in the next edition of the club's employee newsletter.

- Phyllis Vassar, controller, was asked to include the work schedule for the upcoming holiday weekend in the envelope with the employees' paychecks. Vassar argued against this, as she knew from experience that the holiday schedule often led to complaints and questions. She felt that, as a result of attaching the work schedule to the employees' paychecks, complaints and questions would be directed at the controller's office, which is not responsible for establishing work schedules.

Questions

7. For each of the three situations described, evaluate the communication medium proposed to transmit the message. If the medium is inappropriate or insufficient, recommend a better means of communication. Discuss each situation individually.

8. Describe the role of feedback in successful organizational communication.

9. Personal communication (telephone or person-to-person) is frequently used within business organizations. Describe at least two advantages and two disadvantages of personal communication.

Essay Questions 7, 8, 9 — Unofficial Answers

7. An evaluation of each of the three situations described and the recommended means of communication are presented below.

    Job Opening. Using a meeting of the full staff to announce the availability of a clerical position is insufficient and may be inappropriate, as only staff people will know of the vacancy. Jeffrey Stram should have posted the job opening in a location available to all interested parties.

    Staff Training. An announcement in the employee newsletter may not be sufficient notification of an issue that is very important to some of the personnel and may have an important impact on the club. To effectively communicate this information, a letter should be sent to each of the affected employees. It may be necessary to follow the letter with a meeting of these employees to discuss the new requirements and answer employees' questions.

    Holiday Work Schedule. The use of the paycheck envelopes to transmit the holiday work schedule to employees is not appropriate. Holiday schedules should be communicated to the employees by their supervisor. The supervisor should first determine if there are any employees who would volunteer to work on the holiday weekend. Once the schedule is set, it should be posted on the departmental bulletin board.

8. The role of feedback in successful organizational communication encompasses the following:

    a. Feedback allows the sender to determine if the message received was the message intended.

    b. Feedback on performance allows employees to know if they are meeting expectations or should modify behavior. Feedback shows that others are interested and usually results in improved employee attitudes.

    c. The free flow of feedback encourages the presentation of new ideas or differing viewpoints that may result in improvements in current policies or procedures.

9. Two advantages of personal communication include

    a. A fast, efficient way to communicate a message
    b. Facilitating discussion of spontaneous ideas and clarification of complex issues

    Two disadvantages of personal communication include

    a. Forcing parties to make on-the-spot judgments or decisions
    b. Possibly not having the lasting effect or impact of a written communication

---

Consider using Gleim's **CMA Test Prep** for interactive testing with **hundreds of multiple-choice questions** as an additional method of knowledge transfer in your quest to pass Part 4.

STUDY UNIT SIX
BEHAVIOR – ALIGNMENT OF ORGANIZATIONAL GOALS

(5 pages of outline)

The behavioral aspects of the management function of control has the following stages:

1. Develop expectations, standards, budgets, and plans.
2. Undertake activity, production, study, and learning.
3. Measure the activity, production, output, and knowledge.
4. Compare actual activity with expected and budgeted activity.
5. Modify the activity, behavior, or study to better achieve the expected or desired outcome.
6. Revise expectations and standards in light of actual experience.
7. Continue the process or restart the process in the future.

This process is used not only to manage multinational organizations but also to systematize your study of a single study unit.

The seven-step managerial control process is implemented through various organizational arrangements. Furthermore, organizations achieve their objectives by and through people.

Part 4 is specifically concerned with the accountant's role in the management process and the application of the management process to specific situations. Thus, the behavioral issues pertaining to accounting measurements and reports are as critical to accountants as they are to management in general and managers in particular. For that reason, the subject matter of Study Units 6, 7, and 8 add another dimension to issues considered previously in Part 4 and in earlier parts of the CMA examination.

Because of the difficulty of anticipating the specific behavioral concepts that may be tested in Part 4, we ask that readers who have just taken the CMA examination notify us about any concepts not covered in these study units. However, DO NOT disclose information about specific questions. We will post the information on our email update service. Please see page iv.

This study unit is the **first of three** on **behavioral issues**. The three study units are

Study Unit 6: Behavior – Alignment of Organizational Goals
Study Unit 7: Behavior – Budgeting and Standard Setting
Study Unit 8: Behavior – Reporting and Performance Evaluation

After studying the outline and answering the essay questions, you will have the skills necessary to address the following topics listed in the IMA's Learning Outcome Statements:

<u>Part 4 - Section C. Behavioral Issues, 1. Alignment of organizational goals</u>

The candidate should be able to:

  a.   define the concept of goal congruence and explain the concept of agency theory and how it relates to goal congruence

  b.   identify the purposes for goal setting as they relate to employee behavior (motivation)

  c.   explain how goal congruence relates to the success or failure of budgetary plans

  d.   describe the relationship between employee goals and needs and the goals of the firm

  e.   differentiate between responsibility and authority

  f.   demonstrate an understanding of the issues surrounding responsibility without authority

  g.   identify ways in which authority is established (formal and informal)

  h.   evaluate a given management situation for its behavioral implications and suggest alternate approaches

6.1 GOAL CONGRUENCE AND AGENCY THEORY

  1.   A managerial control system should encourage the efficient achievement of organizational objectives. Thus, **goal congruence** and **managerial effort** are aspects of motivation.

      a.   All managers should be motivated to expend the necessary effort to reach common goals. The goals should be set so that they are specific, objective, and verifiable. Conversely, a control system should discourage effort directed toward incongruent goals.

      b.   A key issue for organizations is how to promote goal congruence while securing the benefits of appropriate decentralization. Providing subunit managers with significant autonomy may result in greater awareness of the needs of important constituencies (e.g., customers, suppliers, and employees), faster decisions, more rapid management development, and greater management initiative.

  2.   To achieve organizational objectives, behavior management can be used.

      a.   **Behavior management** (also referred to as positive reinforcement) provides positive motivation through **rewards and punishment**. This technique operates under the assumption that changing consequences is the key to changing behavior.

          1)   Behavior management focuses on using reinforcements, such as praise and bonuses, to increase the likelihood of desired behaviors.

          2)   Sometimes punishments must be used to curtail undesired behavior.

  3.   A means of attaining goal congruence is to **harmonize the measures** used to evaluate managers with the measures used in top management's decision models.

      a.   For example, the transfer price charged by a selling division to a buying division of a company should be set so that individual managers acting in their own best interests will further the objectives of the company. This result will be reached when maximizing the performance measure for a manager also provides the greatest benefit for the organization.

      b.   A budget is one of the ways that management communicates goals.

          1)   Thus, a budget is an important goal-congruence tool. In fact, the overall success of a budget is often dependent upon how good of a goal congruence tool that it is. With a budget, employees in every department are looking at the same goals.

          2)   For instance, if salesmen wanted to optimize inventories, they would want maximum levels so that no sales would ever be lost; whereas financial administrators would want the inventory at zero to avoid carrying costs. The budget conveys to everyone what the company's objectives are regarding inventory levels.

4. **Agency theory** explains how to organize relationships in which one party (the principal) determines the work that another party (the agent) performs.

   a. Agency theory argues that under conditions of incomplete information and uncertainty (or information asymmetries), which characterize most business settings, two agency problems arise: adverse selection and moral hazard.

      1) **Adverse selection** is the condition under which the principal cannot ascertain whether the agent accurately represents his/her ability to do the work for which (s)he is being paid.

      2) **Moral hazard** is the condition under which the principal cannot ascertain whether the agent has put forth maximal effort.

   b. The theory assumes that when information asymmetries exist, individuals will pursue their own self-interest with guile. In other words, a conflict of interest may exist between the owners and management of a firm. The goals of ownership (principal) and management (agent) may not be congruent.

   c. The problems of adverse selection and moral hazard mean that fixed wage contracts are not always the best way to organize relationships between principals and agents. A fixed wage might create an incentive for the agent to **shirk** because his/her compensation will be the same regardless of the quality and quantity of work or level of effort.

      1) When agents have incentive to shirk, it is often more efficient to replace fixed wages with compensation based on residual profits of the firm. The provision of ownership rights (e.g., stock options) reduces the incentive for agents' adverse selection and moral hazard because it makes their compensation dependent upon their performance.

   d. Because constant monitoring is expensive and infeasible, accounting information provides a control over the actions of the agent. The principal is willing to incur monitoring and auditing costs to ensure performance by the agent.

      1) The costs of the agency relationship can be both direct (audits) and indirect (the lost opportunities caused by the restrictions imposed by monitoring).

   e. Agency theory has ramifications for the degree of decentralization appropriate in an organization. When information asymmetry is exploited properly, the result is a flexibility gain to the organization. If this gain exceeds the agency costs, a given degree of decentralization or employee empowerment is beneficial.

5. **Goal-setting theory** is another attempt to explain motivation. According to Edwin Locke's goal-setting theory, specific, difficult goals to which the employee is committed provide the best motivation tool.

   a. Performance improves when goals are specific rather than general, difficult rather than easy, and self-set rather than imposed by others.

   b. Furthermore, feedback, especially self-generated feedback, also improves performance compared with lack of feedback.

   c. Commitment to goals, that is, a determination not to reduce or abandon them, and self-efficacy, that is, a belief in one's ability to accomplish the task, are additional qualities that result in better performance.

6.2 AUTHORITY AND RESPONSIBILITY

1. The relationships present in the structure of an organization include authority, responsibility, and accountability. Classical theory stresses the need for balance between authority and responsibility.

2. The greater the sources of power possessed by a manager, the more likely an employee will be inclined to accept his/her authority. In other words, a manager who has both formal and informal sources of power will be more influential than someone with only one source.

3. **Authority** is the right to direct and exact performance from others, including the right to prescribe the means and methods by which the work will be done. The right to direct should be distinguished from the ability (the power) to accomplish tasks.

    a. Under the classical approach, the right to exercise authority is deemed to be vested in the position. Based on objective criteria, the organization rationally determines where a decision is best made, gives the authority to make the decision to that position, and fills the position with the most suitable person.

    b. Under the behavioral approach, the right to direct is deemed to be only as good as the receiver's willingness to accept direction from another.

        1) It emphasizes the willingness of followers to be directed as opposed to the classical focus on the right of a leader to command.

        2) Belief in this approach necessitates a change in the attitude of the leader toward subordinates by focusing on the leader's need to secure compliance from followers rather than an assumption of blind obedience to commands.

4. **Responsibility** is the obligation to perform.

    a. In the classical view, this obligation is formally imposed by a superior and is inherent in any job.

    b. In the behavioral view, responsibility must and should be delegated; there is a successive dividing and passing down of obligation.

        1) The appropriate amount of authority or power must be delegated with the responsibility.

        2) However, a higher position cannot escape ultimate responsibility.

5. **Accountability** is the duty to account for the fulfillment of the responsibility. In practice, accountability is

    a. The duty to report performance to one's superior

        1) The principle of single accountability or unity of command means that each subordinate should report to only one superior.

        2) Unity of command permits more than one person to act as a subordinate's superior only when coordination of plans is so complete that no conflicting instructions are given.

    b. The physical means for reporting or being able to substantiate performance, i.e., record keeping

6. The alignment of managerial with organizational goals requires assigning responsibility for activities, delegating the authority to perform necessary tasks, and establishing accountability. The result is a structure within which individual efforts can be coordinated to attain ultimate organizational goals.

7. Some degree of controllability is necessary before a manager can influence activities.

8. Larger companies are usually divided into multiple segments, with the amount of autonomy of the divisions reflecting the **decentralization** of the company.

    a. Along with enhancing managerial morale and development, decentralization allows top management to concentrate on a long-range focus and encourages division managers to look outside the company to meet operational needs.

    b. Disadvantages include greater difficulty in achieving goal congruence, duplication of effort, and lack of communication among segment managers.

6.3 CORE CONCEPTS

Goal Congruence and Agency Theory

- A managerial control system should encourage the efficient achievement of organizational objectives. Thus, **goal congruence** and **managerial effort** are aspects of motivation.

- To achieve organizational objectives, behavior management can be used. **Behavior management** (also referred to as positive reinforcement) provides positive motivation through **rewards and punishment**. This technique operates under the assumption that changing consequences is the key to changing behavior.

- A means of **attaining goal congruence** is to harmonize the measures used to evaluate managers with the measures used in top management's decision models.

- **Agency theory** explains how to organize relationships in which one party (the principal) determines the work that another party (the agent) performs. Agency theory argues that under conditions of incomplete information and uncertainty (or information asymmetries), which characterize most business settings, **two agency problems** arise: adverse selection and moral hazard.

- The problems of adverse selection and moral hazard mean that **fixed wage contracts** are not always the best way to organize relationships between principals and agents.

- Agency theory has ramifications for the **degree of decentralization** appropriate in an organization. When information asymmetry is exploited properly, the result is a flexibility gain to the organization.

- **Goal-setting theory** is another attempt to explain motivation. According to Edwin Locke's goal-setting theory, specific, difficult goals to which the employee is committed provide the best motivation tool. Performance improves when goals are specific rather than general, difficult rather than easy, and self-set rather than imposed by others.

Authority and Responsibility

- The relationships present in the structure of an organization include authority, responsibility, and accountability. Classical theory stresses the need for **balance between authority and responsibility**.

- **Authority** is the right to direct and exact performance from others, including the right to prescribe the means and methods by which the work will be done. The right to direct should be distinguished from the ability (the power) to accomplish tasks.

- **Responsibility** is the obligation to perform. In the classical view, this obligation is formally imposed by a superior and is inherent in any job. In the behavioral view, responsibility must and should be delegated; there is a successive dividing and passing down of obligation.

- **Accountability** is the duty to account for the fulfillment of the responsibility. In practice, accountability is the duty to report performance to one's superior and the physical means for reporting or being able to substantiate performance, i.e., record keeping.

6.4 ESSAY QUESTIONS

Recall that your CMA Part 4 exam will probably contain six scenarios, with about three questions per scenario. There will be a recommended time allocation of 20 minutes, 30 minutes, or 45 minutes for each scenario and related questions.

One scenario will involve ethics, and probably one or two scenarios will include calculations and responses on a worksheet. Also, expect at least one scenario on organizational/behavioral topics. The remaining scenarios cover Parts 1, 2, and 3.

Scenario Title	Subtopic	Questions	Suggested Time
VitaCo	Behavior and Strategic Planning	1, 2, 3	30 minutes
Uniservo	Behavior and Responsibility Accounting	4, 5	30 minutes

Scenario for Essay Questions 1, 2, 3

VitaCo has produced and sold games and party favors to department and toy stores since its incorporation in 1950. Annual sales increased slowly and reached $20 million in 2000. In that year, VitaCo developed and marketed "Know and Win," which became the most popular board game in the U.S. in the years 2004-2005. VitaCo's sales reached $120 million in 2005. This growth was accomplished without a significant increase in capital spending and with little increase in management staff.

VitaCo is operating Zupar as an independent division. None of Zupar's top management was retained. A general manager from VitaCo was put in charge of production operations while Zupar middle managers retained direct responsibility for the sales, marketing, and finance functions. In spite of the estimate of significant short-term growth, Zupar had excess capacity that is now being used to produce some items for VitaCo. The Zupar acquisition had further burdened VitaCo's lean organization even though Zupar had well-conceived systems and controls and outstanding middle managers. VitaCo has forecasted continued popularity for "Know and Win," but the demand simply disappeared in the fall of 2004. VitaCo's Marketing Vice-President estimated that 12 months would be needed to design, produce, and market a replacement.

John Grieg, VitaCo's President, has evaluated the impact of all organizational changes before they have been implemented, but VitaCo did not have formal strategic planning. The acquisition of Zupar and the outlook for reduced sales for at least 1 year has made Grieg aware of the need for strategic planning. Although Grieg intends to begin the strategic planning process now, he believes certain decisions cannot await the completion of a formal strategic plan.

Grieg has scheduled a meeting of top management to discuss the consolidation of the managements and to begin the strategic planning process. With respect to the consolidation, he has asked each meeting participant to come prepared to discuss the items listed below regarding the decision to integrate the sales, marketing, finance, and production functions of VitaCo and Zupar.

1. The cost savings from subleasing production and storage facilities that VitaCo had just leased for 5 years

2. The costs of personnel relocation in the case of organizational consolidation

3. The costs associated with continued duplication of some organizational functions

4. Future plans for product lines

5. Resource availability, both human and physical

6. The incremental costs of each alternative

7. The opportunity cost of each alternative

Questions

1. What are the objectives of strategic planning?

   a. Identify the major factors that would be considered in developing a strategic plan for a company. For each major factor identified, indicate whether the factor is within the control of the company and should be recognized in the assignment of responsibilities.

2. For each of the seven items that VitaCo's President wished to be addressed by his staff, explain whether the item is relevant to a decision to integrate the sales, marketing, finance, and production functions of VitaCo and Zupar Games.

3. Identify the advantages to VitaCo of integrating the sales, marketing, finance, and production functions of the two companies.

Essay Questions 1, 2, 3 — Unofficial Answers

1. The purpose of strategic planning is to select the future course for a company. In order to facilitate this process, a company would establish:

   - Financial goals and objectives
   - The area of business in which it will operate
   - The basic organizational structure to carry out its plans

   a. Major factors that are within the control of a company that would be considered in developing a strategic plan would include:

      - Identification of the current status of the company
      - Identification and evaluation of future business opportunities
      - Determination of an acceptable level of risk

   Major factors that are outside the control of a company that would be considered in developing a strategic plan would include:

   - Market growth
   - Changes in technology
   - Economic conditions

2. Any item that is different between the alternatives of integrating and not integrating the sales, marketing, finance, and production functions of VitaCo and Zupar Games is relevant to the decision. Thus, all of the items that VitaCo's President wished to be addressed except item 1 could be relevant to the decision.

   a. The cost savings from subleasing production and storage facilities is a short-run, immediate operating problem that has nothing to do with integrating the functions of the two companies. VitaCo has excess capacity and needs to address this problem now.

   b. Costs of personnel relocation are relevant to the decision because they would be incurred only in the case of organizational consolidation.

   c. Costs associated with duplication of organizational functions are relevant to the decision because these costs can be reduced or avoided in the case of organizational consolidation.

   d. Future plans for product lines are relevant to the decision because:

      - They may not be able to be implemented if the functions are integrated.
      - They may have to be altered if the functions are integrated.

   e. The availability of human and physical resources are relevant to the decision because resource availability may preclude or necessitate organizational consolidation.

   f. Incremental costs are costs that are different between the alternatives, and therefore relevant to the decision.

   g. Opportunity costs are relevant to the decision because the choice of one course of action precludes all others. No decision can be made without generating opportunity costs.

3. The advantages of integrating the sales, marketing, finance, and production functions of the two companies include the following:

   - Economies of scale
   - Improved coordination and communication
   - Use of the best people in each function

This page intentionally left blank.

Scenario for Essay Questions 4, 5

Uniservo is an equipment maintenance company and has recently undergone a management buyout. The management team is replacing the centralized corporate financial control system with a responsibility accounting system that will increase overall participation in the budgeting process. The company is segregated into three geographical profit centers: Eastern, Central, and Western, and each center is responsible for the following:

- Obtaining new business and maintaining profitable contracts with older customers.

- Depreciation for both existing and new assets. Included among the existing assets are technologically obsolete, but underdepreciated, maintenance and repair parts that will continue to be depreciated as a profit-center expense until disposal. This assignment of responsibility to the profit centers is to minimize the reoccurrence of this obsolescence problem. Any new capital asset acquisitions are to be approved by the corporate staff in order to control the cash supply.

- Recommending and implementing real estate changes or consolidations except where long-term leases are in effect. The field offices are in close proximity to the customer base. The majority of leases are annual; however, responsibility for the more costly and longer term contracts in high-rent districts has been assigned to the corporate Real Estate Department. Property taxes are related to the real estate leases. All insurance is negotiated by the corporate Insurance Department to obtain the best national coverage at the most reasonable cost.

Each region's general manager, along with the subordinate managers, is required to develop an annual budget and submit it to the corporate staff for review and consolidation into an overall company budget. After the initial corporate review, the budgets are returned to the general managers who then revise their submissions in order to reach corporate sales and profit objectives. For the coming year, the general managers and corporate staff have agreed on the corporate budget below.

	Uniservo	Eastern Region	Central Region	Western Region
Net sales	$52.8	$22.2	$11.7	$18.9
Controllable costs:				
Salaries				
-Field technicians	22.2	9.3	4.9	8.0
-Supervision	3.5	1.5	.7	1.3
Selling expense	2.5	1.1	.5	.9
Training	.9	.4	.2	.3
Repairs & maintenance	4.0	1.7	.9	1.4
Rents	6.3	2.6	1.4	2.3
Property taxes	1.3	.5	.3	.5
Depreciation	.8	.3	.2	.3
Total controllable expenses	41.5	17.4	9.1	15.0
Controllable contribution	11.3	4.8	2.6	3.9
Expenses controllable by others:				
Insurance	.5	.2	.1	.2
Corporate general and administrative	3.6	1.5	.8	1.3
Total expenses controlled by others	4.1	1.7	.9	1.5
Total contribution	$ 7.2	$ 3.1	$ 1.7	$ 2.4

Uniservo
Consolidated Operating Budget
For the Year Ending December 31, 2005
($ in millions)

Questions

4. Responsibility accounting is widely used by many companies.

   a. Define responsibility accounting.

   b. Discuss the advantages a company attains through the use of responsibility accounting.

   c. Describe how the use of responsibility accounting is advantageous to the managers of the company.

5. Based on the situation presented, evaluate the budget process by considering the following:

   a. Discuss why the budget process and presentation are likely to obtain the managers' support.

   b. Discuss the aspects of the budget presentation that managers are likely to find objectionable, and explain how these aspects can be improved.

Essay Questions 4, 5 — Unofficial Answers

4. a. Responsibility accounting is a system that recognizes various decision or responsibility centers throughout an organization, and reflects the plans and actions of each of these centers by assigning responsibility for particular revenues and costs (as well as assets and liabilities where pertinent) to the individual managers primarily responsible for making decisions about these revenues and costs. Costs are classified into controllable and non-controllable categories with the responsibility center only charged with costs under its control.

    b. The advantages a company attains through the use of responsibility accounting include the following:

    - Participation in the planning process enhances the acceptance and achievability of the guidelines established by the company.
    - Responsibility plans provide clear guidelines to managers for day-to-day decisions and free management from daily operations.
    - More involvement will lead to better decision making.

    c. The use of responsibility accounting is advantageous to the managers in the following ways:

    - Responsibility accounting facilitates delegation of decision-making and, therefore, managers are afforded greater freedom of action without daily supervision. This results in greater job satisfaction and higher motivation to improve performance.
    - Managers are aware of the basis of their performance evaluations.

5. a. The reasons the budget process and presentation are likely to obtain the managers' support include the following:

    - As a result of the active participation of the managers in the budget preparation process they are more likely to support the budget.
    - Any changes required to the submitted budgets were referred back to the managers for their evaluation and suggested revisions to meet the corporate objectives.
    - The budget is segregated into controllable and non-controllable costs, and, in general, the managers are responsible only for items that they control

    b. The aspects of the budget presentation that the managers are likely to find objectionable, and how these aspects can be improved, include the following:

    - Rents for locations under long-term leases are essentially controlled by the corporate Real Estate Department and, therefore, should be reflected below the controllable expenses section, i.e., they should be included in "Expenses controllable by others."
    - Property taxes should be segregated so that those taxes associated with long-term leases are included in the "Expenses controllable by others" category of the operating budget inasmuch as the regions cannot authorize lease cancellations.
    - Depreciation should be included in the "Expenses controllable by others" category as the acquisition of assets is under corporate control.
    - Costs associated with the technologically impaired assets should be moved to the "Expenses controllable by others" category.

STUDY UNIT SEVEN
BEHAVIOR – BUDGETING AND STANDARD SETTING

(7 pages of outline)

This study unit is the **second of three** on **behavioral issues**. The three study units are

Study Unit 6: Behavior – Alignment of Organizational Goals
Study Unit 7: Behavior – Budgeting and Standard Setting
Study Unit 8: Behavior – Reporting and Performance Evaluation

After studying the outline and answering the essay questions, you will have the skills necessary to address the following topics listed in the IMA's Learning Outcome Statements:

Part 4 - Section C. Behavioral Issues, 2. Issues in budgeting and standard setting

The candidate should be able to:

a.   differentiate between authoritative (top-down) and participative (bottom-up) processes for developing budgets and standards

b.   identify the advantages and disadvantages of authoritative budget/standards development

c.   describe the likely behavior of employees responsible for implementing and achieving authoritative budgets and standards

d.   describe the role that top management should play in an effective participative budgeting process

e.   identify the advantages and disadvantages of participative budget and standards development

f.   describe the likely behavior of employers responsible for implementing and achieving participative budgets and standards

g.   demonstrate an understanding of the role that communication plays in effective budgeting and standard setting

h.   define the term budgetary slack

i.   describe how budgetary slack can have both positive and negative effects on the budgeting process

j.   describe the behavioral issues that should be considered when adopting ideal (theoretical) standards

k.   describe the likely behavior of employees being measured by practical (currently attainable) standards

l.   evaluate a given management situation for its behavioral implications and suggest alternate approaches

7.1 DEVELOPMENT OF BUDGETS

1. **Budgets and other standards**, including standard costs, are formalized estimates of future performance used to plan and control operations.

   a. Budgets may **provide feedback** that allows management to develop long-term strategies. Budgets and standards also promote congruence with organizational goals by communicating them to all who need to know. A comprehensive budget thereby facilitates coordination of organizational activities.

   b. Furthermore, budgets and standards are **motivational tools**, particularly if employees have participated in their development and view them as realistic.

   c. Achievement of challenging goals has positive effects on employee performance and self-esteem.

2. The budget is a **communication** tool.

   a. A budget can help tell employees what objectives the firm is attempting to accomplish.

      1) If the firm does not have an overall budget, each department tends to pursue its own objectives without regard to what is good for the firm as a whole. Thus, a budget promotes **goal congruence**. The planning process coordinates the efficient allocation of organizational resources.

      2) For example, the sales department may want to keep as much inventory as possible so that no sales will be lost, but the treasurer may want to keep the inventory as low as possible so that cash need not be spent any sooner than necessary. If the budget specifies the level of inventory, all employees can work toward the same goals.

   b. Budgets facilitate **coordination** of the activities of a firm. The overall budget, often called the **master** or **comprehensive budget**, encompasses both the **operating and financial** budget processes.

   c. An example of a coordination activity is the purchasing of raw materials.

      1) Materials are needed prior to production, but the proper quantity to buy cannot be determined until it is determined how many units of product are to be manufactured.

      2) Thus, a production budget (in units) is a prerequisite to the preparation of a materials purchases budget.

      3) Similarly, a direct labor budget is based on how many units are to be produced and how fast the workers are.

         a) Labor standards are also complex in that they must consider the impact of the learning curve on productivity.

3. The budget is a **motivational** tool.

   a. A budget helps to motivate employees to pursue the organization's objectives.

      1) A budget must be seen as realistic by employees before it can become a good motivational tool.

      2) Employees are particularly motivated if they help prepare the budget. Thus, the budgeting and standard-setting processes are considered better if they are participative.

      3) A manager who is asked to prepare a budget for his/her department will work hard to stay within the budget.

      4) Achievement of challenging goals has positive effects on employee performance and self-esteem.

      b.   Budgets also may reveal the progress of highly effective managers.

          1)   Consequently, managers should not view budgets negatively. A budget is just as likely to help as to hinder a manager's career.

          2)   A manager also may use a budget as a personal self-evaluation tool.

      c.   Unfortunately, the budget is not always viewed in a positive manner. Some managers view a budget as a restriction.

      d.   Employees are more apt to have a positive feeling toward a budget if some degree of flexibility is allowed.

4.   The budget is an **evaluative** tool.

      a.   Comparing actual results to the budget allows managers at all levels to evaluate their own performance, as well as evaluate the performance of subordinate managers.

      b.   **Controllability** is a key concept in the use of budgets and other standards to evaluate performance.

          1)   Controllability is the extent to which a manager can influence activities and related revenues, costs, or other items.

              a)   In principle, it is proportionate to, but not coextensive with, responsibility.

          2)   Controllability is difficult to isolate because few costs, revenues, etc., are under the sole influence of one manager.

              a)   Also, separating the effects of current management's decisions from those of former management is difficult.

          3)   If responsibility exceeds the extent to which a manager can influence an activity, the result may be reduced morale, a decline in managerial effort, and poor performance.

              a)   Such a manager encounters greater risk because his/her success depends on uncontrollable factors. Thus, a manager in these circumstances should be compensated for the incremental risk assumed.

          4)   However, if a manager is accountable solely for activities over which (s)he has extensive influence, the manager may develop too narrow a focus.

              a)   For example, the manager of a cost center may make decisions based only on cost efficiency and ignore the overall effectiveness goals of the organization. By extending the manager's responsibility to profits as well as costs, the organization may encourage desirable behavior congruent with overall goals, such as improved coordination with marketing personnel, even though the manager still does not control revenues.

              b)   Furthermore, a manager who does not control an activity may nevertheless be the individual who is best informed about it. Thus, a purchasing agent may be in the best position to explain price variances even though (s)he cannot control them.

5.   **Participative budgeting** (grass-roots budgeting) and standard setting use input from lower-level and middle-level employees.

      a.   Participation encourages employees to have a sense of ownership of the output of the process.

          1)   The result is an acceptance of and commitment to the goals expressed in the budget.

          2)   A purely top-down approach (an imposed budget that sets **authoritative** rather than participative standards) is much less likely to foster this sense of commitment.

b.   Participation also enables employees to relate performance to rewards or penalties.

1)   The actual impact of budgetary participation depends on cultural, organizational, interpersonal, and individual variables, such as personality.

c.   A further advantage of participation is that it provides a broader information base.

1)   Lower- and middle-level managers have knowledge that senior managers and staff may lack.

2)   Thus, a key decision in the budget and standard-setting process is to identify who in the organization can provide useful input.

d.   Disadvantages of participative budgeting and standard setting include its cost in terms of time and money.

1)   Furthermore, the quality of participation is affected by the goals, values, beliefs, and expectations of those involved.

a)   A manager who expects his/her request to be reduced may inflate the amount.

b)   If a budget is to be used as a performance evaluator, a manager asked for an estimate may provide one that is easily attained.

e.   Participation in developing a budget may result in a **padding** of the budget, also known as budgetary slack.

1)   **Budgetary slack** is the excess of resources budgeted over the resources necessary to achieve organizational goals.

a)   The natural tendency of a manager is to negotiate for a less stringent measure of performance so as to avoid unfavorable variances from expectations.

2)   Management may create slack by overestimating costs and underestimating revenues.

a)   A firm may decrease slack by emphasizing the consideration of all variables, holding in-depth reviews during budget development, and allowing for flexibility in making additional budget changes.

3)   The existence of slack can have both positive and negative effects on the budgeting process. The existence of slack can reduce the planning benefits of a budget since the budget may not be entirely accurate. For example, a cash budget might show that $500,000 needs to be borrowed this month, whereas the money is not really needed because managers were just being cautious. Alternatively, the lack of slack may discourage managers from implementing new programs, or might cause managers to avoid routine maintenance when the budget does not show funds available in a particular period.

6.   **Management-by-objectives (MBO)** is a behavioral, communications-oriented, responsibility-focused, and participative approach to management and employee self direction. Accordingly, MBO stresses the need to involve all affected parties in the budgeting process.

a.   MBO is a top-down process because the organization's objectives are restated for each lower level.

1)   For example, the budgets (quantitative statements of objectives) at each successive level of the organization have a **means-end relationship**. One level's ends provide the next higher level's means for achieving its objectives.

2)   Ideally, the means-end chain ties together the parts of the organization so that the various means all focus on the same ultimate ends (objectives).

    b.   MBO is based on the philosophy that employees want to work hard if they know what is expected, like to understand what their jobs actually entail, and are capable of self-direction and self-motivation.

        1)   Thus, MBO is also a **bottom-up process** because of the participation of subordinates.

    c.   The following are the four **common elements** of MBO programs:

        1)   Establishment of objectives jointly by the superior and subordinate.

        2)   Specificity of objectives. Multiple performance measures are agreed upon so that the subordinate will not neglect other facets of his/her job to concentrate on a single objective.

        3)   Specificity of the time within which objectives are to be achieved.

        4)   Ongoing feedback that permits an individual to monitor and adjust his/her performance.

    d.   The following are **benefits** of MBO:

        1)   Opens up communication between manager and subordinate

        2)   Allows subordinate to participate in setting job objectives

        3)   Forces specification of organizational objectives throughout the organization

        4)   Allows subordinates to be measured on what they do, not on personality traits

        5)   Facilitates employee development

    e.   The following are **limitations** of MBO:

        1)   Failure of managers to accept the philosophy behind MBO

        2)   Failure to give objectives-setters adequate guidelines

        3)   Difficulty in setting truly verifiable objectives

        4)   Tendency for objectives to be short-term only

        5)   Tendency for plans under MBO to become inflexible, making it difficult to adapt to change

        6)   Lack of precise management knowledge of a task, resulting in a supervisor's allowing a subordinate to set inappropriate objectives

        7)   Emphasis on quantitative factors, causing employees to focus on the ends rather than the means, thus possibly jeopardizing the quality of the output

7.   **Management by exception**. Variance analysis is an important tool of the management accountant in that it enables responsibility to be assigned. It also permits management by exception. Management by exception is the practice of giving attention only to those situations in which large variances occur, thus allowing upper-level management to devote its time to problems of the business, not just routine supervision of subordinates. Variance analysis will become familiar to anyone working in industry, whether as an accountant, a manager, a department supervisor, or a marketing person. Variances affect everyone.

7.2 STANDARD SETTING

1. **Standard costs** are budgeted unit costs established to motivate optimal productivity and efficiency. A standard-cost system is designed to alert management when the actual costs of production differ significantly from target or standard costs.

    a. Standard costs are monetary measures with which actual costs are compared.

    b. A standard cost is not just an average of past costs but an objectively determined estimate of what a cost should be. For example, it may be based on accounting, engineering, or statistical quality control studies.

    c. A standard-cost system may be used with both job-order and process costing systems to isolate variances.

    d. Because of the impact of fixed costs in most businesses, a standard costing system is usually not effective unless the company also has a flexible budgeting system. Flexible budgeting uses standard costs to prepare budgets for multiple activity levels.

2. When actual costs and standard costs differ, the difference is a **variance**.

    a. A favorable variance arises when actual costs are less than standard costs.

    b. An unfavorable variance occurs when the actual costs are greater than standard.

    c. EXAMPLE: Management has calculated that, under efficient conditions, a worker should be able to complete one unit of product per hour. If workers are normally paid $6 per hour, the standard labor cost per unit is $6 per unit.

        1) If the actual per-unit amounts for a 1-week period were 1.1 hours at $6.25 per hour, or $6.88 per unit, the variance is $.88 per unit.

        2) The variance is unfavorable because the actual cost exceeded the standard cost.

        3) Management is signaled that corrective action may be needed.

    d. The purpose of identifying and assigning responsibility for variances is to determine who is likely to have information that will enable management to find solutions. The constructive approach is to promote learning and continuous improvement in manufacturing operations, not to assign blame. However, information about variances may be useful in evaluating managers' performance.

3. **Ideal (perfection, theoretical, or maximum efficiency) standards** are standard costs that are set for production under optimal conditions.

    a. They are based on the work of the most skilled workers with no allowance for waste, spoilage, machine breakdowns, or other downtime.

    b. Tight standards can have positive behavioral implications if workers are motivated to strive for excellence. However, they are not in wide use because they can have negative behavioral effects if the standards are impossible to attain.

    c. Ideal, or tight, standards are ordinarily replaced by currently attainable standards for cash budgeting, product costing, and budgeting departmental performance. Otherwise, accurate financial planning will be impossible.

    d. Ideal standards have been adopted by some companies that apply continuous improvement and other TQM principles.

4. **Practical or currently attainable standards** may be defined as the performance that is reasonably expected to be achieved with an allowance for normal spoilage, waste, and downtime.

    a. An alternative interpretation is that practical standards represent possible but difficult to attain results.

5. Standard costs must be kept current. If prices have changed considerably for a particular raw material, there will always be a variance if the standard cost is not changed. Much of the usefulness of standard costs is lost if a large variance is always expected. The primary reason for computing variances is to let management know whenever an unusual event has occurred.

6. In a decentralized organization, standard **transfer prices** (see Subunit 8.6) may have an important effect on behavior. If transfer prices are appropriate, management will maintain its autonomy while achieving goal congruence.

   a. Transfer pricing also may foster internal competition, preventing complacency among managers. Moreover, management needs to be encouraged to use idle internal capacity and superior internally generated products instead of external sources.

7.3 CORE CONCEPTS

Development of Budgets

- Budgets may provide **feedback** that allows management to develop long-term strategies. Budgets and standards also promote **congruence with organizational goals** by communicating them to all who need to know.

- **Participative budgeting** (grass-roots budgeting) and standard setting use input from lower-level and middle-level employees. Participation encourages employees to have a sense of ownership of the output of the process. Participation also enables employees to relate performance to rewards or penalties.

- Participation in developing a budget may result in a padding of the budget, also known as **budgetary slack**, consisting of the excess of resources budgeted over the resources necessary to achieve organizational goals. The existence of slack can have both positive and negative effects on the budgeting process.

- Budgets and standards are often the result of a formal **management-by-objectives (MBO)** program. MBO is a top-down process because the organization's objectives are successively restated into objectives for each lower level. However, it is also a bottom-up process because of the participation of subordinates.

- **Variance analysis** is an important tool of the management accountant in that it enables responsibility to be assigned. It also permits **management by exception**, the practice of giving attention only to those situations in which large variances occur, thus allowing upper-level management to devote its time to problems of the business, not just routine supervision of subordinates.

Standard Setting

- **Standard costs** are budgeted unit costs established to motivate optimal productivity and efficiency. A standard-cost system is designed to alert management when the actual costs of production differ significantly from target or standard costs.

- Standard costs are monetary measures with which actual costs are compared. When actual costs and standard costs differ, the difference is a **variance**.

- **Ideal (perfection, theoretical, or maximum efficiency) standards** are standard costs that are set for production under optimal conditions. They are based on the work of the most skilled workers with no allowance for waste, spoilage, machine breakdowns, or other downtime.

- **Practical or currently attainable standards** may be defined as the performance that is reasonably expected to be achieved with an allowance for normal spoilage, waste, and downtime.

- In a decentralized organization, standard **transfer prices** may have an important effect on behavior. If transfer prices are appropriate, management will maintain its autonomy while achieving goal congruence.

This page intentionally left blank.

7.4 ESSAY QUESTIONS

Recall that your CMA Part 4 exam will probably contain six scenarios, with about three questions per scenario. There will be a recommended time allocation of 20 minutes, 30 minutes, or 45 minutes for each scenario and related questions.

One scenario will involve ethics, and probably one or two scenarios will include calculations and responses on a worksheet. Also, expect at least one scenario on organizational/behavioral topics. The remaining scenarios cover Parts 1, 2, and 3.

Scenario Title	Subtopic	Questions	Suggested Time
Rouge Corporation	Behavior and Budgeting	1, 2	30 minutes
Jasper Corporation	Behavior and MBO	3, 4, 5	30 minutes
Scott Weidner	Behavior and Participative Budgeting	6, 7	30 minutes
Kacie Hengel	Behavior and Governmental Budgeting	8, 9, 10	30 minutes

Scenario for Essay Questions 1, 2

Rouge Corporation is a medium-size company in the steel fabrication industry with six divisions located in different geographical sectors of the United States. Considerable autonomy in operational management is permitted in the divisions due in part to the distance between corporate headquarters in St. Louis and five of the six divisions. Corporate management establishes divisional budgets using prior year data adjusted for industry and economic changes expected for the coming year. Budgets are prepared by year and by quarter, with top management attempting to recognize problems unique to each division in the divisional budget-setting process. Once the year's divisional budgets are set by corporate management, they cannot be modified by division management.

The budget for the next calendar year projects total corporate net income before taxes of $3,750,000 for the year, including $937,500 for the first quarter. Results of first quarter operations presented to corporate management in early April showed corporate net income of $865,000, which was $72,500 below the projected net income for the quarter. The St. Louis Division operated at 4.5% above its projected divisional net income, while the other five divisions showed net incomes with variances ranging from 1.5 to 22% below budgeted net income.

Corporate management is concerned with the first quarter results because they believe strongly that differences between divisions had been recognized. An entire day in late November of last year had been spent presenting and explaining the corporate and divisional budgets to the division managers and their division controllers. A mid-April meeting of corporate and division management has generated unusual candor. All five outstate division managers cited reasons why first quarter results in their respective divisions represented effective management and was the best that could be expected. Corporate management has remained unconvinced and informs division managers that "results will be brought into line with the budget by the end of the second quarter."

Questions

1. Identify and explain the major disadvantages in the procedures employed by Rouge Corporation's corporate management in preparing and implementing the divisional budgets.

2. Discuss the behavioral problems that may arise by requiring Rouge Corporation's division managers to meet the quarterly budgeted net income figures as well as the annual budgeted net income.

Essay Questions 1, 2 — Unofficial Answers

1. The major disadvantages in the procedures employed by Rouge Corporation in preparing and implementing the divisional budgets include the following:

    a. The procedure is top-down versus a bottom-up approach. The budget is prepared by top management and imposed on the divisions. The divisions do not participate in the budget preparation. This lack of participation inhibits goal congruence.

    b. Corporate management says differences between divisions are factored into the budget process. However, problems unique to each division are best recognized by division managers. These managers should be allowed to communicate problems to top management. Additionally, division managers should be allowed to suggest modifications to the budget during the budget period.

    c. The budget is not flexible. The budget is set for the entire year and is not modified as circumstances change.

2. Behavioral problems that may arise due to Rouge Corporation's insistence upon meeting budgeted targets include

    a. Division managers may attempt to manipulate transactions to assist them in meeting the budget. Techniques which can be used include adjusting discretionary expenses and adjusting the timing of capital acquisitions.

    b. Division managers may attempt to manipulate accounting information to distort quarterly performance such as capitalizing expenses and overstating inventory.

    c. Division managers may develop a lack of motivation and initiative to achieve the goals represented in the budget. This may result from a lack of goal congruence because they do not participate in developing the budget.

Scenario for Essay Questions 3, 4, 5

At a meeting of Jasper Corporation's division managers just prior to the beginning of the fiscal year, it was announced that "management by objectives" (MBO) was to be implemented in all the divisions. Increases in division contributions to Jasper's profit targets were established at the meeting; the increase assigned to the Palmer Division was 15%.

On his return from the meeting, Rob Sumner, manager of the Palmer Division, reported to his management team that the division would be operating under the MBO system. Sumner relayed the goal of a 15% increase in contribution to corporate profits and stated that he expected all managers to do their share in helping Palmer meet this goal.

After the first 5 months of the year, Sumner was disappointed with the division's results as it appeared that the 15% objective would not be met. Sumner called a meeting of the management team to review the situation and attempt to identify the reasons for the poor results. The following comments were made during the course of the meeting.

Sales manager: "I realized that in order to reach the objective, we would need a sizeable increase in sales. To achieve this increase, I instituted quantity discounts on several products, and sales of these products have increased dramatically. I don't understand why we have a problem."

Production manager: "We have been able to increase production to keep up with the increased sales. In addition, we have been able to make on-time deliveries for all orders by enlarging the second shift crew and having some key employees work additional hours. Production has kept pace; we're not the problem."

Division controller: "Unfortunately, the products selected for the discounts already had relatively low contribution margins. With the addition of increased production costs caused by overtime payments and shift premiums, these products are scarcely at the breakeven point. To make matters worse, the attention given to these discounted products diverted promotion efforts away from products with higher contribution margins."

Questions

3. Define the goal-setting approach known as management by objectives (MBO).

4. In every MBO implementation, there are problems and solutions.

   a. Discuss at least three reasons why the MBO process at the Palmer Division of Jasper Corporation was not successful.

   b. Describe at least three ways that the Palmer Division could improve its MBO system.

5. Describe several benefits that a company should expect to derive from the successful implementation of an MBO system.

Essay Questions 3, 4, 5 — Unofficial Answers

3.   Management by objectives (MBO) is a formalized goal-setting approach based on the belief that joint subordinate-superior participation in translating overall company objectives into individual objectives will have a positive influence on employee performance. The goals of each layer of the organization should be integrated into the overall company plan, and the results obtained should be measured against the plan.

4.   a.   Three of the several reasons why the MBO process at the Palmer Division of Jasper Corporation was not successful are as follows:

1)   Top management should have ensured overall coordination and integration of functional goals. The flaw in the selection of products to discount would have been avoided in this manner.

2)   There was insufficient communication and coordination among subordinates.

3)   There was insufficient and infrequent feedback. The division manager did not meet with the management team for five months to discuss results.

b.   Three of the several ways that the Palmer Division could improve its MBO system are as follows:

1)   Top management should clearly communicate the division goals to all departmental managers.

2)   The division manager should request all departmental goals in writing, and ensure that the departmental goals support and enhance the division goals.

3)   There should be frequent reviews of progress toward objectives, and timely corrective action should be taken when problems arise.

5.   Several benefits that a company should expect to derive from the successful implementation of an MBO system include the following:

a.   Enhancement of communication through the goal-setting process, plan discussion, and collaboration.

b.   Improved planning as employees are forced to deal with future objectives during the goal-setting process.

c.   Improved employee motivation from participation in the MBO process.

d.   Improved management control as the process of monitoring progress toward goal attainment provides periodic feedback on performance.

Scenario for Essay Questions 6, 7

Scott Weidner, the Controller in the Division of Social Services for the state, recognizes the importance of the budgetary process for planning, control, and motivation purposes. He believes that a properly implemented participative budgeting process for planning purposes and a management by exception reporting process based upon the participative budget will motivate his subordinates to improve productivity within their particular departments. Based upon this philosophy, Weidner has implemented the following budget procedures:

- An appropriation target figure is given to each department manager. This amount is the maximum funding that each department can expect to receive in the next fiscal year.
- Department managers develop their individual budgets within the following spending constraints as directed by the controller's staff.

    1) Expenditure requests cannot exceed the appropriation target.
    2) All fixed expenditures should be included in the budget. Fixed expenditures would include such items as contracts and salaries at current levels.
    3) All government projects directed by higher authority should be included in the budget in their entirety.

- The controller's staff consolidates the departmental budget requests from the various departments into one budget that is to be submitted for the entire division.
- Upon final budget approval by the legislature, the controller's staff allocates the appropriation to the various departments on instructions from the division manager. However, a specified percentage of each department's appropriation is held back in anticipation of potential budget cuts and special funding needs. The amount and use of this contingency fund is left to the discretion of the division manager.
- Each department is allowed to adjust its budget when necessary to operate within the reduced appropriation level. However, as stated in the original directive, specific projects authorized by higher authority must remain intact.
- The final budget is used as the basis of control for a management by exception form of reporting. Excessive expenditures by account for each department are highlighted on a monthly basis. Department managers are expected to account for all expenditures over budget. Fiscal responsibility is an important factor in the overall performance evaluation of department managers.

Weidner believes his policy of allowing the department managers to participate in the budget process and then holding them accountable for their performance is essential, especially during these times of limited resources. He further believes the department managers will be motivated positively to increase the efficiency and effectiveness of their departments because they have provided input into the initial budgetary process and are required to justify any unfavorable performances.

Questions

6. Explain the operational and behavioral benefits that generally are attributed to a participative budgeting process.

7. Identify deficiencies in Scott Weidner's participative budgetary policy for planning and performance evaluation purposes. For each deficiency identified, recommend how the deficiency can be corrected. Use the following format in preparing your response:

Deficiencies	Recommendations
1.	1.

Essay Questions 6, 7 — Unofficial Answers

6. Operational benefits that accrue to an organization from a participative budgeting process include the following:

    a. The participant has the greatest knowledge, both general and detailed, about the activities covered by a specific budget.

    b. Goals are more appropriate to specific situations leading to goal congruence.

    c. Participative budgets may improve productivity.

    Behavioral benefits for participants with a participative budgeting process include

    a. A sense of belonging to the management team.

    b. A sense of satisfaction in helping to set performance levels and provide information.

    c. A better knowledge of what is expected so that improved motivation and morale results.

7.

Deficiencies	Recommendations
1. Setting an upper spending constraint gives indirect approval to spending up to that level whether justified or not.	1. Weidner could institute zero-base budgeting, which would provide that all expenditures be substantiated.
2. Setting prior constraints such as maximum limits and inclusion of noncontrollable fixed expenditures prior to departmental input defeats the purpose of participative management.	2. Divisional constraints should be known to managers prior to budgeting, but individual limits should be determined with the input of managers.
3. Arbitrary allocation of the approved budget defeats the purpose of a participative budget process.	3. The department managers should be involved in the reallocation of the approved budget.
4. The division manager holds back a specified percentage of each department's appropriation for discretionary use.	4. Contingency funds should not be part of a departmental budget. These funds should be identified and provided for before the allocation process to departments.
5. Exception form reporting and evaluation based on performance to budget must be accompanied by rewards.	5. Recognition should be given to those attaining budget goals, not just exceptions.

Scenario for Essay Questions 8, 9, 10

Kacie Hengel, a former corporate controller, has recently moved from private industry into governmental accounting. In both instances, she has had or will have budgeting responsibilities.

The term "budget" and the concept of budgeting can have different connotations depending upon the use and situation. A fundamental difference between governmental and business budgets lies in the appropriation nature of the governmental budget. However, a business organization could choose to base its budgeting process on a basis similar to the governmental approach.

Questions

8. Describe the characteristics which exist in the governmental sector that encourage or require the use of appropriation budgeting.

9. If a business were to adopt an appropriation basis for its budgeting process,

    a. Describe the probable effect on a manager's behavior, and

    b. Explain why a manager would behave in this manner.

10. Explain how governmental budgeting could be modified in order to be more effective for managerial control purposes.

Essay Questions 8, 9, 10 — Unofficial Answers

8.   An appropriation budget is one that establishes fixed amounts which can be applied to achieve the objectives of the organizational unit for the period specified. Several factors exist in the governmental area that cause appropriation budgets to be used.

    a.   The stewardship function is very strong. The government is spending the taxpayers' funds. The stewardship function is symbolized by spending limits. The revenue sources of government are limited and fixed for selected time periods. Thus, many expenditures cannot be based on changing demands for services because the revenues do not vary with the demand for services.

    b.   Specific revenues (taxes) are earmarked for specific activities by taxpayer vote or legislative action and the expenditures on such activities are limited to the available revenues.

9.   a.   The appropriation budget concept would probably lead managers to

        1)   Focus more toward spending resources rather than obtaining results.

        2)   Spend the appropriation amounts, even if they were not needed.

        3)   Think in terms of incremental increases in the budget amounts rather than consider the services offered.

    b.   The appropriation budget concept directs attention to spending up to the limit of the appropriation. Financial performance evaluation would be on the spending limit aspect of activities rather than on the cost/output relationship. Thus, managers would be motivated to act in ways that would result in favorable evaluation regarding the spending limit. Further, failure to spend to the allowable limit implies the amount is not needed, leading to reduced future limits.

10.   The most important step that can be taken to modify governmental budgeting to make it more effective for management control is to introduce the cost/output concept, i.e., relate costs to the outputs (results) produced.

There are several methods used in the governmental area to introduce the cost/output concept of management control. The most common form is performance budgeting. Performance budgeting attempts to evaluate management by evaluating performance in conjunction with the financial requirements. Program budgeting, a technique which attempts to describe program objectives and match them with the costs to achieve them, also would improve management control. The zero based budgeting (ZBB) system also could be considered. ZBB calls for a reevaluation of all activities and their costs on a regular basis. The focus in ZBB, similar to program budgeting, is on the objectives the organization hopes to accomplish.

Consider using Gleim's ***CMA Test Prep*** for interactive testing with **hundreds of multiple-choice questions** as an additional method of knowledge transfer in your quest to pass Part 4.

STUDY UNIT EIGHT
BEHAVIOR – REPORTING AND PERFORMANCE EVALUATION

(16 pages of outline)

This study unit is the **last of three** on **behavioral issues**. The three study units are

Study Unit 6: Behavior – Alignment of Organizational Goals
Study Unit 7: Behavior – Budgeting and Standard Setting
Study Unit 8: Behavior – Reporting and Performance Evaluation

After studying the outline and answering the essay questions, you will have the skills necessary to address the following topics listed in the IMA's Learning Outcome Statements:

Part 4 - Section C. Behavioral Issues, 3. Issues in reporting and performance evaluation

The candidate should be able to:

a. identify and explain the objectives of management compensation/recognition

b. identify and define the various types of management compensation/recognition

c. describe how the various types of compensation affect employee behavior

d. discuss the importance of management compensation plans being grounded in the firm's strategic direction and life cycle

e. identify timely feedback as the link between planning, control, and evaluation

f. describe the purposes of feedback and identify alternative means of feedback such as reports, interviews, and team meetings

g. demonstrate an understanding of the issues surrounding the controllability of costs, motivation, and performance evaluation

h. demonstrate an understanding of how the methods used to allocate common costs can affect behavior and performance

i. describe the role of a flexible budgeting process and variance analysis in performance evaluation

j. explain that there is a hierarchy to variances and that the investigation of variances should positively influence behavior rather than fix blame

k. identify the advantages and disadvantages of using multiple performance measures

l. explain that goal congruence will more likely be optimized by using a combination of both financial and nonfinancial performance measures

m. demonstrate an understanding of how the method used to establish transfer prices can affect motivation and divisional performance

n. describe the likely behavior of employees under varying types of transfer pricing

o. evaluate a given management situation for its behavioral implications and suggest alternate approaches

8.1 COMPENSATION AND BENEFITS

1. **Compensation and benefits** are extrinsic rewards. They should satisfy individual needs, encourage positive expectations (see expectancy theory in Subunit 4.3), be equitable, and be related to performance.

2. **Total employee compensation** can be subdivided into three categories: base pay, incentive compensation, and fringe benefits. Each compensation plan has its own **advantages and disadvantages**.

    a. **Base pay**
        1) Annual salaries
        2) Hourly wages
        3) Overtime and holiday pay
            a) Base pay plans have the great advantage of being easy to administer, but they provide little incentive to the employee to put out any effort.

    b. **Incentive compensation**
        1) Piecework rates motivate the employee to produce a higher level of output, but they carry connotations of sweatshops and lack of attention to quality.
        2) Sales commissions motivate sales personnel to move product out the door, but they can easily focus on revenues at the cost of profitability.
        3) Merit pay rewards salaried employees for extra effort, but can lead to morale problems since evaluation criteria tend to be subjective.
        4) Profit sharing motivates employees to focus on company profitability, but not all employees put out equal effort toward that goal.
        5) Sharing of productivity gains or cost savings motivates employees to pay attention to the efficiency and effectiveness of operations, but the necessary tracking system can have very high administrative costs.
        6) Pay increases for skills mastered or degrees earned motivate employees to keep their skillsets current and engage in lifelong learning, but they can be quite expensive for the organization.
        7) Employee stock-ownership plans give individual employees a stake in the firm's long-term health, but they can lead to morale problems among those who are not eligible.

    c. **Fringe benefits**
        1) Flexible scheduling, such as the four-day, 10-hour-per-day workweek, can increase both productivity and morale for certain employees, but can lead both to morale problems among those who cannot take advantage of such schedules and to difficulties in task coverage.
        2) Company-provided exercise and child day care facilities also can be morale boosters, but can be quite expensive to the organization.
        3) Tax-deferred or -exempt benefits are an extremely common form of fringe benefit.
            a) They qualify for favorable tax benefits under the Internal Revenue Code. In effect, the company can provide these benefits to employees using before-tax dollars.
            b) Many organizations offer cafeteria plans, which allow employees to individually design packages of compensation and benefits.
            c) The most common fringe benefits include:
                i) Pensions and other post-retirement benefits, including 401(k) plans
                ii) Health insurance
                iii) Group-term life insurance
                iv) Discounts on company merchandise

3.   **Deferred Compensation**

a.   Under a **deferred compensation plan**, an executive elects to defer compensation into an account in the expectation of receiving the deferrals plus earnings at retirement. Such a plan may involve company contributions.

1)   **Non-qualified plans** are benefit plans that do not qualify for favorable tax treatment but have far fewer restrictions than qualified plans. Non-qualified plans are unsecured and subject to risks. They must remain "unfunded" to avoid current taxation.

2)   A **Rabbi Trust** is a trust owned by the company that holds assets to help meet non-qualified benefit payments. Rabbi trusts are taxable trusts, and trust assets must be available to corporate creditors in the event of a bankruptcy.

3)   According to **APB Opinion 25**, *Accounting for Stock Issued to Employees*, a **compensatory stock option plan** involves the issuance of stock in whole or in part for employee services rendered. The accounting is based on an **intrinsic-value-based** method.

a)   The compensation cost should be recognized as an expense when the employee performs services. It is ordinarily measured by the quoted market price at the measurement date minus the amount, if any, the employee must pay. (If the option price equals or exceeds the market price at the measurement date, there is no compensation expense.)

b)   If the grant precedes the services, the debit is to deferred compensation expense (a contra equity account). This amount is amortized as services are rendered and expenses are recognized. The credit is to stock options outstanding (an equity account).

c)   When the services are rendered, deferred compensation expense is credited and compensation expense is debited.

d)   Upon exercise, the entry is to debit cash and options outstanding and to credit common stock and additional paid-in capital.

e)   If stock options are not exercised, the balance in stock options outstanding is transferred to a paid-in capital account.

f)   The measurement date is the first date on which the number of shares to which an employee is entitled and the option or purchase price, if any, are known. This date is usually the **grant date**.

g)   When the measurement date is later than the grant date, compensation expense in periods prior to the measurement date is based on the stock's quoted market price at the end of each period.

h)   The measurement date may be later than the grant date because a stock option plan has variable terms; e.g., the amount of stock or the price may depend upon future events.

b.   **SFAS 123**, *Accounting for Stock-Based Compensation*, is an alternative to APB Opinion 25. It applies to stock purchase plans, stock options, restricted stock, and stock appreciation rights.

    1)   Fair-value-based accounting for stock compensation plans is not required. An entity may continue to apply APB Opinion 25. Nevertheless, the fair-value-based method is preferable for purposes of justifying a change in accounting principle. However, initial adoption of an accounting principle for a new transaction is not a change in principle.

    2)   The fair-value-based method measures compensation cost at the grant date based on the value of the award. Recognition is over the service period.

    3)   APB Opinion 25 measures compensation cost based on intrinsic value (quoted market price -- amount to be paid).

    4)   Many stock option plans have no intrinsic value at grant date, and consequently no compensation cost is recognized under APB Opinion 25.

    5)   The fair value of stock options is determined using an option-pricing model. The stock price at the grant date, the exercise price, the expected life of the option, the volatility of the stock and its expected dividends, and the risk-free interest rate over the expected life of the option are elements of the model.

    6)   Nonpublic entities may exclude the volatility factor, which results in measurement at minimum value. The fair value of an option is not adjusted for changes in the model.

c.   An employee stock purchase plan that allows purchase at a discount is not compensatory if the discount is small (5% or less meets the condition automatically), substantially all full-time employees may participate, and the plan has no option features. An example of an option feature is a provision that allows an employee to purchase shares at a fixed discount from the lesser of the market price at grant date or date of purchase.

d.   **Stock appreciation rights (SARs)** permit employees to receive cash equal to the excess of the market price of the company's stock over a specified amount.

    1)   Under **FASB Interpretation 28**, *Accounting for Stock Appreciation Rights and Other Variable Stock Option or Award Plans*, compensation equals the excess of the quoted market value over the value specified.

    2)   The charge to expense is accrued over the service period. If the SARs are for past services and are exercisable immediately, there is no service period.

        a)   Accrued compensation is adjusted (but not below zero) in subsequent periods up to the measurement date for changes in the quoted market value, and the adjustment is reflected in income in the period of the change.

        b)   SFAS 123 adopts a fair-value-based method of accounting for stock appreciation rights. Nevertheless, it permits the continued application of APB Opinion 25 and FASB Interpretation 28.

e.   An **employee stock ownership plan (ESOP)** is defined in the Employee Retirement and Income Security Act of 1974 as a stock bonus plan, or a combination stock bonus and money purchase pension plan, designed to invest primarily in the employer's stock.

    1)   Leveraged ESOPs are allowed to borrow, either from the sponsor (with or without an outside loan) or directly from an outside lender, to acquire employer securities, with the shares usually serving as collateral.

        a)   These shares are held in a suspense account until the debt is repaid, ordinarily from employer contributions and dividends. As the debt is repaid, the shares are released and allocated to individual accounts. Any outside loan is usually guaranteed by the employer-sponsor.

2) The employer records a debit to unearned ESOP shares (a contra equity account) when shares are issued or treasury shares are sold to the ESOP. Even if the ESOP buys on the market, the employer debits unearned shares and credits cash or debt, depending on whether the ESOP is internally or externally leveraged.

    a) When ESOP shares are committed to be released, unearned shares is credited at cost and, depending on the purpose of the release, compensation cost, dividends payable, or compensation liability is debited for the fair value of the shares. The difference between cost and fair value is ordinarily an adjustment of additional paid-in capital.

    b) Dividends on unallocated shares reduce liabilities or serve as compensation to participants. Dividends on allocated shares are debited to retained earnings.

    c) Redemptions of ESOP shares are treasury stock purchases.

    d) If the ESOP has a direct outside loan, the sponsor reports a liability. It also accrues interest cost. Furthermore, it reports cash payments to the ESOP to be used for debt service as reductions of the debt and accrued interest. If the ESOP has an indirect loan (a loan from the sponsor who in turn has an outside loan), essentially the same accounting is followed. If an employer loan is made to the ESOP without an outside loan, the employer does not record the ESOP's note payable, the employer's note receivable, interest cost, or interest income.

3) If the ESOP is not leveraged, shares must be allocated at fiscal year-end. Employer compensation cost is reported equal to the cash or shares (at fair value) contributed or committed to be contributed as provided for in the plan. Dividends are debited to retained earnings.

8.2 PERFORMANCE EVALUATION AND FEEDBACK

1. **Evaluation**

    a. An important aspect of management is the evaluation of employees.

        1) Evaluations are important to the employee, the employer, and the company as a whole.

        2) Evaluations provide an opportunity for growth of the employee and, when done properly, can be instrumental in the prevention of future disputes.

            a) Documentation must be complete, accurate, and consistent.

            b) Employees should be notified of appraisals and given an opportunity to discuss them.

            c) Different techniques are necessary to accommodate different employee performance levels.

    b. **Purposes of Evaluation**

        1) Uses performance criteria to identify job-related abilities necessary to do the job

        2) Uses performance goals to help employees direct their energies toward what the organization expects without constant supervision

        3) Uses performance outcomes to allow employee satisfaction in knowing when jobs are completed and done well

        4) Distinguishes effective from ineffective job performance

        5) Helps employer and organization develop employee strengths and identify weaknesses

        6) Helps in the setting of base pay levels

c.   **Problems of Evaluation**

1)   Design of appraisal system can be faulty if the

a)   Criteria for evaluations are poor or inappropriate

b)   Technique is cumbersome or not understood by users

c)   Criteria focus on wrong attributes causing emphasis on wrong things (e.g., personal appearance rather than job accomplishments)

d)   Top management does not lend support

d.   Evaluation-Based Problems

1)   **Halo effect.** Manager's judgment on one positive trait affects rating on other traits. The opposite of the halo effect wherein the manager lets one negative trait influence other traits is called a **horn effect**.

2)   **Central tendency.** All personnel are rated within the same narrow range; e.g., "All my people are good." In a sense, this means all employees are rated as being average. The **forced normal distribution method** essentially results in central tendency since most employees must be rated average.

3)   **Recency effect.** Most recent behavior overshadows overall performance.

4)   **Differing standards.** Some managers have stricter standards than others, making cross-departmental comparisons difficult.

5)   **Personal bias.** Traits may not reflect actual job performance, so appraisal can be biased by the degree to which the manager likes the subordinate.

6)   **Leniency error** is when a manager fails to give a negative evaluation because of fear of damaging a good working relationship with a worker.

7)   **Contrast error** is the tendency to rate people relative to other people, rather than to performance standards. If most employees are mediocre, a person performing at what might be only an average level is rated as "outstanding." That same person might be rated as "poor" in another department where most workers are superstars. Although at times it may be appropriate to compare people, the normal rating process should compare a worker's performance to job requirements, and not to the performance of others.

8)   Traits like dependability or industriousness may have very little to do with the job expected of an employee and are too subjective to be measured.

9)   Trait scales tend to equate subjectively both pertinent and nonperformance traits (e.g., quality of work and appearance get equal points toward total appraisal score on many scales).

10) The once-a-year process tends to affect the usefulness and accuracy of any job-related information.

11) According to **attribution theory**, people attempt to determine whether observed behavior is internally or externally caused.

a)   Behavior that is unusual for a particular individual is perceived to be externally caused. If it is not unusual, causation is ordinarily perceived to be internal.

b)   If everyone in similar circumstances behaves in a certain way, causation is believed to be external. Otherwise, causation is deemed to be internal.

c)   However, biases may distort attributions.

12) **Fundamental attribution error** is a bias in judgments about the behavior of other people. This bias is a tendency to overestimate internal factors and underestimate external factors.

13) **Self-serving bias** is the tendency to attribute one's successes to internal factors (e.g., diligence and talent) and failures to external factors (e.g., bad luck).

14) **Major types of appraisals**

    a) **Rating scales** on personal traits

    b) **Management by objectives (MBO)** -- behavioral, communications-oriented, responsibility approach to employee self-direction

        i) MBO is based on the philosophy that employees

            • Want to work hard if they know what is expected
            • Like to understand what their jobs actually entail
            • Are capable of self-direction and self-motivation

    c) **Critical incident technique** -- list of critical aspects of job which evaluator uses to evaluate employee performance

    d) **Behaviorally anchored rating scales (BARS)** -- similar to critical incident technique in which descriptions of good and bad performance are developed for a number of specific job-related behaviors and then used for evaluation of employees

15) **Characteristics of effective evaluation systems**

    a) Relevant. Criteria should be reliable and valid. They should relate to employee functions, that is, to activities over which the employees exert control.

    b) Unbiased. Systems should be based on performance of job, not on unrelated personal characteristics.

    c) Significant. Systems should focus on the important part of the job rather than whatever is convenient to evaluate. This avoids misdirection or confusion of employee effort.

    d) Practical. System should be as objective, easy to use, clearly understood, and efficient as possible.

16) **Criteria for effective appraisal**

    a) Employees must understand the appraisal.
    b) They must feel the appraisal is fair.
    c) They must feel it is important to them and their job.

17) A manager can make appraisals easier and more effective by being involved in employee affairs.

    a) Spending a little time with each employee each day and offering praise as well as constructive criticism facilitates acceptance of appraisals.

18) A **360° performance appraisal** is a model for employee assessment in the age of teamwork. It is based on giving workers feedback from peers, customers, supervisors, and those who work for the employee. Feedback is typically provided anonymously.

    a) Appraisal is typically subjective, and popularity is sometimes more important than performance.

    b) Evaluations do not have copies of the employee's job description or performance goals.

19) **Team ratings** are necessary anytime that a company uses teamwork as a part of the work process. Team ratings can be handled in much the same way as individual performance appraisals, but many firms argue that a different method is needed when evaluating teamwork. Thus, team ratings are often conducted by someone other than management, such as the teams themselves or customers. The first step is to define excellence in team performance. This definition is made available to the team members in the form of a **team agreement**, which sets out how the team operates. Without a definition of good performance, a team's performance cannot be evaluated. Teams are jointly accountable for their work. Thus, if any member of the team falls down, everyone else has to ask how they could have helped.

   a) A good team rating system should separate feedback sessions from salary reviews. People may not be as candid with a teammate if they think that something they say could affect the other person's salary.

   b) Team evaluations should be conducted in a "safe" environment, which means with managers not present. Often a neutral facilitator will lead the discussions.

2. Effective management control requires **performance measurement** and **feedback**. This process affects allocation of resources to organizational subunits. It also affects decisions about managers' compensation, advancement, and future assignments.

   a. Furthermore, evaluating their performance serves to **motivate managers** to optimize the measures in the performance evaluation model. However, that model may be inconsistent with the organization's model for managerial decision making.

      1) To achieve goal congruence, the models should be synchronized. For example, if top management wishes to maximize results over the long term, subordinates should be evaluated over the long term.

      2) Unfortunately, information systems seldom provide information on the outcomes of individual decisions, and top managers may be unaware of desirable options not chosen. Moreover, performance feedback usually applies to specific responsibility centers for specific periods. The result is that use of the same criteria for decision making and managerial evaluation may be difficult.

3. Human reactions to **feedback** should be considered in setting performance standards and designing control systems.

   a. The nature of the feedback should motivate employees to improve their performance and reach the planned objectives, rather than offend or intimidate them.

   b. The timing, form, and content of the information on deviations should be considered in order to obtain maximum compliance by those affected.

4. Feedback regarding managerial performance may take the form of **financial and nonfinancial measures** that may be internally or externally generated. Moreover, different measures have a **long-term or short-term emphasis**.

   a. An example of an external financial measure is stock price.

   b. Examples of external nonfinancial measures are market share, customer satisfaction, and delivery performance.

   c. Examples of internal financial measures are cost variances, return on investment, residual income, return on sales, and other financial ratios.

   d. Examples of internal nonfinancial measures are product quality, new product development time, and manufacturing lead time (cycle time).

5. Many forms of performance feedback are based on **accounting information**. The particular measures to be chosen are dependent on a five-stage process:

   a. Top management must determine what measure is consistent with its objectives.

    b.   The elements of the measure must be specified; e.g., calculation of residual income requires a definition of the items to be included in investment. A manager will therefore be motivated to avoid actions that increase the investment base.

    c.   The basis for determining the dollar values of the elements of the measure must also be specified. For example, in a residual income calculation based on an investment base defined as total assets, present value, current cost, current disposal price, or historical cost may be the attribute used to specify the dollar value of the investment.

        1)   Historical cost creates comparability issues because returns on significantly depreciated assets may be higher than those on newer assets that have been acquired using inflated dollars. Thus, otherwise similarly situated managers may report different operating results. Moreover, managers may be reluctant to replace aging assets.

    d.   A standard must be established to provide a basis for comparison.

        1)   One issue is the difficulty of the standard.

        2)   A second issue is whether individual managers should have unique performance goals. Because different managers may face widely varying problems, establishing challenging but attainable goals tailored to individual circumstances is preferable.

    e.   The frequency of performance feedback depends on many factors, such as the nature of the information, its cost, the design of the accounting information system, the level of management receiving the feedback, and the usefulness of the information.

6.   Organizational mechanisms for performance feedback should satisfy the behavioral criteria of goal congruence and managerial effort. However, they should not encroach on the desired level of autonomy granted to a subunit manager.

7.   Top management should be aware of the **limitations of accrual-accounting measures**. For example, cash-based and accrual-based measures may yield different results, so a manager may reject a project with a positive net present value because its effect on accounting income is initially negative.

8.3 CONTROLLABILITY AND COMMON COSTS

1.   **Controllability** is the extent to which a manager can influence activities and related revenues, costs, or other items. In principle, controllability is proportionate to, but not coextensive with, responsibility.

    a.   Controllability is difficult to isolate because few costs are under the sole influence of one manager. Thus, separating the effects of current management's decisions from those of former management is difficult.

    b.   If responsibility exceeds the extent to which a manager can influence an activity, the result may be reduced morale, a decline in managerial effort, and poor performance. Such a manager encounters greater risk because his/her success depends on uncontrollable factors. Thus, a manager in these circumstances should be compensated for the incremental risk assumed.

    c.   However, if a manager is accountable solely for activities over which (s)he has extensive influence, the manager may develop too narrow a focus.

        1)   For example, the manager of a cost center may make decisions based only on cost efficiency and ignore the overall effectiveness goals of the organization. By extending the manager's responsibility to profits as well as costs, the organization may encourage desirable behavior congruent with overall goals, such as improved coordination with marketing personnel, even though the manager still does not control revenues.

      2) Furthermore, a manager who does not control an activity may nevertheless be the individual who is best informed about it. Thus, a purchasing agent may be in the best position to explain price variances even though (s)he cannot control them.

2. Common costs are the costs of products, activities, facilities, services, or operations shared by two or more cost objects.

    a. The term "joint costs" is frequently used to describe the common costs of a single process that yields two or more joint products.

3. The difficulty with common costs is that they are indirect costs whose allocation may be arbitrary.

    a. A direct cause-and-effect relationship between a common cost and the actions of the cost object to which it is allocated is desirable. Such a relationship promotes acceptance of the allocation by managers who perceive the fairness of the procedure, but identification of cause and effect may not be feasible.

    b. An alternative allocation criterion is the benefit received. For example, advertising costs that do not relate to particular products may increase sales of all products. Allocation based on the increase in sales by organizational subunits is likely to be accepted as equitable despite the absence of clear cause-and-effect relationships.

    c. Two specific approaches to common cost allocation are the stand-alone method and the incremental method.

        1) The **stand-alone method** allocates a common cost on a proportionate basis using data regarding each cost object. For example, if the common cost of providing service to customers A and B is $10,000, and the stand-alone costs of servicing customers A and B are $6,000 and $6,000, respectively, A and B should be assigned $5,000 of common costs each.

        2) The **incremental method** requires ranking the users of the cost object. The primary party is then allocated its stand-alone cost, with the secondary party receiving the balance of the common costs. In the preceding example, if customer A is deemed to be the primary user, the allocation will be $6,000 to A and $4,000 to B.

4. Cost allocation is necessary for making economic decisions, e.g., the price to charge for a product or whether to make or buy a part.

5. Cost allocation is also necessary for external financial reporting and for calculation of reimbursements, such as those involved in governmental contracting.

6. Furthermore, cost allocation serves as a motivator. For example, designers of products may be required to include downstream costs, such as servicing and distribution, in their cost projections to fix their attention on how their efforts affect the total costs of the company.

    a. Another example of the motivational effects of cost allocation is that it tends to encourage marketing personnel to emphasize products with large contribution margins.

7. A persistent problem in large organizations is the treatment of the costs of headquarters and other central support costs. Such costs are very frequently allocated.

    a. Research has shown that central support costs are allocated to departments or divisions for the following reasons:

        1) The allocation reminds managers that support costs exist and that the managers would incur these costs if their operations were independent.

        2) The allocation also reminds managers that profit center earnings must cover some amount of support costs.

        3) They should be motivated to use central support services appropriately.

4) Managers who must bear the costs of central support services that they do not control may be encouraged to exert pressure on those who do. Thus, they may be able to restrain such costs indirectly.

8. Negative behavioral effects may arise from arbitrary cost allocations.

a. Managers' morale may suffer when allocations depress operating results.

b. Dysfunctional conflict may arise among managers when costs controlled by one are allocated to others.

c. Resentment may result if cost allocation is perceived to be arbitrary or unfair. For example, an allocation on an ability-to-bear basis, such as operating income, penalizes successful managers and rewards underachievers and may therefore have a demotivating effect.

8.4 FLEXIBLE VS. STATIC BUDGETS

1. A **static budget** is based on only one level of sales or production.

a. It is not very useful if the expected level is not reached or is exceeded.

b. EXAMPLE: Assume that a company budgeted sales at $80,000 and supplies expense at $6,000. What can be said about the efficiency of management if supplies expense is actually $480 when sales are only $40,000? Management cannot evaluate the variance unless it has a budget for a sales level of $40,000.

2. A **flexible budget** is actually a series of several budgets prepared for many levels of activity.

a. At the end of the period, management can compare actual costs or performance with the appropriate budgeted level in the flexible budget.

b. New columns can be developed easily by interpolation or extrapolation.

c. A flexible budget is designed to allow adjustment of the budget to the actual level of activity before comparing the budgeted activity with actual results.

1) In the following example, assume that the $175,000 estimate of variable manufacturing costs was based on expected production of 25,000 units at $7 per unit, but actual production was 25,500 units. Production cost should have been $178,500 (25,500 × $7).

	Static Budget	Flexible Budget	Actual	Variance	
Var. mfg. costs	$175,000	$178,500	$178,000	$ 500	favorable
Selling & admin.	85,000	85,000	83,000	2,000	favorable
	$260,000	$263,500	$261,000	$2,500	favorable

2) The report now reflects the actual level of activity.

3. The virtue of flexible budgeting is that it permits the development of an intricate set of variances to facilitate management planning and control. Variance analysis, which is discussed in Gleim's *CMA Review, Part 2*, Study Unit 9, helps to evaluate performance, to identify certain types of performance gaps, and to provide a starting point for improvement.

4. Although some aspects of planning and control may be formalized, such as a budget, overformalization may be disadvantageous. Inflexibility may limit an organization's performance.

a. Budgets should serve as an aid to decision making. Hence, they must have a sufficient degree of informality to permit the organization to change its plans depending on the circumstances. Such budgets are referred to as informal budgets.

8.5 MULTIPLE MEASURES OF PERFORMANCE

1. The trend in managerial performance evaluation is the **balanced scorecard** approach. Multiple measures of performance permit a determination as to whether a manager is achieving certain objectives at the expense of others that may be equally or more important. For example, an improvement in operating results at the expense of new product development would be apparent using this approach.

    a. The scorecard is a goal congruence tool that informs managers about the nonfinancial factors that top management believes to be important.

    b. As mentioned previously, measures may be financial or nonfinancial, internal or external, and short term or long term.

    c. A typical balanced scorecard classifies objectives into one of **four perspectives** on the business: financial, customer satisfaction, internal business processes, and learning and growth.

        1) Each of the business **objectives** on the scorecard is associated with one or more **measures** that permit the organization to gauge progress toward the objective.

        2) Achievement of the objectives in each perspective makes it possible to achieve the objectives in the next higher perspective.

8.6 TRANSFER PRICING

1. The whole area of centralization versus decentralization is a behavioral issue, as is the related subject of transfer pricing. Transfer pricing is more concerned with goal congruence and motivational issues than with cost issues.

2. Transfer prices are the amounts charged by one segment of an organization for goods and services it provides to another segment of the same organization.

    a. Transfer prices are used by profit and investment centers, but a cost center's costs are allocated to producing departments.

        1) The problem is the determination of the transfer price when one responsibility center purchases from another.

        2) In a decentralized system, each responsibility center theoretically may be completely separate. Thus, Division A should charge the same price to Division B as would be charged to an outside buyer. The reason for decentralization is to motivate managers, and the best interests of Division A may not be served by giving a special discount to Division B if the goods can be sold at the regular price to outside buyers. However, having A sell at a special price to B may be to the company's advantage.

    b. A transfer price should permit a segment to operate as an independent entity and achieve its goals while functioning in the best interests of the company. Hence, transfer pricing should motivate managers; it should encourage goal congruence and managerial effort.

        1) Goal congruence is agreement regarding the goals of the organization or the segment by both supervisors and subordinates. Performance is assumed to be optimized when the parties understand that personal and segmental goals should be consistent with those of the organization.

        2) Managerial effort is the extent to which a manager attempts to accomplish a goal. Managerial effort may include psychological as well as physical commitment to a goal.

3) Motivation is the desire of managers to attain a specific goal (goal congruence) and the commitment to accomplish the goal (managerial effort). Managerial motivation is therefore a combination of managerial effort and goal congruence.

c. Transfer prices can be determined in a number of ways. They may be based on

1) A market price, assuming that a market exists
2) Differential outlay cost plus opportunity cost to the seller

    a) For example, if a good costing $4 can be sold for $10, the outlay cost is $4 and the seller's opportunity cost is $6 (given no idle capacity).

3) Full absorption cost

    a) Full-cost price includes materials, labor, and full allocation of manufacturing overhead.

4) Cost plus a lump sum or a markup percentage

    a) Cost may be either the standard or the actual cost. The former has the advantage of isolating variances. Actual costs give the selling division little incentive to control costs.

    b) A cost-based price ignores market prices and may not promote long-term efficiencies.

5) Negotiation

    a) A negotiated price may result when organizational subunits are free to determine the prices at which they buy and sell internally. Hence, a transfer price may simply reflect the best bargain that the parties can strike between themselves. It need not be based directly on particular market or cost information. A negotiated price may be especially appropriate when market prices are subject to rapid fluctuation.

3. The choice of a transfer pricing policy (which type of transfer price to use) is normally decided by top management at the corporate level. The decision will typically include consideration of the following:

a. **Goal congruence factors.** Will the transfer price promote the goals of the company as a whole?

b. **Segmental performance factors.** The segment making the transfer should be allowed to recover its incremental cost plus its opportunity cost of the transfer. The opportunity cost is the benefit forgone by not selling to an outsider.

1) For this purpose, the transfer should be at market price.
2) The selling manager should not lose income by selling within the company.
3) Properly allocating revenues and expenses through appropriate transfer pricing also facilitates evaluation of the performance of the various segments.

c. **Negotiation factors.** If the purchasing segment could purchase the product or service outside the company, it should be permitted to negotiate the transfer price.

1) The purchasing manager should not have to incur greater costs by purchasing within the company.

d. **Capacity factors.** Does the seller have excess capacity?

1) If Division A has excess capacity, it should be used for producing products for Division B.
2) If Division A is operating at full capacity and selling its products at the full market price, profitable work should not be abandoned to produce for Division B.

e.   **Cost structure factors.** What portions of production costs are variable and fixed?

   1)   If Division A has excess capacity and an opportunity arises to sell to Division B at a price in excess of the variable cost, the work should be performed for Division B because a contribution to cover the fixed costs will result.

f.   **Tax factors.** A wide range of tax issues on the interstate and international levels may arise, e.g., income taxes, sales taxes, value-added taxes, inventory and payroll taxes, and other governmental charges.

   1)   In the international context, exchange rate fluctuations, threats of expropriation, and limits on transfers of profits outside the host country are additional concerns.

g.   EXAMPLE: Division A produces a small part at a cost of $6 per unit. The regular selling price is $10 per unit. If Division B can use the part in its production, the cost to the company (as a whole) will be $6. Division B has another supplier who will sell the item to B at $9.50 per part. Division B wants to buy the $9.50 part from the outside supplier instead of the $10 part from Division A, but making the part for $6 is in the company's best interest. What amount should Division A charge Division B?

   1)   The answer is complicated by many factors. For example, if Division A has excess capacity, B should be charged a lower price. If it is operating at full capacity, B should be charged $10.

   2)   Another question to consider is what portion of Division A's costs is fixed. For example, if a competitor offered to sell the part to B at $5 each, can Division A advantageously sell to B at a price lower than $5? If Division A's $6 total cost is composed of $4 of variable costs and $2 of fixed costs, it is beneficial for all concerned for A to sell to B at a price less than $5. Even at a price of $4.01, the parts would be providing a contribution margin to cover some of A's fixed costs.

4.   **Dual pricing** is another internal price-setting alternative. For example, the seller could record the transfer to another segment at the usual market price that would be paid by an outsider. The buyer, however, would record a purchase at the variable cost of production.

   a.   Each segment's performance would be improved by the use of a dual-pricing scheme.

   b.   The company would benefit because variable costs would be used for decision-making purposes. In a sense, variable costs would be the relevant price for decision-making purposes, but the regular market price would be used for evaluation of production divisions.

   c.   Under a dual-pricing system, the profit for the company will be less than the sum of the profits of the individual segments.

   d.   In effect, the seller is given a corporate subsidy under the dual-pricing system.

   e.   The dual-pricing system is rarely used because the incentive to control costs is reduced. The seller is assured of a high price, and the buyer is assured of an artificially low price. Thus, neither manager must exert much effort to show a profit on segmental performance reports.

8.7 CORE CONCEPTS

Compensation and Benefits

- **Compensation and benefits** are extrinsic rewards. They should satisfy individual needs, encourage positive expectations, be equitable, and be related to performance.

- **Total employee compensation** can be subdivided into three categories: base pay, incentive compensation, and fringe benefits. Each compensation plan has its own **advantages and disadvantages**.

- Under a **deferred compensation plan**, an executive elects to defer compensation into an account in the expectation of receiving the deferrals plus earnings at retirement. Such a plan may involve company contributions.

- **Non-qualified plans** are benefit plans that do not qualify for favorable tax treatment but have far fewer restrictions than qualified plans. Non-qualified plans are unsecured and subject to risks. They must remain "unfunded" to avoid current taxation.

- A **compensatory stock option plan** involves the issuance of stock in whole or in part for employee services rendered. The accounting is based on an **intrinsic-value-based** method.

- **Stock appreciation rights (SARs)** permit employees to receive cash equal to the excess of the market price of the company's stock over a specified amount.

- An **employee stock ownership plan (ESOP)** is a stock bonus plan, or a combination stock bonus and money purchase pension plan, designed to invest primarily in the employer's stock.

Performance Evaluation and Feedback

- An important aspect of management is the **evaluation of employees**. Evaluations are important to the employee, the employer, and the company as a whole. Evaluations provide an opportunity for growth of the employee and, when done properly, can be instrumental in the prevention of future disputes.

- **Evaluation-based problems** include the halo effect, a central tendency, the recency effect, differing standards, personal bias, the leniency error, and the contrast error.

- **Characteristics** of effective evaluation systems are that they are relevant, unbiased, significant, and practical.

- A **360° performance appraisal** is a model for employee assessment in the age of teamwork. It is based on giving workers feedback from peers, customers, supervisors, and those who work for the employee. Feedback is typically provided anonymously.

- **Team ratings** are necessary anytime that a company uses teamwork as a part of the work process. Team ratings can be handled in much the same way as individual performance appraisals, but many firms argue that a different method is needed when evaluating teamwork.

- Effective management control requires **performance measurement** and **feedback**. This process affects allocation of resources to organizational subunits. It also affects decisions about managers' compensation, advancement, and future assignments. Feedback regarding managerial performance may take the form of **financial and nonfinancial measures** that may be internally or externally generated. Moreover, different measures have a **long-term or short-term emphasis**.

- Organizational mechanisms for performance feedback should satisfy the behavioral criteria of **goal congruence and managerial effort**. However, they should not encroach on the desired level of autonomy granted to a subunit manager.

Controllability and Common Costs

- **Controllability** is the extent to which a manager can influence activities and related revenues, costs, or other items. In principle, controllability is proportionate to, but not coextensive with, responsibility.
- **Common costs** are the costs of products, activities, facilities, services, or operations shared by two or more cost objects. The difficulty with common costs is that they are indirect costs whose allocation may be arbitrary.
- Two specific **approaches to common cost allocation** are the stand-alone method and the incremental method. Cost allocation is necessary for making economic decisions, e.g., the price to charge for a product or whether to make or buy a part.
- A persistent problem in large organizations is the treatment of the costs of **headquarters and other central support costs**. Such costs are very frequently allocated. Negative behavioral effects may arise from arbitrary cost allocations.

Flexible vs. Static Budgets

- A **static budget** is based on only one level of sales or production. It is not very useful if the expected level is not reached or is exceeded.
- A **flexible budget** is actually a series of several budgets prepared for many levels of activity. At the end of the period, management can compare actual costs or performance with the appropriate budgeted level in the flexible budget. A flexible budget is designed to allow adjustment of the budget to the actual level of activity before comparing the budgeted activity with actual results.

Multiple Measures of Performance

- The trend in managerial performance evaluation is the **balanced scorecard** approach. Multiple measures of performance permit a determination as to whether a manager is achieving certain objectives at the expense of others that may be equally or more important.
- The scorecard is a **goal congruence tool** that informs managers about the nonfinancial factors that top management believes to be important. Measures may be financial or nonfinancial, internal or external, and short term or long term.
- A typical balanced scorecard includes measures in **four categories**: financial, customer satisfaction, internal business processes, and learning and innovation.

Transfer Pricing

- **Transfer prices** are the amounts charged by one segment of an organization for goods and services it provides to another segment of the same organization.
- A transfer price should permit a segment to operate as an independent entity and achieve its goals while functioning in the best interests of the company. Hence, transfer pricing should motivate managers; it should encourage **goal congruence and managerial effort**.
- The choice of a **transfer pricing policy** is normally decided by top management at the corporate level. The decision will typically include consideration of the following: goal congruence factors, segmental performance factors, negotiation factors, capacity factors, cost structure factors, and tax factors.
- **Dual pricing** is another internal price-setting alternative. For example, the seller could record the transfer to another segment at the usual market price that would be paid by an outsider. The buyer, however, would record a purchase at the variable cost of production. Each segment's performance would be improved by the use of a dual-pricing scheme. However, the dual-pricing system is **rarely used** because the incentive to control costs is reduced.

8.8 ESSAY QUESTIONS

Recall that your CMA Part 4 exam will probably contain six scenarios, with about three questions per scenario. There will be a recommended time allocation of 20 minutes, 30 minutes, or 45 minutes for each scenario and related questions.

One scenario will involve ethics, and probably one or two scenarios will include calculations and responses on a worksheet. Also, expect at least one scenario on organizational/behavioral topics. The remaining scenarios cover Parts 1, 2, and 3.

Scenario Title	Subtopic	Questions	Suggested Time
Employee Retention	Employee Retention	1, 2, 3	30 minutes
Royal Industries	Behavior and Performance Measures	4, 5, 6, 7	30 minutes

Scenario for Essay Questions 1, 2, 3

The retention of experienced employees is of great importance to most business firms. The costs associated with training new employees are high; in some cases, replacing those experienced employees who have a "feel" for their jobs is very difficult. Demographics indicate that the rate of growth in the workforce will decrease each year through 2007 and then decline sharply for the next 10 years. U.S. businesses are already beginning to prepare for the labor shortages ahead by developing innovative programs that encourage experienced employees to continue working.

Those firms that experience sudden growth frequently find themselves with a very young workforce. Experienced employees are a particular asset to these firms, and they have implemented special incentives to encourage long-time employees to extend their services to the company and alter retirement patterns. Other companies that experience layoffs caused by seasonal production or temporary business downturns have implemented "short-time" compensation programs to retain experienced employees.

Questions

1. In order to improve the retention of employees in general, discuss incentives other than wage rates that companies can implement.

2. Describe specific programs that a company experiencing sudden growth could use to motivate long-time, older employees to extend their employment.

3. Define "short-term" compensation, and explain how this program helps companies retain experienced employees.

Essay Questions 1, 2, 3 — Unofficial Answers

1. Incentives other than wage rates that companies can implement to improve the retention of employees include the following:

    a. A company could offer and/or increase other extrinsic rewards such as promotions, employee bonuses, equity participation, and improved benefits.

    b. Job design programs could be implemented which instill employee involvement in creating individual job satisfaction.

    c. The company could set up an MBO (Management by Objectives) program which would ensure an employee's perception and participation of his/her role in the organization and establish expectations (goals) for empirical measurement of individual performance.

    d. An individual could be offered the opportunity to participate in the management of the company through assignments on group projects and special projects.

    e. A program could be instituted in individual career planning, training, and assurance of in-house promotions.

2. Programs that companies experiencing sudden growth could implement to motivate long-time, older employees to extend their employment include the following:

    a. Introduce job sharing where an older employee works part-time, sharing job responsibilities with someone who is younger.

    b. Switch employees from an operational role to a training role.

    c. Eliminate mandatory retirement age.

    d. Introduce flex hours and shorter work weeks with full benefit packages.

    e. Use the employees' experience and knowledge by having them participate in the organization's decision-making process.

3. "Short-time" compensation is a relatively new concept whereby the reduction in work hours due to lower production demands is shared among all the existing employees instead of just a few. All employees will work a shorter work week. There is job security, continued employment, and uninterrupted benefits. The reduction of salaries and wages is sometimes supplemented by state unemployment benefits. No one is released from employment; thus, experienced and junior employees are maintained, minimizing hiring and training costs to the company when work resumes.

Scenario for Essay Questions 4, 5, 6, 7

The Star Paper Division of Royal Industries is located outside Los Angeles. A major expansion of the division's only plant was completed in April of Year 4. The expansion consisted of an addition to the existing building, additions to the production-line machinery, and the replacement of obsolete and fully depreciated equipment that was no longer efficient or cost-effective.

On May 1, Year 4, George Harris became manager of Star. Harris had a meeting with Marie Fortner, vice president of operations for Royal, who explained to Harris that the company measured the performance of divisions and division managers on the basis of return on gross assets (ROA). When Harris asked if other measures were used in conjunction with ROA, Fortner replied, "Royal's top management prefers to use a single performance measure. There is no conflict when there is only one measure. Star should do well this year now that it has expanded and replaced all of that old equipment. You should have no problem exceeding the division's historical rate. I'll check with you at the end of each quarter to see how you are doing."

Fortner called Harris after the first quarter results were completed because Star's ROA was considerably below the historical rate for the division. Harris told Fortner that he did not believe that ROA was a valid performance measure for Star. Fortner indicated that she would discuss this with others at headquarters and get back to Harris. However, there was no further discussion of the use of ROA, only reports on divisional performance at the end of the second and third quarters. Now that the fiscal year has ended, Harris has received the memorandum shown below.

> To: George Harris, Star Paper Division
> From: Marie Fortner, Royal Industries
> Subject: Divisional Performance
>
> The operating results for the fourth quarter and for our fiscal year ended on April 30 are now complete. Your fourth quarter return on gross assets was only 9%, resulting in a return for the year of slightly under 11%. I recall discussing your low return after the first quarter and reminding you after the second and third quarters that this level of return is not considered adequate for the Star Paper Division.
>
> The return on gross assets at Star has ranged from 15% to 18% for the past 5 years. An 11% return may be acceptable at some of Royal's other divisions, but not at a proven winner like Star, especially in light of your recently improved facility. Please arrange to meet with me in the near future to discuss ways to restore Star's return on gross assets to its former level.

Harris is looking forward to meeting with Fortner as he plans to pursue the discussion about the appropriateness of ROA as a performance measure for Star. While the ROA for Star is below historical levels, the division's profits for the year are higher than at any previous time. Harris is going to recommend that ROA be replaced with multiple criteria for evaluating performance, namely, dollar profit, receivable turnover, and inventory turnover.

Questions

4. Identify general criteria that should be used in selecting performance measures to evaluate operating managers.

5. Describe the probable cause of the decline in the Star Paper Division's return on gross assets during the fiscal year ended April 30, Year 5.

6. On the basis of the relationship between Marie Fortner and George Harris, as well as the memorandum from Fortner, discuss apparent weaknesses in the performance evaluation process at Royal Industries.

7. Discuss whether the multiple performance evaluation criteria suggested by George Harris would be appropriate for the evaluation of the Star Paper Division.

Essay Questions 4, 5, 6, 7 — Unofficial Answers

4. General criteria that should be used in selecting performance measures to evaluate operating managers include the following. The measures should

    a. Be controllable by the manager and reflect the actions and decisions made by the manager in the current period.

    b. Be mutually agreed upon, clearly understood, and accepted by all the parties involved.

    c. Address the efficiency and effectiveness of operations.

5. A major expansion of Star Paper's plant was completed in April of Year 4. This expansion included additions to the production-line machinery and the replacement of obsolete and fully depreciated equipment. As a result, the value of the division's asset base increased considerably. While productivity undoubtedly increased during the first year in the expanded plant, the increase was not immediate nor sufficient to offset the increase in the asset base, as there is likely to be a "catch-up" period.

6. Apparent weaknesses in the performance evaluation process at Royal Industries include the following:

    a. There was no mutual agreement on the use of return on assets (ROA) as the only measurement of performance.

    b. The feedback from Fortner was insufficient. Fortner indicated that she would get back to Harris about his questions concerning ROA but she did not do so.

    c. There is only one single measure of performance which may give a distorted picture of actual performance, as is the case with Star Paper. In addition, a single measure could encourage division management to make poor decisions, i.e., delaying the purchase of equipment so that ROA will remain high.

7. Multiple performance evaluation criteria would be appropriate for the evaluation for the Star Paper Division. The criteria suggested by George Harris would take into account more of the results of the key decisions being made by the manager, are not conflicting, and emphasize the balance of profits with the control of current assets. These three measures are controllable by the manager and, in conjunction with ROA, would be more representative of the success of the business.

Consider using Gleim's **CMA Test Prep** for interactive testing with **hundreds of multiple-choice questions** as an additional method of knowledge transfer in your quest to pass Part 4.

STUDY UNIT NINE
ETHICS AS TESTED ON THE CMA EXAM

(9 pages of outline)

ETHICS

Questions containing ethical issues will appear on every examination, presented within the context of specific subject areas. Candidates should be familiar with:

Statement on Management Accounting Number 1C (Revised), *IMA Statement of Ethical Professional Practice*, Institute of Management Accountants, Montvale, N.J., August 2005.

Current references to business ethics are also found in recent periodicals and newspapers.

After studying the outline and answering the essay questions, you will have the skills necessary to address the following topics listed in the IMA's Learning Outcome Statements:

Part 4 - Section D. Ethical considerations

Ethics may be tested in conjunction with any topic area.

1. Provisions of IMA's Statement of Ethical Professional Practice
2. Corporate responsibility for ethical conduct
3. Evaluation and resolution of ethical issues

Using the standards outlined in the *IMA's Statement of Ethical Professional Practice*, the candidate should be able to:

a. evaluate a given business situation for its ethical implications

b. identify specific standards that may have been violated in a given business situation

c. recommend a course of action for management accountants or financial managers to take when confronted with an ethical dilemma in the business environment

d. discuss corporate responsibility for ethical conduct

e. evaluate and propose resolutions for ethical issues such as fraudulent reporting, manipulation of analyses and results, unethical behavior in developing budgets and standards, manipulation of decision factors, and other unethical conduct in a business environment

9.1 ETHICS IN GENERAL

1. **Definitions**

   a. Corporate ethics -- an organization's policies and standards established to assure certain kinds of behavior by its members

   b. Individual ethics -- principles of conduct adhered to by an individual

2. **Increased Concern for Business Ethics**

   a. Electrical-equipment conspiracy cases in 1960 caused public concern and creation of the Business Ethics Advisory Council (BEAC) in 1961 under the Secretary of Commerce.

   b. BEAC pointed out areas needing self-evaluation by the business community:

      1) General business understanding of ethical issues.
      2) Compliance with laws.
      3) Conflicts of interest.
      4) Entertainment and gift expenses.
      5) Relations with customers and suppliers. Should gifts or kickbacks be given or accepted?
      6) Social responsibilities.

   c. BEAC's recommendations generated business interest, especially from big business, in problems of ethical behavior.

   d. More than 40 years later, business ethics is even more in the news than it was in the early 1960s.

      1) In late 2001 and 2002, a wave of improper practices came to light. The following table summarizes some of the more prominent ones:

Scandal Became Public	Company	Details
Oct 2001	Enron	Hid debt of over $1 billion in improper off-the-books partnerships
Nov 2001	Arthur Andersen	Shredded documents related to audit of scandal-plagued client Enron
Feb 2002	Global Crossing	Inflated revenues, shredded accounting-related documents
Feb 2002	Qwest	Inflated revenues
Mar 2002	WorldCom	Booked operating expenses as capital expenses; large off-the-books payments to founder
Apr 2002	Adelphia	Booked operating expenses as capital expenses; hid debt
Jun 2002	Xerox	Inflated revenues

      2) In response to these and many other disclosures, Congress passed the **Corporate and Criminal Fraud Accountability Act of 2002**, also called **Sarbanes-Oxley**.

         a) Among the provisions of Sarbanes-Oxley is a requirement that the chief executive officer and chief financial officer of publicly traded companies certify as to the fair presentation of their financial statements.

      3) Both the financial media and the general press have devoted a great deal of coverage in recent years to business ethics (or the lack thereof).

3. **Factors That May Lead to Unethical Behavior**

   a. In any normal population, some people have less than desirable levels of ethics. If these people hold leadership positions, they will adversely influence subordinates.

   b. Organizational factors may lead to unethical behavior.

      1) Pressures for **short-run performance** in decentralized return on investment (ROI) centers may inhibit ethical behavior.

      2) Emphasis on strict adherence to chain-of-command authority may provide excuses for ignoring ethics when **following orders**.

      3) Informal **work-group loyalties** may subvert ethical behavior.

      4) Committee decision processes may make it possible to abstain from or dodge ethical obligations.

   c. External factors may lead to unethical behavior.

      1) Pressure of competition may compromise ethics in the interest of survival.

      2) Unethical behavior of others may force a compromise of ethics.

      3) Definitions of ethical behavior may vary from one culture to another.

         a) Bribes to overseas officials or buyers may be consistent with some countries' customary business practices, but such a practice is not considered ethical among U.S. purchasing agents.

            i) The propriety of imposing our cultural ethical standards (by refusing to bribe) on another culture may be controversial.

         b) The Foreign Corrupt Practices Act of 1977 prohibits American firms, whether registered with the SEC or not, from paying bribes to any foreign official or foreign political candidate.

            i) Only political payments to foreign officials are prohibited. Payment to foreign business owners or corporate officers are not addressed by the FCPA.

4. **General Guides to Ethics**

   a. Golden Rule -- Do unto others as you would have others do unto you.

   b. Maximize good -- Act to provide the greatest good for the greatest number.

   c. Fairness -- Act in ways that are fair or just to all concerned.

   d. Maximize long-run outcomes -- Act to provide the best long-range benefits to society and its resources.

   e. General respect -- Act to respect the planet all humans share and the rights of others because corporate and individual decisions affect them.

5. **Simplified Criteria for Evaluating Ethical Behavior**

   a. Would this behavior be acceptable if people I respect knew I was doing this?

   b. What are the consequences of this behavior for myself, other employees, customers, and society?

6. **Forces Shaping Personal Ethics**

   a. Ethics are individual and personal, influenced by

      1) Life experiences (rewards for doing right, punishment for doing wrong).

      2) Friendship groups (professional associations, informal groups).

      3) Organizational pressures (responsibilities to superiors and the organization).

b.   Some commentators have pointed out that many of the corporate executives who were indicted for corporate ethics lapses in the early part of the 21st century also had marital problems. These observers argue that an executive who would cheat on his/her spouse (or life partner) would have no difficulty stealing from faceless shareholders and then lying about it to auditors. In other words, executives who are going to be unethical in their personal lives will probably also be unethical in their professional lives.

9.2 CODES OF ETHICAL CONDUCT

1.   An organization's code of ethical conduct is the established general value system the organization wishes to apply to its members' activities through

a.   Communicating organizational purposes and beliefs
b.   Establishing uniform ethical guidelines for members

1)   Including guidance on behavior for members in making decisions

2.   Laws and written rules cannot cover all situations. However, organizations can benefit from having an established ethical code because it

a.   Effectively communicates acceptable values to all members

1)   Including recruits and subcontractors

b.   Provides a method of policing and disciplining members for violations

1)   Through review panels (formal)
2)   Through group pressure (informal)

c.   Establishes high standards against which individuals can measure their own performance

d.   Communicates to those outside the organization the value system from which the organization's members must not be asked to deviate

3.   A typical code for accounting activities (note similarities to the Standards for the Professional Practice of Internal Auditing, codes of ethics of state boards of accountancy, GAAS, etc.) holds that a financial manager must have

a.   Independence from conflicts of economic interest
b.   Independence from conflicts of professional interest

1)   Responsibility to present information fairly to shareholders/owners and not intentionally protect management

2)   Responsibility to present data to all appropriate managers and not play favorites with information or cover up bad news

3)   Responsibility to exercise an ethical presence in the conduct of professional activities

a)   Ensuring organizational compliance with spirit as well as letter of pertinent laws and regulations

b)   Conducting oneself according to the highest moral and legal standards

c)   Reporting to appropriate internal or external authority any illegal or fraudulent organizational act

c.   Integrity in not compromising professional values for the sake of personal goals
d.   Objectivity in presenting information, preparing reports, and making analyses

9.3 THE IMA STATEMENT OF ETHICAL PROFESSIONAL PRACTICE

1. The Institute of Management Accountants (IMA) published its Statement on Management Accounting 1C (Revised), *IMA Statement of Ethical Professional Practice*, in August 2005. The Statement contains four overarching principles, four specific standards, and a section of guidance on the resolution of ethical conflicts.

    a. The four **principles** can be remembered with the mnemonic HFOR (honesty, fairness, objectivity, and responsibility).

    b. The four **standards** can be remembered with the mnemonic CCIC (competence, confidentiality, integrity, and credibility).

    c. The final section, **Resolution** of Ethical Conflict, is especially significant and has been the subject of many CMA Examination questions over the years. One of the most common questions asked deals with the individual to whom a problem should be reported.

2. NOTE: The IMA has an ethics hotline for members who wish to discuss ethical conflicts. It is reached at 1-800-245-1383.

3. The Statement is printed below and on the following page in its entirety.

IMA STATEMENT OF ETHICAL PROFESSIONAL PRACTICE

Members of IMA shall behave ethically. A commitment to ethical professional practice includes overarching principles that express our values, and standards that guide our conduct.

Principles

IMA's overarching ethical principles include: Honesty, Fairness, Objectivity, and Responsibility. Members shall act in accordance with these principles and shall encourage others within their organizations to adhere to them.

Standards

A member's failure to comply with the following standards may result in disciplinary action.

Section I. COMPETENCE

Each practitioner has a responsibility to:

1. *Maintain an appropriate level of professional expertise by continually developing knowledge and skills.*

2. *Perform professional duties in accordance with relevant laws, regulations, and technical standards.*

3. *Provide decision support information and recommendations that are accurate, clear, concise, and timely.*

4. *Recognize and communicate professional limitations or other constraints that would preclude responsible judgment or successful performance of an activity.*

Section II. CONFIDENTIALITY

Each practitioner has a responsibility to:

1. *Keep information confidential except when disclosure is authorized or legally required.*

2. *Inform all relevant parties regarding appropriate use of confidential information. Monitor subordinates' activities to ensure compliance.*

3. *Refrain from using confidential information for unethical or illegal advantage.*

Section III. INTEGRITY

Each practitioner has a responsibility to:

1. *Mitigate actual conflicts of interest. Regularly communicate with business associates to avoid apparent conflicts of interest. Advise all parties of any potential conflict.*

2. *Refrain from engaging in any conduct that would prejudice carrying out their duties ethically.*

3. *Abstain from engaging in or supporting any activity that might discredit the profession.*

Section IV. CREDIBILITY

Each practitioner has a responsibility to:

1. *Communicate information fairly and objectively.*

2. *Disclose all relevant information that could reasonably be expected to influence an intended user's understanding of the reports, analyses, or recommendations.*

3. *Disclose delays or deficiencies in information, timeliness, processing, or internal controls in conformance with organization policy and/or applicable law.*

RESOLUTION OF ETHICAL CONFLICT

In applying the Standards of Ethical Professional Practice, you may encounter problems in identifying unethical behavior or in resolving an ethical conflict. When faced with ethical issues, you should follow the organization's established policies on the resolution of such conflict. If these policies do not resolve the ethical conflict, you should consider the following courses of action:

1. *Discuss the issue with your immediate superior except when it appears that the supervisor is involved. In that case, present the issue to the next level. If you cannot achieve a satisfactory resolution, submit the issue to the next management level. If your immediate superior is the chief executive officer or equivalent, the acceptable reviewing authority may be a group such as the audit committee, executive committee, board of directors, board of trustees, or owners. Contact with levels above the immediate superior should be initiated only with your superior's knowledge, assuming he or she is not involved. Communication of such problems to authorities or individuals not employed or engaged by the organization is not considered appropriate, unless you believe there is a clear violation of the law.*

2. *Clarify relevant ethical issues by initiating a confidential discussion with an IMA Ethics Counselor or other impartial advisor to obtain a better understanding of possible courses of action.*

3. *Consult your own attorney as to legal obligations and rights concerning the ethical conflict.*

9.4 CONFLICT OF INTEREST

1. Conflict of interest is a conflict between the private and the official responsibilities of a person in a position of trust, sufficient to affect judgment, independence, or objectivity in conducting the affairs of the business.

2. **Examples of Conflict of Interest**

    a. Having a substantial financial interest in a supplier, customer, or distributor

    b. Using privileged information gained from one's official position to enter transactions for personal gain

3. **Methods for Control**

    a. Provide a code of conduct provision applying to conflicts of interest.

    b. Require full financial disclosure by managers.

    c. Require prior notification of any transaction that may raise conflict of interest.

    d. Prohibit financial ties to any supplier, customer, or distributor.

    e. Encourage adherence to strong ethical behavior through corporate actions, policies, and public communications.

9.5 LEGAL ASPECTS OF SOCIAL RESPONSIBILITY

1. In addition to individual ethical responsibility, it is important for the candidate to recognize corporate responsibility for ethical conduct. The concept of corporate social responsibility involves more than serving the interests of the organization and its shareholders. Rather, it is an extension of responsibility to embrace service to the public interest in such matters as environmental protection, employee safety, civil rights, and community involvement.

2. A common argument against corporate involvement in socially responsible behavior is that in a competitive market, such behavior incurs costs that place the company at a disadvantage. Socially responsible behavior clearly has immediate costs to the entity, for example, the expenses incurred in affirmative action programs, pollution control, and improvements in worker safety. When one firm incurs such costs and its competitor does not, the other may be able to sell its products or services more cheaply and increase its market share at the expense of the socially responsible firm. The rebuttal argument is that in the long run the socially responsible company may maximize profits by creating goodwill and avoiding or anticipating governmental regulation.

3. The **Racketeer Influenced and Corrupt Organization Act (RICO)** was passed in 1970 as an attempt to combat the problem of organized crime and its infiltration of legitimate enterprises.

    a. Its goals were to eliminate organized crime by concentrating on the illegal monies through the use of civil and criminal forfeitures.

    b. Criminal penalties can be levied up to $25,000 and 20 years in jail. Civil penalties include the awarding of treble damages and attorney's fees to the successful plaintiff.

    c. RICO specifically makes the following activities unlawful:

        1) Using income derived from a pattern of racketeering activity to acquire an interest in an enterprise.

        2) Acquiring or maintaining an interest in an enterprise through a pattern of racketeering activity.

        3) Conducting the affairs of an enterprise through a pattern of racketeering activity.

        4) Conspiring to commit any of these offenses.

    d.   RICO has been used against white-collar criminals, terrorists, Wall Street insider trading, anti-abortion protesters, local law enforcement agencies, and public accounting firms -- none of which was intended by Congress when the law was passed.

4.   The **Foreign Corrupt Practices Act of 1977 (FCPA)** regulates payments by U.S. firms operating in other nations.

    a.   The act is a reaction to publicity over questionable foreign payments by U.S. companies.

    b.   The FCPA makes it a criminal offense to make payments to a foreign government or representative thereof to secure or retain business.

    c.   It prohibits payments of sales commissions to independent agents, if the commissions are knowingly passed to foreign officials.

    d.   Corporations are required to establish internal accounting controls to assure that all overseas payments are proper.

    e.   The FCPA applies even if payment is legal in the nation where it is made.

    f.   The rationale for the FCPA is that the international reputation of the United States is affected by its international business conduct, which should reflect the best of the United States' ethics.

5.   The SEC mandates that the composition of boards of directors include outside directors to create diversity and broaden the overview of a company's place in the market and in society.

6.   Courts are increasingly willing to hold boards of directors and auditors liable for problems.

9.6 CORE CONCEPTS

Ethics

- **Corporate ethics** are embodied in an organization's policies and standards, which are established to assure certain kinds of behavior by its members. **Individual ethics** are principles of conduct adhered to by an individual.

- Electrical-equipment conspiracy cases in 1960 caused public concern and creation of the **Business Ethics Advisory Council (BEAC)** in 1961 under the Secretary of Commerce. More than 40 years later, business ethics is even more in the news than it was in the early 1960s.

- In **late 2001 and 2002**, a wave of improper practices came to light. In response to these and many other disclosures, Congress passed the **Corporate and Criminal Fraud Accountability Act of 2002**, commonly known as **Sarbanes-Oxley**.

- Among the factors that may lead to unethical behavior are **pressures for short-run performance** and an emphasis on strict adherence to chain-of-command authority. The pressure of external competition may compromise ethics in the interest of survival.

- **Two simplified criteria** for evaluating ethical behavior are: "Would this behavior be acceptable if people I respect knew I was doing this?" and, "What are the consequences of this behavior for myself, other employees, customers, and society?"

Codes of Ethical Conduct

- An organization's code of ethical conduct is the **established general value system** the organization wishes to apply to its members' activities through communicating organizational purposes and beliefs and establishing uniform ethical guidelines for members.

- **Laws and written rules** cannot cover all situations. However, organizations can benefit from having an established ethical code.

- A typical code for accounting activities (note similarities to the Standards for the Professional Practice of Internal Auditing, GAAP, GAAS, etc.) holds that a financial manager must have **independence** from conflicts of economic interest; **independence** from conflicts of professional interest; **integrity** in not compromising professional values for the sake of personal goals; and **objectivity** in presenting information, preparing reports, and making analyses.

IMA Statement of Ethical Professional Practice

- The Institute of Management Accountants (IMA) published its Statement on Management Accounting 1C (Revised), ***IMA Statement of Ethical Professional Practice***, in August 2005.

- The Statement contains four overarching **principles**, four specific **standards**, and a section of guidance on the **resolution** of ethical conflicts. The four **principles** can be remembered with the mnemonic HFOR (honesty, fairness, objectivity, and responsibility). The four **standards** can be remembered with the mnemonic CCIC (competence, confidentiality, integrity, and credibility).

- The final section, **Resolution** of Ethical Conflict, is especially significant in regard to the proper person in an organization to whom a problem should be reported. The IMA has an **ethics helpline** for members who wish to discuss ethical conflicts.

Conflict of Interest

- **Conflict of interest** is a conflict between the private and the official responsibilities of a person in a **position of trust**, sufficient to affect judgment, independence, or objectivity in conducting the affairs of the business.

- Conflicts can be **controlled** by, among other things, providing a code of conduct provision applying to conflicts of interest, requiring full financial disclosure by managers, and requiring prior notification of any transaction that may raise conflict of interest.

Legal Aspects of Social Responsibility

- The **Racketeer Influenced and Corrupt Organization Act (RICO)** was passed in 1970 as an attempt to combat the problem of organized crime and its infiltration of legitimate enterprises. However, it has been used against white-collar criminals, terrorists, Wall Street insider trading, anti-abortion protesters, local law enforcement agencies, and public accounting firms -- none of which was intended by Congress when the law was passed.

- The **Foreign Corrupt Practices Act of 1977 (FCPA)** regulates payments by U.S. firms operating in other nations. The Act makes it a criminal offense to make payments to a foreign government or representative thereof to secure or retain business. It does not apply to payments made to foreign business owners. Corporations are required to establish internal accounting controls to assure that all overseas payments are proper.

- The **Securities and Exchange Commission** mandates that the composition of boards of directors include outside directors to create diversity and broaden the overview of a company's place in the market and in society.

This page intentionally left blank.

9.7 ESSAY QUESTIONS

Recall that your CMA Part 4 exam will probably contain six scenarios, with about three questions per scenario. There will be a recommended time allocation of 20 minutes, 30 minutes, or 45 minutes for each scenario and related questions.

One scenario will involve ethics, and probably one or two scenarios will include calculations and responses on a worksheet. Also, expect at least one scenario on organizational/behavioral topics. The remaining scenarios cover Parts 1, 2, and 3.

Scenario Title	Subtopic	Questions	Suggested Time
American Corporation	Ethics and Pressure to Achieve Goals	1, 2	30 minutes
GroChem, Inc.	Ethics and Discovery of Illegal Acts	3, 4, 5	30 minutes
Heart Health Procedures	Ethics and Financial Reporting	6, 7, 8	30 minutes
Northern Paperboard, Inc.	Ethics and Professional Responsibility	9, 10, 11	30 minutes
JLS Corporation	Ethics and Corporate Social Responsibility	12, 13, 14, 15	30 minutes

Scenario for Essay Questions 1, 2

A large American corporation participates in a highly competitive industry. In order to meet this competition and achieve profit goals, the company has chosen the decentralized form of organization. Each manager of a decentralized profit center is measured on the basis of profit contribution, market penetration, and return on investment. Failure to meet the objectives established by corporate management for these measures was not accepted and usually resulted in demotion or dismissal of a profit center manager.

An anonymous survey of managers in the company revealed that the managers felt the pressure to compromise their personal ethical standards to achieve the corporate objectives. For example, at certain plant locations there was pressure to reduce quality control to a level which could not assure that all unsafe products would be rejected. Also, sales personnel were encouraged to use questionable sales tactics to obtain orders, including gifts and other incentives to purchasing agents.

The chief executive officer is disturbed by the survey findings. In his opinion, such behavior cannot be condoned by the company. He concludes that the company should do something about this problem.

Questions

1. Discuss what might be the causes for the ethical problems described.

2. Outline a program that could be instituted by the company to help reduce the pressures on managers to compromise personal ethical standards in their work.

Essay Questions 1, 2 — Unofficial Answers

1. Corporate management has established an environment in which there is an incompatibility (lack of goal congruence) between the achievement of corporate objectives and personal ethics. Under the current situation, severe penalties have been imposed by top management whenever subordinates do not achieve the high levels of performance established by the predetermined objectives. This has caused lower level management to take unethical courses of action.

    Corporate management apparently utilizes an authoritarian, nonparticipative management style which does not consider contributions from lower level management. As a result of this type of management style, top management may have established unreasonable expectations and may not recognize the need to change the expectations in light of changing circumstances. These factors may result in subordinates choosing any means to reach the objectives.

    The penalty and reward system appears to be inappropriate. There is no positive feedback or encouragement for effective performance and the penalties are heavy for failure to meet objectives. No code of ethics exists, and penalties are apparently nonexistent or minor for violation of acceptable business practices that are compatible with personal ethical standards.

2. A company program to reduce the pressures on lower level management who violate the personal ethical standards and acceptable business practices might include the following actions:

    a. Adopt a participative style of management. Encourage each lower level manager to contribute to the establishment of the goals by which (s)he is to be judged.

    b. Expand the feedback system to recognize and reward good performance, allow for investigation and explanation for substandard performance, and adjust for changing conditions.

    c. Adopt a corporate code of ethics or code of acceptable business practices.

    d. Display top management support for the code evidenced by words and actions.

Scenario for Essay Questions 3, 4, 5

Adam Williams was recently hired as assistant controller of GroChem, Inc. which processes chemicals for use in fertilizers. Williams was selected for this position because of his past experience in the chemical processing field. During his first month on the job, Williams made a point of getting to know the people responsible for the plant operations and learning how things are done at GroChem.

During a conversation with the plant supervisor, Williams asked about the company procedures for handling toxic waste materials. The plant supervisor replied that he was not involved with the disposal of wastes and suggested that Williams might be wise to ignore this issue. This response strengthened Williams' determination to probe this area further to be sure that the company was not vulnerable to litigation.

Upon further investigation, Williams discovered evidence that GroChem was using a nearby residential landfill to dump toxic wastes. It appeared that some members of GroChem's management team were aware of this situation and may have been involved in arranging for this dumping; however, Williams was unable to determine whether his superior, the controller, was involved.

Uncertain how he should proceed, Williams began to consider his options by outlining the following three alternative courses of action:

- Seek the advice of his superior, the controller.
- Anonymously release the information to the local newspaper.
- Discuss the situation with an outside member of the board of directors with whom he is acquainted.

Questions

3. Discuss why Adam Williams has an ethical responsibility to take some action in the matter of GroChem, Inc. and the dumping of toxic wastes. Refer to the specific standards (competence, confidentiality, integrity, and/or credibility) of Statement on Management Accounting Number 1C (Revised), *IMA Statement of Ethical Professional Practice*, to support your answer.

4. For each of the three alternative courses of action that Adam Williams has outlined, explain whether or not the action is appropriate. Use SMA 1C to support your answer.

5. Without prejudice to your answer in Question 4, assume that Adam Williams sought the advice of his superior, the controller, and discovered that the controller was involved in the dumping of toxic wastes. Using SMA 1C to support your answer, describe the steps that Williams should take to resolve this situation.

Essay Questions 3, 4, 5 — Unofficial Answers

3.   Adam Williams has an ethical responsibility to take some action in the matter of GroChem, Inc. and the dumping of toxic wastes because in accordance with Statement on Management Accounting Number 1C (Revised), management accountants should not condone the commission of acts by their organization that violate the standards of ethical conduct. The specific standards of SMA 1C that apply are as follows:

    a.   **Competence.** Management accountants have a responsibility to perform their professional duties in accordance with relevant laws, regulations, and technical standards.

    b.   **Confidentiality.** Management accountants must refrain from disclosing confidential information unless legally obligated to do so. Adam Williams may have a legal responsibility to take some action.

    c.   **Integrity.** Management accountants have a responsibility to refrain from engaging in any conduct that would prejudice carrying out duties ethically.

    d.   **Credibility.** Management accountants have a responsibility to disclose all relevant information that could reasonably be expected to influence an intended user's understanding of the reports, analyses, or recommendations.

4.   In accordance with SMA 1C, the first alternative being considered by Adam Williams, seeking the advice of his boss, is appropriate. To resolve an ethical conflict, the first step recommended by SMA 1C is to discuss the problem with the immediate superior, unless it appears that this individual is involved in the conflict. In this case, it does not appear that Williams' boss is involved.

Communication of confidential information to anyone outside the company is inappropriate unless there is a legal obligation to do so, in which case Williams should contact the proper authorities.

Contacting a member of the board of directors would be an inappropriate action at this time. In accordance with SMA 1C, Williams should report the conflict to successively higher levels within the organization and turn only to the board of directors if the problem is not resolved at lower levels.

5.   Adam Williams should follow the established policies of the organization bearing on the resolution of such conflict. If these policies do not resolve the ethical conflict, Williams should report the problem to successively higher levels of management up to the board of directors until it is satisfactorily resolved. There is no requirement for Williams to inform his immediate superior of this action because he is involved in the conflict. If the conflict is not resolved after exhausting all course of internal review, Williams may have no other recourse than to resign from the organization and submit an informative memorandum to an appropriate member of the organization.

Scenario for Essay Questions 6, 7, 8

The external auditors for Heart Health Procedures (HHP) are currently performing the annual audit of HHP's financial statements. As part of the audit, the external auditors have prepared a representation letter to be signed by HHP's Chief Executive Officer (CEO) and Chief Financial Officer (CFO). The letter provides, among other items, a representation that appropriate provisions have been made for

- reductions of any excess or obsolete inventories to net realizable values, and
- losses from any purchase commitments for inventory quantities in excess of requirements or at prices in excess of market.

HHP began operations by developing a unique balloon process to open obstructed arteries to the heart. In the last several years, HHP's market share has grown significantly because its major competitor was forced to cease its balloon operations by the Food and Drug Administration (FDA). HHP purchases the balloon's primary and most expensive component from a sole supplier. Two years ago, HHP entered into a 5-year contract with this supplier at the then current price with inflation escalators built into each of the 5 years. The long-term contract was deemed necessary to assure adequate supplies and discourage new competition. However, during the past year, HHP's major competitor developed a technically superior product, which utilizes an innovative, less costly component. This new product was recently approved by the FDA and has been introduced to the medical community, receiving high acceptance. It is expected that HHP's market share, which has already seen softness, will experience a large decline, and that the primary component used in the HHP balloon will decrease in price as a result of the competitor's use of its recently developed superior, cheaper component. The new component has been licensed by the major competitor to several outside sources of supply to maintain available quantity and price competitiveness. At this time, HHP is investigating the purchase of this new component.

HHP's officers are on a bonus plan that is tied to overall corporate profits. Jim Honig, vice president of manufacturing, is responsible for both manufacturing and warehousing. During the course of the audit, he advised the CEO and CFO that he was not aware of any obsolete inventory nor any inventory or purchase commitments where current, or expected prices, were significantly below acquisition or commitment prices. Honig took this position even though Marian Nevins, assistant controller, had apprised him of both the existing excess inventory attributable to the declining market share and the significant loss associated with the remaining years of the 5-year purchase commitment.

Nevins has brought this situation to the attention of her superior, the controller, who also participates in the bonus plan and reports directly to the CFO. Nevins works closely with the external audit staff and subsequently ascertains that the external audit manager was unaware of the inventory and purchase commitment problems. Nevins is concerned about the situation and is not sure how to handle the matter.

Questions

6. Assuming that the controller did not apprise the CEO and CFO of the situation, explain the ethical considerations of the controller's apparent lack of action by discussing specific standards (competence, confidentiality, integrity, and credibility) of Statement on Management Accounting Number 1C (Revised), *IMA Statement of Ethical Professional Practice*.

7. Assuming Marian Nevins believes the controller has acted unethically and not apprised the CEO and CFO of his findings, describe the steps that she should take to resolve the situation. Use SMA 1C to support your answer.

8. Describe actions that Heart Health Procedures can take to improve the ethical situation within the company.

Essay Questions 6, 7, 8 — Unofficial Answers

6.   Assuming the controller did not apprise the CEO and CFO of the situation, the ethical considerations of the controller's apparent lack of action, as covered in Statement on Management Accounting Number 1C (Revised), are as follows:

    a.   **Competence.** Management accountants have a responsibility to perform their professional duties in accordance with the relevant laws, regulations, and technical standards, and to provide decision support information and recommendations that are accurate, clear, concise, and timely. The controller's apparent lack of action regarding the overstatement of inventory and lack of provision for potential purchase commitment losses do not comply with generally accepted accounting principles.

    b.   **Confidentiality.** This standard does not apply to the situation.

    c.   **Integrity.** Management accountants have a responsibility to mitigate actual conflicts of interest, to refrain from engaging in any activity that would prejudice carrying out duties ethically, and to abstain from engaging in or supporting any activity that might discredit the profession.

    d.   **Credibility.** Management accountants have a responsibility to communicate information fairly and objectively; to disclose all relevant information that could reasonably be expected to influence an intended user's understanding of the reports, analyses, or recommendations; and to disclose delays or deficiencies in information, timeliness, processing, or internal controls in conformance with organization policy and/or applicable law.

7.   The recommended course of action that Marian Nevins should take, as described in Statement on Management Accounting Number 1C (Revised), is as follows:

    a.   Consult company policies and procedures regarding ethical conflict. If the company does not have adequate procedures in place to resolve the conflict, then Nevins should discuss the problem with her immediate supervisor, the controller. However, as the controller is apparently involved in the matter and she has already spoken to him, it would not be necessary to inform him that she is taking the situation to the CFO.

    b.   As the issue is still not resolved, she should consult the next higher level of management, the CFO, particularly since he will be one of the signers of the representation letter.

    c.   During this process Nevins could clarify relevant concepts by confidential discussion with an objective adviser to obtain an understanding of possible courses of action.

    d.   If the issue remains unresolved, Nevins should continue to take the problem to the next higher levels of authority which may include the audit committee, executive committee, and/or the board of directors.

    e.   If the ethical conflict still exists, after exhausting all levels of internal review, Nevins should resign and submit an informative memorandum to an appropriate representative of the organization.

    f.   Except where legally prescribed, communication of these issues to outsiders (the media, regulatory bodies, etc.) by Nevins is not considered appropriate.

8.   The actions that Heart Health Procedures can take to improve the ethical situation within the company, include

    a.   setting the tone at the top for control consciousness of the people in the organization

    b.   establishing an audit committee within the board of directors and providing an avenue for communication free of reprisals within the company

    c.   adopting performance-based, long-term financial incentive plans

Scenario for Essay Questions 9, 10, 11

Northern Paperboard, Inc. (NPI) manufactures paperboard for industry users but has not been a participant in waste paper recycling due to the lack of a sufficient marketplace for recycled materials. However, with the growing consumer concerns over environmental issues, Don Sumner, chairman of NPI, is concerned with NPI's social responsibility. Consequently, Sumner assembled a management task force to review the feasibility of NPI entering the waste paper recycling process, particularly as he foresees the continuing closures of dumping grounds around the country. Sumner believes there are considerable public relations benefits to be gained and that favorable actions by NPI could forestall government intervention.

After completion of their review, the task force compiled a confidential company report concluding that an investment of $21,000,000 would be required to construct a state-of-the-art recycling plant. The report further concluded that as demand for recycled paperboard increases, the plant would be profitable within a three-year period. After considering his perception of NPI's social responsibility, the favorable financial forecasts, and the growing environmental concerns, Sumner endorsed the proposal.

Anne Jurgens, controller, was part of the task force but did not agree with the report's forecasts for growth in the marketplace for recycled products. Jurgens' department prepared cost estimates for the start-up operation that were more conservative than other estimates submitted to the task force. The majority of the task force chose to use the costs associated with the three-year payback period despite Jurgens' objections. At a recent professional meeting, Jurgens stated to a few of her professional colleagues that NPI was actively pursuing the waste paper recycling program only to obtain favorable community reaction.

Questions

9. Explain what is meant by the term "corporate social responsibility."

10. Identify at lease three advantages and at least three disadvantages that a corporation might experience by fulfilling its social responsibility.

11. Referring to the specific standards of competence, confidentiality, integrity, and credibility in Statement on Management Accounting Number 1C (Revised), *IMA Statement of Ethical Professional Practice*, explain whether Anne Jurgens' discussion with her professional colleagues is in violation of SMA 1C.

Essay Questions 9, 10, 11 — Unofficial Answers

9. Corporate social responsibility refers to corporations' responsibilities for the effect their actions have on people, their communities, and their environment. It refers to the moral and ethical aspects of corporate decisions and represents what corporations give back to society for using society's resources.

10. At least three advantages and at least three disadvantages that a corporation might experience from fulfilling its social responsibilities include the following:

    a. Advantages

        1) Benefits long-term interests of working in a better community by extending social well-being and cultural capabilities to the community
        2) Improved recruitment and increased loyalty of current employees
        3) Improved public image (may result in increased sales and/or product loyalty)

    b. Disadvantages

        1) Loss of efficiency through utilization of resources to pursue such efforts which may tend to dilute the company's primary purpose
        2) Conflicting public perceptions where there is concern for corporate cultural contributions but products are perceived as detrimental to health and the environment
        3) Involvement with issues that are too complex or for which the company lacks talent for solving

11. Referring to the specific standards of competence, confidentiality, integrity, and credibility in the Statement on Management Accounting No. 1C (Revised), *IMA Statement of Ethical Professional Practice*, an explanation of whether Anne Jurgens' discussion with her peers is in violation of SMA 1C is presented below.

Competence. A competent controller would be an effective member of the task force and would be expected to issue complete and clear reports and recommendations after appropriate analysis. Consequently, Jurgens perhaps should have issued a report indicating her position that she considered the revenue forecasts a little soft, as well as her concern for the level of costs for a start-up operation.

Confidentiality. Jurgens failed to refrain from disclosing confidential information acquired in the course of her work.

Integrity. Jurgens, by not objecting to the report, has violated the rule to refrain from engaging in any conduct that would prejudice carrying out her duties ethically.

Credibility. Jurgens, by not objecting to the report, has failed to communicate information fairly and objectively.

Scenario for Essay Questions 12, 13, 14, 15

JLS Corporation is a large, publicly owned manufacturing company specializing in the production of appliance parts. Mark Howard, the President and Chief Executive Officer, is philanthropic and socially conscious. He wants JLS Corporation to be recognized as a socially conscious and responsible company. To promote this image, JLS Corporation has donated well over one million dollars during the last two years to the local symphony, the parks department, various charities, and other civic groups. Furthermore, Howard encourages executives to participate in civic activities, i.e., United Fund, school boards and school parent/teacher organizations, service clubs, etc., and gives executives released time to participate in these activities.

Howard recently read a professional monograph on corporate social performance. The monograph identified four areas used to evaluate the company's level of social responsibility:

1. Community involvement
2. Human resources
3. Physical resources and environmental contributions
4. Product or service contributions

Howard believes that the activities JLS has supported seem to concentrate on community involvement. However, he is uncertain whether JLS conducts any activities related to the other three areas of social responsibility.

Questions

12. Explain the meaning of the term "corporate social responsibility."

13. List the issues for and against the social responsibility concept.

14. Identify and explain social responsibility activities that JLS Corporation could be doing currently or could do in the future in the following three areas:

    a. Human resources
    b. Physical resources and environmental contributions
    c. Product or service contributions

15. Mark Howard wants JLS Corporation's shareholders to be aware of the company's commitment to social responsibility. Discuss how the corporation's achievements in the area of social responsibility could be communicated to its shareholders.

Essay Questions 12, 13, 14, 15 — Unofficial Answers

12. The term "corporate social responsibility" is used to describe the extension of a corporation's responsibility in society beyond its obligation to earn a profit for the stockholders. This extension requires a corporation to include activities and objectives in addition to earning a profit for stockholders.

13. Arguments for corporate social responsibility include the following:

    a. Socially responsible activities are in the long-run self-interest of the corporation.
    b. Acceptance of corporate social responsibility may tend to discourage governmental intervention and regulation.
    c. A favorable public image can be created and maintained.

    Arguments against corporate social responsibility include the following:

    a. The primary goal of profit maximization is congruent with society's best interests.
    b. The corporation's goal is satisfaction of the economic goals of the stockholders. The stockholders and their corporate managers are the social beings, not the corporate entity.
    c. Social considerations divert the attention and resources of the corporation to the disadvantage of all.

14. Activities in which JLS could engage to meet a social responsibility with respect to the three areas identified include the following:

    a. Human resources

        1) Contribute to the educational development of people through improved training and career advancement programs for current employees
        2) Provide for the well-being of employees by maintaining safe working conditions

    b. Physical resources and environmental contributions

        1) Contribute to improvement in the environment by reducing company pollution of air and water
        2) Contribute to energy conservation by taking the lead in promoting community-wide energy conservation

    c. Product or service contributions

        1) Design and manufacture safe or better quality products
        2) Respond quickly to customer complaints
        3) Develop clear and concise labels and instructions for product uses

15. Achievements in social responsibility could be included either in a separate section of the annual report or in a special report to the stockholders. Ongoing activities can be reported in company newsletters or magazines, presentations at stockholders' meetings, news releases, and other public relations forums.

Consider using Gleim's **CMA Test Prep** for interactive testing with **hundreds of multiple-choice questions** as an additional method of knowledge transfer in your quest to pass Part 4.

STUDY UNIT TEN
CMA PART 1 REVIEW – BUSINESS ECONOMICS AND GLOBAL BUSINESS

(20 pages of outline)

Part 1 of the CMA exam is titled **Business Analysis**. This study unit is a review of these sections:

A.   **Business Economics.** Factors affecting the individual firm including demand, supply, and elasticity; consumption of goods; production factors and their cost; market structures and pricing; issues in macroeconomics such as inflation, employment, and economic growth; GDP; the nature of business cycles; fiscal and monetary policies.

B.   **Global Business.** Comparative advantages of trade; free trade and protectionism; barriers to international trade; nature and theory of foreign exchange; international capital investments; financing international trade; legal and ethical issues.

This study unit presents the IMA's Learning Outcome Statements and Gleim Core Concepts relevant to these sections. Bear in mind that **all topics** on Part 4 of the exam are tested at **skill level C** (all six skill types required).

10.1 BUSINESS ECONOMICS REVIEW

Part 1 – Section A.1. Factors affecting the individual firm

The candidate should be able to:

a.   demonstrate an understanding of the laws of supply and demand

b.   interpret a graph of supply and demand

c.   demonstrate an understanding of how prices are determined by the interaction of supply and demand

d.   differentiate between changes in demand and changes in the quantity demanded

e.   differentiate between changes in supply and changes in the quantity supplied

f.   identify the market equilibrium price

g.   demonstrate an understanding of how surpluses and shortages affect the market price

h.   calculate the price elasticity of demand

i.   define elastic and inelastic demand and identify each on a graph

j.   estimate total revenue given changes in prices and demand as well as elasticity coefficients

k.   calculate the price elasticity of supply

l.   calculate the cross elasticity of demand and the income elasticity of demand

m.   define externalities and identify their impacts

n.   apply the law of supply and demand and the concepts of elasticity of supply and demand to government intervention in the market, such as price supports, minimum wages, rent control, mandated regulation, etc.

o.   identify the major provisions of U.S. Federal antitrust legislation, including the Sherman Act, the Clayton Act, the Robinson-Patman Act, the Federal Trade Commission Act, and other relevant legislation

p.   list the objectives of antitrust legislation

q.   identify antitrust enforcement sanctions available to the Federal government

r.   demonstrate an understanding of government regulation of natural monopolies

s.   identify the impact of antitrust regulation on a firm

t.   identify the impact of antitrust regulation on an industry

u.   identify the impact of government regulation on a firm's sales, prices, and costs

v.   identify the impact of government regulation on an industry

w.   determine the impact of economic factors on the demand for a firm's product

x.   determine the impact of economic factors on the market price and supply of a firm's factors of production (labor, materials, services, etc.)

Core Concepts for Factors Affecting the Individual Firm

- **Demand** is a schedule of the amounts of a good or service that consumers are willing and able to purchase at various prices during a period of time.

  - **The law of demand:** describes the general tendency of consumers to demand more of a good only when the price is reduced. For this reason, demand is depicted graphically as a downward sloping curve. **Quantity demanded** is any specific point along this curve. **A change in price** thus results in a movement along the demand curve to a new quantity demanded point.

  - **A change in one of the determinants** of demand results in a change in demand, i.e., a shift of the demand curve itself, to the left or right. The determinants of demand are **any factors other than price** that affect the amount of a commodity that consumers purchase: consumer incomes, consumer taste and preference, prices of related goods, consumer expectations, and number of consumers.

- **Supply** is a schedule of the amounts of a good that producers are willing and able to offer to the market at various prices during a specified period of time.

  - **The law of supply** describes the general tendency of producers to supply more of a good only when the price is raised. For this reason, supply is depicted graphically as an upward sloping curve. **Quantity supplied** is any specific point along this curve.

  - **A change in price** thus results in a shift to a different point along the supply curve. **A change in one of the determinants** of supply results in a change in supply, i.e., a shift of the supply curve itself. The determinants of supply are **any factors other than price** that affect the amount of a commodity that producers offer: costs of inputs, change in efficiency of the production process, expectations about price changes, the passage of time, and taxes and subsidies.

- **Market equilibrium** is the combination of price and quantity at which the market demand and market supply curves intersect. Because everything offered for sale is bought at the price-quantity combination, equilibrium is referred to as the **market-clearing price** and the **market-clearing quantity**.

- **Price elasticity of demand** measures the sensitivity of the quantity demanded of a product to a change in its price. It is calculated as follows:

$$\frac{Percentage\ change\ in\ quantity\ demanded}{Percentage\ change\ in\ price}$$

- When the coefficient is greater than one, demand is in a **relatively elastic range**, meaning a small change in price results in a large change in quantity demanded. When the coefficient is less than one, demand is in a **relatively inelastic range**, meaning a large change in price results in a small change in quantity demanded.

- Related coefficients are

  - **Cross-elasticity of demand**, which measures the percentage change in demand for one good given a percentage change in the price of another good
  - **Income elasticity of demand**, which measures the percentage change in quantity demanded given a percentage change in income
  - **Price elasticity of supply**, which measures the sensitivity of the quantity supplied of a product to a change in its price

- **Externalities**, or spillover effects, are costs or benefits affecting third parties. The third party bears a cost or receives a benefit as part of a transaction in which (s)he did not participate.

  - A classic private-sector **spillover cost** is pollution.
  - **Spillover benefits** are most noticeably embodied by public goods, such as education, national defense, and environmental protection.

- **Price controls** are attempts by government to remedy perceived unfairness in the marketplace. They often backfire.

  - **Price ceilings** result in shortages because the market is unwilling to supply all that is demanded at the (government-mandated) artificially low price. Rent controls are an example.
  - **Price floors** result in surpluses because producers are encouraged by the (government-mandated) artificially high price to generate more than the market is willing to absorb. Price supports for agricultural products are an example.

- The **Sherman Act of 1890** is the foundation of all subsequent antitrust law in the U.S.

  - Section 1 makes illegal every contract, combination, or conspiracy in restraint of trade in interstate or foreign commerce. **Price-fixing** is an agreement by the violators that they will not compete on price. This is the most often prosecuted violation under the Sherman Act. The **rule of reason** applies to possible violations that can only be adjudged after thorough analysis of the case. Under this doctrine, only unreasonable restraints of trade are considered illegal.
  - Section 2 of the Sherman Act prohibits the acts of monopolizing or attempting to monopolize. **Monopoly** is the power to control prices or exclude competition.

- Other federal antitrust laws followed:

  - The **Clayton Act of 1914** dealt with price discrimination and tie-in sales.
  - The **Federal Trade Commission Act of 1914** prohibits "unfair methods of competition in commerce" and created the Federal Trade Commission (FTC).
  - The **Wheeler-Lea Amendment of 1938** gave the FTC additional authority.
  - The **Robinson-Patman Act of 1936** further restricted price discrimination.
  - The **Celler-Kefauver Act of 1950** sought to further protect against monopoly creation.
  - The **Antitrust Improvements Act of 1976** required that prior notification of mergers be made to the Justice Department.

- A **natural monopoly** exists when economies of scale are so great in an industry that the lowest per-unit cost can be achieved only if one firm produces all of the output demanded. The usual approach of antitrust law is counterproductive in such cases; fostering competition leads to higher costs passed on to consumer. Regulation of natural monopolies tends to focus on setting price ceilings.

Part 1 - Section A.2. Consumption of goods

The candidate should be able to:

   a.   define the term utility

   b.   differentiate between total utility and marginal utility and show the difference between the two on a graph

   c.   demonstrate an understanding of the law of diminishing marginal utility

   d.   analyze the relationship of marginal utility theory to the demand curve and to the price elasticity of demand

   e.   identify the point of utility maximization

   f.   demonstrate an understanding of indifference curves, including the marginal rate of substitution and the consumer's equilibrium position

Core Concepts for Consumption of Goods

   ▪   **Utility** is the degree to which a good or service provides **satisfaction** to a given consumer. This satisfaction is subjective. **Total utility** is the full degree of satisfaction received by a customer from all the units of a good or service consumed. **Marginal utility** is the additional (subjective) benefit derived from obtaining one more unit of the good or service.

   ▪   The **law of diminishing marginal utility** helps to explain why the demand curve is downward sloping. Additional consumption of a good or service results in successively smaller additions of utility to the consumer. Thus, a consumer will purchase more of a product only if the price decreases.

   ▪   The points on an **indifference curve** represent the combinations of two goods that give equal total utility to a given consumer. Indifference curves are negatively sloped because some of one good must be given up to obtain more of the other. The slope reflects the **marginal rate of substitution (MRS)**. A consumer's downward sloping **budget line** (consumption opportunity line) depicts all combinations of two goods that can be purchased with a given income at the given prices of the two goods.

   ▪   **Utility is maximized** when the budget line is tangent to the highest possible indifference curve. At that point, the consumer receives the highest level of utility possible with the given income.

Part 1 – Section A.3. Production cost functions

The candidate should be able to:

   a.   define explicit and implicit costs

   b.   demonstrate an understanding of normal profit as a cost

   c.   identify and calculate economic profit

   d.   differentiate short-run costs from long-run costs

   e.   distinguish between fixed costs and variable costs

   f.   identify and calculate total product, marginal product, and average product

   g.   define the law of diminishing returns and graphically identify the point of diminishing return

   h.   identify and calculate total cost, average fixed cost, average variable cost, and average total cost

   i.   identify and calculate marginal cost

   j.   interpret the graphical relationship of marginal cost, average variable cost, average fixed cost, and average total cost

   k.   demonstrate an understanding of the long-run average total cost curve

   l.   define economies of scale, constant returns to scale, and diseconomies of scale

   m.   identify and calculate fixed costs and variable costs

   n.   contrast economic profit with accounting profit and calculate economic profit given financial statement information and opportunity costs

Core Concepts for Production Cost Functions

- **Explicit costs (accounting costs)** are those requiring actual cash disbursements. **Implicit costs (opportunity costs)** are those costs not recognized in a concern's formal accounting records. A normal profit is a crucial implicit cost. **Economic costs** are total costs. The true hurdle for an economic decision is whether the revenues from the venture will cover all costs, both explicit and implicit.

    - **Accounting profits** are earned when the (book) income of an organization exceeds the (book) expenses.
    - **Economic profits** are a significantly higher hurdle. They are not earned until the organization's income exceeds not only costs as recorded in the accounting records, but the firm's implicit costs as well.

- **The law of diminishing returns.** Each additional unit of input leads to increased production, but the increase is smaller with each unit, i.e., the "bang for the buck" steadily diminishes.

    - This phenomenon can be depicted graphically as follows: the **slope of the total product curve** begins to flatten out once the point of diminishing marginal returns is passed. The slope turns negative once the point of negative returns is passed.

- The shape and position of a firm's **short-run average total cost (SRATC) curve** is determined by the productivity of its current manufacturing plant. There are as many SRATC curves as there are possible plant setups. A firm's **long-run average total cost (LRATC) curve** is therefore extrapolated from all its possible SRATC curves.

    - **Economies of scale** (increasing returns to scale) describes the situation in which, as production increases, average costs of production decrease.
    - **Constant returns to scale** describes the situation in which an increase in the level of production results in no change in average costs.
    - **Diseconomies of scale** (decreasing returns to scale) describes the situation in which an increase in the level of production leads to an increase in the marginal cost of production.

Part 1 – Section A.4. Market structures and pricing

The candidate should be able to:

a. identify the defining characteristics of pure competition, monopoly, monopolistic competition, and oligopoly
b. differentiate the demand curve of an individual firm in a purely competitive market from the demand curve of the market itself
c. identify, calculate, and graphically represent average, total, and marginal revenue for a firm in a purely competitive market
d. identify and define the point of profit maximization for the purely competitive firm in the short run
e. identify, calculate, and graphically represent average, total, and marginal cost for a firm in a purely competitive market
f. demonstrate an understanding of the short-run equilibrium price for the firm and for the industry in a purely competitive market
g. demonstrate an understanding of profit maximization in the long run for the purely competitive firm
h. identify, calculate, and graphically represent the demand, marginal revenue, and total revenue of a pure monopolist
i. determine the point of profit maximization for a monopolist
j. determine the economic consequences of monopoly
k. identify and graphically represent the demand curve for a monopolistically competitive firm

l.   identify and define the point of profit maximization for a monopolistically competitive firm in the short run

m. explain the long-run profit for a monopolistically competitive firm

n.   identify forms of non-price competition

o.   demonstrate an understanding of the kinked demand curve of an oligopoly

p.   predict the likely effects of boycotts and cartels on prices and output

q.   demonstrate an understanding of the factors impacting a firm in an oligopoly

r.   determine the impact of market structures on a firm

Core Concepts for Market Structures and Pricing

- As with any normal good, the demand curve for the product of an **industry in perfect competition** is downward sloping (if the industry as a whole expects to increase sales, it must lower price).

  - However, since each **individual firm** can satisfy only a small part of the demand facing the industry, its **demand curve is perfectly elastic** (horizontal). Firms in perfect competition are therefore called price takers because they must sell at the market price.

- **Short-run profit maximization** is achieved when the excess of total revenue (TR) over total cost (TC) is largest. A second method applied to short-run production decisions is to compare marginal revenue (MR) and marginal cost (MC).

- For **all market structures**, a firm that does not shut down should produce the level of output at which **MR = MC**. As long as the next unit of output adds more in revenue (MR) than in cost (MC), the firm will increase total profit or decrease total losses.

- In the **long run**, the entry of new firms will eliminate economic profits by driving down the market price as the supply curve shifts to the right. If firms are incurring losses, some will leave the industry. The resulting leftward shift of the supply curve will increase the market price.

- A **natural monopoly** exists when economic or technical conditions permit only one efficient supplier. Examples are utilities, such as electricity and gas distribution.

- The **demand curve** facing a monopolist is downward sloping because, as with any normal good, the monopolistic firm can only sell more product by lowering price.

  - However, unlike a competitive firm, which faces only a very small portion of the whole industry's demand curve, the monopolistic firm's demand curve is the **entire industry's demand curve**.

- **Revenue maximization** is irrelevant to a monopolist. The rational choice is to maximize profits. The monopolist has the power to set output at the level where profits are maximized, that is, where MR = MC. The corresponding price is found with reference to the (downward-sloping) demand curve. This is called **price searching**.

- To maximize profits (or minimize losses) in the short run or long run, a firm in monopolistic competition produces at the level of output at which **MR = MC**.

- In the **long run**, a firm in monopolistic competition tends to earn only a normal profit.

- The price rigidity normally found in oligopolistic markets can be explained in part by the **kinked demand curve theory**. The essence of the theory is that firms will follow along with a price decrease by a competitor but not a price increase.

  - A firm that **raises price** will move into the **elastic portion** of the demand curve. Competitors have little incentive to follow suit, so the price-raising firm loses market share.

  - On the other hand, if the firm cuts price, it enters the **inelastic portion** of the demand curve. Competitors must cut their prices as well so that the first firm gains no market share.

- Price and quantity will therefore remain **"sticky"** at the original point on the demand curve.
- A **cartel** arises when a group of oligopolistic firms join together for price-fixing purposes. This practice is illegal except in international markets. A cartel is a **collusive oligopoly**. Its effects are similar to those of a monopoly.

Part 1 – Section A.5. The economy as a system of markets

The candidate should be able to:

a. explain the nature and significance of resource planning
b. define derived demand
c. define and calculate marginal revenue product and marginal revenue cost
d. identify the determinants of resource demand
e. define substitution resources and complementary resources
f. apply the principles of elasticity to resource demand
g. demonstrate an understanding of the profit maximizing combination of resources
h. contrast nominal wages and real wages
i. describe how productivity affects the level of wages
j. compare labor demand and labor supply in a purely competitive market and in a monopoly
k. determine the impact of unions on the level of wages
l. demonstrate an understanding of the issues related to the minimum wage
m. identify the impact of unionization on a firm
n. identify the extent to which the minimum wage impacts a firm

Core Concepts for the Economy as a System of Markets

- **Derived demand** is the demand for the inputs to the production process (sometimes called factors) derived from the demand for the outputs of the process (i.e., final goods).
- **Marginal productivity theory** applies the law of diminishing marginal returns to determine the optimal quantity and cost of resources. A firm will continue adding inputs to its production process as long as the marginal revenue gained by the additional input exceeds the marginal cost.

  - **Marginal revenue product (MRP)** equals marginal revenue times marginal product.
  - **Marginal resource cost (MRC)** is the additional cost incurred from the addition of a unit of input.
  - Just as a firm produces at the level of output where MR equals MC, a firm will continue to add inputs **until marginal revenue product equals marginal resource cost (MRP = MRC)**.

- Resources can be combined with one of two goals in mind:

  - The **cost of production is minimized** in the long run when the marginal product per dollar of every input is the same.
  - The formula for **profit-maximization** reflects both least-cost production and optimal output.

- Many firms are competing for a large number of equally skilled workers who provide their services independently, so neither firms nor workers can affect the **market rate for labor**. Thus, both firms and workers are necessarily **price takers**.
- The **supply curve for labor** facing a single firm is perfectly elastic, and MRC (the resource price) is therefore the same for all amounts of labor hired. The intersection of the supply curve (MRC) and the demand curve (MRP) is the profit maximization point.
- In some labor markets, workers only have the option of a **single employer**, as in the case of a company town. A market such as this, in which all sellers must sell to a single buyer, is called a **monopsony**.

- ■ A union may increase the **derived demand for labor** by increasing the demand for the firm's products, cooperate with management to enhance labor productivity, or work to raise the price of substitute resources.
- ■ Another union strategy is to **limit the supply** of labor. Thus, unions traditionally oppose immigration and support child labor laws and shorter work weeks.
  - ● One aspect of this approach, typically adopted by skilled workers, is **exclusive unionism**. An employer can hire only union members, and entry into the union is restricted. The wage rate rises and total employment falls.
  - ● An **inclusive unionism** approach attempts to expand membership to virtually all workers in an industry.

Part 1 – Section A.6. Issues in macroeconomics

The candidate should be able to:

a. identify the controversies surrounding the issues of inflation, unemployment, and economic growth

b. define the rate of inflation

c. distinguish nominal from real income

d. list the macroeconomic effects of inflation

e. define demand-pull inflation and cost-push inflation

f. define the unemployment rate

g. identify and define the different types of unemployment, including frictional unemployment, structural unemployment, and cyclical unemployment

h. explain full employment, including the concepts of the natural rate of unemployment and the economy's potential output

i. describe the macroeconomic effects of unemployment

j. interpret the graphical representation of the trade-off between inflation and unemployment

k. demonstrate an understanding of aggregate demand and aggregate supply both in the short run and long run, including the graphical representation of both

l. define economic growth and explain why it is an economic goal

m. interpret the production possibilities curve

n. demonstrate an understanding of demand-side and supply-side policies as used to increase economic growth and identify the limitations of each

o. determine the impact of demand-side and supply-side policies on a firm

p. determine the impact of inflation on the demand for and price of a firm's output

q. determine the impact of inflation on the supply and cost of a firm's factors of production

Core Concepts for Issues in Macroeconomics

- ■ The challenge of macroeconomics is to **balance inflation, unemployment, and growth**.
- ■ The **rate of inflation** is calculated by comparing the change in the two years' indexes:

$$\frac{Current\ year\ price\ index\ -\ Prior\ year\ price\ index}{Prior\ year\ price\ index}$$

  - ● **Demand-pull inflation** is generated by demand outpacing the supply of goods to satisfy it.
  - ● **Cost-push inflation** is generated by increased per-unit production costs, which are passed on to consumers in the form of higher prices.

■ The **unemployment rate** equals:

$$\frac{Number\ of\ unemployed}{Size\ of\ labor\ force} \times 100$$

■ **Excluded from the denominator** are the following:

  ● Those who are (1) under the age of 16 or (2) incarcerated or institutionalized.
  ● Homemakers, full-time students, retirees, and discouraged workers.

■ Among those who remain in the denominator, no distinction is made between **full- and part-time workers**; they are all considered equally employed. The numerator consists of those who are willing and able to work and who are seeking employment.

  ● **Frictional unemployment** is the amount of unemployment caused by the normal workings of the labor market.
  ● **Structural unemployment** results when the composition of the workforce does not match the need. It is the result of changes in consumer demand, technology, and geographical location.
  ● **Cyclical unemployment** is directly related to the level of an economy's output. For this reason, it is sometimes called deficient-demand unemployment.

■ The **natural rate of unemployment** consists of frictional and structural unemployment combined. Economists consider the economy to be at **full employment** when all unemployed workers fall into only these two categories. The rate varies over time because of demographic and institutional changes in the economy.

■ **Economic growth** takes place when both the aggregate demand and aggregate supply curves are driven to the right. Both the level of output and the price level increase. Growth is a major macroeconomic goal because when an economy grows, workers earn higher real wages and have access to a richer variety, and greater quantity, of goods and services. This is the essence of a **rising standard of living**.

■ **Productivity** is measured by the ratio of real output per unit of input. Productivity consists of three factors: the amount of capital, the state of technology, and workforce competence.

■ In modern economies, the government can deploy **demand-side policies** to either stimulate or suppress demand (depending on whether a recessionary or inflationary environment looms, respectively).

  ● The principal tools of **fiscal policy** used by government to stimulate aggregate demand are cutting personal taxes, increasing government spending, and increasing transfer payments.
  ● The principal tools of **monetary policy** used by government to stimulate aggregate demand are lowering the federal funds rate, making money easier to obtain; lowering the discount rate, making money easier to obtain; and buying back government securities on the open market, injecting cash into the economy.
  ● A **limitation** of all demand-side policies is that they may stimulate demand too much and lead to excessive inflation.

■ The government can also implement **supply-side policies**, which are intended to increase the country's stock of investment capital.

  ● The principal **tools** to stimulate aggregate supply are cutting business taxes, cutting capital gains taxes, and cutting taxes on income from savings.
  ● A **limitation** of all supply-side policies is that they may generate government budget deficits and may stimulate supply too much and lead to overcapacity.

Part 1 – Section A.7. Domestic output, national income, and price levels

The candidate should be able to:

    a.   define gross domestic product (GDP) and demonstrate an understanding of its components

    b.   calculate GDP using the expenditures approach and the income approach

    c.   define net domestic product (NDP), national income (NI), personal income (PI), and disposable income (DI)

    d.   distinguish among GDP, NDP, NI, PI, and DI and calculate one from another given relevant data

    e.   demonstrate an understanding of the importance of GDP as a measure of a country's economic prosperity

    f.   identify the challenges inherent in the calculation of GDP, including data collection and accuracy limitations

    g.   demonstrate an understanding of the price level and how it affects the measures of domestic output and national income

    h.   define the Consumer Price Index (CPI)

    i.   differentiate between nominal GDP and real GDP

    j.   demonstrate an understanding of the index of leading economic indicators as a forecast of GDP

Core Concepts for Domestic Output, National Income, and Price Levels

- **Gross domestic product (GDP)** is the principal measure of national economic performance.

    - GDP is the total market value of all **final goods and services** produced within the boundaries of the U.S. by **domestic- or foreign-owned sources** during a specified period of time (usually a year).

    - GDP is calculated without regard to the **ownership** of productive resources. Thus, the value of the output of a U.S.-owned factory abroad is excluded, but the output of a foreign-owned factory in the U.S. is included.

- Two approaches to calculating GDP:

Expenditures Approach:	**Income Approach:**
Consumption by households	Wages
+ Investment by businesses	+ Rents
+ Government purchases	+ Interest
+ Net exports	+ Profits
Gross domestic product	**National income**
	+ Indirect business taxes
	+ Net foreign-factor income
	Net domestic product
	+ Depreciation
	Gross domestic product

- To facilitate year-to-year comparisons, **nominal GDP** is adjusted for changes in the general price level so it can be reported in constant dollars. **Real GDP** = Nominal GDP ÷ Price index. The **Consumer Price Index (CPI)** is the most common price index for adjusting nominal GDP.

- Economists use the Conference Board's **index of leading indicators** to help them forecast future economic trends. The index is an aggregate of ten measures of economic activity. Each measure is meaningless in isolation; it is only the composite index which has predictive value.

Part 1 – Section A.8. Business cycles

The candidate should be able to:

- a.   define the term business cycle
- b.   define and identify on a graph the phases of the business cycle, including the peak, recession, the trough, and recovery
- c.   identify and describe possible causes of business cycles
- d.   describe the macroeconomic characteristics of the different phases of the business cycle
- e.   determine the impacts of business cycles on a firm's prices and output

Core Concepts for Business Cycles

- At a **peak**, the economy is at or near full employment and at or near maximum output for the current level of resources and technology. During a **recession**, income, output, and employment fall. In a **trough**, economic activity reaches its lowest ebb. During a **recovery**, output and employment rise. Eventually, the price level rises also.
- If businesses **cut back on their spending** during a downturn, their suppliers are forced to lay off large numbers of workers. If unemployment becomes widespread, it creates a cycle leading to more unemployment.
- Cycles are considered an **inherent aspect** of a capitalist system under classical economic theory.
- **Investment expenditure is a focal point** used by economists to explain business cycles.

Part 1 – Section A.9. Fiscal policy

The candidate should be able to:

- a.   define fiscal policy and distinguish discretionary from non-discretionary fiscal policy
- b.   identify the tools of fiscal policy
- c.   infer the macroeconomic consequences of both expansionary and contractionary fiscal policies, including the effect on aggregate demand when the level of government spending and/or taxes are changed
- d.   interpret the graphical representation of expansionary and contractionary actions
- e.   explain the effects of changes in taxation policies, including the effect on the distribution of income and the effect on resource allocation
- f.   explain the effects of public expenditure on the economy, including the redistribution of income and the impact on resource allocation
- g.   differentiate a budget deficit from a budget surplus
- h.   identify means of financing a budget deficit
- i.   define and identify built-in stabilizers
- j.   demonstrate an understanding of how a progressive tax system acts as a built-in stabilizer
- k.   compare and contrast cyclical and structural deficits
- l.   define recognition lag and the crowding-out effect
- m.   demonstrate an understanding of how inflation can arise from an expansionary fiscal policy
- n.   define supply-side fiscal policy
- o.   determine the impact that fiscal policies have on a firm (supply, demand, prices, and costs)

Core Concepts for Fiscal Policy

- **Fiscal policy** defines the government as one of the players in the marketplace, taking in revenues (taxes) and making purchases (the annual budget).
- When the current level of output and spending is less than the amount of which the economy is capable at full employment of all its resources, a **recessionary gap** is said to exist. In response, the government institutes **expansionary fiscal policies**, stimulating aggregate demand.
  - Taxes can be cut, putting more money in the hands of consumers.
  - Government can increase its spending, generating demand for goods and services from the private sector.
  - Transfer payments can be increased, putting more money in the hands of consumers.
- When the current level of output and spending exceeds the full-employment level, an **inflationary gap** exists. In response, the government institutes **contractionary fiscal policies**, suppressing aggregate demand.
  - Taxes can be increased, giving consumers less disposable income.
  - Government can cut its spending, reducing demand for goods and services from the private sector.
  - Transfer payments can be decreased, giving consumers less disposable income.
- As a dollar is spent and respent in the economy, it has a cumulative effect greater than the single amount. With each round of earning and spending, the effect of the dollar diminishes. This **multiplier effect** can be simplified as the reciprocal of the marginal propensity to save.
- **Keynesian theory** calls for expansionary fiscal policy during times of recession (to stimulate aggregate demand) and contractionary policy during boom times (to prevent inflation).
- The **budget deficit** is the sum of the cyclical deficit and the structural deficit.
  - A **cyclical deficit** is one that results from economic downturns and not from government action.
  - A **structural deficit** is the deficit that would exist at full employment if there was no downturn in the economy.
- **Recognition lag** is the time it takes for macroeconomists to recognize that a recession (or inflation) is occurring. **Administrative lag** is the time it takes for the government to act on macroeconomic changes. **Operational lag** is the time it takes for the changes implemented by the government to take effect; also called **response lag**.
- The theory behind **supply-side economics** is that **reducing taxes** makes more money available to businesses for capital investment, driving the aggregate supply curve to the right. The model used by supply-siders to explain this is called the **Laffer Curve**. The model holds that within certain ranges, lowering tax rates will actually generate more revenue for the government because output and national income will increase.

Part 1 – Section A.10. Money and monetary policy

The candidate should be able to:

a.   define the nature of money, including its functions as a medium of exchange, a unit of account, and a store of value

b.   demonstrate an understanding of the relationship between the interest rate and the demand for money

c.   define and identify the components of M1, M2, and M3

d.   define the velocity of money

e.   identify the role and functions of the Federal Reserve System (the Fed), including the Board of Governors and the Federal Open Market Committee, and demonstrate an understanding of how the Fed operates

f.   demonstrate an understanding of the commercial banking system and the creation of money

g.   define required reserves and excess reserves

h.   explain the monetary multiplier

i.   identify the goal of monetary policy as achieving a full-employment, noninflationary level of total output

j.   list the tools of monetary policy

k.   define money supply and be able to identify the graphical representation of the supply of and demand for money

l.   demonstrate an understanding of how open-market operations, a change in the reserve requirements ratio, and/or a change in the discount rate affect the money supply

m.   identify both the strengths and weaknesses of monetary policy

n.   determine the impact of monetary policy on a firm's availability and cost of funds

Core Concepts for Money and Monetary Policy

- The three most widely used metrics for the **supply of money** are M1, M2, and M3. Each successive category includes less and less liquid forms.

  - **M1** includes only the most liquid forms of money: currency (paper money & coins) and checking accounts.

  - **M2** adds the following to M1: savings accounts including money market accounts, small (<$100,000) time deposits, and money market mutual funds.

  - **M3** adds the following to M2: large (≥ $100,000) time deposits.

- The **velocity of money** is the number of times the average dollar is spent in a single year. A corollary of this idea is the **equation of exchange**: the amount expended during a year must be equal to the money supply (M) times the velocity (V): *Nominal GDP = M × V.*

- The **Federal Reserve System** was established in 1913. Instead of a single central bank as in many other countries, the United States has **twelve regional** Federal Reserve Banks. The Federal Reserve is independent of the rest of the federal government. This independence, and the long terms of its members, insulate the Fed's decisions from political pressures. The **Federal Open Market Committee (FOMC)** is responsible for administering monetary policy.

- **Roles of the Fed** include the following: open market operations, setting reserve requirements, serving as the bankers' bank, overseeing check collection, issuing currency, serving as fiscal agent for the U.S. government, and examining banks.

- The U.S. Bureau of Engraving and Printing does not create all the money there is. In addition to the federal government, **banks create money**. For example, a bank customer deposits $1,000 and the bank then loans out $800 of it. The depositor has a statement showing that (s)he has a claim on $1,000 of cash and the borrower has $800 of cash in his/her hand. $1,800 now exists where there was only $1,000 previously. The bank has just created $800.

- The Fed attempts to **balance the goals** of gradual, steady economic growth and price stability (manageable inflation). The Fed has **three tools** of monetary policy at its disposal to achieve these goals: open-market operations, the required reserve ratio, and the discount rate.

  - **Open-market operations** are the Fed's **most valuable tool**. When the Fed wishes to loosen the money supply, it purchases U.S. Treasury securities from commercial banks. When the Fed wishes to tighten the money supply, it sells Treasury securities to commercial banks.

    - These sales or purchases result in a shift of the **Federal funds rate**, which is the rate banks charge each other for overnight loans. When the Fed buys Treasury securities, the Federal funds rate falls. When the Fed sells Treasury securities, the Federal funds rate rises.

  - Changes in the **required reserve ratio** are used less frequently. Requiring banks to leave more funds in (noninterest-bearing) reserve accounts has a dramatic effect on profits.

  - The **discount rate** has come to reflect, rather than enact, changes the Fed wishes to make. The discount rate is the rate Federal Reserve banks charge to commercial banks that need loans.

    - After the Fed has put money into the economy by buying Treasury securities, the market reacts by lowering interest rates (since money is now easier to come by). The Fed then lowers the discount rate to match the interest rate action of the market.

10.2 BUSINESS ECONOMICS ESSAY QUESTIONS

Recall that your CMA Part 4 exam will probably contain six scenarios, with about three questions per scenario. There will be a recommended time allocation of 20 minutes, 30 minutes, or 45 minutes for each scenario and related questions.

One scenario will involve ethical issues, and probably one or two scenarios will include calculations and responses on a worksheet. Also, expect at least one scenario on organizational/behavioral topics. The remaining scenarios cover Parts 1, 2, and 3.

Scenario Title	Subtopic	Questions	Suggested Time
Minimum Wage Need	Minimum Wage and the Demand for Labor	1, 2, 3, 4	30 minutes
Soda Ash Need	Taxation and the Demand for Resources	5, 6	20 minutes
Miller Products Company	Labor Costs, Productivity, and Costs of Production	7, 8, 9	30 minutes
Ward Company	Effect of Tax Rebates on the Economy	10, 11, 12	20 minutes
Economic Theory	Supply, Demand, and Production Capacity	13, 14, 15	30 minutes
Keep Safe, Inc.	Elasticity and Price Setting	16, 17, 18, 19	30 minutes

Scenario for Essay Questions 1, 2, 3, 4

Your company manufactures butter and utilities in a labor-intensive production process. Oleo-margarine serves as a close substitute for your product and is produced through a capital-intensive process. Congress is considering a new measure that will raise the minimum wage from $5.15 to $7.25 over a one-year period. You are gravely concerned because the bulk of your workers are currently earning $5.15 per hour; very few oleo workers earn less than $7.25.

Questions

Present a thorough analysis of each of the following statements:

1. "All workers in the butter industry will clearly gain if the measure is passed."

2. "Butter will be priced out of the market."

3. "The workers who will really benefit are those in the oleo-margarine sector."

4. "Historically, employment in the butter industry has gone up with each increase in the minimum wage. This proves there are no adverse employment effects."

Essay Questions 1, 2, 3, 4 — Unofficial Answers

1. Only those butter workers who still have their jobs will gain. Since margarine is a close substitute, butter producers have little ability to raise prices. Producers' major buffer would likely be a substitution of capital for labor. Price increase or substitution means less employment. The exact response depends upon the elasticity of demand for butter workers, which in turn depends upon the elasticity of demand for butter.

2. Butter will tend to rise in price as producers attempt to recover higher costs. The demand curve for butter will not permit the price increase without a corresponding decrease in butter consumption. Producers will therefore reduce the supply of butter. On the other hand, the higher butter price will increase the demand for margarine, which also will tend to drive its price up. Finally, while butter and margarine may be close substitutes, they are certainly not perfect substitutes. The demand elasticity for butter will be limited by the many buyers who consider it to be a superior good, and who will continue to buy it even at a considerable price increase.

3. The increased demand for oleo would increase the derived demand for oleo workers and would tend to drive up their wages and employment.

4. No, this does not prove the nonexistence of adverse employment effects. These adverse effects may have been offset by:

    a. An increase in demand caused by such things as population increases and changing taste.

    b. The price of capital and land also going up. This increases the oleo-margarine price and reduces the incentive for consumers to switch from butter to oleo-margarine. In addition, the incentive for butter producers to substitute capital for labor is reduced.

Scenario for Essay Questions 5, 6

Soda ash is a raw material required for the production of glass. Soda ash can be manufactured synthetically by a procedure called the solvay process or mined as a natural soda ash, also referred to as trona.

The domestic sources of soda ash are adequate to supply all domestic glass production. The price of foreign soda ash is considerably higher; consequently, foreign sources of soda ash do not affect the domestic market.

The domestic soda ash industry has many firms and can be regarded as purely competitive. Consequently, no single firm in the industry can exert any degree of influence over the market price of soda ash. The short-run cost functions (fixed, variable, marginal, total) are identical for both solvay and trona producers.

The Environmental Protection Agency (EPA) is concerned with the pollutants being dumped into streams and rivers by solvay plants. EPA has received the suggestion that a $10-per-ton penalty tax be imposed on the output of producers employing the solvay process.

All firms in the domestic soda ash industry are earning a normal profit. Solvay producers could absorb the $10-per-ton penalty tax in the short run.

Questions

5. Explain the short-run effect a $10-per-ton penalty tax would have on the average fixed cost, average variable cost, average total cost, and marginal cost of solvay producers.

6. If the $10-per-ton penalty tax were imposed on solvay producers, explain the impact it would have on

    a. The supply curves of solvay and trona producers in the short run.
    b. Solvay producers in the long run.

Essay Questions 5, 6 — Unofficial Answers

5.   The $10-per-ton penalty tax levied on solvay production is a per-unit tax on variable cost which has no effect on average fixed cost. However, the tax will raise average variable cost by $10 per ton. The average total cost (average fixed cost plus average variable cost) will also increase $10 per ton due to the tax. Because each additional ton of solvay output will be taxed at $10, the marginal cost will rise $10.

6.   a.   The supply curve for a firm is that portion of the marginal cost curve which lies above the average variable cost curve. The $10-per-ton penalty tax would result in higher marginal costs for solvay producers in the short run which means that the supply curve of solvay producers will decline or shift upward and to the left. Trona producers will be unaffected in the short run, because their costs remain unchanged; therefore, their supply curve remains unchanged.

    b.   In the long run, solvay producers will exit from the market. Even though prices will rise in the short run because supply is reduced with demand unchanged, this will not be adequate to provide a normal return to solvay producers in the long run. Trona producers will earn an above normal profit, this will attract new trona producers, the industry supply curve will increase, and the price will return to the level that existed before the tax was imposed. At this price, with the added tax costs, solvay producers will earn less than a normal return and will leave the industry.

Scenario for Essay Questions 7, 8, 9

Miller Products Company is a medium-sized manufacturer of durable goods. Nearly half of Miller's costs are associated with the wages and employee benefits of its labor force. Miller Products is one of 15 firms in its industry, all with similar labor-intensive production methods.

Industry wages and benefits are set in industry-wide bargaining with a labor union. The settlements have led to rapidly escalating labor costs for several years. The current contract continues the 10% increase for wages and benefits for each of the next two years. Because there was industry-wide bargaining, all of Miller's competitors face similar labor cost problems.

However, labor productivity advances have varied within the industry. Miller's productivity increase, which has averaged one percent per year over the past five years, is much lower than the average three percent advance in the industry. Miller's management is distressed about the increased labor cost and lower relative increase in productivity and is attempting to evaluate the effect on Miller's costs, profitability, and position within the industry.

Questions

7. Discuss the interrelationships among labor costs, productivity, and cost of production. Specifically define the marginal productivity of labor and marginal cost of production as a part of your discussion.

8. Explain the impact the lower relative increase in productivity is likely to have on Miller Products Company's

   a. Costs,
   b. Profitability, and
   c. Position within the industry.

9. Identify alternative actions the management of Miller Products Company could undertake to correct its dilemma of increased labor cost and lower relative increase in productivity. Explain how the actions you identify would affect the results of the company's operations.

Essay Questions 7, 8, 9 — Unofficial Answers

7. The cost of production is increased by increased labor cost and decreased by reduced labor cost. The cost of production is increased by lower productivity and decreased by improved productivity. Changes in the cost of labor (an input) and the quantity of labor required per unit of output (productivity) interact resulting in change in the cost of production.

    The marginal productivity of labor is the increase in output that results from the addition of one unit of labor. The marginal cost of production is the total costs of the additional inputs required to produce one additional unit of output.

8. Miller's labor costs are rising faster than labor productivity, thus production costs will rise. Because productivity is rising at a slower rate than that of most competitors and labor cost increases are similar, Miller's production cost pressures will be more severe than competitors' pressures. This will mean declining profitability and likely a decline in Miller's position within the industry. The relatively higher increase in Miller's marginal cost may cause the firm to price its products slightly above competition, thus reducing market share. The relatively higher production cost increase probably will result in a narrower profit margin.

9. The feasible options available to Miller Products include:

    a. Upgrade the quality of workers hired.
    b. Improve training procedures for new and current employees.

    The above two items should improve productive because the workers will be able to do the tasks more efficiently.

    a. Install an employee bonus plan based upon productivity.
    b. Install an employee profit-sharing plan.

    The above two items should encourage the labor force to make an effort to do the tasks more efficiently because there is a monetary benefit from such effort.

    a. Replace old equipment with new, more efficient equipment.
    b. Redesign the manufacturing process to replace labor with capital equipment.

    The above two items should improve labor productivity by aiding the work force in production.

Scenario for Essay Questions 10, 11, 12

Ward, Inc. is a medium-sized durable goods manufacturing firm located in the midwest. During the past several years, Ward's business has been sluggish and production has been well below capacity. Ward's experience has reflected the disappointing growth of real gross domestic product (GDP) and the high unemployment rates that have existed in the U.S. economy.

Several members of the U.S. Congress have contemplated co-sponsoring a bill which would give an income tax rebate to individual taxpayers in an attempt to promote economic growth and reduce unemployment. The rebate would not apply to corporate taxpayers. The representatives are attempting to evaluate the expected impact of such a tax rebate on the U.S. economy.

Questions

10. Assume that the average taxpayer would receive a $250 income tax rebate and has a marginal propensity to consume disposable income of 0.8. Explain the effect the rebate can be expected to have on the average consumer's spending.

11. Assume that total rebates to be paid to all individual taxpayers in the United States would amount to $25 billion. Explain the effect the total rebates would be expected to have on (1) the U.S. gross domestic product and (2) the rate of unemployment in the United States.

12. Discuss the impact the proposed personal income tax rebate could be expected to have on the capacity, utilization of capacity, and earnings of a company such as Ward, Inc.

Essay Questions 10, 11, 12 — Unofficial Answers

10. The average consumer's disposable income would rise by $250, which will result in a $200 increase in spending when the marginal propensity to consume is considered.

11. An income tax rebate or a reduction in taxes, like an increase in investment, will raise the level of aggregate demand and set off the multiplier effect. The proper multiplier for tax charges is the ordinary multiplier minus 1 or 4 in this situation.

$$\frac{1}{1 - MPC} - 1 = \frac{1}{1 - .8} - \frac{.2}{.2} = \; = \frac{.8}{1 - .8} = \frac{.8}{.2} = 4$$

The gross domestic product will increase $100 billion ($25 billion × 4).

This increase in GDP will be associated with more production and employment. Therefore, the unemployment rate can be expected to decline.

12. The proposed tax rebate can be expected to have a significant positive impact on durable goods manufacturers such as Ward, Inc. The increase purchases will increase capacity utilization and the additional volume should result in increased earnings. If the increased economic activity can be sustained, this will result in an expansion in total production capacity.

Scenario for Essay Questions 13, 14, 15

Economic theory hypothesizes that the levels of output and prices are determined by the interaction of aggregate demand and aggregate supply. The downsloping aggregate demand curve represents the real national output that will be purchased by consumers, businesses, and governments at each possible price level. The aggregate supply curve represents the level of real national output that would be produced at each price level. The intersection of the aggregate demand curve (AD) and the aggregate supply curve (AS) determines the level of output and price level.

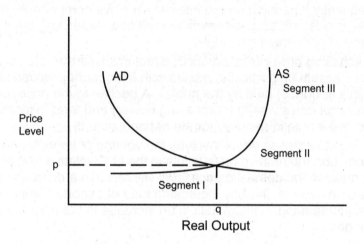

Questions

13. The downsloping aggregate demand curve implies that there is an inverse relationship between the price level and the level of real national output. The explanation for this relationship is based on three factors:

    a.   Real interest rate effect
    b.   Purchasing power (real balance) effect
    c.   Foreign purchases effect

    Using two of these factors, explain why the aggregate demand curve is downsloping.

14. The upsloping aggregate supply curve is envisioned as having three segments: *Segment I* with significant unused capacity, *Segment II* approaching full employment, and *Segment III* where full employment of resources is assumed. Briefly explain

    a.   Why the aggregate supply curve tends to slope upward to the right
    b.   The significance of the three segments of the aggregate supply curve

15. Describe the impact of two of the following economic changes on real national output as it relates to the aggregate supply (*Segment II*) and/or aggregate demand curves.

    a.   A decline in interest rates due to an increase in the money supply
    b.   An increase in personal income taxes
    c.   An increase in imports

Essay Questions 13, 14, 15 — Unofficial Answers

13.   The downsloping aggregate demand (AD) curve implies that there is an inverse relationship between the price level and the level of real national output. This relationship is primarily based on three factors, as explained below:

   a.   The real interest rate effect suggests that the rationale for the downsloping AD curve lies in the impact of the changing price level upon interest rates and in turn upon consumption and investment spending. This will allow interest rates to fall and, consequently, spending on the interest sensitive components of aggregate demand (capital goods, housing, automobiles) will rise, increasing the aggregate quantity demanded of the nation's output.

   b.   The purchasing power (real balance) effect involves the real value of the accumulated financial assets (in particular, assets with fixed money values such as savings accounts or bonds) held by the public. A decline in the price level will increase the real value of one's wealth (purchasing power) and tend to increase spending which, in turn, will increase demand for the nation's output.

   c.   The foreign purchases effect involves the volume of imports and exports, which depend upon the relative price levels in the U.S. relative to those in foreign countries. A decrease in the domestic price level will result in a decrease in imports and an increase in exports, thereby increasing the net exports component of the U.S. aggregate demand. This results in an increase in the aggregate U.S. goods demanded.

14.   a.   The reason the aggregate supply curve tends to slope upward to the right is that there is a positive relationship between the price level and the amount of real output that producers are willing to supply. The basic assumption is that per-unit production costs (average cost) of output increase as firms try to supply the growing market.

   b.   The significance of the three segments of the aggregate supply curve are as follows:

   1)   Segment I is horizontal and occurs when the real levels of national output are substantially lower than the full-employment output level and, therefore, significant amounts of unused machinery and equipment and unemployed workers are available.

   2)   Segment II is upward sloping. As the economy expands, some industries that require certain types of workers may encounter shortages while other industries are faced with substantial unemployment. In addition, raw-material shortages or other similar production bottlenecks may begin to appear. Some firms will be forced to use older and less efficient machinery as they approach capacity production and may hire less capable workers. Thus, the rising real output is accompanied by higher per-unit production costs and rising price levels.

   3)   Segment III is vertical and occurs once full employment is reached in all sectors and output cannot be further expanded. Individual firms will bid away resources from competing firms resulting in an increase in the price level.

15.   The impact of the following economic changes on the real national output, as it relates to the aggregate supply and/or aggregate demand curves, is as follows:

   a.   A decline in interest rates due to an increase in the money supply would have its initial impact on aggregate demand. Lower interest rates would stimulate business investment, as well as housing and durable expenditures.

   b.   An increase in personal taxes will decrease disposable income which, in turn, reduces aggregate demand and national output.

   c.   An increase in imports will decrease domestic net exports and decrease aggregate demand for U.S. products, and real output will decline.

Scenario for Essay Questions 16, 17, 18, 19

Keep Safe, Inc. manufactures computer disk drives. Its customers are virtually "locked in" to Keep Safe as their supplier, effectively giving the company a monopoly in this market. Keep Safe charges a premium price for its products; however, it does currently have one favored customer which is granted a discounted price.

Kevin Mitchell, Keep Safe's accounting manager, has a brother-in-law who is a top executive at Data Key, Inc., a large, well-established computer company. Data Key is planning to enter the market for notebook computers as a competitively priced, high-quality supplier. Mitchell approached Frederick Taylor, Keep Safe's sales manager, with the following proposal.

If Keep Safe will sell its disk drives to Data Key at the same discount that the favored company receives, Data Key will pay Taylor, personally, a fee for his service. The discount would be hidden from Keep Safe's top management and the competitors of Data Key. This discount would give Data Key a competitive advantage. There would be no rational business reason for this discount, since the cost to make these disk drives would be the same as for any other customer. Also, the volume would not be large enough to warrant a quantity discount. Mitchell says he will record the full amount of the sale and then "bury" the difference in accounts such as bad debts, returns, and quantity discounts.

The graphs below illustrate the two distinct markets for Keep Safe's disk drives.

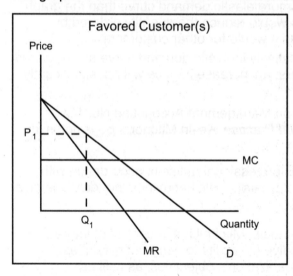

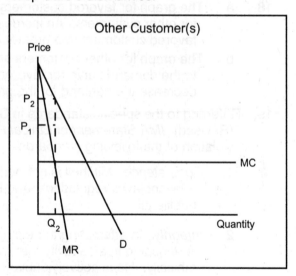

Questions

16. Identify the conditions that must be present for price discrimination to be possible.

17. The Robinson-Patman Act of 1936 prohibits price discrimination and other exclusionary practices that substantially lessen competition. Discuss the objectives of this law and how it might be applicable to Keep Safe, Inc. if Taylor were to pursue Mitchell's proposal to discount the drives sold to Data Key, Inc.

18. By referring to the different elasticities of demand shown in the two graphs above, describe how an increase in price would affect the quantity ordered for the following:

    a. Favored customer(s)
    b. Other customers

19. Referring to the specific standards (competence, confidentially, integrity, and credibility) in Statement on Management Accounting No. 1C, (Revised) *IMA Statement of Ethical Professional Practice*, discuss whether or not Mitchell's behavior is ethical and give the reasons for your conclusion.

Essay Questions 16, 17, 18, 19 — Unofficial Answers

16. The conditions that must be present for price discrimination to be possible are

   a. The seller must have market power and control over prices; i.e., a downward sloping demand curve.

   b. Buyers must have different elasticities of demand.

   c. Different buyers must be kept distinct, so that the low-price buyer does not resell to the high-price customer.

17. The objectives of the Robinson-Patman Act of 1936 are to maintain competition by protecting small business and maintaining equitable prices among buyers who compete with each other. The act prohibits any form of interstate price discrimination if the end result is to lessen competition. Further, the act specifically prohibits quantity discounts unless such discounts can be justified on the basis of cost differences to the manufacturer. If Keep Safe, Inc. were to provide the discount, it would likely be in violation of the Robinson-Patman Act. Keep Safe would be giving Data Key, Inc. a discriminatory price. There is no cost difference in providing disks to Data Key, and there are no other competitors offering a lower price.

18. a. The graph for favored customers shows a more elastic demand curve than the graph for other customers. An increase in price would reduce the quantity ordered by favored customers to a greater extent than it would for other customers.

   b. The graph for other customers shows a relatively inelastic demand curve as compared to the demand curve for favored customers; an increase in price will not significantly decrease the demand for the product.

19. Referring to the specific standards in Statement on Management Accounting No. 1C (Revised), *IMA Statement of Ethical Professional Practice*, Kevin Mitchell's behavior is in violation of the following standards.

   1. *Competence.* Mitchell is not performing his professional duties in accordance with relevant laws, regulations, and technical standards. His behavior is not only unethical but illegal.

   2. *Integrity.* In attempting to help his brother-in-law, Mitchell has a conflict of interest. He is engaging in an activity that would prejudice his ability to carry out his duties ethically. He is actively subverting the organization's objectives, as well as discrediting the profession.

   3. *Credibility.* Since Mitchell intends to "bury" the difference, he will not be communicating information fairly and objectively, he will not be disclosing all the relevant information, and he will not be disclosing deficiencies in information and internal controls.

10.3 GLOBAL BUSINESS REVIEW

<u>Part 1 – Section B.1. Global trade</u>

The candidate should be able to:

  a.   define terms commonly associated with global trade, including net exports and net imports
  b.   define and demonstrate an understanding of the terms of trade (or exchange ratio)
  c.   interpret the production possibilities curves and determine the cost ratio for the two products on the graph
  d.   determine the gains from trade and the resulting trading possibilities curve
  e.   define and demonstrate an understanding of the principle of comparative advantage
  f.   identify the advantages and disadvantages of free trade from the point of view of a country and the point of view of an individual firm
  g.   define protectionism and identify the barriers to free trade
  h.   define and analyze effects of tariffs, import quotas, nontariff barriers, voluntary export restrictions, trigger pricing, and antidumping rules on a country, an industry, and an individual firm
  i.   analyze domestic policies to promote exports, including export subsidies
  j.   identify the function of the Export-Import Bank
  k.   discuss the arguments used to support protectionism
  l.   identify the economic and social costs of protectionism
  m.   estimate the impact of protectionism on industries and firms
  n.   graphically analyze the supply and demand of exports and imports
  o.   differentiate among a customs union, a common market, and an economic union
  p.   identify the key international agreements on trade including the European Union, General Agreement on Tariffs and Trade (GATT), North American Free Trade Agreement (NAFTA), and the World Trade Organization (WTO)

Core Concepts for the Advantages of Trade

  ■   The laws of supply and demand affect imports and exports in the same way that they affect domestic goods. The term **net exports** refers to the amount of a country's exports minus its imports. Conversely, a nation can have **net imports** if its imports exceed its exports.

  ■   **Terms of trade** (the exchange ratio) is the ratio of a country's export price index to its import price index, multiplied by 100. When the ratio falls, a country is said to have deteriorating terms of trade. When the ratio is less than 100, the country is an overall loser in terms of world trade.

  ■   **Countries vary greatly** in their efficiency in producing certain goods because of the immobility of resources. This variation can be largely attributed to differences from country to country in the following five factors: climatic and geographical conditions, human capacities, supply and type of capital accumulation, proportions of resources, and political and social climates.

  ■   Given these differences, it is clear that countries can **mutually benefit from trade**. The greatest advantage from trade is obtained when **each nation specializes** in producing what it can produce most efficiently or, more precisely, least inefficiently. If nations specialize and then exchange with others, more is produced and consumed than if each nation tries to be self-sufficient.

- The explanatory mechanism for this phenomenon is **comparative advantage**. This principle is based on relative opportunity costs. A country has a comparative advantage in a given product when its opportunity cost for generating that product is lower than another country's, that is, when it has to give up fewer units of some other product in order to increase production. The principle of comparative advantage is so powerful, it even applies when one country has an **absolute advantage** in both products.

- If two countries specialize in generating the product in which each has a comparative advantage and then engage in trade, the world has more of both products than if they did not specialize. Thus, **specialization and trade** enhance world output without changing total inputs. Moreover, the greater abundance of affordable goods means that workers in both countries experience **higher real wages**.

- **Developing countries** exporting primarily raw materials are dependent on vibrant economies in developed (importing) countries. Even when one country is technologically superior in all industries, one of the industries will go out of business when free trade takes place. Therefore, **technological superiority** is no guarantee of continuing operation in a case of free trade. A country must have a comparative advantage in the production of a good, not necessarily an absolute advantage, to guarantee continuing production when free trade exists.

- A high-wage country with a comparative advantage for a product will see that product survive even though the laborers in the developing country have lower wages. Thus, a **knowledge of wage rates is not sufficient** information to determine which country's industry would decline under free trade.

- For nations to receive the full advantages of international specialization and exchange, free trade **must be allowed among all countries**. Trade barriers cause **resources to be misallocated** in the country that established the barrier because inputs are used to produce products that could be produced more economically in other countries.

Core Concepts for Trade Barriers

- Even though individuals (on the whole) are best off under free trade, **governments** often establish policies designed to **interfere** in the workings of the marketplace. Until the free-trade movement in the late 18th and early 19th centuries, it was the policy of governments around the world to actively impede trade.

- Trade barriers take many forms:

  - **Protectionism** is any measure taken by a government to protect domestic producers. Protectionism takes many forms.

  - **Tariffs** are consumption taxes designed to restrict imports, e.g., a tax on German beer. Governments raise tariffs to discourage consumption of imported products.

  - **Import quotas** set fixed limits on different products, e.g., French wine.

  - **Domestic content rules** require that at least a portion of any imported product be constructed from parts manufactured in the importing nation.

  - **Voluntary export restrictions** are agreements entered into by exporters to reduce the number of products made available in a foreign country in an attempt to avoid official sanctions.

  - A **trigger price mechanism** automatically imposes a tariff barrier against unfairly cheap imports by levying a duty (tariff) on all imports below a particular reference price (the price that "triggers" the tariff).

  - **Antidumping rules** prevent foreign producers from "dumping" excess goods on the domestic market at less than cost to squeeze out competitors and gain control of the market.

  - **Exchange controls** limit foreign currency transactions and set exchange rates. The purpose is to limit the ability of a firm selling in a country to repatriate its earnings.

  - **Export subsidies** are payments by the government to producers in certain industries in an attempt to increase exports.

- **Special tax benefits to exporters** are an indirect form of export subsidy. Certain exports may require **licenses.**

- The **Export-Import Bank**, or Ex-Im, is the federal government's official export credit agency. While initially designed to support the credit needs of exporters and to promote exports, the organization has also, at various times, served as a policy tool of the White House. By the 1990s, the guaranteeing of loans made by other financial institutions had become the primary activity of the Ex-Im.

- The **economic effects of tariffs and quotas** can be summarized as follows:

  - **Workers are shifted** from relatively efficient export industries into less efficient protected industries. Real wages decline as a result, as does total world output.

  - Under a **tariff**, the excess paid by the customer for an imported good goes into government coffers where it can be spent on domestic concerns. Under a **quota**, prices are also driven up (by the induced shortage), but the excess goes to the exporter in the foreign country.

  - A **tariff** is laid on all importers equally; thus, the more efficient ones will still be able to set their prices lower than the less efficient ones. An import **quota**, on the other hand, does not affect foreign importers equally and import licenses can be assigned as much for political favoritism as on any other grounds.

- Advocates of trade barriers advance three basic **arguments in favor** of protectionism: reducing imports protects domestic jobs; certain industries are essential to national security; and infant industries need protection in the early stages of development.

- Considering two nations and one product, **global equilibrium** cannot be at the equilibrium point of either of the two countries. This is because for world trade to take place, one country must have an excess supply and the other must have excess demand. By definition, world exports must equal world imports.

Core Concepts for Trade Agreements

- **Economic integration** is the joining of the markets from two or more nations into a free-trade zone. Examples of economic blocs of trading nations are the European Union and the North American Free Trade Agreement (NAFTA). Generally, the trading bloc provides trading incentives to member nations and discriminates against nonmember nations.

- The **European Union (EU)** is an economic and political association of European countries. Currently, the EU consists of 25 member states. It provides a **single market for goods and services** without any economic barriers.

- Under the **General Agreement on Tariffs and Trade (GATT)**, the signatory countries agreed to equal treatment of all member nations, multilateral negotiations to reduce tariffs, and the abolition of import quotas. However, GATT has now been replaced by the **World Trade Organization (WTO)**. The WTO Agreement is a permanent set of commitments by more than 120 nations designed to prohibit trade discrimination among member nations and between imported and domestic products. Most of the rules of GATT are still applicable with respect to trade in goods. The WTO provides for a multilateral **dispute settlement** apparatus.

- The **North American Free Trade Agreement (NAFTA)** basically provides for free trade among the U.S., Canada, and Mexico. NAFTA arranged for the gradual phasing-out over a period of 15 years of tariffs on almost all products sold between the three countries. Unlike the European Union, NAFTA did not create a new set of administrative bodies to oversee the trading activities of the three member nations. It simply removed barriers to trade.

- The **theory** behind free trade zones is that they benefit consumers by lowering prices and that manufacturers and workers gain from expanded markets for the items each country produces most efficiently.

Part 1 – Section B.2. Foreign exchange

The candidate should be able to:

a.   demonstrate an understanding of a nation's balance of payments

b.   define and identify the components of the current account, the capital account, and the official reserves account

c.   define trade deficits, identify their causes, and explain their implications

d.   calculate the balance of payment deficit or surplus

e.   compare and contrast a flexible or floating exchange-rate system and a fixed exchange-rate system

f.   graphically determine the exchange rate under a flexible exchange-rate system

g.   calculate whether a currency has depreciated or appreciated against another currency over a period of time

h.   infer the effect on the price of goods with a change in the exchange rate

i.   calculate the effective interest rate on a foreign currency loan

j.   identify the determinants of exchange rates under a flexible exchange-rate system

k.   list the advantages and disadvantages of a flexible exchange-rate system

l.   explain the methods used to maintain a fixed exchange rate system, including the use of reserves, trade policies, exchange controls, exchange rationing, and domestic macroeconomic adjustments

m.   describe managed floating exchange rates

n.   analyze the impact of changes in foreign exchange rates on a firm

o.   identify mechanisms available to firms to mitigate the impact of changes in exchange rates

Core Concepts for the Balance of Payments

- A country's **balance of payments** is the combination of two accounts, the current account and the capital account.

  - The **current account** records the net of all cross-border exchanges of goods, services, interest and dividends payments, and non-reciprocal transfers such as foreign aid and transmittals to relatives.

  - The **capital account** records the net of all cross-border exchanges of capital assets and financial instruments.

  - A third account is the **official reserves account**, which keeps track of transactions involving the central bank and its official reserve assets, such as gold and foreign currency.

- To summarize:

  - Balance of trade = Exports of goods – Imports of goods
  - Balance on goods and services = Exports of services – Imports of services
  - Balance on current account   = Balance of trade
                                    + Balance on goods and services
                                    + Net investment income
                                    + Net transfers

  - Balance on capital account = Capital inflows + Capital outflows
  - Balance of payments = Balance on current account + Balance on capital account
  - Official reserves account offsets balance of payments

- A country has an **unfavorable balance** of payments when money flowing to other countries exceeds money flowing in. To compensate for the unfavorable balance, the central bank must hold **reserves of its own currency**. This depletes the reserves of foreign currency and ties up domestic funds that could be used for other purposes.

Core Concepts for Foreign Currency Rates and Markets

- In general, when the **demand for a country's merchandise**, capital assets, and financial instruments rises, **demand for its currency rises**. The **exchange rate** is the price of one country's currency in terms of another country's currency.

- By 1973, it was clear that any governmental intervention in currency markets was unworkable and a **floating exchange rate system** was established. Despite this, some countries continue to fix their currencies (e.g., the Saudi riyal and the Chinese yuan).

- As exchange rates **fluctuate**, buying power rises and falls. Currency appreciates when it can buy more units of another currency. Currency depreciates when it can purchase fewer units of another currency. **Equilibrium exchange rates** in floating markets are determined by the supply of and demand for the currencies.

- During periods of extreme fluctuation in the value of a nation's currency, intervention by governments or central banks may occur to maintain fairly stable exchange rates. This is called a **managed float**. Floating rates permit adjustments to eliminate balance of payments deficits or surpluses.

  - **Long-term** exchange rates are dictated by the purchasing-power parity theorem. In the long run, real prices should be the same worldwide for a given good. Exchange rates will adjust until purchasing-power parity is achieved.

  - **Medium-term** exchange rates are dictated by the economic activity in a country. If more goods are exported because of an increased preference for U.S. goods, the demand curve for dollars shifts to the right, causing upward pressure on the value of the dollar.

  - **Short-term** exchange rates are dictated by interest rates. Big corporations and banks invest their large reserves of cash where the real interest rate is highest. A rise in the real interest rate in a country will lead to an appreciation of the currency because it will be demanded for investment at the higher real interest rate.

- To determine the **effective interest rate on a foreign currency loan**, multiply the amount lent by the conversion rate in effect at the time. Next, multiply the maturity amount (principal + interest) by the conversion rate in effect on the date of maturity. Divide the difference in these two amounts by the first amount. The result is the effective rate.

- The **spot rate** is the exchange rate paid for immediate delivery of a currency. The **forward exchange rate** is the future price of the currency. If the forward rate in foreign currency units per dollar is greater than the spot rate, the dollar is selling at a **premium** in the forward market. If the spot rate in foreign currency units per dollar is greater than the forward rate, the dollar is selling at a **discount** in the forward market.

Part 1 – Section B.3. Other global topics

The candidate should be able to:

a. summarize the functions of the World Bank and the International Monetary Fund
b. define direct foreign investment and demonstrate an understanding of how it can benefit a firm
c. define an American depository receipt (ADR)
d. identify and explain the benefits of international diversification
e. define direct foreign investment
f. identify the risks of direct foreign investment, including political risk and exchange rate risk
g. demonstrate an understanding of the issues inherent in multinational capital budgeting and financing
h. calculate the overall expected return and variance of a "portfolio" of projects
i. identify and explain methods of payment for international trade, including prepayment, letters of credit, sight drafts, time drafts, consignment, and open account

j.   identify and explain common trade financing methods, including cross-border factoring, letters of credit, banker's acceptances, forfaiting, and countertrade

k.   demonstrate an understanding of how transfer pricing is used by multinational firms to manage their effective worldwide tax rate

l.   identify legal and ethical issues in conducting business worldwide

Core Concepts for Other Global Topics

- From 1944 until 1971, a system of fixed exchange rates based on a modified gold standard was in use. International reserves in this system included foreign currencies and the right to borrow in specified situations. The **Bretton Woods Conference**, where this system was agreed to, also led to the **formation of two important bodies** still in existence today:

  - Resources of the **International Monetary Fund (IMF)** consist of a pool of currency from which participating countries can draw during short-term balance of payments difficulties.

  - The **World Bank**'s purpose is to provide credit for development purposes to underdeveloped countries.

- **Eurodollars** are U.S. dollars held at banks outside of the U.S., either foreign banks or branches of U.S. banks. The growth in the use of Eurodollars has been spectacular because they facilitate the exchange of goods between other nations (often the exchanges use dollars even if the U.S. is not involved in the transaction).

- **Eurobonds** are sold in one country but denominated in the currency of another country. Their advantage is that they are usually less stringently regulated than most other bonds. Thus, transaction costs are lower. They are not always denominated in Eurodollars.

- The **euro** (€) is the new common currency adopted by most members of the European Union. Its phase-in period began in 1999. It is not to be confused with the Eurodollar.

- **Methods of payment** for international trade include prepayment, letters of credit, sight drafts, time drafts, consignment, and open account.

- **Methods of financing** international trade include cross-border factoring, banker's acceptances, forfaiting, and countertrade.

- **Multinational corporations** have both benefits for and adverse effects on both their home and host countries.

- A **direct foreign investment** involves buying equipment and buildings in a foreign country for a new company. The advantages of a direct foreign investment include lower taxes in the foreign nation, annual depreciation allowances for the amount invested, and access to foreign capital sources.

- When determining whether to operate a foreign subsidiary, a company must take the following **factors** into account: tax differences, restrictions on remittances, administrative fees, currency fluctuations, salvage value, host-country government policies, and any nonfinancial considerations.

- Multinational corporations frequently derive income from several countries. The government of each country in which a corporation does business may enact statutes imposing one or more types of **tax** on the corporation. **Transfer pricing** is an important aspect of the tax calculation for multinational corporations that transfer inventories between branches in different countries.

- The **Foreign Corrupt Practices Act (FCPA)**, a federal law passed in 1977, makes it a requirement for firms to have adequate internal control systems. The Act amends the Securities Exchange Act of 1934 to make certain payments to foreign officials and other foreign persons unlawful, and to require maintenance of accurate records. It also makes the offer, payment, or authorization of any gift of value to foreign officials and other persons for corrupt purposes unlawful by any domestic concern.

10.4 GLOBAL BUSINESS ESSAY QUESTIONS

Recall that your CMA Part 4 exam will probably contain six scenarios, with about three questions per scenario. There will be a recommended time allocation of 20 minutes, 30 minutes, or 45 minutes for each scenario and related questions.

One scenario will involve ethical issues, and probably one or two scenarios will include calculations and responses on a worksheet. Also, expect at least one scenario on organizational/behavioral topics. The remaining scenarios cover Parts 1, 2, and 3.

Scenario Title	Subtopic	Questions	Suggested Time
Trade Barriers	Protectionism	1, 2, 3	30 minutes
Balance of Payments	Balance of payments	4, 5, 6	30 minutes
Deerfield Devices, Inc.	Investing in Foreign Countries	7, 8, 9	30 minutes
Multinational Corporation	Investing in Foreign Countries	10, 11	30 minutes

Scenario for Essay Questions 1, 2, 3

In the early 1930s, as countries sought to increase employment by raising tariffs, world-wide protectionism reached a new high. Since then, there has been a downward trend in tariffs resulting from many international and regional agreements. On January 1, 1995, the World Trade Organization (WTO) replaced the General Agreement on Tariffs and Trade (GATT) as the main international agreement enabling free trade. The WTO is a permanent set of commitments by more than 120 nations designed to prohibit trade discrimination among member nations and between imported and domestic products.

In addition to the global agreement embodied in the WTO, groups of neighboring countries have formed regional agreements. Examples of regional agreements include the 1993 North American Free Trade Agreement joining Canada, Mexico, and the United States as a tariff-free trading zone, and the 1957 Treaty of Rome which was the beginning of the European Union. The European Union, a common market or customs union, not only provides for free trade among its members but also facilitates the free movement of labor and capital. Despite these efforts to increase free trade, protectionist sentiments remain strong in both the United States and Europe.

Questions

1. Increased tariffs were used in the 1930s in an effort to increase employment. Discuss why this may not be a valid argument for the use of tariffs or other trade barriers.

2. In conjunction with the reduction in tariffs and quotas in the 1970s and 1980s, there has been an increase in the use of nontariff barriers to trade. Identify and describe at least two nontariff barriers to international trade.

3. Discuss at least five arguments, other than increased employment, that are used to justify protectionism.

Essay Questions 1, 2, 3 — Unofficial Answers

1. The long-run impact of tariffs is not to increase domestic employment but to reallocate workers away from export industries toward protected domestic industries. For example, if U.S. imports are restricted, foreign nations will no longer have dollars with which to purchase U.S. exports and may choose to purchase goods from countries with no tariff restrictions. As a consequence, export industries are likely to decline while the protected domestic industries may increase. Because the export industries that decline tend to be more efficient (due to comparative advantages) than the protected industries that expand, this shift implies a less efficient use of resources and may cause higher prices.

2. At least two nontariff barriers to international trade include

   a. Import quotas, i.e., limiting the amount of imported goods that can enter the domestic market. Quotas are targeted by product.

   b. Local content requirements which generally specify that a certain percentage of a finished good must be made from domestically produced parts in order for the finished product to be considered domestically produced.

3. At least five arguments, other than increased employment, that are used to justify protectionism include the following:

   a. To promote greater diversification and insulate the domestic economy from international political developments, depressions abroad, and social and cultural adversities.

   b. To preserve or strengthen industries producing strategic goods and materials essential for defense or technological advancements.

   c. To protect research and development investments and "infant industries" to allow them to establish themselves. This could foster inefficient production. It could also limit the market to the industry's domestic market.

   d. To counter stiff competition from foreign markets and persistent trade deficits which could adversely affect the domestic economy. The balance of payments is favorably affected by a country with trade barriers.

   e. To retaliate against trading partners that restrict the sale of U.S. products in their countries. Protection against unfair or predatory trade practices.

Scenario for Essay Questions 4, 5, 6

As the world has evolved into a global economy, a country's balance of payments has taken on increasing significance as it tracks the nation's financial and competitive position. As a result, there is a greater need to understand how governments record international trade and investments. In recent years, the United States, once the world's largest creditor nation, has had a negative net foreign investment balance and become the world's largest debtor nation.

Questions

4. Define each of the components of the balance of payments listed below and describe the U.S. experience in the last decade.

   a. The trade balance in the current account
   b. The balance of the capital account
   c. The reserves in the official financing account

5. Explain why the U.S. dollar has had a high value relative to other currencies and how this has helped to contribute to the United States becoming a debtor nation.

6. Discuss how being a debtor nation has affected U.S. competitiveness in the global marketplace.

Essay Questions 4, 5, 6 — Unofficial Answers

4.   a.   The trade balance in the current account records all international transactions involving the purchase or sale of physical products between domestic and foreign residents. Sales to residents of foreign countries are recorded as merchandise exports; purchases by domestic residents are considered merchandise imports. The trade balance is sometimes referred to as the merchandise trade balance, meaning that service exports and imports are not included. Throughout most of the 1980s, the U.S. trade balance had an increasing deficit year by year; however, in recent years, this trend has reversed and the U.S. trade balance has shown a lowering of yearly deficits.

       b.   The balance of the capital account reflects international capital flows involving the purchase or sale of real and financial assets. Real assets include real estate and equipment, while financial assets include stocks and bonds. The capital account reports the purchase and sale of these assets located in other countries by Americans, as well as the purchase and sale of U.S. assets by foreign citizens. Over the past decade, the U.S. capital account has reflected a surplus balance; this is often the case when there is a deficit in the trade account as the deficit in the trade account is financed by the surplus in the capital account. As the trade deficit has decreased in recent years, so have the annual changes to the surplus in the capital account.

       c.   The official financing account records all of the international financial transactions between the monetary authorities and the central banks of foreign countries. When monetary authorities intervene in the currency markets by buying or selling dollars, this is reflected as a net change in the reserves of the official financing account. This account is used to settle net differences between the current account and the capital accounts, and the official reserves are held by the central banks in the form of foreign currencies. During the early 1980s, monetary authorities tended not to intervene in the currency market with respect to the dollar. However, in recent years the U.S. has been actively buying and selling dollars on the currency markets as the current account deficit has exceeded the capital account surplus.

5.   The high value of the U.S. dollar during the 1980s can be attributed to the relatively high real interest rates in the U.S. when compared to other regions of the world. Foreign investors were attracted to the higher rates of return earned in the U.S., which created a large demand for dollars on the exchange markets as foreigners had to convert their currencies into dollars in order to buy U.S. investments. The elevated value of the U.S. dollar contributed to the current account deficit by raising the price of U.S. exports and lowering the price of foreign imports. Since U.S. exports did not earn sufficient foreign exchange to pay for foreign imports, the U.S. borrowed from the rest of the world to finance the current account deficit. The financing of large trade deficits caused foreigners to accumulate a larger volume of claims against U.S. assets than the U.S. had against foreign assets. As a result, the U.S. became a net debtor with the rest of the world in the late 1980s.

6.   As a result of the U.S. status as a debtor nation, the continuing trade deficits, and the high value of the dollar, U.S. firms are at a competitive disadvantage against foreign goods and services. A high value for the dollar causes the foreign price of U.S. exports to increase and the dollar price of U.S. imports to fall. These factors have caused reduced aggregate demand for U.S. goods and services, resulting in lower levels of real national output and employment. Also, the high debt payments paid by the U.S. leave fewer dollars available to invest in capital spending.

Scenario for Essay Questions 7, 8, 9

Deerfield Devices, Inc., a U.S. manufacturer of computer peripheral equipment, is considering establishing an overseas manufacturing facility. The reduced costs of this facility, particularly lower wage rates, would allow Deerfield to compete more effectively as the company has become vulnerable to lower-cost, imported peripheral equipment. Deerfield has investigated many opportunities over the past year and has now narrowed the field to the following three alternatives.

- The government of Brazil has expressed interest in having Deerfield locate its plant in Brasilia, and Deerfield is interested in increasing its presence in the South American market. However, Brazil's trade regulations regarding the type of investment being proposed by Deerfield require that Deerfield form a joint venture with a local partner. Deerfield would have a minority share in the joint venture but would maintain operating control by controlling the technology. In addition, Deerfield would have to operate under foreign exchange regulations that would restrict the amount of profits the company would be allowed to repatriate each year.

- Nigeria has made an attractive offer to Deerfield that includes support from the local government, local investment in the building of the facility, and the purchase of a portion of the plant's output. In return, Deerfield must enter into a countertrade agreement with Nigeria whereby Deerfield would accept payment in the form of goods for the peripheral equipment purchased by Nigeria.

- Deerfield is also interested in locating its plant in Mexico City as distribution throughout the United States would be less difficult than from the other locations being considered. In addition, the plant would be close to Deerfield's headquarters in Houston, Texas. Mexico has offered both tariff and tax relief as well as local equity investment to encourage Deerfield to locate there. However, Deerfield must enter into a buy-back arrangement whereby the company would agree to purchase 75% of the total output of the manufacturing plant for the next 4 years.

Questions

7. Discuss the reasons a host country would

   a. Require foreign investors to form joint ventures with local nationals
   b. Restrict the repatriation of profits

8. Explain why some host countries insist on countertrade agreements.

9. Describe several benefits investing companies expect to receive when agreeing to participate in countertrade and buy-back arrangements.

Essay Questions 7, 8, 9 — Unofficial Answers

7. a. The reasons a host country would require foreign investors to form joint ventures with local nationals include

    1) Participation in dividend policies, transfer pricing decisions, and other strategic control issues

    2) Promotion of the transfer of technology and increased employment

    3) Sharing in the profits from foreign investment

    4) Retaining control of their industries and resources

    b. The reasons a host country would restrict the repatriation of profits include

    1) Reduction of the drain on foreign reserves from the host country that are needed to buy other necessities

    2) Retention of the profits for a longer period of time to improve chances of success

    3) Protection of local investment and encouragement for foreign investors to stay longer

8. Host countries insist on countertrade agreements to

    a. Stimulate their own economies

    b. Act as a positive influence on their balance of payments transactions

    c. Gain access to new markets by using the marketing skills and outlets of the purchasing companies

9. Benefits investing companies expect to receive when agreeing to participate in countertrade and buy-back arrangements include

    a. Gaining access to new international markets

    b. Gaining new sources of supply such as natural resources

    c. Obtaining lower costs and increased profits from lower wages and other production costs

    d. Relief from local taxes

    e. Capital loans and equity investments to defray start-up costs

Scenario for Essay Questions 10, 11

Almost all major United States companies have production facilities and marketing outlets throughout the world, and the pace of multinationalism has accelerated in recent years. By the early 1970s, United States multinationals conducted one-quarter of the world's merchandise export trade. During the period from 1999 to 2003, direct investment in the U.S. by foreign companies fluctuated between about $50 billion and about $330 billion. Investment abroad by U.S. companies ranged from about $120 billion to about $255 billion. A few U.S. corporations have more than half of their assets in foreign countries. In aggregate terms, roughly 400 multinational enterprises produce perhaps as much as one-third of the free world's industrial output.

Multinational corporations have wholly-owned foreign subsidiaries, partially-owned foreign joint ventures, and/or patent and trademark licensing agreements abroad. Some of the more sophisticated corporations have foreign research and development activities and multinational management organizations.

Questions

10. Describe the reasons why firms decide to become multinational.

11. Identify and describe both the advantages and disadvantages of multinational corporations from the point of view of the

    a. Home country
    b. Host country

Essay Questions 10, 11 — Unofficial Answers

10. Most firms become multinational to expand markets and improve profit potential. Many multinational firms began with efforts to secure national resources that were not available in the home country. These firms were seeking long-term security rather than cost savings. Expansion into foreign markets often occurs where firms have a monopolistic advantage over the foreign competition. This advantage is associated with advanced technology, strong product differentiation, or economies of scale, and is frequently protected by proprietary knowledge or trademarks. Without these special advantages, the foreigner would be at a disadvantage as local firms would be more familiar with local markets, laws, and customs. Because of import tariffs, high transportation costs, and national purchasing policies, firms frequently have difficulty increasing market share in foreign countries. Rather than contend with these barriers, firms establish production facilities and distribution centers in the foreign countries, thereby overcoming economic disadvantages. To improve their competitive position, many firms establish foreign facilities to take advantage of less expensive resources.

11. a. The advantages of multinational corporations from the point of view of the country include the following: Direct foreign investment often has a favorable balance of payments effect from profits, dividends, and patent royalties. While there may be an initial transfer of capital abroad, this capital does not always come from the home country. In addition, many multinationals export components for assembly abroad, and these exports help the home country's balance of payments. Multinationals promote international trade, contribute to the effectiveness of international monetary arrangements, and help maintain liberal trade policies. The profits and knowledge gained from foreign operations may be used to expand or improve home industries.

   The disadvantages of multinational corporations from the point of view of the home country include the following: Because the foreign investment of some multinationals replaces exports from the home country, there is a negative effect on the balance of payments. When factories are built abroad, jobs are exported, and corporations have the option of moving additional operations out of the country. Multinationalism may give a corporation certain advantages in its home market that purely domestic rivals cannot match. The advantages include vertical integration, the spreading of joint costs over many markets, and the use of foreign profits to boost the home market position. Multinationals may be subject to the risk of foreign expropriation of assets.

   b. The advantages of multinational corporations from the point of view of the host country include: Multinationals can promote economic development and prosperity in the host country. The infusion of capital can mobilize host country resources, boosting output and efficiency. Expanding exports improve the host country's balance of payments. The introduction of new technology by multinationals saves less-developed countries the costs of developing technology and adds to the country's productive capabilities. Local employment usually increases and results in an improved standard of living. Multinationals provide training for skilled workers and managers.

   The disadvantages of multinational corporations from the point of view of the host country include the following: Multinationals may contribute to a net capital outflow in the host country as profits are repatriated and royalties are paid. Capital outflow problems can be aggravated by arbitrary transfer prices among multinational subsidiaries. This is done to move profits to those countries where taxes are low or to evade laws restricting repatriation of profits. Multinationals may cause inappropriate technology to be introduced. Most advanced technology is capital-intensive and labor-saving, and may not be in the best interests of less-developed countries where labor is abundant.

STUDY UNIT ELEVEN
CMA PART 1 REVIEW – INTERNAL CONTROLS AND QUANTITATIVE METHODS

(12 pages of outline)

Part 1 of the CMA exam is titled **Business Analysis**. This study unit is a review of these sections:

C. **Internal Controls.** Internal control environment, procedures, and standards; responsibility and authority for internal auditing; types of audits; assessing the adequacy of the accounting information system.

D. **Quantitative Methods.** Quantitative methods and techniques including regression analysis, learning curves, linear programming, sensitivity analysis, network analysis, probability concepts, expected values, decision trees, simulation, and other appropriate aids to decision making.

This study unit presents the IMA's Learning Outcome Statements and Gleim Core Concepts relevant to these sections. Bear in mind that **all topics** on Part 4 of the exam are tested at **skill level C** (all six skill types required).

11.1 INTERNAL CONTROLS REVIEW

Part 1 – Section C.1. Risk assessment and controls

The candidate should be able to:

a. demonstrate an understanding of internal control risk assessment and the management of internal control risk

b. explain how a company's organizational structure, policies, objectives, and goals, as well as its management philosophy and style, influence the scope and effectiveness of the control environment

c. demonstrate an understanding of how the organizational structure defines the key areas of authority and responsibility

d. identify the Board of Directors' responsibilities with respect to ensuring that the company is operated in the best interest of shareholders

e. describe how internal controls are designed to provide reasonable assurance regarding achievement of an entity's objectives involving (i) effectiveness and efficiency of operations, (ii) reliability of financial reporting, and (iii) compliance with applicable laws and regulations

f. identify reasons why personnel policies and procedures, particularly with the employment and promotion of competent personnel, are integral to an efficient control environment

g. define and give examples of segregation of duties

h. identify and explain why the following four types of functional responsibilities should be performed by different organizations or people: (i) authority to execute transactions, (ii) recording transactions, (iii) custody of assets involved in the transactions, and (iv) periodic reconciliations of the existing assets to recorded amounts

i. demonstrate an understanding of the importance of independent checks and verification

j. identify examples of safeguarding controls

k. explain how the use of pre-numbered forms, as well as specific policies and procedures detailing who is authorized to receive specific documents, is a means of control

l.   define inherent risk, control risk, and detection risk

m.   demonstrate an understanding that risk encompasses both the total dollar value of assets that are exposed to loss, as well as the probability that such a loss will occur

n.   state that controls designed to prevent fraud make perpetration of fraud more difficult, but they are not complete insurance against fraud

o.   identify the major internal control provisions of the Foreign Corrupt Practices Act

p.   identify the major internal control provisions of Sarbanes-Oxley

Core Concepts for Risk Assessment and Controls

- All systems of internal control involve **tradeoffs between cost and benefit**. For this reason, no system of internal control can be said to be "100% effective." Organizations accept the fact that risk can only be **mitigated, not eliminated**.

- **Risk can be quantified** as a combination of two factors: the severity of consequences and the likelihood of occurrence. The expected value of a loss due to a risk exposure can thus be stated numerically as the product of the two factors.

- An organization establishes a **system of internal control** to help it manage many of the risks it faces. The IMA refers to internal control as "the whole system of controls (financial and otherwise) ..." The proper design and operation of an organization's system of internal controls is the **responsibility of management**.

- An organization's **control environment** encompasses the **attitudes and actions** of the board of directors and upper management regarding the significance of control, i.e., the "tone at the top." The components include organizational structure, policies, objectives and goals, management philosophy and operating style, and assignment of authority and responsibility.

- The **audit committee** is a subcommittee of the board of directors whose purpose is to help keep the external auditors independent of management. This is accomplished by assigning the selection, compensation, and oversight of the external auditors to the audit committee. Many stock exchanges require a listed organization to have an audit committee.

- In its 1992 publication *Internal Control – Integrated Framework*, the Committee of Sponsoring Organizations of the Treadway Commission **(COSO)** defined internal control as providing reasonable assurance about the achievement of objectives in the areas of **effectiveness and efficiency** of operations, **reliability** of financial reporting, and **compliance** with applicable laws and regulation. Note that the Framework specifically cites reasonable, not absolute, assurance about the achievement of management's objectives.

- **Control activities** are designed and placed in operation to ensure that management's directives are executed. **Control procedures** are implemented to manage or limit risk in accordance with the entity's risk assessments whenever risk exposures exist that threaten loss of assets or misstatements of accounting or management information.

- Controls can be identified in **these areas**: segregation of duties, including the four basic functional responsibilities; independent checks and verification; safeguarding controls; prenumbered forms; and specific document flow.

- **Segregation of duties** involves assigning different employees to perform functions such that an employee acting alone is prevented from committing an error or concealing a fraud in the normal course of his/her duties. **Four types** of functional responsibilities should be segregated: the authority to execute transactions, the recording of transactions, custody of the assets affected by the transactions, and periodic reconciliation of the existing assets to recorded amounts.

- **Compensating controls** replace the normal controls, such as segregation of duties, when the latter cannot feasibly be implemented. For example, in the finance and investment cycle, top management may authorize and execute investments and have access to the records, stock certificates, etc. The compensating control in this case is for at least two people to perform each function.

- **Fraud** differs from error because it is intentional. It typically involves pressures or incentives to engage in wrongdoing and a perceived opportunity to do so. Examples are fraudulent financial reporting and misappropriation of assets. Internal controls are designed to, among other things, prevent fraud. However, because of the concealment aspects of fraudulent activity (e.g., collusion or falsification of documents), the controls cannot give absolute assurance that material fraud will be prevented or detected.

- The **Foreign Corrupt Practices Act (FCPA)** is designed to prevent secret payments of corporate funds for purposes that Congress has determined to be contrary to public policy. The Act prohibits bribery of any foreign **official**, foreign **political party** or official thereof, or **candidate for political office** in a foreign country. Only political payments to foreign officials are prohibited. Payment to foreign business owners or corporate officers are not addressed by the FCPA.

- Regardless of whether they have foreign operations, the FCPA requires all public companies to make and keep **books, records, and accounts in reasonable detail** that accurately and fairly reflect transactions and dispositions of assets. All public companies must devise and maintain a **system of internal accounting control** sufficient to provide reasonable assurance that the basic goals of transaction authorization, financial reporting, and safeguarding of assets are achieved.

- The **Sarbanes-Oxley Act of 2002** applies to issuers of publicly traded securities subject to federal securities laws. The Act requires that each member of the **audit committee**, including at least one who is a financial expert, be an **independent** member of the issuer's board of directors. An independent director is not affiliated with, and receives no compensation (other than for service on the board) from, the issuer.

- **Section 404** of the Act requires management to **establish and document internal control procedures** and to include in the annual report a report on the company's internal control over financial reporting. The **external auditor must attest** to and report on management's assessment.

Part 1 - Section C.2. Internal auditing

The candidate should be able to:

- a. define the internal audit function and identify its functions
- b. demonstrate an understanding of the scope of internal auditing
- c. identify incidents that internal auditors should report to management or the Board of Directors
- d. define a compliance audit and identify its objectives
- e. define an operational audit and identify its objectives

Core Concepts for Internal Auditing

- An adequate **internal audit activity (IAA)** is now considered to be so basic to the governance of a modern corporation that some stock exchanges require all companies registering to trade their stock to have one.

- The Institute of Internal Auditors (The IIA) provides the following definition: "Internal auditing is an **independent, objective assurance and consulting activity** designed to add value and improve an organization's operations."

- The internal audit activity must be **organizationally independent** of the activities under audit. In addition, individual internal auditors must maintain an **attitude of objectivity** in carrying out their duties. Independence, therefore, is an attribute of the internal audit department as a whole, while objectivity is an attribute of the auditors themselves.

- Generally, the internal audit function is headed by the **chief audit executive (CAE)** who reports directly to the chief executive officer (CEO). The CAE also should have direct, unhindered access to the board of directors. The purpose, authority, and responsibility of the IAA should be defined in a **written charter**.

- The **three principal functions** of internal auditing within a modern organization are to aid (1) upper management in the maintenance of the firm's system of internal control, (2) upper management in improving the efficiency of the firm's operations, and (3) the external auditors in the conduct of the audit of financial statements.

- The internal audit activity **must report** certain types of **incidents** that come to its attention to upper management and the board of directors. They include fraud, illegal acts, material weaknesses and significant deficiencies in internal control, and significant penetrations of information security systems.

- Internal auditors should **assess compliance** in specific areas as part of their role in organizational governance. They also should conduct follow-up and report on management's response to **regulatory body reviews**. Given the ever-expanding scope of governmental regulation, these duties of internal auditors have assumed increased importance.

- **Operational auditing** is a review of a function within an enterprise to appraise the **efficiency** and economy of operations and the **effectiveness** with which those functions achieve their objectives.

Part 1 – Section C.3. Systems controls and security measures

The candidate should be able to:

a.   identify threats to information systems, including input manipulation, program alteration, direct file alteration, data theft, sabotage, viruses, Trojan horses, and theft

b.   demonstrate an understanding of how systems development controls are used to enhance the accuracy, validity, safety, security, and adaptability of systems input, processing, output, and storage functions

c.   identify procedures to limit access to physical hardware

d.   identify means by which management can protect programs and databases from unauthorized use

e.   identify input controls, processing controls, and output controls and describe why each of these controls is necessary

f.   identify the similarities and relationships between output controls and input controls

g.   identify and describe the types of storage controls and demonstrate an understanding of when and why they are used

h.   outline the inherent risks of using the Internet as compared to data transmissions over secured transmission lines

i.   define data encryption and describe why there is a much greater need for data encryption methods when using the Internet

j.   identify a firewall and its uses

k.   demonstrate an understanding of how flowcharts of activities are used

l.   outline the reasons why all program and data files should be backed up regularly and frequently and stored at a secure remote site

m.   develop an outline of a disaster recovery plan

n.   define the objective of a disaster recovery plan

Core Concepts for Systems Controls and Security Measures

- The three **goals** of information security are **availability, confidentiality, and integrity**.
- **Threats** to information systems include input manipulation, program alteration, direct file alteration, data theft, sabotage, viruses / logic bombs / worms / Trojan horses (known collectively as malware), back doors, and theft.
- **Physical controls** limit physical access and environmental damage to computer equipment and important documents. They consist of
  - **Physical access** (i.e., who can get into a room with computer equipment), and
  - **Environmental controls** (i.e., maintaining the computer equipment room with a constant level of temperature and humidity, and a fire-suppression system).
- **Logical controls** are established to limit access in accordance with the principle that all persons should have access only to those elements of the organization's information systems that are necessary to perform their job duties. Logical controls have a double focus:
  - **Authentication** is the act of assuring that the person attempting to access the system is in fact who (s)he says (s)he is. The most widespread means of achieving this is through the use of IDs and passwords.
  - **Authorization** is the practice of assuring that, once in the system, the user can only access those programs and data elements necessary to his/her job duties. In many cases, users should be able to view the contents of some data fields but not be able to change them.
- **Input, Processing, and Output Controls**
  - **Input controls** vary depending on whether input is entered in online or batch mode. **Online input controls** can be used when data are keyed into an input screen. Among them are preformatting, edit checks, limit (reasonableness) checks, and check digits. **Batch input controls** can be used when data are grouped for processing in "batches." Commonly used ones are management release, record counts, financial totals, and hash totals.
  - **Processing controls** include validation, completeness, arithmetic controls, sequence checks, run-to-run control totals, and key integrity.
  - **Output controls** include a complete audit trail and error listings.
- **Storage controls** consist of dual write routines, validity checks, and physical controls.
- Certain security **risks are inherent** in use of the **Internet**. Listed here are some of the forms that attacks over the Internet can take.
  - **Password attacks.** A brute-force attack uses password cracking software to try large numbers of letter and number combinations to access a network. Passwords also may be compromised by Trojan horses, IP spoofing, and packet sniffers.
  - A **man-in-the-middle attack** takes advantage of networking packet sniffing and routing and transport protocols.
  - A **denial-of-service (DoS)** attack is an attempt to overload an organization's network with so many messages that it cannot function (i.e., induce a system crash).

- **Data encryption** is a very powerful tool in counteracting Internet attacks. Encryption technology converts data into a code. Two major types of encryption software exist.

  - **Public-key**, or **asymmetric**, encryption is the more secure of the two because it requires two keys: The public key for coding messages is widely known, but the private key for decoding messages is kept secret by the recipient. The parties who wish to transmit coded messages must use algorithmically-related pairs of public and private keys. Neither party knows the other's private key. The related public key and private key pair is issued by a certificate authority; the private key is issued only to one party.

  - **Private-key**, or **symmetric**, encryption is less secure because it requires only a single key for each pair of parties that want to send each other coded messages.

- A **firewall** is a combination of hardware and software that separates an internal network from an external network, such as the Internet, and prevents passage of specific types of traffic. A firewall alone is not an adequate defense against computer viruses. Specialized anti-virus software is a must.

- **Flowcharting** is the representation of a process using pictorial symbols.

  - **Vertical flowcharts** present successive steps in a top-to-bottom format.

  - **Horizontal flowcharts**, also called systems flowcharts, depict areas of responsibility (departments or functions) in vertical columns. Activities and documents flow back and forth between departments across the page.

- **Periodic backup and rotation** are essential. The offsite location must be temperature- and humidity-controlled and guarded against physical intrusion. Just as important, it must be geographically remote enough from the site of the organization's main operations that it would not be affected by the same natural disaster.

- A typical **backup routine** involves duplicating all data files and application programs once a month. Incremental changes, that is, only those data elements and programs that have changed since the last full monthly backup, are backed up every week and kept at the main processing center.

- **Disaster recovery** planning is also called **contingency** planning. Disaster recovery is the process of resuming normal information processing operations after the occurrence of a major interruption. Business continuity is the continuation of business by other means during the period in which computer processing is unavailable or less than normal. **Two major types** of contingencies must be planned for: those in which the data center is physically available (power failure, viruses, hacking) and those in which it is not (floods, fires, hurricanes, earthquakes).

- An **alternate processing facility** is a physical location maintained by an outside contractor for the express purpose of providing processing facilities for customers in case of disaster. The recovery center, like the offsite storage location for backup files, must be far enough away that it will likely be unaffected by the same natural disaster that forced the abandonment of the main facility. Usually, companies contract for backup facilities in another city.

11.2 INTERNAL CONTROLS ESSAY QUESTIONS

Recall that your CMA Part 4 exam will probably contain six scenarios, with about three questions per scenario. There will be a recommended time allocation of 20 minutes, 30 minutes, or 45 minutes for each scenario and related questions.

One scenario will involve ethical issues, and probably one or two scenarios will include calculations and responses on a worksheet. Also, expect at least one scenario on organizational/behavioral topics. The remaining scenarios cover Parts 1, 2, and 3.

Scenario Title	Subtopic	Questions	Suggested Time
Wooster Company	Controls over Purchasing Cycle	1, 2	30 minutes
Micro Dynamics	System of Internal Control	3, 4, 5	30 minutes
Leigh Industries	Internal Audit Function	6, 7, 8	30 minutes
Employee and Management Fraud	Detecting Errors and Irregularities	9, 10, 11	30 minutes
Sachem Manufacturing Company	Auditing Computer Environments	12, 13	30 minutes

Scenario for Essay Questions 1, 2

Wooster Company is a beauty and barber supplies and equipment distributorship servicing a five-state area. Management generally has been pleased with the overall operations of the company to date. However, the present purchasing system has evolved through practice rather than having been formally designed. Consequently, it is inadequate and needs to be redesigned.

A description of the present purchasing system is as follows. Whenever the quantity of an item is low, the inventory supervisor phones the purchasing department with the item description and quantity to be ordered. A purchase order is prepared in duplicate in the purchasing department. The original is sent to the vendor, and the copy is retained in the purchasing department filed in numerical order. When the shipment arrives, the inventory supervisor sees that each item received is checked off on the packing slip which accompanies the shipment. The packing slip is then forwarded to the accounts payable department. When the invoice arrives, the packing slip is compared with the invoice in the accounts payable department. Once any difference between the packing slip and the invoice are reconciled, a check is drawn for the appropriate amount and is mailed to the vendor with a copy of the invoice. The packing slip is attached to the invoice and filed alphabetically in the paid invoice file.

Questions

Wooster Company intends to redesign its purchasing system from the point in time when an item needs to be ordered until payment is made. The system should be designed to ensure that all of the proper controls are incorporated into the system.

1. Identify the internally and externally generated documents that would be required to satisfy the minimum requirements of a basic system, and indicate the number of copies of each document that would be needed.

2. Explain how all of these documents should interrelate and flow among Wooster's various departments, including the final destination or file for each copy.

Essay Questions 1, 2 — Unofficial Answers

1. The documents that would be required to satisfy the minimum requirements of a basic system and the minimum number of copies are:

    <u>Internally generated documents</u>

    - Purchase requisition -- 2 copies
    - Purchase order -- 4 copies
    - Receiving report -- 2 copies
    - Payment voucher -- 2 copies
    - Check -- 2 copies

    <u>Externally generated documents</u>

    - Invoice -- 2 copies
    - Packing slip -- 1 or 2 copies

2. How these documents flow among Wooster's departments is detailed below.

    <u>Purchase Requisition (2 copies)</u>
    This document is generated by the inventory supervisor. Copies are distributed as follows:

    Original -- Sent to Purchasing as a formal request for an order; filed in Purchasing.

    Copy -- Filed in Stores/Inventory Department.

    <u>Purchase Order (4 copies)</u>
    This document is generated by the Purchasing Department with distribution as follows:

    Original -- Vendor

    Copy -- Sent to the Stores/Inventory Department to check with order received.

    Copy -- Sent to Accounts Payable to be matched with the invoice from vendor and receiving report from Stores/Inventory Department.

    Copy -- Retained in Purchasing Department and filed by vendor.

    <u>Receiving Report (2 copies)</u>
    This report is generated by the Stores/Inventory Department and completed as follows:

    Original -- The report is completed in the Stores/Inventory Department and forwarded to Accounts Payable to compare with the invoice and purchase order.

    Copy -- Retained in Stores/Inventory Department.

    <u>Payment Voucher (2 copies) and Check</u>
    The voucher and check are prepared by Accounts Payable and routed as follows:

    Originals -- Voucher and check with supporting documents (invoice, purchase order, receiving report) sent to the controller or treasurer for signature; check sent to vendor; approved payment voucher returned to Accounts Payable.

    Voucher Copy -- Retained in Accounts Payable.

    Check Copy -- Retained by the controller or treasurer.

    <u>Invoice (2 copies)</u>
    This document is generated by the vendor. Both copies go to Accounts Payable where the invoice is compared with the receiving report, purchase order, and packing slip.

    Original -- Forwarded to controller or treasurer with support documents and with voucher and check for approval; returned to Accounts Payable after approval and filed.

    Copy -- Retained in Accounts Payable and filed by vendor.

    <u>Packing Slip (2 copies)</u>
    The packing slip is generated by the vendor and included with the shipment of goods.

    Original -- Compare with what was actually received and also compare to the Purchase Order. It should then be filed by Stores/Inventory Department.

    Copy -- Sent with Receiving Report to Accounts Payable.

Scenario for Essay Questions 3, 4, 5

Micro Dynamics, a developer of database software packages, is a publicly-held company whose stock is traded over the counter. The company recently received an enforcement release proceeding through an SEC Administrative Law Judge that cited the company for inadequate internal controls. In response, Micro Dynamics has agreed to establish an internal audit function and strengthen its audit committee.

A manager of the Internal Audit Department was recently hired as a result of the SEC enforcement action to establish an internal audit function. In addition, the composition of the audit committee has been changed to include all outside directors. Micro Dynamics has held its initial planning meeting to discuss the roles of the various participants in the internal control and financial reporting process. Participants at the meeting included the company president, the chief financial officer, a member of the audit committee, a partner from Micro Dynamics' external audit firm, and the newly appointed manager of the Internal Audit Department. Comments by the various meeting participants are presented below.

President: "We want to ensure that Micro Dynamics complies with the SEC's enforcement release, and that we don't find ourselves in this position again. The Internal Audit Department should help to strengthen our internal control system by correcting the problems. I would like your thoughts on the proper reporting relationship for the manager of the Internal Audit Department."

Chief financial officer: "I think the manager of the Internal Audit Department should report to me since much of the department's work relates to financial issues. The audit committee should have oversight responsibilities."

Audit committee member: "I believe we should think through our roles more carefully. The Treadway Commission has recommended that the audit committee play a more important role in the financial reporting process; the duties of today's audit committee have expanded beyond the rubber-stamp approval. We need to have greater assurance that controls are in place and being followed."

External audit partner: "We need a close working relationship among all of our roles. The Internal Audit Department can play a significant role monitoring the control systems on a continuing basis and should have strong ties to your external audit firm."

Internal Audit Department manager: "The Internal Audit Department should be more involved in operational auditing, but also should play a significant monitoring role in the financial reporting area."

Questions

3. Describe the role of each of the following in the establishment, maintenance, and evaluation of Micro Dynamics' system of internal control.

    a. Management
    b. Audit committee
    c. External auditor
    d. Internal Audit Department

4. Describe the responsibilities that Micro Dynamics' audit committee has in the financial reporting process.

5. Discuss the characteristics of an audit committee in terms of the following.

    a. Composition, size, and term of membership
    b. Relationship with management, the external auditor, and the internal auditor

Essay Questions 3, 4, 5 — Unofficial Answers

3.   a.   Management has the overall responsibility for protecting company assets and, therefore, for establishing, maintaining, and evaluating the internal control system.

b.   The audit committee's primary responsibility involves assisting the board of directors in carrying out their responsibilities as they relate to the organization's accounting policies, internal control, and financial reporting practices. The audit committee assists management and the board in fulfilling their fiduciary and accountability responsibilities, and helps maintain a direct line of communication between the board and the external and internal auditors.

c.   The external auditor reviews the organization's control structure, including the control environment, accounting systems, and control procedures, in order to assess the control risks for financial statement assertions. In addition, the external auditor would inform the company of any material weaknesses found during the review.

d.   The Internal Audit Department performs both operational and financial audits to determine compliance with established policies and procedures, and reports its findings and recommendations to management or the audit committee for evaluation and corrective action. The Internal Audit Department may also assist the external auditors with their review of the internal control system.

4.   The responsibilities of the Micro Dynamics' audit committee in the financial reporting process include:

a.   Obtaining assurance that the organization's control system is adequate and effective, identifying risk and exposure, and assuring that the financial disclosures made by management reasonably reflect the financial position, results of operations, and changes in cash flow

b.   Reviewing the progress of the audit and the final audit findings

c.   Acting as a liaison between the auditors and the board of directors

5.   a.   The audit committee should consist of at least three independent, outside directors. The maximum size may vary but normally three to five members would be sufficient to allow each member to play an active role. The term is set by the board of directors and may vary but should include an arrangement to allow continuity to be maintained while rotating the membership.

b.   The audit committee is selected by the board of directors and assists the board of directors in carrying out their responsibilities concerning the organization's accounting policies, internal control, and financial reporting practices. The audit committee's oversight responsibilities that relate to the activities of management, the external auditor, and the internal auditor provide assurance to management and the public regarding the reliability and integrity of financial information. The audit committee also has the responsibility of selecting the external auditors, helping to resolve problems arising during the audit, and discussing the audit results with management and the external auditor.

Scenario for Essay Questions 6, 7, 8

Leigh Industries has an Internal Audit Department consisting of a director and four staff auditors. The director of internal audit, Diane Bauer, reports to the corporate controller who receives copies of all internal audit reports. In addition, copies of all internal audit reports are sent to the audit committee of the board of directors and the individual responsible for the area or activity being audited.

In the past, the company's external auditors have relied on the work of the Internal Audit Department to a substantial degree. However, in recent months, Bauer has become concerned that the objectivity of the internal audit function is being affected by the amount of non-audit work being performed by the department. This possible loss of objectivity could result in more extensive testing and analysis by the external auditors. The percentage of non-audit work performed by the internal auditors has steadily increased to the point where it now represents about 25% of the total hours worked. A sample of five recent non-audit activities is presented below.

a. One of the internal auditors assisted in the preparation of policy statements on internal control. These statements included such things as policies regarding sensitive payments and the safeguarding of assets.

b. The bank statements of the corporation are reconciled each month as a regular assignment for one of the internal auditors. The corporate controller believes this strengthens the internal control function because the internal auditor is not involved in either the receipt nor the disbursement of cash.

c. The internal auditors are asked to review the annual budget each year for relevance and reasonableness before the budget is approved. At the end of each month, the corporate controller's staff analyzes the variances from budget and prepares explanations of these variances. These variances and explanations are then reviewed by the internal audit staff.

d. One of the internal auditors has been involved in the design, installation, and initial operation of a new computerized inventory system. The auditor was primarily concerned with the design and implementation of internal accounting controls and conducted the evaluation of these controls during the test runs.

e. The internal auditors are sometimes asked to make the accounting entries for complex transactions as the employees in the Accounting Department are not adequately trained to handle such transactions. The corporate controller believes this gives an added measure of assurance to the accurate recording of these transactions.

Questions

6. Define objectivity as it relates to the internal audit function.

7. For each of the five situations outlined above, explain whether the objectives of Leigh Industries' Internal Audit Department has been materially impaired. Consider each situation independently.

8. The director of internal audit reports directly to the corporate controller.

   a. Does this reporting relationship affect the objectivity of the Internal Audit Department? Explain your answer.

   b. Would your answer to the evaluation of the five situations in the question above change if the director of internal audit reported to the audit committee of the board of directors? Explain your answer.

Essay Questions 6, 7, 8 — Unofficial Answers

6. The internal auditor must have and maintain objectivity, which implies no subordination of judgment to another and arises from an independent mental attitude which views events on a factual basis without influence from feelings, prejudice, opinions, or interests.

7. a. The internal auditor's objectivity is not impaired by the preparation of policy statements on internal control. The preparation of policy statements to guide others in the development and implementation of internal controls is a responsibility of the internal audit staff.

    b. The internal auditor's objectivity is impaired. In order to maintain objectivity, the auditor should not perform operational assignments that are included as part of the independent evaluation and verification of a proper system of internal control. Separation of duties must be maintained.

    c. Objectivity is not impaired in the review of the budget for relevance and reasonableness if the internal auditor has no responsibility for establishing or implementing the budget. However, the review of variances and explanations would impair objectivity as this is an area that would normally be reviewed during an operational audit.

    d. Objectivity is impaired to the extent that the internal auditor has been involved in the design and installation of internal accounting controls, as there will be little confidence in audit findings issued by the individual who designed and installed the system being audited.

    e. The preparation of accounting records will materially impair the internal auditor's objectivity by involving the auditor in day-to-day operations.

8. a. This reporting relationship adversely affects the objectivity of the Internal Audit Department. The corporate controller is responsible for the accounting system and related operational transactions. The internal audit staff is responsible for the independent and objective review and examination of the accounting system and related operational transactions. Independence and objectivity may not exist because the internal audit staff is responsible for reviewing the work of the corporate controller, the person to whom it reports.

    b. No, the responses for the above question would not be affected by the internal audit staff reporting to an audit committee rather than the corporate controller. In order to maintain objectivity, the internal audit staff should refrain from performing non-audit functions such as management decision-making, design and installation of systems, recordkeeping, operational duties, etc.

Scenario for Essay Questions 9, 10, 11

The impact of employee and management fraud is staggering both in terms of dollar costs and its effect on the victims. Presented below are three independent cases of employee wrongdoing.

A retail store that was part of a national chain experienced an abnormal inventory shrinkage in its audiovisual department. The internal auditors, noting this shrinkage, included an in-depth evaluation of the department in the scope of their audit of the store. During their review, the auditors were "tipped" by an employee that a particular customer bought a large number of small electronic components and that the customer always went to a certain cashier's checkout line. The auditors' work revealed that the cashier and the customer had colluded to steal a number of electronic components. The cashier did not record the sale of several items the customer took from the store.

Internal auditors discovered a payroll fraud in a large hospital when, on a surprise basis, they observed the distribution of paychecks. The supervisors of each department distributed paychecks to employees and were supposed to return unclaimed checks to the payroll department. When the auditors took control of, and followed up on, an unclaimed paycheck for an employee in the food service department, they discovered that the employee had quit 4 months previously. The employee and the supervisor had argued, and the employee had simply left and never returned. The supervisor had continued to turn in a time card for the employee and, when the paychecks came for distribution, had taken the unclaimed checks and cashed them.

While performing an audit of cash disbursements in a manufacturing firm, internal auditors discovered a fraud perpetrated by an accounts payable clerk. The clerk had made copies of supporting documents and used the copies to support duplicate payments to a vendor of materials used in the manufacturing process. The clerk, who had opened a bank account in a name similar to that of the vendor, took the duplicate checks and deposited them in the bank account.

Questions

9. Explain the internal auditor's general role in detecting errors and irregularities.

10. Discuss the steps that an internal auditor should take when fraud is suspected.

11. For each of the three situations presented above, describe the recommendations that the internal auditors should make to prevent similar problems in the future.

Essay Questions 9, 10, 11 — Unofficial Answers

9. The internal auditor's general role in detecting errors and irregularities, as set forth in the Standards for the Professional Practice of Internal Auditing, should include the following responsibilities.

    a. Internal auditors should have sufficient knowledge of fraud to enable them to identify indications of fraud.

    b. In exercising due professional care, internal auditors should be alert to the possibility of intentional wrongdoing, errors, omissions, inefficiency, waste, ineffectiveness, and conflicts of interest.

    c. Internal auditors should be alert to opportunities, such as control weaknesses, that could allow fraud. If significant control weaknesses are detected, additional tests conducted by internal auditors should include tests directed toward identification of other indicators of fraud.

    d. Internal auditors should evaluate the indicators that fraud may have been committed and decide whether any further action is necessary or whether an investigation should be recommended.

    e. Internal auditors should notify the appropriate authorities within the organization if a determination is made that there are sufficient indicators of the commission of a fraud to recommend an investigation.

10. When fraud is suspected, the internal auditor should:

    a. Inform the appropriate authorities within the organization.

    b. Recommend whatever investigation is considered necessary in the circumstances.

    c. Have the authority to inform higher levels of management, e.g., the audit committee or outside directors, if no action is taken in resolving suspected wrongdoing.

11. **Inventory** -- The inventory shrinkage problem is an example of collusion. While collusion is often difficult to prevent, the store could improve its control system by:

    a. Implementing job rotation so that the same employees are not always performing the same duties

    b. Separating the payment for expensive items from the pickup of these items at a separate location

    Payroll -- The payroll fraud described could be prevented through the introduction of better internal controls including:

    a. Separation of duties. A supervisor with the authority to sign time cards should not be allowed to distribute paychecks. An individual with no other payroll-related duties should be given the responsibility for distributing checks.

    b. Periodic floor checks for employees on the payroll.

    Accounts Payable -- In order to prevent further occurrences of accounts payable fraud, the company should implement and enforce a policy that prohibits the payment of invoices based on copies of supporting documents. Should a situation arise where payment on the basis of copies of supporting documents is necessary, specific authorization to do so should be required for each individual case.

Scenario for Essay Questions 12, 13

The Internal Audit Department of Sachem Manufacturing Company is considering the purchase of computer software that will aid in the auditing process. Sachem's financial and manufacturing control systems are completely automated on a large mainframe computer. Melinda Robinson, the director of internal audit, believes that Sachem should acquire computer audit software to assist in the financial and procedure audits that her department conducts. The types of software packages that Robinson is considering are described below:

- A generalized audit software package that assists in basic audit work such as the retrieval of live data from large computer files. The department would review this information using conventional audit investigation techniques. More specifically, the department could perform criteria selection, sampling, basic computations for quantitative analysis, record handling, graphical analysis, and the printing of output (i.e., confirmations).

- An integrated test facility package (ITF) that uses, monitors, and controls "dummy" test data through existing programs and checks the existence and adequacy of program data entry controls and processing controls.

- A control flowcharting package that provides a graphical presentation of the data flow of information through a system, pinpointing control strengths and weaknesses.

- A program (parallel) simulation and modeling package that uses actual data to conduct the same systemized process by using a different computer-logic program developed by the auditor. The package can also be used to seek answers to difficult audit problems (involving many comparisons and computations) within statistically acceptable confidence limits.

Questions

12. Without regard to any specific computer audit software, identify the general advantages to the internal auditor of using computer audit software to assist with audits.

13. Describe the audit purpose facilitated and the procedural steps to be followed by the internal auditor to use a(n)

    a. Generalized audit software package
    b. Integrated test facility package
    c. Control flowcharting package
    d. Program (parallel) simulation and modeling package

Essay Questions 12, 13 — Unofficial Answers

12. General advantages to the internal auditor of using computer audit software to assist with audits include the following:

    a. Audits can be more efficient, saving labor time spent on routine calculations. The routine operations of footing extensions, transcription between reports, and report generation are computer generated as a result of the software.

    b. The auditor's time spent on the audit is more analytical than clerical.

    c. The auditor is able to examine more records and extract desired data more readily through ad hoc reporting.

    d. Computer-generated reports and schedules are more objective and professional, improving data communication.

    e. Audit sampling is improved. Any bias in sample selection is eliminated because of assured randomness. This has a direct effect on sampling precision, reliability, and audit accuracy.

13. a. The purpose of generalized audit software programs is to perform a variety of auditing operations on the computer files used to store the information. The steps to be followed by the internal auditor to use generalized computer audit software would include

    1) Planning and designing the audit application.

    2) Ensuring that the output and final reports are generated from the files being tested.

    b. The purpose of integrated test facility (ITF) packages is to test both source data controls and processing controls. The steps to be followed by the internal auditor to use an ITF include

    1) Selection and preparation of the test transactions to be passed through the ITF. These transactions must be representative of all of the transactions the dummy unit emulates. All types of valid and invalid transactions must be used and blended with regular transactions over time to properly test the system under normal conditions.

    2) Review of all output and processing routines including a comparison of actual results to predetermined results.

    c. The purpose of a control flowcharting package is to interpret the program source code and generate a program flowchart corresponding to it in order to facilitate the review of internal controls. The steps to be followed by the internal auditor to use a control flowcharting package would include the following:

    1) Establish the audit objective by identifying the systems and program to be tested.

    2) Review manuals and documentation of the system and interview involved personnel to get an overview of the operations to be tested.

    d. The purpose of a parallel simulation package is to ensure that organizational objectives are being met, ensure compliance to technical standards, and detect unauthorized program changes. The steps to be followed by the internal auditor to use a parallel simulation package include the following:

    1) Run the same data used in the company's current application program using the "simulated" application program.

    2) Compare the results from the "simulated" application with the results from the company's current application program to verify that objectives are being met.

11.3 QUANTITATIVE METHODS REVIEW

Part 1 – Section D.1. Forecasting analysis

The candidate should be able to:

a. demonstrate an understanding of a simple regression equation and the measures associated with it

b. define a multiple regression equation

c. identify the assumptions of simple and multiple regression analyses

d. calculate the result of a simple regression equation as applied to a specific situation

e. demonstrate an understanding of learning curve analyses

f. calculate the results under a cumulative average-time learning model and under an incremental unit-time learning model

g. demonstrate an understanding of exponential smoothing and calculate a forecast using this method

h. demonstrate an understanding of time series analyses, including objectives and patterns, i.e., trend, cyclical, seasonal, and irregular

i. list the benefits and shortcomings of regression analysis, learning curve analysis, and time series analysis

Core Concepts for Forecasting Analysis

- **Forecasts** are the basis for business plans. Forecasts are used to project product demand, inventory levels, cash flow, etc. **Qualitative methods** of forecasting rely on the manager's experience and intuition.

- **Correlation analysis** is the foundation of any quantitative method of forecasting. Correlation is the strength of the **linear relationship** between two variables, expressed mathematically in terms of the coefficient of correlation (r). It can be graphically depicted by plotting the values for the variables on a graph in the form of a scatter diagram. The value of r ranges from 1 (perfect direct relationship) to –1 (perfect inverse relationship).

- The **coefficient of determination** (r^2), or the coefficient of correlation squared, is a measure of how good the fit is between the two variables. Mathematically, the coefficient of determination is the proportion of the total variation in the dependent variable that is accounted for by the independent variable.

- **Regression analysis**, also called **least-squares analysis**, is the process of deriving the linear equation that describes the relationship between two variables with a nonzero coefficient of correlation. Simple regression is used when there is one independent variable. The simple regression equation is, obviously, the algebraic formula for a straight line: $y = a + bx$. Regression analysis is particularly valuable for budgeting and cost accounting purposes.

- **Learning curve analysis** reflects the increased rate at which people perform tasks as they gain experience. The time required to perform a given task becomes progressively shorter during the early stages of production. The curve is usually expressed as a percentage of reduced time to complete a task for each doubling of cumulative production. The most common percentage used in practice is 80%. **Two methods** of applying learning curve analysis are in common use:

  - The **cumulative average-time learning model** projects the reduction in the cumulative average time it takes to complete a certain number of tasks. The time spent on the most recent unit is treated as if it were the average for all units so far.

  - The **incremental unit-time learning model** projects the reduction in the incremental time it takes to complete the last task. The time spent on all units so far is accumulated and the average taken.

- **Time series analysis** projects future trends based on past experience (for this reason, it is also called trend analysis). Time series/trend analysis encompasses **three main techniques**:

  - **Simple moving average** is appropriate when, for instance, the demand for a product is relatively stable and not subject to seasonal variations. The data points are summed and divided by the number of time periods. This process is repeated for successive groups of time periods.

  - **Weighted moving average** allows a firm to give each data point a weight indicating its relative importance in determining the outcome.

  - **Exponential smoothing** is a widespread technique for making projections because it requires less data be kept on hand than the moving average methods.

    - Step 1 – Develop some forecasts using a more data-intensive method such as one of the two moving average methods.
    - Step 2 – Set the smoothing factor (alpha) between 0 and 1. The closer it is set to 1, the more weight is put on recent data.
    - Step 3 – Calculate the next period's forecast. Each forecast is the sum of the current period's actual results multiplied by the smoothing factor, and the current period's forecast multiplied by the smoothing factor's complement.

Part 1 – Section D.2. Linear programming

The candidate should be able to:

- a. demonstrate an understanding of the objectives of linear programming
- b. define and identify the objective function
- c. demonstrate an understanding of the mathematical formulation of a constraint
- d. calculate the optimal solution by the use of linear programming using the graphical method and the algebraic method
- e. identify the benefits and shortcomings of linear programming

Core Concepts for Linear Programming

- Linear programming is a technique used to **optimize a linear function** subject to certain **constraints**. The objective of linear programming is to choose the best solution from a potentially infinite number of possibilities. Applied to business, linear programming is a way of **maximizing revenue or profit**, or minimizing cost, given limited resources.

- Managers are often faced with problems of selecting the most profitable or least costly way to use available resources. The **objective function** is the statement of the problem for which a solution is sought.

- To begin, the constraints are stated in business terms, e.g., the minimum size of a production run to make setup costs worthwhile. Next, the constraints must be translated into mathematical formulas, e.g., Output $\geq$ 500.

- The **graphical method** involves plotting the linear functions represented by the constraint formulas. First, the mathematical statements of the constraints are restated as linear equations. Then, the constraints are graphed. The region enclosed by the graphed functions is the feasible region. The optimal solution is at the intersection of two or more constraint equations.

- The **algebraic method** complements the graphical method. The combination of the two products that maximizes the objective function is at one of the corners of the feasible region. The Cartesian coordinates of the intersections of the constraint lines can be determined by solving simultaneously the relevant pairs of equations.

- The **advantage** of linear programming is its applicability to many types of problems and its usefulness for sensitivity analysis. A major **disadvantage** is the restrictiveness of its linear assumptions, for example, that all costs are variable or fixed.

Part 1 – Section D.3. Network analysis

The candidate should be able to:

a. define PERT and explain how it is used for scheduling projects
b. develop a project network analysis
c. identify the critical path after a network is developed
d. calculate the critical path through a network and all the related start, finish, and slack times
e. demonstrate an understanding of what makes critical activities different from other activities
f. demonstrate an understanding of the cost impact of shortening a critical path
g. identify the benefits and shortcomings of network analysis

Core Concepts for Network Analysis

- **Gantt charts** are the **simplest** of the project management tools. Each component task of a project is shown as a horizontal bar, the length of which depicts the length of time estimated to complete the task. The major disadvantage of the Gantt chart arises when attempting to use one for a very large-scale project.

- **Network analysis techniques** are aids in the management of large-scale projects with many interrelated activities. Also called **critical path scheduling**, network analysis depicts the totality of a project as a set of nodes representing the component tasks, connected by a web of lines representing the required sequence of the tasks.

  - **The critical path is the longest path** in time through the network. It is critical because, if any activity on the critical path takes longer than expected, the entire project will be delayed. Every network has at least one critical path. Some have more than one.

- **Program Evaluation and Review Technique (PERT)** is the most prominent network analysis technique. To perform a PERT analysis:

  - Enumerate the **tasks** making up the project.
  - Determine the **dependencies** among the tasks.
  - Create a **network diagram** of the interdependencies.
  - Determine the **critical path**.
  - Determine **early start and finish times** for each task.
  - Determine **late start and finish times** for each task.
  - Determine **slack times** for each noncritical task.

    - The slack time for any activity is the amount of time the start of that activity can be delayed without delaying the completion of the project as a whole. Slack time equals late start minus early start.

- **Critical activities** are those on the critical path. By definition, they have no slack time.

- **Activity times** in PERT analysis can be **weighted** to include probabilistic estimates. The expected time for each task is the result of this weighting operation. Three time estimates are made: **optimistic, most likely,** and **pessimistic**. The traditional weighting is to 1:4:1.

- Time is not a project manager's only consideration. In practice, managers seek the optimum **tradeoff between cost and time** in project management. A project can be expedited at the cost of devoting additional resources to it. This is referred to as **crashing the network**, and involves the calculation of crash costs and **crash time** for each activity.

- **Steps** in crashing the network:
  - Step 1 – Prepare a crash cost figure and crash time for each activity.
  - Step 2 – Calculate the cost per unit of time to expedite each activity:

    [(Crash cost – Normal cost) ÷ (Normal time – Crash time)]
  - Step 3 – Shorten the critical path at the lowest cost.
  - Step 4 – Determine the new critical path.
  - Step 5 – Repeat steps 3 and 4.

Part 1 – Section D.4. Probability concepts

The candidate should be able to:

a. demonstrate an understanding as to why probabilities for all values of a random variable must equal one

b. develop and interpret a probability distribution table

c. calculate the expected value of random variables

d. identify the benefits and shortcomings of probability concepts and expected value techniques

Core Concepts for Probability Concepts

- **Probability** is the process of **quantifying the likelihood** of a future event. The probability of an event varies from 0 to 1, with 0 meaning the event definitely will not occur, and 1 meaning the event is certain. Thus, the sum of the probabilities for all possible values for a random variable must equal 1.
- Four terms deal with probability: **certainty** (all the facts surrounding a decision are known exactly, and each alternative is associated with only one possible outcome), **uncertainty** (the probabilities of the possible outcomes are unknown and must be subjectively determined), **risk** (the probabilities of the possible outcomes are known and can be mathematically stated), and **states of nature** (the set of possible outcomes of a future event).
- Types of probability. Two events are **mutually exclusive** if they cannot occur simultaneously. Two events are **independent** if the occurrence of one has no effect on the probability of the other. The **conditional probability** of two events is the probability that one will occur given that the other has already occurred. The **joint probability** for two events is the probability that both will occur.

Part 1 – Section D.5. Decision tree analysis

The candidate should be able to:

a. construct a decision tree analysis, analyze decisions, and infer results based on the decision tree

b. define and identify the assumptions of the decision tree analysis technique

c. explain the relationship between decision trees and investment decisions

d. describe the process used to estimate the cash flow and probability values used in decision tree analysis

e. identify the benefits and shortcomings of a decision tree analysis

Core Concepts for Decision Tree Analysis

- **Expected value** is a means of associating a **dollar amount** with each of the possible outcomes of a probability distribution. The outcome yielding the highest expected value (which may or may not be the most likely one) is the optimal alternative. The expected value of an event is calculated by multiplying the probability of each outcome by its payoff and summing the products. A calculation such as this is often referred to as a **payoff table**. A **criticism** of expected value is that it is based on repetitive trials, whereas many business decisions involve only one trial.

- A **decision tree** graphically displays the contents of a payoff table. The decision tree depicts the sequence of events over time. Accordingly, the decision tree displays all potential sequences. The **decision** is under the manager's control. The **state of nature** is the future event whose outcome the manager is attempting to predict. The **payoff** is the financial result of the combination of the manager's decision and the actual state of nature.

- **Perfect information** is the certain knowledge of which state of nature will occur. The expected value of perfect information (EVPI) is the additional expected value that could be obtained if a decision maker knew ahead of time which state of nature would occur. It is the monetary difference between the expected value of a transaction made with perfect information and the best choice without perfect information.

Part 1 – Section D.6. Other quantitative techniques

The candidate should be able to:

a. identify the uses of sensitivity analysis
b. identify situations when sensitivity analysis is useful
c. perform a sensitivity analysis with different values for the probabilities of the states of nature and/or the payoffs
d. identify the benefits and shortcomings of sensitivity analysis
e. demonstrate an understanding of the uses of simulation models, including the Monte Carlo technique
f. define controllable inputs and probabilistic inputs
g. demonstrate an understanding of the simulation approach called what-if analysis
h. demonstrate an understanding of how simulations can be used to model and learn about the behavior of complex systems
i. identify the benefits and shortcomings of simulation models
j. define and identify applications of queuing theory and Markov analysis

Core Concepts for Other Quantitative Techniques

- **Sensitivity analysis** reveals how sensitive expected value calculations are to the accuracy of the initial estimates. Sensitivity analysis is thus useful in determining whether expending additional resources to obtain better forecasts is justified. If a change in the probabilities assigned to the various states of nature results in large changes in the expected values, the decision maker is justified in expending more effort to make better predictions about the outcomes.

- **Simulation** is a technique for experimenting with logical and mathematical models using a computer. The technique answers the question of how the results change when the assumptions change. **Physical models** include automobile mock-ups, airplane models used for wind-tunnel tests, and breadboard models of electronic circuits. **Abstract models** may be pictorial (architectural plans), verbal (a proposed procedure), or logical-mathematical.

- The simulation procedure has **five steps**:
  - Define the objectives.
  - Formulate the model.
  - Validate the model.
  - Design the experiment.
  - Conduct the simulation and evaluate the results.

- The **Monte Carlo technique** is often used in simulation to generate the individual values for a random variable. A random number generator is used to produce numbers with a uniform probability distribution (equal likelihoods of occurrence). The second step is to transform these numbers into values consistent with the desired distribution. The performance of a quantitative model may be investigated by randomly selecting values for each of the variables in the model (based on the probability distribution of each variable) and then calculating the value of the solution. If this process is performed a large number of times, the distribution of results from the model will be obtained.

■ **Queuing theory** is one technique for workflow analysis. An organization can improve throughput by carefully designing the way inputs arrive at workstations and how they are processed upon arrival.

- The most significant aspects of queuing theory are the **number of lines** and the **service facility structure**.

  - Single channel, single phase (ATM, bank lobby)
  - Single channel, multiple phase (fast-food drive-through)
  - Multiple channel, single phase (big-box retail checkout)
  - Multiple channel, multiple phase (hospital)

- As capacity utilization increases, so does customer waiting time. Thus, management must strike a delicate balance between customers who walk away and overcapacity.

■ **Markov analysis** is useful in decision problems in which the probability of the occurrence of a future state depends only on the current state. A characteristic of the Markov process is that the initial state matters less and less as time goes on because the process will eventually reach its steady state.

11.4 QUANTITATIVE METHODS ESSAY QUESTIONS

Recall that your CMA Part 4 exam will probably contain six scenarios, with about three questions per scenario. There will be a recommended time allocation of 20 minutes, 30 minutes, or 45 minutes for each scenario and related questions.

One scenario will involve ethical issues, and probably one or two scenarios will include calculations and responses on a worksheet. Also, expect at least one scenario on organizational/behavioral topics. The remaining scenarios cover Parts 1, 2, and 3.

Scenario Title	Subtopic	Questions	Suggested Time
Steven Company	Expected Value and Decision Trees	1, 2, 3	45 minutes
Video Recreation, Inc.	Forecasting	4	30 minutes
Miller, Lombardi, and York	Linear Programming	5, 6, 7, 8	30 minutes
Leastan Company	Linear Programming	9, 10, 11	30 minutes
Henderson Equipment	Learning Curves and Outsourcing	12, 13, 14	45 minutes

Scenario for Essay Questions 1, 2, 3

Steven Company plans to introduce a high-speed back-up unit for networked servers in the near future.

Steven's R&D and Market Research Departments have been working on this project for an extended period and the combined development costs incurred to date amount to $1,500,000. R&D designed several designs for the back-up units. Three of the designs were approved for development into prototypes, and from these only one will be manufactured. Market Research has determined that the appropriate selling price would be $400 per unit, regardless of the model selected.

The estimated demand schedule for three market situations is shown below. These three demand levels are the only ones the company considers feasible, and other demand levels are not expected to occur. Steven can meet all demand levels because its plant currently is below full capacity.

	Unit Sales	Probability of Occurrence
Light demand	20,000	25%
Moderate demand	80,000	60
Heavy demand	120,000	15

Costs for the three models are presented below. Manufacturing overhead, 40% of which is variable, is applied to Steven's products using a plant-wide application rate of 250% of direct labor dollars.

Unit costs	Model A	Model B	Model C
Direct material	$150	$100	$114
Direct labor	40	50	48
Manufacturing overhead	100	125	120
Total unit costs	$290	$275	$282
Other costs			
Tooling and advertising	$3,000,000	$4,500,000	$4,100,000
Incurred development costs	1,500,000	1,500,000	1,500,000

Steven has decided to employ an expected value model in his analysis to reach a decision as to which of the three prototypes to manufacture and sell.

Questions

1. Develop a payoff table to determine the expected monetary value for each of the three models Steven Company could manufacture. Based on your analysis, identify the prototype model Steven should manufacture and sell.

2. Steven Company's costs for a back-up unit design that was not developed into a prototype were estimated as follows:

Unit costs	
Direct materials	$130
Direct labor	46
Manufacturing overhead	115
Total unit costs	$291
Other costs	
Tooling and advertising	$4,000,000
Incurred development costs	1,500,000

    If this design had been developed into a viable model, it would have sold for $400 and had the same expected demand as the other models. Steven's management eliminated this model from consideration because it was considered an inadmissible act, i.e., the calculation of its payoff would have been irrelevant. Explain why the model design was considered an inadmissible act, thus making the calculation of its payoff irrelevant.

3. Steven Company could have employed a decision tree model in this situation. Explain how the decision tree model could have been employed in making this decision.

Essay Questions 1, 2, 3 — Unofficial Answers

1. Steven Company should manufacture and sell Model B because this model provides the greatest expected profit ($9,700,000). Supporting calculations are presented below.

Unit Contribution Margin Calculation

	Model A	Model B	Model C	Undeveloped Prototype (Requirement b)
Selling price	$400	$400	$400	$400
Variable costs				
Direct material	150	100	114	130
Direct labor	40	50	48	46
Manufacturing overhead				
Variable	40	50	48	46
Fixed	0	0	0	0
Total variance costs	230	200	210	222
Contribution margin	$170	$200	$190	$178

Total Contribution Margin Calculation by Volume Level ($000 omitted)

Volume Level		Model A	Model B	Model C	Prototype (Requirement b)
Demand	Units				
Light	20,000	$ 3,400	$ 4,000	$ 3,800	$ 3,560
Moderate	80,000	13,600	16,000	15,200	14,240
Heavy	120,000	20,400	24,000	22,800	21,360
Fixed costs					
Tooling and advertising		3,000	4,500	4,100	4,000

Development – sunk cost – not relevant

Payoff Table of Conditional Profit (Loss) by Model ($000 omitted)

Volume Level		Model A	Model B	Model C	Prototype
Demand	Units				
Light	20,000	$ 400	$ (500)	$ (300)	$ (440)
Moderate	80,000	10,600	11,500	11,100	10,240
Heavy	120,000	17,400	19,500	18,700	17,360

Expected Monetary Value ($000 omitted)

Demand	Probability	Model A	Model B	Model C
Light	.25	$ 100	$ (125)	$ (75)
Moderate	.60	6,360	6,900	6,660
Heavy	.15	2,610	2,925	2,805
Expected monetary value		$9,070	$9,700	$9,390

2. The undeveloped prototype model was considered an inadmissible act because the conditional profit (loss), or payoff, at each level of demand (light, moderate, heavy) for this model was less than Model C (see calculations for Question 1).

3. A decision tree could have been developed for this decision. The alternatives -- Models A, B, C -- could have been represented as branches from the decision point (square node). For each alternative, branches representing the possible events (demand levels) would be extended from event nodes (circles). The conditional profit or loss resulting from each possible demand level would appear at the end of the event branch. Each conditional profit (loss), for each event of each alternative, would be weighted by its probability and then summed to determine the expected monetary value (EMV) for each alternative. The alternative with the greatest EMV would be selected.

Scenario for Essay Question 4

Video Recreation, Inc. (VRI) is a supplier of video games and equipment such as large-screen televisions and DVD players. The company has recently concluded a major contract with Sunview Hotels to supply games for the hotel video lounges. Under this contract, a total of 4,000 games will be delivered to Sunview Hotels throughout the western United States, and all of the games will have a warranty period of 1 year for both parts and labor. The number of service calls required to repair these games during the first year after installation is estimated as follows:

Number of Service Calls	Probability
400	.1
700	.3
900	.4
1,200	.2

VRI's Customer Service Department has developed three alternatives for providing the warranty service to Sunview. These three plans are presented below.

Plan 1: VRI would contract with local firms to perform the repair services. It is estimated that six such vendors would be needed to cover the appropriate areas and that each of these vendors would charge an annual fee of $15,000 to have personnel available and to stock the appropriate parts. In addition to the annual fee, VRI would be billed $250 for each service call and would be billed for parts used at cost plus a 10% surcharge.

Plan 2: VRI would allow the management of each hotel to arrange for repair service when needed and then would reimburse the hotel for the expenses incurred. It is estimated that 60% of the service calls would be for hotels located in urban areas where the charge for a service call would average $450. At the remaining hotels, the charges would be $350. In addition to these service charges, parts would be billed at cost.

Plan 3: VRI would hire its own personnel to perform repair services and to do preventive maintenance. Nine employees located in the appropriate geographical areas would be required to fulfill these responsibilities, and their average salary would be $24,000 annually. The fringe benefit expense for these employees would amount to 35% of their wages. Each employee would be scheduled to make an average of 200 preventive maintenance calls during the year; each of these calls would require $15 worth of parts. Because of this preventive maintenance, it is estimated that the expected number of hotel calls for repair service would decline 30%, and the cost of parts required for each repair service call would be reduced by 20%.

VRI's Accounting Department has reviewed the historical data on the repair costs for equipment installations similar to those proposed for Sunview Hotels and found that the cost of parts required for each repair occurred in the following proportions:

Parts Cost per Repair	Proportion
$30	15%
$40	15%
$60	45%
$90	25%

Question

4. Video Recreation, Inc. wishes to select the least costly alternative to fulfill its warranty obligations to Sunview Hotels. Recommend which of the three plans presented above should be adopted by VRI. Support your recommendation with appropriate calculations and analysis.

Essay Question 4 — Unofficial Answers

4.   Video Recreation, Inc. should adopt Plan 3 as the least costly alternative. Calculations for all three plans are as follows:

Expected Number of Service Calls

Number of Service Calls	×	Probability	=	Expected Calls
400		.1		40
700		.3		210
900		.4		360
1,200		.2		240
		1.0		850

Expected Value of Parts Costs

Parts Cost per Repair	×	Proportion	=	Expected Cost
$30		.15		$ 4.50
40		.15		6.00
60		.45		27.00
90		.25		22.50
		1.00		$60.00

Plan 1

Vendor fees (6 × $15,000)	$ 90,000
Service calls (850 × $250)	212,500
Parts ($60 × 850 × 1.1)	56,100
Estimated total cost	$358,600

Plan 2

Urban service calls (850 × .6 × $450)	$229,500
Rural service calls (850 × .4 × $350)	119,000
Parts ($60 × 850)	51,000
Estimated total cost	$399,500

Plan 3

Employee salaries (9 × $24,000)	$216,000
Fringe benefits (.35 × $216,000)	75,600
Preventive maintenance parts (200 × 9 × $15)	27,000
Repair parts (850 × .7)($60 × .8)	28,560
Estimated total cost	$347,160

Scenario for Essay Questions 5, 6, 7, 8

The firm of Miller, Lombardi, and York was recently formed by the merger of two companies providing accounting services. York's business was providing personal financial planning, while Miller and Lombardi conducted audits of small governmental units and provided tax planning and preparation for several commercial firms. The combined firm has leased new offices and acquired several laptop computers that are used by the professional staff in each area of service. However, in the short run, the firm does not have the financial resources to acquire computers for all of the professional staff.

The expertise of the professional staff can be divided into three distinct areas that match the services provided by the firm, i.e., tax preparation and planning, insurance and investments, and auditing. However, since the merger, the new firm has had to turn away business in all three areas of service. One of the problems is that, while the total number of staff seems adequate, the staff members are not completely interchangeable. Limited financial resources do not permit hiring any new staff in the near future and, therefore, the supply of staff is restricted in each area.

Rich Oliva has been assigned the responsibility of allocating staff and computers to the various engagements. Management has given Oliva the objective of maximizing revenues in a manner consistent with maintaining a high level of professional service in each of the areas of service. Management's time is billed at $160 per hour, and the staff's time is billed at $100 per hour for those with experience, and $80 per hour for inexperienced staff. Pam Wren, a member of the staff, recently completed a course in quantitative methods at the local university. She suggested to Oliva that he use linear programming to assign the appropriate staff and computers to the various engagements.

Questions

5. Identify and discuss the assumptions underlying the linear programming model.

6. Explain the reasons why linear programming would be appropriate for Miller, Lombardi, and York to use in making staff assignments.

7. Identify and discuss the data that would be needed to develop a linear programming model for Miller, Lombardi, and York.

8. Discuss objectives other than revenue maximization that Rich Oliva should consider before making staff allocations.

Essay Questions 5, 6, 7, 8 — Unofficial Answers

5.   The linear programming model starts with an objective or goal to be achieved subject to a set of limiting factors called constraints. The linear programming model allows the user to optimize (maximize or minimize) the objective function subject to the constraints. The central assumptions in all linear programming models are linearity, certainty, and non-negativity. The linearity assumption means that the objective function and the constraints in the model can be expressed in the form of linear equations. The constraints can be in the form of strict equalities or upper and lower bounds, i.e., less than or greater than. The certainty assumption means that the numerical value of any factor in the problem will not vary significantly. The non-negativity assumption limits the solution to positive numbers with real meaning, e.g., the staff cannot work negative hours.

6.   Linear programming methods are applied mainly to allocation problems, that is, allocating scarce resources among alternative uses according to some objective. The scarce resources for a business firm may include personnel, material, equipment, or capital. The objective function may take the form of profit maximization or some other measure of desired performance. In this particular case, linear programming is appropriate since the firm of Miller, Lombardi, and York has an objective in the form of profit maximization subject to restricted resources, i.e., staff available in the short run is restricted in each area.

7.   The following data would be needed to develop the linear programming model for Miller, Lombardi, and York.

   a.   Total management hours available in each category of service provided

   b.   Total hours by each type of staff, i.e., experienced and without experience, available for each category of service provided

   c.   Number of microcomputers and hours available

   d.   Billing rates for management and staff

8.   Rich Oliva should consider the following alternative objectives before making the staff allocations:

   a.   Maximize the computer hours available

   b.   Minimize total variable costs consistent with maintaining a high level of professional service

   c.   Nonquantitative objectives such as the preferences of individuals in management to be in specific areas of service

Scenario for Essay Questions 9, 10, 11

Leastan Company manufactures a line of carpeting which includes a commercial carpet and a residential carpet. Two grades of fiber, heavy-duty and regular, are used in manufacturing both types of carpeting. The mix of the two grades of fiber differs in each type of carpeting, with the commercial grade using a greater amount of heavy-duty fiber.

Leastan will introduce a new line of carpeting in two months to replace the current line. The present fiber in stock will not be used in the new line. Management wants to exhaust the present stock of regular and heavy-duty fiber during the last month of production.

Data regarding the current line of commercial and residential carpeting are presented below.

	Commercial	Residential
Selling price per roll	$1,000	$800
Production specifications per roll of carpet:		
Heavy-duty fiber, lb.	80	40
Regular fiber, lb.	20	40
Direct labor hours	15	15
Standard cost per roll of carpet:		
Heavy-duty fiber ($3/lb.)	$240	$120
Regular fiber ($2/lb.)	40	80
Direct labor ($10/hour)	150	150
Variable manufacturing overhead		
(60% of direct labor cost)	90	90
Fixed manufacturing overhead		
(120% of direct labor cost)	180	180
Total standard cost per roll	$700	$620

Leastan has 42,000 pounds of heavy-duty fiber and 24,000 pounds of regular fiber in stock. All fiber not used in the manufacture of the present types of carpeting during the last month of production can be sold as scrap at $.25 a pound.

There is a maximum of 10,500 direct labor hours available during the month. The labor force can work on either type of carpeting.

Sufficient demand exists for the present line of carpeting so that all quantities produced can be sold.

Questions

9. Calculate the number of rolls of commercial carpet and residential carpet Leastan Company must manufacture during the last month of production to completely exhaust the heavy-duty and regular fiber still in stock.

10. Can Leastan Company manufacture these quantities of commercial and residential carpeting during the last month of production? Explain your answer.

11. A member of Leastan Company's cost accounting staff has stated that linear programming should be used to determine the number of rolls of commercial and residential carpeting to manufacture during the last month of production.

   a. Explain why linear programming should be used in this application.
   b. Formulate the objective and constraint functions so that this application can be solved by linear programming.

Essay Questions 9, 10, 11 — Unofficial Answers

9.   Let C = Rolls of commercial carpet;
        R = Rolls of residential carpet

Heavy-duty fiber constraint (80C + 40R = 42,000 pounds)
Regular fiber constraint (20C + 40R = 24,000 pounds)

Solving by simultaneous equations

$$
\begin{array}{rl}
80C + 40R &= 42,000 \\
-\ (20C + 40R &= 24,000) \\
\hline
60C &= 18,000
\end{array}
$$

Commercial Carpet = 300 Rolls

$$
\begin{array}{rl}
20(300) + 40R &= 24,000 \\
6,000 + 40R &= 24,000 \\
40R &= 18,000
\end{array}
$$

Residential Carpet = 450 Rolls

10.   No. Leastan Company cannot manufacture these quantities of commercial and residential carpeting because the direct labor constraint will be exceeded as shown in the following calculation:

Labor constraint: 15C + 15R = 10,500

Using the solution from Question 9 above (e.g., C = 300, R = 450):

        15(300) + 15(450) = 11,250 > 10,500

The direct labor hour constraint is exceeded by 750 hours.

11.   a.   Linear programming is a mathematical model for solving two or more unknowns in two or more equations. Linear programming is used to determine a mix of products which will maximize the contribution margin or minimize costs by identifying inputs, outputs, and their related assumptions and limitations (constraints) and combining them in the model. Linear programming can be used to allocate limited facilities and resources among their many alternative uses in such a way that optimum benefit is derived from their utilization.

    b.   Let C = Rolls of commercial carpet
        R = Rolls of residential carpet
        S_1 = Pounds of scrap of heavy-duty fiber
        S_2 = Pounds of scrap of regular fiber

Maximize $Z = 760C + 560R + .25S_1 + .25S_2$

Constraints:

Heavy-duty fiber	$80C + 40R + S_1 = 42,000$ lbs.
Regular fiber	$20C + 40R + S_2 = 24,000$ lbs.
Direct labor	$15C + 15R \leq 10,500$ hours
Non-negativity	$C, R, S_1, S_2 \geq 0$

Scenario for Essay Questions 12, 13, 14

The Henderson Equipment Company has produced a pilot run of 50 units of a recently developed cylinder used in its finished products. The cylinder has a 1-year life, and the company expects to produce and sell 1,650 units annually. The pilot run required 14.25 direct labor hours for the 50 cylinders, averaging .285 direct labor hours per cylinder. The last cylinder in the pilot run required .194 direct labor hours. Henderson has experienced an 80% learning curve on the direct labor hours needed to produce new cylinders. Past experience indicates that learning tends to cease by the time 800 parts are produced.

Henderson's manufacturing costs for cylinders are presented below:

Direct labor	$12.00 per hour
Variable overhead	10.00 per direct labor hour
Fixed overhead	16.60 per direct labor hour
Materials	4.05 per unit

When pricing products, Henderson factors in selling and administrative expenses at $12.70 per direct labor hour.

Henderson has received a quote of $7.50 per unit from the Lytel Machine Company for the additional 1,600 cylinders needed. Henderson frequently subcontracts this type of work and has always been satisfied with the quality of the units produced by Lytel.

Questions

12. If the cylinders are manufactured by Henderson Equipment Company, determine

    a. The average direct labor hours per unit for the first 800 cylinders (including the pilot run) produced. Round calculations to three decimal places.

    b. The total direct labor hours for the first 800 cylinders (including the pilot run) produced.

    c. The marginal direct labor hours for the 800th cylinder produced. Round calculations to three decimal places.

13. After completing the pilot run, Henderson Equipment Company must manufacture an additional 1,600 units to fulfill the annual requirement of 1,650 units. Without prejudice to your answer in Question 12, assume that

    • The first 800 cylinders produced (including the pilot run) required 100 direct labor hours, and

    • The 800th unit produced (including the pilot run) required .079 hours.

    Calculate the total manufacturing costs for Henderson to produce the additional 1,600 cylinders required.

14. In order to maximize profits, determine whether Henderson Equipment Company should manufacture the additional 1,600 cylinders or purchase the cylinders from Lytel Machine Company. Support your answer with appropriate calculations.

Essay Questions 12, 13, 14 — Unofficial Answers

12. If the cylinders are manufactured by Henderson Equipment Company, the direct labor hour computations are as follows:

   a. For the first 800 cylinders (including the pilot run) produced, the average direct labor hour per unit equals .117.

   b. For the first 800 cylinders (including the pilot run) produced, the total direct labor hours amount to 93.60.

   c. For the 800th cylinder produced, the marginal direct labor hour equals .079.

Formulas:

1. Average direct labor hours per unit   = Prior production run's direct labor hours per unit × .8
2. Total direct labor hours   = Average direct labor hours per unit × cumulative units
                                                     of production
3. Marginal direct labor hours   = Prior production run's marginal direct labor hours × .8

Cumu- lative Output		Average DL Hours per Unit		Total DL Hours		Marginal DL Hours
50		.285		14.25		.194
100	(.8 × .285)	.228	× 100	22.80	(.8 × .194)	.155
200	(.8 × .228)	.182	× 200	36.40	(.8 × .155)	.124
400	(.8 × .182)	.146	× 400	58.40	(.8 × .124)	.099
800	(.8 × .146)	.117	× 800	93.60	(.8 × .099)	.079

13. The total costs to produce the additional 1,600 cylinders required, assuming the first 800 cylinders produced (including the pilot run) required 100 direct labor hours and the 800th unit produced required .079 direct labor hour, amounts to $12,381.94, calculated as follows:

- Total units to be produced   =   1,650
- Additional units required   =   1,600 (1,650 – Pilot Run of 50)
- Units available to meet the 1,600 requirement   =   750 (800 – Pilot Run of 50)
- Additional production requirement   =   850 (1,600 – 750)

Direct labor hours consumed	= 85.75 hours (100 hours – Pilot Run of 14.25 hours)	
Direct labor	= 85.75 hours × $12.00/hour	$1,029.00
Variable overhead	= 85.75 hours × $10.00/hour	857.50
Fixed overhead	= 85.75 hours × $16.60/hour	1,423.45
Material	= 750 units × $4.05/unit	3,037.50

Last 850 units

Aggregate cost 850 units × [.079 ($12.00 + 10.00 + 16.60) + 4.05]	6,034.49
Total manufacturing costs for remaining 1,600 units	$12,381.94

14. To maximize profits, Henderson Equipment Company should manufacture the additional 1,600 cylinders. The cost to manufacture is $2,156.20 less than the cost to purchase from Lytel Machine Company, calculated as shown below.

Purchase cost (1,600 units @ $7.50 per unit)			$12,000.00
Manufacturing cost: Question 13 above		$12,381.94	
Less: Fixed overhead 750 units (85.75 hours × $16.60)	$1,423.45		
850 units (850 × .079 × $16.60)	1,114.69	2,538.14	9,843.77
Savings by manufacturing			$ 2,156.20

STUDY UNIT TWELVE
CMA PART 1 REVIEW –
FINANCIAL STATEMENT ANALYSIS

(12 pages of outline)

Part 1 of the CMA exam is titled **Business Analysis**. This study unit is a review of this section:

E.   **Financial Statement Analysis.** Development of accounting standards; financial statement assurance; interpretation and analysis of financial statements including ratio analysis and comparative analysis; limitations of ratio analysis; market value vs. book value; international issues.

This study unit presents the IMA's Learning Outcome Statements and Gleim Core Concepts relevant to this section. Bear in mind that **all topics** on Part 4 of the exam are tested at **skill level C** (all six skill types required).

12.1   FINANCIAL STATEMENT ANALYSIS REVIEW

Part 1 – Section E.1. Development of accounting standards

The candidate should be able to:

   a.   demonstrate an understanding of the development of U.S. accounting standards

   b.   describe the organizational structure of the Financial Accounting Standards Board (FASB)

   c.   identify the due process steps of developing U.S. accounting standards

   d.   identify the qualitative characteristics of accounting information

   e.   distinguish between the primary qualities of relevance and reliability and the secondary qualities of comparability and consistency

   f.   identify the ingredients of each of the primary qualities

   g.   identify the user groups that influence accounting standards, including the investing public and financial community, business entities and industrial associations, the Institute of Management Accountants (IMA), the American Institute of Certified Public Accountants (AICPA), CPA firms, government agencies, the American Accounting Association (AAA), the Financial Executive Institute (FEI), and other professional accounting and finance organizations

   h.   demonstrate an understanding of the FASB's relationship with the Securities and Exchange Commission (SEC) and the SEC's role in standard setting

   i.   identify the different types of statements that constitute U.S. Generally Accepted Accounting Principles (GAAP) and identify which is most authoritative

   j.   describe in general terms the structure and work products of the International Accounting Standards Board (IASB) and its relationship with the FASB

Core Concepts for the Development of U.S. Accounting Standards

- The **Securities and Exchange Commission (SEC)** has the authority to promulgate accounting rules for publicly held companies. The SEC in turn delegated rule-making authority to the American Institute of Accountants, later the **American Institute of Certified Public Accountants (AICPA)**.

- The AICPA established the **Financial Accounting Standards Board (FASB)**, which promulgates generally accepted accounting principles (GAAP) for U.S. businesses. As of March 2008, the FASB had issued 160 **Statements of Financial Accounting Standards (SFASs)**.

- The **FASB has historically had seven salaried members**, all having extensive experience in financial accounting, with four required to be CPAs. Each member severs all other business affiliations during his/her term. A simple majority of the FASB decides its agenda. The members determine which subjects require attention and the order of their importance. The number of board members is being reduced to five on July 1, 2008.

- **FASB procedures** may be summarized as follows:

  Step 1   A project is placed on the agenda.
  Step 2   A task force of experts defines specific problems and alternatives.
  Step 3   The FASB technical staff conducts research and analysis.
  Step 4   A discussion memorandum is drafted and released.
  Step 5   At least 60 days later, a public hearing is held.
  Step 6   Public response is evaluated.
  Step 7   The FASB deliberates on the various issues raised.
  Step 8   The FASB releases an exposure draft of a proposed statement.
  Step 9   At least a 30-day waiting period is allowed for public comment.
  Step 10 All letters and comments are evaluated.
  Step 11 The FASB revises the draft if necessary.
  Step 12 The entire FASB gives final consideration to the draft.
  Step 13 The FASB takes a final vote.

- If **four or more affirmative votes** are cast, a Statement of Financial Accounting Standards (SFAS) is issued. All dissenting opinions of board members must be published along with the statement.

- The hierarchies for U.S. GAAP are presented in Statement on Auditing Standards 69 (as amended), which is codified in AICPA Professional Standards as section AU 411. Category (a), with the **highest degree of authoritativeness**, contains FASB Standards and Interpretations; APB Opinions; and Accounting Research Bulletins (the latter two as long as they have not been superseded by SFASs).

Core Concepts for Qualitative Characteristics of Accounting Information

- The FASB's **Statement of Financial Accounting Concepts (SFAC) 2**, *Qualitative Characteristics of Accounting Information*, describes the qualities or characteristics of accounting information that make it **useful for decision making**.

- **Understandability** and **decision usefulness** are user-specific qualities.

- Relevance is the first primary decision-specific quality. The two principal ingredients of relevance are

  - **Feedback value** and
  - **Predictive value**.
  - **Timeliness** is an ancillary aspect of relevance.

- **Reliability** is the other primary decision-specific quality. The three principal ingredients of reliability are

  - **Representational faithfulness**
  - **Verifiability**
  - **Neutrality**

- **Comparability and consistency** are the secondary and interactive qualities.
- **Costs and benefits** is the pervasive constraint, i.e., the cost of providing a piece of financial information should not outweigh the benefit that a decision maker can gain from it.
- **Materiality** is the threshold for recognition. Materiality is "the magnitude of an omission or misstatement of accounting information that, in the light of surrounding circumstances, makes it probable that the judgment of a reasonable person relying on the information would have been changed or influenced by the omission or misstatement."

Core Concepts for Groups Involved in Standard Setting

- Groups of users differ in their needs for financial reporting. Because of their varying interests, these **user groups attempt to influence the standard setting process**, seeking to have transactions and events reported in the particular way most useful for their purposes.
- The **principal groups** interested in standard setting are
  - The investing public and the financial community
  - Business entities and industrial associations
  - Institute of Management Accountants (IMA)
  - American Institute of Certified Public Accountants (AICPA)
    - Accounting Standards Executive Committee (AcSEC)
  - Larger CPA firms
  - Governmental bodies
    - Governmental Accounting Standards Board (GASB)
    - Federal Accounting Standards Advisory Board (FASAB)
    - Cost Accounting Standards Board (CASB)
  - U.S. Congress
  - Internal Revenue Service
  - American Accounting Association (AAA)
  - Financial Executives International (FEI)
- The **Sarbanes-Oxley Act of 2002** led to the creation of the the **Public Company Accounting Oversight Board (PCAOB)**. The PCAOB will establish by rule auditing, quality control, ethics, independence, and other standards relating to the preparation of audit reports for public entities. The PCAOB is required to cooperate with the AICPA and other groups in setting auditing standards and may adopt their proposals. Nevertheless, the PCAOB is authorized to amend, modify, repeal, or reject any such standards.
- The **International Accounting Standards Board (IASB)** cooperates with national accounting standard-setters to achieve convergence in accounting standards around the world. The IASB has issued 8 International Financial Reporting Standards (IFRSs). IFRSs were recognized by the European Union as of January 1, 2005, and by the U.S. SEC in 2007 (but for now, only for non-U.S.-based companies).

Part 1 – Section E.2. Financial statement assurance

The candidate should be able to:

a. demonstrate an understanding of the distinct responsibilities of management and of independent auditors for the financial statements

b. identify the type of audit report that would be issued given a specific set of facts

c. identify related provisions of the Sarbanes-Oxley Act of 2002 and the related rulings of the Public Company Accounting Oversight Board (PCAOB)

Core Concepts for Financial Statement Assurance

- **Certified Public Accountants (CPAs)** offer a variety of services. The traditional **financial statement audit** is the most important assurance service that CPAs provide. Audited GAAP-based financial statements are a must for such purposes as filing with the Securities and Exchange Commission (SEC) and applying for lines of credit with banks.

- A traditional audit provides the **highest level of assurance**. Specifically, the auditor states that the entity's financial statements are presented fairly in accordance with generally accepted accounting principles (GAAP), and that the auditor is reasonably sure that the statements contain no material misstatements.

- A radical change in the traditional practice of auditing was brought about by the **Sarbanes-Oxley Act of 2002**. The Act established the **Public Company Accounting Oversight Board (PCAOB)** "to oversee the auditors of public companies in order to protect the interests of investors and further the public interest in the preparation of informative, fair, and independent audit reports."

- PCAOB Auditing Standard 2 requires that an **audit of internal control** be **integrated** with the audit of financial statements.

- Although auditors are allowed to issue separate reports on the audits of financial statements and internal controls, in practice they are most **often combined into a single report**. The wording and structure of audit reports have been standardized in order to avoid misinterpretations.

  - The **introductory paragraph**
  - The **scope paragraph**
  - The **definition paragraph**
  - The **inherent limitations paragraph**
  - The **opinion paragraph**

- The Five Types of Audit Reports

  - A **standard unqualified opinion**
  - An **unqualified opinion with explanatory language**
  - A **qualified opinion**
  - An **adverse opinion**
  - A **disclaimer of opinion**

- The **Sarbanes-Oxley Act of 2002** contains provisions that impose **new responsibilities** on publicly traded companies and their auditors. Among these, the chief executive officer (CEO) and chief financial officer (CFO) of the issuer must certify that the issuer's financial statements and disclosures "fairly present, in all material respects, the operations and financial condition of the issuer." This statement must accompany the audit report.

- **Section 404** of the Sarbanes-Oxley Act requires management to establish and document internal control procedures and to include in the annual report a **report on the company's internal control** over financial reporting. The **auditor must attest** to and report on management's assessment. The auditor's report also must describe any material weaknesses in the controls.

Part 1 – Section E.3. Short-term liquidity

The candidate should be able to:

- a. define and calculate current assets, current liabilities, and working capital
- b. analyze working capital by calculating the current ratio, the quick (acid test) ratio, the cash ratio, the cash flow ratio, and the cash to current liabilities ratio
- c. calculate and interpret accounts receivable turnover and inventory turnover and demonstrate an understanding of the effects on these ratios of changes in one or more elements in the financial statement

d. calculate and interpret days sales outstanding in receivables, days sales in inventory, and days purchases in accounts payable
e. define the operating cycle of a firm
f. demonstrate an understanding of the liquidity of current liabilities
g. identify the liquidity index as a measure of short-term liquidity

Core Concepts for Short-Term Liquidity

- **Liquidity** is a firm's ability to pay its current obligations as they come due and thus remain in business in the short run. Liquidity measures the ease with which assets can be converted to cash.
- **Liquidity ratios** measure this ability by relating a firm's liquid assets to its current liabilities.
  - The **current ratio**

    Current assets ÷ Current liabilities
  - The **quick (acid test) ratio**

    (Cash and equivalents + Marketable securities + Net receivables) ÷ Current liabilities
  - The **cash ratio**

    (Cash and equivalents + Marketable securities) ÷ Current liabilities
  - The **cash-to-current-liabilities ratio**

    Cash and equivalents ÷ Current liabilities
  - The **cash flow ratio**

    Cash flow from operations ÷ Current liabilities
- **Activity ratios** measure how quickly the two major noncash assets are converted to cash. They measure results over a period of time, and thus draw information from the firm's income statement.
  - **Accounts receivable turnover**

    Net credit sales ÷ Average trade receivables (net)
  - **Inventory turnover**

    Cost of goods sold ÷ Average inventory
  - **Accounts payable turnover**

    Purchases ÷ Average accounts payable
  - **Days sales outstanding in receivables**

    365 ÷ Accounts receivable turnover
  - **Days purchases in accounts payable**

    365 ÷ Accounts payable turnover
- **Overall Liquidity Concepts**
  - A firm's **operating cycle** is the amount of time that passes between the acquisition of inventory and the collection of cash on the sale of that inventory.

    Days sales in receivables + Days sales in inventory
  - The **cash cycle** is that portion of the operating cycle that is not days purchases in accounts payable. This is somewhat counterintuitive because the cash cycle is the portion of the operating cycle when the company does not have cash, i.e., when cash is tied up in the form of inventory or accounts receivable.

    Operating cycle – Days purchases in payables
  - The **liquidity of current liabilities** is the ease with which a firm can issue new debt or raise new structured (convertible, puttable, callable, etc.) funds. The **liquidity index** is a measure of the proportion that the two major noncash current assets (weighted) make up of all liquid assets.

Part 1 – Section E.4. Capital structure and solvency

The candidate should be able to:

a.   define capital structure

b.   define solvency

c.   distinguish debt from equity and demonstrate an understanding of the effect on the capital structure and solvency of a company with a change in the composition of debt vs. equity

d.   define operating leverage and financial leverage

e.   calculate and interpret the financial leverage ratio and identify the effects on this ratio with changes in capital structure

f.   calculate and interpret the following ratios: total debt to total capital, total debt to equity capital, equity capital to total debt, long-term debt to equity capital (debt to equity ratio), and debt to total assets

g.   demonstrate an understanding of the effect on these capital structure ratios with a change in one or more elements of the financial statement

h.   define, calculate, and interpret common-size statements

i.   define asset coverage

j.   calculate and interpret the following ratios: fixed assets to equity capital, net tangible assets to long-term debt, and total liabilities to net tangible assets

k.   calculate and interpret the following ratios: earnings to fixed charges, times interest earned, and cash flow to fixed charges

l.   discuss how capital structure decisions affect the risk profile of a firm

Core Concepts for Capital Structure and Solvency

- **Solvency** is a firm's ability to pay its noncurrent obligations as they come due and thus remain in business in the long run (contrast with liquidity). The key ingredients of solvency are the firm's capital structure and degree of leverage.

- A firm's **capital structure** includes its sources of financing, both long- and short-term. These sources can be in the form of debt (external sources) or equity (internal sources). Debt is the creditor interest in the firm. Equity is the ownership interest in the firm.

- A firm's **leverage** is the relative amount of the fixed cost of capital, principally debt, in a firm's capital structure. Leverage, by definition, creates financial risk, which relates directly to the question of the cost of capital. The more leverage, the higher the financial risk, and the higher the cost of debt capital.

  - **Operating leverage**

    Contribution margin ÷ Operating income

  - **Financial leverage**

    Operating income ÷ Net income

  - The **financial leverage ratio**, also called the equity multiplier

    %Δ in Net income ÷ %Δ in EBIT

- **Capital structure ratios** report the relative proportions of debt and equity in a firm's capital structure.

  - The **total debt to total capital ratio**

    Total debt ÷ Total capital

  - The **total debt to equity capital ratio**

    Total debt ÷ Stockholders' equity

  - The **equity capital to total debt ratio**

    Stockholders' equity ÷ Total debt

- • The **long-term debt to equity capital ratio** (also called the debt to equity ratio)

  Long-term debt ÷ Stockholders' equity

- • The **debt to total assets ratio** (also called the debt ratio)

  Total liabilities ÷ Total assets

- ■ **Asset coverage** is the extent to which a firm's liabilities are covered by its assets. Assets are the source of earning power. Their liquidation value also serves as security, whether explicit or implicit, for the firm's debts.

  - • The ratio of **fixed assets to equity capital** indicates the extent to which shareholders have financed a firm's fixed assets.

    Property, plant, and equipment (net) ÷ Stockholders' equity

  - • The ratio of **net tangible assets to long-term debt** is a more conservative measure. It reflects the amount of liquidatable assets available for debt payment in the event of default.

  - • The ratio of **total liabilities to net tangible assets** measures the security provided to all creditors, not just long-term, by the firm's more readily realizable assets.

- ■ **Earnings coverage** is a creditor's best measure of a firm's ongoing ability to generate the earnings that will allow it to satisfy its long-term debts and remain solvent.

  - • The **times interest earned ratio** is an income statement approach to evaluating a firm's ongoing ability to meet the interest payments on its debt obligations.

    EBIT ÷ Interest expense

  - • The **earnings to fixed charges ratio** (also called the fixed charge coverage ratio) extends the times-interest-earned ratio to include the interest portion associated with long-term lease obligations.

  - • The **cash flow to fixed charges ratio** removes the difficulties of comparing amounts prepared on an accrual basis.

Part 1 – Section E.5. Return on invested capital

The candidate should be able to:

- a. identify and define the components of return on invested capital (ROI)
- b. identify uses for ROI
- c. demonstrate an understanding of the factors that contribute to inconsistent definitions of "invested capital" and "return" when using ROI to measure performance
- d. identify and calculate adjustments that should be made to capital and income
- e. calculate and interpret the return on total assets ratio and return on common equity ratio
- f. analyze return on assets and return on equity using the DuPont model
- g. calculate and interpret profit margin on sales and total asset turnover and demonstrate an understanding of the relationship between these two ratios
- h. infer the effect on return on total assets of a change in one or more elements of the financial statements
- i. disaggregate return on common equity into profit margin on sales, total asset turnover, and equity multiplier (leverage) and be able to calculate these ratios given financial statement data
- j. calculate and interpret sustainable equity growth, dividend yield, and the dividend payout ratio
- k. calculate and interpret return on common equity

Core Concepts for Return on Invested Capital

- **Return on invested capital** (also called return on investment or **ROI**) is an umbrella concept for measures that reflect how efficiently a company is using the monies contributed by its shareholders to generate a profit.

- **Return on total assets (ROTA)** is the most common ratio for reporting ROI. It is sometimes referred to simply as **return on assets (ROA)**.

  `Net income ÷ Average total assets`

- **Inconsistent definitions** complicate comparisons of ROI. Many analysts consider the calculation presented above to be far too simplistic. The wide variety of definitions in use for the terms "return" and "investment" creates difficulties in comparability.

- **Return on common equity (ROCE)** is probably the most common adjusted ROI measure.

  `(Net income – Preferred dividends) ÷ Average common equity`

- The **DuPont model** begins with the standard equation for return on total assets and breaks it down into two component ratios, one that focuses on the income statement and one that relates income to the balance sheet:

  `Net profit margin  ×   Total asset turnover`

- **Return on common equity can be disaggregated** into three components, similar to the DuPont model's two for ROTA. The numerator (net income minus preferred dividends) can be thought of as income available to common shareholders (IACS).

  `Net profit margin ×  Total asset turnover  × Equity multiplier`

- **Increasing shareholder wealth** is the fundamental goal of any corporation. Three common ratios measure the success of this goal:

  - The **dividend payout ratio** measures what portion of accrual-basis earnings was actually paid out to common shareholders in the form of dividends.

    `Dividends to common shareholders ÷ IACS`

  - A related ratio is the **dividend yield**:

    `Dividend per share ÷ Market price per share`

  - The **sustainable equity growth rate** is the highest growth rate a company can sustain without increasing leverage.

    `ROCE × (1 – Dividend payout ratio)`

Part 1 – Section E.6. Profitability analysis

The candidate should be able to:

a.   identify factors to be considered in measuring income, including estimates, accounting methods, disclosure incentives, and the different needs of users

b.   explain the importance of the source, stability, and trend of sales and revenue

c.   demonstrate an understanding of the relationship between revenue and receivables and revenue and inventory

d.   infer the effect on revenue with changes in revenue recognition and measurement methods

e.   analyze company cost of sales by calculating and interpreting the gross profit margin

f.   interpret changes in gross profit

g.   analyze company expenses using common-size income statements

h.   identify and define the major expense categories for a company, including selling expenses, depreciation expense, maintenance, amortization, general and administrative expenses, financing expenses, and income taxes

   i.   infer reasons for increases over time in any of these expenses as a percent of revenue

   j.   distinguish between gross profit margin, operating profit margin, and net profit margin, and analyze the effects of changes in the components of each

   k.   calculate and interpret book value per share

Core Concepts for Profitability Analysis

- **Profitability analysis** must address the many factors involved in measuring the firm's income; the stability, sources, and trends of revenue; revenue relationships; and expenses, including cost of sales. This analysis attempts to answer questions about the relevant income measure, income quality, the persistence of income, and the firm's earning power.

- **Income** equals the sum of revenues and gains minus the sum of expenses and losses.

- **Cost of goods sold** is the **single largest cost element** for any seller of merchandise and thus has the greatest impact on profitability. A company's gross profit margin is the percentage of its net sales that it is able to keep after paying for merchandise.

- Three common percentages **measure profitability** directly from the income statement: gross profit margin, operating profit margin, and net profit margin is what percentage remains after other gains and losses (including interest expense) and income taxes have been added or deducted.

- **Book value per share** equals the amount of net assets available to the shareholders of a given type of stock divided by the number of those shares outstanding.

    (Total equity – Liquidation value of preferred equity) ÷ Common shares outstanding

Part 1 – Section E.7. Earnings-based analysis

The candidate should be able to:

   a.   identify the determinants and indicators of earnings quality

   b.   define earnings persistence and identify its determinants

   c.   recast earnings to show persistent earnings for a company, excluding erratic, unusual, and nonrecurring items

   d.   demonstrate an understanding of the relationship between accounting data and stock prices

   e.   calculate and interpret the fundamental valuation multiples of the market/book ratio and the price/earnings ratio

   f.   calculate and interpret basic and diluted earnings per share

   g.   define the concept of earnings power

   h.   calculate and interpret earnings yield, dividend yield, and dividend payout

Core Concepts for Earnings-Based Analysis

- **Earnings quality** is the degree to which a firm's reported earnings represent a reliable measure of its performance.

- **Earnings persistence** is the degree of predictability and stability of the elements, sources, amount, and trend of earnings.

- **Recasting earnings** is the process of separating persistent from nonpersistent items, i.e., from the random, erratic, unusual, and nonrecurring items.

- **Adjusting earnings** and its elements is the process of moving items to the periods most affected for analytical purposes.

- **Fundamental Valuation Multiples**
  - A high **market/book ratio** reflects the stock market's positive assessment of the firm's asset management. It measures how much an investor must spend to "own" a dollar of net assets.
  - A high **price/earnings ratio** reflects the stock market's positive assessment of the firm's earnings quality and persistence. It measures how much an investor must spend to "buy" a dollar of earnings.
- **Earnings per share (EPS)** is probably the most heavily relied-upon performance measure used by investors. EPS states the amount of current-period earnings that can be associated with a single share of a corporation's common stock. EPS is only calculated for **common stock** because common shareholders are the residual owners of a corporation.
  - **Basic Earnings Per Share (BEPS)**

$$\frac{Income\ available\ to\ common\ shareholders}{Weighted\text{-}average\ number\ of\ common\ shares\ outstanding}$$

  - Two BEPS amounts are reported, one using income from continuing operations and one using net income.
  - **Diluted Earnings Per Share (DEPS)**
  - The numerator is increased by the amounts that would not have had to be paid if dilutive potential common stock had been converted, namely, dividends on convertible preferred stock and after-tax interest on convertible debt.
  - The denominator is increased by the weighted-average number of additional shares of common stock that would have been outstanding if dilutive potential common stock had been converted.
- **Earnings power**, also called earnings coverage, is the capacity of the firm's operations to produce cash inflows. A predictably stable pattern of earnings is the optimal source of funds for payment of long-term debt and other fixed charges. It also enhances the firm's credit standing, allowing it to borrow on favorable terms when its cash balance is low.
- **Earnings yield** is the rate of return on the fair value of a share of common stock. It is the reciprocal of the P-E ratio and thus measures the amount of earnings an investor expects to receive per dollar invested.

  Earnings per share ÷ Market price per share

Part 1 – Section E.8. Other analytical issues

The candidate should be able to:

- a.   analyze common-size financial statements
- b.   identify other factors in financial statement analysis, including international considerations, inflation, and nonfinancial considerations
- c.   demonstrate the impact of inflation and foreign exchange fluctuations on financial ratios
- d.   identify limitations of ratio analysis
- e.   distinguish between accounting profit and economic profit
- f.   distinguish between book value and market value

Core Concepts for Other Analytical Issues

- **Comparative analysis** involves both horizontal and vertical analysis. Horizontal (trend) analysis compares analytical data over a period of time. Vertical analysis makes comparisons among a single year's data.

- Comparing a company's performance with respect to its **industry** may identify the company's strengths and weaknesses.

- **Common-size financial statements** are used to compare firms of different sizes. Items on common-size financial statements are expressed as percentages of corresponding base-year figures. The base amount is assigned the value of 100%.

- **Inflation** is an increase and **deflation** is a decrease in the general price level. The more common occurrence is inflation. The general price level is inversely related to the purchasing power of money.

- Tools for **Measuring Price Level Changes**

  - The **Consumer Price Index (CPI)** measures price level by a monthly pricing of a specified set of goods and services purchased by a typical urban consumer.

  - The **gross domestic product (GDP) price index (GDP deflator)** includes the prices of all goods and services produced in the U.S.

  - The **Producer Price Index (PPI)** measures the prices of specified commodities at the time of their first commercial sale.

- **Impact of Inflation** on Financial Management

  - Interest rates include an inflation premium
  - Inflation increases resource prices
  - Taxpayers may be pushed into higher brackets
  - Profits are distorted
  - The accuracy of forecasts required for business planning is reduced

- Inflation is an **arbitrary redistribution of income** that does not reflect the operations of the free market or the government's attempt to alter income distribution. Inflation hurts creditors, fixed-income groups, and savers. But inflation benefits debtors because they pay back their debts in less valuable units of money.

- **Two approaches** to accounting for price-level changes can be used. Both methods require classifying balance sheet items as monetary or nonmonetary. **Monetary items** include cash, receivables, and payables. They require no adjustment because they automatically reflect their real purchasing power and "replacement cost" as of the balance sheet date. **Nonmonetary items** include inventories; property, plant, and equipment; intangible assets; unearned income; and equity items.

  - The **constant dollar/purchasing power approach** involves restating nonmonetary items to account for the effects of inflation. Each nonmonetary item is multiplied by a conversion percentage calculated as follows:

    Price index at reporting date ÷ Price index at time of original transaction

  - The **current cost approach** involves restating nonmonetary balance sheet items at their current (replacement) cost.

- The FASB grappled with the issue of price-level accounting but met with resistance from issuers of financial statements. Under **GAAP**, therefore, financial statements must adhere to the principle of **historical cost**.

Core Concepts for Limitations of Ratio Analysis

- Although ratio analysis provides useful information pertaining to the efficiency of operations and the stability of financial condition, it has **inherent limitations**.
  - Comparison with industry averages is more useful for firms that operate within a particular industry than for conglomerates.
  - The effects of inflation on fixed assets and depreciation, inventory costs, long-term debt, and profitability cause misstatement of a firm's balance sheet and income statement.
  - Ratio analysis may be affected by seasonal factors.
  - A firm's management has an incentive to window dress financial statements to improve results.
  - Comparability of financial statement amounts and the ratios derived from them is impaired if different firms choose different accounting policies.
  - Generalizations regarding which ratios are strong indicators of a firm's financial position may change from industry to industry, firm to firm, and division to division.
  - Ratios are based on accounting data, much of which is subject to estimation.
  - Managers may be induced to manipulate accounting data as a means of enhancing stock prices.
  - Earnings quality is the precision of the "noise" term contained in earnings. It is the inverse of the variance in earnings. If earnings have a high degree of variability, many ratios will become less meaningful.

12.2 FINANCIAL STATEMENT ANALYSIS ESSAY QUESTIONS

Recall that your CMA Part 4 exam will probably contain six scenarios, with about three questions per scenario. There will be a recommended time allocation of 20 minutes, 30 minutes, or 45 minutes for each scenario and related questions.

One scenario will involve ethical issues, and probably one or two scenarios will include calculations and responses on a worksheet. Also, expect at least one scenario on organizational/behavioral topics. The remaining scenarios cover Parts 1, 2, and 3.

Scenario Title	Subtopic	Questions	Suggested Time
Meyers and Richardson	Types of Audit Opinions	1, 2	45 minutes
Politicization of Standard Setting	Politicization of Standard Setting	3, 4, 5	30 minutes
GASB	Role of GASB	6, 7, 8, 9	30 minutes

Scenario for Essay Questions 1, 2

An independent auditing firm, Meyers and Richardson (M&R), recently encountered the following situations on five engagements:

- Myracle Corporation has been an audit client with M&R for over 10 years. In the past 4 years, the financial condition of Myracle has steadily declined to the point that M&R substantially doubts the company's ability to continue in existence. There were no other problems noted during the audit.

- Parker Corporation has decided to value fixed assets using replacement costs and to record inventory at the selling price rather than the original cost (both practices produce a higher cost and were significant in nature). Parker believes that this better suits the information needs of shareholders. After M&R informed Parker that these practices were departures from generally accepted accounting principles, Parker insisted that, if the information is allowed in supplemental reporting, it should be permitted in the body of the statements.

- Eaton Industries has been an audit client for 3 years. Eaton's operations are profitable, and business is accelerating. Since it is 85 days after the end of Eaton's fiscal year, management is urging M&R to prepare the auditor's report. Eaton's net inventory balance is 20% of total assets, but Eaton's management has not authorized the taking of a physical inventory because it would disrupt company activities to the extent that sales would be lost. M&R has been unable to verify the inventory balance using alternative methods and believes there is not sufficient evidence to form an opinion.

- Carter Corporation has recently sold common stock to the public and has hired M&R as the auditor. After completion of the field work, M&R was told that the company does not wish to issue a statement of cash flows, as Carter's management believes it is misleading and not necessary to evaluate company activities. No other problems were noted during the audit.

- Markay Corporation has been a client for several years and has received a "clean opinion" on every engagement. During the current year, Markay changed the estimates used in the depreciation of its major assets because of new engineering information. This change increased Markay's net income and is disclosed in a footnote to the financial statements.

At the conclusion of a financial audit, the auditor usually issues an Independent Auditor's Report to be included in the client's annual report and attached to the Securities and Exchange Commission's Form 10-K. The most prevalent type of auditor's report that is issued is the standard report.

Questions

1. Briefly describe the purpose and content of each of the three paragraphs that an independent auditor includes in the standard Independent Auditor's Report.

2. Identify the type of opinion Meyers and Richardson (M&R), the independent audit firm, would render for

    a. Myracle Corporation
    b. Parker Corporation
    c. Eaton Industries
    d. Carter Corporation
    e. Markay Corporation

    Be sure to explain the rationale for the type of opinion selected.

Essay Questions 1, 2 — Unofficial Answers

1.   The purpose and content of each of the three paragraphs that an independent auditor includes in the standard Independent Auditor's Report are as follows:

    a.   The first or introductory paragraph

        1)   Identifies the financial statements that have been audited.

        2)   Delineates the time period of the financial statements.

        3)   Describes management's responsibility for the financial statements.

        4)   Defines the auditor's responsibility for expressing an opinion on the financial statements.

    b.   The second or scope paragraph states that

        1)   The audit was conducted in accordance with generally accepted auditing standards.

        2)   The audit was planned to obtain reasonable assurance that the statements are free of material misstatements.

        3)   Tests were used to identify material misstatements.

        4)   The accounting principles and significant estimates used by management were evaluated.

        5)   The audit conducted provides a reasonable basis for the opinion given.

    c.   The third or opinion paragraph states that the financial statements

        1)   Present fairly, in all material aspects, the financial position, results of operations, and the cash flows of the company.

        2)   Are in accordance with generally accepted accounting principles.

2.   The types of opinions that Meyers and Richardson (M&R) would render for each of the firms are presented as follows:

    a.   Myracle Corporation – M&R would render the Auditor's Standard Report (unqualified opinion) with additional explanatory language. Since there were no other problems noted during the audit of Myracle Corporation, a standard unqualified opinion could be given for the existing circumstances. However, since there is doubt as to the future existence of the company, an explanatory paragraph must be added regarding the company's ability to continue as a going concern.

    b.   Parker Corporation – In this case, M&R would most likely render an adverse opinion. The recording of both fixed assets at replacement cost and inventory at selling price are departures from generally accepted accounting principles. Since the sum of inventory and fixed assets generally represents a material portion of a firm's assets and should have a pervasive effect on the income statement, an adverse opinion would be appropriate.

    c.   Eaton Industries – In this case, M&R would issue a disclaimer of an opinion due to scope limitation. Since the auditor has been prevented by the firm from confirming the value of the inventory, there is insufficient evidence on which to base an opinion.

    d.   Carter Corporation – By omitting the statement of cash flows, Carter Corporation is not in conformity with generally accepted accounting principles. M&R would issue a qualified report with a third paragraph explaining the omission and the company's failure to comply with GAAP.

    e.   Markay Corporation – M&R would issue an unqualified report for Markay Corporation. The change in the estimated life of assets is a change in accounting estimate and is treated as a prospective change. If the footnote disclosure is adequate, no other reference to the change is required. Only the comparability of the company's financial statements will be affected.

Scenario for Essay Questions 3, 4, 5

Some accountants have said that politicization in the development and acceptance of generally accepted accounting principles (i.e., standard-setting) is taking place. Some use the term "politicization" in a narrow sense to mean the influence by governmental agencies, particularly the Securities and Exchange Commission, on the development of generally accepted accounting principles. Others use it more broadly to mean the compromising that takes place in bodies responsible for developing generally accepted accounting principles because of the influence and pressure of interested groups (SEC, American Accounting Association, businesses through their various organizations, Institute of Management Accountants, financial analysts, bankers, lawyers, etc.).

Questions

3. The Committee on Accounting Procedures of the AICPA was established in the mid to late 1930s and functioned until 1959, at which time the Accounting Principles Board came into existence. In 1973, the Financial Accounting Standards Board was formed and the APB went out of existence. Do the reasons these groups were formed, their methods of operation while in existence, and the reasons for the demise of the first two indicate an increasing politicization (as the term is used in the broad sense) of accounting standard-setting? Explain your answer by indicating how the CAP, the APB, and the FASB operated or expect to operate. Cite specific developments which tend to support your answer.

4. What arguments can be raised to support the "politicization" of accounting standard-setting?

5. What arguments can be raised against the "politicization" of accounting standard-setting?

Essay Questions 3, 4, 5 — Unofficial Answers

3.   CAP. The Committee on Accounting Procedure, CAP, which was in existence from 1938 to 1959, was a natural outgrowth of AIA committees in existence during the period 1933 to 1938. The committee was formed in response to the criticism received by the accounting profession during the financial crises of 1929 and the years thereafter. As a general rule, CAP directed its attention almost entirely to resolving specific accounting problems and topics rather than to the development of GAAP. The demise of the CAP could be traced to four factors: (1) the narrow nature of the subjects covered, (2) the lack of theoretical groundwork in establishing the procedures, (3) the lack of any real authority by the CAP in prescribing adherence to the procedures, and (4) the lack of any formal representation on the CAP of interest groups.

APB. The objectives of the APB were formulated to correct the deficiencies of the CAP. The APB was charged with the responsibility of developing written expression of GAAP through consideration of the research done by other members of the AICPA in preparing Accounting Research Studies. The demise of the APB occurred because the purposes for which it was created were not being accomplished. Interest groups outside of the accounting profession questioned the appropriateness of having the AICPA responsible for the establishment of GAAP. Politicization of the establishment of GAAP had become a reality because of the far-reaching effects involved in the questions being resolved.

FASB. The FASB represents an attempt to vest the responsibility of establishing GAAP in an organization representing the diverse interest groups affected by the use of GAAP. It is independent, in fact, of any private or governmental organization.

Conclusion: The evolution of the current FASB certainly does represent "increasing politicization of accounting standard-setting." Many of the efforts extended by the AICPA can be attributed to the desire to satisfy the interests of many groups within society.

4.   Arguments for politicization of the accounting rule-making process.

   a.   Accounting depends on public confidence for success. Critical issues are not solely technical, so those having an interest should have influence on that output.

   b.   There are conflicts between the various interest groups. Compromise is necessary, particularly since the critical issues in accounting are value judgments, not the type which are solvable using deterministic models. Only in this way (reasonable compromise) will the financial community have confidence in the fairness of accounting rule-making.

   c.   Over the years, accountants have been unable to establish, on the basis of technical accounting elements, rules which would bring about the desired uniformity and acceptability. This inability itself indicates that rule-setting is consensus in nature.

   d.   The public accounting profession makes rules which business enterprises and individuals "have" to follow. For many years, these businesses and individuals had little say as to what the rules would be, in spite of the fact that their economic well-being was influenced by those rules.

5.   Arguments against the politicization of the accounting rule-making process.

   a.   Many feel that accounting is technical in nature. They feel that substantive, basic research by objective, independent researchers will result in the best solutions to critical issues, such as the concepts of income and capital.

   b.   Even if it is accepted that there are no "absolute truths" as far as critical issues are concerned, many feel that accountants, taking into account the diverse interests of the groups using accounting information, are in the best position because of their independence, education, training, and objectivity, to decide what GAAP ought to be.

   c.   The complex situations that arise in the business world require that trained accountants develop the appropriate accounting principles.

   d.   This approach would lead to "lobbying" to influence the principles.

Scenario for Essay Questions 6, 7, 8, 9

The Financial Accounting Standards Board (FASB) and the organizations that preceded the FASB have generally devoted their efforts to establishing financial reporting requirements for the private sector of the economy, i.e., to enterprises that were engaged in trade or business to earn a profit. Thus, a void existed for the establishment of reporting standards for governmental units.

The Government Finance Officers Association (GFOA) of the United States and Canada created a committee that eventually become the National Council on Governmental Accounting (NCGA). The purpose of the NCGA was to address accounting issues and reporting problems of governmental units. The NCGA issues several statements and interpretations.

The Governmental Accounting Standards Board (GASB) was established in 1984 to succeed the NCGA, which was dissolved in June of the same year. The Financial Accounting Foundation (FAF) oversees the GASB as well as the FASB. Similar to the FASB, the GASB has a Governmental Accounting Advisory Council. The GASB has a full-time chairman and consists of a five-member board, each of whom is appointed for a 5-year term.

Questions

6. Discuss how the operations of governmental units are unique and differ from the operations of enterprises in the private sector.

7. Discuss how governmental financial reporting is different from private-sector reporting.

8. The creation of the Governmental Accounting Standards Board (GASB) has been controversial. Which governmental units must comply with the pronouncements issued by the GASB?

9. Explain the hierarchy of GASB and FASB pronouncements in terms of their application to governmental entities.

Essay Questions 6, 7, 8, 9 — Unofficial Answers

6. The ways operations of governmental units are different from private enterprise include:

    a. The private sector operates to make a profit for the owners, while the governmental units lack a profit motive and exist to provide services to its citizens.

    b. Governmental units are extensively regulated by constitutions, charters, and statutes, many of which pertain to financial accounting areas.

    c. The performance of governmental units is not subject to the test of direct competition in markets as are business enterprises.

    d. Government operations are diverse and include such activities as the judicial system, social services, and public safety. Government operations also include fiduciary operations in which assets are held by governmental units as a trustee or agent. Some proprietary operations of the governmental units do resemble commercial activities, but they emphasize service rather than maximum profit.

    e. The citizens subject to a governmental unit's jurisdiction provide resources to the governmental unit principally through taxation. Many of these taxes are paid on a self-assessment basis; no comparable revenue source exists for businesses.

7. The major differences between governmental financial reporting and private-sector reporting include the following:

    a. Governmental units use fund accounting, while business entities emphasize the economic entity as the accounting unit.

    b. Governmental units emphasize accountability and stewardship of resources entrusted to public officials rather than earning profit for the benefit of the owners.

    c. Governmental reporting must reflect the legal restrictions placed on both the raising and spending of revenues.

    d. The presentation of accounting information differs from that of the private sector, and some statements are not prepared in accordance with generally accepted accounting principles.

8. The GASB issues Statements of Governmental Accounting Standards, a subdivision of the Financial Accounting Foundation (FAF), which establishes financial accounting and reporting standards for state and local governmental units, including governmental hospitals, colleges and universities, and nonprofit organizations. Agencies of the federal government need not comply.

9. The hierarchy of GASB and FASB pronouncements in terms of their application to governmental entities is essentially as follows:

    a. GASB Statements and Interpretations are the most authoritative sources of generally accepted accounting principles (GAAP) applicable to government entities.

    b. If the GASB has not issued a Statement or Interpretation that addresses the issue, FASB Statements and Interpretations should be researched next for guidance.

    c. If neither the GASB nor the FASB has addressed the matter in a Statement or Interpretation, the pronouncements of other bodies composed of expert accountants apply. Examples of pronouncements at this level include GASB and FASB Technical Bulletins, AICPA audit and accounting guides and Statements of Position, and pronouncements of the hospital and college and university accounting standards committees.

    d. If guidance is not found from the above sources, then what has become accepted in practice should be researched for guidance.

Consider using Gleim's ***CMA Test Prep*** for interactive testing with **hundreds of multiple-choice questions** as an additional method of knowledge transfer in your quest to pass Part 4.

STUDY UNIT THIRTEEN
CMA PART 2 REVIEW – BUDGET PREPARATION AND COST MANAGEMENT

(15 pages of outline)

Part 2 of the CMA exam is titled **Management Accounting and Reporting**. This study unit is a review of these sections:

A. **Budget Preparation.** Planning process, purposes of planning and budgeting; budgeting concepts; annual profit plans and supporting schedules; types of budgets, including activity-based budgeting, kaizen budgeting, project budgeting, and flexible budgeting.

B. **Cost Management.** Cost concepts, flows and terminology; alternative cost objectives; cost measurement concepts; cost accumulation systems including a job order costing, process costing, and activity-based costing; overhead cost allocation.

This study unit presents the IMA's Learning Outcome Statements and Gleim Core Concepts relevant to these sections. Bear in mind that **all topics** on Part 4 of the exam are tested at **skill level C** (all six skill types required).

13.1 BUDGET PREPARATION REVIEW

Part 2 – Section A.1. Budgeting concepts

The candidate should be able to:

a. demonstrate an understanding of the role that budgeting plays in the overall planning and performance evaluation process of an organization

b. demonstrate an understanding of the interrelationships between economic conditions, industry situation, and a firm's plans and budgets

c. identify the role that budgeting plays in formulating short-term objectives and planning and controlling operations to meet those objectives

d. identify the characteristics that define successful budgeting processes

e. demonstrate an understanding of the role that budgets play in measuring performance against established goals

f. explain how the budgeting process facilitates communication among organizational units and enhances coordination of organizational activities

g. describe the concept of a controllable cost as it relates to both budgeting and performance evaluation

h. prepare an operational budget

i. prepare a capital expenditure budget

j. demonstrate an understanding of the concept of management-by-objective and how it relates to performance evaluation

k. identify the benefits and limitations of management-by-objective

l. demonstrate an understanding of how the planning process coordinates the efficient allocation of organizational resources

m. identify the appropriate time frame for various types of budgets

n.   identify who should participate in the budgeting process for optimum success

o.   describe the role of top management in successful budgeting

p.   identify the role of top management or the budget committee in providing appropriate guidelines for the budget and identify items that should be included in these guidelines

q.   demonstrate an understanding of the use of cost standards in budgeting

r.   differentiate between ideal (theoretical) standards and currently attainable (practical) standards

s.   differentiate between authoritative standards and participative standards

t.   identify the steps to be taken in developing standards for both direct material and direct labor

u.   define the role of benchmarking in standard setting

v.   demonstrate an understanding of the techniques that are used to develop standards such as activity analysis and the use of historical data

w.   discuss the importance of a policy that allows budget revisions that accommodate the impact of significant changes in budget assumptions

x.   demonstrate an understanding of the role of budgets in monitoring and controlling expenditures to meet strategic objectives

Core Concepts for Budgeting Concepts

- **The budget is a formal quantification of management's plans.** A budget lays out in specific terms an organization's expectations about the consumption of resources and the resulting outcomes.

- The budget lays out the **specific revenue targets** and expense limitations for each functional area and department of the organization on a month-by-month basis. A budget cannot simply be a lump-sum total for a year. **Incremental goals** must be achieved each month or week. This is especially true in seasonal businesses such as agricultural supply.

- **Controllability** is the extent to which a manager can influence activities and related revenues and costs. Controllable costs are those that are under the discretion of a particular manager. Noncontrollable costs are those to which another level of the organization has committed, removing the manager's discretion. The principle of controllability must be kept in mind when the budget is used as the basis for managerial evaluation.

- **Management-by-objectives (MBO)** is a comprehensive approach to management with two hallmarks: Objectives are expressed in measurable terms, and those held responsible for achieving them participate in setting them. MBO is a top-down process. The organization's overall objectives are formulated by the board and upper management, then restated for each lower level.

- The planning process **coordinates the efficient allocation** of organizational resources.

- **Participation** in the budget preparation process is up and down the organization.

- **Standard costs** are predetermined expectations about how much a unit of input, a unit of output, or a given activity should cost. The use of standard costs in budgeting allows the standard-cost system to alert management when the actual costs of production differ significantly from the standard.

  - A purely **top-down (authoritative)** approach to standard setting has the advantage of ensuring total consistency across all functional areas. It is also far less complex and time-consuming than coordinating input from the middle and lower levels.

  - **Participative (grass-roots)** standard setting uses input from middle- and lower-level employees. Participation encourages employees to have a sense of ownership of the output of the process. The result is an acceptance of, and commitment to, the goals expressed in the budget.

- **Benchmarking** is the continuous process of comparing an organization's performance metrics with those of others in the same industry, or even of other industries. The goal is to set standards with an eye to those of the best-in-class organization.
  - Often an organization will find that the assumptions under which the budget was prepared undergo **significant change** during the year. A policy must be in place to accommodate revisions to the budget resulting from these changes.

Part 2 – Section A.2. Budget systems

For each of the budget systems identified (annual/master budgets, project budgeting, activity-based budgeting, zero-based budgeting, continuous budgeting, kaizen budgeting, and flexible budgeting), the candidate should be able to:

  a.   define its purpose, appropriate use, and time frame
  b.   identify the budget components and explain the interrelationships among the components
  c.   demonstrate an understanding of how the budget is developed
  d.   compare and contrast the benefits and limitations of the budget system
  e.   calculate budget components on the basis of information presented
  f.   evaluate a business situation and recommend the appropriate budget solution

Core Concepts for Budget Systems

- The **master budget**, also called the comprehensive budget or annual profit plan, encompasses the organization's **operating and financial** plans for a specified period (ordinarily a year or single operating cycle).
- In the **operating budget**, the emphasis is on obtaining and using current resources. It contains the
  - Sales budget
  - Production budget
  - Direct materials budget
  - Direct labor budget
  - Manufacturing overhead budget
  - Ending finished goods inventory budget
  - Cost of goods sold budget
  - Nonmanufacturing budget
  - Pro forma income statement
- In the **financial budget**, the emphasis is on obtaining the funds needed to purchase operating assets. It contains the
  - Capital budget
  - Projected cash disbursement schedule
  - Projected cash collection schedule
  - Cash budget
  - Pro forma balance sheet
  - Pro forma statement of cash flows
- A **project budget** consists of all the costs expected to attach to a particular project, such as the design of a new airliner or the building of a single ship.
- **Activity-based budgeting** applies activity-based costing principles to budgeting. It focuses on the numerous activities necessary to produce and market goods and services and requires analysis of cost drivers.
- **Zero-based budgeting (ZBB)** is a budget and planning process in which each manager must justify his/her department's entire budget every budget cycle.
- A **continuous (rolling) budget** is one that is revised on a regular (continuous) basis. Typically, a company continuously extends such a budget for an additional month or quarter in accordance with new data as the current month or quarter ends.

- The Japanese term kaizen means continuous improvement, and **kaizen budgeting** assumes the continuous improvement of products and processes. Accordingly, kaizen budgeting is based not on the existing system but on changes yet to be made.

- A **static budget** is based on only one level of sales or production. The level of production and the containment of costs are, though related, two separate managerial tasks. Contrast this with a **flexible budget**, which is a series of budgets prepared for many levels of activity. At the end of the period, management can compare actual performance with the appropriate budgeted level in the flexible budget.

- A **life-cycle** budget estimates a product's revenues and expenses over its entire life cycle beginning with research and development and ending with the withdrawal of customer support. Life-cycle budgeting is intended to account for the costs at all stages of the value chain (R&D, design, production, marketing, distribution, and customer service).

Part 2 – Section A.3. Annual profit plan and supporting schedules

The candidate should be able to:

a.   demonstrate an understanding of the role the sales budget plays in the development of an annual profit plan

b.   identify the factors that should be considered when preparing a sales forecast and evaluate the feasibility of the sales forecast based on business and economic information provided

c.   identify the components of a sales budget and prepare a sales budget based on relevant information provided

d.   demonstrate an understanding of the relationship between the sales budget and the production budget

e.   identify the role that inventory levels play in the preparation of a production budget and define other factors that should be considered when preparing a production budget

f.   prepare a production budget based on relevant information provided and evaluate the feasibility of achieving sales goals on the basis of production plans

g.   demonstrate an understanding of the relationship between the direct materials budget, the direct labor budget, and the production budget

h.   define the use of inventory levels and procurement policies in developing a direct materials budget and the role that labor skills, union contracts, and hiring policies play in the development of a direct labor budget

i.   prepare direct materials and direct labor budgets based on relevant information provided and evaluate the feasibility of achieving production goals on the basis of these budgets

j.   prepare a forecast of employee related costs and benefits such as employer contributions to Social Security, employment related taxes, health and life insurance, and pension contributions based on relevant information provided

k.   demonstrate an understanding of alternative ways of allocating employee benefit expense, e.g., as a portion of direct labor expense or as overhead, and the effect that allocation has on the financial statements

l.   demonstrate an understanding of the relationship between the overhead budget and the production budget

m.   identify the fixed and variable expenses in an overhead budget

n.   define the components of overhead expense and prepare an overhead budget based on relevant information provided

o.   identify the components of the cost of goods sold budget and demonstrate an understanding of the relationship between the cost of goods sold budget, the pro forma income statement, and the pro forma statement of financial position

p.   demonstrate an understanding of contribution margin per unit and total contribution margin, identify the appropriate use of these concepts, and calculate both unit and total contribution margin

q.   prepare a cost of goods sold budget based on relevant information provided

r. identify the components of the selling and administrative budget and demonstrate an understanding of the nature of these expenses

s. describe the relationship between the selling and administrative budget, the pro forma income statement, and the pro forma statement of financial position

t. demonstrate an understanding of how specific components of the selling and administrative budget may affect the contribution margin

u. demonstrate an understanding of the relationship between the budget for acquisition of capital assets, the cash budget, and the pro forma financial statements

v. define the purposes of the cash budget and describe the relationship between the cash budget and all other budgets

w. identify the elements of a cash budget and demonstrate an understanding of the relationship between credit policies and purchasing (payables) policies and the cash budget

x. prepare a cash budget from information given and recommend the optimal investment/financing strategy

y. define the purpose of a pro forma income statement, a pro forma statement of financial position, and a pro forma cash flow statement and understand the relationship among these statements and all other budgets

z. prepare a pro forma income statement, a pro forma statement of financial position, and a pro forma cash flow statement from relevant information provided

Core Concepts for Annual Profit Plan and Supporting Schedules

- The **sales budget**, also called the revenue budget, is the **starting point** for the massive cycle that produces the annual profit plan (i.e., the master budget).

  - The sales budget is an outgrowth of the **sales forecast**. The sales forecast distills recent sales trends; overall conditions in the economy and industry; market research; activities of competitors; and credit and pricing policies.

- The **production budget** follows directly from the sales budget.

  - The production budget is concerned with **units only**.

- The **direct materials and direct labor budgets** follow directly from the production budget.

  - The direct materials budget is concerned with **both units and input prices**.

  - The **cost of fringe benefits** must be derived once the cost of wages has been determined. Whether employee fringes are included in direct labor costs or treated as overhead, the effect on cost of goods sold is the same.

- The **manufacturing overhead budget** reflects the nature of overhead as a mixed cost, i.e., one that has a variable component and a fixed component.

  - **Variable overhead** contains those elements that vary with the level of production (indirect materials, indirect labor, variable factory operating costs).

  - **Fixed overhead** contains those elements that remain the same regardless of the level of production (real estate taxes, insurance, depreciation).

- The **ending finished goods inventory budget** can be prepared now that the components of finished goods cost have been projected.

- The **cost of goods sold budget** combines the results of the projections for the three major inputs (materials, labor, overhead).

- The **nonmanufacturing budget** consists of the individual budgets for R&D, design, marketing, distribution, customer service, and administrative costs.

  - The **variable and fixed portions** of selling and administrative costs must be treated separately.

- The **pro forma income statement** is the culmination of the operating budget process. The pro forma income statement is used to decide whether the budgeted activities will result in an acceptable level of income.

13.2 BUDGET PREPARATION ESSAY QUESTIONS

Recall that your CMA Part 4 exam will probably contain six scenarios, with about three questions per scenario. There will be a recommended time allocation of 20 minutes, 30 minutes, or 45 minutes for each scenario and related questions.

One scenario will involve ethical issues, and probably one or two scenarios will include calculations and responses on a worksheet. Also, expect at least one scenario on organizational/behavioral topics. The remaining scenarios cover Parts 1, 2, and 3.

Scenario Title	Subtopic	Questions	Suggested Time
Wielson Company	Flexible Budgeting and Selling Expenses	1, 2, 3	30 minutes
Watson Corporation	Projections and Pro Forma Statements	4, 5	30 minutes
Healthful Foods, Inc.	Ethics and Budgeting	6, 7, 8	30 minutes

Scenario for Essay Questions 1, 2, 3

Wielson Company employs flexible budgeting techniques to evaluate the performance of several of its activities. The selling expense flexible budgets for three representative monthly activity levels are shown below.

Representative Monthly Flexible Budgets for Selling Expenses

Activity measures:			
Unit sales volume	400,000	425,000	450,000
Dollar sales volume	$10,000,000	$10,625,000	$11,250,000
Number of orders	4,000	4,250	4,500
Number of salespersons	75	75	75
Monthly expenses:			
Advertising and promotion	$1,200,000	$1,200,000	$1,200,000
Administrative salaries	57,000	57,000	57,000
Sales salaries	75,000	75,000	75,000
Sales commissions	200,000	212,500	225,000
Salesperson travel	170,000	175,000	180,000
Sales office expense	490,000	498,750	507,500
Shipping expense	675,000	712,500	750,000
Total selling expenses	$2,867,000	$2,930,750	$2,994,500

The following assumptions were used to develop the selling expense flexible budgets:

- The average size of Wielson's sales force during the year was planned to be 75 people.
- Salespersons are paid a monthly salary plus commission on gross dollar sales.
- Travel costs are best characterized as a step variable cost. The fixed portion is related to the number of salespersons while the variable portion tends to fluctuate with dollar sales.
- Sales office expense is a mixed cost with the variable portion related to the number of orders processed.
- Shipping expense is a mixed cost with the variable portion related to number of units sold.

A salesforce of 80 persons generated a total of 4,300 orders resulting in a sales volume of 420,000 units during November. The gross dollar sales amount to $10.9 million. The selling expenses incurred for November were as follows:

Advertising and promotion	$1,350,000
Administrative salaries	57,000
Sales salaries	80,000
Sales commissions	218,000
Salesperson travel	185,000
Sales office expense	497,200
Shipping expense	730,000
Total	$3,117,200

Questions

1. Explain why flexible budgeting is a useful management tool.

2. Explain why the selling expense in flexible budgets presented above would not be appropriate for evaluating Wielson Company's November selling expenses, and indicate how the flexible budget would have to be revised.

3. Prepare a selling expense report for November that Wielson can use to evaluate control over selling expenses. The report should have a line for each selling expense item showing the budgeted amount, the actual selling expense, and the monthly dollar variation.

Essay Questions 1, 2, 3 — Unofficial Answers

1. A flexible budget allows management to directly compare the actual cost of operations with budgeted costs for the activity achieved. It assists management in evaluating the effects of varying levels of activity on costs, profits, and cash position, thus aiding in the choice of the level of operation for planning purposes.

2. The flexible budgets presented are based on three different activity measures, none of which coincide with the actual level of performance for November. The budget must be restated to a level of activity that matches the actual results. The fixed and variable components of the mixed costs must be segregated and a budgeted cost calculated for the level of activity attained.

3. Selling expense report is presented below:

Wielson Company
Selling Expense Report
November

Monthly Expense	Budget	Actual	Variance
Advertising and promotion	$1,200,000	$1,350,000	$150,000 U
Administrative salaries	57,000	57,000	---
Sales salaries[1]	80,000	80,000	---
Sales commissions[2]	218,000	218,000	---
Salesperson travel[3]	183,200	185,000	1,800 U
Sales office expense[4]	500,500	497,200	(3,300) F
Shipping expense[5]	705,000	730,000	25,000 U
Total	$2,943,700	$3,117,200	$173,500 U

U = unfavorable, or over budget.
F = favorable, or under budget.

Supporting Calculations

[1] $\left(\dfrac{\$75,000}{75}\right) \times 80 = \$80,000$

[2] $\left(\dfrac{\$200,000}{\$10,000,000}\right) \times \$10,900,000 = \$218,000$

[3] Change in cost: $175,000 – $170,000 = $5,000
Change in sales dollars: $10,625,000 – $10,000,000 = $625,000
Variable cost per dollar of sales = change in cost divided by change in activity level:
    $5,000 ÷ $625,000 = $.008 per dollar of sales
Fixed cost at 75 person level: $170,000 – ($10,000,000 × .008) = $90,000
Fixed cost at 80 person level: $\left(\dfrac{\$90,000}{75}\right) \times 80 = \$96,000$

Total travel budget: $96,000 fixed + ($10,900,000 × .008) variable = $183,200

[4] Change in cost: $498,750 – $490,000 = $8,750
Change in number of orders: 4,250 – 4,000 = 250
Variable cost per order: $8,750 ÷ 250 = $35
Fixed cost: $490,000 – (4,000 × $35) = $350,000
Total office expense budget: $350,000 + (4,300 × $35) – $500,500

[5] Change in cost: $712,500 – $675,000 = $37,500
Change in number of units: 425,000 – 400,000 = 25,000
Variable cost per unit: $37,500 ÷ 25,000 = $1.50
Fixed cost: $675,000 – (400,000 × $1.50) = $75,000
Total shipping expense budget: $75,000 + (420,000 × $1.50) = $705,000

Scenario for Essay Questions 4, 5

Watson Corporation manufactures and sells extended keyboard units. Robin Halter, budget analyst, coordinated the preparation of the annual budget for the year ending August 31, Year 7. The budget was based on the prior year's activity. The pro forma statements of income and cost of goods sold are presented below.

Watson Corporation Pro Forma Statement of Income For the Year Ending August 31, Year 7 ($000 omitted)		
Net sales		$25,550
Cost of goods sold		16,565
Gross profit		8,985
Operating expenses		
Marketing	$3,200	
General and administrative	2,000	5,200
Income from operations before income taxes		$ 3,785

Watson Corporation Pro Forma Statement of Cost of Goods Sold For the Year Ending August 31, Year 7 ($000 omitted)		
Direct materials:		
Materials inventory, 9/1/Year 6	$ 1,200	
Materials purchased	11,400	
Materials available for use	12,600	
Materials inventory, 8/31/Year 7	1,480	
Direct materials consumed		$11,120
Direct labor		980
Factory overhead:		
Indirect materials	1,112	
General factory overhead	2,800	3,912
Cost of goods manufactured		16,012
Finished goods inventory, 9/1/Year 6		930
Cost of goods available for sale		16,942
Finished goods inventory, 8/31/Year 7		377
Cost of goods sold		$16,565

On December 10, Year 6, Halter met with Walter Collins, vice president of finance, to discuss the results. After their discussion, Collins directed Halter to reflect the following changes to the budget assumptions in revised pro forma statements.

- The estimated production in units for the fiscal year should be revised from 140,000 to 145,000 units with the balance of production being scheduled in equal segments over the last 9 months of the year. The actual first quarter's production was 25,000 units.

- The planned inventory for finished goods of 3,300 units at the end of the fiscal year remains unchanged and will be valued at the average manufacturing cost for the year. The finished goods inventory of 9,300 units on September 1, Year 6, and dropped to 9,000 units by November 30, Year 6.

- Due to a new labor agreement, the labor rate will increase 8% effective June 1, Year 7, the beginning of the fourth quarter, instead of the previously anticipated effective date of September 1, Year 7, the beginning of the next fiscal year.

- The assumptions remain unchanged for direct materials inventory at 16,000 units for the beginning inventory and 18,500 units for the ending inventory. Direct materials inventory is valued on a first-in, first-out basis. During the first quarter, direct materials for 27,500 units of output were purchased for $2,200,000. Although direct materials will be purchased evenly for the last 9 months, the cost of the direct materials will increase by 5% on March 1, Year 7, the beginning of the third quarter.
- Indirect material costs will continue to be 10% of the cost of direct materials.
- One-half of general factory overhead and all of the marketing and general and administrative expenses are fixed.

Questions

4. Based on the revised data presented, calculate Watson Corporation's projected sales for the year ending August 31, Year 7, in

   a. Number of units to be sold.
   b. Dollar volume of net sales.

5. Prepare the pro forma statement of cost of goods sold for the year ending August 31, Year 7.

Essay Questions 4, 5 — Unofficial Answers

4. a. Based on the revised data presented, Watson Corporation's projected unit sales for the year ending August 31, Year 7, are 151,000 units calculated as follows:

Beginning inventory -- finished goods	9,300
Planned production	145,000
Units available for sale	154,300
Ending inventory -- finished goods	3,300
Units to be sold	151,000

   b. Based on the revised data presented, Watson Corporation's projected dollar volume of net sales for the year ending August 31, Year 7, is $26,425,000 calculated as follows:

Selling price per unit

$$= \frac{Original\ projected\ sales\ dollars}{Original\ projected\ unit\ sales}$$

$$= \frac{\$25,550,000}{(9,300 + 140,000 - 3,300)}$$

$$= \underline{\$175}\ per\ unit$$

Dollar volume of projected net sales $= \$175/\text{unit} \times 151,000 \text{ units}$
$= \underline{\$26,425,000}$

5. Based on the revised data presented, Watson Company's pro forma statement of costs of goods sold for the year ending August 31, Year 7, is presented below. Supporting calculations are on the next page.

Watson Corporation
Pro Forma Statement of Cost of Goods Sold
For the Year Ending August 31, Year 7

Direct materials		
Materials inventory, 9/1/Year 6		$ 1,200,000
Materials purchased[1]		12,120,000
Materials available for use		13,320,000
Materials inventory, 8/31/Year 7[2]		1,554,000
Direct materials consumed		11,766,000
Direct labor[3]		1,037,400
Factory overhead		
Indirect material[4]	$1,176,600	
General factory overhead[5]	2,850,000	
Factory overhead applied		4,026,600
Cost of goods manufactured		16,830,000
Finished goods inventory, 9/1/Year 6		930,000
Cost of goods available for sale		17,760,000
Finished goods inventory, 8/31/Year 7[6]		383,028
Cost of goods sold		$17,376,972

Supporting Calculations

[1]Materials purchased:

27,500 units @ $80 per unit*	$2,200,000
40,000 units @ $80 per unit	3,200,000
80,000 units @ $84 per unit**	6,720,000
	$12,120,000

*$2,200,000 ÷ 27,500 units
**$80.00 × 1.05

[2]Materials inventory, 8/31/Year 7:
18,500 units × $84 $ 1,554,000

[3]Direct labor:

25,000 units @ $7 per unit*	$ 175,000
80,000 units @ $7 per unit	560,000
40,000 units @ $7.56 per unit**	302,400
	$ 1,037,400

*$980,000 ÷ 140,000 units
**$7.00 × 1.08

[4]Indirect materials:
$11,766,000 × .10 $ 1,176,600

[5]General factory overhead:

$2,800,000 ÷ 2	$1,400,000
	1,450,000

$$\frac{\$1,400,000}{140,000 \ units} \times 145,000 \ units$$

$ 2,850,000

[6]Finished goods inventory, 8/31/Year 7:
Average cost per unit

$$\frac{\$16,830,000}{145,000 \ units} = \$116.07 \ per \ unit$$

Finished goods
3,300 × $116.07 $ 383,028

Scenario for Essay Questions 6, 7, 8

Healthful Foods, Inc., a manufacturer of breakfast cereals and snack bars, has experienced several years of steady growth while maintaining a relatively low level of debt. The Board of Directors has adopted a long-run strategy to maximize the value of the shareholders' investment. To achieve this goal, the Board of Directors established the following five-year financial objectives:

- Increase sales by 12% per year
- Increase income before taxes by 15% per year
- Increase dividends by 12% per year
- Maintain long-term debt at a maximum 16% of assets

These financial objectives have been attained for the past three years. At the beginning of last year, the president, Andrea Donis, added a fifth financial objective of maintaining cost of goods sold at a maximum of 70% of sales, and this goal was attained last year. The budgeting process at Healthful Foods is to be directed toward attaining these goals for the forthcoming year, a difficult task with the economy in a recession. In addition, the increased emphasis on eating healthful foods has driven up the price of ingredients significantly faster than the rate of inflation.

John Winslow, cost accountant at Healthful Foods, has responsibility for the preparation of the profit plan for next year. Winslow assured Donis that he could present a budget that achieved all of the financial objectives. Winslow believed that he could overestimate the ending inventory and reclassify fruit and grain inspection costs as administrative rather than manufacturing costs to attain the desired objective. Presented below are the statements for Year 5 and the budgeted statements for Year 6.

Healthful Foods, Inc.
Income Statement

	Year 5 Actual	Year 6 Budget
Sales	$850,000	$947,750
Variable costs:		
Cost of goods sold:	510,000	574,725
Selling & Administrative	90,000	87,500
Contribution margin	250,000	285,525
Fixed costs:		
Manufacturing	85,000	94,775
Selling & Administrative	60,000	70,000
Income before taxes	$105,000	$120,750

Healthful Foods, Inc.
Statement of Financial Position
(in thousands)

	Year 5 Actual	Year 6 Budget
Assets:		
Cash	$ 10	$ 17
Accounts receivable	60	68
Inventory	300	365
Plant & equipment (net)	1,630	1,600
Total	$2,000	$2,050
Liabilities:		
Accounts payable	$ 110	$ 122
Long-term debt	320	308
Shareholders' equity:		
Common stock	400	400
Retained earnings	1,170	1,220
Total	$2,000	$2,050

The company paid dividends of $27,720 in Year 5, and the expected tax rate for Year 6 is 34%.

Questions

6. Describe the relationship between strategic planning and budgeting.

7. For each of the five financial objectives, determine whether Winslow's budget attains these objectives. Support your conclusion in each case by presenting calculations, and use the following format:

   Objective   Attained/Not Attained   Calculations

8. Explain why the adjustments contemplated by Winslow are unethical, citing the standards of competence, confidentiality, integrity, and/or credibility from Statement on Management Accounting No. 1C (Revised), *IMA Statement of Ethical Professional Practice*.

Essay Questions 6, 7, 8 — Unofficial Answers

6.   Strategic planning identifies the overall objectives of an organization and generally considers the impact of external factors such as competitive forces, market demand, and technological changes when identifying overall objectives.

Budgeting is the quantitative expression of plans evolving from strategic planning. The time horizon for budgeting is generally a year, or an operating cycle, and greater attention is focused on internal factors than external factors.

7.   For each of the following financial objectives established by the Board of Directors and president of Healthful Foods, Inc., the calculations to determine whether John Winslow's budget attains these objectives are presented in Exhibit 1 below.

Exhibit 1

Healthful Foods, Inc.
Calculation of Financial Objectives

Objective	Attained/ Not Attained	Calculations
Increase sales by 12% $850,000 \times 1.12 = \$952,000$	Not Attained	$(\$947,750 - \$850,000) \div \$850,000 = 11.5\%$
Increase income before taxes by 15% $\$105,000 \times 1.15 = \$120,750$	Attained	$(\$120,750 - \$105,000) \div \$105,000 = 15\%$
Increase dividends by 12% $[(\$27,720 + \text{effect of additional shares}) \times 1.12 = \$31,046]$	Not Attained	$\$120,750 \times (1 - t) - \text{Change in retained earnings} = \text{Dividends}$ $\$120,750 \times .66 - \$50,000 = \$29,695$ $(\$29,695 - \$27,720) \div \$27,720 = 7\%$
Maintain long-term debt at or below 16% $\$2,050,000 \times .16 = \$328,000$	Attained	$\$308,000 \div \$2,050,000 = 15.0\%$
Maintain COGS at or below 70% of sales $\$947,750 \times .70 = \$663,425$	Attained	$\$574,725 \div \$947,750 = 60.6\%$

8.   The accounting adjustments contemplated by Winslow are unethical because they will result in intentionally overstating income by understating the cost of sales. The specific standards of Statement on Management Accounting Number 1C (Revised), *IMA Statement of Ethical Professional Practice* violated by Winslow are presented below.

Competence – By making the accounting adjustments, Winslow violated the competency standard by not preparing financial statements in accordance with technical standards.

Integrity – Winslow violated the integrity standard by engaging in an activity that prejudices his ability to carry out his duties ethically by not communicating unfavorable as well as favorable information and by engaging in an activity that appears to be a conflict of interest.

Credibility – By overstating the inventory and reclassifying certain costs, Winslow has violated the credibility standard. He has failed to communicate information fairly and objectively, has failed to fully disclose all relevant information that would influence the users' understanding of the report, and has failed to disclose deficiencies in information and internal controls.

13.3 COST MANAGEMENT REVIEW

Part 2 – Section B.1. Terminology

The candidate should be able to:

    a.   identify and differentiate all cost items reported on the income statement

    b.   identify and calculate those costs incurred to complete a product and reported as cost of goods sold

    c.   identify and calculate those costs incurred for current operations (period costs) but not included in cost of goods sold

    d.   identify and calculate the components of cost concepts such as prime cost, conversion cost, overhead cost, carrying cost, sunk cost, discretionary cost, and opportunity cost

    e.   demonstrate an understanding of the characteristics that differentiate fixed costs, variable costs, and mixed costs and evaluate the effect that changes in production volume have on these costs

    f.   identify, differentiate, and calculate direct vs. indirect costs

    g.   describe the importance of timely and accurate costing information as a tool for strategic planning and management decision making

Core Concepts for Cost Management Terminology

- A **cost object** is any entity to which costs can be attached. A **cost driver** is the basis used to assign costs to a cost object. The cost driver is the cause of the cost.

- The **costs of manufacturing** a product can be classified as one of **three types**: direct materials, direct labor, and manufacturing overhead. Overhead typically consists of indirect materials, indirect labor, and factory operating costs.

- Manufacturing costs are often grouped as either **prime costs** (direct materials plus direct labor) or **conversion costs** (direct labor plus manufacturing overhead).

- Operating a manufacturing concern also requires the incurrence of **nonmanufacturing costs**, consisting of selling (marketing) costs and administrative expenses.

- **Product costs** (also called inventoriable costs) are capitalized as part of finished goods inventory. They eventually become a component of cost of goods sold. **Period costs** are expensed as incurred, i.e., they are not capitalized in finished goods inventory and are thus excluded from cost of goods sold.

- For **external reporting, all manufacturing costs** (direct materials, direct labor, variable overhead, and fixed overhead) must be treated as product costs, and all selling and administrative (S&A) costs must be treated as period costs. This approach is called absorption costing (also called full costing).

- For **internal reporting, only variable manufacturing costs** are capitalized as product costs. All other costs (variable S&A and the fixed portion of both production and S&A expenses) are treated as period costs. This approach is called variable costing (also called direct costing).

- **Direct costs** are ones that can be associated with a particular cost object in an economically feasible way, i.e., they can be **traced** to that object. **Indirect costs** are ones that cannot be associated with a particular cost object in an economically feasible way and thus must be **allocated** to that object.

- To simplify the allocation process, **indirect costs** are often collected in **cost pools**. A cost pool is an account into which a variety of similar cost elements with a common cause are accumulated. Manufacturing overhead is a commonly used example.

Core Concepts for Cost Behavior and Relevant Range

- The **relevant range** defines the limits within which per-unit variable costs remain constant and fixed costs are not changeable. It is synonymous with the **short run**.

    - **Variable cost per unit** remains constant in the short run regardless of the level of production. **Variable costs in total**, on the other hand, vary directly and proportionally with changes in volume.

    - **Fixed costs in total** remain unchanged in the short run regardless of production level. **Fixed cost per unit**, on the other hand, varies indirectly with the activity level.

    - **Mixed (semivariable) costs** combine fixed and variable elements.

- **Marginal cost** is the cost incurred by a one-unit increase in the activity level of a particular cost driver. Necessarily then, marginal cost remains **constant across the relevant range**.

Core Concepts for Cost Classification

- Cost of goods sold is a straightforward computation for a **retailer** because retailers have only a **single class of inventory**. The calculation is more complex for a **manufacturer** because manufacturers have **three distinct classes of inventory**. The manufacturer's cost of goods manufactured is analogous to the retailer's purchases account.

- Costs can be defined in **conceptual groupings**.

    - Controllable vs. noncontrollable costs
    - Avoidable vs. committed costs
    - Incremental vs. differential cost
    - Engineered vs. discretionary costs
    - Outlay vs. opportunity cost (explicit vs. implicit)
    - Economic vs. imputed cost
    - Relevant vs. sunk costs (historical cost is a sunk cost)

- **Manufacturing processes** their own particular cost groups.

    - Joint costs, separable costs, and by-products
    - Normal vs. abnormal spoilage
    - Rework, scrap, and waste

- **Other manufacturing concepts** include

    - Just-in-time (JIT) manufacturing systems and backflush costing
    - Kaizen (continuous improvement)
    - Kanban (ticket)
    - Manufacturing cell

Part 2 – Section B.2. Measurement concepts

The candidate should be able to:

a. demonstrate an understanding of the behavior of fixed and variable costs in the long and short terms and how a change in assumptions regarding cost type or relevant range affects these costs

b. identify cost objects and cost pools and assign costs to appropriate activities

c. demonstrate an understanding of the nature and types of cost drivers and the causal relationship that exists between cost drivers and costs incurred

d. demonstrate a thorough understanding of the various methods for measuring costs and accumulating work-in-process and finished goods inventories and a basic understanding of how inventories are relieved

e. identify and calculate the components of cost measurement techniques such as actual costing, normal costing, and standard costing; identify the appropriate use of each technique; and describe the benefits and limitations of each technique

f. demonstrate an understanding of the characteristics of variable costing and absorption costing and the benefits and limitations of these measurement concepts

g. calculate inventory costs using both variable costing and absorption costing

h. demonstrate an understanding of how the use of variable costing or absorption costing affects the value of inventory, cost of goods sold, and operating income

i. determine the appropriate use of joint product and by-product costing and demonstrate an understanding of concepts such as split-off point and separable costs

j. determine the allocation of joint product and by-product costs using the physical measure method, the sales value at split-off method, gross profit (gross margin) method, and the net realizable value method; and describe the benefits and limitations of each method

k. demonstrate an understanding of costing systems used by service sector companies

Core Concepts for Costing Techniques

- Absorption vs. Variable Costing

  - **Absorption costing** treats all manufacturing costs as product costs. The inventoried cost of the product thus includes all production costs, whether variable or fixed. This technique is required under GAAP.

  - **Variable costing** considers only variable manufacturing costs to be product costs, i.e., inventoriable. Fixed manufacturing costs are considered period costs and are thus expensed as incurred. This technique is permitted for internal reporting only.

- Normalized Costing

  - **Actual costing** is the most accurate, but also the least timely and most volatile, method of accumulating costs.

  - **Normal costing** charges actual direct materials and direct labor to a cost object, but applies overhead on the basis of budgeted (normalized) rates.

  - **Extended normal costing** extends the use of normalized rates to manufacturing overhead so that all three major input categories use normalized rates.

- Cost Accumulation Systems

  - **Job-order costing** for manufacturing customized products
  - **Process costing** for mass production
  - **Activity-based costing (ABC)** when overhead is a high proportion of the total cost
  - **Life-cycle costing** to track a product's lifetime costs
  - **Operation costing** when production is a hybrid of custom and mass production
  - **Backflush costing** when just-in-time inventory is used

- **Standard costing** is a system designed to alert management when the actual costs of production differ significantly from target ("standard") costs. Standard costs are predetermined, attainable unit costs.

- Four methods for **allocating joint costs** are

  - Physical unit method
  - Sales-value at split-off method
  - Estimated net realizable value (NRV) method
  - Constant gross-margin percentage NRV method

- Three methods for **allocating service department costs** are in common use:

  - Direct method
  - Step-down method
  - Reciprocal method

Part 2 – Section B.3. Accumulation systems

For each cost accumulation system identified (job-order costing, process costing, activity-based costing, life-cycle costing), the candidate should be able to:

a. define the nature of the system, understand the cost flows of the system, and recognize its appropriate use

b. calculate inventory values and cost of goods sold

c. demonstrate an understanding of the proper accounting for normal and abnormal spoilage

d. discuss the strategic value of cost information regarding products and services, pricing, overhead allocations, and other issues

e. identify the benefits and limitations of each cost accumulation system

For the following specific cost accumulation systems, the candidate should be able to:

f. demonstrate an understanding of the concept of equivalent units in process costing and calculate the value of equivalent units

g. define the elements of activity-based costing such as cost pool, cost driver, resource driver, activity driver, and value-added activity

h. calculate product cost using an activity-based system and compare and analyze the results with costs calculated using a traditional system

i. demonstrate an understanding of the concept of the life-cycle costing and the strategic value of including upstream costs, manufacturing costs, and downstream costs

j. describe how operation costing is a hybrid cost system utilizing characteristics of both job costing and process costing and identify industry settings where operation costing is appropriate

k. demonstrate an understanding of backflush costing and describe why it is appropriate in a just-in-time setting where manufacturing cells are utilized

l. demonstrate an understanding of how activity based costing can be utilized in service firms

Core Concepts for Job-Order Costing

- **Job-order costing** is concerned with accumulating costs by specific job. This method is appropriate when producing **products with individual characteristics** or when identifiable groupings are possible, e.g., yachts, jewelry.

  - **Direct costs** (direct materials and direct labor) are charged at the actual amounts incurred.

  - **Manufacturing overhead** is charged using an estimated rate. Overhead costs are applied to ("absorbed" by) each job based on a predetermined overhead application rate for the year. At the end of the period, overhead may have been overapplied or underapplied.

- Output that does not meet the quality standards for salability is considered spoilage.

  - If the spoilage is the amount expected in the ordinary course of production, it is considered **normal spoilage** and treated as a **product cost**.

  - If the spoilage is over and above the amount expected in the ordinary course of production, it is considered **abnormal spoilage** and is treated as a period cost.

Core Concepts for Process Costing

- Process cost accounting is used to assign costs to relatively **homogeneous products** that are **mass produced** on a continuous basis (e.g., petroleum products, thread, computer monitors).
- **Direct materials** are used by the first department in the process. **Conversion costs** are the sum of direct labor and manufacturing overhead. The products move from one department to the next. Each department adds more direct materials and more conversion costs.
- **Equivalent units of production (EUP)** is the number of complete goods that could have been produced using the inputs consumed during the period.
  - The EUP conversion is a two-phase process: First, the equivalent units are determined, then the per-unit cost is calculated.
  - The two calculations are made separately for direct materials and conversion costs (transferred-in costs are by definition 100% complete). Conversion costs are assumed to be uniformly incurred.
- **Two methods** of calculating EUP are in common use:
  - Under the **weighted-average** method, units in beginning work-in-process inventory are treated as if they were started and completed during the current period.
  - Under the **first-in, first-out (FIFO)** method, units in beginning work-in-process inventory are part of the EUP calculation. The calculation is thus more complex than weighted-average but tends to be more accurate.

Core Concepts for Activity-Based Costing

- **Activity-based costing (ABC)** is a response to the significant increase in the incurrence of **indirect costs** resulting from the rapid advance of technology. ABC is a refinement of an existing costing system (job-order or process).
- **Volume-based systems** involve: accumulating costs in general ledger accounts (utilities, taxes, etc.), using a single cost pool to combine the costs in all the related accounts, selecting a single driver to use for the entire indirect cost pool, and allocating the indirect cost pool to final cost objects.
- **Activity-based systems**, by contrast, involve: identifying organization activities that constitute overhead, assigning the costs of resources consumed by the activities, and assigning the costs of the activities to final cost objects.
- **Activities** are classified in a hierarchy according to the level of the production process at which they take place: unit-level activities, batch-level activities, product-sustaining (or service-sustaining) activities, and facility-sustaining activities.
- Once the activities are designated, the next step in enacting an ABC system is to **assign the costs of resources to the activities**. This is termed first-stage allocation. A separate accounting system may be necessary to track resource costs separately from the general ledger.
- Once the resources have been identified, resource drivers are designated to allocate resource costs to the activity cost pools. Resource drivers are measures of the resources consumed by an activity.
- The final step in enacting an ABC system is **allocating the activity cost pools to final cost objects**. This is termed second-stage allocation. Costs are reassigned to final-stage (or, if intermediate cost objects are used, next-stage) cost objects on the basis of activity drivers. Activity drivers are measures of the demands made on an activity by next-stage cost objects, such as the number of parts in a product used to measure an assembly activity.

- A **cost object** may be a job, product, process, activity, service, or anything else for which a cost measure is desired. **Intermediate cost objects** receive temporary accumulations of costs as the cost pools move from their originating points to the final cost objects. For example, work-in-process is an intermediate cost object, and finished salable goods are final cost objects.

Core Concepts for Life-Cycle Costing

- A **life-cycle approach** to budgeting estimates a product's revenues and expenses over its **entire sales life cycle** beginning with research and development, proceeding through the introduction and growth stages into the maturity stage, and finally into the harvest or decline stage. Accordingly, life-cycle costing takes a **long-term view** of the entire cost life cycle, also known as the value chain.

- Life-cycle costing emphasizes the relationships among costs incurred at **different value-chain stages**, for example, the effect of reduced design costs on future customer-service costs. Because it makes a distinction between **incurring costs** (actually using resources) and **locking in (designing in) costs**, life-cycle costing highlights the potential for cost reduction activities during the upstream phase of the value chain.

- Essentially, life-cycle costing requires the **accumulation of all costs over a product's lifetime**, from inception of the idea to the abandonment of the product. These costs are then allocated to production on an expected unit-of-output basis.

Core Concepts for Operation Costing

- **Operation costing** is a **hybrid** of job-order costing and process costing that emphasizes physical processes (operations) for cost management and control purposes. Operation costing is appropriate when similar products are produced in different models or styles or otherwise have distinctive traits.

- Operation costing accumulates total conversion costs and determines a **unit conversion cost** (total conversion cost ÷ total units passing through the operation) for each operation as in process costing. Production is controlled using work orders, and direct materials costs are charged specifically to products as in job-order systems. **More work-in-process accounts** are needed because one is required for each operation.

Core Concepts for Backflush Costing

- **Backflush costing** is often used by firms that have adopted a **just-in-time (JIT)** production philosophy. A JIT system treats carrying inventory as a nonvalue-adding activity. Hence, components are made available just in time to be used in the production process. Backflush costing complements JIT because it simplifies costing.

- Backflush costing treats the detailed recording of inventory data as a nonvalue-adding activity. **Work-in-process is usually eliminated**, journal entries to inventory accounts may be delayed until the time of product completion or even the time of sale, and standard costs are used to assign costs to units when journal entries are made, that is, to "flush" costs out of the system to the points at which inventories remain.

Part 2 – Section B.4. Overhead costs

The candidate should be able to:

- a.　demonstrate an understanding of the fixed and variable nature of overhead expenses
- b.　determine the appropriate time frame for classifying both variable and fixed overhead expenses
- c.　demonstrate an understanding that overhead rates can be determined in a variety of ways (e.g., plant-wide rates, departmental rates, and individual cost driver rates), and describe the benefits and limitations of each of these methods
- d.　identify the components of variable overhead expense
- e.　determine the appropriate allocation base for variable overhead expenses
- f.　calculate the per unit variable overhead expense
- g.　identify the components of fixed overhead expense
- h.　identify the appropriate allocation base for fixed overhead expense and demonstrate an understanding that because the allocation base is generally variable (e.g., direct labor hours), fixed overhead is often over or under applied
- i.　calculate the fixed overhead application rate
- j.　demonstrate an understanding of overhead control accounts, overhead allocation accounts, and the expensing of over or under applied overhead expenses
- k.　compare and contrast traditional overhead allocation with activity-based overhead allocation
- l.　calculate overhead expense in an activity-based setting and describe the benefits derived from activity-based overhead allocation
- m.　demonstrate an understanding of the need to allocate the cost of service departments such as human resources or information technology to divisions, departments, or activities
- n.　demonstrate an understanding of the direct method, the reciprocal method, and the step-down method to allocate service or support department costs

Core Concepts for Absorption (Full) vs. Variable (Direct) Costing

- ■　Under **absorption costing** (sometimes called full or full absorption costing), the **fixed portion of manufacturing overhead** is "absorbed" into the cost of each product.
  - ●　Product cost thus includes all manufacturing costs, both fixed and variable. Absorption-basis cost of goods sold is subtracted from sales to arrive at **gross margin**.
  - ●　This method is **required under GAAP** for external reporting purposes and under the Internal Revenue Code for tax purposes.
- ■　**Variable costing** (sometimes called direct costing) is more appropriate for **internal reporting**.
  - ●　Product cost includes **only variable manufacturing costs**. Variable-basis cost of goods sold and the variable portion of S&A expenses are subtracted from gross margin to arrive at **contribution margin**.
- ■　When production exceeds sales, operating income is higher under absorption costing. This is the **perverse incentive** inherent to absorption costing and reveals why many companies prefer variable costing for internal reporting. A production manager can increase absorption-basis operating income merely by increasing production, whether there is any customer demand for the additional product or not.

Core Concepts for Joint Product and By-Product Costing

- When two or more separate products are produced by a **common manufacturing process** from a common input, the outputs from the process are joint products. Joint (common) costs are those costs incurred up to the point where the products become separately identifiable, called the **split-off point**.

    - At the split-off point, the joint products acquire separate identities. Costs incurred after split-off are **separable costs**.

- **Several methods** are available to **allocate joint costs**.

    - A physical measure-based approach employs a physical measure such as volume, weight, or a linear measure. The **physical-unit method** allocates joint production costs to each product based on their relative proportions of the measure selected.

    - The **sales-value at split-off method** is based on the relative sales values of the separate products at split-off.

    - The **estimated net realizable value (NRV) method** also allocates joint costs based on the relative market values of the products.

    - The **constant gross-margin percentage NRV method** is based on allocating joint costs so that the gross-margin percentage is the same for every product.

- **By-products** are one or more products of relatively small total value that are produced simultaneously from a common manufacturing process with products of greater value and quantity. They can be sold or discarded.

Core Concepts for Overhead Costs and Normal Costing

- Whenever **overhead** is to be allocated, as in job-order costing and activity-based costing, an **appropriate allocation base** must be chosen. In traditional cost accounting, allocation bases include direct labor hours, direct labor cost, machine hours, materials cost, and units of production. The crucial quality of an allocation base is that it be a **cost driver** of the costs in the pool to be allocated.

- Overhead is usually allocated to products based upon the **level of activity**. For example, if overhead is largely made up of machine maintenance, the activity base may be machine hours. The predetermined overhead application rate equals budgeted overhead divided by the budgeted activity level (measure of capacity).

- Inevitably, the overhead amounts applied throughout the year will vary from the amount actually incurred, which is only determinable once the job is complete. This **variance** is called **over- or underapplied overhead**.

- During times of **low production**, per-unit overhead charges will **skyrocket**. This leads to higher product costs during years of lower production and to distortions in the financial statements.

- To **prevent these distortions** in the financial statements, **normal costing** derives the overhead application rate by looking at several years at a time, not just one. **Extended normal costing** applies the use of a normalized rate to direct costs as well as to manufacturing overhead.

Core Concepts for Allocation of Service Department Costs

- **Service (support) department** costs are considered part of overhead (indirect costs). Thus, they cannot feasibly be traced to cost objects and therefore **must be allocated** to the operating departments that use the services. When service departments also render services to each other, their costs may be allocated to each other before allocation to operating departments.
- **Three methods** of service department allocation are in general use.
  - The **direct method** is the simplest. The direct method allocates service department costs directly to the producing departments without regard for services rendered by service departments to each other. Service department costs are allocated to production departments based on an allocation base appropriate to each service department's function.
  - The **step** or **step-down method** allocates some of the costs of services rendered by service departments to each other. The step method derives its name from the procedure involved: The service departments are allocated in order, from the one that provides the most service to other service departments down to the one that provides the least.
  - The **reciprocal method** is the most complex and the most theoretically sound of the three methods. It is also known as the simultaneous solution method, cross allocation method, matrix allocation method, or double distribution method. The reciprocal method recognizes services rendered by all service departments to each other.

13.4 COST MANAGEMENT ESSAY QUESTIONS

Recall that your CMA Part 4 exam will probably contain six scenarios, with about three questions per scenario. There will be a recommended time allocation of 20 minutes, 30 minutes, or 45 minutes for each scenario and related questions.

One scenario will involve ethical issues, and probably one or two scenarios will include calculations and responses on a worksheet. Also, expect at least one scenario on organizational/behavioral topics. The remaining scenarios cover Parts 1, 2, and 3.

Scenario Title	Subtopic	Questions	Suggested Time
Kristina Company	Process Costing	1, 2, 3	30 minutes
Northcoast Manufacturing Company	Overhead Application	4, 5	30 minutes
Wood Glow Manufacturing Company	Process Costing	6, 7, 8	30 minutes
Tastee-Treat Company	Overhead Application	9, 10	30 minutes
Bonn Company	Service Department Allocation	11, 12	30 minutes
Daniels Tool and Die Corporation	Absorption vs. Variable Costing	13, 14, 15	30 minutes
Talor Chemical Company	Joint Product Costing	16, 17	30 minutes
Huber Corporation	Absorption vs. Variable Costing	18, 19	30 minutes
Sun Company	Budgeting and Changing Cost Structure	20, 21, 22, 23	30 minutes

Scenario for Essay Questions 1, 2, 3

Kristina Company, which manufactures quality paint sold at premium prices, uses a single production department. Production begins with the blending of various chemicals, which are added at the beginning of the process, and ends with the canning of the paint. Canning occurs when the mixture reaches the 90% stage of completion. The gallon cans are then transferred to the Shipping Department for crating and shipment. Labor and overhead are added continuously throughout the process. Factory overhead is applied on the basis of direct labor hours at the rate of $3.00 per hour.

Prior to May, when a change in the process was implemented, work-in-process inventories were insignificant. The change in the process enables greater production but results in material amounts of work-in-process for the first time. The company has always used the weighted average method to determine equivalent production and unit costs. Now, production management is considering changing from the weighted average method to the first-in, first-out method.

The following data relate to actual production during the month of May:

Costs for May

Work-in-process inventory, May 1 (4,000 gallons 25% complete)	
Direct materials-chemicals	$ 45,600
Direct labor ($10 per hour)	6,250
Factory overhead	1,875
May costs added	
Direct materials-chemicals	228,400
Direct materials-cans	7,000
Direct labor ($10 per hour)	35,000
Factory overhead	10,500

Units for May

	Gallons
Work-in-process inventory, May 1 (25% complete)	4,000
Sent to Shipping Department	20,000
Started in May	21,000
Work-in-process inventory, May 31 (80% complete)	5,000

Questions

1. Prepare a schedule of equivalent units for each cost element for the month of May using the

   a. Weighted average method
   b. First-in, first-out method

2. Calculate the cost (to the nearest cent) per equivalent unit for each cost element for the month of May using the

   a. Weighted average method
   b. First-in, first-out method

3. Discuss the advantages and disadvantages of using the weighted average method versus the first-in, first-out method, and explain under what circumstances each method should be used.

Essay Questions 1, 2, 3 — Unofficial Answers

1. a. The equivalent units for each cost element, using the weighted average method, are presented below.

	Direct Materials		
	Chemicals	Cans	Conversion
Units completed and transferred to Shipping	20,000	20,000	20,000
Work-in-process at 5/31			
Chemicals (100%)	5,000		
Cans (0%)		0	
Conversion costs (80%)			4,000
Equivalent units	25,000	20,000	24,000

   b. The equivalent units for each cost element, using the first-in, first-out method, are presented below.

	Direct Materials		
	Chemicals	Cans	Conversion
Transferred to Shipping from 5/1 work-in-process			
(4,000 @ 25%)			
Chemicals (0%)	0		
Cans (100%)		4,000	
Conversion costs (75%)			3,000
Current production transferred to Shipping (100%)	16,000	16,000	16,000
5/31 work-in-process (5,000 @ 80%)			
Chemicals (100%)	5,000		
Cans (0%)		0	
Conversion costs (80%)			4,000
Equivalent units	21,000	20,000	23,000

2. a. The cost per equivalent unit for each cost element, using the weighted average method, is presented below.

	Direct Materials		
	Chemicals	Cans	Conversion*
Work-in-process at 5/1	$ 45,600	$ 0	$ 8,125
May costs added	228,400	7,000	45,500
Total costs	$274,000	$ 7,000	$53,625
+ Weighted average Equivalent units	25,000	20,000	24,000
Cost per Equivalent units	$ 10.96	$ .35	$ 2.23

   Conversion cost = Direct labor + Factory overhead

   b. The cost per equivalent unit for each cost element, using the first-in, first-out method, is presented below.

	Direct Materials		
	Chemicals	Cans	Conversion
May costs incurred	$228,400	$ 7,000	$45,500
+ First-in, first-out Equivalent units	21,000	20,000	23,000
Cost per Equivalent units	$ 10.88	$ .35	$ 1.98

3. The weighted average method is easier to use as the calculations are simpler. This method tends to obscure current period costs as the cost per equivalent unit includes both current costs and prior costs that were in the beginning inventory. This method is most appropriate when conversion costs, inventory levels, and raw material prices are stable.

   The first-in, first-out method is based on the work done in the current period only. This method is most appropriate when conversion costs, inventory levels, or raw material prices fluctuate. In addition, this method should be used when accuracy in current equivalent unit costs is important or when a standard cost system is used.

Scenario for Essay Questions 4, 5

Northcoast Manufacturing Company, a small manufacturer of parts used in appliances, has just completed its first year of operations. The company's controller, Vic Trainor, has been reviewing the actual results for the year and is concerned about the application of factory overhead. Trainor is using the following information to assess operations:

- Northcoast's equipment consists of several machines with a combined cost of $2,200,000 and no residual value. Each machine has an output of five units of product per hour and a useful life of 20,000 hours.

- Selected actual data of Northcoast's operations for the year just ended is presented below.

Products manufactured	650,000 units
Machine utilization	130,000 hours
Direct labor usage	35,000 hours
Labor rate	$15 per hour
Total factory overhead	$1,130,000
Cost of goods sold	$1,720,960
Finished goods inventory (at year-end)	$430,240
Work-in-process inventory (at year-end)	$0

- Total factory overhead is applied to direct labor cost using a predetermined plant-wide rate.

- The budgeted activity for the year included 20 employees each working 1,800 productive hours per year to produce 540,000 units of product. The machines are highly automated, and each employee can operate two to four machines simultaneously. Normal activity is for each employee to operate three machines. Machine operators are paid $15 per hour.

- Budgeted factory overhead costs for various levels of activity are shown in the table below.

Northcoast Manufacturing Company
Budgeted Annual Costs for Total Factory Overhead

Units of product	360,000	540,000	720,000
Labor hours	30,000	36,000	42,000
Machine hours	72,000	108,000	144,000
Total factory overhead costs:			
Plant supervision	$ 70,000	$ 70,000	$ 70,000
Plant rent	40,000	40,000	40,000
Equipment depreciation	288,000	432,000	576,000
Maintenance	42,000	51,000	60,000
Utilities	144,600	216,600	288,600
Indirect material	90,000	135,000	180,000
Other costs	11,200	16,600	22,000
Total	$685,800	$961,200	$1,236,600

Questions

4. Based on Northcoast Manufacturing Company's actual operations for the past year,

   a. Determine the dollar amount of total over/underapplied factory overhead and explain why this amount is material.

   b. Prepare the journal entry to close out Northcoast's total factory overhead account.

5. Vic Trainor believes that Northcoast Manufacturing Company should be using machine hours to apply total factory overhead. Using the data given,

   a. Determine the dollar amount of total over/underapplied factory overhead if machine hours had been used as the application base.

   b. Explain why machine hours would be a more appropriate application base.

Essay Questions 4, 5 — Unofficial Answers

4.   a.   Northcoast's underapplied factory overhead was $195,500, calculated as follows:

$$\text{Predetermined overhead application rate} = \frac{\$961,200}{36,000 \times \$15} = 1.78 \text{ or } 178\%$$

Actual applied overhead [(35,000 × $15) × 1.78]	$ 934,500
Actual incurred overhead	1,130,000
Underapplied overhead	$ 195,500

The reasons the amount of underapplied factory overhead, amounting to $195,500, could be considered material include the fact that underapplied overhead represents

- Over 11% of cost of goods sold ($195,500 ÷ $1,720,960).
- Over 17% of actual factory overhead costs ($195,500 ÷ $1,130,000).

    b.   Since the amount of underapplied overhead is material, the accounting treatment is to prorate this amount to work-in-process, finished goods, and cost of goods sold. Since there is no work-in-process, the journal entry would be:

	Debit	Credit
Factory overhead applied	$934,500	
Cost of goods sold	156,400	
Finished goods inventory	39,100	
Factory overhead control		$1,130,000

To record factory overhead allocated on the following basis.

• Cost of goods sold	$1,720,960
Finished goods	430,240
Total	$2,151,200

• Cost of goods sold	=	$1,720,960 ÷ $2,151,200
	=	.80 × $195,500
	=	$156,400

• Finished goods	=	$430,240 ÷ $2,151,200
	=	.20 × $195,500
	=	$39,100

5.   a.   If machine hours were used as the application base, Northcoast Manufacturing Company would have had the following results:

• Predetermined overhead rate	=	$\dfrac{\$961,200}{108,000}$
	=	$8.90 per machine hour

• Actual applied overhead	=	$8.90 × actual machine hours
	=	$8.90 × 130,000
	=	$1,157,000

• Overapplied overhead	=	Applied overhead – Actual overhead
	=	$1,157,000 – $1,130,000
	=	$27,000 overapplied

    b.   Machine hours would be a more appropriate application base for Northcoast's factory overhead inasmuch as Northcoast appears to have a capital intensive manufacturing process where each direct laborer is able to operate two to four machines. The use of machines drives a large portion of overhead costs, i.e., depreciation, maintenance, and utility expense. Using the basic driver of overhead costs as the application base results in more reliable cost information and better decisions.

Scenario for Essay Questions 6, 7, 8

Wood Glow Manufacturing Co. produces a single product, a wood refinishing kit that sells for $17.95. The final processing of the kits occurs in the Packaging Department. An internal quilted wrap is applied at the beginning of the packaging process. A compartmented outside box printed with instructions and the company's name and logo is added when units are 60% through the process. Conversion costs consisting of direct labor and applied overhead occur evenly throughout the packaging process. Conversion activities after the addition of the box involve package sealing, testing for leakage, and final inspection. Rejections in the Packaging Department are rare and may be ignored. The following data pertain to the activities of the Packaging Department during the month of October:

- Beginning work-in-process inventory was 10,000 units, 40% complete as to conversion costs.
- 30,000 units were started and completed in the month.
- There were 10,000 units in ending work-in-process, 80% complete as to conversion costs.

The Packaging Department's October costs were

Quilted wrap	$80,000
Outside boxes	50,000
Direct labor	22,000
Applied overhead ($3.00 per direct labor dollar)	66,000

The costs transferred in from prior processing were $3.00 per unit. The cost of goods sold for the month was $240,000, and the ending finished-goods inventory was $84,000. Wood Glow uses the first-in, first-out method of inventory valuation.

Wood Glow's controller, Mark Brandon, has been asked to analyze the activities of the Packaging Department for the month of October. Brandon knows that in order to properly determine the department's unit cost of production, he must first calculate the equivalent units of production.

Questions

6. Prepare an equivalent units of production schedule for the October activity in the Packaging Department. Be sure to account for the beginning work-in-process inventory, the units started and completed during the month, and the ending work-in-process inventory.

7. Determine the cost per equivalent unit of the October production.

8. Assuming that the actual overhead incurred during October was $5,000 more than the overhead applied, describe how the value of the ending work-in-process inventory would be determined.

Essay Questions 6, 7, 8 — Unofficial Answers

6.   The equivalent units of production schedule for the Packaging Department's October activity is as follows:

| | | Equivalent Units | | | |
	Whole Units	Quilted Wrap	Boxes	Direct Labor	Overhead
To complete beginning WIP inventory	10,000	0	10,000	6,000	6,000
Started and completed	30,000	30,000	30,000	30,000	30,000
Ending WIP inventory	10,000	10,000	10,000	8,000	8,000
Equivalent units of production		40,000	50,000	44,000	44,000

7.   Cost per equivalent unit of October production is as follows:

	October Costs	÷	Equivalent Units	=	Unit Costs
Quilted wrap	$80,000		40,000		$2.00
Boxes	50,000		50,000		1.00
Direct labor	22,000		44,000		.50
Applied overhead	66,000		44,000		1.50
Equivalent unit cost					$5.00

8.   If $5,000 is considered an immaterial amount for Wood Glow Manufacturing, the additional overhead incurred would be charged to the cost of goods sold for the month of October. If $5,000 is material, the underapplied overhead should be prorated among the cost of goods sold, work-in-process inventory, and finished goods inventory.

Scenario for Essay Questions 9, 10

Tastee-Treat Company prepares, packages, and distributes six frozen vegetables in two different sized containers. The different vegetables and different sizes are prepared in large batches. The company employs an actual cost job order costing system. Manufacturing overhead is assigned to batches by a predetermined rate on the basis of direct labor hours. The manufacturing overhead costs incurred by the company during two recent years (adjusted for changes using current prices and wage rates) are presented below.

	Year 1	Year 2
Direct labor hours worked	2,760,000	2,160,000
Manufacturing overhead costs incurred:*		
Indirect labor	$11,040,000	$ 8,640,000
Employee benefits	4,140,000	3,240,000
Supplies	2,760,000	2,160,000
Power	2,208,000	1,728,000
Heat and light	552,000	552,000
Supervision	2,865,000	2,625,000
Depreciation	7,930,000	7,930,000
Property taxes and insurance	3,005,000	3,005,000
Total overhead costs	$34,500,000	$29,880,000

* (adjusted for changes in current prices and wage rates)

Questions

9. Tastee-Treat Company expects to operate at a 2,300,000 direct labor hour level of activity in the current year. Using the data from two recent years, calculate the rate Tastee-Treat should employ to assign manufacturing overhead to its products.

10. Explain how the company can use the information it developed for calculating the overhead rate for

   a. Evaluation of product pricing decisions

   b. Cost control evaluation

   c. Development of budgets

Essay Questions 9, 10 — Unofficial Answers

9.   Calculate the cost and volume differentials to determine the variable overhead rate:

$$\frac{\$34,500,000}{2,760,000} - \frac{\$29,880,000}{2,160,000} = \frac{\$4,620,000}{600,000}$$

$$= \$7.70/direct\ labor\ hour$$

Total overhead -- Year 2	$34,500,000
Total variable overhead (2,760,000 × $7.70)	(21,252,000)
Total fixed overhead	$13,248,000

Total overhead costs at 2,300,000 direct labor hours:

Total variable overhead (2,300,000 × $7.70)	$17,710,000
Total fixed overhead	13,248,000
Total overhead	$30,958,000

$$Total\ overhead\ rate = \frac{\$30,958,000}{2,300,000}$$

$$= \$13.46\ per\ hour$$

10.   a.   Evaluation of product pricing decisions -- Tastee-Treat products are sold in a highly competitive market with little product differentiation possible. Thus, the prices it can charge will be based largely on market factors rather than the company's cost. The calculation of the overhead rate required the company to estimate the variable costs. In short-term price-cutting situations, the price set should cover at least the variable material, labor, and overhead costs. For the longer term, the total overhead costs assigned to the various types of vegetables and container sizes may provide some basis for price differentials among the items.

b.   Cost control evaluation -- The calculation of the overhead rates required the company to estimate the fixed overhead costs and the variable overhead costs per direct labor hour. The amounts are estimates of what the costs should or will be during Year 3. The amounts can be used as the basis for preparation of a flexible budget to be compared to actual costs incurred. Any difference between the flexible budget amounts and actual costs would be a measure of the effectiveness of overhead cost control.

c.   Development of budgets -- The estimates of fixed overhead costs and the variable overhead cost per direct labor hour are useful in budget development. They permit the company to calculate the estimated factory overhead costs for different activity levels that are being considered as the budget is developed.

Scenario for Essay Questions 11, 12

Bonn Company recently reorganized its data processing activities. The small installations located within the accounting departments at its plants have been replaced with a single IT department at corporate headquarters. Because the department has focused its activities on converting applications to the new system and producing reports for the plant and subsidiary managements, little attention has been devoted to the costs of the department. Now company management has requested that the departmental manager recommend a cost accumulation system to facilitate cost control and the development of suitable rates to charge users for service.

For the past two years, the departmental costs have been recorded in one account. The costs have then been allocated to user departments on the basis of computer time used. The schedule below reports the costs for the current year.

	Data Processing Department Costs for the Year Ended December 31		Computer hours for user processing* Hourly rate ($1,176,000 ÷ 2,750)	2,750 $428
(1)	Salaries and benefits	$ 622,600	*Use of available computer hours	
(2)	Supplies	40,000	Testing and debugging programs	250
(3)	Equipment maintenance contract	15,000	Set-up of jobs	500
(4)	Insurance	25,000	Processing jobs	2,750
(5)	Heat and air-conditioning	36,000	Down-time for maintenance	750
(6)	Electricity	50,000	Idle time	742
(7)	Equipment and furniture depreciation	285,400		4,992
(8)	Building improvements depreciation	10,000		
(9)	Building occupancy and security	39,300		
(10)	Corporate administrative charges	52,700		
	Total costs	$1,176,000		

The manager recommends that costs be accumulated by five activity centers within the department: Systems Analysis, Programming, Data Preparation, Computer Operations (processing), and Administration. He then suggests that the costs of Administration should be allocated to the other four activity centers before a separate rate for charging users is developed for the first four activities.

The manager made the following observations regarding the charges to the several subsidiary accounts after reviewing the details of the accounts:

1. Salaries and benefits – records salary and benefits of all employees in the department.
2. Supplies – records paper costs for printers and a small amount for other costs.
3. Equipment maintenance contracts – records charges for maintenance contracts.
4. Insurance – records costs of insurance covering the equipment and furniture.
5. Heat and air-conditioning – records a charge from the corporate heating and air-conditioning department for the incremental costs to meet special needs of the computer department.
6. Electricity – records the charge for electricity based upon a separate meter within the department.
7. Equipment and furniture depreciation – records the depreciation charges for all owned equipment and furniture within the department.
8. Building improvements – records the amortization charges for the building changes required to provide proper environmental control and electrical service for the computer equipment.
9. Building occupancy and security – records the computer department's share of the costs of the building allocated to the department on the basis of square feet occupied.
10. Corporate administrative charges – records the computer department's share of the corporate administrative costs allocated on the basis of number of employees.

Questions

11. For each of the ten cost items, state whether it should be distributed to the five activity centers and, for each cost item that should be distributed, recommend the basis upon which it should be distributed. Justify your conclusion in each case.

12. Assume the costs of the Computer Operations (processing) activity will be charged to the user departments on the basis of computer hours. Using the analysis of computer utilization shown in the problem, determine the total number of hours that should be employed to determine the charge rate for Computer Operations. Justify your answer.

Essay Questions 11, 12 — Unofficial Answers

11. The ten cost items can be categorized into four basic groups for purposes of discussion:

Item	Allocation	Allocation Method	Justification
I. All items in this category should be distributed.			
1. Salaries	yes	Direct	The costs of these two items are directly incurred by the activity centers and can be controlled by the supervisor. A part of the salaries and benefits might be excluded from a marginal cost charging rate.
2. Supplies	yes	Direct	
II. All items in this category should be distributed because a direct causal basis exists, but they should be excluded from a marginal cost charging rate.			
3. Equipment maintenance	yes	Direct	The costs of these items are directly incurred by the activity centers but are controlled by corporate policy. They would be included in a full cost charging rate and excluded from a marginal cost charging rate.
4. Insurance	yes	Direct	
7. Equipment, furniture, and depreciation	yes	Direct	The costs of these items are directly incurred by the activity centers. They are not controllable costs in the usual sense. They would be included in a full cost rate and excluded from a marginal cost charging rate.
5. Heat and air conditioning	yes	Direct (one center only)	
8. Building improvements and depreciation	yes	Direct (one center only)	
III. All items should be distributed because a reasonable measure for estimating the causal relationship exists.			
6. Electricity	yes	Equipment usage and wattage ratings	A reasonable estimate can be made of the electrical charges, and they can be controlled by efficient use of equipment. The cost should be included in a full cost and marginal cost charging rate.
IV. The following items should be distributed only if a full cost charging rate is required.			
9. Building occupancy and security	yes (only for full cost charging rate)	Square feet	There is no cost control benefit from allocation of these costs. The only reason to allocate is for a full cost charging rate.
10. Corporation administrative charges	yes (only for full cost charging rate)	Number of employees or some other general basis	

12. The number of hours selected for determining the charging rate depends upon the purpose of establishing the rate. If the objective is to charge user departments for all of the costs of Computer Operations, the actual hours which can be identified with the user departments will be included in the base hours. This amounts to 3,500 hours as shown below.

In order to promote cost control, Bonn Company might consider a dual charging rate whereby the marginal costs would be charged over actual user time (3,500 hours) and fixed costs over available time (4,242 hours).

Actual User Time		Available Time	
Testing and debugging	250	Testing and debugging	250
Set-up	500	Set-up	500
Processing	2,750	Processing	2,750
		Idle time	742
	3,500		4,242

Scenario for Essay Questions 13, 14, 15

The Daniels Tool & Die Corporation has been in existence for a little over 3 years; sales have been increasing each year. A job order cost system is used. Factory overhead is applied to jobs based on direct labor hours, utilizing the absorption (full) costing method. Overapplied or underapplied overhead is treated as an adjustment to cost of goods sold. The company's income statements for the last 2 years are presented below.

Daniels Tool & Die Corporation
Year 3-Year 4 Comparative Income Statements

	Year 3	Year 4
Sales	$840,000	$1,015,000
Cost of goods sold		
Finished goods, 1/1	$ 25,000	$ 18,000
Cost of goods manufactured	548,000	657,600
Total available	$573,000	$ 675,600
Finished goods, 12/31	18,000	14,000
Cost of goods sold before overhead adjustment	$555,000	$ 661,600
Underapplied factory overhead	36,000	14,400
Cost of goods sold	$591,000	$ 676,000
Gross profit	$249,000	$ 339,000
Selling expenses	$ 82,000	$ 95,000
Administrative expenses	70,000	75,000
Total operating expenses	$152,000	$ 170,000
Operating income	$ 97,000	$ 169,000

Daniels Tool & Die Corporation
Inventory Balances

	1/1/Year 3	12/31/Year 3	12/31/Year 4
Raw material	$22,000	$30,000	$10,000
Work-in-process costs	$40,000	$48,000	$64,000
Direct labor hours	1,335	1,600	2,100
Finished goods costs	$25,000	$18,000	$14,000
Direct labor hours	1,450	1,050	820

Daniels used the same predetermined overhead rate in applying overhead to production orders in both Year 3 and Year 4. The rate was based on the following estimates:

Fixed factory overhead	$ 25,000
Variable factory overhead	$155,000
Direct labor hours	25,000
Direct labor costs	$150,000

In Year 3 and Year 4, actual direct labor hours expended were 20,000 and 23,000, respectively. Raw materials put into production were $292,000 in Year 3 and $370,000 in Year 4. Actual fixed overhead was $37,400 for Year 4 and $42,300 for Year 3, and the planned direct labor rate was the direct labor rate achieved.

For both years, all of the reported administrative costs were fixed, while the variable portion of the reported selling expenses result from a commission of 5% of sales revenue.

Questions

13. For the year ended December 31, Year 4, prepare a revised income statement utilizing the variable (direct) costing method. Be sure to include contribution margin.

14. Prepare a numerical reconciliation of the difference in operating income between Daniels' Year 4 income statement prepared on the basis of absorption costing and the revised Year 4 income statement prepared on the basis of variable costing.

15. Describe both the advantages and disadvantages of using variable costing.

Essay Questions 13, 14, 15 — Unofficial Answers

13.

Daniels Tool & Die Corporation
Variable Costing Income Statement
For the year ended December 31, Year 4

Sales		$1,015,000
Finished goods, 1/1/Year 4	$ 16,950	
Work-in-process 1/1/Year 4	46,400	
Manufacturing costs incurred	650,600	
Total available	$713,950	
Work-in-process 12/31/Year 4	(61,900)	
Finished goods 12/31/Year 4	(13,180)	
Variable manufacturing cost of goods sold	$638,870	
Variable selling expenses	50,750	
Total variable costs		(689,620)
Contribution margin		$ 325,380
Fixed factory overhead	$ 37,400	
Fixed selling expenses	44,250	
Fixed administrative expenses	75,000	
Total fixed costs		(156,650)
Operating income		$ 168,730

14. The difference in the operating income of $270 is caused by the different treatment of fixed manufacturing overhead. Under absorption costing, fixed overhead costs are assigned to inventory and are not expensed until the goods are sold. Under variable costing, these costs are treated as expenses in the period incurred. Since the direct labor hours in the work-in-process and finished goods inventories had a net increase of 270 hours, the absorption costing operating profit is higher because the fixed factory overhead associated with the increased labor hours in inventory is not expensed under absorption costing.

	1/1/Year 4 Inventories	12/31/Year 4 Inventories	Difference
Work-in-process	1,600	2,100	500
Finished goods	1,050	820	(230)
Total	2,650	2,920	270

15. The advantages of using variable costing follow.

   a. The fixed manufacturing costs are reported at incurred values, not at absorbed values, which increases the likelihood of better control over fixed costs.

   b. Profits are directly influenced by changes in sales volume and not by changes in inventory levels.

   c. Contribution margin by product line, territory, department, or division is emphasized.

The disadvantages of using variable costing follow.

   a. Variable costing is not acceptable for tax reporting, for SEC reporting, nor for external financial reporting; therefore, companies need to keep two sets of records.

   b. Costs other than variable costs, i.e., fixed costs and total production costs, may be ignored when making decisions, especially long-term decisions.

   c. With the movement toward a fully automated factory, fixed factory overhead may be a significant portion of production costs. To ignore these significant costs in inventory valuation may not be acceptable.

Scenario for Essay Questions 16, 17

Talor Chemical Company is a highly diversified chemical processing company. The company manufactures swimming pool chemicals, chemicals for metal processing companies, specialized chemical compounds for other companies, and a full line of pesticides and insecticides.

Currently, the Noorwood plant is producing two derivatives, RNA-1 and RNA-2, from the chemical compound VDB developed by Talor's research labs. Each week 1,200,000 pounds of VDB is processed at a cost of $246,000 into 800,000 pounds of RNA-1 and 400,000 pounds of RNA-2. The proportion of these two outputs is fixed and cannot be altered because this is a joint process. RNA-1 has no market value until it is converted into a product with the trade name Fastkil. The cost to process RNA-1 into Fastkil is $240,000. Fastkil wholesales at $50 per 100 pounds.

RNA-2 is sold as is for $80 per hundred pounds. However, Talor has discovered that RNA-2 can be converted into two new products through further processing. The further processing would require the addition of 400,000 pounds of compound LST to the 400,000 pounds of RNA-2. The joint process would yield 400,000 pounds each of DMZ-3 and Pestrol -- the two new products. The additional raw material and related processing costs of this joint process would be $120,000. DMZ-3 and Pestrol would each be sold for $57.50 per 100 pounds. Talor management has decided not to process RNA-2 further based on the analysis presented in the schedule below. Talor uses the physical method to allocate the common costs arising from joint processing.

		Process Further		
	RNA-2	DMZ-3	Pestrol	Total
Production in pounds	400,000	400,000	400,000	
Revenue	$320,000	$230,000	$230,000	$460,000
Costs				
VDB costs	$ 82,000	$ 61,500	$ 61,500	$123,000
Additional raw materials (LST) and processing of RNA-2		60,000	60,000	120,000
Total costs	$ 82,000	$121,500	$121,500	$243,000
Weekly gross profit	$238,000	$108,500	$108,500	$217,000

A new staff accountant who was to review the analysis above commented that it should be revised and stated, "Product costing of products such as these should be done on a net relative sales value basis, not a physical-volume basis."

Questions

16. Discuss whether the use of the net relative-sales-value method would provide data more relevant for the decision to market DMZ-3 and Petrol.

17. Critique the Talor Company's analysis and make any revisions that are necessary. Your critique and analysis should indicate

    a. Whether Talor Chemical Company made the correct decision.

    b. The gross savings (loss) per week of Talor's decision not to process RNA-2 further, if different from the company-prepared analysis.

Essay Questions 16, 17 — Unofficial Answers

16. The net relative sales value method does not provide additional data for the marketing decision. Joint cost allocation is necessarily arbitrary and, although useful for financial accounting purposes, is not relevant to the decision to market DMZ-3 and Pestrol. The joint or common costs are irrelevant to this decision because they are incurred in both cases, i.e., the method of cost allocation has no impact on the differential profit. Talor Company should calculate the differential profit of its alternate choices by comparing the differential revenues and differential costs.

17. a. Talor Company's analysis is incorrect because it incorporates allocated portions of the common costs of VDB. The weekly cost of VDB ($246,000) will be incurred whether or not RNA-2 is converted through further processing. Thus, any allocation of the common cost of VDB is strictly arbitrary and not relevant to the decision to market DMZ-3 and Pestrol.

  b. Talor Company's decision not to process RNA-2 further is incorrect. The decision resulted in a loss of $20,000 in gross profit per week as indicated by the following analysis

     Revenue from further processing of RNA-2:

DMZ-3 (400,000 × $57.50 ÷ 100)	$230,000
Pestrol (400,000 × $57.50 ÷ 100)	230,000
Total revenue from further processing	$460,000
Less revenue from sale of RNA-2	320,000
Incremental revenue	$140,000
Less incremental cost	120,000
Incremental profit	$ 20,000

     The cost of VDB is not relevant and thus is omitted from the solution.

Scenario for Essay Questions 18, 19

The Vice President for Sales of Huber Corporation has received the Income Statement for July Year 1. The statement has been prepared on the direct cost basis and is reproduced below. The firm has just adopted a direct costing system for internal reporting purposes.

Huber Corporation
Income Statement
For the Month of July Year 1
($000 omitted)

Sales		$2,400
Less: Variable standard cost of goods sold		1,200
Manufacturing margin		$1,200
Less: Fixed manufacturing costs at budget	$600	
Fixed manufacturing cost spending variance	0	600
Gross margin		$ 600
Less: Fixed selling & administrative costs		400
Net income before taxes		$ 200

The controller attached the following notes to the statements.

- The unit sales price for July averaged $24.
- The standard unit manufacturing costs for the month were

Variable cost	$12
Fixed cost	4
Total cost	$16

The unit rate for fixed manufacturing costs is a predetermined rate based upon a normal monthly production of 150,000 units.

- Production for July was 45,000 units in excess of sales.
- The inventory at July 31 consisted of 80,000 units.

Questions

18. The Vice President for Sales is not comfortable with the direct cost basis and wonders what the net income would have been under the prior absorption cost basis.

    a. Present the November income statement on an absorption cost basis.

    b. Reconcile and explain the difference between the direct costing and the absorption costing net income figures.

19. Explain the features associated with direct cost income measurement that should be attractive to the Vice President for Sales.

Essay Questions 18, 19 — Unofficial Answers

18.   a.

Huber Corporation
Income Statement (Absorption Cost Basis)
For the Month of July Year 1
($000 omitted)

Sales (100,000 units @ $24 per unit)		$2,400
Less cost of goods sold:		
Variable cost per unit	$ 12	
Fixed cost per unit	4	
Total unit cost	$ 16	
Volume in units	× 100,000	
Cost of goods sold at standard	$ 1,600	
Production volume variation (5,000 units @ $4)	20	1,620
Gross margin		$ 780
Less: Fixed selling & administrative costs		400
Net Income before taxes		$ 380

   b.

Reconciliation of Net Income Before Taxes,
Direct and Absorption Costing Methods
($000 omitted)

	Direct Costing	Absorption Costing
Reported net income before taxes	$200	$380

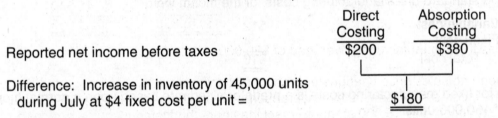

Difference: Increase in inventory of 45,000 units during July at $4 fixed cost per unit =	$180

Absorption costing attaches a $4 fixed manufacturing cost per unit to each unit produced in July. Because the production during July (145,000 units) exceeded sales of July (100,000 units), the fixed cost assigned to the 45,000 unit increase in the inventory balance results in $180,000 (45,000 units @ $4 fixed cost per unit) less fixed costs being charged to the income statement in July and the resultant increase of $180,000 in net income before taxes.

19.   The Vice President for Sales should find the direct costing approach to income determination desirable for many reasons, including

   a.   Direct costing income varies with units sold, not units produced.

   b.   Fixed manufacturing costs are charged against revenue in the period in which they were incurred; consequently, manufacturing cost per unit does not change with a change in production levels.

   c.   The contribution margin offers a useful tool for making decisions which consider changes in cost/volume/profit relationships.

Scenario for Essay Questions 20, 21, 22, 23

Sun Company, a subsidiary of Guardian, Inc., produces and sells three product lines. The company employs a standard cost accounting system for record keeping purposes. At the beginning of the current year, the president of Sun Company presented the budget to the parent company and accepted a commitment to contribute $15,800 to Guardian's consolidated profit for the year. The president has been confident that the year's profit would exceed budget target, since the monthly sales reports that he has been receiving have shown that sales for the year will exceed budget by 10%. The president is both disturbed and confused when the controller presents an adjusted forecast as of November 30 indicating that profit will be 11% under budget. The two forecasts are presented below:

Sun Company
Forecasts of Operating Results

	1/1	11/30
Sales	$268,000	$294,800
Cost of sales at standard	212,000	233,200
Gross margin at standard	$ 56,000	$ 61,600
Over- (under-) absorbed fixed manufacturing overhead	--	(6,000)
Actual gross margin	$ 56,000	$ 55,600
Selling expenses	$ 13,400	$ 14,740
Administrative expenses	26,800	26,800
Total operating expenses	$ 40,200	$ 41,540
Earnings before tax	$ 15,800	$ 14,060

*Includes fixed manufacturing overhead of $30,000.

There have been no sales price changes or product mix shifts since the 1/1 forecast. The only cost variance on the income statement is the underabsorbed manufacturing overhead. This arose because the company produced only 16,000 standard machine hours (budgeted machine hours were 20,000) during the year as a result of a shortage of raw materials while its supplier was closed by a strike. Fortunately, Sun Company's finished goods inventory was large enough to fill all sales orders received.

Questions

20. Analyze and explain why the profit has declined in spite of increased sales and good control over costs.

21. What plan, if any, could Sun Company adopt during December to improve their reported profit at year end? Explain your answer.

22. Illustrate and explain how Sun Company could adopt an alternative internal cost reporting procedure that would avoid the confusing effect of the present procedure.

23. Would the alternative procedure described in Question 22 be acceptable to Guardian, Inc. for financial reporting purposes? Explain.

Essay Questions 20, 21, 22, 23 — Unofficial Answers

20. Because Sun Company uses absorption costing, the net income is influenced by both sales volume and production volume. Sales volume was increased in the 11/30 forecast, and at standard gross profit rates this would increase earnings before taxes by $5,600. However, during this same period production volume was below the 1/1 forecast, causing an unplanned volume variance of $6,000. The volume variance and the increased selling expenses (due to the 10% increase in sales) overshadowed the added profits from sales as shown below:

Increased sales		$26,800
Increased cost of sales at standard		21,200
Increased gross margin at standard		5,600
Less:		
Volume variance	$6,000	
Increased selling expenses	1,340	7,340
Decrease in earnings		$ 1,740

21. The basic cause of the lower forecast of profits is low production. If raw materials can be obtained, and if it is reasonable in light of expected future sales, Sun Company could schedule heavy production which would reduce the volume variance.

22. Sun Company could adopt direct costing. Under direct costing, fixed manufacturing costs would be treated as period costs and would not be assigned to production. Consequently, earnings would not be affected by production volume but only by sales volume. Statements prepared on a direct costing basis are illustrated below.

Sun Company
Forecasts of Operating Results

	Forecasts as of	
	1/1	11/30
Sales	$268,000	$294,800
Variable costs		
Manufacturing	$182,000	$200,200
Selling expenses	13,400	14,740
Total variable costs	$195,400	$214,940
Contribution margin	$ 72,600	$ 79,860
Fixed costs		
Manufacturing	$ 30,000	$ 30,000
Administration	26,800	26,800
Total fixed costs	$ 56,800	$ 56,800
Earnings before taxes	$ 15,800	$ 23,060

23. Direct costing would not be acceptable for financial reporting purposes because generally accepted accounting principles seem to require the allocation of some fixed manufacturing costs to inventory.

Consider using Gleim's **CMA Test Prep** for interactive testing with **hundreds of multiple-choice questions** as an additional method of knowledge transfer in your quest to pass Part 4.

STUDY UNIT FOURTEEN
CMA PART 2 REVIEW –
INFORMATION MANAGEMENT AND
PERFORMANCE MEASUREMENT

(15 pages of outline)

Part 2 of the CMA exam is titled **Management Accounting and Reporting**. This study unit is a review of these sections:

C.   **Information Management.** Nature of management and accounting information systems; systems development and design; techniques and terminology applicable to the development of computer-based accounting information systems; networks and client/server systems; electronic commerce; ERP systems.

D.   **Performance Measurement.** Factors to be analyzed for control and performance evaluation including revenues, costs, profits, and investment in assets; variance analysis based on flexible budgets and standard costs; responsibility accounting for revenue, cost, contribution, and profit centers; balanced scorecard; quality considerations.

This study unit presents the IMA's Learning Outcome Statements and Gleim Core Concepts relevant to these sections. Bear in mind that **all topics** on Part 4 of the exam are tested at **skill level C** (all six skill types required).

14.1   INFORMATION MANAGEMENT REVIEW

Part 2 – Section C.1. Nature and purpose of an information system

The candidate should be able to:

a.   identify the different types of business information systems, e.g., transaction processing, management information, decision support, etc.

b.   explain the functions of information systems, including business processing and data analysis

c.   differentiate between centralized and decentralized information systems and identify the advantages and disadvantages of each

d.   identify and define the two basic ways that transaction processing systems process data; i.e., (i) batch processing and (ii) real-time processing

e.   explain how information systems are used for competitive advantage in organizations by solving temporal and financial problems

Core Concepts for the Nature and Purpose of an Information System

- An information system performs four major tasks: **input**, **transformation**, **output**, and **storage**.
- The functions of information systems can be grouped into two major categories: **business processing** and **data analysis**.
- Each **organizational level** uses information systems appropriate to its functions:
    - At the **strategic** level, high-level executives use **executive support systems**.
    - At the **management** level, middle managers use **decision support systems** and **management information systems**.
    - At the **knowledge** level, knowledge workers such as engineers and accountants use **knowledge work systems** and **office automation systems**.
    - At the **operational** level, operational managers and bookkeepers use **transaction processing systems**.
- **Batch processing** is the accumulation and grouping of transactions for processing on a **delayed basis**.
- **Online processing** involves direct communication with the computer, giving the system the capability to handle transactions **as they are entered**.
    - **Real-time processing** involves processing an input record and **receiving the output** soon enough to affect a current decision-making process.
- Batch and online modes are commonly **combined** in a single application, to permit continuous **entry** of transactions throughout the workday in online mode and periodic **posting** of the transactions to the master files in batch mode.
- The advent of cheaper and smaller computers has permitted the development of a hybrid of centralization and decentralization called **distributed processing**. The decision is then not whether an application should run centrally or locally, but rather, which **parts of the application** should run on which platforms.

Part 2 - Section C.2. Systems development and design

The candidate should be able to:

a. explain why end-users and information technology specialists should design information systems based on an analysis of an organization's business processes and information requirements and that the business process should be well defined and documented

b. define a systems development life cycle (SDLC)

c. outline the steps of an SDLC and explain how they are related

d. define prototyping as a systems development tool and demonstrate when prototyping techniques are preferable to traditional SDLC techniques

e. define rapid application development (RAD) tools

f. define object-oriented analysis and design (OOAD)

g. demonstrate an understanding of systems feasibility studies, i.e., cost/benefit analyses which include both tangible and intangible benefits

h. identify both the tangible and intangible benefits of a cost/benefit analysis

Core Concepts for Systems Development and Design

- Some **approaches** to developing new information systems include prototyping, rapid application development (RAD), object-oriented analysis and design (OOAD), and the classic systems development life cycle (SDLC).
- Positive results are more frequently obtained if the systems development process is **formally structured, documented, and subject to management controls**.
- The typical **steps in the systems development process** are project definition, feasibility study, cost-benefit analysis, project initiation, existing system analysis, new system design, physical database design, program development, installation and operation, and system maintenance.
- The **cost-benefit analysis** that accompanies any large-scale systems development project should examine both tangible and intangible benefits as well as tangible costs.

Part 2 – Section C.3. Technology of information systems

The candidate should be able to

a. identify the advantages of using telecommunications systems, which allow companies to move data from distant points and process information on a global basis at multiple locations, generally at relatively low cost

b. demonstrate an understanding of the different types of communications networks

c. describe a wide area network (WAN) and local area network (LAN)

d. demonstrate an understanding of client/server networks

e. define "peer to peer" networks

f. distinguish between mainframe systems and client/server applications and identify the advantages and disadvantages of each

g. demonstrate an understanding of a database management system and describe its characteristics

h. distinguish between a flat database and a relational database

i. demonstrate an understanding of a relational database system

j. demonstrate an understanding of Decision Support Systems, how they operate, and the types of decisions that these systems support

k. define Artificial Intelligence, including expert systems, fuzzy logic, neural networks, etc., and explain how they can capture management reasoning in software

l. demonstrate how to use a spreadsheet for business analysis, planning, and modeling

m. construct a spreadsheet used for accounting, business, reporting, or analysis purposes

n. analyze the details of a spreadsheet report and determine which formulas are causing errors and how to correct the formulas

o. describe the internet and identify the components of the internet's backbone

p. define "browser" software

q. define the term intranet and explain its uses

r. identify how intranets enable companies to share expertise among the organizational units

s. define a virtual private network and identify how it can be used

Core Concepts for Technology of Information Systems

- **Decentralization** has been the theme throughout the electronic data processing era. Originally, highly centralized mainframe computers were the only option.

- The development of the **local area network** (LAN) allowed for huge productivity gains by allowing workers to share information without the need for the high expense and specialized staff of a mainframe.

- In a **client/server network**, the devices play specialized roles. This configuration allows for each function in the network to be performed by the most appropriate hardware platform.

  - A **client** is any device that uses the resources of another object, whether that other object be another device or a software program.

  - A **server** is a device or program that provides services for other devices and programs.

- Public switched networks, value-added networks, and virtual private networks are possible configurations for **wide area networks** (WAN), i.e., networks used by organizations that span more than a single building.

- Networks consist of client devices, a transmission medium, and one or more protocols.

  - A **client device** can be anything from a mainframe computer to an MP3 player.

  - Among the **physical media** used to connect the devices on a network are twisted pair wire and coaxial cable. Hubs, bridges, switches, routers, and gateways are devices used to link the various pieces of physical media.

  - A **protocol** is the set of standards for message transmission among the devices on the network. Examples are Ethernet and TCP/IP.

  - **Wireless networks** use the atmosphere as a transmission medium.

- A **database** is a series of related files combined to **minimize redundancy** of data items.

- Early solutions such as **flat files** and **network databases** were **awkward to maintain** and required high machine overhead.

- The **relational database** has been the most cost-effective architecture. Relational databases employ **normalization techniques** to ensure that data items are stored with as little redundancy as possible. Also, relational databases have very powerful search features.

- A **database management system** is an **integrated set of computer programs** that centralize and greatly ease the tasks of administering the database.

- A **database administrator** is the individual with overall responsibility for developing and maintaining the database and for establishing controls to protect its integrity.

- A **decision support system** (DSS) is an interactive system that is useful in solving **semistructured and unstructured problems**, that is, those requiring a decision-maker to exercise judgment and to control the process.

- Model-driven, data-driven, document-driven, and knowledge-driven are possible **configurations** for decision support systems.

- **Artificial intelligence** (AI) is computer software designed to perceive, reason, and understand.

- In the business arena, emphasis has been on the particular form of AI termed **expert systems**. Expert systems rely on a computer's ability to think and make decisions in a human way.

- The power of spreadsheets comes from their ability to perform arithmetic operations on **large amounts of data**, to **quickly report** these results, and to perform **what-if operations**.

- **Errors** are common in spreadsheets, and they are not always obvious because they are embedded in formulas which lie "behind the scenes."

- The **Internet** is a **network of networks** all over the world.

- The Internet facilitates **inexpensive communication and information transfer** among computers, with gateways allowing mainframe computers to interface with personal computers.
- An **intranet** permits sharing of information throughout an organization by applying Internet connectivity standards and Web software (e.g., browsers) to the organization's internal network.

Part 2 – Section C.4. Electronic commerce

The candidate should be able to

a.   define and identify major characteristics of electronic data interchange (EDI)
b.   explain how EDI differs from Internet-based electronic commerce applications
c.   define public key cryptography and identify how it is used within networks
d.   define business-to-business (B2B) commerce and its characteristics
e.   summarize the importance of the Internet for B2B commerce
f.   demonstrate an understanding of how B2B electronic commerce has affected the supply chain
g.   demonstrate an understanding of other e-commerce technologies, including online transaction processing and electronic funds transfer

Core Concepts for Electronic Commerce

- **E-business** is an umbrella term referring to all methods of conducting business electronically.
- **E-commerce** is a narrower term referring to financial transactions with outside parties, e.g., the purchase and sale of goods and services.
- **Electronic data interchange** (EDI) is the leading method of carrying on e-commerce. It involves the communication of data in standardized format directly from a computer in one entity to a computer in another entity.
- EDI services are often provided by third-party communications vendors through services known as **value-added networks** (VANs).
- **Encryption** technology is vital for the security and therefore the success of electronic commerce, especially with regard to transactions carried out over public networks.
    - **Private-key**, or symmetric, encryption is the less secure of the two because there is only one key. The single key must be revealed to both the sender and recipient.
    - **Public-key**, or asymmetric, encryption is more secure. The public key used by the sender for encoding is widely known, but the related private key used by the recipient for decoding is known only to the recipient.
- **Business-to-business** (B2B) involves communications with vendors, distributors, and other businesses over the Internet.
- **Benefits** of working with suppliers and business customers over the Internet include reduced purchasing costs and increased market efficiency.
- **Electronic funds transfer** (EFT) is the movement of cash from one bank to another by purely electronic means.

Part 2 – Section C.5. Integrated enterprise-wide data model

The candidate should be able to:

a.   define enterprise-wide planning (ERP) and its characteristics, including its reliance on an enterprise-wide database

b.   explain why business processes must generally be reengineered and highly integrated to utilize ERP

c.   describe an enterprise-wide database (data warehouse)

d.   define data mining

e.   demonstrate an understanding of how data warehousing facilitates data mining

f.   define data marts

g.   define object-oriented databases

h.   demonstrate an understanding of how Structured Query Language (SQL) is used to retrieve, update, and append information to a relational database

i.   define online analytical processing

Core Concepts for Integrated Enterprise-Wide Data Model

- **Enterprise resource planning** (ERP) is intended to integrate enterprise-wide information systems by creating one database linked to all of an organization's applications.

- A **data warehouse** is a central database for transaction-level data from more than one of the organization's systems.

- A **data mart** is subset of an enterprise-wide data warehouse.

- A data warehouse enables **data mining**, i.e., the search for unexpected relationships between data.

14.2 INFORMATION MANAGEMENT ESSAY QUESTIONS

Recall that your CMA Part 4 exam will probably contain six scenarios, with about three questions per scenario. There will be a recommended time allocation of 20 minutes, 30 minutes, or 45 minutes for each scenario and related questions.

One scenario will involve ethical issues, and probably one or two scenarios will include calculations and responses on a worksheet. Also, expect at least one scenario on organizational/behavioral topics. The remaining scenarios cover Parts 1, 2, and 3.

Scenario Title	Subtopic	Questions	Suggested Time
PWR Instruments	IT Governance	1, 2, 3, 4	30 minutes
Sullivan Sport	Computer-Based Accounts Receivable	5, 6	30 minutes
Marshall Associates	Systems Development	7, 8, 9	30 minutes
Morgan Electrical Supplies, Inc.	Database Management Systems	10, 11, 12	30 minutes

Scenario for Essay Questions 1, 2, 3, 4

PWR Instruments is a manufacturer of precision nozzles for fire hoses. The company was started by Ronald Paige who has an engineering background and who serves as PWR's president. This closely-held corporation has been very successful and has experienced steady growth.

Reporting to Paige are six vice presidents representing the company's major functions -- marketing, production, research and development, information services, finance, and personnel. The Information Services Department was established during the fiscal year just ended when PWR began developing a new computer-based information system. The new database system employs a powerful server connected by a local area network to dedicated terminals, desktop computers, and laptops in each of the six departments. For example, analysts in the Finance Department are able to access the data stored on the main computer through the microcomputers and use the microcomputers as smart terminals on a stand-alone basis. PWR is still in the process of designing and developing new applications for its computer system.

Paige has recently received the management letter which was prepared by the company's external audit firm at the conclusion of the annual audit and has called a meeting with his vice presidents to review the recommendations. One of the major items that Paige wants to discuss with his management team is the recommendation that PWR form an information systems steering committee.

Questions

1. Explain why the external auditor would recommend that PWR Instruments establish an information systems steering committee and discuss the specific responsibilities of an information systems steering committee.

2. Identify the individuals at PWR Instruments who would most likely serve on the information systems steering committee.

3. Explain several advantages that PWR Instruments might realize from the establishment of an information systems steering committee.

4. An information systems steering committee must be familiar with the general systems development life cycle. Identify the steps in a systems development life cycle.

Essay Questions 1, 2, 3, 4 — Unofficial Answers

1. The external auditor would recommend the establishment of an information systems steering committee so that the company, from an overall organizational perspective, focuses on

   a. A coordinated planning effort with all functional areas represented.
   b. Setting priorities to ensure that the highest priority items are considered first.

   The specific responsibilities of the steering committee include

   a. Developing a strategic system plan which incorporates both short-term and long-term goals.
   b. Reviewing all major systems project proposals, including cost-benefit analyses, for approval or rejection.
   c. Assuring internal control considerations.

2. The individuals who should most likely serve on the information systems steering committee include the six vice presidents or their representatives, who should be high level managers knowledgeable about the company's plans and the information systems area; one or more members of the Information Systems Organization; and perhaps a member of the Financial and/or Internal Audit Organizations.

3. The advantages that might be realized from the establishment of an information systems steering committee include

   a. Top management involvement in the information systems plan and function
   b. Facilitating the coordination and integration of departments/functions and improving interdepartmental communications
   c. Providing more effective management control over the allocation of systems resources

4. The steps of a systems development life cycle include

   a. Identification and definition of user needs, problems, and opportunities
   b. Feasibility studies and cost/benefit analyses
   c. Systems analysis, including data flow diagrams, as well as inputs/outputs
   d. Systems design and preparation of systems flowcharts
   e. Hardware and software acquisitions, requests for proposals, and completion of in-house programming
   f. Implementation, i.e., debugging, module testing, system testing, file conversions, training, documentation, location and method of input/output, internal controls, parallel operation, etc.
   g. Systems audit, i.e., is the system meeting the intended objectives
   h. Maintenance, feedback, improvements, and enhancements

Scenario for Essay Questions 5, 6

Sullivan Sport is a distributor of recreational equipment. Sales are made on account with terms of net 30 days from the date of shipment. The number of delinquent accounts and uncollectible accounts has increased during the last twelve months. Customers complain of errors in their accounts. Management believes that the information generated is inadequate and untimely.

The current accounts receivable system was developed when Sullivan began operations in 1993. A new computer was installed 18 months ago. The accounts receivable application was not revised at that time because other applications were considered more important. Management has now asked the Systems Department to design a new accounts receivable system to satisfy these objectives.

- Produce current and timely reports about customers that will

  - Aid in controlling bad debts.
  - Notify the Sales Department of delinquent customer accounts (those which should lose credit privileges).
  - Notify the Sales Department of customers with uncollectible accounts (accounts to be closed and written off).

- Notify customers on a timely basis regarding

  - Amounts owed to Sullivan.
  - Changes in account status (loss of charge privileges).

- Minimize the chance for errors in customers' accounts.

Input data for the system will be taken from four source documents–credit applications, sales invoices, cash payment remittances, and credit memoranda. The accounts receivable master file will be maintained on a machine-readable file by customer account number.

The preliminary design of the new receivables system has been completed by the Systems Department. A description of the proposed reports and other output generated by the system are detailed below.

1. Accounts Receivable Register. A daily alphabetical listing of all customer accounts that shows the balance as of the last statement, activity since the last statement, and the current account balance.

2. Customer Statements. Monthly statements for each customer showing activity since the last statement and new account balance; the top portion of the statement is to be returned with the payment and serves as the cash payment remittance.

3. Activity Reports. Monthly reports that show

    a. Customers who have not purchased any merchandise for 90 days.
    b. Customers whose account balances exceed their credit limit.
    c. Customers who have current sales on account but are delinquent.

4. Delinquency and Write-off Register. A monthly alphabetical listing of delinquent or closed customers' accounts.

Questions

5. Identify the data that Sullivan Sport should capture and store in the computer-based accounts receivable file records for each customer.

6. a. Review the proposed reports to be generated by Sullivan's new accounts receivable system, and discuss whether these reports are adequate to satisfy the objectives designated by management.

    b. Recommend changes, additions, and/or deletions that should be made to the reporting structure to be generated from Sullivan's new system.

Essay Questions 5, 6 — Unofficial Answers

5.   The data that Sullivan Sport should capture and store in the computer-based accounts receivable file records for each customer include the following:

   a.   Customer identification data, such as account number (primary key), name, and address.

   b.   Credit data, such as credit limit, credit available, current credit status (current, days past due, delinquent, etc.), and outstanding balance.

   c.   Related transaction data, such as transaction date, dollar amount of each transaction, date of last sale, salesperson assigned to the account, and delinquency (collection) notices.

6.   a.   In general, the proposed reports do not appear to be adequate to satisfy all of management's objectives.

     1)   The Accounts Receivable Register will provide timely information on customer account balances. However, the report does not contain any credit information or aging of outstanding balances and will not satisfy the management objective of providing information to aid in controlling bad debts or recognizing delinquent accounts.

     2)   The Customer Statements will provide timely notices to customers regarding amounts owed. However, the statements do not contain any aging information or notification of any change in credit status.

     3)   The information in the Activity Reports should help control bad debts by notifying the Sales Department about customers who have exceeded their credit limit or are continuing to place orders when they are considered delinquent.

     4)   The Delinquency and Write-off Register will satisfy the management objective of notifying the Sales Department of customer accounts that are delinquent and/or closed.

   b.   The proposed reporting structure at Sullivan Sport should be changed in the following ways:

     1)   The Accounts Receivable Register should be expanded to include more information about each customer, i.e., account status, credit limit, aging of the account balance, etc.

     2)   The Customer Statements should also include additional data about the account, i.e., an aging schedule to show the customer the status of the current balance, notification of when payment is due, credit limit available, etc.

     3)   The Activity Reports need to be run on a more timely basis, as a monthly report does not provide sufficient notification of delinquent customers or customers who have exceeded their credit limit. The information on customers who have not purchased any merchandise for 90 days is not appropriate for this report and should be included in a sales report, possibly coded to individual salespeople or territories.

     4)   The Delinquency and Write-off Register should be run on a more timely basis to allow management and the Sales Department to react to situations where new orders should not be accepted.

     5)   Reports allowing the reconciliation of the subsidiary ledgers with the general ledger should be generated.

<u>Scenario for Essay Questions 7, 8, 9</u>

Marshall Associates, a sports gear manufacturer, is planning to install a new computer system to integrate Marshall's marketing, accounting, and customer information. At a recent meeting of Marshall's management, there was discussion about how to proceed with this project, as well as questions about the project's economic feasibility. The roles of management and users in the development of this project were also discussed. Marshall's management identified the four phases of the systems development life cycle as

- Systems Analysis
- Systems Design
- Systems Acquisition
- Systems Implementation

Questions

7. a. Describe the role of management in the development and design of a new system.
    b. Describe the role of users in the development and design of a new system.

8. Describe at least three benefits of installing a new computer system at Marshall Associates.

9. Identify at least three distinct and mutually exclusive types of documentation that would be used in each one of the four life cycle phases described (e.g., three types for Systems Analysis, etc.).

Essay Questions 7, 8, 9 — Unofficial Answers

7.   a.   Included in its role in the development and design of a new system, management should

      1)   Establish and participate on a steering committee to partake in major decisions, establish or approve project schedules/timetables, and monitor the project as it progresses

      2)   Outline the types of information needed to make management decisions

      3)   Select key personnel to lead the project

      4)   Provide a motivational "tone at the top" and endorse an adequate organizational communication program to complete the systems progress

  b.   Included in their role in the development and design of a new system, the users should

      1)   Identify the information flows and the shortcomings of the existing systems

      2)   Participate in the determination of information requirements and report formats

      3)   Effectively communicate with the systems organization and other users on a regular basis and provide feedback

      4)   Assist in establishing internal controls for the new system

8.   At least three benefits of installing a new computer system at Marshall Associates are

  a.   Better service to customers comprehending faster product deliveries, better on-hand inventory information, fewer product stockouts, timely records of customer requests and inquiries, and timely credit information

  b.   An increase in productivity, efficiency, and effectiveness, as there will be improved job satisfaction and morale due to the automation of otherwise mundane work, allowing the employees to work on more meaningful, challenging, and creative projects

  c.   More reliable, accurate, and timely information providing better decision making

  d.   Integrated data processing applications

9.   At least three distinct and mutually exclusive types of documentation that would be used in each one of the four life cycle phases include the following:

Systems analysis includes

  a.   The feasibility study
  b.   An outline of the present system flow diagrams, input/output formats, etc.
  c.   Formal systems requirements report

Systems design includes

  a.   Data flow diagrams and systems flow diagrams
  b.   Internal control and security documentation
  c.   Input and output specifications

Systems acquisition includes

  a.   Systems specifications outlining required memory, processing speeds, capacity, etc.
  b.   Comparing cost/benefit analyses of hardware/software alternatives
  c.   Service and/or maintenance agreements

Systems implementation includes

  a.   Implementation and conversion plans, including PERT diagrams and other scheduling documents
  b.   Systems testing documentation
  c.   Follow-up or post-installation analysis documentation which documents the system's effectiveness as compared to requirements and actual processing outputs

Scenario for Essay Questions 10, 11, 12

Morgan Electrical Supplies, Inc. distributes components to the construction industry. As the business grew and the variety of components to be stocked expanded, Morgan acquired a computer and implemented an inventory control system. Other applications, such as accounts receivable, accounts payable, payroll, and sales analysis, were gradually computerized as each function expanded. The inventory system has been upgraded to an online system while all the other applications are operating in batch mode. Over the years, Morgan has developed or acquired more than 100 application programs and maintains 150 files. At a management meeting, the sales manager complained about the difficulty in obtaining current information to respond to customer inquiries. As a result, the controller engaged a consulting firm to explore the situation. The consultant recommended installing a database management system (DBMS), and Morgan proceeded on this course, employing Jack Gibbons as the database administrator.

At a meeting, Gibbons presented an overview of the DBMS using the chart below. Gibbons explained that the database approach assumes an organizational, data-oriented viewpoint, as it recognizes that a centralized database represents a vital resource. Instead of being assigned to applications, information is more appropriately used and managed for the entire organization. Both the roles of the application programs and query software and the tasks of the application programmers and users are simplified. Under the database approach, the data are available to all users within security guidelines.

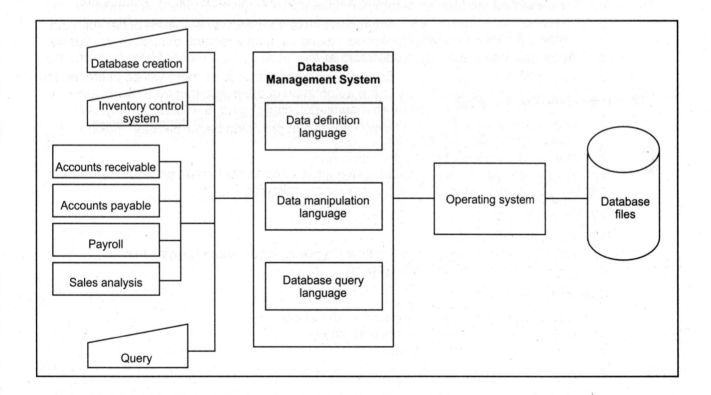

Questions

10. Explain the basic difference between a file-oriented system and a database management system.

11. Describe at least three advantages and at least three disadvantages of the database management system.

12. Describe the duties and responsibilities of Jack Gibbons, the database administrator.

Essay Questions 10, 11, 12 — Unofficial Answers

10. The basic differences between a file-oriented system and a database management system (DBMS) include the following:

    a.   The file-oriented system focuses on individual applications, each with its own set of files and with each file physically separate from the other files.

    b.   In the database management system, the focus is on data rather than a particular application. This leads to data independence, data standardization, one-time data entry, data security, and shared data ownership.

11. At least three advantages of a database management system are

    a.   Reduced data redundancy and inconsistencies.

    b.   Ability to expand data fields without affecting application programs; instead, simple alterations are needed only in the DBMS.

    c.   Data accessibility increases the timeliness, effectiveness, and availability of information.

At least three disadvantages of a database management system are

    a.   More highly trained technical personnel are required.

    b.   Increased vulnerability as a common database is highly integrated. A breakdown in hardware or software has a much more severe effect than in a system having separate files and applications.

    c.   Audit trails being somewhat obscured as the result of movement of data from one file to another.

12. The duties and responsibilities of the database administrator include

    a.   Design and control of a firm's database. This responsibility includes ensuring application independence and backup and recovery procedures.

    b.   Definition and control of the data dictionary.

    c.   Assignment of user codes and maintenance of other security measures.

    d.   Control of all changes in data and in programs that use the database.

14.3 PERFORMANCE MEASUREMENT REVIEW

Part 2 – Section D.1. Cost and variance measures

The candidate should be able to:

- a. analyze performance against operational goals using a variety of methods, including measures based on revenue, manufacturing costs, non-manufacturing costs, and profit depending on the type of center or unit being measured

- b. explain why performance evaluation measures should be directly related to strategic and operational goals and objectives and why timeliness of feedback is critical

- c. explain the reasons for variances (as opposed to only generating numerical results) within a performance monitoring system

- d. explain why performance measures should be related to the factors that drive the element being measured, e.g., cost drivers and revenue drivers

- e. recommend performance measures and a periodic reporting methodology given operational goals and actual results

- f. prepare a performance analysis by comparing actual results to the master budget, calculate favorable and unfavorable variances from budget, and provide explanations for variances based on the situation presented

- g. identify the benefits and limitations of measuring performance by comparing actual results to the master budget

- h. prepare a flexible budget based on actual sales (output) volume

- i. determine the sales-volume variance and the sales-price variance by comparing the flexible budget to the master (static) budget

- j. determine the flexible-budget variance by comparing actual results to the flexible budget

- k. investigate the flexible-budget variance to determine individual differences between actual and budgeted input prices and input quantities

- l. explain management by exception and demonstrate how budget variance reporting is utilized in this environment

- m. define a standard cost system and identify the reasons for adopting a standard cost system

- n. demonstrate an understanding of price (rate) variances and calculate the price variances related to direct material and direct labor inputs

- o. demonstrate an understanding of efficiency (usage) variances and calculate the efficiency variances related to direct material and direct labor inputs

- p. demonstrate an understanding of spending and efficiency variances as they relate to fixed and variable overhead

- q. calculate a sales-mix variance and explain its impact on revenue and contribution margin

- r. demonstrate an understanding that the efficiency (usage) variances can be further analyzed as mix and yield variances

- s. explain how a mix variance results from using direct material and/or labor inputs in a ratio that differs from standard specifications and calculate a mix variance

- t. calculate a yield variance

- u. demonstrate how price, efficiency, spending, and mix variances can be applied in service companies as well as manufacturing companies

- v. analyze variances, identify causes, and recommend corrective actions

Core Concepts for Cost and Variance Measures

- The starting point for variance analysis is the **static budget variance**, which measures the difference between the static (master) budget amount and the actual results.
- The static budget variance consists of **two components**:
  - The **flexible budget variance** measures the difference between the actual results and the amount expected for the achieved level of activity (the flexible budget).
  - The **sales volume variance** measures the difference between the static budget and the amount expected for the achieved level of activity (the flexible budget).
- This **three-way variance analysis** can be computed for any of the elements of operating income.
- Besides the three-way breakdown (static budget variance/flexible budget variance/sales volume variance), the direct materials variance can also be decomposed into the **materials price variance** and the **materials quantity variance**.
- The materials quantity variance can be further broken down into the **direct materials mix variance** and the **direct materials yield variance**.
- Besides the three-way breakdown (static budget variance/flexible budget variance/sales volume variance), the direct labor variance can also be decomposed into the **labor rate variance** and the **labor efficiency variance**.
- The labor efficiency variance can be further broken down into the **direct labor mix variance** and the **direct labor yield variance**.
- A partial productivity measure is the **ratio** of output quantity to input quantity for a **single factor of production**.
- Total productivity is the **ratio** of output to the cost of **all inputs used**.
- A manufacturing concern's total overhead variance is composed of **variable and fixed portions**.
- Besides the three-way breakdown (static budget variance/flexible budget variance/sales volume variance), the **variable overhead variance** can also be decomposed into the **variable overhead spending variance** and the **variable overhead efficiency variance**.
- In the standard three-way breakdown, the **sales volume variance component** of the **fixed overhead variance** is **always $0** because fixed costs are by their nature unchanging within the relevant range of the budgeting cycle.
- The flexible budget variance component can be decomposed into a **fixed overhead spending variance** and a **fixed overhead volume variance**.
- Variances usually **do not appear** on the **financial statements**. They are recorded in the ledger accounts but are only used for **managerial control**.
- If a firm's **sales differ from the amount budgeted**, the difference could be attributable to either the sales price variance or the sale volume variance.
- For a single-product firm, the **sales price variance** is the change in the contribution margin attributable solely to the change in selling price.
- For a single-product firm, the **sales volume variance** is the change in the contribution margin caused by the difference between the actual and budgeted volume.
- If a company produces two or more products, the **multiproduct sales variances** reflect not only the effects of the change in total unit sales but also any difference in the mix of products sold.

Part 2 – Section D.2.   Responsibility centers and reporting segments

The candidate should be able to:

a. identify and explain the different types of responsibility centers (strategic business units)

b. recommend appropriate responsibility centers given a business scenario

c. demonstrate an understanding of contribution margin reporting as used for performance evaluation

d. analyze a contribution margin report and evaluate performance

e. identify segments that organizations evaluate, including product lines, geographical areas, or other meaningful segments

f. explain why the allocation of common costs among segments can be an issue in performance evaluation

g. identify methods for allocating common costs, such as stand-alone cost allocation and incremental cost allocation

h. define transfer pricing and identify the objectives of transfer pricing

i. identify the methods for determining transfer prices and list the advantages and disadvantages of each method

j. explain how transfer pricing is affected by business issues such as the presence of outside suppliers and the opportunity costs associated with capacity usage

k. describe how special issues such as tariffs, exchange rates, and the availability of materials and skills affect performance evaluation in multinational companies

l. describe how special issues such as taxes, currency restrictions, and expropriation risk affect transfer pricing in multinational companies

Core Concepts for Responsibility Centers and Reporting Segments

- A well-designed responsibility accounting system establishes **responsibility centers** (also called **strategic business units**)

  - A **cost center**, e.g., a maintenance department, is responsible for costs only.
  - A **revenue center**, e.g., a sales department, is responsible for revenues only.
  - A **profit center**, e.g., an appliance department in a retail store, is responsible for revenues and expenses.
  - An **investment center**, e.g., a branch office, is responsible for revenues, expenses, and invested capital.

- **Goal congruence** is promoted by encouraging cooperation among organizational functions (production, marketing, and support). **Suboptimization** occurs when one segment of a firm takes action that is in its own best interests but is detrimental to the firm as a whole.

- The **contribution margin approach** to performance evaluation is emphasized in responsibility accounting because it focuses on controllability, as opposed to the gross margin approach which is used for external reporting. The contribution margin approach lends itself to relevant revenue and relevant cost analysis.

  - **Contribution margin** = Revenues – Variable costs, both manufacturing and S&A
  - **Gross margin** = Revenues – Manufacturing costs, both variable and fixed

- A **segment** is a product line, geographical area, or other meaningful subunit of the organization.

- **Allocation of central administration costs** is a fundamental issue in responsibility accounting. It is usually made based on budgeted revenue or contribution margin. If central administrative or other fixed costs are not allocated, responsibility centers might reach their revenue or contribution goals without covering all fixed costs.

- ■ **Common costs** are the costs of products, activities, facilities, services, or operations shared by two or more cost objects. The difficulty with common costs is that they are indirect costs whose allocation may be arbitrary. **Two specific approaches** to common cost allocation are in general use:

  - The **stand-alone method** allocates a common cost to each cost object on a proportionate basis.
  - The **incremental method** allocates the common cost up to the amount of each cost object's traceable cost total.

- ■ A persistent problem in large organizations is the treatment of the **costs of headquarters** and other central support costs. Such costs are frequently allocated.

- ■ **Transfer prices** are the amounts charged by one segment of an organization for goods and services it provides to another segment of the same organization. Transfer pricing should motivate managers by encouraging goal congruence and managerial effort. **Three basic methods** for determining transfer prices are in common use:

  - **Cost plus pricing** sets price at the selling division's full cost of production plus a reasonable markup.
  - **Market pricing** uses the price the selling division could obtain on the open market.
  - **Negotiated pricing** gives the divisions the freedom to bargain between themselves and come to their own agreement regarding price.

- ■ The **minimum price** that a selling division is willing to accept is the sum of the incremental cost of producing the unit so far plus the opportunity cost of selling the unit internally. The **opportunity cost of selling internally** varies depending on two factors: the existence of an external market for the product and whether the selling division has excess capacity.

Part 2 – Section D.3. Financial measures

The candidate should be able to:

  a. demonstrate an understanding of the issues involved in determining product profitability, business unit profitability, and customer profitability, including cost measurement, cost allocation, investment measurement, and valuation
  b. calculate product-line profitability, business unit profitability, and customer profitability given a set of data and assumptions
  c. evaluate customers and products on the basis of profitability and identify ways to improve profitability and/or drop unprofitable customers and products
  d. define and calculate return on investment (ROI)
  e. calculate ROI based on the Dupont Model and describe how this model enhances the analysis of ROI calculations
  f. analyze and interpret ROI calculations and evaluate performance on the basis of the analysis
  g. define and calculate residual income (RI)
  h. analyze and interpret RI calculations and evaluate performance on the basis of the analysis
  i. compare and contrast the benefits and limitations of ROI and RI as measures of performance
  j. define economic value added (EVA®) and calculate it based on a simple (non-complex) scenario
  k. compare and contrast ROI measures using corporation data and external market data
  l. demonstrate an understanding of how EVA® differs from ROI and residual income measures
  m. define market value added

n.   explain how revenue and expense recognition policies may affect the measurement of income and reduce comparability among business units and companies

o.   explain how inventory measurement policies, joint asset sharing, and overall asset measurement may affect the measurement of investment and reduce comparability among business units and companies

p.   define cash flow return on investment

q.   demonstrate an understanding of the effect international operations can have on performance measurement

Core Concepts for Financial Measures

- **Performance measures** are means of revealing how efficiently an investment center is deploying the capital that has been invested in it to produce income for the owners.

    - **Return on investment (ROI)** is the key performance measure of an investment center.

        Net income ÷ Average total assets

    - The well-known **DuPont method** restates the ROI formula as the product of total asset turnover and profit margin.

        Total asset turnover = Sales ÷ Average total assets

        Profit margin = Net income ÷ Sales

    - **Residual income** is a dollar measure rather than a percentage rate. The target rate is ordinarily the weighted-average cost of capital, but it may be an arbitrary hurdle rate.

        Net income – (Total investment × Target rate of return)

    - **Economic value added (EVA®)** is a more specific version of residual income. EVA® represents a business unit's true economic profit primarily because a charge for the cost of equity capital is implicit in the cost of capital.

        After-tax OI – [After-tax WACC × (Total assets – Current liabilities)]

- Other measures of managerial performance regarding the creation of shareholder wealth include

    - The **equity spread** calculates equity value creation.

        Beginning equity capital × (ROI – % cost of equity)

    - **Total shareholder return** is calculated as follows:

        (Change in stock price + Dividends per share) ÷ Initial stock price

    - The most straightforward calculation of **market value added (MVA)** determines the wealth created during a stated period as the difference between the market value of equity (shares outstanding × market price) and the adjusted equity supplied by shareholders. MVA reflects the evaluation of the firm's future performance by the securities markets.

Part 2 – Section D.4.　Balanced scorecard

The candidate should be able to:

    a.　define the concept of a balanced scorecard and identify its components

    b.　define critical success factors and discuss the importance of these factors in evaluating a firm

    c.　identify financial measures, such as operating income, revenue growth, revenues from new products, gross margin percentage, cost reductions, EVA®, ROI, RI, etc., and evaluate their relevance in a specific corporate situation

    d.　identify customer satisfaction measures, such as market share, retention, response time, delivery performance, defects, lead time, etc., and evaluate their relevance in a specific corporate situation

    e.　identify internal business process measures, such as new product introductions, technological capability, cycle time, etc., and evaluate their relevance in a specific corporate situation

    f.　identify innovation and learning measures, such as employee skill sets, organizational learning, industry leadership, etc., and evaluate their relevance in a specific corporate situation

    g.　describe the characteristics of successful implementation and use of a balanced scorecard

    h.　analyze and interpret a balanced scorecard and evaluate performance on the basis of the analysis

Core Concepts for the Balanced Scorecard

- **Critical success factors (CSFs)** are specific, measurable financial and nonfinancial elements of a firm's performance that are vital to its competitive advantage. A firm identifies its CSFs by means of a **SWOT analysis** that addresses internal factors (its strengths and weaknesses) and external factors (its opportunities and threats).

- Once the firm has identified its CSFs, it must establish **specific, measurable ways** for each CSF that are both relevant to the success of the firm and reliably stated. Measures must be both financial and nonfinancial, short-term and long-term.

- A typical balanced scorecard classifies objectives into one of four perspectives on the business: **financial, customer satisfaction, internal business processes, and learning and growth**.

  - Each **objective** is **associated with** one or more **measures** that permit the organization to gauge progress toward the objective.

  - Achievement of the objectives in each perspective makes it possible to achieve the objectives in the **next higher perspective**.

Part 2 – Section D.5.　Quality considerations

The candidate should be able to:

    a.　identify the core principles of total quality management (TQM)

    b.　identify the opportunity costs associated with poor quality management

    c.　demonstrate an understanding of the role that communication and training play in successful TQM programs

    d.　describe the relationship between quality management and productivity and explain why misconceptions about this relationship can lead to poor decisions

    e.　demonstrate an understanding of methods to analyze quality problems such as control charts, Pareto diagrams, and cause-and-effect (fishbone) diagrams

    f.　identify how quality considerations factor into the firm's overall performance measurement and evaluation process

g.   identify the purpose of quality audits and gap analyses

h.   define quality as it relates to customer expectations

i.   define conformance as it relates to quality and identify the characteristics of goalpost quality conformance and absolute quality conformance

j.   describe and identify the components of the costs of quality commonly referred to as prevention costs, appraisal costs, internal failure costs, and external failure costs

Core Concepts for Quality Considerations

- One of the dimensions of quality is **conformance**, or how well a product and its components meet applicable standards.

  - The **traditional view** is that conforming products are those with characteristics that lie within an acceptable specified range of values that includes a target value.

  - The traditional view was superseded by the **zero-defects** (goalpost conformance) approach that sought to eliminate all nonconforming output.

- **Processes** for improving quality include: policy deployment, quality function deployment including the Plan-Do-Check-Act Cycle, kaizen, employee involvement, quality circles, suppliers' management, competitive benchmarking, quality training, reward and recognition, and customer retention.

- SMA 4R lists **four categories of costs of quality**: prevention, appraisal, internal failure, and external failure. An organization should attempt to minimize its total cost of quality.

- **Conformance costs** include prevention and appraisal, which are both financial measures of internal performance.

  - **Prevention** attempts to avoid defective output. These costs include preventive maintenance, employee training, review of equipment design, and evaluation of suppliers.

  - **Appraisal** embraces such activities as statistical quality control programs, inspection, and testing.

- **Nonconformance costs** include costs of internal failure (a financial measure of internal performance) and external failure costs (a financial measure of customer satisfaction).

  - **Internal failure** costs occur when defective products are detected before shipment.

  - **External failure**, or lost opportunity, costs include lost profits from a decline in market share as dissatisfied customers make no repeat purchases and return products for refunds.

- In 1987, the International Organization for Standardization (ISO) introduced **ISO 9000**, a "family" of 11 standards and technical reports that provide guidance for establishing and maintaining a quality management system. The intent of the standards is to ensure the quality of the **process, not the product**. The marketplace determines whether a product is good or bad.

  - ISO 9000 has given birth to a **new industry of consultants** who advise companies on how to meet the standards and obtain registration.

  - These consultants conduct **quality audits** to help companies determine whether they have a sufficiently adequate quality system to apply for ISO 9001:2000 certification.

- One of the first steps in implementing an improved **quality management system (QMS)** is to compare the current QMS to the requirements of the ISO 9000 or Malcolm Baldridge Award standards. This procedure is most commonly called a **gap analysis**.

- **Measures** of quality include: quality cost indices, nonfinancial measures of internal performance (e.g., manufacturing cycle efficiency), nonfinancial measures of customer satisfaction (e.g., delivery cycle time), and nonquantitative factors (e.g., customer goodwill).

- **Management of time** is important to any quality improvement program. Measures include product development and delivery time, breakeven time, customer-response time, manufacturing cycle (throughput) time, and queuing (waiting-line) theory.
- **Tools for the measurement of quality** include statistical control charts, Pareto (80:20) diagrams, histograms, fishbone (Ishikawa) diagrams, and the Taguchi quality loss function.
- The emergence of the **total quality management (TQM)** concept is one of the most significant developments in managerial accounting. TQM recognizes that quality improvement can increase revenues and decrease costs significantly.
- TQM's **core principles** or critical factors are emphasis on the customer, satisfaction of external customers, satisfaction of internal customers, requirements for external suppliers, and requirements for internal suppliers.
- **Continuous improvement** is a never-ending process, not a destination. TQM is a **comprehensive approach** to quality. It treats the pursuit of quality as a basic organizational function that is as important as production or marketing.
- TQM is the **continuous pursuit of quality** in every aspect of organizational activities through a philosophy of doing it right the first time, employee training and empowerment, promotion of teamwork, improvement of processes, and attention to satisfaction of customers, both internal and external.

14.4 PERFORMANCE MEASUREMENT ESSAY QUESTIONS

Recall that your CMA Part 4 exam will probably contain six scenarios, with about three questions per scenario. There will be a recommended time allocation of 20 minutes, 30 minutes, or 45 minutes for each scenario and related questions.

One scenario will involve ethical issues, and probably one or two scenarios will include calculations and responses on a worksheet. Also, expect at least one scenario on organizational/behavioral topics. The remaining scenarios cover Parts 1, 2, and 3.

Scenario Title	Subtopic	Questions	Suggested Time
Measuring Entity Performance	Performance Measures	1, 2, 3	30 minutes
Tonya Maloney	Performance Measurement and Motivation	4, 5, 6	30 minutes
LAR Chemical Company	Direct Materials Variances	7, 8	30 minutes
Romano Foods, Inc.	Process Costing and Spoilage	9, 10, 11	30 minutes
Mountain View Hospital	Direct Labor Variances	12, 13, 14	30 minutes
Ajax Consolidated	Transfer Pricing	15, 16, 17, 18	30 minutes
Reid Corporation	Operational Design and Motivation	19, 20, 21, 22	30 minutes
TQM	Total Quality Management	23, 24, 25	30 minutes

Scenario for Essay Questions 1, 2, 3

The Institute of Management Accountants has issued Statements on Management Accounting Number 4D, *Measuring Entity Performance*, to help management accountants deal with the issues associated with measuring entity performance. Managers can use these measures to evaluate their own performance or the performance of subordinates, to identify and correct problems, and to discover opportunities. To assist management in measuring achievement, there are a number of performance measures available. To present a more complete picture of performance, it is strongly recommended that several of these performance measures be utilized and that they be combined with nonfinancial measures such as market share, new product development, and human resource utilization. Five commonly used performance measures that are derived from the traditional historical accounting system are listed below.

- Gross profit margin (percent)
- Cash flows
- Return on the investment in assets
- Residual income
- Total asset turnover

Questions

For each of the five performance measures identified above:

1. Describe how the measure is calculated.
2. Describe the information provided by the measure.
3. Explain the limitations of this information.

Essay Questions 1, 2, 3 — Unofficial Answers

1.   How the measure is calculated:

   a.   Gross profit margin is determined by dividing gross profit by net sales. Gross profit is determined by subtracting cost of goods sold from net sales.

   b.   Cash flow is determined by adding net cash flows from operating activities to the net cash flows from investing activities and financing activities for a period of time. This information is generally presented as part of the primary financial statements of a company.

   c.   Return on the investment in assets is determined by dividing net income (before nonrecurring items) by average total assets.

   d.   Residual income is operating income less an imputed interest for invested capital. This imputed interest is calculated by multiplying net assets times the firm's required rate of return or cost of capital.

   e.   Total asset turnover is determined by dividing net sales by average total assets.

2.   Information provided by the measure:

   a.   Gross profit margin is a measure of profitability and indicates how much is left of each sales dollar to cover operating expenses and profit.

   b.   Cash flow can be used to evaluate cash management performance and measure a company's ability to remain solvent during a particular period.

   c.   Return on assets is a profitability measure and can be used to evaluate the efficiency of asset usage and management, and the effectiveness of business strategies to create profits.

   d.   Residual income measures the amount of operating income earned above the imputed cost of capital for the operating unit. If the measure is positive, returns exceed the cost of financing the operating unit.

   e.   Total asset turnover measures asset activity and the ability of the firm to generate sales through the use of assets. Generally, the more sales dollars generated per dollar of assets used, the better the net income of an entity.

3.   Limitations of this information:

   a.   Gross profit margin is a good measure for trend analysis of a particular company, but variable ways of calculating cost of goods sold limit its usefulness for comparative analysis.

   b.   Cash flow data states what happened during a particular period but is not an indicator of future performance.

   c.   The calculation of return on assets can be affected by varying accounting assumptions used in the calculation of net income.

   d.   Because of differing costs of capital, the measure cannot be effectively used for comparative analysis.

   e.   When calculating the turnover, total assets may need to be refined by the elimination of assets that do not relate to sales as the inclusion of these items could distort the measure.

Scenario for Essay Questions 4, 5, 6

Tonya Maloney has just been promoted to divisional controller at American Wicker, Inc., and is concerned about the nature of her new reporting responsibilities.

Some executives believe that it is extremely important to manage "by numbers." This form of management requires that all employees with departmental or divisional responsibilities spend time understanding the company's operations and how they are reflected by the company's financial reports. Because of the manager's increased comprehension of the financial reports and the activities that they represent, his/her subordinates will become more attuned to the meaning of financial reports and the important signposts that can be detected in these reports. Companies utilize a variety of numerical measurement systems including standard costs, financial ratios, human resource forecasts, and operating budgets.

Questions

4. a. Discuss the characteristics that should be present in a standard cost system in order to encourage positive employee motivation.

    b. Discuss how a standard cost system should be implemented to positively motivate employees.

5. The use of variance analysis often results in "management by exception."

    a. Explain the meaning of "management by exception."
    b. Discuss the behavioral implications of "management by exception."

6. Explain how employee behavior could be adversely affected when "actual to budget" comparisons are used as the basis for performance evaluation.

Essay Questions 4, 5, 6 — Unofficial Answers

4. a. The characteristics that should be present in a standard cost system in order to encourage positive employee motivation include

    1) Participation in setting standards from all levels of the organization including purchasing, engineering, manufacturing, and accounting
    2) The integration of organizational communication by translating the organizational goals and objectives into monetary terms for the employees
    3) Support of the standard cost system by management
    4) Incorporation of standards that are perceived as achievable and accurate and apply to controllable costs

    b. A standard cost system should be implemented to positively motivate employees by

    1) Communicating the corporate objectives of a standard cost system
    2) Soliciting from employees standards for which they will be held accountable
    3) Tying the individual's performance in the standard cost system to the individual's performance review and reward system

5. a. Under "management by exception," management's attention is focused only on those items that deviate significantly from the standard. The assumption is that managers will allocate their time and energy most efficiently and effectively by addressing the most significant problems.

    b. The behavioral implications of "management by exception" include both positive and negative implications.

    On the positive side, this technique increases management efficiency by concentrating only on material variances, allowing time for the manager to concentrate on other activities.

    On the negative side, managers tend only to focus on the negative variances rather than positive ones limiting their employee interactions to negative reinforcement or punishment. This technique may not indicate detrimental trends at an early stage and fragmentation of efforts can occur from dealing only with the specific problems rather than global issues.

6. Employee behavior could be adversely affected when "actual to budget" comparisons are used as the basis for performance evaluation. Employees may subvert the system and submit budgets that are low so they can meet or exceed the budget favorably, thereby averting negative reinforcement for varying unfavorably to budget. There can be a minimal level of motivation since exceptional performance is not rewarded. Employees may strive for mediocrity and not work up to their full potential.

Scenario for Essay Questions 7, 8

The LAR Chemical Co. manufactures a wide variety of chemical compounds and liquids for industrial uses. The standard mix for producing a single batch of 500 gallons of one liquid is as follows:

Liquid Chemical	Quantity (in gallons)	Cost (per gallon)	Total Cost
Maxan	100	2.00	$200
Salex	300	.75	225
Cralyn	225	1.00	225
	625		$650

There is a 20% loss in liquid volume during processing due to evaporation. The finished liquid is put into 10 gallon bottles for sale. Thus, the standard material cost for a 10-gallon bottle is $13.00.

The actual quantities of raw materials and the respective cost of the materials placed in production during November were as follows:

Liquid Chemical	Quantity (in gallons)	Total Cost
Maxan	8,480	$17,384
Salex	25,200	17,640
Cralyn	18,540	16,686
	52,220	$51,710

A total of 4,000 bottles (40,000 gallons) were produced during November.

Questions

7. Calculate the total raw material variance for the liquid product for the month of November and then further analyze the total variance into

    a. Material price variance
    b. Material mix variance
    c. Material yield variance

8. Explain how LAR Chemical Co. could use each of the three material variances – price, mix, yield – to help control the cost to manufacture this liquid compound.

Essay Questions 7, 8 — Unofficial Answers

7. Total variance

Actual Cost	Standard Cost	Total Variance
$51,710	$52,000[1]	$290 F

a. Material price variance

	Actual	AQ × SP	Variance
Total material price variance	$51,710	$54,400[2]	$2,690 F

[1] $650 × 80 batches or $1.04 × 50,000 gallons

		Gallons		Std. cost gal.		Total
[2]	Maxan	8,480	×	$2.00	=	$16,960
	Salex	25,200	×	.75	=	18,900
	Cralyn	18,540	×	1.00	=	18,540
						$54,400

b. Material mix variance

$$\frac{\text{(Standard weighted average cost per input gallon)}}{\text{(Standard proportion)}} = \frac{\$650}{625} = \$1.04 \text{ per input gallon}$$

Actual gallons × standard cost (actual proportion from 7.a.)	$54,400.00
Less actual quantity × standard weighted average cost per input gallon (standard proportion) (52,220 × $1.04)	54,308.80
Total mix variance	$ 91.20 U

c. Material yield variance

Actual production	40,000 gallons
Standard expected input for actual productions	50,000 gallons
Actual input	52,220 gallons
Variance in input	2,220 gallons
Standard weighted average cost per input gallon (standard proportion)	× $1.04
Total yield variance	$2,308.80 U

8. Before management can control costs, they need to know which costs are out of line, within whose area of responsibility has the variance appeared, what is the cause of the variance, and who has the responsibility to correct the cause. Variances help management to answer these issues. Specifically, the variances indicate where management should begin its investigation:

a. Price variation – the information to identify the causes of the price variance usually can be obtained in the purchasing department. A review of purchasing procedures and records would disclose whether the variances were caused by permanent changes in prices, poor purchasing practices or poor production scheduling requiring incurrence of extra costs to expedite shipments. The information obtained will identify the department responsible for the extra cost and provide clues to improve the control.

b. Mix and yield variances – the information to identify the cause of these variances can be obtained in production. A review of material records and handling procedure would disclose whether the mix variance was caused by the use of wrong proportions, entering excess materials into the process because of carelessness, or adjustment of the mix to accommodate off-standard material quality. Yield variance would often be explained by the same information. Nonstandard proportions would result in nonstandard yields and excess material inputs. The information obtained would identify the department responsible and provide clues to improve control.

Scenario for Essay Questions 9, 10, 11

Romano Foods, Inc. manufactures Roman Surprise Frozen Pizzas that are 12 inches in diameter and retail for $4.69 to $5.99, depending upon the topping. The company employs a process costing system in which the product flows through several processes. Joe Corolla, vice president of production, has had a long-running disagreement with the controller, Sue Marshall, over the handling of spoilage costs. Corolla resists every attempt to charge production with variance responsibilities unless they are favorable. Spoilage costs have not been significant in the past, but, in November, the Mixing Department had a large amount of spoilage. Traditionally, Romano Foods has treated 10% of good output as normal spoilage. The department input 120,000 units of ingredients, and 13,000 dough units were rejected at inspection. Marshall is concerned about the abnormal spoilage and wants Corolla to take corrective steps. Corolla, on the other hand, maintains that the Mixing Department is operating properly. He has prepared the following report to support his contention.

Romano Foods – Mixing Department
Production Cost Report
Month ended November 30, Year 1

Input Units	Total Cost	Good Output Units	10% Normal Spoilage	Abnormal Spoilage	Good Units Cost
120,000	$45,360	107,000	12,000	1,000	$.42

Budgeted unit cost	$0.435
Actual cost per good unit	0.420
Favorable variance	$0.015

Cost Reconciliation

Cost of 107,000 good units @ $.42 each	$44,940
Abnormal spoilage (charge to purchasing for buying inferior materials):	
1,000 units @ $.42 each	420
Total cost	$45,360

Questions

9. Revise Joe Corolla's production cost report for November Year 1 by calculating the

   a. Number of units of normal spoilage
   b. Number of units of abnormal spoilage
   c. Total and unit costs of the Mixing Department's production of good units in November
   d. Total and unit costs of abnormal spoilage

10. Prepare the journal entry to transfer costs for the Mixing Department for November to the Assembly Department.

11. Describe how Joe Corolla's production cost report has shown the performance of the Mixing Department to be less favorable than that shown in the revised report.

Essay Questions 9, 10, 11 — Unofficial Answers

9.   The revised production cost report for November Year 1 is as follows:

Romano Foods – Mixing Department Production Cost Report
Month ended November 30, Year 1

Input Units	Total Cost	Good Output Units	10% Normal Spoilage	Abnormal Spoilage	Good Unit Cost
120,000	$45,360	107,000	10,700	2,300	$.4158

Budgeted unit cost	$.4350
Actual cost per good unit	.4158
Favorable variance	$.0192

Cost Reconciliation

Cost of 107,000 good units at $.4158	$44,490.60
Abnormal spoilage (2,300 × $.378)	869.40
Total production costs	$45,360.00

Supporting Calculations

1.   10% of good output = units of normal spoilage
     .10 × 107,000 units = 10,700 units of normal spoilage

2.
Total spoilage	13,000
Less normal spoilage	10,700
Abnormal spoilage	2,300

3.
Total cost of November production	$ 45,360
Divide by total input (units)	÷ 120,000
Unit cost of production	$ .378
Good units completed (107,000 × $.378)	$40,446.00
Normal spoilage (10,700 × $.378)	4,044.60
Total cost of good units	$44,490.60
Unit cost of good units ($44,490.60 ÷ 107,000)	$ .4158

4.
Abnormal spoilage (units)	2,300
Multiplied by unit cost of production	× .378
Total cost of abnormal spoilage	$ 869.40

10.   The journal entry required to transfer costs of the Mixing Department to the Assembly Department charges the cost of good production to the Assembly Department, charges a loss for abnormal spoilage, and credits Mixing with the total cost of production.

	Debit	Credit
Work-in-process assembly	$44,490.60	
Loss from abnormal spoilage	869.40	
Work-in-process mixing		$45,360.00

11.   Corolla's report is less favorable because he ignored normal spoilage in calculating unit cost. In addition, he miscalculated normal spoilage as 10% of total input rather than 10% of good output and, thus, miscalculated abnormal spoilage. Corolla divided November production costs ($45,360) by the good units produced plus the incorrect amount of abnormal spoilage (107,000 + 1,000 = 108,000) to get the $.42 per unit. By ignoring the equivalent units of normal spoilage, he used a higher base for calculating unit cost. Normal spoilage should be incorporated into the equivalent unit calculation to get an accurate unit cost.

Scenario for Essay Questions 12, 13, 14

Mountain View Hospital (MVH) has adopted a standard cost accounting system for evaluation and control of nursing labor. Diagnosis Related Groups (DRGs), instituted by the U.S. government for health insurance reimbursement, are used as the output measure in the standard cost system. A DRG is a patient classification scheme in which inpatient treatment procedures are related to the numbers and types of patient ailments treated. MVH has developed standard nursing times for the treatment of each DRG classification, and nursing labor hours are assumed to vary with the number of DRGs treated within a time period.

The nursing unit on the fourth floor treats patients with four DRG classifications. The unit is staffed with registered nurses (RNs), licensed practical nurses (LPNs), and aides. The standard nursing hours and salary rates are as follows.

Fourth Floor Nursing Unit
Standard Hours

DRG Classification	RN	LPN	Aide
1	6	4	5
2	26	16	10
3	10	5	4
4	12	7	10

Standard Hourly Rates

RN	$12.00
LPN	8.00
Aide	6.00

For the month of May, the results of operations for the fourth floor nursing unit are presented below:

Actual Number of
Patients

DRG 1	250
DRG 2	90
DRG 3	240
DRG 4	140
	720

	RN	LPN	Aide
Actual hours	8,150	4,300	4,400
Actual salary	$100,245	$35,260	$25,300
Actual hourly rate	$12.30	$8.20	$5.75

The accountant for MVH calculated the following standard times for the fourth floor nursing unit for the month of May:

DRG Classification	No. of Patients	Standard Hours per DRG			Total Standard Hours		
		RN	LPN	Aide	RN	LPN	Aide
1	250	6	4	5	1,500	1,000	1,250
2	90	26	16	10	2,340	1,440	900
3	240	10	5	4	2,400	1,200	960
4	140	12	7	10	1,680	980	1,400
					7,920	4,620	4,510

The hospital calculates labor variances using a flexible budgeting approach for each reporting period by labor classification (RN, LPN, Aide), since the hospital does not have data to calculate variances by DRG. Labor mix and yield variances are also calculated, since one labor input can be substituted for another labor input. Variances are used by hospital administration to evaluate performance of nursing labor.

Questions

12. Calculate the total flexible budget variance for the fourth floor nursing unit of MVH for the month of May, indicating how much of this variance is attributed to

    a. Labor efficiency
    b. Rate differences

13. a. Calculate the labor mix variance for the fourth floor nursing unit of MVH. (Use whole hours and whole cents in all calculations.)

    b. Explain the significance of the labor mix variance calculated in Question 13 a.

14. a. Calculate the labor yield variance for the fourth floor nursing unit of Mountain View Hospital. (Use whole hours and whole cents in all calculations.)

    b. Interpret the meaning of the labor yield variance calculated in Question 14 a.

Essay Questions 12, 13, 14 — Unofficial Answers

12. a. and b. The total flexible budget variance for the fourth floor nursing unit of Mountain View Hospital for the month of May is an unfavorable $1,745. Of this amount, $460 favorable is attributable to labor efficiency and $2,205 unfavorable to rate differences. The calculation of these amounts is presented below.

Labor Class	Actual Hours × Actual Rate		
RN	8,150 ×	$12.30 =	$100,245
LPN	4,300 ×	8.20 =	35,260
Aide	4,400 ×	5.75 =	25,300
			$160,805

Labor Class	Actual Hours × Standard Rate		
RN	8,150 ×	$12.00 =	$ 97,800
LPN	4,300 ×	8.00 =	34,400
Aide	4,400 ×	6.00 =	26,400
			$158,600

Labor Class	Standard Hours × Standard Rate		
RN	7,920 ×	$12.00 =	$ 95,040
LPN	4,620 ×	8.00 =	36,960
Aide	4,510 ×	6.00 =	27,060
			$159,060

- Total flexible budget variance
  = $160,805 – $159,000
  = $1,745 unfavorable

- Labor efficiency variance
  = $158,600 – $159,060
  = $460 favorable

- Labor rate variance
  = $160,805 – $158,600
  = $2,205 unfavorable

13. a. The labor mix variance for the fourth floor nursing unit of MVH is an unfavorable $1,406, calculated as follows:

$$\frac{\text{Standard hours by labor class}}{\text{Total standard hours}} \times \text{Actual hours} = \text{Expected actual labor mix}$$

(7,920 ÷ 17,050) × 16,850 = 7,827 RN hours
(4,620 ÷ 17,050) × 16,850 = 4,566 LPN hours
(4,510 ÷ 17,050) × 16,850 = 4,457 Aide hours

(Actual hours – Expected hours) × Standard rate = Labor mix variance

(8,150 – 7,827) × $12.00 =	$3,876 U
(4,300 – 4,566) × 8.00 =	2,128 F
(4,400 – 4,457) × 6.00 =	342 F
Labor mix variance =	$1,406 U

b. The labor mix variance shows the difference between total costs for the actual number of hours used in labor classifications and the cost of the standard proportions designated for these labor types. The mix of staff was such that proportionately more RN time and less LPN and Aide time was used. As RN time costs more, management should use this information to understand the reasons for more RN input, such as availability of Aides and LPNs.

14.   a.   The labor yield variance for the fourth floor nursing unit of MVH is $1,866 favorable, calculated as follows:

$$\frac{Total\ standard\ costs}{Total\ standard\ hours} = Average\ standard\ hourly\ rate$$

$$\$159{,}060 \div 17{,}050 = \underline{\$9.33}$$

$$(Actual\ hours - Standard\ hours) \times Average\ standard\ hourly\ rate = Labor\ yield\ variance$$

$$
\begin{aligned}
(8{,}150 - 7{,}920) &\times \$9.33 = \$2{,}146\ U \\
(4{,}300 - 4{,}620) &\times\ \ 9.33 =\ \ \ 2{,}986\ F \\
(4{,}400 - 4{,}510) &\times\ \ 9.33 =\ \ \ 1{,}026\ F \\
\text{Labor yield variance} &= \underline{\underline{\$1{,}866\ F}}
\end{aligned}
$$

   b.   The yield variance reveals the difference between the standard cost of actual labor (based on the actual labor mix times the average of the standard mix rates) and the standard cost of the standard mix of labor. The favorable yield variance represents efficiencies for the LPN and Aide classifications but indicates that RN labor could have been used more efficiently. This could indicate understaffing in the LPN and Aide classifications that forced RNs to perform duties normally assigned to others.

Scenario for Essay Questions 15, 16, 17, 18

Ajax Consolidated has several divisions; however, only two divisions transfer products to other divisions. The Mining Division refines toldine which is then transferred to the Metals Division. The toldine is processed into an alloy by the Metals Division and is sold to customers at a price of $150 per unit. The Mining Division is currently required by Ajax to transfer its total yearly output of 400,000 units of toldine to the Metals Division at total manufacturing cost plus 10 percent. Unlimited quantities of toldine can be purchased and sold on the open market at $90 per unit. While the Mining Division could sell all the toldine it produces at $90 per unit on the open market, it would have to incur a variable selling cost of $5 per unit.

Brian Jones, manager of the Mining Division, is unhappy with having to transfer the entire output of toldine to the Metals Division at 110 percent of cost. In a meeting with the management of Ajax, he said, "Why should my division be required to sell toldine to the Metals Division at less than market price? For the year just ended, Metals' contribution margin was over $19 million on sales of 400,000 units while Mining's contribution was just over $5 million on the transfer of the same number of units. My division is subsidizing the profitability of the Metals Division. We should be allowed to charge the market price for toldine when transferring to the Metals Division."

Presented below is the detailed unit cost structure for both the Mining and Metals Divisions for the fiscal year ended May 31.

Cost Structure Per Unit

	Mining Division	Metals Division
Transfer price from Mining Division	--	$ 66
Direct material	$12	6
Direct labor	16	20
Manufacturing overhead	32[1]	25[2]
Total cost per unit	$60	$117

[1] Manufacturing overhead cost in the Mining Division is 25% fixed and 75% variable.
[2] Manufacturing overhead cost in the Metals Division is 60% fixed and 40% variable.

Questions

15. Explain why transfer prices based on cost are not appropriate as a divisional performance measure.

16. Using the market price as the transfer price, determine the contribution margin for both the Mining Division and the Metals Division for the year ended May 31.

17. If Ajax Consolidated were to institute the use of negotiated transfer prices and allow divisions to buy and sell on the open market, determine the price range for toldine that would be acceptable to both the Mining Division and the Metals Division. Explain your answer.

18. Identify which one of the three types of transfer prices-- cost-based, market-based, or negotiated-- is most likely to elicit desirable management behavior at Ajax Consolidated and thus benefit overall operations. Explain your answer.

Essay Questions 15, 16, 17, 18 — Unofficial Answers

15. Among the reasons transfer prices based on cost are not appropriate as a divisional performance measure are because they

   a. Provide little incentive for the selling division to control manufacturing costs as all costs incurred will be recovered.

   b. Often lead to suboptimal decisions for the company as a whole.

16. Using the market price as the transfer price, the contribution margin for both the Mining Division and the Metals Division for the year ended May 31 is as calculated in Exhibit 1 below.

   Exhibit 1

   Ajax Consolidated Calculation of
   Divisional Contribution Margin
   For the Year Ended May 31

	Mining Division	Metals Division
Selling price	$ 90	$ 150
Less: Variable costs		
Direct material	12	6
Direct labor	16	20
Manufacturing overhead	24[1]	10[2]
Transfer price		90
Unit contribution margin	$ 38	$ 24
Volume	× 400,000	× 400,000
Total contribution margin	$15,200,000	$9,600,000

   [1] Variable overhead = $32 × 75% = $24.
   [2] Variable overhead = $25 × 40% = $10.

   NOTE: The $5 variable selling cost that the Mining Division would incur for sales on the open market should not be included as this is an internal transfer.

17. If the use of a negotiated transfer price was instituted by Ajax Consolidated, which also permitted the divisions to buy and sell on the open market, the price range for toldine that would be acceptable to both divisions would be determined as follows:

   a. The Mining Division would like to sell to the Metals Division for the same price it can obtain on the outside market, $90 per unit. However, Mining would be willing to sell the toldine for $85 per unit as the $5 variable selling cost would be avoided.

   b. The Metals Division would like to continue paying the bargain price of $66 per unit. However, if Mining does not sell to Metals, Metals would be forced to pay $90 on the open market. Therefore, Metals would be satisfied to receive a price concession from Mining equal to the costs that Mining would avoid by selling internally. Therefore, a negotiated transfer price for toldine between $85 and $90 would benefit both divisions and the company as a whole.

18. A negotiated transfer price is the most likely to elicit desirable management behavior as it will

   a. Encourage the management of the Mining Division to be more conscious of cost control

   b. Benefit the Metals Division by providing toldine at less cost than its competitors

   c. Provide a more realistic measure of divisional performance

Scenario for Essay Questions 19, 20, 21, 22

Reid Corporation, a diversified manufacturing firm, has been experiencing decreasing profits and market share for the past 2 years. The company president, Arthur Johnson, has hired a consultant to report on the operations of three of Reid's manufacturing plants. The consultant has made several visits to each of the plants and has recently compiled his findings in a report to Johnson. The consultant observed that the levels of employee participation vary considerably throughout the organization and presented the following examples.

- At the western plant, where small appliances are manufactured, a standard cost system was recently implemented. The steps used by the plant manager to establish the standards provided for employee participation at all points during the process. Despite these efforts, the employee perception is that the final standards were imposed by top management to satisfy some overall corporate goal.

- At the southern plant, where heavy equipment is assembled, stop buttons have been installed on the assembly line to allow workers to correct problems immediately. This enables the employees to have greater control over their work, and, as a consequence, the workers perceive greater involvement in all facets of decision making.

- At the northern plant, a metal-stamping facility, costs have risen and product quality has declined to the point where the products are no longer competitive. The employees have little sense of commitment to the company as most jobs are routine and uninteresting. There is high employee turnover and excessive absenteeism. Some plant workers have suggested that the formation of quality circles might improve the situation.

Questions

19. Describe four factors that generally determine the level of employee participation in an organization's control systems.

20. Recommend ways to modify the standard cost system at the western plant in order to increase employee participation and gain wider acceptance of the standards.

21. Other than those mentioned above, describe the benefits that have accrued to the southern plant from the installation of the stop buttons on the assembly line.

22. Explain how the northern plant and its employees could benefit from the introduction of quality circles.

Essay Questions 19, 20, 21, 22 — Unofficial Answers

19. Four factors that generally determine the level of employee participation in an organization's control system include management style, organizational environment or culture, performance measures, and the employees' desire to participate.

Managerial style, participative or directive, is a primary determinant in the level of employee participation. Regardless of the organizational environment, directive managers utilize low to medium levels of employee involvement based on the subordinates' desire to participate and the accuracy level of the control. Participative managers need to assess the organizational culture as participative or nonparticipative. Nonparticipative organizational cultures force these managers to maintain low to medium levels of participation (similar to directive managers), while participative organizations allow for medium to high levels of employee participation based on each employee's desire to become involved.

An organizational environment that is subject to turbulent changes may require rapid decision making at lower levels and, consequently, greater employee participation.

20. The current standard cost system at the western plant failed to achieve the desired employee perception of a participatory management style. Ways to improve the situation include:

a. Improving communications with the employees. While employees were involved in developing data for standard setting, their recommendations were not necessarily incorporated.

b. Conducting frequent reviews of the standards to ensure that they are continually revised to attainable levels.

c. Establishing training programs to prepare employees to achieve the standards. The employees' current job skills may not be sufficient to meet management's standards.

d. Having top management explain the company's goals and the desired employee involvement in achieving those goals.

21. In addition to the control over work, other benefits that were derived at the southern plant from the installation of stop buttons include:

a. Safety features that can stop action to avoid serious accidents

b. Cost reductions as errors can be corrected before long runs of defective equipment are turned out

c. Improvement in employee morale, increased concern for quality, and reduced resistance to change

22. The ways that the northern plant and its employees could benefit from the introduction of quality circles include:

a. Establishment of a participatory environment with the employees who would be affected by procedural changes

b. Increased employee self-esteem and interest due to working jointly with management in the review of problems and their solutions

c. More immediate implementation and acceptance of decisions

Scenario for Essay Questions 23, 24, 25

In an increasingly competitive global environment, quality is a powerful competitive weapon. Many top executives regard Total Quality Management (TQM) as a precondition for corporate global success. TQM is a strategic commitment to making quality a guiding factor in everything an organization does.

Quality can be an elusive term and difficult to define. One possible definition is that quality is the total of all features and performance characteristics of a product that conform to specifications and that satisfy customers on a timely basis and at an acceptable price. Quality begins and ends with the customer. The costs of not recognizing this are high; quality costs range from 15 to 20% of sales revenue for many organizations. In some industries, a company can increase its profits 50% or more by simply retaining 10% of their customers.

On June 30, 1993, the Institute of Management Accountants issued Statements on Management Accounting Number 4-R (SMA 4-R), *Managing Quality Improvements*. This statement serves as a guideline for management accountants in employing their skills in the quality management process.

Questions

23. Identify and explain several of the steps that an organization should take for the implementation of a Total Quality Management (TQM) program in order for it to be successful.

24. Identify and explain the components of the cost of quality.

25. One of the tools that managers use in implementing a quality program is competitive benchmarking. Define competitive benchmarking and discuss how it can help an organization implement its quality program.

Essay Questions 23, 24, 25 — Unofficial Answers

23. Among the steps that an organization should take to successfully implement a Total Quality Management (TQM) program include the following:

    a.   Make a strategic commitment, as top management support is critical. Create a CEO/Quality Council and appropriately staff this council.

    b.   Learn, understand, and adopt the new philosophy. Conduct executive quality training programs. Conduct a quality audit to identify strengths and weaknesses versus "best in class."

    c.   Prepare a gap analysis (i.e., determine what the company lacks to become "best in class").

    d.   Develop strategic quality improvement plans.

    e.   Conduct employee communication and training programs encouraging education for everyone.

    f.   Establish quality teams and encourage employee involvement.

    g.   Create a measurement system and set goals and key success factors.

    h.   Revise compensation, appraisal, and recognition systems to reflect emphasis on quality. Eliminate numerical quotas and avoid slogans and targets for the workforce.

    i.   Encourage vendors to adopt the quality concept. End the practice of awarding business to vendors on the basis of price alone.

    j.   Continually review and revise the process. Instill a spirit of continuous improvement.

24. The cost of quality has two basic components, cost of conformance and cost of nonconformance.

    a. **Cost of conformance**

        1) Costs of prevention are costs necessary to ensure that customer requirements and specifications are met. These include product and process design, training, maintenance of equipment, and supplier certification programs

        2) Costs of appraisal are costs necessary to detect output that does not meet customer specifications. These include inspection, testing, and quality control procedures.

    b. **Cost of nonconformance**

        1) Costs of internal failure are costs of not meeting customer requirements. These include rework to correct defects and scrap or waste.

        2) Costs of external failure or lost opportunity are lost profits from not meeting customer requirements. These include returns, field repairs, product liability expenses, warranty expense, lost profits from canceled orders or lost future sales.

25. Competitive benchmarking is the continuous process of measuring an enterprise's products, services, processes, and practices against the "best in class." For a quality program to succeed, it is imperative for a company to look beyond its own past performance. The critical factor is how well the company measures up against the competition in satisfying the customers. Benchmarking provides an objective measure of a company's performance and helps identify the gap between the company's practices and "the best," thereby establishing goals of high performance and the means to accomplish those goals.

Consider using Gleim's **CMA Test Prep** for interactive testing with **hundreds of multiple-choice questions** as an additional method of knowledge transfer in your quest to pass Part 4.

STUDY UNIT FIFTEEN
CMA PART 2 REVIEW –
EXTERNAL FINANCIAL REPORTING I

(11 pages of outline)

Part 2 of the CMA exam is titled **Management Accounting and Reporting**. This study unit is a review of this section:

E. **External Financial Reporting.** Principal financial statements and their purposes; limitations of financial statement information; asset recognition and measurement.

This study unit represents the IMA's Learning Outcome Statements and Gleim Core Concepts relevant to this section. Bear in mind that **all topics** on Part 4 of the exam are tested at **skill level C** (all six skill types required).

15.1 OVERVIEW OF FINANCIAL REPORTING AND ASSETS REVIEW

Part 2 – Sections E.1. Objectives of external financial reporting; and E.2. Financial accounting fundamentals

The candidate should be able to:

a. identify the objectives of external financial reporting, i.e., providing information on resources and obligations, comprehensive income, and cash flow

b. identify and demonstrate an understanding of basic accounting assumptions and conventions, including going concern, historical cost, accrual accounting, and conservatism

c. demonstrate an understanding of recognition and measurement concepts

d. differentiate between realization and recognition

e. identify financial statement elements for each of the financial statements

f. Special topics: business combinations, consolidated financial statements, and accounting for derivatives

For each special topic, the candidate should be able to:

- Define and describe its characteristics
- Demonstrate a basic understanding of the relevant accounting issues
- Describe the impact on a firm's financial statements

Core Concepts for Conceptual Framework Underlying Financial Accounting

- The Financial Accounting Standards Board (FASB) promulgated its **Statements of Financial Accounting Concepts (SFACs)** to provide accountants with "a framework of fundamentals on which financial accounting and reporting standards could be based." Six SFACs are extant.

- "The **function of financial reporting** is to provide information that is useful to those who make economic decisions about business enterprises and about investments in or loans to business enterprises" (SFAC 1).

- The conceptual framework defines **ten interrelated elements** of financial statements that are directly related to measuring performance and status of an entity: assets, liabilities, equity or net assets, investments by owners, distributions to owners, comprehensive income, revenues, expenses, gains, and losses (SFAC 6).

- Four **fundamental recognition criteria** apply to all recognition issues: definition of an element of financial statements, measurability, relevance, and reliability (SFAC 5).
- Different **measurement attributes** of assets and liabilities are used in current practice: historical cost, historical proceeds, current (replacement) cost, current market value (exit value), net realizable value (NRV), net settlement value, and present value (SFAC 5).

Core Concepts for Assumptions, Principles, and Limitations

- Certain **assumptions underlie the environment** in which the reporting entity operates. These assumptions were not promulgated by an official body. They have developed over time and are generally recognized by the accounting profession.
  - The **economic-entity** assumption
  - The **going-concern** (business continuity) assumption
  - The **monetary-unit** (unit-of-money) assumption
  - The **periodicity** assumption
- Certain **principles** provide guidelines that the accountant follows when recording financial information.
  - The **revenue recognition** and **matching** principles were formally incorporated by the FASB as recognition and measurement concepts.
  - The **historical cost principle** holds that transactions should be recorded at cost because that is the most objective determination of value. It is a reliable measure.
  - The **full-disclosure principle** holds that financial statement users should be able to assume that anything they need to know about a company is reported in the financial statements.
- Users of financial statements should be aware of certain **limitations of financial reporting**. Information supplied by financial reporting involves estimation, classification, summarization, judgment, and allocation. Financial statements primarily reflect transactions and events that have already occurred.
- Certain **constraints (doctrines)** circumscribe the process of recognition in the financial statements.
  - The **cost-benefit** and **materiality** constraints were formally incorporated by the FASB as qualitative characteristics of financial reporting.
  - The **industry practices** constraint allows that occasionally GAAP are not followed in an industry because adherence to them would generate misleading or unnecessary information.
  - The conservatism constraint encourages accountants, when faced with two or more acceptable choices, to report the less optimistic figure.

Part 2 – Section E.3. Financial statements and statement users

For the statement of financial position (balance sheet), the statement of earnings (income statement), statement of cash flows, and the statement of changes in shareholders' equity, the candidate should be able to:

a. identify the users of these financial statements and their needs
b. demonstrate an understanding of the purposes and uses of each statement
c. identify the major components and classifications of each statement
d. identify the limitations of each statement
e. identify statement information that requires supplemental disclosure in the body of the statement or in the footnotes
f. recognize the correct format of financial information in each statement
g. calculate and classify components of each financial statement

Core Concepts for Financial Statements and Statement Users

- The **elements** of one statement **articulate** (are interrelated) with those of other statements.
    - The balance sheet reports assets, liabilities, equity, and investments by owners **at a moment in time**.
    - The statement of income and statement of retained earnings report revenues, expenses, gains, losses, and distributions to owners **over a period of time**.
    - The elements of the **balance sheet** are **changed by** those on the **income statement** and are their cumulative result.
- The statement of financial position (balance sheet) "provides information about an entity's **assets, liabilities, and equity** and their relationships to each other at a moment in time."
    - The items in the balance sheet represent the **resources** of the entity and **claims** to those resources.
- The items in the statements of income and retained earnings represent the **effects of transactions** and other events and circumstances that result in changes in the entity's resources and claims to those resources.
    - The statement of income can be presented in the **single-step**, **multi-step**, or **condensed** format.
    - The results of **discontinued operations** and the effects of **extraordinary items** are presented **separately** after income from continuing operations.
- The primary purpose of a statement of cash flows is to provide relevant information about the **cash receipts and payments** of an entity during a period.
    - Cash flows are classified as being from **operating** activities, **investing** activities, or **financing** activities.
    - Cash flows from **operating activities** can be displayed using the **direct method** (income statement approach) or the **indirect method** (reconciliation approach).
    - If the **direct method** is used for reporting operating activities, a **reconciliation** that mimics the indirect method **must be disclosed**.

Part 2 – Section E.4. Recognition, measurement, valuation, and disclosure

For each of the subtopics listed, the candidate should be able to:

a. define the subtopic and describe the characteristics of its components
b. demonstrate an understanding of appropriate valuation techniques for the components of each subtopic
c. demonstrate an understanding of the appropriate accounting conventions for the components of each subtopic
d. compare and contrast valuation techniques and accounting methods
e. show the correct financial statement presentation
f. identify the appropriate disclosure requirements in the body of the financial statements and/or in the footnotes or supplemental schedules

I. Cash and marketable securities

a. subtopic components: cash, cash equivalents, marketable (trading) securities
b. determine when cash is restricted

Core Concepts for Cash, Cash Equivalents, and Marketable Securities

- Cash is the **first item presented** in the assets section of the balance sheet. It is ready money, the **most liquid** of assets.
- **Cash equivalents** are short-term, highly liquid investments. They are readily convertible into known amounts of cash, are so near maturity that interest rate risk is insignificant, and generally have an original maturity of 3 months or less. Common examples are Treasury bills, money market funds, and short-term commercial paper.
- **Trading securities** are bought and held primarily for sale in the near future. They are purchased and sold frequently. Unrealized holding gains and losses on trading securities are included in earnings.

II. Accounts receivable

a. subtopic components: current, noncurrent, trade, and nontrade receivables; trade discounts, cash (sales) discounts, sales returns and allowances, net realizable value, promissory note, factoring receivables, write-offs, and collection of write-offs
b. identify issues related to the valuation of accounts receivable
c. calculate cash discounts using both the gross method and the net method
d. identify two methods of recording uncollectibles and describe why the allowance method is the generally accepted approach
e. calculate the allowance for uncollectibles using both the percentage-of-sales (income statement) approach and the percentage-of-receivables (balance sheet) approach
f. discount a long-term note using the time value of money tables and indicate its correct valuation at time of sale
g. calculate the interest revenue and discount amortized for each time period of the note
h. define and be able to compute an imputed interest rate
i. demonstrate an understanding of receivables when they are used as collateral
j. distinguish between receivables sold on a with-recourse basis and those sold on a without-recourse basis

Core Concepts for Accounts Receivable

- A receivable is a **current** asset if it is reasonably expected to be collected within the longer of 1 year or the entity's normal operating cycle.
  - **Trade receivables**, which constitute the majority of receivables, arise from credit sales to customers as part of the ordinary revenue-producing activities of an entity.
    - **Accounts receivable** are often short-term, unsecured, and informal credit arrangements (open accounts). Most trade receivables are accounts.
    - **Notes receivable** are evidenced by a formal instrument, such as a promissory note.
  - **Nontrade receivables** include all receivables not classified as trade receivables. Examples include lease receivables and interest, dividends, rent, or royalties accrued.
- **Cash discounts** (sales discounts) are a means of accelerating cash collection by rewarding customers for early payment. They can be accounted for in one of two ways:
  - The **gross method** accounts for receivables at their face amount. It is used when customers are not expected to pay soon enough to take the discount.
  - The **net method** records receivables net of the applicable cash (sales) discount allowed for early payment. It is used when customers are expected to pay within the discount period.

- **Sales returns and allowances** constitute a provision must be made for the return of merchandise because of product defects, customer dissatisfaction, etc.
- There are two approaches to **accounting for bad debts**:
  - The **direct write-off method** expenses bad debts when they are determined to be uncollectible. It is only permissible under GAAP when the amount is immaterial.
  - The **allowance method** systematically records bad debt expense as a percentage of either sales or the level of accounts receivable on an annual basis. It is preferred under GAAP. **Two approaches** to calculating the amount charged to bad debt expense are available under the allowance method:
    - Under the **income-statement approach**, the matching principle is applied, and periodic bad debt expense is computed as a percentage of sales.
    - Under the **balance-sheet approach**, accounts receivable are reported at their net realizable value (NRV).
- Occasionally a customer will pay on an **account previously written off**. The first entry is to reestablish the account for the amount the customer has agreed to pay (any remainder remains written off). The second entry records the receipt of cash.
- Companies often use their **accounts receivables as financing tools**, either selling them to improve cash flow or as collateral for loans.
  - In order to improve liquidity, a company will sometimes sell its accounts receivable to a third party who assumes the responsibility of collection. This process is referred to as **factoring**.
  - A **pledge** (a general assignment) is the use of receivables as collateral (security) for a loan.
  - An **assignment** (a specific assignment) is a more formal borrowing arrangement (secured borrowing).
  - **Securitization** is the transfer of a portfolio of financial assets to a special-purpose entity (SPE), often a trust, and the sale of beneficial interests in the SPE to investors.

Core Concepts for Notes Receivable and the Time Value of Money

- A **note receivable** is a debt evidenced by a **two-party writing**, i.e., a promissory note, and thus follows the laws concerning negotiable instruments.
- Receivables should be recorded at the **present value of the expected future cash flows**, and any difference between the proceeds and the face amount, if material, must be recognized as a premium or discount and amortized.
  - A **discount** results when the stated rate is less than the effective rate. A **premium** results when the stated rate is greater than the effective rate.
- A quantity of money to be received or paid in the future is worth less than the same amount now. The difference, called the **time value of money**, is measured in terms of interest calculated using the appropriate discount rate. Interest is the "price of money," i.e., the amount paid by a borrower to a lender for the privilege of borrowing the funds.
  - The **present value** of an amount is the value today of some future payment.
  - The **future value** of an amount is the amount available at a specified time in the future based on a single investment (deposit) today.
  - An **annuity** is usually a series of equal payments at equal intervals of time, e.g., $1,000 at the end of every year for 10 years.
    - An **ordinary annuity** (annuity in arrears) is a series of payments occurring at the end of each period.
    - In an **annuity due** (annuity in advance) the payments are made at the beginning of each period.

- ■   The **effective interest method** or effective rate method of amortizing discount or premium results in a **constant rate of return** on a receivable or payable. Under this method, two calculations are made each period:

$$Interest\ expense\ for\ the\ period = Book\ value \times Effective\ interest\ rate$$

$$Discount/premium\ amortized = Interest\ expense\ - Cash\ interest\ paid$$

- ■   Amortizing discounts and premiums with the effective interest method results in the net carrying amount of the asset (liability) being adjusted over time, **reaching the face amount at maturity**.
- ■   Sometimes notes are issued **without a stated rate** and an unknown effective rate. In these cases, the rate must be **imputed** from other facts surrounding the transaction, e.g., the marketability of the note and the debtor's creditworthiness.
- ■   When a note receivable is **discounted (i.e., sold**, usually at a bank), the gain or loss on disposition of the note must be calculated. The steps in discounting a note are to compute the: (1) total interest receivable on the note, (2) maturity amount, (3) accrued interest receivable, (4) bank's discount, (5) cash proceeds, (6) carrying amount of the note, and (7) gain or loss.

III. Inventories

- a.   subtopic components: raw material inventory, work-in-process inventory, finished goods inventory, merchandise inventory; perpetual, modified perpetual, and periodic inventory systems; cost of goods sold, cost of goods available for sale, goods in transit, and consigned goods
- b.   identify issues in inventory valuation, including which goods to include, what costs to include, and which cost assumption to use
- c.   identify the costs included in inventory
- d.   differentiate between FOB shipping point and FOB destination
- e.   demonstrate an understanding of special sale agreements, including sales with a buyback agreement (product financing arrangement), sales with high rates of returns, and sales on installment
- f.   calculate and indicate the correct entries and financial statement presentation for purchase discounts using the gross method and using the net method
- g.   identify accounting issues related to purchase commitments
- h.   identify and compare cost flow assumptions used in accounting for inventories
- i.   calculate ending inventory and cost of goods sold using the specific identification, average cost, first-in-first-out (FIFO), and last-in-first-out (LIFO) methods
- j.   calculate the effect on income and on assets of using different inventory methods
- k.   analyze the effects of inventory errors
- l.   demonstrate an understanding of the LIFO reserve and LIFO liquidation
- m.   calculate ending inventory and cost of goods sold using dollar-value LIFO
- n.   identify advantages and disadvantages of the different inventory methods
- o.   apply the lower of cost or market rule
- p.   identify when inventories are valued at net realizable value
- q.   demonstrate an understanding of the relative sales value method
- r.   determine ending inventory by using the gross profit method and by using the retail inventory method
- s.   recommend the inventory method and cost flow assumption that should be used for a firm in a specific industry given a set of facts and management goals

Core Concepts for Inventory Accounting -- Fundamentals

- **Inventory** includes items for resale, not long-term assets subject to depreciation.
  - Inventory tracking is simplified for a **retailer** because such entities have only a single class of inventory, that is, merchandise to be sold to the final customer.
  - The classification is more complex for a **manufacturer**, who has three distinct classes of inventory: raw materials, work-in-process, and finished goods.
- **Goods included in inventory** include those physically on hand, certain goods in transit, and goods out on consignment. **All costs necessary** to bring goods to a salable condition are capitalized as part of inventory, i.e., purchase price plus freight-in for a retailer.
- **Three basic systems** are in common use for tracking inventory:
  - A **periodic system** is used by a firm with no need to monitor inventory on a continuous basis. The inventory account maintains the beginning balance throughout the period.
  - A **perpetual system** is used by a firm that requires continuous accurate balances. Acquisitions are added to inventory as they occur.
  - A **modified perpetual system** is a simplified version of the perpetual system that tracks quantities (but not dollars) on a continuous basis.
- Two methods are available for recording **purchase discounts**:
  - The **gross method** accounts for payables at their face amount. It is used when the purchaser does not expect to pay soon enough to take the discount.
  - The **net method** records payables net of the cash (sales) discount for early payment. It is used when the purchaser expects to pay within the discount period. Its advantage is that it isolates purchase discounts lost, which are treated as financing charges.

Core Concepts for Inventory Accounting -- Cost Flow Assumptions

- **Specific identification** involves keeping individual cost records for every item in inventory. This is only practical when the number of items in inventory is small, such as automobiles, heavy equipment, yachts, or jewelry.
- **Average inventory** costing comes in two varieties:
  - The **moving-average** method is used with **perpetual inventory** systems. A new average cost is calculated after each purchase.
  - The **weighted-average** method is used with **periodic inventory** systems. Because perpetual records are not kept, inventory cost is only calculated at the end of each period.
- **First-in, first-out (FIFO)** considers the first goods purchased to be the first goods sold. Accordingly, ending inventory consists of the latest purchases. Cost of goods sold consists of costs carried over in beginning inventory and purchases during the current period.
- **Last-in, first-out (LIFO)** considers the most recent purchases to be sold first. Accordingly, ending inventory is priced at the cost of beginning inventory and the earliest purchases.
  - A **significant advantage** of LIFO is its matching of current revenues with the most recent product costs. LIFO has traditionally been used as a tax-postponement tool.
- **Dollar-value LIFO** overcomes the shortcomings inherent in specific-good LIFO. The key is measuring inventory in terms of total dollars rather than in units.
  - Dollar-value LIFO involves a **double-conversion process**. First, restate each period's ending inventory at its equivalent base-year value, then determine the LIFO cost basis of each year's component of the ending balances.
- In any year when the balance goes down, a portion of the most recent year's layer must be **stripped away** and can never be replaced.

Core Concepts for Inventory Accounting -- Valuation Techniques

- When inventory **declines in value**, the principle of historical cost is abandoned in favor of the constraint of conservatism.

- The **lower of cost or market (LCM)** rule requires that inventory be written down to its replacement value if its utility is no longer as great as its cost. The loss should be recognized in the period in which it occurs, not the period in which the inventory is sold.

  - Market value should not exceed a **ceiling** equal to net realizable value (NRV). Reporting inventory above NRV overstates its utility and will result in a loss at the time of sale.

  - Market should not be less than a **floor** equal to NRV less a normal profit margin.

- **Two methods** are in common practice for recording LCM.

  - Under the **direct method**, the loss is charged as a direct reduction of inventory.

  - Under the **allowance method**, which is the preferred technique, the loss is charged to a valuation account.

- If market declines can reasonably be expected to be restored by year-end, **they should not be recognized**.

- An **estimate of inventory** is often needed because taking a physical count of every item is impractical. Two methods are in common use.

  - The **gross profit method** computes ending inventory given sales and a standard markup. The gross profit is subtracted from sales to determine cost of sales. This method is often used in the preparation of interim statements and when inventory has been destroyed or stolen.

  - The **retail inventory method** converts ending inventory at retail to cost. The advantage of this method is that a physical inventory can be taken at retail. The cost-retail ratio used to convert retail to cost depends upon the flow assumption used. Also, the lower-of-cost-or-market concept may be applied to the retail method.

IV. Investments

a. subtopic components: debt securities: held-to-maturity, trading, and available-for-sale securities; equity securities: less than 20% holdings (available-for-sale and trading), between 20% and 50% holdings, and holdings more than 50%

b. calculate discounts, premiums, and interest on debt securities using the effective interest method and utilizing time value of money tables

c. define holding gain or loss

d. calculate the realized gain/loss on the sale of a debt or equity security

e. calculate the securities fair value adjustment for available-for-sale and trading debt securities

f. identify and describe the fair value method, equity method, and consolidated method for equity securities

g. compare the equity method with the fair value method

h. demonstrate an understanding of reclassification adjustments

i. account for impairment of value and indicate the correct cost basis for the impaired security

j. identify and describe the proper accounting for transfers of investment securities between categories

Core Concepts for Investments

- **Short-term investments** are current assets. They must be readily marketable and be intended to be converted into cash within the next year or operating cycle, whichever is longer.
- When debt or equity securities are acquired, they **should be classified** as one of the following:
  - **Held-to-maturity** securities are debt securities that the reporting enterprise has the positive intent and ability to hold to maturity. Held-to-maturity securities are reported at amortized cost.
  - **Trading securities** can consist of debt securities and equity securities. Trading securities are bought and held primarily for sale in the near term. Unrealized holding gains and losses are included in earnings.
  - **Available-for-sale** securities include both debt securities and equity securities. The accounting is similar to that for trading securities. Unrealized holding gains and losses are reported in other comprehensive income.
- If a **decline in fair value** of an individual held-to-maturity or available-for-sale security below the amortized cost basis is other than temporary (i.e., **impairment**), the cost basis is written down to fair value as a new cost basis. The write-down is a realized loss and is included in earnings.
- When ownership of an investee reaches the level of **significant influence**, the investor must adopt the equity method. A 20% or greater ownership interest is rebuttably presumed to permit such influence.
  - Under the equity method, the investment's carrying amount is increased or decreased by the **investor's proportionate share** of earnings or losses. The investment's carrying amount is also reduced by any dividends received from the investee.
- The **cost method** is used when the investor cannot exercise significant influence over the investee, and the equity securities do not have readily determinable fair values. Thus, it is the default method when the equity method and fair-value accounting are not applicable.

V. Property, plant, and equipment

a. subtopic components: land, buildings, equipment, and self-constructed assets; additions, improvements, replacements, reinstallations, and repairs; nonmonetary exchanges; depreciation; depletion; impairment

b. calculate depreciation using the activity method, the straight-line method, the sum-of-the-years'-digits method, declining-balance method, the group method, and the composite method

c. calculate and record the gain or loss on the disposition of tangible assets

d. identify the basis on which tangible assets would be valued when payment is in the form of stock

e. demonstrate an understanding of the correct accounting treatment for interest costs incurred for the construction or acquisition of tangible assets

f. determine the effect on the financial statements of using different depreciation methods

g. recommend a depreciation method given a set of data and management goals

h. calculate a depletion base given acquisition, exploration, development, and restoration costs

Core Concepts for Property, Plant, and Equipment

- PPE may be either **personal property** (something movable, e.g., equipment) or **real property** (such as land or a building).
- PPE are reported at **historical cost** (net of applicable depreciation in the case of non-land PPE).
- **Site preparation costs**, such as razing old buildings, clearing, filling, and draining, are **costs of the land**, not of the building to be constructed on the land.
- The **cost of a building** includes any liens assumed and any costs of renovation and preparation.
- The **cost of machinery and equipment** includes the purchase price and all installation and start-up costs.
- **Improvements** made to property that is merely being leased, such as buildings constructed on leased land, are accounted for in the same way as property to which title is held (except that the depreciation period generally may not extend beyond the lease term).
- **Subsequent expenditures** are **capitalized** if they provide additional benefits by (a) improving the quality of services rendered by the asset, (b) extending the asset's useful life, or (c) increasing its output.
- When PPE is disposed of in a **partial monetary exchange** (i.e., boot is received), **gain must be recognized** in proportion of the amount of boot to the amount of total assets given up.
- When a long-lived asset is **impaired** (i.e., its fair value is less than its carrying amount), a **loss** equal to the excess is recognized if the amount is not recoverable.
- **Depreciation** is the process of systematically and rationally **allocating the historical cost** of the productive capacity of a tangible capital asset to the periods benefited. It is **not** a process of **valuation**.
- The **straight-line method** is the **simplest**. It allocates the asset's cost at a constant rate over its estimated useful life.
- **Accelerated methods** were popularized when they became allowable on **tax returns**, but the same method need not be used for tax and financial statement purposes. The two major ones are **declining balance** and **sum-of-the-years' digits**.
- **Activity-based methods**, such as **units-of-output**, calculate depreciation as a function of an **asset's use** rather than the time it has been held.
- **Depletion** is similar to depreciation, but the assets involved are **wasting assets**, such as natural resources (petroleum, timber, iron ore, etc.).

VI. Intangibles

a. subtopic components: intangible assets: patents, copyrights, trademarks and trade names, leaseholds, franchises and licensees; purchased intangibles and internally-created intangibles; goodwill; internally created goodwill and purchased goodwill; negative goodwill; amortization; research and development; start-up costs, initial operating losses, advertising costs, and computer software costs

b. demonstrate an understanding of the accounting for impairment of intangible assets

c. determine the effect on the financial statements of various intangible asset transactions

Core Concepts for Intangibles

- **Intangible assets** are nonfinancial assets that **lack physical substance**. They often convey a right to do something that gives its holder some form of **economic benefits**, e.g., patents and copyrights.

- Intangible assets are **not depreciated**. Instead, they are periodically **reviewed for impairment** and written down to fair value.

- **Research and development costs** are expensed as incurred; they may **not** be capitalized.

15.2 OVERVIEW OF FINANCIAL REPORTING AND ASSETS ESSAY QUESTIONS

Recall that your CMA Part 4 exam will probably contain six scenarios, with about three questions per scenario. There will be a recommended time allocation of 20 minutes, 30 minutes, or 45 minutes for each scenario and related questions.

One scenario will involve ethical issues, and probably one or two scenarios will include calculations and responses on a worksheet. Also, expect at least one scenario on organizational/behavioral topics. The remaining scenarios cover Parts 1, 2, and 3.

Scenario Title	Subtopic	Questions	Suggested Time
Jebec Industries	Notes to the Financial Statements	1	30 minutes
Genie Company	Inventory Costing Methods	2, 3, 4	30 minutes
Environmental Engineering Research, Inc.	R&D Expenses	5, 6	30 minutes
Merrimac Corporation	Transactions and Financial Statements	7	30 minutes

Scenario for Essay Question 1

The preliminary draft of the Statement of Financial Position at the end of the current fiscal year for Jebec Industries is presented on the next page. The statement will be incorporated into the annual report to stockholders and will present the dollar amounts at the end of both the current and prior years in a side-by-side comparative basis. The accounts in the statement are properly classified, and the dollar amounts have been determined in accordance with generally accepted accounting principles. The company does not intend to provide any more detailed information in the body of the statement.

JEBEC INDUSTRIES
STATEMENT OF FINANCIAL POSITION
November 30, Year 2
(millions of dollars)

Assets

Current assets	
Cash	$ 9.0
Marketable equity securities	4.5
Accounts receivable – trade (net)	75.3
Inventories	152.0
Prepayments and other	3.2
Total current assets	$244.0
Investments in equity securities	36.8
Plant, property, and equipment (net)	524.7
Total assets	$805.5

Liabilities and Stockholders' Equity

Current liabilities	
Current maturities on long-term debt	$ 24.3
Notes payable	53.0
Accounts payable	93.2
Accrued taxes	28.2
Accrued interest	7.3
Other	2.9
Total current liabilities	$208.9
Long-term debt	318.1
Total liabilities	$527.0
Stockholders' equity	
Preferred stock	$ 20.0
Common stock	51.3
Paid-in capital on common stock	43.6
Retained earnings – appropriated	27.2
Retained earnings – unappropriated	136.4
Total stockholders' equity	$278.5
Total liabilities and stockholders' equity	$805.5

Question

1. Identify the accounts that most likely would require further disclosure in the notes to the financial statements and describe what information would have to be disclosed in those notes by Jebec Industries before the statement can be included as part of the annual report for presentation to its stockholders.

Essay Question 1 — Unofficial Answers

1. The accounts which most likely would require further disclosure in the notes to the financial statements and the information that would have to be disclosed include the following:

    a. Marketable equity securities and investment in equity securities

        1) Disclose, at the date of each Statement of Financial Position presented, the total cost and market value of both current and noncurrent marketable equity securities.

        2) Disclose, at the date of the most recent Statement of Financial Position presented, the total gross unrealized gains and the total gross unrealized losses for both current and noncurrent marketable equity securities.

    b. Accounts receivable -- trade

        1) The accounting method used to estimate uncollectible receivables and the balance in the allowance account should be disclosed.

        2) Any receivables which are assigned or pledged as collateral should be disclosed.

    c. Inventories

        1) Disclose the major classifications of inventory, i.e., finished goods, work-in-process, raw materials.

        2) Disclose the basis of pricing inventories, i.e., lower of cost or market.

        3) Disclose the method of determining inventory cost, i.e., LIFO, FIFO, average.

    d. Plant, property, and equipment

        1) The balances of major classes of depreciable assets by nature or function should be disclosed.

        2) The depreciation amount and the methods used in computing depreciation should be disclosed by major classes.

        3) The accumulated depreciation allowances by classes or in total should be disclosed.

    e. Current liabilities and long-term debt

        1) Maturities, interest rates, and other terms and conditions provided in the loan agreement should be disclosed.

        2) Assets pledged as collateral and covenants to reduce debt, maintain working capital, and/or restrict dividends for specific liabilities, should be disclosed.

    f. Stockholders' equity

        1) For each different class of stock, disclosure should be made regarding the par or stated value and the total number of shares authorized, issued, outstanding, and reserved for stock options. Disclose in summary form terms sufficient to explain pertinent rights and privileges of the various securities.

        2) Any appropriations or restrictions of retained earnings should be described.

Scenario for Essay Questions 2, 3, 4

The Genie Company is considering a change from the first-in, first-out (FIFO) method of inventory valuation to the dollar-value last-in, first-out (LIFO) method for the fiscal year ended May 31, Year 9. Genie manufactures two staplers -- compact and standard -- that would be combined into a single inventory pool if dollar value LIFO is adopted.

Selected financial data for Genie's two products are presented in the schedule shown below. Pretax income for the Year 8-Year 9 fiscal year would be $420,000 using the FIFO method of inventory valuation. Genie is subject to an income tax rate of 40%.

| | Compact Stapler | | |
	Units	Cost per Unit	Total
Ending inventory at May 31, Year 8 (FIFO)	65,000	$4.80	$ 312,000
Add: Years 8-9 fiscal year production*	500,000	$5.52	$2,760,000
Less: Sales	(525,000)		
Ending inventory at May 31, Year 9 (FIFO)	40,000	$5.52	$ 220,800

| | Standard Stapler | | |
	Units	Cost per Unit	Total
Ending inventory at May 31, Year 8 (FIFO)	35,000	$8.00	$ 280,000
Add: Years 8-9 fiscal year production*	600,000	$9.00	$5,400,000
Less: Sales	(583,000)		
Ending inventory at May 31, Year 9 (FIFO)	52,000	$9.00	$ 468,000

*The unit production costs are annual averages.

Questions

2. Discuss the advantages and disadvantages of a switch from the FIFO method of inventory valuation to the LIFO method.

3. Explain the following terms that are commonly used with the LIFO method of inventory valuation:

   a. LIFO pool
   b. Dollar-value method
   c. LIFO increment
   d. LIFO reserve

4. a. Calculate the ending inventory as of May 31, Year 9, for Genie Company using the dollar-value LIFO method of inventory valuation using a single inventory pool.
   b. Calculate the effect the change to dollar-value LIFO inventory method would have on pretax income and on income taxes.

Essay Questions 2, 3, 4 — Unofficial Answers

2.   A switch from the FIFO method to the LIFO method has the following advantages:

   a.   LIFO matches more recent costs with current revenues, providing a better measure of current earnings and more meaningful gross margin analysis.

   b.   LIFO results in greater cost of goods sold, less taxable income, and a deferral of income taxes during periods of increasing prices.

   c.   LIFO minimizes write downs during periods of increasing prices because the older and lower carrying costs are usually less than market value.

   A switch from the FIFO method of inventory valuation to the LIFO method has the following disadvantages:

   a.   LIFO requires complex recordkeeping and computations.

   b.   LIFO does not approximate the physical flow of most items.

   c.   LIFO can lead to profit manipulation or distortion through the timing of purchases.

   d.   LIFO results in lower reported profits and the understatement of inventory on the balance sheet during periods of increasing prices.

3.   a.   A LIFO pool is a group of similar inventory items. Each pool is assumed to be one unit for costing and is used to compare the relative quantity of goods on hand at the end of each year.

   b.   The dollar-value method bases the LIFO inventory computation on dollars of inventory, uses broad inventory pools, and uses specific price indices for each pool every year.

   c.   A LIFO increment is an increase in quantity expressed in base-year prices.

   d.   A LIFO reserve is the difference between the LIFO inventory valuation and some other valuation of the inventory.

4.   a.

	May 31, Year 8 (Base Year) Price	May 31, Year 9 Current Year Ending Inventory
Compact stapler	$4.80	40,000
Standard stapler	8.00	52,000

	Current Year Ending Inventory at Base Year Price
Compact stapler	$192,000
Standard stapler	416,000
May 31, Year 9, inventory at base year prices	$608,000
Less: May 31, Year 8, inventory at base year prices (FIFO) ($312,000 + $280,000)	(592,000)
Current year LIFO increment at base year prices	$ 16,000
Times: Current year price index ($688,800 ÷ $608,000)	×1.13289
Current year LIFO increment at current year prices	18,126
Addback: May 31, Year 8, inventory at base year prices (FIFO)	$592,000
May 31, Year 9, dollar value LIFO Inventory	$610,126

   b.

May 31, Year 9, FIFO inventory ($220,800 + $468,000)	$688,800
Less: May 31, Year 9, dollar value LIFO inventory	(610,126)
Decrease in pretax income due to change	$ 78,674
Times: Income tax rate	× .40
Decrease in income taxes	$ 31,470

Scenario for Essay Questions 5, 6

Environmental Engineering Research, Inc. (EER) manufactures and installs waste disposal systems for private industry and governmental units. Early in the current year, the company completed a large facility devoted to the research and development (R&D) of new solutions to the waste disposal problems encountered around the world. Besides developing systems for sale, the company is engaged in providing R&D services for several companies under contractual arrangements.

The following expenditures apply to the R&D activities of EER for the fiscal year ended May 31.

- The research facility was completed in March for a total cost of $135 million, and it is being used to conduct all of the company's R&D activities, including R&D under contract for others.
- Salaries and wages of the employees engaged in R&D at the new facility were $2,485,000.
- During August of the prior year, the company fabricated equipment specifically for use in a project to develop new methods of cleaning up oil spills. The equipment cost $540,000 and is expected to operate for 4 years. The equipment has no alternative use other than this project.
- The city of Cleveland has contracted with EER to design a pilot plant for removing heavy metal waste from river beds. To date, costs of $496,500 have been expended on the project, which is expected to take 2 more years to complete. The total estimated cost to complete this project is $1,342,000.
- EER acquired sludge and other waste products for use in testing the effectiveness of various R&D projects. The only costs involved in acquiring this material were transportation costs of $25,000.

Questions

5. Statement of Financial Accounting Standards No. 2 (SFAS 2), *Accounting for Research and Development Costs*, requires that all research and development expenditures be expensed in the period incurred.

    a. Explain the rationale underlying the expensing requirement.
    b. Discuss the criticisms of the expensing requirement.

6. Describe how each of the costs described above should be presented on Environmental Engineering Research, Inc.'s financial statements and/or in the footnotes to be in compliance with the requirements of SFAS 2.

Essay Questions 5, 6 — Unofficial Answers

5. a. The reasons that the FASB concluded that all research and development costs should be expensed when incurred include the following:

   1) There is normally a high degree of uncertainty about the future benefits of individual research and development projects.

   2) A direct relationship between research and development costs and specific future revenue generally has not been demonstrated. As a result, the notion of matching cannot be readily applied to research and development costs.

   b. Criticisms of the expensing requirement for research and development costs include the following:

   1) Enterprises undertake research and development activities with the hope of future benefits. There is a high probability of future benefits from an enterprise's total research and development program, even though many individual activities will fail. Therefore, the entire cost of these activities should be capitalized without regard to the certainty of future benefits from individual projects.

   2) Immediate expensing eliminates the possibility of matching future revenues with their associated costs.

6. To be in compliance with the requirements of SFAS 2, each of the costs incurred by Environmental Engineering Research, Inc. should be presented on the financial statements and/or in the footnotes as follows:

   a. The $135 million cost of the research facility that has alternative future uses (R&D plus contract services) should be capitalized as a tangible asset. The portion of the depreciation expense related to research and development activities should be charged to R&D expense and separately disclosed in the footnotes. The portion of the depreciation expense related to R&D performed under contract should be charged to the cost of services provided (cost of goods sold) with a corresponding receivable established since reimbursement is expected.

   b. The salaries and wages of employees engaged in research and development should be charged to income in the period in which the employees worked. The portion related to research and development activities should be charged to R&D expense and separately disclosed in the footnotes. The portion related to R&D performed under contract should be charged to the cost of services provided (cost of goods sold) with a corresponding receivable established since reimbursement is expected.

   c. Since the equipment fabricated has no alternative future use, the cost of the equipment should be charged to R&D expense in the period incurred and separately disclosed in the footnotes.

   d. Total costs of $496,500 incurred for the design of the pilot plant under contract with the city of Cleveland should be charged to the cost of services provided (cost of goods sold) and treated as a receivable since reimbursement is expected. No footnote disclosure is required.

   e. When acquired, the materials should be carried as inventory and allocated to R&D expense as consumed. If it is assumed that the cost is not significant and that allocation for specific activities would be difficult, it would be reasonable to charge the entire amount to R&D expense in the period incurred.

Scenario for Essay Question 7

Merrimac Corporation began manufacturing pinball machines in the mid-fifties. By 1975, the pinball machine market had declined significantly, and Merrimac opened a new division to develop and manufacture video games. The pinball machine division was phased out in 1980, and since then Merrimac has concentrated exclusively on the development and manufacture of video games for both the home and commercial markets. In 1985, Merrimac acquired a chain of video game parlors in a move to expand; this division has shown only moderate success.

James Heuga has been hired as the accounting manager, and he has been assigned the task of preparing the financial statements for the fiscal year ended November 30. Heuga is concerned about the proper financial statement presentation of several transactions that occurred during the year. Bill Werner, controller of Merrimac, has agreed to discuss these transactions with Heuga. The transactions in question include the following:

A.   During the year-end physical inventory, the inventory of replacement parts for a 1998 model video game was determined to be obsolete. The inventory was written down to its salvage value and a $46,000 loss was recorded.

B.   At the beginning of the fiscal year, Merrimac changed the method of calculating depreciation on its building for financial reporting from the sum-of-the-years'-digits method to the straight-line method. If straight-line depreciation had originally been used, the gross cumulative effect on income would be $78,000 as of the beginning of the current fiscal year.

C.   Three years ago, Merrimac acquired the copyright to the software for a new video game. At that time, the total useful life was estimated to be 9 years. Based on recent innovations in video software, the total useful life was changed to 6 years, effective for the current year.

D.   Merrimac warrants its commercial machines for 2 years subsequent to the sale. The warranty costs associated with the current year's sales are estimated to be $104,200.

E.   Merrimac is the plaintiff in a lawsuit that will go to trial early next year. The company's lawyers believe it probable that Merrimac will win a favorable judgment in the amount of $242,000.

F.   Merrimac is the defendant in a lawsuit filed by one of its customers. The company's lawyers believe it probable that Merrimac will lose and estimate the settlement to be approximately $164,000.

Question

7.   For each of the six transactions, explain how and why it affects Merrimac Corporation's

    a.   Income statement,
    b.   Statement of financial position (exclusive of net income effects),
    c.   Cash flow statement (exclusive of net income effects), and/or
    d.   Footnote disclosure.

Essay Question 7 — Unofficial Answers

7.   Each of the six transactions would affect Merrimac Corporation's financial statements as follows:

a.   Transaction A

   1)   The loss due to obsolescence of inventory would appear in other expenses and losses (if immaterial, in cost of goods sold) on the income statement above income before taxes.

   2)   The amount in ending inventory would be less.

   3)   The loss does not affect cash flow unless using the indirect method.

   4)   The write-down of obsolete inventory probably is not significant enough to be disclosed in the footnotes. If material, it must be disclosed in the footnotes.

b.   Transaction B

   1)   The cumulative effect of $78,000 for the change from sum-of-the-years'-digits to straight-line depreciation represents a change in accounting principle and would be reported net of tax.

   2)   The opening balance in accumulated depreciation would be restated as though straight-line depreciation had been used from the beginning.

   3)   The cumulative effect would appear as an adjustment in the reconciliation of net income to cash flow from operating activities.

   4)   The change in accounting principle must be fully described.

c.   Transaction C

   1)   The change in useful life is a change in estimate that affects present and future periods only, and the increased amortization would be reported in operating expenses causing a decline in income. The current amortization should reflect the new estimated useful life.

   2)   The copyright account would be decreased by the higher current period amortization.

   3)   The amortization of the copyright would appear as an adjustment in the reconciliation of net income to cash flow from operating activities.

   4)   If the change in estimate is significant, then it should be described in the footnote detailing amortization methods. Otherwise, it need not be separately disclosed.

d.   Transaction D

   1)   Warranty costs represent a contingent liability considered probable and reasonably estimated. The expense for warranty costs is included within operating expenses.

   2)   The estimated liability for warranty costs is generally considered a current liability.

   3)   The warranty expense does not directly affect cash flow; however, it would appear as an adjustment in the reconciliation of net income to cash flow from operating activities.

   4)   Warranty policies are described in the footnote on revenue recognition methods. If warranty expense is a departure from the amount normally incurred, then it should be described in the footnotes.

e. Transaction E

　　1) In accordance with SFAS 5, *Accounting for Contingencies*, contingencies that might result in gains usually are not reflected in the accounts since to do so might be to recognize revenue prior to its realization. Accordingly, no disclosure in the financial statements is necessary.

f. Transaction F

　　1) This is a loss contingency that is probable and can be reasonably estimated. The loss should appear on the income statement as an "Other gain or loss."

　　2) This event is a loss contingency that is probable and can be reasonably estimated. Therefore, the estimated liability should appear on the statement of financial position.

　　3) The cash flow for the contingent loss would appear as an adjustment in the reconciliation of net income to cash flow from operating activities.

　　4) The lawsuit should be described in the footnotes.

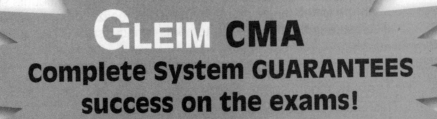
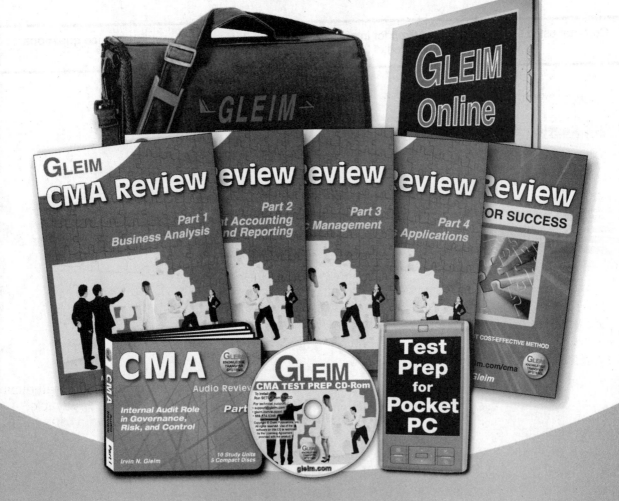

STUDY UNIT SIXTEEN
CMA PART 2 REVIEW –
EXTERNAL FINANCIAL REPORTING II

(10 pages of outline)

Part 2 of the CMA exam is titled **Management Accounting and Reporting.** This study unit is a review of this section:

E. **External Financial Reporting.** Liability recognition and measurement; equity recognition and measurement; revenue, expenses, extraordinary items, and earnings per share; the SEC and its reporting requirements; the annual report.

This study unit presents the IMA's Learning Outcome Statements and Gleim Core Concepts relevant to this section. Bear in mind that **all topics** on Part 4 of the exam are tested at **skill level C** (all six skill types required).

16.1 LIABILITIES, EQUITY, REVENUE RECOGNITION, AND OTHER ISSUES REVIEW

Part 2 – Section E.4. Recognition, measurement, valuation, and disclosure

For each of the subtopics listed, the candidate should be able to:

- define the subtopic and describe the characteristics of its components
- demonstrate an understanding of appropriate valuation techniques for the components of each subtopic
- demonstrate an understanding of the appropriate accounting conventions for the components of each subtopic
- compare and contrast valuation techniques and accounting methods
- show the correct financial statement presentation
- identify the appropriate disclosure requirements in the body of the financial statements and/or in the footnotes or supplemental schedules

VII. Current liabilities

a. subtopic components: current liability: notes payable, accounts payable, current maturities of long-term debt, short-term obligations expected to be refinanced, dividends payable, returnable deposits, unearned (or deferred) revenues, taxes payable, and employee-related liabilities; loss contingencies; warranty costs; premiums and coupons

b. identify the classification issues of short-term debt expected to be refinanced

c. identify the different types of employee-related liabilities

d. apply both the expense warranty approach and the sales warranty approach

Core Concepts for Current Liabilities

- **Accounts payable** arise in the normal course of business to reflect obligations to suppliers. They are classified as current liabilities.
- The **gross method** reports payables at their face amount. It is used when **the company does not expect** to take advantage of any discount allowed for early payment.
- The **net method** reports payables net of the applicable discount. It is used when **the company expects** to pay within the discount period.
- A **note payable** is a debt acknowledged by a **written agreement**.
- Notes payable should be reported at their face amount **net of any premium or discount** arising from a difference between the note's stated rate of interest and the market rate.
- **Other current liabilities** which must be reported are current maturities of long-term debt, short-term obligations expected to be refinanced, deposits and advances received, deferred (unearned) revenues, taxes payable, employee-related liabilities (e.g., compensated absences), loss contingencies, warranty liabilities, and coupons issued.

VIII. Long-term liabilities and bonds payable

a. subtopic components: long-term liabilities/debt: bonds, long-term notes payable, mortgage notes payable, zero-interest-bearing notes, convertible debt

b. calculate interest expense, interest payable, bond discount and premium using the straight-line method and the effective interest method (time value of money tables)

c. identify the proper classification of bond discount and premium as an adjunct account

d. identify the proper accounting treatment of debt issuance expenses

e. define implicit interest rate and imputed interest

f. account for notes issued for property, goods, and services

g. calculate imputed fair value and note discount where the stated interest rate is unreasonable

h. define off-balance sheet financing and identify different forms of this type of borrowing

i. indicate the disclosure requirements for off-balance sheet financing

Core Concepts for Long-Term Liabilities and Bonds Payable

- A **bond** is a **formal (long-term) contractual agreement** to pay an amount of money (the face amount) at the maturity date plus interest at the stated rate at specific intervals.
- Bonds should be reported at their face amount **net of any premium or discount** arising from a difference between the note's stated rate of interest and the market rate.
- Convertible debt issued with stock purchase warrants can be accounted for under the **book-value method** or the **market-value method**.
- A **variable interest entity** is an **off-balance-sheet** arrangement that may take any legal form. The **primary beneficiary consolidates** a variable interest entity.

IX. Equity transactions and earnings per share

a. subtopic components: preferred stock and common stock; capital stock, additional paid-in capital and retained earnings; treasury stock (cost method and par value method); property dividends, scrip dividends; liquidating dividends; stock dividends (large and small); retained earnings

b. apply the accounting procedures for issuing shares of stock, including par value stock, no-par stock, stock sold on a subscription basis, lump sum sales, and stocks issued in noncash transactions

c. apply the accounting procedures for the declaration and payment of common stock and preferred stock dividends

d. define stock options, warrants, and rights and determine the correct presentation in the financial statements for these instruments

e. identify transactions that affect paid-in capital and those that affect retained earnings

f. infer the effect on shareholders' equity of large and small stock dividends

g. define stock split and distinguish from stock dividend

h. identify reasons for the appropriation of retained earnings

i. calculate earnings per share (basic and diluted)

Core Concepts for Equity Transactions and Earnings per Share

- The **equity** of a business enterprise consists of contributed capital, retained earnings, and accumulated other comprehensive income.

- The **common shareholders** are the **owners** of a corporation. The issuance of common stock makes it easy for a business to **raise large amounts of capital** from many disparate parties.

- **Preferred stock** is a **hybrid** of debt and equity, i.e., holders stand higher in priority in bankruptcy than holders of common stock but lower than holders of debt. Also, preferred stock receives a **mandatory dividend**, similar to debt; the payment of dividends on common stock is residual, not mandatory.

- If stock is issued with a **par or stated value**, amounts received upon sale are recorded as **paid-in capital in excess of par**.

- Likewise, when **stock subscriptions** are sold, paid-in capital in excess of par is credited for the amount received that exceeds the par or stated value of the stock subscribed.

- When **different classes of securities** are sold for a **lump sum**, the proceeds should be **allocated** based on the relative fair values of the securities (the **proportional method**). If the fair value of one of the classes of securities is not known, the others are recorded at their fair values and the remainder is credited to the securities for which the fair value is not known (the **incremental method**).

- **Gains and losses may not be recognized** on transactions in a company's **own stock**.

- Treasury stock, i.e., **an entity's own stock reacquired** on the open market, is generally accounted for **at cost**, but the par value method is also acceptable.

- Under the **cost method**, additional paid-in capital is unaffected when treasury stock is acquired; under the **par value method**, additional paid-in capital is reduced.

- Under both methods, **paid-in capital from treasury stock** is recorded when treasury stock is **resold** above cost (under the cost method) or above par (under the par value method).

- Dividends provide information about **a company's health** to the stock market.

- The dividends on **cumulative preferred stock** accumulate during periods when no dividends are paid out. These must be paid before any dividends can be paid on common stock.

- Holders of **participating preferred stock** share in the cash dividends remaining after preferred shareholders have been paid at the preference rate and common shareholders have been paid a basic return.
- **Other types of dividends** are property dividends (distribution of tangible property), scrip dividends (distribution of notes payable), and stock dividends (distribution of the company's outstanding-but-unissued stock).
- A **stock split** is merely an increase in the number of outstanding shares; no journal entry is recorded.
- **Few entries** are made to retained earnings except to record annual income or loss and the declaration of dividends.
- Retained earnings is **sometimes appropriated** to a special account to disclose management's intent that some earnings retained in the business and not paid out as dividends will be used for special purposes. It is important to note that appropriating earnings does not set aside assets.
- **Stock options** give certain employees the option to purchase common stock at a specified price for a specified period of time.
- **Stock warrants** are certificates evidencing options to buy stock at a given price within a certain period. They may be issued to employees and shareholders and may be attached to bonds or preferred stock.
- In a **rights offering**, each shareholder is issued a certificate or warrant that is an option to buy a certain number of shares at a fixed price.
- Earnings per share is presented in **two calculations**.
- **Basic earnings per share** is the income available to common shareholders divided by the **weighted-average number of shares** of common stock outstanding.
- **Diluted earnings per share** increases the numerator of the basic calculation for any **dividends on convertible preferred stock**, and increases the denominator to include the weighted-average number of additional shares of common stock that would have been outstanding if **dilutive potential common stock** had been issued.
- For purposes of determining the **degree of dilution**, the **if-converted method** is applied. The dilutive effect of all dilutive securities is considered to have been effective on the first day of the year.
- Earnings per share data is presented on the **income statement**.

X. Revenues and expenses

a.   apply the revenue recognition principles to various types of transactions
b.   identify issues involved with revenue recognition at point of sale, including sales with buyback agreements, sales when right of return exists, and trade loading (or channel stuffing)
c.   identify instances where revenue is recognized before delivery
d.   distinguish between percentage-of-completion and completed-contract methods for recognizing revenue
e.   apply the percentage-of-completion and the completed-contract methods
f.   compare and contrast the recognition of costs of construction, progress billings, collections, and gross profit recognized under the two long-term contract accounting methods
g.   demonstrate an understanding of the proper accounting for losses on long-term contracts
h.   identify instances where revenue is recognized after delivery
i.   identify the situations in which each of the following revenue recognition methods would be used: installment sales method, cost recovery method, and deposit method
j.   demonstrate an understanding of the accounting procedures under the installment method, the cost recovery method, and the deposit method

k.   define gains and losses and indicate the proper financial statement presentation
l.   discuss the issues and concerns that have been identified with respect to revenue recognition practices
m.   demonstrate an understanding of the matching principle with respect to revenues and expenses and be able to apply it to a specific situation
n.   demonstrate an understanding of expense recognition practices

Core Concepts for Revenue Recognition

- Revenues are normally recognized when they are **realized or realizable and earned**.
- The **installment method** recognizes income on a sale as the related receivable is collected.
- The **cost-recovery method** may be used when receivables are collected over an extended period, considerable doubt exists as to collectibility, and a reasonable estimate of the loss cannot be made.
- Long-term construction contracts can be accounted for under the **completed-contract method**, but the **percentage-of-completion method** is preferable.
- The **percentage-of-completion method** recognizes periodic revenue or gross profit based upon the estimated total revenue or gross profit for the project, the percentage of the project completed, and the revenue or gross profit recognized to date.
- Ordinarily, **progress billings** are made and payments are received during the term of the contract. Construction in progress in excess of billings constitutes a **current asset**. Billings in excess of construction in progress constitute a **current liability**.
- When inventory is **consigned**, title and risk of loss remain with the consignor (owner of the goods). The consignor only **recognizes revenue** when the goods are **sold**.

XI. Comprehensive income

a.   define comprehensive income and other comprehensive income
b.   identify the three alternative ways that other comprehensive income may be displayed in the financial statements
c.   calculate comprehensive income

Core Concepts for Comprehensive Income

- **Comprehensive income** consists of net income and items of other comprehensive income.
- **Items** of other comprehensive income include foreign currency items, minimum pension liability adjustments, unrealized gains and losses on available-for-sale securities, and certain gains and losses on derivatives.
- Comprehensive income and its components **must be displayed** in a financial statement given the same prominence as other statements. No format is specified.
- Among the **possible formats** for reporting comprehensive income are: a separate statement of comprehensive income, a combined statement of income and comprehensive income, and a statement of changes in equity.

XII. Segment reporting

a.   define operating segment
b.   identify the disclosures required for a reportable operating segment
c.   determine if a segment is reportable given a set of data

Core Concepts for Segment Reporting

- **Reportable segments** are those that provide information about the different types of business activities of the entity and the economic environment in which it operates.
- A business unit should be **treated as a reportable segment** if (a) its reported revenues are at least 10% of the combined revenues of all segments, (b) its assets are at least 10% of the combined assets of all operating segments, or (c) the absolute amount of reported profit or loss is at least 10% of the greater of combined segments that reported a loss or combined segments that did not report a loss.

XIII. Multinational considerations

- a. identify the challenges inherent in translating foreign entities' financial statements to the parent's reporting currency
- b. define functional currency
- c. distinguish between the monetary/nonmonetary method and the current rate method
- d. translate a foreign entity's financial statements from the entity's functional currency to the reporting currency
- e. remeasure a foreign entity's financial statement to the functional currency
- f. describe the significance of a foreign currency transaction gain (loss) on the financial statements
- g. define "highly inflationary economy" and identify which currency should be used as the reporting currency for a company in this environment
- h. identify disclosure requirements for translation of foreign currency financial statements

Core Concepts for Foreign Currency Issues

- An entity's **functional currency** is the currency of the primary economic environment in which it operates.
- Financial statement amounts must be measured in the functional currency (i.e., the currency of the country where the subsidiary is doing business) then **translated** using a **current exchange rate** into the **domestic currency** of the parent.
- When the **exchange rate** between the functional and domestic currencies **changes** before a foreign-denominated receivable or payable is settled, a **gain or loss** must be included in net income in the period of the change.

Part 2 – Sections E.1. Objectives of external financial reporting; and E.2. Financial accounting fundamentals

- identify the objectives of external financial reporting, i.e., providing information on resources and obligations, comprehensive income, and cash flow
- identify and demonstrate an understanding of basic accounting assumptions and conventions, including going concern, historical cost, accrual accounting, and conservatism
- demonstrate an understanding of recognition and measurement concepts as they relate to revenue, expenses, fixed assets, current assets, current liabilities, long-term liabilities, and equity transactions
- differentiate between realization and recognition
- identify financial statement elements for each of the financial statements
- Special topics: leases, pensions and other post-retirement benefits, deferred income taxes, stock options, discontinued operations, extraordinary items, accounting changes, early extinguishment of debt, business combinations, consolidated financial statements, and accounting for derivatives

For each special topic, the candidate should be able to:
- Define and describe its characteristics
- Demonstrate a basic understanding of the relevant accounting issues
- Describe the impact on a firm's financial statements

Note: In-depth application knowledge of the accounting rules for these special topic transactions and events is not required. Candidates are, however, expected to have an understanding of the basic concepts.

Core Concepts for Leases

- A lease is an agreement whereby a **lessor (owner) conveys** the right to use specific property for a stated period **to a lessee** in exchange for a stated payment.
- A **lessee** classifies leases as **capital leases** or **operating leases**.
- A **lessee** classifies a lease as a **capital lease** if **any of four criteria** are met at the inception of the lease: a transfer of ownership, a bargain purchase option, the lease term is 75% or more of the asset's estimated economic life, or the present value of the minimum lease payments is at least 90% of the fair value of the leased property.
- The **minimum lease payments** consist of the minimum rental payments and any bargain purchase option.
- A **lessor** determines whether a lease is classified as **capital** using the **same four criteria** as a lessee. A lessor further classifies all capital leases as either **direct financing leases** (lessor recognizes no dealer's profit) or **sales-type leases** (lessor recognizes dealer's profit).
- Leases that **do not meet** any of the four criteria for capitalization are classified as **operating leases** (by both lessors and lessees).

Core Concepts for Pensions and Other Postretirement Benefits

- The **projected benefit obligation** of a **defined benefit plan** is measured using assumptions as to future as well as past and current salary levels.
- The **calculation of the projected benefit obligation** at the end of a period is as follows: beginning PBO plus current service cost, plus prior service cost, minus benefits paid, plus or minus changes in assumption.
- The **accumulated benefit obligation** is the present value of **benefits accrued to date** based on past and current compensation levels.
- The **calculation of the net periodic pension cost** for a period is as follows: service cost plus interest cost, minus return on plan assets, plus and minus gains and losses, plus amortization of prior service cost.
- The **total net liability** reported on the **balance sheet** is the unfunded accumulated benefit obligation minus the fair value of the plan assets.

Core Concepts for Deferred Income Taxes

- Deferred income taxes are the **tax effects** of a current period transaction that **will not be felt** until a later period.
- A **temporary difference** arises when the recovery of an asset or the settlement of a liability has tax consequences.
- Such differences that result in **future taxable amounts** give rise to **deferred tax liabilities** in the balance sheet (e.g., installment sales). Differences that result in **future deductible amounts** give rise to **deferred tax assets** (e.g., subscriptions revenues received).
- A **permanent difference** arises when a difference in tax and GAAP recognition does not result in a balance sheet item (e.g., state and municipal bond interest received). Such a difference does not result in a deferred tax asset or liability.

Core Concepts for Discontinued Operations

- When a segment has been **disposed of** or is classified as **held for sale**, the results of its operations are **reported separately** in the income statement after results from continuing operations.
- The operating results of the disposed segment include any **loss for a writedown** or **gain for a writeup** to fair value of a long-lived asset.

Core Concepts for Extraordinary Items

- An extraordinary item is one that is **unusual in nature** and **infrequent in occurrence**.
- Extraordinary items are **reported separately** in the income statement, net of applicable taxes, after results of discontinued operations.

Core Concepts for Accounting Changes and Error Corrections

- An **accounting change** is (a) a change in accounting principle, (b) a change in the application of a principle, or (c) a change to a generally accepted principle when the principle previously used is no longer generally accepted.
- An accounting change is reported in the **balance sheet** by adjusting the **beginning balances** of assets and liabilities (of the earliest period presented) for the effect of the change **as if the change had been in effect** in earlier periods. (Formerly, the cumulative effect of an accounting change was presented in the income statement.)
- **Prior-period adjustments** are debited or credited, net of tax, to retained earnings and reported as adjustments in the statement of retained earnings.

Core Concepts for Early Extinguishment of Debt

- **Gains or losses** on the extinguishment of debt before maturity are **recognized in income** in the period of the extinguishment.

Core Concepts for Business Combinations

- A **business combination** takes place anytime an entity acquires the net assets or a controlling equity interest in another company.
- All such combinations are accounted for as **purchases**. (Formerly, combinations could, under certain circumstances, be accounted for as poolings-of-interests, in which the existing valuations of assets and liabilities were simply carried over to the new entity.)
- In general, the **cost of the acquired entity** is allocated to the assets acquired and liabilities assumed in accordance with their **fair values** at the acquisition date.
- Specifically, the FASB has provided guidance for the **valuation of individual assets** (work-in-process is booked at estimated selling price minus costs to complete, raw materials are booked at current replacement costs, etc.).
- Any **excess paid** by the acquiring entity over the assessed value of the acquired entity's net assets is recorded as an intangible asset named **goodwill**.

Core Concepts for Consolidated Financial Statements

- **Consolidated statements** are intended to present the results of operations, financial position, and cash flows of a parent and its subsidiaries **as if they were a single economic entity**.
- **Profits and losses** on transactions within the consolidated entity are **completely eliminated**, but the procedure varies depending on whether the transaction was **downstream** (parent to subsidiary) or **upstream** (subsidiary to parent).
- **Interentity debt transactions** are also eliminated.

Core Concepts for Derivatives and Hedging

- A **derivative** is an **investment transaction** in which the buyer purchases the right to a potential gain with a commitment for a potential loss. Examples include call options, forward contracts, futures contracts, interest rate swaps, and put options.
- Derivatives should be **contrasted with financial instruments**, such as cash, accounts receivable, and equity securities.
- Derivatives should be recognized as **assets or liabilities** in the balance sheet. **Fair value** is the only relevant measure for derivatives.
- **Hedging** is the purchase or sale of a derivative or other instrument in order to **neutralize the risk** of another transaction. Types include fair-value hedges and cash-flow hedges.

Part 2 – Section E.5. The SEC and its reporting requirements

The candidate should be able to:

a. identify the two major Acts establishing the SEC and its powers (Securities Act of 1933 and the Securities Exchange Act of 1934); and demonstrate knowledge of the major provisions of each

b. describe the general reporting requirements of public companies

c. define the integrated disclosure system, standardized financial statements, and Management Discussion and Analysis

d. identify other disclosures regarding business operations

e. identify and describe the SEC disclosure requirements, including the registration with the SEC (initial filing and subsequent filings when issuing securities), the annual report to the SEC or Form 10-K, the quarterly report or Form 10-Q, disclosure of material events or Form 8-K, and proxy statements and solicitations

f. identify and explain the major provisions of the Sarbanes-Oxley Act of 2002

g. identify the functions and responsibilities of the Public Company Accounting Oversight Board (PCAOB)

Core Concepts for The SEC and Its Reporting Standards

- The **Securities and Exchange Commission** was created by an Act of Congress to **regulate the trading of securities** and otherwise to enforce securities legislation.
- The **integrated disclosure system** regularizes the information that must be submitted by publicly traded companies.
- **Audited financial statements** along with management's discussion and analysis are inherent parts of the **basic information package**.
- **Form 10** is filed by companies that wish to register securities.
- **Form 10-K** is the annual report to the SEC. It must be certified by an independent accountant and filed within 90 days (60 days for most entities by 2006).
- **Form 10-Q** is the quarterly report. It need not be accompanied by an independent accountant's report, but it must be filed within 45 days (30 days beginning in 2006) of the end of each of the company's first three quarters.
- **Form 8-K** is a current report to disclose material events such as a change in control, bankruptcy or receivership, or the resignation of directors.

Part 2 – Section E.6. The annual report

The candidate should be able to:

    a.   identify audit services related to the annual report

    b.   identify the basic components of the annual report, including management's statement of responsibility for the financial statements and the independent auditor's report

    c.   describe the Audit Committee's level of responsibility for the integrity of the financial information presented in the annual reports

    d.   identify the Audit Committee's functions to include (1) nominating the public accounting firm that will conduct the annual external audit, (2) participating in the process of setting the scope of internal and external audits, and (3) inviting direct audit communications on major problems encountered during the course of internal and external audits

    e.   discuss how the audit opinion letter published in the annual report can impact the market perception of the firm

    f.   identify and describe other sections in the annual report, including the letter to shareholders, management discussion and analysis, and the statement on social responsibility

Core Concepts for The Annual Report

- The SEC generally delegates the authority to **promulgate external reporting standards** (through the FASB) to the accounting profession.

- The **Sarbanes-Oxley Act of 2002** requires public companies to include a statement in the annual reports affirming **management's responsibility** for internal control over financial reporting.

- The financial statements of a publicly traded company are accompanied by the **report of the independent external auditors**.

- The primary function of **external auditors** (independent public accountants) is to **attest** to the fair presentation of financial statements in all material respects in conformity with U.S. GAAP.

- The **standard audit reports** are the unqualified opinion, the unqualified opinion with explanatory language, the qualified opinion, the adverse opinion, and the disclaimer of opinion.

- The **unqualified opinion** asserts the auditors' conclusion that the financial statements are free of material misstatement. The other opinions are departures to varying degrees from this "clean" audit opinion.

- The **Sarbanes-Oxley Act** created the **Public Company Accounting Oversight Board** to register and monitor accounting firms that perform audits of publicly held companies.

- The Act also requires auditors to **attest to** whether **management's assessment** of its system of **internal control** over financial reporting is sound.

- The purpose of an audit committee (a subcommittee of outside directors) is to **help keep external and internal auditors independent of management** and to assure that the directors are exercising due care.

- The **Sarbanes-Oxley Act** requires **each member** of the audit committee, including at least one who is a financial expert, to be an **independent member** of the issuer's board of directors (an independent member is not affiliated with, and receives no compensation from, the issuer).

16.2 LIABILITIES, EQUITY, REVENUE RECOGNITION, AND OTHER ISSUES ESSAY QUESTIONS

Recall that your CMA Part 4 exam will probably contain six scenarios, with about three questions per scenario. There will be a recommended time allocation of 20 minutes, 30 minutes, or 45 minutes for each scenario and related questions.

One scenario will involve ethical issues, and probably one or two scenarios will include calculations and responses on a worksheet. Also, expect at least one scenario on organizational/behavioral topics. The remaining scenarios cover Parts 1, 2, and 3.

Scenario Title	Subtopic	Questions	Suggested Time
Davids Corporation	Leases	1, 2, 3	30 minutes
CJC, Inc.	Financial Reporting	4, 5, 6	30 minutes
DVS Industries	Revenue Recognition	7, 8	30 minutes
Multipro, Inc.	Segment Reporting	9, 10, 11	30 minutes
CDA Corporation	Pensions	12, 13, 14	30 minutes
Carmel Corporation	Reporting Contingencies	15, 16, 17	30 minutes
SEC Filings	SEC Filings	18, 19, 20, 21	30 minutes
Securities Regulation	Securities Regulation	22, 23, 24	30 minutes
Role of the SEC	Role of the SEC	25, 26, 27	30 minutes

Scenario for Essay Questions 1, 2, 3

The Davids Corporation is a diversified company with nationwide interests in commercial real estate developments, banking, copper mining, and metal fabrication. The company has offices and operating locations in major cities throughout the United States. Corporate headquarters for Davids Corporation is located in a metropolitan area of a midwestern state, and executives connected with various phases of company operations travel extensively. Corporate management is evaluating the feasibility of acquiring a business aircraft that can be used by company executives to expedite business travel to areas not adequately served by commercial airlines. Proposals for either leasing or purchasing a suitable aircraft have been analyzed, and the leasing proposal was considered to be more desirable.

The proposed lease agreement involves a twin-engine turboprop Viking that has a fair market value of $900,000. This plane would be leased for a period of 10 years beginning January 1 of next year. The lease agreement is cancelable only upon accidental destruction of the plane. An annual lease payment of $127,600 is due on January 1 of each year; the first payment is to be made on January 1 of next year. Maintenance operations are strictly scheduled by the lessor, and Davids Corporation will pay for these services as performed. Annual maintenance costs are $6,200. The lessor will pay all insurance premiums and local property taxes, which amount to a combined total of $3,600 annually and are included in the annual lease payment of $127,600. Upon expiration of the 10-year lease, Davids Corporation can purchase the Viking for $40,000. The estimated useful life of the plane is 15 years, and its salvage value in the used plane market is estimated to be $100,000 after 10 years. The salvage value probably will never be less than $75,000 if the engines are overhauled and maintained as prescribed by the manufacturer. If the purchase option is not exercised, possession of the plane will revert to the lessor, and there is no provision for renewing the lease agreement beyond its termination.

Davids Corporation can borrow $900,000 under a 10-year term loan agreement at an annual interest rate of 12%. The lessor's implicit interest rate is not expressly stated in the lease agreement, but this rate appears to be approximately 8% based on ten net rental payments of $124,000 per year and the initial market value of $900,000 for the plane. On January 1 of next year, the present value of all net rental payments and the purchase option of $40,000 is $800,000 using the 12% interest rate. The present value of all net rental payments and the $40,000 purchase option on January 1 of next year is $920,000 using the 8% interest rate implicit in the lease agreement. The financial vice-president has established that this lease agreement is a capital lease as defined in SFAS 13, "Accounting for Leases."

Questions

1. What is the appropriate amount that Davids Corporation should recognize for the leased aircraft on its Statement of Financial Position after the lease is signed?

2. Without prejudice to your answer in Question 1, assume that the annual lease payment is $127,600 as stated in the question, that the appropriate capitalized amount for the leased aircraft is $1,000,000 on January 1 of next year, and that the interest rate is 9%. How will the lease be reported in the December 31 of next year Statement of Financial Position and related Income Statement? (Ignore any income tax implications.)

3. Identify and explain the four factors that differentiate a capital lease from an operating lease.

Essay Questions 1, 2, 3 — Unofficial Answers

1.   The appropriate amount for the leased aircraft on Davids' Statement of Financial Position after the lease is signed is $900,000, the fair market value of the plane. In this case, fair market value is less than the present value of the net rental payments plus purchase option ($920,000). When this occurs, the asset is recorded at fair market value.

2.   The aircraft will be reflected on Davids' Statement of Financial Position as follows:

Noncurrent assets:

Leased property under capitalized lease	$1,000,000
Less accumulated amortization	61,667
	$ 938,333

Current liabilities:

Obligations under capitalized lease (Note A)

Interest payable	$ 78,840
Principal	45,160
	$124,000

Noncurrent liabilities:

Obligations under capitalized leases (Note A)	$830,840

The following items relating to the leased aircraft will be reflected on Davids Corporation's Income Statement:

Depreciation expense (Note A)	$61,667
Interest expense	78,840

Note A:

The company leases a Viking Turboprop aircraft under a capital lease. The lease runs until December 31, Year 10. The annual lease payment is paid in advance on January 1 and amounts to $127,600, of which $3,600 is for insurance and property taxes. The aircraft is being depreciated on the straight-line basis over the economic life of the asset. The depreciation on the aircraft included in the current year's depreciation expense and the accumulated amortization on the aircraft amount to $61,667.

Computations

Amortization		
Capitalized amount		$1,000,000
Salvage value		75,000
Depreciation base		$ 925,000
Economic life		15 yrs.
Annual amortization		$ 61,667
Liability amounts		
Lease liability 1/1/Year 1		$1,000,000
Payment 1/1/Year 1		124,000
Lease liability 12/31/Year 1		876,000
Lease payment due 1/1/Year 2	$124,000	
Interest on lease ($876,000 × .09)	78,840	
Reduction of principal		45,160
Noncurrent liability 12/31/Year 3		$ 830,840

3.   The four factors are to ensure that the party making use of the service utility of the asset is the party that carries the asset and any liability on its books. If at the inception of the lease agreement any one of the following four criteria is fulfilled, the lessee shall account for the arrangement as a capital lease.

   a.   <u>Ownership of the property is transferred to the lessee by the lease.</u> Such leases, in effect, are simply installment purchases and should be accounted for as any installment purchase.

   b.   <u>The lease contains a bargain purchase option.</u> A bargain purchase option is a provision allowing the lessee to purchase the property for a price that is enough lower than the expected fair value of the property at the date the option is exercisable to make exercise of the option virtually assured. Such an option makes the lease arrangement essentially an installment purchase.

   c.   <u>The lease term (including any bargain renewal options) is equal to 75% or more of the estimated economic life of the asset.</u> A bargain renewal option is a provision allowing the lessee to renew the lease for a rental which is enough lower than the expected fair rental of the property at the date the option is exercisable, as seen at the inception of the lease, to make exercise of the option virtually assured.

   d.   <u>The present value of the minimum lease payments (excluding executory costs) equals or exceeds 90% of the fair value of the leased property (less any investment tax credits applicable).</u> Minimum lease payments are discounted back at the lessee's incremental borrowing rate or the implicit rate used by the lessor, whichever is less. Such provisions make the lease, in essence, an installment purchase.

Scenario for Essay Questions 4, 5, 6

The owners of CJC, Inc., a privately held company, are considering a public offering of the company's common stock as a means of acquiring additional funding. Preparatory to making a decision about a public offering, the owners had a lengthy conversation with John Duncan, CJC's chief financial officer. Duncan informed the owners of the reporting requirements of the Securities and Exchange Commission, including the necessity for audited financial statements. At the request of the owners, Duncan also discussed the objectives of financial reporting, the sophistication of users of financial information, and the stewardship responsibilities of management, all of which are addressed in Statement of Financial Accounting Concepts No. 1, "Objectives of Financial Reporting by Business Enterprises."

Questions

4. Discuss the primary objectives of financial reporting.

5. Describe the level of sophistication that can be expected of the users of financial information.

6. Explain the stewardship responsibilities of management.

Essay Questions 4, 5, 6 — Unofficial Answers

4. The primary objectives of financial reporting are to provide information that is useful:

    a. To present any potential investors, creditors, and other users of financial statements in making rational investment and credit decisions.

    b. In assessing future cash flows related to the enterprise's operations and its ability to meet financial obligations and pay dividends.

    c. In assessing the economic resources of the enterprise and claims against these resources.

5. Although the level of sophistication related to business and financial accounting matters varies both within and between user groups, users are expected to possess a reasonable understanding of business and economic activities and are expected to be willing to study the information with reasonable diligence. Financial information is intended to be a useful tool to those who are able and willing to use it.

6. One of the results of the corporate form of organization has been the tendency to separate ownership from management. Thus, the stewardship function has been added to the management responsibilities of recording and reporting financial information. The stewardship responsibilities of management include the following:

    a. Periodic accountability to the owners not only for the custody and safekeeping of the company's resources but also for their efficient and profitable use.

    b. Accountability to prospective investors and to the general public when the company's securities are offered to the public.

Scenario for Essay Questions 7, 8

DVS Industries has three operating divisions -- Queenswood Construction Division, Paperback Publishing Division, and Protection Securities Division. Each division maintains its own accounting system and method of revenue recognition.

Queenswood Construction Division. During the fiscal year ended November 30, Queenswood Construction Division had one construction project in process. A $24,000,000 contract for construction of a civic center was granted on June 19, and construction began on August 1. Estimated costs of completion at the contract date were $20,000,000 over a two-year time period from the date of the contract. On November 30, construction costs of $6,000,000 had been incurred and progress billings of $6,600,000 had been made. The construction costs to complete the remainder of the project were reviewed on November 30, and were estimated to amount to only $12,000,000 due to an expected decline in raw materials costs. Revenue recognition is based upon a percentage-of-completion method.

Paperback Publishing Division. The Paperback Publishing Division sells novels to a few book distributors who in turn sell to national chains of bookstores. Paperback allows distributors to return up to 30% of sales, and distributors give the same terms to bookstores. While returns of individual titles fluctuate greatly, the returns from distributors have averaged 20% in each of the past five years. A total of $8,000,000 in paperback novel sales was made to distributors during the current year. On November 30, $3,000,000 of current year sales was still subject to return privileges over the next six months. The remaining $5,000,000 of current year sales had actual returns of 21%. Sales from the prior year totaling $2,000,000 were collected in the current year less 18% returns. This division records revenue according to the method referred to as revenue recognition when the right of return exists.

Protection Securities Division. Protection Securities Division works through manufacturers' agents in various cities. Orders for alarm systems and down payments are forwarded from agents, and the division ships the goods FOB factory directly to customers (usually police departments and security guard companies). Customers are billed directly for the balance due plus shipping costs. The firm received orders for $6,000,000 of goods during the fiscal year ended November 30. Down payments of $600,000 were received and $5,000,000 of goods were billed and shipped. Actual freight costs of $100,000 were billed. Commissions of 10% on product price are paid manufacturing agents after goods are shipped to customers. Such goods are warranted for 90 days after shipment, and warranty returns have been about 1% of sales. Revenue is recognized at the point of sale.

Questions

7. There are a variety of methods for revenue recognition. Define and describe each of the following methods of revenue recognition and indicate whether each is in accordance with generally accepted accounting principles.

     a. Point of sale

     b. Completion of production

     c. Percentage-of-completion

     d. Installment contract

8. Compute the revenue to be recognized in the current year for each of the three operating divisions in accordance with generally accepted accounting principles.

Essay Questions 7, 8 — Unofficial Answers

7. a. Point of sale method recognizes revenue when the earnings process is complete. This can be the date goods are delivered, when title passes, when services are rendered and billable, or as time passes (e.g., rent or royalty income). This method most closely follows the accrual accounting method and is in accordance with GAAP.

    b. The completion of production method recognizes revenue only when the project is complete. This is used primarily with short-term contracts, or long-term contracts when there is difficulty in estimating the costs remaining to complete a project. The advantage is that income is recognized on final results, not estimates. The disadvantage is that when the contract extends over more than one accounting period, performance on the project is not recognized and earnings are distorted.

    c. The percentage-of-completion method of revenue recognition is used on long-term projects, usually construction. To apply it, the following conditions must exist:

    1) A firm contract price with a high probability of collection
    2) A reasonably accurate estimate of costs (and, therefore, of gross profit)
    3) A way to reasonably estimate the extent of progress of the project

    Gross profit is recognized in proportion to the work completed. In the final period, the actual total profit is known, and the difference between this amount and profit recognized to date is shown as profit of the period. The method is in accordance with GAAP for long-term projects when estimates are dependable.

    d. The installment sales method is applicable when the sales price is received over an extended period of time. The installment method recognizes revenue as the cash is collected and is used when the collection of the sales price is not reasonably assured. This method is not in accordance with GAAP because it violates accrual basis accounting. The method can be used where collectibility is unsure.

8. <u>Queenswood Construction.</u> A change of cost estimates calls for a revision of revenue and profit to be recognized in the period in which the change was made.

Contract price		$24,000,000
Actual costs to 11/30	$ 6,000,000	
Estimated costs to complete	12,000,000	
Total cost		18,000,000
Estimated profit		$ 6,000,000
Percentage of contract completed ($6,000,000 ÷ 18,000,000)		33 1/3%
Revenue to be recognized in the current year ($24,000,000 × 1/3)		$ 8,000,000

<u>Paperback Publishing Division</u>

Sales – current year	$ 8,000,000
Less: Sales returns and allowances (20%)	1,600,000
Net sales – revenue to be recognized in the current year	$ 6,400,000

Although distributors can return up to 30% of sales, experience indicates that 20% of sales is the expected amount of returns. The 21% of returns on the initial $5,000,000 of the current year sales confirms that 20% of sales will provide a reasonable estimate.

<u>Protection Securities Division</u>

Revenue for the current year = $5,000,000

The revenue is the amount of goods actually billed and shipped when revenue is recognized at point of sale (terms are FOB factory). Down payments are not sales.

Scenario for Essay Questions 9, 10, 11

Multipro, Inc. manufactures a wide variety of pharmaceuticals, medical instruments, and other related medical supplies. Eighteen months ago, the company developed and began to market a new product line of antihistamine drugs under various trade names. Sales and profitability of this product line during the current fiscal year greatly exceeded management's expectations. The new product line will account for 10% of the company's total sales and 12% of the company's operating income for the fiscal year ending June 30. Management believes sales and profits will be significant for several years.

Multipro is concerned about its market position relative to its competitors should disclosure be made about the volume and profitability of its new product line in its annual financial statements. Management is not sure how the SFAS 14, "Financial Reporting for Segments of a Business Enterprise," applies in this case.

Questions

9. What is the purpose for requiring that segment information be disclosed in financial statements?

10. Identify and explain the factors that should be considered when attempting to decide how products should be grouped to determine a single business segment.

11. What options, if any, does Multipro, Inc. have regarding the disclosure of its new antihistamine product line? Explain your answer.

Essay Questions 9, 10, 11 — Unofficial Answers

9. The purpose for requiring segment information to be disclosed in financial statements is to assist financial statement users in analyzing and understanding the enterprise's financial statement by permitting better assessment of the enterprise's past performances and future prospects.

10. SFAS 14 states that no single set of characteristics is universally applicable in determining the segments of an enterprise nor can any one characteristic be used as the single determining characteristic in all cases. The determination of the segments appropriate for an enterprise is the responsibility of management; i.e., management should use its judgment in deciding how to report its segment information. Specific characteristics or sets of characteristics management can use in determining how to group its products into segments include the following:

   a. Use of existing profit centers.

   b. A segment shall be regarded as significant and identified as a reportable segment if one or more of the following are satisfied:

      1) 10% or more of the total revenue is derived from one segment.
      2) 10% of the operating profit (loss) of the total is contributed by the segment.
      3) 10% of the combined identifiable assets can be associated with the segment.

   c. Products can be grouped by industry classification systems such as the Standard Industrial Classification (SIC) or Enterprise Standard Industrial Classification (ESIC).

   d. Segments can be determined by the nature of the product. Related products and services have similar purposes or end uses. Thus, they may be expected to have similar rates or profitability, similar degrees of risk, and similar opportunities for growth.

11. The options available to Multipro, Inc. are

   a. Segment by product line -- antihistamines. This single product meets the 10% test and can be anticipated as a significant product line in the future.

   b. Segment by product group -- pharmaceuticals, medical instruments, and medical supplies. Antihistamines can be carried as a part of the pharmaceuticals group.

   c. Disaggregate pharmaceuticals into ethical and proprietary drugs and carry antihistamines under whichever industry segment is appropriate (probably proprietary drugs, in this case).

   d. Multipro must report revenue, profitability, and identifiable assets for each business segment. The products can be listed within the segment, however, it is not necessary to list specific sales revenue and net income figures for each product. Therefore, option (1) would disclose details management does not wish to reveal to competitors; options (2) and (3) would meet the segment objectives without revealing individual product data regarded as detrimental to the company.

Scenario for Essay Questions 12, 13, 14

The CDA Corporation, which has been in operation for the past 23 years, decided late last year to adopt, beginning on January 1 of the current year, a funded pension plan for its employees. The pension plan is to be noncontributory and will provide for vesting after 5 years of service by each eligible employee. A trust agreement has been entered into whereby a large national insurance company will receive the yearly pension fund contributions and administer the fund.

Management, through extended consultation with the fund trustee, internal accountants, and independent actuaries, arrived at the following conclusions:

1. The normal pension cost for the current year will be $30,000.

2. The present value of the past service cost at date of inception of the pension plan (January 1 of the current year) is $200,000.

3. Because of the large sum of money involved, the past service costs will be funded at a rate of $23,365 per year for the next fifteen years. The first payment will not be due until January 1 of next year.

4. In accordance with APB Opinion 8, the "unit credit method" of accounting for the pension costs will be followed. Pension costs will be amortized over a ten-year period. The ten-year accrual factor is $29,805 per year. Neither the maximum nor minimum amortization amounts as prescribed by APB Opinion 8 will be violated.

5. Where applicable, an 8% interest rate was assumed.

Questions

12. Define:

   a. Normal pension costs
   b. Past service costs

13. What amounts (use XXX if amount cannot be calculated) will be reported in the company's

   a. Income statement for the current year
   b. Balance sheet as of December 31 of the current year
   c. Notes to the statements

   Give account titles with the amounts.

14. What amounts (use XXX if amount cannot be calculated) will be reported in the company's

   a. Income statement for next year
   b. Balance sheet as of December 31 of next year
   c. Notes to the statements

   Give account titles with the amounts.

Essay Questions 12, 13, 14 — Unofficial Answers

12.   a.   Normal cost -- The annual cost assigned, under the actuarial cost method in use, to years subsequent to the inception of a pension plan or to a particular valuation date.

    b.   Past service cost -- Pension cost assigned, under the actuarial cost method in use, to years prior to the inception of a pension plan.

13.   a.   Pension expense $59,805
         (normal cost $30,000 and past service cost $29,805)

    b.   Deferred past service costs $ 6,440
        Due to pension trustee $53,365

    c.   The notes to the statements should disclose the existence of the plan, the company's accounting and funding policies, and the amount by which vested benefits exceed the total of the pension fund and balance sheet accruals less prepayments or deferred charges. In this case the amount cannot be calculated; therefore, the amount would be $XXX.

14.   a.   Pension expense $59,805
         Interest on unfunded past service costs
           ($6,440 × .08)   515

    b.   Deferred past service costs
         ($6,440 + $6,440 + $515) $13,395
        Due to pension trustee $53,365

    c.   The notes to the statements should disclose the existence of the plan, the company's accounting and funding policies, and the amount by which vested benefits exceed the total of the pension fund and balance sheet accruals less prepayments or deferred charges. In this case, the amount cannot be calculated; therefore, the amount would be $XXX.

Scenario for Essay Questions 15, 16, 17

Carmel Corporation is in the process of preparing its financial statements for the fiscal year ended May 31. The assistant controller, Ron Singleton, has discovered several situations that may require adjustments to Carmel's records.

- Due to political developments in the Middle East, Michael McKeon, division manager of foreign operations, believes the possibility of expropriation of one of its foreign facilities exists. The book value of this facility is $2,400,000.

- Carmel manufactures a car wax. In June of last year, Carmel changed suppliers for one of the ingredients in the car wax. Shortly thereafter, customers began complaining that the wax caused the finish on their cars to become cloudy. In November of last year, the company recalled the products manufactured with this ingredient and changed back to the original supplier. Carmel's lawyers believe it is probable that the company will lose the $2 million class action suit that was filed by a group representing the consumers who use Carmel's car wax. However, the lawyers believe the suit will be settled for $326,000, the estimated cost to correct the problem for the cars affected.

- Carmel is the plaintiff in a lawsuit against the supplier of the defective car wax ingredient. Carmel's lawyers believe it is highly probable that the company will win the suit and recover the $375,000 lost as a result of the customers' lawsuit and other expenses associated with recalling the product.

- Carmel also manufactures portable facsimile machines that sell for $245 each. The machines are covered by an 18-month warranty which includes parts and labor. The Production Department estimates that the warranty cost for machines sold during the fiscal year will be $102,800.

Questions

15. Describe the conditions that existed in financial reporting that resulted in the promulgation of Statement of Financial Accounting Standards No. 5 (SFAS 5), *Accounting for Contingencies*.

16. Using SFAS 5, *Accounting for Contingencies*,

   a. Define the term "contingency" as used in accounting, and
   b. Describe the conditions that must be present for recognition of (a) a gain contingency and (b) a loss contingency.

17. Describe how the situations presented above would be treated in the May 31 financial statements and footnotes of Carmel Corporation based on SFAS 5, *Accounting for Contingencies*.

Essay Questions 15, 16, 17 — Unofficial Answers

15.   Statement of Financial Accounting Standards No. 5 (SFAS 5), *Accounting for Contingencies*, was promulgated as business entities previously tended to refrain from disclosing loss contingencies and to record gains before settlement. In many cases, losses were recorded only when an asset was actually impaired or a liability was actually incurred, while gains were recorded before the actual receipt of an asset or settlement of a contingency. As a result, the users of financial information depended on inflated financial information in making business decisions. In some cases, the adverse effects of these business decisions brought pressure on the accounting profession to require more complete disclosure.

16.   a.   According to SFAS 5, a contingency is defined as an existing condition, situation, or set of circumstances involving uncertainty as to possible gain or loss to an enterprise that will ultimately be resolved when one or more future events occur or fail to occur.

       b.   Gain contingencies should not be recognized in the financial statements because to do so would recognize income prior to realization. Gain contingencies may be disclosed in the footnotes when there is a high probability that the contingency will become a reality.

             An estimated loss from a loss contingency should be recognized in the financial statements if both of the following conditions are met:

             1)   Information available prior to financial statement issuance indicates that it is probable that a liability has been incurred at the date of the financial statements.

             2)   The amount of the loss can be reasonably estimated. Footnote disclosure is required for loss contingencies not meeting both these conditions if there is a reasonable possibility that a loss may have been incurred.

17.   According to SFAS 5, the situations encountered by Carmel Corporation should be treated in the financial statements as follows:

       a.   The contingent loss due to the possible expropriation of foreign facilities should not be recognized in the financial statements since the loss is not described as probable. If the loss is either probable or estimable, but not both, or if there is at least a reasonable possibility that a liability may have been incurred, disclosure should be made in the footnotes of the nature of the contingency and an estimated range of the possible loss or a statement that an estimate cannot be made.

       b.   Because it is probable at the financial statement date that a liability has been incurred and because the amount is subject to reasonable estimation, the contingent liability for the customers' lawsuit should be recognized as an estimated liability and as an estimated loss in the amount of $326,000.

       c.   The contingent gain from the lawsuit against the supplier should not be recognized in the financial statements until a verdict is returned in the lawsuit. However, since it is highly probable that the company will win the lawsuit, the contingency gain may be disclosed in the footnotes, provided the information disclosed is not misleading to the users of the financial statements.

       d.   Carmel Corporation should recognize a contingent liability for the obligations related to product warranties, as it is probable that customers will make claims under the warranty conditions and a reasonable estimate of the costs involved can be made. A warranty expense and an estimated liability for $102,800 should be reasonable.

Scenario for Essay Questions 18, 19, 20, 21

The purpose of the Securities Act of 1933 is to regulate the initial offering of a firm's securities by ensuring that investors are given full and fair disclosure of all pertinent information about the firm. The Securities Exchange Act of 1934 was passed to regulate the trading of securities on secondary markets and to eliminate abuses in the trading of securities after their initial distribution. To accomplish these objectives, the 1934 Act created the Securities and Exchange Commission (SEC). Under the auspices of the SEC, public companies must not only register their securities but must also periodically prepare and file Forms 8-K, 10-K, and 10-Q.

Questions

18. With regard to Form 8-K, discuss the

    a.   Purpose of the report

    b.   Timing of the report

    c.   Format of the report

    d.   Role of financial statements in the filing of the report

19. Identify five circumstances under which the Securities and Exchange Commission requires the filing of Form 8-K.

20. Discuss how the filing of Form 8-K fosters the purpose of the Securities and Exchange Commission.

21. Does the Securities and Exchange Commission pass judgment on securities based on information contained in periodic reports? Explain your answer.

Essay Questions 18, 19, 20, 21 — Unofficial Answers

18.   a.   The purpose of Form 8-K, called the Current Report, is to ensure that any significant event affecting a firm's policies or financial position is immediately reported to the SEC. Covering the period since the filing of the latest annual or quarterly report, Form 8-K provides a continuous stream of material information concerning specified events between filings.

b.   Form 8-K must be filed with the SEC within 15 days after the occurrence of a reportable event (5 business days after a change in independent accountants or the resignation of a director). Violation of the 8-K filing requirement may jeopardize a registrant's status.

c.   Form 8-K is a narrative report with sufficient flexibility to permit management to describe any significant events. The first page must contain the standard 8-K heading identifying the reporting corporation, and the body of the report details the specified event or events in accordance with the disclosure requirements outlined in the regulations for each event. The corporation may include any other information, financial or otherwise, it deems appropriate for a complete description of the event. The report must be signed by an officer of the corporation.

d.   The inclusion of audited and pro forma financial statements is only required when reporting the acquisition of a business. Financial statements may be included in a Form 8-K in order to clarify the effect of any event on the corporation. In general practice, financial statements are included if an event is deemed to have a material financial impact.

19.   Five circumstances under which the Securities and Exchange Commission requires the filing of Form 8-K include

a.   Changes in the control of the registrant
b.   Acquisitions or dispositions of assets
c.   Material legal proceedings
d.   Bankruptcy or receivership
e.   Changes in the registrant's certifying accountants

20.   The role of the SEC is to regulate the issuance and trading of securities. By requiring the disclosure of adequate information, it enables investors to make informed judgments about securities. Form 8-K fosters this purpose by requiring firms to report significant events as they occur to the investing public.

21.   The purpose of the securities laws is not to have the SEC judge the merits of securities offered for sale. Through its strict disclosure and reporting requirements, the SEC attempts to make certain that the investor has the opportunity to judge the merits of securities on the basis of full disclosure of the pertinent facts. The SEC does have the power to suspend trading in securities of companies that fail to make full and accurate reports; however, these actions are not based on the merits of the securities but on the companies' failures to comply with reporting regulations.

Scenario for Essay Questions 22, 23, 24

During the late 1920s, approximately 55% of all personal savings in the United States were used to purchase securities. Public confidence in the business community was extremely high as stock values doubled and tripled in short periods of time. The road to wealth was believed to be through the stock market, and everyone who was able participated. Thus, the public was severely affected when the Dow Jones Industrial Average fell 89% between 1929 and 1933. The public outcry arising from this decline in stock prices motivated the passage of major federal laws regulating the securities industry.

Questions

22. Describe the investment practices of the 1920s that contributed to the erosion of the stock market.

23. Explain the basic objectives of each of the following:

    a. Securities Act of 1933
    b. Securities Exchange Act of 1934

24. More recent legislation has resulted from abuses in the securities industry. Explain the provisions of each of the following:

    a. Foreign Corrupt Practices Act of 1977
    b. Insider Trading Sanctions Act of 1984

Essay Questions 22, 23, 24 — Unofficial Answers

22. Investment practices of the 1920s that contributed to the erosion of the stock market include the following:

   a.   The prices of securities were manipulated through the use of "wash sales" or "matched orders."

   Brokers or dealers engaged in prearranged buy and sell orders that created the impression of activity and drove up prices. When the public began buying, driving prices up even higher, the brokers and dealers would sell, making huge profits before prices fell back to market level.

   b.   False or misleading financial statements were issued to lure unwary investors.

   c.   The excessive use of credit to finance speculative activities served to undermine the market. There was no limit to the amount of credit or "margin" that a broker could extend to a customer. As a result, a slight decline in market prices often caused overextended customers to sell when margins could not be covered, thus further reducing prices.

   d.   Corporate officials and other "insiders" misused information about corporate activities to take advantage of fluctuations in stock prices.

23.   a.   The objectives of the Securities Act of 1933 are to

   1)   Provide investors with financial and other information concerning the initial offering of securities for sale, thus ensuring full and fair disclosure. Companies were required to file a registration statement and a prospectus for review.

   2)   Prohibit misrepresentation, deceit, and other fraudulent acts and practices in the sale of securities.

   b.   The objectives of the Securities Exchange Act of 1934 are to

   1)   Regulate the trading of securities on secondary markets by requiring the registration of securities traded on any national exchange.

   2)   Create a regulatory agency, the Securities and Exchange Commission, to administer the requirements of both the 1933 and 1934 acts.

24.   a.   The provisions of the Foreign Corrupt Practices Act of 1977 include the requirement for public companies to devise and maintain a system of internal accounting controls to provide reasonable assurance that transactions are properly authorized, recorded, and accounted for.

   b.   The provisions of the Insider Trading Sanctions Act of 1984 include increased penalties against persons who profit from illegal use of insider information. Fines of up to three times the profits gained or losses avoided can be imposed on those who misuse nonpublic information.

Scenario for Essay Questions 25, 26, 27

The U.S. Securities and Exchange Commission (SEC) was created in 1934 and consists of five commissioners and a large professional staff. The SEC professional staff is organized into five divisions and several principal offices. The primary objective of the SEC is to support fair securities markets. The SEC also strives to foster enlightened shareholder participation in corporate decisions of publicly traded companies. The SEC has a significant presence in financial markets, the development of accounting practices, and corporation-shareholder relations, and has the power to exert influence on entities whose actions lie within the scope of its authority.

Questions

25. Explain where the Securities and Exchange Commission receives its authority.

26. Describe the official role of the Securities and Exchange Commission in the development of financial accounting theory and practices.

27. Discuss the interrelationship between the Securities and Exchange Commission and Financial Accounting Standards Board with respect to the development and establishment of financial accounting theory and practices.

Essay Questions 25, 26, 27 — Unofficial Answers

25. The Securities and Exchange Commission (SEC) is an independent federal agency that receives authority from federal legislation enacted by Congress. The Securities and Exchange Act of 1934 created the SEC.

26. As a result of the Securities and Exchange Act of 1934, the SEC has legal authority relative to accounting practices. The U.S. Congress has given the SEC broad regulatory power to control accounting principles and procedures in order to fulfill its goal of full and fair disclosure.

27. There is no direct relationship, as the SEC was created by Congress and the Financial Accounting Standards Board (FASB) was created by the private sector. However, the SEC historically has followed a policy of relying on the private sector to establish financial accounting and reporting standards known as generally accepted accounting principles (GAAP). The SEC does not necessarily agree with all of the pronouncements of the FASB. In cases of unresolved differences, the SEC rules take precedence over FASB rules for companies within SEC jurisdiction.

Consider using Gleim's *CMA Test Prep* for interactive testing with **hundreds of multiple-choice questions** as an additional method of knowledge transfer in your quest to pass Part 4.

STUDY UNIT SEVENTEEN
CMA PART 3 REVIEW – STRATEGIC PLANNING
AND STRATEGIC MARKETING

(12 pages of outline)

Part 3 of the CMA exam is titled **Strategic Management**. This study unit is a review of these sections:

A.   **Strategic Planning.** Strategic and tactical planning; manufacturing paradigms such as JIT, MRP, and theory of constraints; value chain analysis; benchmarking; ABM and continuous improvement.

B.   **Strategic Marketing.** Strategic role of marketing; market segmentation; managing products and services; pricing strategies; promotional mix and distribution strategy.

This study unit presents the IMA's Learning Outcome Statements and Gleim Core Concepts relevant to these sections. Bear in mind that **all topics** on Part 4 of the exam are tested at **skill level C** (all six skill types required).

17.1 STRATEGIC PLANNING REVIEW

Part 3 – Section A.1. Strategic and tactical planning

The candidate should be able to:

a.   discuss how strategic planning determines the path an organization chooses for attaining its long-term goals and missions

b.   identify the time frame appropriate for a strategic plan

c.   identify the external factors that should be analyzed during the strategic planning process and understand how this analysis leads to recognition of organizational opportunities, limitations, and threats

d.   identify the internal factors that should be analyzed during the strategic planning process and explain how this analysis leads to recognition of organizational strengths, weaknesses, and competitive advantages

e.   demonstrate an understanding that the analysis of external and internal factors leads to the development of the overall organizational mission and that this mission leads to the formulation of long-term business objectives such as business diversification, the addition or deletion of product lines, or the penetration of new markets

f.   identify the role of capital budgeting and capacity planning in the strategic planning process

g.   explain why short-term objectives, tactics for achieving these objectives, and operational planning (master budget) must be congruent with the strategic plan and contribute to the achievement of long-term strategic goals

h.   explain why performance measurement and other reporting systems must be congruent with and support measurement of progress on strategic and operational measures

i.   identify the characteristics of successful strategic/tactical planning

j.   define contingency planning and discuss its importance, particularly where changes in external factors might adversely impact strategic plans

Core Concepts for Strategic and Tactical Planning

- **Strategic planning** is a function of **strategic management**, which is the continuing process of pursuing a favorable competitive fit between the firm and its dynamic environment.

- A common **classification of strategies** is: corporate strategies, competitive strategies, and functional strategies.

- **Strategic planning** follows a formal five-step process: (1) formulate the mission statement, (2) analyze the firm's internal environment, (3) analyze the firm's external environment, (4) select appropriate strategies and create strategic business units, and (5) implement the chosen strategies.

- A **situational analysis** (also called a SWOT analysis) considers organizational **strengths and weaknesses** and their interactions with **opportunities and threats**.

- Strengths and weaknesses are inherent in the organization's **internal environment**; opportunities and threats are aspects of the **external environment**.

- A firm's **core competencies** are the source of its competitive advantages.

- **Strategic controls** should be established to monitor progress, isolate problems, identify invalid assumptions, and take prompt corrective action.

- **Michael E. Porter's comprehensive model** of the structure of industries and competition provides a tool for understanding the **external factors** analyzed during strategic planning.

- The **five competitive forces** named by Porter are: (1) rivalry among existing firms; (2) threats of, and barriers to, entry; (3) threat of substitute goods and services; (4) threat of buyers' bargaining power; and (5) threat of suppliers' bargaining power.

- **Premises** are the underlying **assumptions** about the expected environment in which plans will operate.

- Managers should ask, "What internal and external factors would influence the actions planned for this organization (division, department, program)?" Premises must be considered at all levels of the organization.

- A **mission statement** is a formal, written document that defines the organization's purpose in society.

- Management's primary task is to **reach organizational objectives** effectively and efficiently.

- **Effectiveness** is the degree to which the objective is accomplished. **Efficiency** is maximizing the output for a given quantity of input.

- Each **subunit** of an organization may have its own objectives. Broad objectives should be established at the top and retranslated in more specific terms as they are communicated downward in a **means-end hierarchy**.

- **Policies** are general statements that guide thinking and action in decision making. **Procedures** are specific directives that define how work is to be done. **Rules** are specific, detailed guides that restrict behavior.

- A **program** is an organized set of objectives, policies, procedures, and rules designed to carry out a given course of action.

- A **budget** is a plan that contains a quantitative statement of expected results. A budget may be defined as a quantified program.

- The **master budget** encompasses the organization's **operating** and **financial plans** for a specified period.

- Budgets serve **multiple functions**, e.g., they quantify objectives and the means for achieving them and provide a means for communicating the organization's objectives to all levels of personnel.

- **Short-range, tactical, or operational planning** is usually considered to be for **one year or less** concerning such matters as production, materials procurement, expenses and revenues, and cash flows.

- **Strategic, or long-range, planning** is for periods from one to **as many as 20 years** (although 10 is more common) concerning such matters as new product development, capital budgeting, major financing, and mergers and acquisitions.

- **Contingency planning** is based on different sets of premises. It stipulates different sets of actions for management based on these premises.

- Although planning and objective-setting are necessarily top-down processes, the **lowest possible** relevant units of management should be **involved in the planning process**.

Part 3 – Section A.2. Manufacturing paradigms

The candidate should be able to:

a. define a just-in-time system and describe its central purpose

b. identify the operational benefits of implementing a just-in-time system

c. define the term kanban and describe how kanban is used in a just-in-time system

d. demonstrate an understanding of work cells and how they relate to just-in-time processes

e. define material resource planning (MRP) and identify its benefits

f. calculate subunits needed to complete an order for a finished product using MRP

g. demonstrate an understanding of the concept of outsourcing and identify the benefits and limitations of choosing this option

h. demonstrate an understanding of the theory of constraints and the steps involved in theory of constraints analysis

i. define and calculate throughput contribution and understand its relationship to the theory of constraints

j. demonstrate an understanding of a drum-buffer-rope system as a tool for managing product flow

k. discuss how the theory of constraints and activity-based costing are complementary analytical tools

l. identify other contemporary productivity concepts such as automation and the use of robots, computer-aided design, computer-integrated manufacturing, and flexible manufacturing systems

Core Concepts for Manufacturing Paradigms

- A just-in-time inventory management system **limits the output** of each function to the immediate demand of the next function. The accompanying **reductions in inventory levels** result in less money invested in idle assets.

- High inventory levels often **mask production problems** because defective parts can be overlooked when plenty of good parts are available.

- Higher productivity, reduced order costs as well as carrying costs, faster and cheaper setups, shorter manufacturing cycle times, better due date performance, improved quality, and more flexible processes are **objectives of JIT methods**.

- **Minimization of inventory** is a goal because many inventory-related activities are viewed as nonvalue-added. JIT is a **pull system**; items are pulled through production by current demand, not pushed through by anticipated demand.

- **Frequent receipt of deliveries** from suppliers often means less need for a sophisticated inventory control system and for control personnel. JIT also may **eliminate central receiving areas**, hard copy receiving reports, and storage areas. A central warehouse is not needed because deliveries are made by suppliers directly to the area of production.

- **Kanban**, a Japanese term meaning ticket, is one of the many elements of the JIT system as it was developed by the Toyota Motor Corporation. Tickets (also described as cards or markers) control the flow of production or parts so that they are **produced or obtained in the needed amounts** at the needed times.

- JIT also encompasses changes in the **production process** itself. To implement this approach and to eliminate waste of materials, labor, factory space, and machine usage, the **factory is reorganized** to permit what is often called **lean production**.

- A **materials requirements planning (MRP)** system enables a company to efficiently fulfill the requirements of the master production schedule by coordinating both the manufacture of component parts for finished goods and the arrival of the raw materials necessary to create the intermediate components.

- MRP is a **push system**, that is, the demand for raw materials is driven by the forecasted demand for the final product, which can be programmed into the computer.

- **Manufacturing resource planning (MRP II)** is a closed-loop manufacturing system that integrates all facets of a manufacturing business, including production, sales, inventories, schedules, and cash flows. The **same system** is used for both the **financial reporting and managing operations** (both use the same transactions and numbers).

- **Outsourcing** is the management or day-to-day execution of an entire business function by a third-party service provider. Outsourced services may be provided on or off premises, in the same country, or in a separate country.

- The basic premise of the **theory of constraints (TOC)** as applied to business is that improving any process is best done not by trying to maximize efficiency in every part of the process, but by focusing on the **handful of factors** that are crucial, called **constraints**. Increasing the efficiency of processes that are not constraints merely creates backup in the system.

- The **steps in a TOC analysis** are: identify the bottleneck operation (the constraint); determine the most profitable profit mix given the constraint; maximize product flow through the bottleneck; increase capacity at the bottleneck; and redesign the manufacturing process.

- A basic principle of TOC analysis is that short-term profit maximization requires maximizing the **contribution margin through the constraint**, called the **throughput contribution** or throughput margin.

- **Throughput costing**, sometimes called **supervariable costing**, recognizes **only direct materials costs** as being truly variable and thus relevant to the calculation of throughput contribution. All other manufacturing costs are ignored because they are considered fixed in the short run.

- Production flow is managed using the **drum-buffer-rope** (DBR) system. The drum is the bottleneck operation, the buffer is the minimal amount of work-in-process input to the drum, and the rope is the sequence of activities preceding and including the bottleneck that must be coordinated.

- Modern manufacturing environments impose control and improve quality through **automation**, or the substitution of machines for humans. An example of the use of automation and advanced technologies is **flexible manufacturing**, which is the capacity of computer-controlled machinery to perform many different programmed functions.

- A **computer-integrated manufacturing (CIM)** system involves designing products using **computer-aided design (CAD)**, testing the design using computer-aided engineering (CAE), manufacturing products using computer-aided manufacturing (CAM), and integrating all components with a computerized information system.

- CIM entails a **holistic approach** to manufacturing in which design is translated into product by **centralized processing and robotics**.

Part 3 – Section A.3. Business process performance

The candidate should be able to:

a.   define value chain analysis

b.   identify the steps in value chain analysis

c.   demonstrate an understanding of how value chain analysis is used to better understand a firm's competitive advantage

d.   define a value-added activity and explain how the value-added concept is related to improving performance

e.   demonstrate an understanding of process analysis and how to improve business process performance through business process reengineering

f.   analyze a sequence of tasks, activities, and processes

g.   define the Pareto principle

h.   demonstrate an understanding of benchmarking process performance

i.   identify the benefits of benchmarking in creating a competitive advantage

j.   apply activity-based management principles to recommend process performance improvements

k.   demonstrate an understanding of the relationship among continuous improvement techniques, activity-based management, and quality performance

l.   demonstrate an understanding of the concept of continuous improvement (kaizen) and how it relates to implementing ideal standards and quality improvements

m.   define best practice analysis and discuss how it can be used by an organization to improve performance

Core Concepts for Business Process Performance

- The **value chain** is a model for depicting the way in which every function in a company adds value to the final product. **Primary activities** (R&D, manufacturing, etc.) deal with the product directly. **Support activities** (human resources, inventory management, etc.) lend aid to the primary activity functions.

- The **supply chain** is the flow of materials and services from their original sources to final consumers. Moreover, it usually encompasses more than one firm.

- **Value engineering** is a means of reaching targeted cost levels. It is a systematic approach to assessing all aspects of the value chain cost buildup for a product. The purpose is to minimize costs without sacrificing customer satisfaction. Value engineering requires distinguishing between **cost incurrence** and **locked-in costs**.

- **Cost incurrence** is the actual use of resources, but **locked-in (designed-in)** costs will result in the use of resources in the future as a result of past decisions. Thus, value engineering emphasizes **controlling costs at the design stage**, that is, before they are locked in.

- **Life-cycle costing** is sometimes used as a basis for cost planning and product pricing. Life-cycle costing estimates a product's revenues and expenses over its expected life cycle. The result is to **highlight upstream and downstream costs** that often receive insufficient attention in the cost planning process.

- **Process value analysis** is a comprehensive understanding of how an organization generates its output. It involves a determination of which activities that use resources are **value-adding** or **nonvalue-adding** and how the latter may be reduced or eliminated.

- Technological advances have increased the popularity of **total quality management (TQM)** techniques and **business process reengineering**. Reengineering should be contrasted with **process improvement**, which consists of incremental but constant changes that improve efficiency.

- **Pareto analysis** is based on the concept that about 80% of results or effects are caused by about 20% of people or events. Thus, managers should concentrate on the relatively few people or events that have the **most significant effects**.

- **Benchmarking** is an ongoing process that entails quantitative and qualitative measurement of the difference between the company's performance of an activity and the performance by the best in the world.

- **Kaizen** is the Japanese word for the continuous pursuit of improvement in every aspect of organizational operations.

- The trend in managerial performance evaluation is the **balanced scorecard** approach. Multiple measures of performance permit a determination as to whether a manager is achieving certain objectives at the expense of others that may be equally or more important. The scorecard is a **goal congruence tool** that informs managers about the nonfinancial factors that top management believes to be important.

17.2 STRATEGIC PLANNING ESSAY QUESTIONS

Recall that your CMA Part 4 exam will probably contain six scenarios, with about three questions per scenario. There will be a recommended time allocation of 20 minutes, 30 minutes, or 45 minutes for each scenario and related questions.

One scenario will involve ethical issues, and probably one or two scenarios will include calculations and responses on a worksheet. Also, expect at least one scenario on organizational/behavioral topics. The remaining scenarios cover Parts 1, 2, and 3.

Scenario Title	Subtopic	Questions	Suggested Time
Bio-Cure, Inc.	Strategic Planning	1, 2, 3, 4	30 minutes
Megafilters, Inc.	Just-In-Time Manufacturing	5, 6, 7	30 minutes
Bakker Industries	Production Capacity and Demand	8, 9	30 minutes

Scenario for Essay Questions 1, 2, 3, 4

Bio-Cure, Inc. (BCI) was established 5 years ago by several medical scientists who developed a potential cure for Acquired Immune Deficiency Syndrome (AIDS). As a by-product of their experimentation, they also developed several other vaccines that could have relatively significant market potential. BCI was originally funded by the founding scientists who planned BCI's activities at periodic brainstorming sessions.

During the past year, BCI was in need of additional financing to continue its research efforts as the company's products have not yet been brought to market. A major financial institution brought BCI and a venture capital group together. The venture capital group provided a sizable capital infusion for a controlling interest in BCI. As part of its normal management procedures to control its investments, the venture capital group developed a formal strategic plan for BCI, which included a mission statement and strategic goals for each functional area of BCI. The president of the venture capital group forwarded the strategic plan by mail to BCI's management.

Questions

1. Identify at least four advantages of planning through brainstorming sessions.

2. Identify at least four advantages of formal organizational planning.

3. Provide at least three reasons why the management group of Bio-Cure, Inc. is likely to resist the change in planning technique.

4. Recommend at least two ways that communication could have been improved, thereby making the change in planning technique more acceptable to Bio-Cure, Inc.'s management group.

Essay Questions 1, 2, 3, 4 — Unofficial Answers

1. At least four advantages of planning through brainstorming sessions include

    a. Ideas that are valuable and often better in quality than those generated separately, as one idea leads to another or pieces of one combine with another

    b. Using other people for ideas by bringing the talents of various individuals with different backgrounds together

    c. Participation leading to more ideas that will give rise to more alternatives

    d. Clustering of ideas before evaluation, i.e., short improvements, capital requirements, employee knowledge, attitudes, etc.

2. At least four advantages of formal organizational planning include

    a. Providing structure to the company, assigning responsibilities, and focusing energy and efforts. A chain of command is in place.

    b. Encouraging an analysis of the organization's environment, i.e., concepts of market and technology translated into specific products, estimates of product demand, and governmental impacts.

    c. Encouraging analyses of organizational strengths and weaknesses, i.e., product and market capabilities, production capacity, technical skills, organizational structure, and human resources.

    d. Generating, evaluating, and selecting alternative strategies in order to take advantage of opportunities.

3. At least three reasons why the management group of Bio-Cure, Inc. is likely to resist the change in the planning technique include

    a. A general feeling that the plan is imposed by outsiders, which could lead to anger, fear, and mistrust

    b. Displeasure, as the imposed plan may stymie the flexibility and creativity that apparently existed before, particularly from a scientific-oriented research group

    c. A change in organizational culture

4. At least two ways that communication could have been improved, thereby making the change in planning technique more acceptable to Bio-Cure, Inc.'s management group, include

    a. The president of the venture capital group calling a meeting of everyone to explain the overriding organizational, functional, and integration strategies and that planning is a dynamic process requiring revision as new information is developed

    b. Encouraging feedback and participation from the managers responsible for implementing the plans

Scenario for Essay Questions 5, 6, 7

The management at Megafilters, Inc. has been discussing the possible implementation of a just-in-time (JIT) production system at its Illinois plant, where oil filters and air filters for heavy construction equipment and large, off-the-road vehicles are manufactured. The Metal Stamping Department at the Illinois plant has already instituted a JIT system for controlling raw materials inventory, but the remainder of the plant is still discussing how to proceed with the implementation of this concept. Some of the other department managers have grown increasingly cautious about the JIT process after hearing about the problems that have arisen in the Metal Stamping Department.

Robert Goertz, manager of the Illinois plant, is a strong proponent of the JIT production system and recently made the following statement at a meeting of all departmental managers: "Just-in-time is often referred to as a management philosophy of doing business rather than a technique for improving efficiency of the plant floor. We will all have to make many changes in the way we think about our employees, our suppliers, and our customers if we are going to be successful in using just-in-time procedures. Rather than dwelling on some of the negative things you have heard from the Metal Stamping Department, I want each of you to prepare a list of things we can do to make a smooth transition to the just-in-time philosophy of management for the rest of the plant."

Questions

5. The just-in-time (JIT) management philosophy emphasizes objectives for the general improvement of a production system. Describe several important objectives of this philosophy.

6. Discuss several actions that Megafilters, Inc. can take to ease the transition to a just-in-time (JIT) production system at the Illinois plant.

7. In order for the just-in-time (JIT) production system to be successful, Megafilters, Inc. must establish appropriate relationships with its vendors, employees, and customers. Describe each of these three relationships.

Essay Questions 5, 6, 7 — Unofficial Answers

5. The objectives for the general improvement of a production system as emphasized in the just-in-time (JIT) management philosophy include

    a. Flowing product continuously through the plant and minimizing the investment in raw materials, work-in-process, and finished goods inventories

    b. Making production operations in the plant more efficient by redesigning work stations, simplifying the environment, and reducing both set-up and lead times

    c. Increasing the attention to quality control, reducing obsolescence and waste, and identifying non-value-added cost drivers (i.e., nonproductive labor, insurance, taxes) that can be eliminated

6. Megafilters, Inc. can take the following actions to ease the transition to a just-in-time (JIT) production system at the Illinois plant:

    a. Communicate to employees, customers, and vendors the corporate objectives and plans for implementing the JIT production system.

    b. Elicit employee participation in implementing the JIT system and train employees on the necessary tools (i.e., computers).

    c. Chart the production-process flows through the plant and develop statistical measurement and control procedures. Simplify processing and identify and alleviate cost drivers, non-value-added activities, and waste.

    d. Obtain competitive bids and JIT proposals from several vendors for each material, selecting the few who will reduce lead times, increase the quality of raw materials, and comply with strict delivery schedules.

7. Megafilters, Inc. must establish the following appropriate relationships in order to successfully implement the just-in-time (JIT) production system:

    a. Vendors

        1) Reduce the number of vendors to those who will be highly dependable and reliable.

        2) Commit the vendor to high quality standards by shifting responsibility for production problems to the suppliers (i.e., defective parts).

    b. Employees

        1) Develop trust and communication with the employees to obtain team participation in the initial plan and elicit feedback in the future.

        2) Increase the employees' responsibility to assist in improving operations and quality while reducing cost drivers.

        3) Treat employees as partners in the process, eliciting their commitment.

    c. Customers

        1) Develop trust and communication for including the customers' participation in the initial plan and eliciting feedback in the future.

        2) Ensure that Megafilters is fulfilling the customers' needs and demands.

        3) Build a team spirit through assurances that the company will meet the customers' demands at a competitive price. Employ the customer as a partner in the process (i.e., wait together for delayed deliveries, in order to keep costs at a minimum).

Scenario for Essay Questions 8, 9

Bakker Industries sells three products (Products 611, 613, and 615) that it manufactures in a factory consisting of four departments (Departments 1 through 4). Both labor and machine times are applied to the products in each of the four departments. Neither machines nor labor can be switched from one department to another.

Bakker's management is planning its production schedule for the next several months. There are labor shortages in the community. Some of the machines will be out of service for overhauling. Available machine and labor time by department for each of the next six months is listed below.

		Depart	ment	
Monthly Capacity Availability	1	2	3	4
Normal machine capacity in machine hours	3,500	3,500	3,000	3,500
Capacity of machines being repaired in machine hours	(500)	(400)	(300)	(200)
Available machine capacity in machine hours	3,000	3,100	2,700	3,300
Labor capacity in direct labor hours	4,000	4,500	3,500	3,000
Available labor in direct labor hours	3,700	4,500	2,750	2,600

Labor and Machine Specifications per Unit of Product

Product	Labor and Machine Time				
611	Direct labor hours	2	3	3	1
	Machine hours	2	1	2	2
613	Direct labor hours	1	2	--	2
	Machine hours	1	1	--	2
615	Direct labor hours	2	2	1	1
	Machine hours	2	2	1	1

The Sales Department's forecast of product demand over the next six months is presented below.

Product	Monthly Sales Volume (Units)
611	500
613	400
615	1,000

Bakker's inventory levels will not be increased or decreased during the next six months. The unit price and cost data valid for the next six months are presented below.

	Product		
	611	613	615
Unit costs:			
Direct material	$ 7	$ 13	$ 17
Direct labor			
Department 1	12	6	12
Department 2	21	14	14
Department 3	24	--	16
Department 4	9	18	9
Variable overhead	27	20	25
Fixed overhead	15	10	32
Variable selling	3	3	4
Unit selling price	$196	$123	$167

Questions

8. Determine whether the monthly sales demand for the three products can be met by Bakker Industries' factory. Use the monthly requirement by department for machine hours and direct labor hours for the production of Products 611, 613, and 615 in your calculations.

9. What monthly production schedule should Bakker Industries select in order to maximize its dollar profits? Support the schedule with appropriate calculations, and present a schedule of the contribution to profit that would be generated by the production schedule selected.

Essay Questions 8, 9 — Unofficial Answers

8.   Bakker will not be able to meet the monthly demand for the three products because of insufficient machine capacity in Department 1. However, there is sufficient capacity for both labor and machine hours in all other departments as shown below.

Bakker Industries
Sales Demand vs. Machine and Labor Hour Capacities

	Departments			
	1	2	3	4
Machine hours needed (Hours × Demand)				
Product: 611	1,000	500	1,000	1,000
613	400	400	--	800
615	2,000	2,000	1,000	1,000
Total hours required	3,400	2,900	2,000	2,800
Machine hours available	3,000	3,100	2,700	3,300
Excess (Deficiency)	(400)	200	700	500
Labor hours needed (Hours × Demand)				
Product: 611	1,000	1,500	1,500	500
613	400	800	--	800
615	2,000	2,000	1,000	1,000
Total hours required	3,400	4,300	2,500	2,300
Labor hours available	3,700	4,500	2,750	2,600
Excess (Deficiency)	300	200	250	300

9.   Bakker has a scarce resource: machine capacity in Department 1. Thus, the company should maximize contribution per machine hour to maximize overall profit, as calculated below.

Contribution Maximization Calculation

- Calculation of contribution per machine hour:

	Product		
	611	613	615
Unit selling price	$196.00	$123.00	$167.00
Less: variable costs	(103.00)	(73.00)	(97.00)
Contribution per unit	$ 93.00	$ 50.00	$ 70.00
Machine hours in Department 1	÷ 2	÷ 1	÷ 2
Contribution per machine hour	$ 46.50	$ 50.00	$ 35.00

- Use available machine capacity to maximize contribution per machine hour:

Machine hours available in Department 1	3,000
Use 400 hours to produce 400 units of Product 613	(400)
	2,600
Use 1,000 hours to produce 500 units of Product 611	(1,000)
Use remaining hours to produce 800 units of Product 615	1,600

- Contribution from this production schedule:

Product 613 (400 × $50)	$ 20,000
Product 611 (500 × $93)	46,500
Product 615 (800 × $70)	56,000
Total contribution	$122,500

17.3 STRATEGIC MARKETING REVIEW

Part 3 – Section B.1. Strategic role within the firm

The candidate should be able to:

a. identify the interrelationships between a firm's overall strategy and its marketing process

b. demonstrate an understanding of the process of setting company marketing strategies, as well as the objectives and tactics to reach those strategic marketing goals

c. demonstrate an understanding of strengths/weaknesses/opportunities/threats (SWOT) analysis

d. explain the critical importance of identifying customer needs and providing value to satisfy those customer needs

e. define and demonstrate an understanding of business portfolio concepts

f. demonstrate an understanding of the marketing process, including analyzing marketing opportunities, selecting target markets, developing the marketing mix, and managing the marketing effort

g. demonstrate an understanding of the interrelationships among marketing analysis, planning, implementation, and control

h. define strategic groups within industries and discuss why they require unique marketing strategies

i. identify Porter's three generic strategies

j. demonstrate an understanding of competitive changes during an industry's evolution

k. differentiate among embryonic industries, growth industries, industry shakeout, mature industries, and declining industries

l. demonstrate an understanding of the effect of globalization on industry structure

m. identify internal competitive advantage and its components, including efficiency, quality, innovation, and customer satisfaction

n. demonstrate an understanding of the value creation chain

o. identify distinctive competencies, resources, and capabilities

p. identify reasons that marketing strategies fail and identify ways to sustain competitive advantage, including continuous improvement and benchmarking

Core Concepts for Marketing's Strategic Role within the Firm

- The **marketing process** involves: analyzing marketing opportunities, choosing target markets, formulating marketing strategies, planning the marketing program and mix, and managing the marketing effort.

- Businesses should be **defined in market terms**, that is, in terms of needs and customer groups.

- The **scope of marketing** may be broadly defined as demand management.

- The **business-process approach** to value creation and delivery is to involve marketing in all phases, including strategic planning.

- The analysis of **marketing opportunities** begins with market-oriented strategic planning. It addresses the structural analysis of industries and competition, including the five **competitive forces**, the nature of a firm's **competitive advantages** (its competencies, resources, and capabilities), and the **generic strategies** based on those advantages.

- One way to describe an industry considers the **number of sellers** and the **extent of differentiation** of products and services, an approach used in microeconomics.

- Another way to characterize an industry is by reference to its **entry, exit, or mobility barriers**.

- A **strategic group** consists of firms in an industry that have adopted **similar competitive strategies**. Hence, a potential entrant into an industry must consider which strategic group to target.

- Michael E. Porter describes **four generic strategies** to be applied to business units: cost leadership, differentiation, cost focus, and focused differentiation.

- Porter's generic strategies are responses to the **five competitive forces**: rivalry among existing firms; threats of, and barriers to, entry; the threat of substitutes; buyers' bargaining power; and the threat of suppliers' bargaining power.

- The **growth-share matrix**, created by the Boston Consulting Group, plots a firm's SBUs relative to two variables, market growth rate (high or low) and relative market share (high or low). The interaction of these two factors allows the firm to classify its SBUs into four categories: dogs, question marks, cash cows, and stars.

- The other most frequently used portfolio model was developed by **General Electric**. The two variables are business strength (strong, medium, or weak) and market attractiveness (high, medium, or low). A firm can determine the proper strategy for an SBU after plotting into which of three zones the SBU is classified.

- The **five competitive forces** and the basic, underlying structural factors **are the same** in global competition as in national competition.

- **Global competitive advantage** may be gained by, for example, economies of scale in centralized production, product differentiation, and mobility of production.

- **Impediments** to global competition include high transportation and storage costs; the need for a direct sales force; difficulty of responding to changes in fashion, technology, etc.; and governmental impediments.

- **Strategic alternatives in global industries** include broad line global competition, a global focus strategy, a national focus strategy, a protected niche strategy, and transnational coalitions.

Part 3 – Section B.2. Managing marketing information

The candidate should be able to:

a. identify marketing information needs

b. demonstrate an understanding of the marketing information development process, including internal data collection, marketing intelligence, and marketing research

c. define customer relationship management

d. identify efficient methods of compiling, distributing, and using marketing information

Core Concepts for Managing Marketing Information

- Each firm has unique requirements for **information about customer needs and wants**, preferences, and behavior in all of its markets, including those abroad.

- **Sales information systems** and **databases** of customers and products may be analyzed and combined.

- **Marketing research** is defined by Philip Kotler as "the systematic design, collection, analysis, and reporting of data and findings relevant to a specific marketing situation."

- The **six steps** in the marketing research process are: (1) define the task, (2) develop a research plan, (3) collect the data, (4) analyze the data, (5) report the findings, and (6) make a decision.

- A **competitive intelligence system** should be established to, among other things, identify competitor strategies and monitor their new product introductions.

- A starting point for competitive intelligence is **customer value analysis (CVA)**, the premise being that customers choose from competitors' products or services the brands that provide the greatest customer value.

- A marketer responds to **customer needs** by stating a **value proposition**, that is, the benefits offered to satisfy those needs. The value proposition is an attempt to affect customer **wants** (needs focused on particular satisfiers).

- **Value** is an aggregate of the elements of the **customer value triad**: quality, service, and price.

- **Customer satisfaction** is the relation between the offering's perceived performance and the customer's expectations. High customer satisfaction tends to create high customer loyalty that results in repurchases.

- Kotler defines **customer relationship management** as "the process of managing detailed information about individual customers and carefully managing all the customer 'touchpoints' with the aim of maximizing customer loyalty."

- The firm should seek to minimize customer churn (customer loss) because **customer retention** through customer satisfaction is a key to profitability.

- **Customer equity** is the sum of the customer lifetime values for all firm customers. According to Rust, Zeithaml, and Lemon, it has certain drivers (value, brand, and relationship equity) and subdrivers.

- The **marketing communications mix** consists of **five promotional tools** or media chosen as the means of reaching current stakeholders (customers, employees, shareholders, suppliers, etc.), possible future stakeholders, and the public. The **five tools** are advertising, sales promotion, public relations, personal selling, and direct marketing.

- **Marketing communications** will be **efficient and effective** if target audiences are properly identified, objectives are clearly defined, messages are well designed, communication channels are appropriate, the total budget is adequate but not excessive, and the right marketing communications mix is chosen.

- The **advertising process** may be defined in terms of the **5 Ms**: mission, money, message, media, and measurement.

- **Sales promotion tools** vary: Consumer tools include gifts, coupons, rebates, etc.; trade tools include, e.g., bulk discounts; and business and sales force tools include contests, specialty items, conventions, and trade shows.

- **Public relations tools** include publishing newsletters, reports, etc.; holding special events; inducing news media to cover the firm; sponsoring sports teams, etc.; performing community service activities; providing speakers; and using identity media, such as logos, stationery, etc.

- **Personal selling** is the most basic (and the oldest) form of direct marketing. The great majority of industrial firms use a professional sales force or hire manufacturers' representatives or other agents to perform the in-person task of selling.

- **Direct marketing** employs means of access to potential customers that bypass marketing intermediaries.

Part 3 – Section B.3. Market segmentation, targeting, and positioning

The candidate should be able to

a. identify target marketing steps, including market segmentation, targeting, and positioning

b. identify and define mass marketing, segment marketing, niche marketing, and micromarketing

c. demonstrate an understanding of segmenting consumer markets, business markets, and international markets

d. identify requirements for effective segmentation

e. demonstrate an understanding of market targeting, including evaluating and selecting market segments

f. define positioning strategy

Core Concepts for Market Segmentation, Targeting, and Positioning

- **Mass marketing** groups people into large categories based solely on their demographic traits, e.g., age, income, gender, or education level. **Segment marketing** focuses on people who share particular wants, such as married, first-time homeowners buying kitchen appliances on limited budgets.
- **Segmenting** can be done on the basis of geography, demographics, psychographics, behavior, or on a multiattribute basis. Once market segments have been identified, the firm selects its **target(s)**.
- **Positioning** establishes a distinct and favorable place for the firm's offering and image in the minds of customers. Positioning is the basis for the marketing mix.

Part 3 – Section B.4. Managing products and services

The candidate should be able to:

a.   distinguish between products and services

b.   classify products and services, including consumer products, industrial products, and other marketable entities

c.   demonstrate an understanding of product attributes, branding, packaging, labeling, and product support services

d.   demonstrate an understanding of product line decisions and product mix decisions

e.   demonstrate an understanding of services marketing, including the nature and characteristics of service marketing strategies

f.   demonstrate an understanding of new product development strategy and product life-cycle strategies

Core Concepts for Managing Products and Services

- A **product strategy** should align the approaches taken to choosing the product mix and product lines, branding, packaging, and labeling.
- Products are commonly **classified** in three categories: durability and tangibility, consumer goods, and industrial goods.
- **Branding** is the development, maintenance, and protection of a unique identity for the selling firm.
- According to Philip Kotler, **brand equity** is "the positive differential effect that knowing the brand name has on customer response to the product or service."
- A product mix contains **product lines**. Analysis of a product line should provide a basis for decisions about **product-line strategies**, such as building, maintaining, harvesting, or divesting a product line.
- Services are **intangible**, so customers need tangible evidence of their quality. The three Ps are: people, physical evidence and presentation, and process.
- Companies can expand into **international markets** through several means, including licensing, exporting, local component assembly, joint venture, and direct investment.
- **Strategies** for a global marketing organization include a multinational strategy (portfolio approach), a global strategy (regarding the world as one market), and a glocal strategy (combining elements of local responsiveness with global integration).
- **Global firms** are primarily managed from one central country. **Transnational firms** lack a national identity.

Part 3 – Section B.5. Pricing strategy

The candidate should be able to:

a. identify internal and external factors affecting pricing decisions

b. demonstrate an understanding of general pricing approaches, including cost-based pricing, value-based pricing, and competition-based pricing

c. discuss the role of the management accountant in pricing decisions

d. demonstrate an understanding of new product pricing strategies, including market skimming pricing and market penetration pricing

e. demonstrate an understanding of product mix pricing strategies, including product line pricing, optional product pricing, captive product pricing, by-product pricing, and product bundle pricing

f. demonstrate an understanding of price adjustment strategies including discount and allowance pricing, segmented pricing, psychological pricing, promotional pricing, geographical pricing, and international pricing

g. demonstrate an understanding of how elasticity and the bargaining power of either the buyer or seller can impact the price

Core Concepts for Pricing Strategy

- **Pricing** is the element of the 4 Ps of marketing that generates revenues, not costs.
- A firm's **steps** in the pricing process are: determine its pricing objectives; estimate demand at each price; estimate learning curves and costs for different outputs; estimate costs of different marketing offers; consider competitors' actions (costs, prices, and offers); choose a pricing strategy; and establish a price.
- A thorough test marketing of pricing alternatives enables management to estimate the demand curve and the **price elasticity of demand** for a particular product. Without a knowledge of price elasticity, a firm may not charge the price that will maximize profits.
- A product's position in its **life cycle** should be considered when establishing a price (introduction, growth, maturity, decline).
- **Cost-based pricing** begins with a cost determination followed by setting a price that will recover the value chain costs and provide the desired return on investment (also called target-return pricing).
- **Product-mix pricing** systems include product-line pricing, optional-product pricing, captive-product pricing, byproduct pricing, and product-bundle pricing.
- **Market-based pricing** determines prices according to the product's perceived value and competitors' actions rather than the seller's cost.
- **Value-based pricing** charges relatively low prices relative to the quality delivered.
- **Geographical pricing** is a means of differentiating prices by geographic region.

Part 3 – Section B.6. Promotional mix and distribution strategy

The candidate should be able to:

a. define marketing communication mix

b. demonstrate an understanding of the integrated marketing communication process, including the need for integrated marketing communications

c. identify and define the components of the overall communication mix, including advertising, sales promotion, public relations, and personal selling

d. demonstrate an understanding of the advertising process, including setting advertising objectives, setting the advertising budget, developing advertising strategy, and advertising evaluation

e. demonstrate an understanding of the sales promotion process, including sales promotion objectives, tools, strategy, and evaluation

f. demonstrate an understanding of public relations and identify related tools

g. demonstrate an understanding of the role of the personal selling process as an element of promotional mix

h. identify the most effective component of the marketing mix (advertising, sales promotion, public relations, or personal selling) to use in a given situation

i. define relationship marketing

j. demonstrate an understanding of the direct marketing model, its benefits, forms of direct marketing, integrated campaign process, and ethical issues

k. define the nature and functions of distribution channels

l. demonstrate an understanding of distribution channel behavior and organizations, including vertical, horizontal, and hybrid marketing systems and channel disintegration trends

m. demonstrate an understanding of distribution channel design decisions, including analysis of consumer service needs, defining channel objectives and constraints, identifying and evaluating major alternatives, and global implementations

Core Concepts for Promotional Mix and Distribution Strategy

- Selecting distribution channels is an important decision because it affects the basic way a firm does business. It influences product development, marketing communication strategy, sales force size, and pricing. Essentially, the choice of distribution channels represents the **foundation for a firm's other marketing policies**.

- A **conventional marketing system** consists of separate, independent members that do not control the others.

- A **vertical marketing system** differs because it is a coordinated system with a channel captain that has substantial ability to control other members' behavior. The effect is to eliminate members' pursuit of conflicting objectives. Use of VMSs is the norm in the U.S. consumer market.

- A **horizontal marketing system** is a group of unrelated firms that share resources to exploit a marketing opportunity. An example is a fast-food company setting up stores in a Wal-Mart.

- A **multichannel marketing system** is a hybrid in which a firm uses multiple channels to reach market segments. Advantages are better coverage of markets, lower costs, and specialized selling.

- **Channel design** may involve the degree of emphasis on a **push strategy** (inducing intermediaries to promote and sell the firm's products) versus a **pull strategy** (motivating customers to pressure intermediaries to sell the firm's products).

17.4 STRATEGIC MARKETING ESSAY QUESTIONS

Recall that your CMA Part 4 exam will probably contain six scenarios, with about three questions per scenario. There will be a recommended time allocation of 20 minutes, 30 minutes, or 45 minutes for each scenario and related questions.

One scenario will involve ethical issues, and probably one or two scenarios will include calculations and responses on a worksheet. Also, expect at least one scenario on organizational/behavioral topics. The remaining scenarios cover Parts 1, 2, and 3.

Scenario Title	Subtopic	Questions	Suggested Time
Grobert, Inc.	Internal Expansion and External Acquisition	1, 2	30 minutes

Scenario for Essay Questions 1, 2

Grobert, Inc. is a closely held public company that produces premium ice cream. Grobert started as a family-owned ice cream parlor in Chicago. Because of the superior taste and quality of its high-cream-content product, the company's reputation grew, and Grobert began packaging its ice cream for distribution through local stores in the adjoining communities. Several years later, the company incorporated and sold a limited number of shares to finance market expansion in four contiguous states.

The sons of the founder returned to the business after college and have convinced the family-dominated management team that further expansion should be undertaken to take advantage of Grobert's solid reputation. The sons have developed the following two mutually exclusive alternatives for expansion. Either plan will be financed by long-term debt.

- Grobert would expand internally by adding a line of low-fat ice cream to penetrate the health-conscious marketplace. It has been determined that the existing plant could accommodate the additional equipment required for low-fat production. The technical expertise to develop and start up this new product line is considered to be available in the current work force, but some additional employment would be required to handle increased volume.

- Grobert would acquire Delicious Add-Ons (DAO), a producer of specialty toppings for ice cream sundaes. DAO is located in San Francisco, and its specialty toppings are distributed through supermarkets and delicatessens in several large cities. DAO, which maintains a direct selling force in these metropolitan locations, would continue to operate as a separate division. However, it is expected that over a period of 2 years, Grobert would be able to absorb the administrative, financial, and data processing functions of DAO into the existing Grobert departments.

Questions

1. Identify the economic advantages and disadvantages of Grobert, Inc.'s plan to expand internally by developing the new line of low-fat ice cream to complement its quality, high-cream-content product.

2. Identify the advantages and disadvantages of Grobert, Inc.'s plan to expand through the external acquisition of Delicious Add-Ons. Be sure to address economic, operational, and marketing considerations.

Essay Questions 1, 2 — Unofficial Answers

1.   The economic advantages and disadvantages of Grobert, Inc.'s plan to expand internally through developing a new line to complement its quality, high-cream-content product include the following:

   a.   Advantages

      1)   Brand loyalty (recognition) and a similar customer base would ease market penetration by providing a vehicle for reaching consumers with changing tastes and/or concerns from a health aspect for high-cream-content products.

      2)   Operational efficiencies and cost savings would result from reduced or no learning curve and further usage of available plant space.

      3)   The company can use existing management and technical expertise to launch the new product line.

   b.   Disadvantages

      1)   New product developments require up-front outlays for research, new facilities, test marketing, etc., prior to any revenue recognition. This could cause earnings declines initially and could affect dividend payouts.

      2)   There is the risk of entering the low-fat market too late, especially if there are product development delays.

      3)   The low-fat product may be perceived as a substitute product, competing with other low-fat products of lesser quality and, thus, bring price pressures that could carry over to the established product. Furthermore, if the low-fat product is more moderately priced, it could lead to a diversion of consumers from the higher priced established product.

2.   The advantages and disadvantages of Grobert, Inc.'s plan to expand through the external acquisition of Delicious Add-Ons (DAO), taking into consideration the economic, operational, and marketing aspects, include the following:

   a.   Advantages

      1)   The acquisition would provide immediate and quantifiable earnings and cash flow that would aid in offsetting the cost.

      2)   The management experience and technical expertise required to run this business segment are already in place.

      3)   DAO has existing distribution channels, a direct sales force, and metropolitan locations, with large concentrations of consumers who can provide markets for Grobert, Inc.'s other established and successful products.

      4)   The acquisition would diversity Grobert's product base and at the same time add a complementary product.

   b.   Disadvantages

      1)   Grobert lacks knowledge of the acquired products and markets. While it is assumed that the acquired management will remain, if there is an exodus of key personnel, Grobert would be immediately responsible for the success or failure of the acquisition.

      2)   Allowing the acquired company to operate independently for at least 2 years could result in decisions being made that are not in concert with Grobert's strategies.

      3)   The new product may not be of good or consistent quality.

Consider using Gleim's **CMA Test Prep** for interactive testing with **hundreds of multiple-choice questions** as an additional method of knowledge transfer in your quest to pass Part 4.

STUDY UNIT EIGHTEEN
CMA PART 3 REVIEW –
CORPORATE FINANCE

(8 pages of outline)

Part 3 of the CMA exam is titled **Strategic Management**. This study unit is a review of this section:

C.   **Corporate Finance.** Types of risk; measures of risk; portfolio management; options and futures; capital instruments for long-term financing; dividend policy; factors influencing the optimum capital structure; cost of capital; and managing and financing working capital.

This study unit represents the IMA's Learning Outcome Statements and Gleim Core Concepts relevant to this section. Bear in mind that **all topics** on Part 4 of the exam are tested at **skill level C** (all six skill types required).

18.1 CORPORATE FINANCE REVIEW

Part 3 – Section C.1. Risk and return

The candidate should be able to:

a.   calculate rates of return

b.   identify and demonstrate an understanding of the different types of risk [systematic (market), unsystematic (company), industry, country, etc.]

c.   demonstrate an understanding of the relationship between risk and return

d.   calculate expected return, standard deviation of return, and coefficient of variation

e.   identify the different types of attitudes toward risk and infer how attitude might affect the management of risk

f.   define a portfolio and distinguish between individual security risk and portfolio risk

g.   define value at risk (VAR)

h.   demonstrate an understanding of diversification

i.   differentiate between systematic and unsystematic risk

j.   demonstrate an understanding of how individual securities affect portfolio risk

k.   define beta and identify the meaning of a security's beta

l.   calculate the expected risk-adjusted returns using the capital asset pricing model (CAPM) and arbitrage pricing theory (APT)

m.   define hedging and demonstrate how hedging can be used to manage financial risk

Core Concepts for Risk and Return

- A **return** is the amount received by an investor as compensation for taking on the risk of the investment. The **rate of return** is the return stated as a percentage of the amount invested, calculated as follows: (amount received – amount invested) ÷ amount invested.
- The **expected rate of return** on an investment is determined using an **expected value** calculation. It is an average of the outcomes weighted according to their probabilities.
- The **greater the standard deviation** of the expected return, the **riskier the investment**.
- The **coefficient of variation** is useful when the rates of return and standard deviations of two investments differ. It measures the risk per unit of return because it divides the standard deviation by the expected return.
- Specific **types of investment risks** include interest-rate risk, purchasing-power risk, default risk, market (systematic) risk, nonmarket (diversifiable) risk, portfolio risk, total risk, liquidity risk, business risk, exchange rate risk, commodities risk, and political risk.
- **Leverage** is the relative amount of the fixed cost of capital, principally debt, in a firm's capital structure.
- The **degree of financial leverage** is the ratio of operating income to net income. If the return on assets exceeds the cost of debt, additional leverage is favorable.
- The **degree of operating leverage** is the ratio of contribution margin to operating income. It measures the extent to which a firm incurs fixed rather than variable costs in operations.
- The **degree of total leverage** is the degree of financial leverage times the degree of operating leverage. Firms with a high degree of operating leverage do not usually employ a high degree of financial leverage and vice versa. One of the most important considerations in the use of financial leverage is operating leverage.
- **Riskier investments** have higher potential rates of return.
- A **risk averse** investor is one with a diminishing marginal utility for wealth, i.e., the potential gain is not worth the additional risk. A **risk neutral** investor adopts an expected value approach. A **risk-seeking** investor has an optimistic attitude toward risk.
- **Risk and return** should be evaluated for a firm's **entire portfolio**, not for individual assets.
- Thanks to the diversification effect, **combining securities** results in a **portfolio risk that is less** than the average of the standard deviations because the returns are imperfectly correlated.
- Given **perfect negative correlation** of the prices of two stocks, risk would in theory be eliminated.
- An important measurement used in portfolio analysis is the **covariance**. It measures the **volatility** of returns together with their correlation with the returns of other securities.
- A feasible portfolio that offers the highest expected return for a given risk or the least risk for a given expected return is an **efficient portfolio**. A portfolio that is selected from the efficient set of portfolios because it is tangent to the investor's highest indifference curve is the **optimal portfolio**.
- A company's investment in securities should be based on **expected net cash flows** and **cash flow uncertainty evaluations**. Arranging a portfolio so that the maturity of funds will coincide with the need for funds will maximize the average return on the portfolio and provide increased flexibility.
- **Portfolio theory** concerns the composition of an investment portfolio that is efficient in balancing the risk with the rate of return of the portfolio. **Asset allocation** is a key concept in financial planning and money management.

- **Specific risk**, also called diversifiable risk, unsystematic risk, residual risk, and unique risk, is the risk associated with a specific investee's operations: new products, patents, acquisitions, competitors' activities, etc. Specific risk is the risk that can be **potentially eliminated by diversification**.
- **Market risk**, also called undiversifiable risk and systematic risk, is the risk of the stock market as a whole. Some conditions in the national economy **affect all businesses**, which is why equity prices so often move together.
- The effect of an individual security on the volatility of a portfolio is measured by its sensitivity to movements by the overall market. This sensitivity is stated in terms of a stock's **beta coefficient**.
- The stock can have the same **volatility** as the overall market (beta = 1.0), be more volatile than average (beta > 1.0), or be less volatile than average (beta < 1.0).
- The **capital asset pricing model** relates the risk of a security, as measured by its beta coefficient, to the rate of return expected on that security. The **security market line** graphically depicts market risk premium.
- **Arbitrage pricing theory** is based on the assumption that an asset's return is a function of multiple systematic risk factors. In contrast, the CAPM is a model that uses just one systematic risk factor to explain the asset's return.
- **Hedging** is defined in *The CPA Letter* as "a defensive strategy designed to protect an entity against the risk of adverse price or interest-rate movements on certain of its assets, liabilities, or anticipated transactions. A hedge is used to avoid or reduce risks . . ."

Part 3 – Section C.2. Financial instruments

The candidate should be able to:

a. define and identify the characteristics of bonds, common stock, and preferred stock
b. identify and describe the basic features of a bond such as maturity, par value, coupon rate, provisions for redeeming, covenants, options granted to the issuer or investor, indentures, and restrictions
c. define the different types of dividends, including cash dividends, stock dividends, and stock splits
d. demonstrate an understanding of the dividend payment process for both common and preferred stock
e. value bonds, common stock, and preferred stock using discounted cash flow methods
f. demonstrate an understanding of the dividend discount model
g. demonstrate an understanding of relative or comparable valuation methods, such as price/earnings (P/E) ratios, price/book ratios, and price/sales ratios
h. recognize various forms of loan covenants, restrictions, and indentures
i. demonstrate an understanding of duration as a measure of bond interest rate sensitivity
j. demonstrate an understanding of how income taxes impact financing decisions
k. define and demonstrate an understanding of derivatives, their payoff structures, and their uses
l. distinguish between futures and forwards
m. demonstrate an understanding of options
n. demonstrate a basic understanding of the Black-Scholes and the binomial option-valuation models
o. define and identify characteristics of other sources of long-term financing, such as leases, convertible securities, warrants, and retained earnings

Core Concepts for Financial Instruments

- A firm may have long-term financing requirements that it cannot, or does not want to, meet using retained earnings. A firm must in such cases issue **debt**, **common stock**, or **preferred stock** (a hybrid of the first two).

- **Advantages** of issuing **common stock** include the fact that common stock does not require a fixed dividend and that there is no fixed maturity date for repayment of the capital. **Disadvantages** include the dilution of control (voting rights), the dilution of earnings available for distribution, and high underwriting costs.

- **Preferred stock** is a hybrid of debt and equity. It has a fixed charge and increases leverage, but payment of dividends is not an obligation. Also, preferred shareholders stand ahead of common shareholders in priority in the event of corporate bankruptcy.

- **Bonds** are long-term debt instruments. They are similar to term loans except that they are usually offered to the public and sold to many investors. **Advantages** include not having to share basic control of the firm with debtholders and that the interest paid on debt is tax deductible as an expense. **Disadvantages** include the fact that debt has a fixed charge and that debt adds risk to a firm.

- **Dividend policy** determines what portion of a corporation's net income is distributed to shareholders and what portion is retained for reinvestment.

- The desire for stability has led theorists to propound the **information content** or **signaling hypothesis**, which states that "a change in dividend policy is a signal to the market regarding management's forecast of future earnings."

- **Important dates** concerning the declaration of dividends are: (1) the date of declaration, (2) the date of record, (3) the date of payment, and (4) the ex-dividend date.

- Dividends can take the form of **cash** or **stock**.

- A quantity of money to be received or paid in the future is worth less than the same amount now. The difference, called **the time value of money**, is measured in terms of interest calculated using the appropriate **discount rate**.

- **Per-share ratios** relate company financial information to the market price per share.

- **Earnings per share** equals net income available to common shareholders divided by the average number of shares outstanding for the period.

- **Book value per share** equals the amount of net assets available to the shareholders of a given type of stock divided by the number of those shares outstanding.

- **Dividend yield** equals the annual dividend payment divided by the market value per share.

- The **price-earnings (P-E) ratio** equals the market price per share of common stock divided by EPS.

- **Price-book ratio** equals the market price per share of common stock divided by the book value per share.

- **Price-sales ratio** equals the market price per share of common stock divided by sales per share.

- A bond's **duration** is the average time until each payment, weighted for the proportion of the total stream that each payment constitutes.

- A **derivative** is defined informally as an investment transaction in which the buyer purchases the right to a potential gain with a commitment for a potential loss. It is a wager on whether the value of something will go up or down. The purpose of the transaction is either to **speculate** (incur risk) or to **hedge** (avoid risk).

- **Options and futures** are derivative securities. They are not claims on business assets, such as those represented by equity securities. Instead, they are created by the parties who trade in them.

- A **call option** is the most common type of option. It gives the owner the right to purchase the underlying asset at a fixed price. Thus, it represents a long position because the owner gains from a price increase.

- A **put option** gives the owner the right to sell the underlying asset for a fixed price. It represents a short position because the owner benefits from a price decrease.

- The value of a call option is based on its exercise price, its expiration date, the price of the underlying asset, the variability of that asset, and the risk-free interest rate. The well-known **Black-Scholes Option-Pricing Model** uses these factors.

- The **binomial methods** are based on upward and downward stock price movements comparable to the standard deviation in the Black-Scholes formula.

- A futures contract is a specific kind of **forward contract**, which is simply an executory contract. The parties to a forward contract agree to the terms of a purchase and sale, but performance, that is, payment, by the buyer and delivery by the seller is deferred.

- A **futures contract** is a definite agreement that allows a trader to purchase or sell an asset at a fixed price during a specific future month. Futures contracts for agricultural commodities, metals, oil, and financial assets are traded on numerous exchanges.

- Corporations have certain methods of making their debt and equity issues more **attractive to investors**.

- **Stock rights** evidenced by **warrants** are options that are distributed with debt or preferred stock. They permit a holder to share in a company's prosperity through a future purchase of stock at a special low price.

- **Convertible bonds** or **convertible preferred stock** may be exchangeable by the investor for common stock under certain conditions.

- **Employee stock ownership plans** acquire shares in the company's stock and hold them in the name of the company's employees.

- Under a **dividend reinvestment plan**, any dividends due to shareholders are automatically reinvested in shares of the same corporation's common stock.

- A firm's first issuance of securities to the public is called an initial public offering, known as **going public**. When a firm goes public, it issues its securities on a new issue or IPO market (a primary market).

Part 3 – Section C.3. Cost of capital

The candidate should be able to:

a. define the cost of capital and demonstrate an understanding of its applications in capital structure decisions

b. determine the weighted average (historical) cost of capital and the cost of its individual components

c. calculate the marginal cost of capital and demonstrate an understanding of the significance of using the marginal cost as opposed to the historical cost

d. demonstrate an understanding of the use of the cost of capital in capital investment decisions

e. demonstrate an understanding of how income taxes impact capital structure and capital investment decisions

Core Concepts for the Cost of Capital

- The **weighted-average cost of capital** weights the cost of each debt and equity component by the percentage of that component in the financial structure.

- Each **component of the firm's capital structure** (debt, preferred stock, common stock, retained earnings) is weighted for its proportion of the total. These weights are then applied to each component's after-tax rate (for debt) or expected rate of return (for equity). The total of the resulting percentages is the firm's WACC.

- Standard financial theory provides a model for the **optimal capital structure** of every firm. This model holds that shareholder wealth-maximization results from minimizing the weighted-average cost of capital.

- The stock price is affected by the **dividend-payout ratio** because some investors may want capital gains, but others may prefer current income. Thus, investors will choose stocks that give the proper mix of capital gains and dividends.

- A firm cannot continue to raise unlimited amounts of new funds at its historical cost of capital. At some point, the costs of servicing new sources of funding will increase a firm's cost of capital. The **marginal cost of capital (MCC)** is the cost to a firm of the next dollar of new capital raised.

- The **marginal efficiency of investment** is the decrease in return on additional dollars of capital investment because the most profitable investments are made initially.

Part 3 – Section C.4. Managing current assets

The candidate should be able to:

a. define working capital and identify its components

b. explain the benefit of short-term financial forecasts in the management of working capital

c. identify factors influencing the levels of cash

d. identify and explain the three motives for holding cash

e. demonstrate an understanding of how firms monitor cash inflows and outflows and prepare forecasts of future cash flows

f. identify methods of speeding up cash collections

g. calculate the net benefit of a lockbox system

h. define concentration banking and discuss how firms utilize it

i. demonstrate an understanding of the uses of compensating balances

j. identify methods of slowing down disbursements

k. define payable through draft and zero balance account

l. demonstrate an understanding of disbursement float and overdraft systems

m. define electronic commerce and discuss its use by firms

n. define the different types of marketable securities, including money market instruments, T-bills, Treasury notes, Treasury bonds, repurchase agreements, Federal agency securities, bankers' acceptances, commercial paper, negotiable CDs, Eurodollars, and other marketable securities

o. demonstrate an understanding of the variables in marketable security selections, including safety, marketability, yield, maturity, and taxability

p. demonstrate an understanding of the risk and return trade-off in the selection of marketable securities

q. list reasons for holding marketable securities

r. identify reasons for carrying accounts receivable and the factors influencing the level of receivables

s. demonstrate an understanding of the impact of changes in credit terms

t. define default risk

u. demonstrate an understanding of the factors involved in determining an optimal credit policy

v. calculate the average collection period

w. identify reasons for carrying inventory and the factors influencing its level

x. identify and calculate the costs related to inventory

y. define lead time and safety stock

z. demonstrate an understanding of economic order quantity (EOQ) and how a change in one variable would affect the EOQ (calculation not required)

aa. define just-in-time and kanban inventory management systems

Core Concepts for Managing Current Assets

- Management must make **investment decisions** to obtain a proper mix of productive assets. Also, it must secure financing for these assets with the objective of maximizing shareholders' wealth.

- The **investing and financing** decisions are not independent. The amount and composition of assets are directly related to the amount and composition of financing.

- **Taxes** (federal, state, local, and foreign) are an important consideration because they are frequently 25% to 50% of all costs.

- **Working capital finance** concerns the optimal level, mix, and use of current assets and current liabilities. The objective is to minimize the cost of maintaining liquidity while guarding against the possibility of technical insolvency.

- **Solvency ratios**, such as the current ratio and quick ratio, measure the short-term viability of the business, i.e., the firm's ability to continue in the short term by paying its obligations.

- **Activity ratios**, such as the inventory turnover ratio and receivables turnover ratio, measure the firm's use of assets to generate revenue and income.

- **Three motives** for holding cash are: as a medium of exchange, as a precautionary measure, and for speculation.

- **Cash collections** should be **expedited**. Thus, invoices should be mailed promptly; credit terms must be competitive but should encourage prompt payment; and a lockbox system may be used.

- **Slowing cash disbursements** increases available cash. Cash flow considerations sometimes make it necessary to forgo the discounts offered for early settlement of trade payables. Payment by draft (usually in the form of a check) is a means of slowing cash outflows.

- **Models for cash management**, such as the Baumol and Miller-Orr models, provides a firm with guidelines for holding the correct amount of cash, such that enough is available to pay current liabilities but not so much that interest revenue is forgone.

- As temporary investments, marketable securities may be purchased with **maturities timed** to meet seasonal fluctuations, to pay off a bond issue, to make tax payments, or otherwise to satisfy anticipated needs. Marketable securities should be chosen with a view to their degree of safety, that is their default risk.

- The **money market** is the market for short-term investments where companies invest their temporary surpluses of cash.

- Some **common money market instruments** are: U.S. Treasury obligations, repurchase agreements, federal agency securities, bankers' acceptances, commercial paper, and certificates of deposit.

- The objective of managing accounts receivable is to have both the **optimal amount** of receivables outstanding and the optimal amount of bad debts. This balance requires a trade-off between the benefits of credit sales, such as more sales, and the costs of accounts receivable, e.g., collection, interest, and bad debt costs.

- Receivables management seeks to maximize the accounts-receivable-turnover ratio, that is, to **shorten the average time receivables are held**. A common analytical tool is an aging schedule.

- The firm should **minimize total inventory costs**. These include ordering costs (the costs of placing and receiving orders) and carrying costs (the costs of storage, insurance, security, etc.).

- The firm must also **minimize stockout costs** (the lost sales and lost goodwill incurred when an entity does not have products demanded by customers) and **safety stock** (the quantity held for sale during the lead time).

- The **order point** is the time an order should be placed to insure receiving the inventory before stockout occurs. The traditional inventory management approach uses the basic economic order quantity model to minimize the sum of ordering and carrying costs.

- The traditional inventory management approach uses the basic **economic order quantity model** to minimize the sum of ordering and carrying costs.

Part 3 – Section C.5. Financing current assets

The candidate should be able to:

a. demonstrate an understanding of how risk affects a firm's approach to its current asset financing policy (aggressive, conservative, etc.)

b. describe the different types of short-term credit, including trade credit, short-term bank loans, commercial paper, lines of credit, and bankers' acceptances and identify their advantages and disadvantages

c. estimate the annual cost and effective annual interest rate of not taking a cash discount

d. calculate the effective annual interest rate of a bank loan with a compensating balance requirement and/or a commitment fee

e. describe the different types of secured short-term credit, including accounts receivable financing and inventory financing

f. demonstrate an understanding of factoring accounts receivable and calculate the cost of factoring

g. demonstrate an understanding of the maturity matching or hedging approach to financing

Core Concepts for Financing Current Assets

- Short-term credit is debt scheduled to be **repaid within 1 year**. It often involves a lower interest rate and is more readily available than long-term credit.

- The major **sources of short-term credit** are: accrued expenses, trade credit, short-term bank loans, commercial paper, lines of credit, and bankers' acceptances.

- Before deciding whether to take a **trade discount**, the firm should have calculated the annualized cost of not taking the discount. The cost of a bank loan can be calculated using simple formulas.

- **Secured** forms of short-term credit include pledged receivables, warehouse financing, and trust receipts.

- Cash gain can be obtained by **factoring** (selling) receivables to a third party.

18.2 CORPORATE FINANCE ESSAY QUESTIONS

Recall that your CMA Part 4 exam will probably contain six scenarios, with about three questions per scenario. There will be a recommended time allocation of 20 minutes, 30 minutes, or 45 minutes for each scenario and related questions.

One scenario will involve ethical issues, and probably one or two scenarios will include calculations and responses on a worksheet. Also, expect at least one scenario on organizational/behavioral topics. The remaining scenarios cover Parts 1, 2, and 3.

Scenario Title	Subtopic	Questions	Suggested Time
ProCorp, Inc.	Inventory Management	1, 2, 3	30 minutes
Attract-One, Inc.	Cash Management	4, 5, 6, 7	30 minutes
Abid & Co.	Receivables Management	8, 9	30 minutes
Comfort Gear	Working Capital Management	10, 11	30 minutes
Safe-T-Systems	Cost of Capital	12, 13, 14	30 minutes
Lever Corporation	Leverage	15, 16, 17	30 minutes

Scenario for Essay Questions 1, 2, 3

John Holster, controller for ProCorp, Inc., has been examining all phases of ProCorp's manufacturing operations in order to reduce costs and improve efficiency. The reason for urgency is that the company's sales force has been complaining about lost sales due to product stockouts, and the production people are unhappy about downtime caused by shortages of raw materials. Holster believes the company may be losing as much as $200,000 in revenue as a result of these problems.

ProCorp manufactures only one product, boomerangs (trademark, Boomers). The single raw material used in making Boomers is plastic, with each Boomer requiring 8 ounces of red plastic. ProCorp expects to manufacture 300,000 Boomers this year with a steady demand through the entire year. The ordering costs for clerical processing are $30 per order of plastic. There is a 3-day delay between placement of an order and receipt of the inventory. The constant carrying costs for storage, handling, insurance, and interest are $.72 per Boomer unit per year.

Questions

1. Discuss the general benefits of a well-managed inventory policy.

2. By using the economic order quantity formula, ProCorp, Inc. determined that the optimal economic order quantity is 2,500 pounds of plastic which will produce 5,000 units.

   a. Discuss how an increase in annual sales demand, ordering costs, and carrying costs will affect the economic order quantity.

      1) Annual sales demand
      2) The ordering costs
      3) The carrying costs for storage, handling, insurance, and interest

   b. Determine the number of times ProCorp will order plastic during the year.

3. ProCorp, Inc., while reviewing its safety stock policy, has determined that an appropriate safety stock level is 1,250 pounds of plastic, which will produce 2,500 units.

   a. Describe the factors that affect an appropriate safety stock level.

   b. List the effects of maintaining an appropriate safety stock level on ProCorp's short-term and long-term profitability.

   c. Identify the effect that a well-implemented just-in-time inventory procedure will have on the safety stock level, and explain why.

Essay Questions 1, 2, 3 — Unofficial Answers

1.   The general benefits of a well-managed inventory policy include the following:

    a.   Reduces risks from theft, damage, obsolescence, style changes, and deterioration

    b.   Enhances customer service level and maximizes sales by avoiding stockouts

    c.   Minimizes invested working capital, interest, taxes, and insurance costs due to lower inventory levels

2.   a.   An increase in each of the following components will affect the economic order quantity as follows:

        1)   Increased annual sales demand will cause the economic order quantity to increase.

        2)   Increased ordering costs would cause the economic order quantity to increase.

        3)   Increased carrying costs for storage, handling, insurance, and interest would cause the economic order quantity to decrease.

    b.   ProCorp would order plastic 60 times a year (300,000 units ÷ 5,000 units).

3.   a.   The factors that affect an appropriate safety stock level include

        1)   Reliability of supply
        2)   Sales demand fluctuations
        3)   Reliability of production and order lead times
        4)   Customer dissatisfaction resulting from stockouts

    b.   The effects of maintaining an appropriate safety stock level on ProCorp's short-term and long-term profitability include the following:

        1)   Short term

            a)   Decreased inventory investment and storage costs
            b)   Reduced manufacturing costs through reduced overtime

        2)   Long term

            a)   Better customer relations by minimizing stockouts, which should lead to increasing sales and profitability

    c.   A well-implemented just-in-time (JIT) inventory procedure will reduce the safety stock level close to zero as JIT is based on producing to actual customer orders using small batches. This is possible because JIT requires development of better supplier relations, reduced lead times, improved production and inventory planning, and improved sales forecasts.

Scenario for Essay Questions 4, 5, 6, 7

Attract-One, Inc. (AOI), a moderately profitable producer of fragrances, has been in business for a number of years and sells its products through its U.S. retailer network. In the last year, AOI has developed and introduced a line of fragrances that has had wide public acceptance. Retailer remittances have grown to an average of $200,000 each business day, with additional collections of $1,250,000 a day for each 4-day period following the special occasions of Valentine's Day, Mother's Day, June graduations, and Christmas.

AOI is continuing to expand its network of retail outlets and introduce new lines of consumer products, fully expecting continued growth of the company. As a result, Steve Louhan, treasurer, has been hired to direct AOI's cash management function. After reviewing the company's centralized operations, Louhan found that retailer remittances take an average of 5 mail days to reach AOI. An additional 2 days are needed for in-house processing before bank deposits are made.

Louhan has investigated various regional lockbox arrangements as a means to accelerate this cash collection process. Louhan determined that with a three-bank system, one each in the eastern, central, and western regions of the U.S., mail times could be reduced by 2 days. In addition, the in-house check processing would be eliminated. The banks would provide AOI with a listing of daily transactions and any supporting documents that retailers submit with payments. The lockbox service charges would be $1,000 per month for each bank, and Louhan estimates that 6% interest could be earned on short-term investments.

Louhan is also considering various ways of investing available funds, including the use of marketable securities. He believes this is particularly important during the peak periods when cash inflows are large.

Questions

4. Briefly describe the responsibilities of the cash management function.

5. Identify and describe at least two motives for a company to hold cash.

6.   a. Identify and explain at least three characteristics of marketable securities that a company should consider when investing.

     b. Identify at least three types of financial instruments that would meet Attract-One, Inc.'s cash and investing needs.

7. Recommend whether or not Attract-One, Inc. should implement a lockbox system by preparing an analysis using a 360-day year.

Essay Questions 4, 5, 6, 7 — Unofficial Answers

4. The responsibilities of the cash management function include planning and controlling cash collections, disbursements, and cash balances in order to maintain liquidity, as well as develop banking relationships.

5. At least two motives for a company to hold cash include using cash for

   a. Transactions, since cash is necessary to conduct business, such as purchases, paying wages, taxes, or dividends

   b. Precautions against unexpected needs, as cash inflows and outflows are unpredictable

6. a. At least three characteristics that a firm should consider when investing in marketable securities include

   1) Default risk, as safety of principal is an important concern for investments that are to be included in the short-term portfolio

   2) Marketability, as the securities should be easy to sell for cash liquidity needs

   3) Maturity, as yields are generally higher, but riskier for longer-term investment

   b. At least three types of financial instruments that would meet Attract-One, Inc.'s cash and investing needs include

   1) U.S. Treasury bills
   2) Negotiable certificates of deposit
   3) Prime commercial paper

7. The company should implement the lockbox system as the total time savings would be 4 days (2 days mail time and 2 processing days), and the opportunity cost of the current system is $51,333, which is greater than the $36,000 cost of implementing the lockbox system, as calculated below.

   a. Cost of implementing the lockbox system

3 banks × $1,000 per month × 12 months	=	$36,000

   b. Interest income from lockbox implementation

   1) Interest income from average daily balances

   Time savings × Daily average collections = Reduction in cash balance × Annual interest = Interest income

4 days saved × $200,000 × .06	=	$48,000

   2) Interest income from additional holiday volume

[(4 holidays × 4 days saved × $1,250,000) ÷ 360] × .06	=	3,333

   3) Total interest income | = | $51,333

   NOTE: Interest income from time savings of daily average collections alone exceeds cost of implementation. Interest income associated with holiday savings is an additional benefit.

Scenario for Essay Questions 8, 9

Abid & Co. manufactures pumps that it distributes through plumbing supply houses as well as manufacturer's representatives. Accounts receivable have grown due to creeping extensions of time that customers have been taking in remitting payments for supplies. Bad debts have grown to 3 percent of sales. Abid's president has hired Joe Jackler to improve Abid's liquidity position. Jackler met with Dorretta Mooney, Abid's controller, and learned that Abid's (1) sales prices have a 20 percent margin over the sum of direct operating costs and all selling costs, (2) production is less than full capacity, (3) terms are 2/12, net 45, which is in line with industry practices, and (4) dunning notices are sent monthly on past due accounts. On average, customers pay 35 days after the sale. Delinquent accounts are sent to collection agencies when reaching a past due status of 12 months. Customers owing over $2,000 will be contacted monthly via telephone. In the past, this was only done for customers owing over $8,000. Jackler was able to group Abid's customers into risk classes according to the probability of loss as follows:

Risk Class Number	Probable Loss Ratio (in Percentages)
1	0
2	0 – .5
3	.6 – 1
4	2 – 3
5	4 – 6
6	7 – 12
7	13 – 20
8	over 20

After considering the available alternatives, Jackler has implemented the following changes to Abid's credit policies to improve cash flow.

- Credit terms will change to 2/10, net 30. Jackler believes the current customers will accept this change and there will be minimal effect on sales. The overall effects of this change will be to improve accounts receivable turnover, reduce the opportunity costs of carrying receivables, and identify potentially troubled accounts sooner.

- Customers in risk groups 1 through 5 will continue to have the customer credit extended to them; selling to groups 6 and 7 will be under more stringent terms, such as cash on delivery; and sales to group 8 will require advance payments. This change will cause a reduction in sales; however, this reduction will come from the high-risk customer.

- Collection efforts will be increased to ensure compliance with the new credit terms. Accounts outstanding 9 months or more will be turned over to a collection agency. Jackler believes this action will reduce bad debts to a level of 1 to 1.5 percent of sales.

Mooney is responsible for extending credit to customers who deal directly with the company and for establishing guidelines for manufacturer's representatives. Mooney performed her own risk study. She concluded that Jackler's "classifications" were inappropriate and believes that some of the larger customers are better risks than indicated in Jackler's analysis. Mooney did not share her findings with Abid's president or Jackler. She decided that to follow the policies would reduce sales more than Jackler estimates. Consequently, Mooney does not intend to comply totally with the new policies.

Questions

8. Describe and evaluate the probable effects on sales and cash flows of each of the changes recommended by Joe Jackler to be made to Abid & Co.'s credit and collection policies.

    a.   Collection procedures
    b.   Customer credit terms to 2/10, net 30
    c.   Credit status by risk grouping

9. Referring to all of the specific standards (competence, confidentiality, integrity, and/or credibility) in Statement on Management Accounting No. 1C (Revised), *IMA Statement of Ethical Professional Practice*, evaluate Mooney's decision not to comply fully with the changes in the credit and collection policies implemented by Joe Jackler.

Essay Questions 8, 9 — Unofficial Answers

8.   The probable effects on sales and cash flows on each of the changes recommended by Joe Jackler to be made to Abid & Co.'s credit and collection policies are as follows:

  a.   The probable effects of the recommended changes to collection procedures include

   1)   A decrease in sales because customers may become irritated by the new procedures, particularly those customers who have been taking 45 days to pay or with balances in the $2,000 to $8,000 range. Customers may move to competitors with more relaxed credit terms.

   2)   An increase in cash flow because of accelerated collections, as well as reduced accounts receivable balances as a result of the shortened collection cycle (30 versus 45 days). Also, there will be a reduction in the time frame in which delinquent accounts are turned over to collection agencies.

   3)   A reduction in bad debts as troubled accounts will be identified sooner and have credit curtailed earlier.

  b.   The probable effects of changes to the customer credit terms to 2/10, net 30 include

   1)   A decrease in sales as customers switch to competitors with more relaxed credit terms.

   2)   The number of past due accounts increasing as the payment period has been shortened.

   3)   Accelerated cash flow as customers meet the new discount policy and 30-day payment period, which would also result in a reduction of short-term financing and opportunity costs.

  c.   The probable effects of the recommended changes to the credit status by risk grouping include

   1)   A decrease in sales because the extension of customary credit has become more stringent and/or denied to the higher risk customers.

   2)   An increase in cash flow due to a curtailing of risky accounts, as well as a decrease in bad debts because high risk customers must pay on delivery or in advance.

9.   Mooney's decision not to comply fully with the changes in the policies implemented by Jackler are in violation of the specific standards in Statement on Management Accounting No. 1C (Revised), *IMA Statement of Ethical Professional Practice*, as outlined below.

  a.   **Competence**

   1)   Mooney did not prepare clear, complete reports and/or recommendations, after appropriate analyses of relevant and reliable information, for review by the president of Abid & Co. or Jackler.

  b.   **Integrity**

   1)   Mooney did not avoid actual or apparent conflicts of interest and advise all appropriate parties of conflicts of interest. She has a conflict in implementing company policies that affect her relationships with customers.

   2)   Mooney's actions also are in conflict with the specific standard of refraining from subverting the organization's legitimate and ethical objectives.

  c.   **Credibility**

   1)   Mooney did not communicate information fairly and objectively, nor did she disclose all relevant information.

Scenario for Essay Questions 10, 11

Daniel Greenfield, treasurer of Comfort Gear Corporation, has been negotiating a new term loan with Midland Bank. Comfort Gear, a manufacturer of ski equipment, has decided to introduce a line of tennis equipment. The proceeds of the loan will be used to finance the start-up of this new line.

Greenfield is considering a $6 million loan for 3 years. The loan would be effective on July 1, Year 5, and would be payable June 30, Year 8. The loan agreement offered by Midland contains protective covenants. Greenfield is concerned that Comfort Gear will be unable to achieve its growth objectives and remain within the limits of the covenants. The covenants are:

- Comfort Gear must maintain working capital of at least $6 million throughout the term of the loan, and current liabilities cannot be more than 40% of total assets. Midland Bank and Comfort Gear have agreed to consider all of the company's loans as long-term throughout the life of the loans even though portions of these loans would normally be classified as a current liability.

- Cash dividends cannot exceed 10% of profits in any given year, and Comfort Gear cannot repurchase any of its shares without the prior approval of Midland.

- Comfort Gear's ratio of total debt to net equity, which will be 4.0 after the loan, must show a 0.5 improvement in each year of the loan, indicating a reduction in the firm's overall risk.

- Comfort Gear cannot incur any additional long-term debt nor can it pledge or mortgage any assets.

In each of the next 3 years, the planned asset growth rate for Comfort Gear is 10% for current assets and 10% for net fixed assets. Revenues are planned to expand 30% in each year with after-tax profits forecasted to be 20% of sales. Maximum cash dividends will be paid each year to maintain investor interest. Comfort Gear plans to pay its outstanding $4 million long-term debt on June 30, Year 7.

Comfort Gear's income statement for the year ended June 30, Year 5, and its condensed statement of financial position as of July 1, Year 5, incorporating the proceeds of the new term loan, are as shown.

Comfort Gear Corporation Income Statement For the Year Ended June 30, Year 5 (In thousands of dollars)		
Sales		$10,000
Cost of sales		5,900
Gross margin		4,100
Selling and administrative expense	$800	
Interest expense	300	1,100
Income before taxes		3,000
Income taxes		1,200
Net income		$ 1,800

Comfort Gear Corporation Condensed Statement of Financial Position July 1, Year 5 (In thousands of dollars)	
Current assets	$12,000
Net fixed assets	8,000
Total assets	$20,000
Current liabilities	$ 6,000
Long-term debt	10,000
Net equity	4,000
Total liabilities and shareholders' equity	$20,000

Questions

10. Based on management's assumptions, prepare an analysis as of June 30 for each year of the loan showing whether Comfort Gear will be able to achieve its growth expectations and meet the protective covenants. Indicate whether the following covenants are met.

    a. Working capital requirement
    b. Current liability restriction
    c. Improvement in the ratio of total debt to net equity

11. Discuss the specific risks of loaning funds to Comfort Gear that would be reduced for Midland Bank by including the following types of protective covenants in the loan.

    a. Working capital requirement
    b. Long-term debt restriction
    c. Loan proceeds restriction

Essay Questions 10, 11 — Unofficial Answers

10. Comfort Gear will be able to achieve its growth expectations and meet the protective covenants during the life of the new term loan with the exception of the working capital requirement at June 30, Year 7. Supporting calculations appear in Exhibit 1 below.

Exhibit 1

	Beginning	6/30/Year 6	6/30/Year 7	6/30/Year 8
Calculation of net equity				
Sales (30% growth per year)	$10,000	$13,000	$16,900	$21,970
Net income (20% of sales)		$ 2,600	$ 3,380	$ 4,394
Less: Cash dividend (10% of net income)		260	338	439
Change in net equity		2,340	3,042	3,955
Beginning net equity		4,000	6,340	9,382
Net equity	$ 4,000	$ 6,340	$ 9,382	$13,337
Calculation of financial position				
Current assets (10% growth per year)	$12,000	$13,200	$14,520	$11,572
Less: Payment of long-term debt			4,000	
Net fixed assets (10% growth per year)	8,000	8,800	9,680	10,648
Total assets	20,000	22,000	20,200	22,220
Less: Long-term debt	10,000	10,000	6,000	6,000
Net equity	4,000	6,340	9,382	13,337
Current liabilities	$ 6,000	$ 5,660	$ 4,818	$ 2,883
Covenant compliance				
Working capital				
Current assets – current liabilities				
(must be ≥ $6,000)	$ 6,000	$ 7,540	$ 5,702	$ 8,689
Current liabilities				
Current liabilities ÷ total assets				
(must be ≤ 40% of total assets)	30%	26%	24%	13%
Debt-to-equity ratio				
Total liabilities ÷ net equity				
(must improve .5 per year)	4.00	2.47	1.15	0.67

11. The specific risks of loaning funds to Comfort Gear that would be reduced by including the protective covenants specified by Midland Bank include the following.

   a. The working capital requirement

     1) Reduces the risk of non-liquidity

     2) Ensures that Comfort Gear will continue to be a going concern during the term of the loan

     3) Reduces the risk of overexpansion and unnecessary spending, reserving a greater portion of generated revenue for working capital purposes

   b. The long-term debt restriction

     1) Ensures that Comfort Gear does not incur interest payments that overburden the company's ability to pay

     2) Reduces the risks associated with overexpansion

     3) Reduces the risk that assets will be secured by a creditor with a greater claim than Midland Bank

   c. The loan proceeds restriction

     1) Assures that the risks in the loan-granting process are the risks being taken

     2) Assures that the proceeds are not being used to fund current operations or other projects

Scenario for Essay Questions 12, 13, 14

Safe-T-Systems (STS) has developed safety devices marketed to manufacturing facilities in the midwest. STS's limited product line has been well accepted and the company is experiencing favorable profits and cash flow. The research staff is developing four new products that it believes will gain market acceptance. The marketing staff advised that there is good revenue potential for each proposed product where anticipated revenues and profits are equal relative to the level of investment. These products are independent of each other so that STS can invest in any combination of the four products, or only in a single product. The investment required for each project is as follows:

Product	Investment (in millions)
Foot pedal release	$ 2.4
Power tool safety lock	1.7
Stationary machine retraction	4.6
Overhead machine retraction	3.3
Total	$12.0

STS's capital structure is currently composed of 60% long-term debt and 40% common equity (common stock and retained earnings), and management believes these contemplated transactions will maintain these capital ratios in the future. The weighted average cost of capital in this capital structure is 13.2%. The annual cost of internally generated funds from operations is 12%.

STS's cash flow in the current year will generate an estimated $2 million of funds which will be used first for product investment. STS can raise $3 million through privately placed short-term notes at a constant interest rate of 9%. Any product investments beyond $5 million ($2 million of current year cash flow and $3 million of privately placed notes) would have to be financed by a combination of long-term bonds and issuance of additional common stock. STS's effective tax rate is 40%.

	Proportion	Cost
Long-term bonds	60	10%
Common stock	40	13

Questions

12. a. Explain the difference between weighted average cost of capital and weighted marginal cost of capital.
    b. Explain why the weighted marginal cost of capital should be used instead of the weighted average cost of capital when evaluating product investment opportunities in discounted cash flow analyses.

13. If Safe-T-Systems plans to invest up to $5 million in the development of new products during the current year, calculate the weighted marginal cost of capital for this transaction.

14. Assume Safe-T-Systems (STS) already invested $5 million in power tool safety locks and overhead machine retraction devices this year. STS is now considering investing additional funds at the same debt to equity proportions in foot pedal releases and stationary machine retraction devices. Calculate the cost of capital STS should use in its analysis.

Essay Questions 12, 13, 14 — Unofficial Answers

12. a. The weighted average cost of capital is based on historical costs, and thus reflects a composite rate of past financing decisions. Weighted marginal cost of capital measures the cost of new, additional capital at current rates.

    b. When evaluating product investment opportunities in discounted cash flow analyses, the weighted marginal cost of capital should be used where the concern is what rates are presently available and can be used for future, new investments rather than how the capital was raised in the past. The weighted average cost of capital reflects historical rates from past decisions as well as present rates. Whereas the weighted marginal cost of capital reflects current market conditions in obtaining incremental financing and allows an evaluation of capital structure based on future events and opportunity costs.

13. The weighted marginal cost of capital for the first $5 million of new funds is 8.04 percent, calculated as follows:

Type of Financing	After-Tax Cost	Weight	Weighted Marginal Cost of Capital
Retained earnings	12.0%	40	4.80%
Debt = X(1 – tax rate) = 9% × .60	5.4%	60	3.24%
Weighted marginal cost of capital			8.04%

14. The weighted marginal cost of capital that STS should use in evaluating foot pedal releases and stationary machine retraction devices is 8.80 percent, calculated as follows:

Type of Financing	After-Tax Cost	Weight	Weighted Marginal Cost of Capital
Equity common stock	13.0%	40	5.20%
Debt = X(1 – tax rate) = 10% × .60	6.0%	60	3.60%
Weighted marginal cost of capital			8.80%

The weighted marginal cost of capital for an investment in excess of the first $5 million has increased because of the higher market cost of new equity capital and additional long-term bonds. In order to increase the firm's value, foot pedal releases and stationary machine retraction devices would have to earn a return that exceeds 8.80%, the incremental marginal cost of capital.

Scenario for Essay Questions 15, 16, 17

Lever Corporation manufactures fuel injectors and is located in the midwest. Its products are used by automobile, truck, boat, and airplane manufacturers. The president of the company, Lisa McDermott, is considering the assumption of additional debt to purchase more highly automated equipment in order to expand Lever's operations and increase its current productivity.

McDermott has asked the company's financial team to assemble data and analyze different alternatives at various levels of operating and financial leverage.

The following three alternatives are being considered by Christian Smyth, chief financial officer: In Alternative 1, Lever would continue to operate with its current equipment and not incur any debt. In Alternative 2, Lever would assume debt and upgrade some of its equipment. In Alternative 3, Lever would replace equipment with more highly automated equipment, and increase its debt significantly. The company is subject to an effective corporate income tax rate of 40 percent.

	Alternative 1	Alternative 2	Alternative 3
Debt	$ 0	$ 40,000	$200,000
Equity	$200,000	$200,000	$200,000
Interest Rate	10%	10%	10%
Fuel Injector			
Selling price per unit	$ 50.00	$ 50.00	$ 50.00
Variable costs per unit	35.00	30.00	20.00
Fixed costs	30,000	60,000	90,000
Units sold – prior year	12,000	12,000	12,000

The forecasted range of sales for all three alternatives is 12,000 to 13,200 units.

Questions

15. Operating and financial leverage are factors influencing the firm's optimum capital structure. Define the following terms:

  a. Operating leverage
  b. Financial leverage

16. For Alternative 3 being considered by Lever Corporation, calculate the degree of operating leverage at 12,000 units. Calculate your answer to three decimal points.

17. Discuss at least two implications to Lever Corporation of increasing operating and financial leverage.

Essay Questions 15, 16, 17 — Unofficial Answers

15. a. Operating leverage refers to the level of fixed assets in a firm and the decrease in variable costs as fixed costs increase. It is calculated as the percentage change in operating income divided by the percentage change in revenue.

  b. Financial leverage is the ratio of debt to the total value of the firm, referring to the degree to which the assets of the firm are financed with debt and subsequent effect of interest payments. It can be calculated as the percentage change in net income divided by the percentage change in operating income.

16. The degree of operating leverage at 12,000 units for Alternative 3 is 1.333, calculated as follows:

$$Operating\ leverage = \frac{Percent\ change\ in\ operating\ income}{Percent\ change\ in\ total\ revenue}$$

Alternative 3

Revenue (12,000 units × $50)	$600,000
Less: Variable costs (12,000 units × $20)	240,000
Contribution margin	360,000
Less: Fixed costs	90,000
Operating income	$270,000

Assuming a one unit change in units sold, the change in revenue is $50 and the change in operating income is $30 ($50 – $20 variable costs).

Degree of Operating Leverage =

$$\frac{Unit\ contribution \div operating\ income}{Unit\ sales\ price \div total\ revenue}$$

$$= \frac{\$30 \div \$270,000}{\$50 \div \$600,000} = 1.333$$

17. At least two implications of increasing operating and financial leverage include the following:

  a. The firm's competitiveness and market share may increase. In many firms, higher volumes with lower prices are only possible with investments in automation.

  b. With a high degree of leverage, particularly financial leverage, lenders will require a higher interest rate due to the perceived increase in risk, therefore increasing the cost of debt to the firm.

Consider using Gleim's **CMA Test Prep** for interactive testing with **hundreds of multiple-choice questions** as an additional method of knowledge transfer in your quest to pass Part 4.

STUDY UNIT NINETEEN
CMA PART 3 REVIEW –
DECISION ANALYSIS

(5 pages of outline)

Part 3 of the CMA exam is titled **Strategic Management**. This study unit is a review of this section:

D. **Decision Analysis.** Logical steps to reach a decision; relevant data concepts; cost-volume-profit analysis; marginal analysis; cost-based pricing; income tax implications for operational decision analysis.

This study unit presents the IMA's Learning Outcome Statements and Gleim Core Concepts relevant to this section. Bear in mind that **all topics** on Part 4 of the exam are tested at **skill level C** (all six skill types required).

19.1 DECISION ANALYSIS REVIEW

Part 3 – Section D.1. Decision process

The candidate should be able to:

    a.   identify and demonstrate an understanding of the steps needed to reach a decision, i.e., (i) obtain information, (ii) identify alternative courses of action, (iii) make predictions about future scenarios, (iv) choose and justify an alternative, (v) implement a decision, and (vi) evaluate performance to provide feedback

    b.   demonstrate an understanding of how management should evaluate decision results

Core Concepts for the Decision-Making Process

- Rational decision making involves these **steps**: defining the problem, obtaining information, identifying alternative courses of action, making predictions about future costs, choosing and justifying an alternative, implementing the decision, and evaluating performance to provide feedback.

- The most common difficulty in problem solving is **defining the problem**.

- Among the **methods** that can be used to **search for a solution** are attribute listing, blast! then refine, brainstorming, creative leap, and Delphi technique.

- Among the **models** that can be used for **evaluating alternatives** are simulation, linear programming, and the Monte Carlo method.

- Choosing a course of action involves not only comparing the **future cash flows** of the potential courses of action, but also considering **qualitative factors**, such as relationships with employees, and **nonfinancial quantitative factors**, such as the rate of defective output.

- **Three problems** in decision making are framing error, escalation, and overconfidence.

Part 3 - Section D.2. Relevant data concepts

The candidate should be able to:

- a.   differentiate between economic concepts of revenues and costs and accounting concepts of revenues and costs
- b.   define relevant revenues (expected future revenues) and relevant costs (expected future costs)
- c.   identify cost behavior patterns, define cost traceability, and demonstrate an understanding of cost relevance as it relates to various cost objects for which decisions are to be made
- d.   demonstrate an understanding of various costs incurred in the value chain and the composition of such costs for decisions such as pricing, alternative manufacturing options, contracts negotiations, and outsourcing decisions
- e.   differentiate between costs that are avoidable or unavoidable in a decision process setting
- f.   identify relevant costs as the incremental, marginal, or differential costs among alternative courses of action and calculate the relevant costs given a numerical scenario
- g.   define sunk costs and explain why they are not relevant
- h.   distinguish between quantitative factors (e.g., cost of direct labor) and qualitative factors (e.g., reduction in new-product development time)
- i.   define qualitative factors as outcomes that cannot be measured in numerical terms, e.g., employee morale
- j.   demonstrate an understanding of opportunity costs as the contribution to income that is forgone by not using a limited resource in its best alternative use
- k.   demonstrate an understanding of the impact of income taxes on the relevant revenue and cost data employed in the decision process

Core Concepts for Relevant Data Concepts

- ■   The **accounting concept** of costs includes only explicit costs, i.e., those that represent actual outlays of cash, the allocation of outlays of cash, or commitments to pay cash. The **economic concept** of costs includes both explicit and implicit (i.e., opportunity) costs.

- ■   In decision making, an organization must focus on only **relevant revenues and costs**. To be relevant, revenues and costs must be made in the future and differ among the possible alternative courses of action.

- ■   A vital concept in decision making is that of **relevant range**, i.e., the range of activity over which fixed costs remain fixed. Relevant range is synonymous with the short run.

- ■   **Cost behavior** does not necessarily determine the relevance of costs.

- ■   **Cost traceability** allows decision makers to associate costs with a cost object in an economically feasible way. Costs which cannot be traced must be allocated. An allocated cost may still be relevant.

- ■   The **impact of income taxes** on a company's earnings must be considered in any business decision.

Part 3 – Section D.3. Cost-volume-profit analysis

The candidate should be able to:

a. demonstrate an understanding of how cost-volume-profit (CVP) analysis (breakeven analysis) is used to examine the behavior of total revenues, total costs, and operating income as changes occur in output levels, selling prices, variable costs per unit, or fixed costs

b. differentiate between costs that are fixed and costs that are variable with respect to levels of output

c. demonstrate an understanding of the behavior of total revenues and total costs in relation to output within a relevant range

d. explain why the classification of fixed vs. variable costs is affected by the timeframe being considered

e. demonstrate an understanding of how contribution margin per unit is used in CVP analysis

f. calculate contribution margin per unit and total contribution margin

g. calculate the breakeven point in units and dollar sales to achieve targeted operating income or targeted net income

h. demonstrate an understanding of how changes in unit sales mix affect operating income in multiple-product situations

i. demonstrate an understanding of why there is no unique break-even point in multiple-product situations

j. analyze and recommend a course of action using CVP analysis

k. demonstrate an understanding of the impact of income taxes on CVP analysis

Core Concepts for Cost-Volume-Profit (CVP) Analysis

- **Cost-volume-profit analysis** (also called breakeven analysis) is a tool for understanding the interaction of revenues with fixed and variable costs.
- The **break-even point** is the level of output at which total revenues equal total expenses; that is, the point at which operating income is zero.
- The **contribution income statement** with per unit amounts is an integral part of break-even analysis. Every unit sold contributes a certain percentage of its sales revenue to covering fixed costs. Once fixed costs are fully covered, all additional revenue contributes to profit.
- The break-even model can be used to find **target operating income**, or to find the break-even point for **multiple products**, or to determine the profitability of a **special order**.

Part 3 – Section D.4. Marginal analysis

The candidate should be able to:

a.   demonstrate proficiency in the use of marginal analysis for decisions such as (a) introducing a new product or changing output levels of existing products, (b) accepting or rejecting special orders, (c) making or buying a product or service, (d) selling a product or performing additional processes and selling a more value-added product, and (e) adding or dropping a segment

b.   identify relevant information as the future revenues and future costs that will differ between the decisions in any type of marginal analysis

c.   explain why any cost, including any allocated costs, that does not differ between alternatives, should be ignored in marginal decision analyses

d.   demonstrate an understanding of opportunity cost in marginal analysis

e.   calculate the effect of opportunity cost in a marginal analysis decision

f.   recommend a course of action using marginal analysis

g.   calculate the effect on operating income when changes in output levels occur

h.   calculate the effect on operating income of a decision to accept or reject a special order when there is idle capacity and the order has no long-run implications

i.   identify qualitative factors in make-or-buy decisions, such as product quality and dependability of suppliers

j.   calculate the effect on operating income of a decision to make-or-buy a product or service

k.   differentiate between avoidable and unavoidable costs in the decision to drop or add a segment

l.   demonstrate an understanding of the impact of income taxes on marginal analysis decisions

Core Concepts for Marginal Analysis

■   The typical problem for which **marginal (differential or incremental) analysis** can be used involves choices among courses of action. The focus is on incremental revenues and costs, not the totals of all revenues and costs for the given option.

■   A special order which might at first be rejected could turn out to be profitable after marginal analysis. Marginal analysis emphasizes incremental costs, highlighting the ability of marginal revenue to **cover fixed costs**.

■   The key variable in a **make-or-buy** (insource vs. outsource) decision is total relevant costs, not total costs.

■   Marginal analysis also applies to decisions regarding **which products and services** to sell and in what quantities to sell them given the known demand and resource limitations.

■   In general, if the marginal cost of a project exceeds the marginal revenue, the firm should **disinvest** in a particular operation or product line.

Part 3 – Section D.5. Cost-based pricing

The candidate should be able to:

a. demonstrate an understanding of cost-behavior patterns, cost traceability, cost drivers, and cost relevance in measuring the costs of products

b. demonstrate an understanding of how the pricing of a product or service is affected by the demand for the product or service, as well as the supply availability

c. discuss how pricing decisions in the short-run can differ from pricing decisions in the long-run

d. calculate the relevant costs associated with short-run special product purchase orders

e. discuss the importance of stable and predictable costs over an extended time period for long-run pricing decisions

f. demonstrate an understanding of the market-based approach to the pricing decision

g. differentiate between a cost-based approach and a market-based approach to setting prices

h. explain why market-based pricing strategies are generally used when operating in a competitive commodities type market

i. define and demonstrate an understanding of target pricing and target costing

j. identify techniques used to set prices based on understanding customers' perceptions of value, competitors' technologies, products, costs, and financial conditions

k. identify the main steps in developing target prices and target costs

l. define value engineering

m. calculate the target operating income per unit and target cost per unit

n. define and distinguish between a value-added cost and a nonvalue-added cost

o. define the pricing technique of cost plus target rate of return

p. define a product life cycle and life-cycle costing

q. define peak-load pricing

r. evaluate and recommend pricing strategies under specific market conditions or opportunities

Core Concepts for Cost-Based Pricing

- **Pricing objectives** include profit maximization, target margin maximization, volume-oriented objectives, image-oriented objectives, and stabilization objectives

- **Factors** to consider in pricing decisions are: supply and demand; internal factors such as marketing-mix strategy and relevant costs; and external factors such as market type (pure competition, monopolistic competition, etc.) and customer perceptions.

- **Pricing approaches** include cost-based pricing, market-based pricing, competition-based pricing, new product pricing, pricing by intermediaries, and product-mix pricing.

- A **target price** is the expected market price for a product or service, given the company's knowledge of its consumers' perceptions of value and competitors' responses.

- **Life-cycle costing** estimates a product's revenues and expenses over its expected life cycle, from R&D all the way through product phaseout.

19.2 DECISION ANALYSIS ESSAY QUESTIONS

Recall that your CMA Part 4 exam will probably contain six scenarios, with about three questions per scenario. There will be a recommended time allocation of 20 minutes, 30 minutes, or 45 minutes for each scenario and related questions.

One scenario will involve ethical issues, and probably one or two scenarios will include calculations and responses on a worksheet. Also, expect at least one scenario on organizational/behavioral topics. The remaining scenarios cover Parts 1, 2, and 3.

Scenario Title	Subtopic	Questions	Suggested Time
Award Plus Co.	Ethics and Outside Purchasing	1, 2, 3, 4	20 minutes
Sonimad Mining Corporation	Sell-or-Process-Further	5, 6	30 minutes
Sommers Company	Special Orders	7, 8, 9, 10	30 minutes
Marcus Fibers, Inc.	Pricing and Bidding	11, 12, 13	30 minutes
Don Masters	Breakeven Analysis	14, 15	30 minutes
Pralina Products Company	Cost-Volume-Profit Analysis	16, 17, 18	30 minutes

Scenario for Essay Questions 1, 2, 3, 4

Award Plus Co. manufactures medals for winners of athletic events and other contests. Its manufacturing plant has the capacity to produce 10,000 medals each month; current monthly production is 7,500 medals. The company normally charges $175 per medal. Variable costs and fixed costs for the current activity level of 75% are shown below.

Current Product Costs	
Variable costs	
Manufacturing	
Labor	$ 375,000
Material	262,500
Marketing	187,500
Total variable costs	825,000
Fixed costs	
Manufacturing	275,000
Marketing	175,000
Total fixed costs	450,000
Total costs	$1,275,000
Unit variable costs	$ 110
Unit fixed costs	60
Average unit costs	$ 170

Award Plus has just received a special onetime order for 2,500 medals at $100 per medal. For this particular order, no variable marketing costs will be incurred. Cathy Senna, a management accountant with Award Plus, has been assigned the task of analyzing this order and recommending whether or not the company should accept or reject it. After examining the costs, Senna suggested to her supervisor, Gerard LePenn who is the controller, that they request competitive bids from vendors for the raw materials as the current quote seems high. LePenn insisted that the prices are in line with other vendors and told her that she was not to discuss her observations with anyone else. Senna later discovered that LePenn is a brother-in-law of the owner of the current raw materials supply vendor.

Questions

1. Identify and explain the costs that will be relevant to Cathy Senna's analysis of the special order being considered by Award Plus Co.

2. Determine if Award Plus Co. should accept the special order. In explaining your answer, compute both the new average unit cost for Award Plus and the incremental unit cost for the special order.

3. Discuss at least three other considerations that Cathy Senna should include in her analysis of the special order.

4. Using the steps described in Statement on Management Accounting Number 1C (Revised), *IMA Statement on Ethical Professional Practice*, explain how Cathy Senna should try to resolve the ethical conflict arising out of the controller's insistence that the company avoid competitive bidding.

Essay Questions 1, 2, 3, 4 — Unofficial Answers

1. Costs that will be relevant are those expected future costs applicable to a particular decision (the costs that will differ between the alternatives). Only the variable costs of labor and materials are relevant. Because the order was received directly by Award Plus, variable marketing is not relevant because additional marketing costs will not be incurred. Fixed costs are also not relevant because no capital investments are needed to meet the order.

2. Award Plus Co. should accept the offer. Although the average unit cost of $148.75 is higher than the price offered, the unit incremental cost is only $85. Accepting the special order will result in a contribution per unit of $15 ($100 less $85) and a total additional contribution margin of $37,500 (2,500 units × $15), as shown below.

	Current Monthly Production	Special Order	Combined Production
Units produced	7,500	2,500	10,000
Sales	$1,312,500 [1]	$250,000 [2]	$1,562,500
Variable costs			
Labor	375,000	125,000 [3]	500,000
Materials	262,500	87,500 [4]	350,000
Marketing	187,500	--	187,500
Total variable costs	825,000	212,500	1,037,500
Fixed costs			
Manufacturing	275,000	--	275,000
Marketing	175,000	--	175,000
Total fixed costs	450,000	--	450,000
Total costs	1,275,000	212,500	1,487,500
Income before tax	$ 37,500	$ 37,500	$ 75,000
Costs per unit			
Variable [5]	$ 110.00	$ 85.00	$ 103.75
Fixed [6]	60.00	--	45.00
Average unit costs [7]	$ 170.00	$ 85.00	$ 148.75

[1] 7,500 units × $175	=	$1,312,500
[2] 2,500 units × $100	=	250,000
[3] 2,500 units × ($375,000 ÷ 7,500 units)	=	125,000
[4] 2,500 units × ($262,500 ÷ 7,500 units)	=	87,500
[5] Total variable costs ÷ units produced	=	variable/incremental cost per unit
[6] Total fixed costs ÷ units produced	=	fixed cost per unit
[7] Total costs ÷ units produced	=	average cost per unit

3. At least three other considerations that Senna should include in her analysis include

   a. Possible problems with other customers who want similar treatment.

   b. The short-term nature of differential profit analysis; such analyses are not valid in the long run, where all costs, including fixed costs, must be recovered.

   c. The future customer potential of the buyer generating additional revenues.

4. In accordance with Statement on Management Accounting Number 1C (Revised), *IMA Statement on Ethical Professional Practice*, Senna should try to resolve the ethical conflict by taking the following steps:

   a. Follow Award Plus Co.'s established policies on such matters.

   b. If such policies do not exist, she should discuss the situation with her manager unless, as in this case, the manager is involved in the conflict. Then, she should discuss the situation with the manager's supervisor, probably the CFO.

   c. If the CFO cannot help resolve the matter, then she should continue going to the next higher managerial level, including the audit committee of the board of directors.

   d. Senna should clarify relevant concepts by confidential discussions with an objective advisor to obtain an understanding of possible courses of action.

   e. If the ethical conflict still exists after exhausting all avenues of internal review, then she may have to resign and submit an informative memorandum to the board.

Scenario for Essay Questions 5, 6

Sonimad Mining Company produces and sells bulk raw coal to other coal companies. Sonimad mines and stockpiles the coal; it is then passed through a one-step crushing process before being loaded onto river barges for shipment to customers. The annual output of 10 million tons, which is expected to remain stable, has an average cost of $20 per ton with an average selling price of $27 per ton.

Management is evaluating the possibility of further processing the coal by sizing and cleaning to expand markets and enhance product revenue. Management has rejected the possibility of constructing a sizing and cleaning plant, which would require a significant long-term capital investment.

Bill Rolland, controller of Sonimad, has asked Amy Kimbell, mining engineer, to develop cost and revenue projections for further processing the coal through a variety of contractual arrangements. After extensive discussions with vendors and contractors, Kimbell has prepared the following projections of incremental costs of sizing and cleaning Sonimad's annual output.

Sonimad Mining Company Sizing and Cleaning Processes	
	Incremental Costs
Direct labor (employee leasing)	$600,000 per year
Supervisory personnel (employee leasing)	100,000 per year
Heavy equipment rental, operating, and maintenance costs	25,000 per month
Contract sizing and cleaning	3.50 per ton
Outbound rail freight (per 60-ton rail car)	240 per car

In addition to the preceding cost information, market samples obtained by Kimbell have shown that electrical utilities enter into contracts for sized and cleaned coal similar to that mined by Sonimad at an expected average price of $36 per ton.

Kimbell has learned that 5% of the raw bulk output that enters the sizing and cleaning process will be lost as a primary product. Normally, 75% of this product loss can be salvaged as coal fines. These are small pieces ranging from dust-like particles up to pieces 2 inches in diameter. Coal fines are too small for use by electrical utilities but are frequently sold to steel manufacturers for use in blast furnaces.

Unfortunately, the price for coal fines frequently fluctuates between $14 and $24 per ton (FOB shipping point), and the timing of market volume is erratic. While companies generally sell all their coal fines during a year, it is not unusual to stockpile this product for several months before making any significant sales.

Questions

5. Prepare an analysis to show whether it would be more profitable for Sonimad Mining Company to continue to sell the raw bulk coal or to process it further through sizing and cleaning. (Note: Ignore any value related to the coal fines in your analysis.)

6. a. Taking into consideration any potential value to the coal fines, prepare an analysis to show if the fines would affect the results of your analysis prepared in Question 5.

    b. What other factors should be considered in evaluating a sell-or-process-further decision?

Essay Questions 5, 6 — Unofficial Answers

5. The analysis shown below indicates that it would be more profitable for Sonimad Mining
    company to continue to sell raw bulk coal without further processing. (This analysis ignores
    any value related to coal fines.)

    Incremental Sales Revenue:
    Sales revenue after further processing

(9,500,000 tons × $36)	$342,000,000
Sales revenue from bulk raw coal	
(10,000,000 tons × $27)	270,000,000
Incremental sales revenue	72,000,000

    Incremental costs:

Direct labor	600,000
Supervisory personnel	100,000
Heavy equipment costs ($25,000 × 12 months)	300,000
Sizing and clearing (10,000,000 tons × $3.50)	35,000,000
Outbound rail freight (9,500,000 tons ÷ 60 tons) × $240 per car	38,000,000
Incremental costs	74,000,000
Incremental gain (loss)	$ (2,000,000)

6. a. The analysis shown below indicates that the potential revenue from the coal fines
        by-product would result in additional revenue, ranging between $5,250,000 and
        $9,000,000, depending on the market price of the fines.

        1) Coal fines   = 75% of 5% of raw bulk tonnage
                          = .75 × (10,000,000 × .05)
                          = 375,000 tons

        Potential additional revenue:

	Market price	
	Minimum	Maximum
	$14 per ton	$24 per ton
Additional revenue	$5,250,000	$9,000,000

        Since the incremental loss is $2 million, as calculated in Question 5 above,
        including the coal fines in the analysis indicates that further processing provides
        a positive result and is, therefore, favorable.

    b. Other factors that should be considered in evaluating a sell-or-process-further decision
        include the

        1) Stability of the current customer market and how it compares to the market for
            sized and cleaned coal
        2) Storage space needed for the coal fines until they are sold and the handling
            costs of coal fines
        3) Reliability of cost (e.g., rail freight rates) and revenue estimates, and the risk of
            depending on these estimates
        4) Timing of the revenue stream from coal fines and impact on the need for liquidity
        5) Possible environmental problems, i.e., dumping of waste and smoke from
            unprocessed coal

Scenario for Essay Questions 7, 8, 9, 10

The Sommers Company, located in Wisconsin, manufactures a variety of industrial valves and pipe fittings that are sold to customers in nearby states. Currently, the company is operating at about 70% capacity and is earning a satisfactory return on investment.

Management has been approached by Glasgow Industries Ltd. of Scotland with an offer to buy 120,000 units of a pressure valve. Glasgow Industries manufactures a valve that is almost identical to Sommers' pressure valve; however, a fire in Glasgow Industries' valve plant has shut down its operations. Glasgow needs the 120,000 valves over the next 4 months to meet commitments to its regular customers; the company is prepared to pay $19 each for the valves, FOB shipping point.

Sommers' product cost, based on current attainable standards, for the pressure valve is

Direct materials	$ 5.00
Direct labor	6.00
Manufacturing overhead	9.00
Total cost	$20.00

Manufacturing overhead is applied to production at the rate of $18 per standard direct labor hour. This overhead rate is made up of the following components.

Variable factory overhead	$ 6.00
Fixed factory overhead-direct	8.00
Fixed factory overhead-allocated	4.00
Applied manufacturing overhead rate	$18.00

Additional costs incurred in connection with sales of the pressure valve include sales commissions of 5% and freight expense of $1.00 per unit. However, the company does not pay sales commissions on special orders that come directly to management.

In determining selling prices, Sommers adds a 40% markup to product cost. This provides a $28 suggested selling price for the pressure valve. The Marketing Department, however, has set the current selling price at $27 to maintain market share.

Production management believes that it can handle the Glasgow Industries order without disrupting its scheduled production. The order would, however, require additional fixed factory overhead of $12,000 per month in the form of supervision and clerical costs.

If management accepts the order, 30,000 pressure valves will be manufactured and shipped to Glasgow Industries each month for the next 4 months.

Questions

7. Determine how many additional direct labor hours would be required each month to fill the Glasgow Industries order.

8. Prepare an incremental analysis showing the impact of accepting the Glasgow Industries order.

9. Calculate the minimum unit price that Sommers' management could accept for the Glasgow Industries order without reducing net income.

10. Identify the factors, other than price, that Sommers Company should consider before accepting the Glasgow Industries order.

Essay Questions 7, 8, 9, 10 — Unofficial Answers

7. The manufacturing overhead rate is $18.00 per standard direct labor hour and the standard product cost includes $9.00 of manufacturing overhead per pressure valve. Accordingly, the standard direct labor hour per finished valve is 1/2 hour ($9 ÷ $18). Therefore, 30,000 units per month would require 15,000 direct labor hours.

8. The incremental analysis of accepting the Glasgow Industries' order of 120,000 units is presented below.

	Per unit	Totals for 120,000 units
Incremental revenue	$19.00	$2,280,000
Incremental costs		
Variable costs		
Direct materials	5.00	600,000
Direct labor	6.00	720,000
Variable overhead	3.00	360,000
Total variable costs	$14.00	1,680,000
Fixed overhead		
Supervisory and clerical costs		
(4 months @ $12,000)		48,000
Total incremental costs		1,728,000
Incremental profit before tax		$552,000

The following costs are irrelevant to the incremental analysis:

a. Shipping
b. Sales Commission
c. Fixed Factory Overhead - Direct, Allocated

9. The minimum unit price that Sommers could accept without reducing net income must cover variable costs plus the additional fixed costs.

Variable unit costs		
Direct materials	$5.00	
Direct labor	6.00	
Variable overhead	3.00	$14.00
Additional fixed cost ($48,000 ÷ 120,000)		.40
Minimum unit price		$14.40

10. Sommers should consider the following factors before accepting the Glasgow order.

a. The effect of the special order on Sommers' sales at regular prices
b. The possibility of future sales to Glasgow Industries and the effects of participating in the international marketplace
c. The company's relevant range of activity and whether or not the special order will cause volume to exceed this range
d. The impact on local, state, and federal taxes
e. The effect on machinery or the scheduled maintenance of equipment

Scenario for Essay Questions 11, 12, 13

Marcus Fibers, Inc. specializes in the manufacture of synthetic fibers that the company uses in many products such as blankets, coats, and uniforms for police and firefighters. Marcus has been in business since 1975 and has been profitable each year since 1983. The company uses a standard cost system and applies overhead on the basis of direct labor hours.

Marcus has recently received a request to bid on the manufacture of 800,000 blankets scheduled for delivery to several military bases. The bid must be stated at full cost per unit plus a return on full cost of no more than 9% after income taxes. Full cost has been defined as including all variable costs of manufacturing the product, a reasonable amount of fixed overhead, and reasonable incremental administrative costs associated with the manufacture and sale of the product. The contractor has indicated that bids in excess of $25.00 per blanket are not likely to be considered.

In order to prepare the bid for the 800,000 blankets, Andrea Lightner, cost accountant, has gathered the information presented below about the costs associated with the production of the blankets.

Raw material	$1.50 per pound of fibers
Direct labor	$7.00 per hour
Direct machine costs*	$10.00 per blanket
Variable overhead	$3.00 per direct labor hour
Fixed overhead	$8.00 per direct labor hour
Incremental administrative costs	$2,500 per 1,000 blankets
Special fee**	$.50 per blanket
Material usage	6 pounds per blanket
Production rate	4 blankets per direct labor hour
Effective tax rate	40 percent

* Direct machine costs consist of items such as special lubricants, replacement of needles used in stitching, and maintenance costs. These costs are not included in the normal overhead rates.

** Marcus recently developed a new blanket fiber at a cost of $750,000. In an effort to recover this cost, Marcus has instituted a policy of adding a $.50 fee to the cost of each blanket using the new fiber. To date, the company has recovered $125,000. Lightner knows that this fee does not fit within the definition of full cost as it is not a cost of manufacturing the product.

Questions

11. Calculate the minimum price per blanket that Marcus Fibers, Inc. could bid without reducing the company's net income.

12. Using the full cost criterion and the maximum allowable return specified, calculate Marcus Fibers, Inc.'s bid price per blanket.

13. Without prejudice to your answer in Question 12, assume that the price per blanket that Marcus Fibers, Inc. calculated using the cost-plus criterion specified is greater than the maximum bid of $25.00 per blanket allowed. Discuss the factors that Marcus Fibers, Inc. should consider before deciding whether to submit a bid at the maximum acceptable price of $25.00 per blanket.

Essay Questions 11, 12, 13 — Unofficial Answers

11. The minimum price per blanket that Marcus Fibers, Inc. could bid without reducing the company's net income is $24.00 calculated as follows:

Raw materials (6 lb. @ $1.50/lb.)	$ 9.00
Direct labor (.25 hr. @ $7.00/hr.)	1.75
Machine time ($10.00/blanket)	10.00
Variable overhead (.25 hr. @ $3.00/hr.)	.75
Administrative cost ($2,500 ÷ 1,000)	2.50
Minimum bid price	$24.00

12. Using the full cost criterion and the maximum allowable return specified, Marcus Fibers, Inc.'s bid price per blanket would be $29.90, calculated as follows:

Relevant costs from Question 11	$24.00
Fixed overhead (.25 hr. @ $8.00/hr.)	2.00
Subtotal	26.00
Allowable return (.15* × $26.00)	3.90
Bid price	$29.90

*9% ÷ (1 – tax rate of 40%)

13. Factors that Marcus Fibers, Inc. should consider before deciding whether to submit a bid at the maximum acceptable price of $25.00 per blanket include the following:

a. The company should be sure there is sufficient excess capacity to fulfill the order and that no additional investment is necessary in facilities or equipment which would increase the fixed expense.

b. If the order is accepted at $25.00 per blanket, there will be a $1.00 contribution per blanket to fixed costs. However, the company should consider whether there are other jobs that would make a greater contribution.

c. Acceptance of the order at a low price could cause problems with current customers who might demand a similar pricing arrangement.

Scenario for Essay Questions 14, 15

Don Masters and two of his colleagues are considering opening a law office in a large metropolitan area that would make inexpensive legal services available to those who could not otherwise afford these services. The intent is to provide easy access for their clients by having the office open 360 days per year, 16 hours each day from 7:00 a.m. to 11:00 p.m. The office would be staffed by a lawyer, paralegal, legal secretary, and clerk-receptionist for each of the two 8-hour shifts.

To determine the feasibility of the project, Masters hired a marketing consultant to assist with market projections. The results of this study show that, if the firm spends $500,000 on advertising the first year, the number of new clients expected each day would have the following probability distribution.

Number of New Clients per Day	Probability
20	.10
30	.30
55	.40
85	.20

Masters and his associates believe these numbers are reasonable and are prepared to spend the $500,000 on advertising. Other pertinent information about the operation of the office is given below.

- The only charge to each new client would be $30 for the initial consultation. All cases that warranted further legal work would be accepted on a contingency basis with the firm earning 30% of any favorable settlements or judgments. Masters estimates that 20% of new client consultations will result in favorable settlements or judgments averaging $2,000 each. It is not expected that there will be repeat clients during the first year of operations.

- The hourly wages of the staff are projected to be $25 for the lawyer, $20 for the paralegal, $15 for the legal secretary, and $10 for the clerk-receptionist. Fringe benefit expense will be 40% of the wages paid. A total of 400 hours of overtime is expected for the year; this will be divided equally between the legal secretary and the clerk-receptionist positions. Overtime will be paid at one and one-half times the regular wage, and the fringe benefit expense will apply to the full wage.

- Masters has located 6,000 square feet of suitable office space which rents for $28 per square foot annually. Associated expenses will be $22,000 for property insurance and $32,000 for utilities.

- It will be necessary for the group to purchase malpractice insurance, which is expected to cost $180,000 annually.

- The initial investment in office equipment will be $60,000; this equipment has an estimated useful life of 4 years.

- The cost of office supplies has been estimated to be $4 per expected new client.

Questions

14. Determine how many new clients must visit the law office being considered by Don Masters and his colleagues for the venture to break even during its first year of operations.

15. Using the information provided by the marketing consultant, determine if it is feasible for the law office to achieve breakeven operations.

Essay Questions 14, 15 — Unofficial Answers

14. In order to break even during the first year of operations, 10,220 clients must visit the law office being considered by Don Masters and his colleagues, as calculated below.

Breakeven Calculations for First Year of Operations

Fixed expenses:		
Advertising		$ 500,000
Rent (6,000 × $28)		168,000
Property insurance		22,000
Utilities		32,000
Malpractice insurance		180,000
Depreciation ($60,000 ÷ 4)		15,000
Wages & fringe benefits		
Regular wages:		
($25 + $20 + $15 + $10)		
× 16 hours × 360 days	$403,200	
Overtime wages:		
(200 × $15 × 1.5) +		
(200 × $20 × 1.5)	7,500	
Total wages	410,700	
Fringe benefits @ 40%	164,280	574,980
Total fixed expenses		$1,491,980

$$\text{Breakeven point} = \text{Revenue} - \text{Variable cost} - \text{Fixed cost}$$
$$= \$30X + (\$2,000 \times .2X \times .30) - \$4X - \$1,491,980$$
$$= \$30X + \$120X - \$4X - \$1,491,980$$
$$146X = \$1,491,980$$
$$X = 10,219.04 \text{ or } \underline{10,220} \text{ clients}$$

15. Based on the report of the marketing consultant, the expected number of new clients during the first year is 18,000, as calculated below. Therefore, it is feasible for the law office to break even during the first year of operations as the breakeven point is 10,220 clients.

Expected value	= (20 × .10) + (30 × .30) + (55 × .40) + (85 × .20)
	= 50 clients per day
Annual clients	= 50 × 360 days
	= 18,000 clients per year

Scenario for Essay Questions 16, 17, 18

Pralina Products Company is a regional firm which has three major product lines -- cereals, breakfast bars, and dog food. The income statement for the year ended April 30, Year 4, is shown below; the statement was prepared using absorption (full) costing. Explanatory data appear following the statement.

Pralina Products Company
Income Statement
For the Year Ended April 30, Year 4
(000 omitted)

	Cereals	Breakfast Bars	Dog Food	Total
Sales in pounds	2,000	500	500	3,000
Revenue from sales	$1,000	$400	$200	$1,600
Cost of sales				
Raw materials	$ 330	$160	$100	$ 590
Direct labor	90	40	20	150
Factory overhead	108	48	24	180
Total cost of sales	$ 528	$248	$144	$ 920
Gross margin	$ 472	$152	$ 56	$ 680
Operating expenses				
Selling expenses				
Advertising	$ 50	$ 30	$ 20	$ 100
Commissions	50	40	20	110
Salaries and related benefits	30	20	10	60
Total selling expenses	$ 130	$ 90	$ 50	$ 270
General and Administrative expenses				
Licenses	$ 50	$ 20	$ 15	$ 85
Salaries and related benefits	60	25	15	100
Total general and administrative expenses	$ 110	$ 45	$ 30	$ 185
Total operating expenses	$ 240	$135	$ 80	$ 455
Operating income before taxes	$ 232	$ 17	$ (24)	$ 225

Other Data

1. <u>Cost of sales</u>. The company's inventories of raw materials and finished products do not vary significantly from year to year. The inventories at April 30, Year 4, were essentially identical to those at April 30, Year 3. Factory overhead was applied to products at 120% of direct labor dollars. The factory overhead costs for the Year 3-4 fiscal year were as follows:

Variable indirect labor and supplies	$ 15,000
Variable employee benefits on factory labor	30,000
Supervisory salaries and related benefits	35,000
Plant occupancy costs	100,000
	$180,000

2. <u>Advertising</u>. The company has been unable to determine any causal relationship between the level of sales volume and the level of advertising expenditures. Because management believes advertising is necessary, an annual advertising program is implemented for each product line. Each product line is advertised independently.

3. <u>Commissions</u>. Sales commissions are paid to the sales force at the rates of 5% on the cereals and 10% on the breakfast bars and dog food.

4. <u>Licenses</u>. Licenses are required for each product line. These are renewed annually.

5. <u>Salaries and related benefits</u>. Sales and administrative personnel devote time to all product lines. Their salaries are allocated on the basis of estimates of time spent on each line.

Questions

The controller of Pralina Products is going to prepare a report explaining cost-volume-profit (CVP) analysis. Identify and explain the following points, which the controller should include in the report:

16. The advantages that CVP analysis can provide to a company.
17. The difficulties Pralina could experience in the calculations involved in CVP analysis.
18. The dangers that Pralina should be aware of in using data derived from CVP analysis.

Essay Questions 16, 17, 18 — Unofficial Answers

16.   Advantages that CVP analysis could provide include

    a.   Determining the marginal contribution of products which can assist management in planning sales volume and profitability including the calculation of a breakeven point

    b.   Identifying products which can support heavy sales promotion expenditures

    c.   Assisting in decisions related to eliminating a product

    d.   Accepting a special order at a discounted price

17.   Difficulties Pralina Products could expect to have on the CVP calculations include

    a.   Separating mixed costs into their fixed and variable components

    b.   Determining how to treat joint or common costs

    c.   Determining efficiency and productivity within the relevant range

    d.   Determining a constant sales mix within the relevant range

18.   Pralina Products should be aware of the following dangers when using CVP analysis:

    a.   The use of inaccurate assumptions for the calculations

    b.   CVP analysis tends to focus on the short term

    c.   CVP analysis tends to focus on incremental variable costs, but fixed costs must be managed and controlled

---

Consider using Gleim's **CMA Test Prep** for interactive testing with **hundreds of multiple-choice questions** as an additional method of knowledge transfer in your quest to pass Part 4.

STUDY UNIT TWENTY
CMA PART 3 REVIEW –
INVESTMENT DECISIONS

(7 pages of outline)

Part 3 of the CMA exam is titled **Strategic Management**. This study unit is a review of this section:

E.   **Investment Decisions.** Cash flow estimates; time value of money; discounted cash flow concepts; net present value; internal rate of return; non-discounting analysis techniques; income tax implications for investment decision analysis; ranking investment projects; risk analysis; real options.

This study unit represents the IMA's Learning Outcome Statements and Gleim Core Concepts relevant to this section. Bear in mind that **all topics** on Part 4 of the exam are tested at **skill level C** (all six skill types required).

20.1 INVESTMENT DECISIONS REVIEW

Part 3 – Section E.1. Capital budgeting process

The candidate should be able to:

   a.   define capital budgeting

   b.   demonstrate an understanding of capital budgeting applications in making decisions for project investments

   c.   identify the steps or stages undertaken in developing and implementing a capital budget for a project

   d.   identify and calculate the relevant cash flows of a capital investment project on both a pretax and after-tax basis

   e.   demonstrate an understanding of how income taxes affect cash flows

   f.   distinguish between cash flows and accounting profits and discuss the relevance to capital budgeting of the following: incremental cash flow, sunk cost, and opportunity cost

   g.   explain the importance of changes in net working capital in the capital budgeting process

   h.   discuss how the effects of inflation are reflected in capital budgeting analysis

   i.   describe the role of the post-audit in the capital budgeting process

Core Concepts for the Capital Budgeting Process

- Capital budgeting is the process of **planning and controlling** investments for **long-term projects**. By their nature, capital projects affect **multiple accounting periods** and will constrain the organization's financial planning well into the future. Once made, capital budgeting decisions tend to be relatively inflexible.

- **Stages** in the capital budgeting process are:

  - Identification and definition
  - Search for potential investments
  - Information acquisition
  - Selection
  - Financing
  - Implementation
  - Monitoring

- A **common misstep** in regard to capital budgeting is the temptation to gauge the desirability of a project by using accrual accounting numbers instead of cash flows. The measure usually produced this way is called **book rate of return** or accrual accounting rate of return. Book rate of return is considered an **unsatisfactory guide** to selecting capital projects for multiple reasons.

  GAAP net income from investment ÷ Book value of investment

- **Relevant cash flows** are a much more reliable guide when judging capital projects, since only they provide a true measure of a project's potential to affect shareholder value. The relevant cash flows can be divided into three categories:

  - **Net initial investment**

    - Purchase of new equipment
    - Initial working capital requirements
    - After-tax proceeds from disposal of old equipment

  - **Annual net cash flows**

    - After-tax cash collections from operations excluding depreciation effect
    - Tax savings from depreciation deductions

  - **Project termination cash flows**

    - After-tax proceeds from disposal of new equipment
    - After-tax proceeds from recovery of working capital

- Three crucial terms relevant to capital budgeting:

  - An **incremental cash flow** is the difference in cash received or disbursed resulting from selecting one option instead of another.

  - A **sunk cost** is one that is either already paid or irrevocably committed to be incurred. Because it is unavoidable and will therefore not vary with the option chosen, it is not relevant to future decisions.

  - An **opportunity cost** is the maximum benefit forgone by using a scarce resource for a given purpose and not for the next-best alternative. In capital budgeting, the most basic application of this concept is the desire to place the company's limited funds in the most promising capital project(s).

Part 3 - Section E.2. Discounted cash flow analysis

The candidate should be able to:

a.   demonstrate an understanding of the two main discounted cash flow (DCF) methods, net present value (NPV) and internal rate of return (IRR)

b.   demonstrate an understanding of the weighted average cost of capital approach to NPV calculations

c.   calculate the NPV and IRR using time value of money tables

d.   demonstrate an understanding of the decision criteria used in NPV and IRR analyses to determine acceptable projects

e.   compare NPV and IRR focusing on the relative advantages and disadvantages of each method, particularly with respect to independent versus mutually exclusive projects, the "multiple IRR problem" and the cash flow pattern that causes the problem, and why NPV and IRR methods can produce conflicting rankings for capital projects if not applied properly

f.   identify assumptions of the different methods of evaluating capital investment projects

g.   recommend project investments on the basis of DCF analysis

Core Concepts for Discounted Cash Flow Analysis

- When analyzing capital projects, the management accountant must **discount the relevant cash flows** using the time value of money. A firm's goal is for its discount rate to be **as low as possible**. The lower the firm's discount rate, the lower the "hurdle" the company must clear to achieve profitability. For this reason, the rate is sometimes called the **hurdle rate**.

  - The two most widely used rates in capital budgeting are the firm's weighted-average cost of capital and the shareholders' opportunity cost of capital.

- A **common pitfall** in capital budgeting is the tendency to use the company's current rate of return as the benchmark. This can lead to rejecting projects that should be accepted.

  - For example, a firm's current rate of return on all projects is 12%. Its shareholders' opportunity cost of capital is 10%. The company incorrectly rejects a project earning 11%.

- The **net present value (NPV) method** for projecting the profitability of an investment expresses a project's return in dollar terms. NPV nets the expected cash streams related to a project (inflows and outflows), then discounts them at the hurdle rate, also called the desired rate of return.

  - If the NPV of a project is positive, the project is desirable because it has a higher rate of return than the company's desired rate.

- The **internal rate of return (IRR) method** expresses a project's return in percentage terms. The IRR of an investment is the discount rate at which the investment's NPV equals zero. In other words, it is the rate that makes the present value of the expected cash inflows equal the present value of the expected cash outflows.

  - If the IRR is higher than the company's desired rate of return, the investment is desirable.

- **IRR used in isolation** is seldom the best route to a sound capital budgeting decision.

  - When the **direction of the cash flows** changes, focusing simply on IRR can be misleading. This effect is known as the multiple IRR problem. Essentially, there are as many solutions to the IRR formula as there are changes in the direction of the net cash flows.

  - Focusing only on IRR **when capital is limited** can lead to unsound decisions. A project with a lower rate of return may actually add more shareholder value.

- A project's NPV can easily be determined using different desired rates of return for different periods. The IRR is **limited to a single summary rate** for the entire project.
- IRR rates **cannot simply be added** as NPV dollars can. The IRR for the whole is not the sum of the IRRs for the parts.

■ Often a decision maker must choose between two mutually exclusive projects, one whose inflows are **higher in the early years** but fall off drastically later and one whose inflows are **steady throughout** the project's life.

- The higher a firm's hurdle rate, the more quickly a project must pay off.
- Firms with low hurdle rates prefer a slow and steady payback.

Part 3 – Section E.3. Payback and discounted payback

The candidate should be able to:

a. demonstrate an understanding of the payback method
b. identify the advantages and disadvantages/limitations of the payback method
c. calculate payback periods and discounted paybacks
d. identify the advantages and disadvantages/limitations of the discounted payback method

Core Concepts for Payback and Discounted Payback

■ The **payback period** is the number of years required to return the original investment; that is, the time necessary for a new asset to pay for itself. Note that no consideration is made for the time value of money under this method.

■ Companies using the payback method set a maximum **length of time** within which projects must **pay for themselves** to be considered acceptable. If the cash flows are not constant, the calculation must be in cumulative form. If the cash flows are constant, this formula can be used:

Payback period = Initial net investment ÷ Annual expected cash flow

■ The strength of the payback method is its **simplicity**.

- The payback method is sometimes used for foreign investments if foreign expropriation of firm assets is feared. Even in these circumstances, it is most often used in addition to a more sophisticated method.
- To some extent, the payback period measures risk. The longer the period, the riskier the investment.

■ The payback method has two significant **weaknesses**.

- It disregards all cash inflows after the payback cutoff date. Applying a single cutoff date to every project results in accepting many marginal projects and rejecting good ones.
- It disregards the time value of money. Weighting all cash inflows equally ignores the fact that money has a cost.

■ The **discounted payback method** is sometimes used to overcome the second of the drawbacks inherent in the basic payback method. The net cash flows in the denominator are discounted to calculate the period required to recover the initial investment. Clearly, this is a more conservative technique than the traditional payback method.

- The discounted payback method's advantage is that it acknowledges the time value of money.
- Its drawbacks are that it loses the simplicity of the basic payback method and still ignores cash flows after the arbitrary cutoff date.

- The **bailout payback method** incorporates the salvage value of the asset into the calculation. It measures the length of the payback period when the periodic cash inflows are combined with the salvage value.
- The **payback reciprocal** (1 ÷ payback) is sometimes used as an estimate of the internal rate of return.
- The **breakeven time** is the period required for the discounted cumulative cash inflows on a project to equal the discounted cumulative cash outflows (usually but not always the initial cost).

Part 3 – Section E.4. Ranking investment projects

The candidate should be able to:

a. define capital rationing and mutually exclusive projects
b. rank capital investment projects and recommend optimal investments using the profitability index
c. determine when the profitability index would be recommended over the NPV rule (i.e., independent projects with capital rationing)
d. identify and discuss the problems inherent in comparing projects of unequal scale and/or unequal lives
e. demonstrate an understanding of the advantages and disadvantages of the different methods of evaluating alternate capital investment projects
f. identify alternative solutions to the ranking problem, including internal capital markets and linear programming

Core Concepts for Ranking Investment Projects

- **Capital rationing** exists when a firm sets a limit on the amount of funds to be invested during a given period. In such situations, a firm cannot afford to undertake all profitable projects. **Only those projects** that will return the greatest NPV for the limited capital available in the internal capital market can be undertaken.
- The **profitability index** (or excess present value index) is a method for ranking projects to ensure that limited resources are placed with the investments that will return the highest NPV.

  Profitability index = NPV of future cash flows ÷ Net investment

- **Internal capital market** is a way of referring to the provision of funds by one division of a firm to another division. A division operating in a mature industry that generates a lot of cash can provide funding to another division that is in the cash-hungry development stage.
  - An advantage is the avoidance of stock issue costs or interest costs on new debt.
  - A disadvantage is that calling it a "market" is somewhat misleading. The dynamics of the process are more akin to centralized planning and budgeting than to the workings of a free marketplace.
- **Linear programming** is a technique (now usually computerized) for optimizing resource allocations so as to select the most profitable or least costly way to use available resources. It involves optimizing an objective function subject to the net of constraint equations.
  - For example, a linear programming application can maximize NPV for a group of projects in a capital rationing situation (expenditure constraint).

Part 3 – Section E.5. Risk analysis in capital investment

The candidate should be able to:

    a.   identify alternative approaches to dealing with risk in capital budgeting

    b.   demonstrate an understanding of sensitivity analysis and certainty equivalents

    c.   identify qualitative considerations in making capital investment decisions

    d.   explain why a rate specifically adjusted for risk should be used when project cash flows are more or less risky than is normal for a firm

    e.   distinguish among sensitivity analysis, scenario analysis, and Monte Carlo simulation as risk analysis techniques

    f.   describe how CAPM can be used in the capital budget process

Core Concepts for Risk Analysis in Capital Investment

- **Risk analysis** attempts to measure the likelihood of the variability of future returns from the proposed investment.

- Several approaches can be used to **assess risk**:

- Under the **informal method**, NPVs are calculated at the firm's desired rate of return, and the possible projects are individually reviewed.

- With **risk-adjusted discount rates**, the rate of return is adjusted upward as the investment becomes riskier.

- The **certainty equivalent adjustments** technique forces the decision maker to specify at what point the firm is indifferent to the choice between a certain sum of money and the expected value of a risky sum.

- Under **sensitivity analysis**, forecasts of many calculated NPVs under various assumptions are compared to see how sensitive NPV is to changing conditions. Changing or relaxing the assumptions about a certain variable or group of variables may drastically alter the NPV.

- **Simulation analysis** represents a refinement of standard profitability theory. The computer is used to generate many examples of results based upon various assumptions. Project simulation is frequently expensive.

- The **capital asset pricing model** is derived from the use of portfolio theory. It assumes that the return on each asset in a portfolio has variability. In a portfolio, each security's specific variability is eliminated through diversification, and the only relevant risk is the market component.

Part 3 – Section E.6. Real options in capital investments

The candidate should be able to:

    a.   demonstrate an understanding of the concept of real options in the capital budgeting process

    b.   identify the four common real options, e.g., the option to (a) make follow-on investments if the immediate investment project succeeds, (b) abandon a project, (c) wait and learn before investing, or (d) vary a firm's output or its production methods

    c.   identify these real options as either put or call options

    d.   demonstrate an understanding of the variables and factors that affect the value of options

Core Concepts for Real Options in Capital Investments

- **Real (managerial or strategic) options** reduce the risk of an investment project. A real option is the flexibility to affect the amounts and risk of an investment project's cash flows, to determine its duration, or to postpone its implementation.
- The **value of a real option** is the difference between the project's NPV without the option and its NPV with the option.
- Real options are **not measurable with the same accuracy** as financial options because the formulas applicable to the latter may not be appropriate for the former.
- Management accountants should be able to **determine what real options are embedded** in a project, measure their value, and offer advice about structuring a project to include such options.
- The following are among the types of real options: abandonment, the option of making a follow-up investment, the option to wait and learn, the flexibility option to vary inputs, the capacity option to vary output, the option to enter a new geographical market, and the new product option.

20.2 INVESTMENT DECISIONS ESSAY QUESTIONS

Recall that your CMA Part 4 exam will probably contain six scenarios, with about three questions per scenario. There will be a recommended time allocation of 20 minutes, 30 minutes, or 45 minutes for each scenario and related questions.

One scenario will involve ethical issues, and probably one or two scenarios will include calculations and responses on a worksheet. Also, expect at least one scenario on organizational/behavioral topics. The remaining scenarios cover Parts 1, 2, and 3.

Scenario Title	Subtopic	Questions	Suggested Time
Clewash Linen Supply Co.	Investment Decision Making	1	20 minutes

Scenario for Essay Question 1

Clewash Linen Supply Co. provides laundered items to various commercial and service establishments in a large metropolitan city. Clewash is scheduled to acquire some new cleaning equipment in mid-Year 5 which should provide some operating efficiencies. The new equipment would enable Clewash to increase the volume of laundry it handles without any increase in labor costs. In addition, the estimated maintenance costs in terms of pounds of laundry processed would be reduced slightly with the new equipment.

The new equipment was justified not only on the basis of reduced cost but also on the basis of expected increase in demand starting late in Year 5. However, since the original forecast was prepared, several potential new customers have either delayed or discontinued their own expansion plans in the market area which is serviced by Clewash. The most recent forecast indicates that no great increase in demand can be expected until late Year 6 or early Year 7.

Question

1. Identify and explain the factors Clewash Linen Supply Co. should consider in deciding whether or not to delay the investment in the new cleaning equipment. In the presentation of your response, distinguish between those factors which tend to indicate that the investment should be made as scheduled versus those which tend to indicate that the investment should be delayed.

Essay Question 1 — Unofficial Answers

1.   Some of the factors which affect the decision of whether or not to delay the investment in new cleaning equipment are given below. Each factor can have two sides, i.e., delay versus no delay, depending upon the circumstances involved.

   a.   Unemployment, inflation rate, and business conditions in general. Business outlook improving -- do not delay. Business outlook deteriorating -- delay. Unemployment, inflation rate, and business conditions all affect the climate for business and should be considered.

   b.   Difficulty associated with acquisition and installation of equipment and training of operators. Great difficulty -- do not delay. Little difficulty -- delay. The greater the lead time involved, the sooner the equipment should be acquired so that it is ready when needed.

Consider using Gleim's **CMA Test Prep** for interactive testing with **hundreds of multiple-choice questions** as an additional method of knowledge transfer in your quest to pass Part 4.

APPENDIX A
IMA MEMBERSHIP AND EXAMINATION FORMS

You must apply and become an IMA member in order to participate in the IMA Certification programs. The cost is $195 per year for Regular or International membership. Recent graduates (associates) have discounted fees of $65 their first year out of school and $130 their second year out of school. Full-time faculty dues (in the U.S., Canada, and Mexico) are $98 and dues for full-time students are $39 per year (must carry at least 6 equivalent hours per semester and reside in the U.S., Canada, or Mexico).

The IMA offers three member interest groups at $75 per year: the Controllers Council, the Cost Management Group, and the Small-Business Council. Everyone except students and associates must pay a $15 IMA registration fee.

The following two pages can be photocopied and used to apply for IMA membership, or call the IMA at (800) 638-4427, ext. 510, and ask for a CMA "kit." You also may email the IMA at info@imanet.org to request an information kit or apply online on the IMA's website at www.imanet.org.

Completion of the registration form on the two pages following the IMA membership application is required in order to take any of the examination parts.

NOTE: The ICMA application has been replaced by the IMA Certification Program. You can apply for admission into the Certification Program by checking the appropriate box on either the IMA Membership Application or the Exam Registration Form. The fee is $200 ($75 for students).

INSTITUTE OF MANAGEMENT ACCOUNTANTS®

MEMBERSHIP APPLICATION ✦ ✦ ✦

☐ New Application	**PERSONAL INFORMATION** *(please print)*

☐ **Renewal**

☐ Mr. ☐ Ms. ☐ Mrs. ☐ Miss ☐ Dr.　Last/Family Name/Surname: _____

☐ **Certification**
(IMA membership required)

First/Given Name: _____　Middle Initial: _____ Suffix: _____

Date of Birth (month/day/year): _____ / _____ / _____

Please indicate your contact preference:

☐ **BUSINESS MAILING ADDRESS:**
(See reverse side to enter SIC, job title, and responsibility codes)

Title: _____

Company Name: _____

Street/P.O. Box: _____

_____

City: _____

State/Province: _____

Zip Code/Postal Code: _____

Country: _____

Business Phone: *(Include Country/Area/City Codes)* _____

E-mail Address: _____

☐ **HOME MAILING ADDRESS:**

Street/P.O. Box: _____

_____

City: _____

State/Province: _____

Zip Code/Postal Code: _____

Country: _____

Phone: *(Include Country/Area/City Codes)* _____

Fax: _____

EDUCATION HISTORY

	Name of Institution	Degree	Major	Date Received/Expected
Undergraduate:				
Graduate:				

Professional Designations Earned: ☐ U.S. CPA ☐ CFA ☐ CIA ☐ Other: _____

CHAPTER AFFILIATION
See a list of Regular/Student Chapter options by visiting our website www.imanet.org, or call (800) 638-4427.

Chapter Name: _____　Chapter Number: _____　☐ Member-At-Large (Check here if no chapter affiliation is desired)

☐ International Member-At-Large

A. MEMBERSHIP INFORMATION *(All payments must be in U.S. Dollars)*

☐ **Regular Membership** $195.00
(You must reside in the U.S., Canada, or Mexico)

☐ **International Membership** $195.00
(Available to professionals residing outside the U.S., Canada, or Mexico)

☐ **Student Membership** .... $ 39.00
(You must be taking 6 or more hours per semester and reside in the U.S., Canada, or Mexico)

Expected Graduation Date (Year) _____

☐ **Associate Membership**
(You must apply within 2 years of completing full-time studies and reside in the U.S., Canada, or Mexico)

Select One: ☐ 1st year after graduation .... $ 65.00

☐ 2nd year after graduation $130.00

☐ **Academic Membership** .... $ 98.00
(You must be a full-time faculty member and reside in the U.S., Canada, or Mexico)

B. OPTIONAL SERVICES
(IMA membership required. All payments must be in U.S. Dollars)

☐ **Member Interest Groups** .... $ 75.00 each
　☐ Controllers Council ☐ Cost Management Group ☐ Small Business Council

☐ **CPE Offerings** *(Prices valid through 12/31/08)*

☐ IMA Ethics Series: Success Without Compromise (4 CPE) .... $ 75.00*

☐ IMA Ethics Series: Fraud in Financial Reporting (2 CPE) .... $ 59.00*

☐ IMA Knowledge Exchange　(Unlimited CPE) $274.00**

☐ IMA Advantage　　　　(Unlimited CPE) $274.00**

☐ IMA Knowledge Exchange/Advantage Combo $409.00**

☐ IMA CPEdge (24+ CPE) $187.00**
*Valid for 60 days from date of purchase.　**Valid for 365 days.

☐ **Certification** ☐ CMA

☐ Certification Entrance Fee *(One-time payment)* $200.00

☐ Certification Entrance Fee for students in the U.S., Canada,
　and Mexico *(One-time payment)* $75.00

☐ **Exam Waiver Fee** *(See www.imanet.org for more information)* $190.00

INSTITUTE OF MANAGEMENT ACCOUNTANTS, INC.

• 10 Paragon Drive, Montvale, NJ 07645-1760 • (800) 638-4427 or (201) 573-9000 • fax (201) 474-1600 • ima@imanet.org • www.imanet.org •

C. REGISTRATION FEES

☐ **Membership Registration Fee** $15.00
(All new members except Students and Associates)

☐ **Reinstatement Fee** $15.00
(If your membership has lapsed for 90 days, a $15.00 reinstatement fee applies)

TOTAL DUE (add sections A, B, and C) . . . .$ _____

APPLICANT STATEMENT

☐ Check here if you have ever been convicted of a felony. Please enclose a confidential letter with a brief explanation of circumstances to the attention of President & CEO.

I affirm that the statements on this application are correct, and I agree to abide by the Statement of Ethical Professional Practice.

Signature: _____ Date: _____

IMA occasionally makes available its members' addresses (excluding telephone and e-mail) to vendors who provide products and services to the management accounting and finance community. If you prefer not to be included in these lists, please check this box. ☐

PREFERRED METHOD OF PAYMENT
(All payments must be in U.S. Dollars)

☐ **Wire Payments** . . . .
All wire transfers must be made with bank fees prepaid. Please notify IMA by e-mail (dhuckins@imanet.org) that you are paying by wire transfer. Include your name, amount sent, and wire transfer receipt number.

☐ **Check Payments**
My check for $ _____ , payable to IMA, is enclosed.
No checks drawn on foreign banks will be accepted unless they are payable through U.S. correspondent banks and in U.S. dollars.

☐ **Credit Card Payments**
Charge my credit card: ☐ AMEX ☐ Discover ☐ MasterCard ☐ VISA

Card Number: _____ Exp.: _____

Cardholder Name: _____

Signature: _____

CMA CERTIFICATION PROGRAM

IMA membership required. If you are applying to the certification program for the first time, please check the appropriate box and enclose the Certification Entrance Fee ($200.00) required of new certification applicants only. (Students in the U.S., Canada, and Mexico must pay the reduced fee of $75.00)

☐ Applying as a **Student** (*U.S., Canada, and Mexico only*) — Upon graduation, arrange for an official copy of your transcript to be sent.

☐ Applying as **Faculty** (*U.S., Canada, and Mexico only*) — Please provide a letter on school stationery affirming full-time teaching status.

Please complete the Additional Educational Information below:

ADDITIONAL EDUCATIONAL INFORMATION

Check the appropriate box and make arrangements for supporting documents to be forwarded to the IMA certification department. Only one form of credentials is required.

☐ **Later** — By selecting this option, many applicants choose to provide their educational credentials after completing the exams.

If you would like to have your credentials reviewed prior to taking the exams to ensure that they are acceptable, please select one of the options below. Please note that the educational requirement must be fulfilled prior to certification.

☐ **College Graduate** — Submit official transcript (translated into English) showing university degree conferred and official university seal, or arrange to have proof of degree sent directly from university.

☐ **GMAT or GRE Scores** — Provide copy of scores.

☐ **U.S. CPA Exam, U.S. CFA Exam, or other acceptable certification or license** — Arrange to have proof sent directly from your certifying organization. Acceptable designations are listed at www.imanet.org.

Strategic Finance Magazine
Subscription rates per year:
Members: . . . . $ 48 (Included in dues, nondeductible)
Student Members: . . . . $ 25 (Included in dues, nondeductible)

Management Accounting Quarterly
Subscription rates per year:
Members: . . . . $ 10 (Included in dues, nondeductible)

SIC CODE – STANDARD INDUSTRY CLASSIFICATIONS
(Please Circle One)
01 Education
02 Healthcare
03 Media and Entertainment
16 Construction, Mining, Agriculture
21 Manufacturing
41 Transportation, Communication, Utilities
51 Wholesale/Retail Trades
61 Finance
63 Insurance
81 Business Services
82 Real Estate
86 High Tech
90 Nonprofit
93 Government
96 Pharmaceuticals & Biotechnology
99 Other _____

JOB TITLE CODE
(Please Circle One)
05 Executive Officer
11 Corporate Officer
15 Vice President
31 Controller
33 Chief Financial Officer
35 Director/Manager
41 Supervisor
47 Accountant
51 Analyst
55 Programmer
57 Administrative
59 Consultant
65 Academic
99 Other _____

RESPONSIBILITY CODE
(Please Circle One)
01 General Management
05 Corporate Management
10 Public Accounting
15 General Accounting
20 Personnel Accounting
25 Cost Accounting
30 Government Accounting
33 Environmental Accounting
35 Finance
40 Risk Management
45 Budget and Planning
50 Taxation
55 Internal Auditing
60 Education
65 Information Systems
70 Student
75 Retired
80 Other _____

MEMBER PROFILE

1. Do you have international responsibilities?
☐ Yes ☐ No

2. Does your company have international locations?
☐ Yes ☐ No

3. Who will pay your IMA dues?
☐ Me ☐ My Company

4. What are you looking for most from your IMA Membership?
☐ Career assistance ☐ Professional networking
☐ Certification ☐ Industry news
☐ Education ☐ Leadership training
☐ CPE ☐ Research
☐ Other (please specify) _____

5. Are you a member of any other association?
☐ AAA ☐ AFP ☐ AICPA ☐ ASWA
☐ CFA Institute (AIMR) ☐ FEI ☐ IIA
☐ Other (please specify) _____

6. Is your organization:
☐ Public sector ☐ Nonprofit
☐ Private sector ☐ Government

8. How did you learn about IMA?
☐ Chapter meeting ☐ Marketing piece
☐ IMA educational program ☐ Company recommended
☐ IMA website ☐ Industry associate
☐ Industry publication ☐ Professor
☐ Other _____
☐ Other website _____

9. How many employees are in your company or organization?
☐ Under 50 ☐ 51-100 ☐ 101-200 ☐ 201-500
☐ 501-1,000 ☐ 1,001-10,000 ☐ Over 10,000

10. What is your company's current annual revenue?
☐ Under $1 million ☐ $500 million - $1 billion
☐ $1 - $10 million ☐ $1 billion - $5 billion
☐ $10 - $100 million ☐ $5 billion - $10 billion
☐ $100 - $500 million ☐ Over $10 billion

Please send your completed application and payment (made out to IMA) to:

INSTITUTE OF MANAGEMENT ACCOUNTANTS, INC.

Rev. 0308

· 10 Paragon Drive, Montvale, NJ 07645-1760 · (800) 638-4427 or (201) 573-9000 · fax (201) 474-1600 · ima@imanet.org · www.imanet.org ·

482

Institute of Certified Management Accountants
10 Paragon Drive • Montvale, New Jersey 07645-1759
(201) 573-9000 • (800) 638-4427 • FAX: (201) 474-1600

CMA EXAMINATION REGISTRATION FORM

| PERSONAL INFORMATION | TYPE OR PRINT CLEARLY |

☐ Please check box if you are applying to the ICMA program, complete side two and pay the $200 entrance fee. No exam will be authorized without remitting the entrance fee. If the exam is not completed in four years, fee will expire.

☐ Mr. ☐ Ms. ☐ Miss ☐ Mrs. ☐ Dr.   ☐ IMA Member # _____

Last Name/Family Name   First Name/Surname   Middle Initial   Suffix
☐ Please check box if this is a new address.   Please Specify ☐ Home   ☐ Business

Mailing Address/Street/P.O. Box

City   State/Province/Country   Zip Code/Postal Code

Daytime Telephone (include area code or country/city code)

E-mail   Fax Number: (Include Area/Country/City Codes)

NOTES:
(1) Examination Fees and Certification Entrance Fees are NOT REFUNDABLE.

(2) You are required to take all the parts you register for within the same 120 day authorization period. (For Part 4 your authorization period is the month for which you are registered.)

(3) Parts 1, 2, and 3 must be passed before registering for Part 4.

(4) Part 4 is given the second month of every quarter. (Feb., May, Aug., and Nov.) at Prometric Testing Centers.

| PLACE A CHECK MARK IN THE BOX(ES) BELOW FOR THE PART(S) YOU WISH TO TAKE AT THIS TIME |

| ☐ Entrance Fee | ☐ PART 1 Business Analysis | ☐ PART 2 Management Accounting & Reporting | ☐ PART 3 Strategic Management | ☐ PART 4 Business Applications (Please select a testing window. See Notes 3 & 4 Above) | ☐ February ☐ May ☐ August ☐ November |

TOTAL PARTS _____

$200 Regular Member Entrance Fee if applicable (MUST BE PAID PRIOR TO TAKING FIRST EXAM), expires in 4 years. .... $ _____

$ 75 Student Member Entrance Fee if applicable (U.S., Mexican and Canadian college students) (MUST BE PAID PRIOR TO TAKING FIRST EXAM), expires in 4 years. .... $ _____

$190 Examination Registration Fee per part .... $ _____

Less: Student/Faculty Discount (50% students, 100% faculty) (U.S., Mexican and Canadian college students/faculty only) .... $ _____

Faculty Retakes at 50% of cost .... $ _____

$190 Part I Waiver Fee if applicable (Arrange to have proof sent directly from the certifying organization) .... $ _____

AMOUNT DUE .... $ _____

| PLEASE COMPLETE BOTH SIDES | NOTE: PAYMENT IN FULL MUST ACCOMPANY REGISTRATION FORM - FEES SUBJECT TO CHANGE |

7/08

CERTIFICATION PROGRAM APPLICATION

If you are applying for admission to the certification program, please complete the following.

☐ **Applying as a Student** (U.S., Mexico and Canada) – Upon graduation, arrange for an official copy of your transcript to be sent.

☐ **Applying as Faculty** (U.S., Mexico and Canada) – Please provide a letter on school stationery affirming full-time teaching status.

ADDITIONAL EDUCATIONAL INFORMATION

Check one of the following and make arrangements for supporting documents to be forwarded to the IMA certification department.

☐ **Later** - By selecting this option, applicants choose to provide their educational credentials after completing the exams. If you would like to have your credentials reviewed prior to taking the exams to ensure that they are acceptable, please select one of the options below. Please note that the educational requirement must be fulfilled prior to certification.

☐ **College Graduate** - Submit official transcript showing university degree conferred and official university seal or arrange to have proof of degree sent directly from university.

NOTE: Please pay the entrance fee before submitting your educational credentials.

Name on transcript (if different from front of registration form)

☐ **GMAT or GRE Scores** - Provide copy of scores.

☐ **Professional Certification** – Arrange to have proof of certification sent directly from the certifying organization. See listing of acceptable certifications at http://www.imanet.org/certification_started_education_professional.asp

CONFIDENTIALITY STATEMENT & PAYMENT INFORMATION

I hereby attest that I will not divulge the content of this examination, nor will I remove any examination materials, notes, or other unauthorized materials from the examination room. I understand that failure to comply with this attestation may result in invalidation of my grades and disqualification from future examinations. For those already certified by the Institute of Certified Management Accountants, failure to comply with the statement will be considered a violation of IMA's Statement of Ethical Professional Practice and could result in revocation of the certification.

I affirm that the statements on this registration are correct and agree to abide by IMA's Statement of Ethical Professional Practice.

Signature of Applicant: _____ Date: _____

PREFERRED METHOD OF PAYMENT (All payments must be in U.S. Dollars)

☐ **Wire Payments**

All wire transfers must ne made with banks fees prepaid. Please notify IMA by e-mail (dhuckins@imanet.org) that you are paying by wire transfer. Include your name, amount sent, and wire transfer receipt number.

☐ **Check Payments**

My check for $ _____, payable to ICMA, is enclosed. No checks drawn from foreign banks will be accepted unless they are payable through U.S. correspondent banks and in U.S. dollars.

☐ **Credit Card Payments**

Charge my credit card: ☐ VISA ☐ MasterCard ☐ American Express ☐ Discover

Credit Card Number: __ __ __ __ — __ __ __ __ — __ __ __ __ — __ __ __ __   Expiration Date: ___/___ MM/YY

Card Holder Name: _____

Signature of Card Holder: _____

IMA occasionally makes available its members' addresses (excluding telephone and e-mail) to vendors who provide products and services to the management accounting and finance community. If you prefer not to be included in these lists, please check this box. ☐

PLEASE COMPLETE BOTH SIDES   **NOTE: PAYMENT IN FULL MUST ACCOMPANY REGISTRATION FORM - FEES SUBJECT TO CHANGE**

7/08

INSTITUTE OF MANAGEMENT ACCOUNTANTS
Advancing the Profession™

10 Paragon Drive • Montvale, New Jersey 07645-1760 • www.imanet.org
(201) 573-9000 • (800) 638-4427 • Fax (201) 474-1600

CERTIFIED MANAGEMENT ACCOUNTANT
Professionals Driving Business Performance™

APPENDIX B
ICMA CONTENT SPECIFICATION OUTLINES

The following pages consist of a partial reprint of the ICMA's Content Specification Outlines (CSOs) for Part 4, effective July 1, 2004. Please use these CSOs as reference material only. The ICMA's CSOs have been carefully analyzed and have been incorporated into 20 study units to provide systematic and rational coverage of exam topics.

We are confident that we provide comprehensive coverage of the subject matter tested on the CMA exam. If, after taking the exam, you feel that certain topics, concepts, etc., tested were not covered or were inadequately covered, please call, fax, or email us. We do not want information about CMA questions, only information/feedback about our *CMA Review* system's coverage.

Content Specification Outlines for the
Certified Management Accountant (CMA)
Examinations

The content specification outlines presented below represent the body of knowledge that will be covered on the CMA examinations. The outlines may be changed in the future when new subject matter becomes part of the common body of knowledge.

Candidates for the CMA designation are required to take Parts 1, 2, 3, and 4. Part 4, Business Applications, may only be taken after successful completion of Parts 1, 2, and 3.

Candidates are responsible for being informed on the most recent developments in the areas covered in the outlines. This includes understanding of public pronouncements issued by accounting organizations as well as being up-to-date on recent developments reported in current accounting, financial and business periodicals.

Important additional information about the content specification outlines and the examinations is listed below. [Items 1. through 7. pertain to Parts 1, 2, and 3 of the exam.]

8. Part 4, Business Applications, consists of several essay questions and problems that are delivered in a computer-based format. Both written and quantitative responses will be required. Candidates will be expected to present written answers that are responsive to the question asked, presented in a logical manner, and demonstrate an appropriate understanding of the subject matter. It should be noted that candidates are expected to have working knowledge in the use of word processing and electronic spreadsheets.

9. Ethical issues and considerations will be tested on Part 4, Business Applications. At least one question in this part will be devoted to an ethical situation presented in a business-oriented context. Candidates will be expected to evaluate the issues involved and make recommendations for the resolution of the situation.

In order to more clearly define the topical knowledge required by a candidate, varying levels of coverage for the treatment of major topics of the content specification outlines have been identified and defined. The cognitive skills that a successful candidate should possess and that should be tested on the examinations can be defined as follows:

Knowledge: Ability to remember previously learned material such as specific facts, criteria, techniques, principles, and procedures (i.e., identify, define, list).

Comprehension: Ability to grasp and interpret the meaning of material (i.e., classify, explain, distinguish between).

Application: Ability to use learned material in new and concrete situations (i.e., demonstrate, predict, solve, modify, relate).

Analysis: Ability to break down material into its component parts so that its organizational structure can be understood; ability to recognize causal relationships, discriminate between behaviors, and identify elements that are relevant to the validation of a judgment (i.e., differentiate, estimate, order).

Synthesis: Ability to put parts together to form a new whole or proposed set of operations; ability to relate ideas and formulate hypotheses (i.e., combine, formulate, revise).

Evaluation: Ability to judge the value of material for a given purpose on the basis of consistency, logical accuracy, and comparison to standards; ability to appraise judgments involved in the selection of a course of action (i.e., criticize, justify, conclude).

The three levels of coverage can be defined as follows:

Level A: Requiring the skill levels of knowledge and comprehension.

Level B: Requiring the skill levels of knowledge, comprehension, application, and analysis.

Level C: Requiring all six skill levels, knowledge, comprehension, application, analysis, synthesis, and evaluation.

[All topics on Part 4 of the exam are tested at Level C.]

Part 4 – Business Applications

The final part of the CMA examination is a three-hour test test consisting of several business-oriented essay questions and problems requiring both written and quantitative responses. These questions will include a combination of a variety of topics from the content specifications for Parts 1, 2, and 3 as well as some special topics outlined below. These topics will be presented in realistic business situations, and candidates will be expected to show an understanding of the appropriate principles and practices. It should be noted that Part 4 may only be taken after successful completion of Parts 1, 2, and 3.

In addition to the topics outlined in the content specifications for Parts 1, 2 and 3, the Part 4 examination will include the following topics. There will be at least one question that will be devoted to an ethical situation presented in a business-oriented context.

Additional Part 4 Topics

1. *Organization management*

    a. Organization structures
    b. Jobs and teams
    c. Leadership styles and sources of power
    d. Motivational theories
    e. Diversity issues

2. *Organization communication*

    a. Communication models
    b. Deterrents to effective communication

3. *Behavioral issues*

    a. Alignment of organizational goals
    b. Issues in budgeting and standard setting
    c. Issues in reporting and performance evaluation

4. *Ethical considerations*

    a. Provisions of "Standards of Ethical Conduct for IMA Members"*
    b. Corporate responsibility for ethical conduct
    c. Evaluation and resolution of ethical issues such as

    - Fraudulent reporting
    - Manipulation of analyses and results
    - Unethical behavior in developing budgets and standards
    - Manipulation of decision factors

* Available at www.imanet.org.

APPENDIX C
ICMA SUGGESTED READING LIST

The ICMA suggested reading list that follows is reproduced to give you an overview of the scope of Part 4. You will not have the time to study these texts. Our *CMA Review* system is complete and thorough and is designed to maximize your study time. For all four parts, candidates are expected to stay up-to-date by reading articles from journals, newspapers, and professional publications.

Part 4 – Business Applications

Organization Management

Moorhead, Gregory and Griffin, Ricky W., *Organizational Behavior: Managing People and Organizations*, 8th edition, Houghton Mifflin Company, Boston, MA, 2007.

Robbins, Stephen P., *Organizational Behavior*, 10th edition, Prentice-Hall, Upper Saddle River, NJ, 2002.

Organization Communication

Moorhead, Gregory and Griffin, Ricky W., *Organizational Behavior: Managing People and Organizations*, 8th edition, Houghton Mifflin Company, Boston, MA, 2007.

Robbins, Stephen P., *Organizational Behavior*, 10th edition, Prentice-Hall, Upper Saddle River, NJ, 2002.

Behavioral Issues

Blocher, Edward J., Chen, Kung H., and Lin, Thomas W., *Cost Management: A Strategic Emphasis*, 3rd edition, Irwin/McGraw Hill, New York, NY 2004.

Horngren, Charles T., Foster, George M., and Datar, Srikant, *Cost Accounting: A Managerial Emphasis*, 12th edition, Prentice-Hall Inc., Upper Saddle River, NJ, 2006.

Ethical Considerations

IMA's "Statement of Ethical Professional Practice"

488

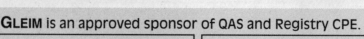

INDEX

COMPLETE GLEIM CPA SYSTEM

All 4 sections, including Gleim Online, books*, *Test Prep CD-Rom*, *Test Prep for Pocket PC*, Audio CDs, plus bonus book bag.

Also available by exam section @ $274.95 (does not include book bag).

*Fifth book: *CPA Review: A System for Success*

☐ $989.95

$_____

COMPLETE GLEIM CMA SYSTEM

Includes: Gleim Online, books*, *Test Prep CD-Rom*, *Test Prep for Pocket PC*, Audio CDs, plus bonus book bag.

Also available by exam part @ $213.95 (does not include book bag).

*Fifth book: *CMA Review: A System for Success*

☐ $739.95

$_____

COMPLETE GLEIM CIA SYSTEM

Includes: Gleim Online, books*, *Test Prep CD-Rom*, *Test Prep for Pocket PC*, Audio CDs, plus bonus book bag.

Also available by exam part @ $224.95 (does not include book bag).

*Fifth book: *CIA Review: A System for Success*

☐ $824.95

$_____

GLEIM EA REVIEW SYSTEM

Includes: Gleim Online, books, *Test Prep CD-Rom*, *Test Prep for Pocket PC*, Audio CDs, plus bonus book bag.

Also available by exam part @ $224.95 (does not include book bag).

☐ $629.95

$_____

"THE GLEIM SERIES" EXAM QUESTIONS AND EXPLANATIONS

Includes: 5 books and *Test Prep CD-Rom*.

Also available by part @ $29.95.

☐ $112.25

$_____

GLEIM ONLINE CPE

Try a FREE 4 hour course at gleim.com/cpe
- Easy-to-Complete
- Informative
- Effective

Contact
GLEIM PUBLICATIONS
for further assistance:

gleim.com
800.874.5346
sales@gleim.com

SUBTOTAL $_____

Complete your
order on the
next page

GLEIM PUBLICATIONS, INC.

P. O. Box 12848   Gainesville, FL 32604

TOLL FREE: 800.874.5346
LOCAL: 352.375.0772
FAX: 352.375.6940
INTERNET: gleim.com
E-MAIL: sales@gleim.com

Customer service is available (Eastern Time):
8:00 a.m. - 7:00 p.m., Mon. - Fri.
9:00 a.m. - 2:00 p.m., Saturday
Please have your credit card ready,
or save time by ordering online!

SUBTOTAL (from previous page) $_____
Add applicable sales tax for shipments within Florida. _____
Shipping (nonrefundable) 25.00

TOTAL $_____

Fax or write for prices/instructions on shipments outside the 48 contiguous states, or simply order online.

NAME (please print) _____

ADDRESS _____ Apt. _____
(street address required for UPS)

CITY _____ STATE_____ ZIP_____

_____ MC/VISA/DISC _____ Check/M.O.   Daytime Telephone (_____)_____

Credit Card No. _____ - _____ - _____ - _____

Exp. _____/_____   Signature _____
   Month / Year

E-mail address _____

1. We process and ship orders daily, within one business day over 98.8% of the time. Call by 3:00 pm for same day service.

2. Please PHOTOCOPY this order form for others.

3. No CODs. Orders from individuals must be prepaid.

4. Gleim Publications, Inc. guarantees the immediate refund of all resalable texts and unopened software and audios if returned within 30 days. Applies only to items purchased direct from Gleim Publications, Inc. Our shipping charge is nonrefundable.

5. Components of specially priced package deals are nonrefundable.

Prices subject to change without notice.
06/08

For updates and other important information, visit our website.

gleim.com

GLEIM
KNOWLEDGE
TRANSFER
SYSTEMS®

Please forward your suggestions, corrections, and comments concerning typographical errors, etc., to **Irvin N. Gleim • c/o Gleim Publications, Inc. • P.O. Box 12848 • University Station • Gainesville, Florida • 32604.** Please include your name and address so we can properly thank you for your interest.

1. _____

2. _____

3. _____

4. _____

5. _____

6. _____

7. _____

8. _____

9. _____

10. _____

11. _____

12. _____

13. _____

14. _____

15. _____

16. _____

17. _____

18. _____

Remember, for superior service: <u>Mail</u>, <u>email</u>, or <u>fax</u> questions about our materials.
<u>Telephone</u> questions about orders, prices, shipments, or payments.

Name: _____

Address: _____

City/State/Zip: _____

Telephone: Home: _____ Work: _____ Fax: _____

Email: _____

GLEIM Bookmark

Dr. Gleim's Advice: Cover the answers and explanations in our book with this bookmark. Answers will not be alongside questions when you take an exam. Use our Online course, Test Prep CD-Rom, and audios to complete your study program. Gleim's Test Prep CD-Rom will emulate actual exam conditions and track your progress.

Professor-Led LIVE Review

• **LIVE weekly study sessions**

• **Leadership of a Professor**

• **Interactive Online Community**

• **Gleim's proven self-study materials**

• **CPA, CMA, CIA, and EA Reviews**

Contact GLEIM for the location nearest you.

800.874.5346
gleim.com

GLEIM KNOWLEDGE TRANSFER SYSTEMS®